OXFORD GUIDES TO CHAUCER

The Canterbury Tales

Oxford Guides to Chaucer

The Canterbury Tales

HELEN COOPER

OXFORD UNIVERSITY PRESS

Oxford University Press, Walton Street, Oxford OX2 6DP
Oxford New York Toronto
Delhi Bombay Calcutta Madras Karachi
Petaling Jaya Singapore Hong Kong Tokyo
Nairobi Dar es Salaam Cape Town
Melbourne Auckland
and associated companies in
Berlin Ibadan

Oxford is a trade mark of Oxford University Press

Published in the United States
by Oxford University Press, New York

First published 1989
First published in paperback with corrections 1991

British Library Cataloguing in Publication Data
Cooper, Helen, 1947–
The Canterbury tales.–(Oxford guides to Chaucer)
1. Poetry in English. Chaucer, Geoffrey,
1340–1400. Canterbury tales
I. Title II. Series
821'.1
ISBN 0–19–811191–6
ISBN 0–19–811978–X (pbk)

Library of Congress Cataloging in Publication Data
Cooper, Helen.
Oxford guides to Chaucer. The Canterbury tales/Helen Cooper.
Bibliography: p.   Includes index.
1. Chaucer, Geoffrey, d. 1400. Canterbury tales.   I. Title.
PR1874.C64 1989   821'.1—dc19   88–35160
ISBN 0–19–811191–6
ISBN 0–19–811978–X (pbk)

Printed in Great Britain
by Biddles Ltd.
Guildford and King's Lynn

FOREWORD

THE idea for a series of guides to Chaucer originated in a sense that medieval studies in general and Chaucerian studies in particular had advanced to a point where a reappraisal of his poetry was both possible and necessary. The three volumes are devoted to the shorter poetry, *Troilus and Criseyde*, and the *Canterbury Tales*. We see these books as fulfilling a role comparable to the introduction to a good edition, but at greater length than would be possible there. The kind of line-by-line expository material that the notes to an edition would contain is included only where such matters are of wider importance for an understanding of the whole text or where recent scholarship has made significant advances. We hope to provide readers of Chaucer with essential and up-to-date information, with the emphasis falling on how the interpretation of that information advances our understanding of his work; we have therefore gone beyond summarizing what is known to suggest new critical readings.

The original plan for the series was designed to provide some degree of consistency in the outline of the volumes, but it was part of the project from the start that there should be plenty of room for each author's individuality. We hope that our sense of common interests and concerns in our interpretation of Chaucer's poetry will provide a deeper critical consistency below the diversity. Such a paradox would, after all, be true to the nature of our subject.

Helen Cooper
A.J. Minnis
Barry Windeatt

ACKNOWLEDGEMENTS

F IVE years ago, when Oxford University Press first asked me to draw up a scheme for a series of Chaucer handbooks, I did not quite realize what I was letting myself in for. It may be that they did not realize either. My part is now complete, and I must pay thanks to their English editor, Kim Scott Walwyn, for her encouragement, patience, and broad-mindedness.

To have asked any of my medievalist friends to comment on the draft of such an extensive work would have been taking unfair advantage of their willingness, so its errors are all on my own head. It could not, however, have been written without outside help. Charlotte Morse generously agreed to take a core sample in the shape of the section on the Clerk's Tale, and if the scholarship is sharper there than elsewhere, it is to her I owe it. V. A. Kolve very kindly gave me access to his unpublished work on the Summoner's Tale. Other colleagues—John Alford, Edwin Craun, Ruth Morse— have commented on other sections; and two of my fellow Fellows from University College, Oxford, have given me the benefit of their expertise, Colin Day on the chemistry behind the Canon's alchemy, and Alexander Murray on all kinds of things from sophisms to suicide. The undergraduates who have cross-examined me on the *Tales* in tutorials, and urged fine readings of their own, have provided a stimulus to excellence of which I can only have fallen short.

My greatest debt, however, is to my husband. That there are far fewer infelicities than in the original drafts I owe to his sharp eyes. He has helped me every page of the way, and has remained sufficiently interested in the *Tales* in spite of it all to reread them at the end. The last word of thanks must go to my children, for their tolerating Chaucer as an extra member of the household for so much of their lives, and for bearing with a mother who, as the youngest described it, 'sits upstairs writing and writing and writing. Her book has taken far too long.'

CONTENTS

FRAGMENT II(B¹)

FRAGMENT III(D)

FRAGMENT IV(E)

FRAGMENT V(F)

ABBREVIATIONS

ChR	*Chaucer Review*
EETS	Early English Text Society
ELH	*English Literary History*
ELN	*English Language Notes*
ELR	*English Literary Renaissance*
ES	*English Studies*
JEGP	*Journal of English and Germanic Philology*
MÆ	*Medium Ævum*
M&H	*Medievalia et humanistica*
MLN	*Modern Language Notes*
MLQ	*Modern Language Quarterly*
MP	*Modern Philology*
MS	*Medieval Studies*
NLH	*New Literary History*
NM	*Neuphilologische Mitteilungen*
N&Q	*Notes and Queries*
PMLA	*Publications of the Modern Languages Association*
RES	*Review of English Studies*
SAC	*Studies in the Age of Chaucer*
SP	*Studies in Philology*
UTQ	*University of Toronto Quarterly*

INTRODUCTION

The object of this book is to give an up-to-date summary of what is known about the *Canterbury Tales*, together with a critical reading of each tale. The whole work and each of the tales are discussed under the following headings (though I sometimes conflate sections if this makes better sense):

Date. Some of the tales are believed to have been written as independent works before the *Tales* itself was conceived; and there are various theories about the progress of composition. I give evidence where this is available, and record hypothesis where it seems plausible.

Text. There are some eighty surviving manuscripts of part or all of the *Tales*, and no two of them say quite the same thing. As it is fearfully easy to base an argument on a passage of doubtful authenticity, or on structural patterns adopted by editors on flimsy manuscript evidence, I try to note those variants that could significantly affect the sense or the style. I also indicate the kind of glosses that accompany each tale, and if these are ever likely to be Chaucer's.

Genre. The *Canterbury Tales* is unique among story-collections for its generic variety—a variety often insisted on in the links between the tales. Some of the most interesting individual tales also mix genres within themselves. A sense of genre, to judge from the many comments made on the subject within the work, was crucial to Chaucer's conception of the *Tales*, and I try to give some indication of its function and effect.

Sources and analogues. Where specific sources are known for the individual tales, I give summaries and an account of Chaucer's use and adaptation of them. I also discuss the sources of illustrative material, authoritative aphorisms, and so on. Where no sources are known, I try to reconstruct the literary context in which he was working.

Structure. The tales are often intriguingly structured, both in the arrangement of their narrative material and in their tendency to play games with fictive forms. I discuss the ground plan of each tale, how structure can affect meaning, and the interest in the process of storytelling that Chaucer shows.

Themes. Chaucer does not write full-scale allegory; he rarely writes a story that does not carry some kind of overt meaning, often expressed in digressions, comments from the narrator, and concluding *moralitees*. In this section, I look at the relation of such matters to the narratives that contain them, and also at the *sentence*, the inner meaning, behind the tales, whether this is made explicit or not. The ways in which tale and teller can affect each other are also discussed here.

The tale in context. The tales of the Canterbury sequence could stand as autonomous short stories or narrative poems, but they do not: they are placed within a larger work, and each tale affects the others and is affected by them. This section studies the additional meanings and resonances that result from their being part of the larger scheme.

Style. The style—or styles—of each tale can be as distinctive as its genre or its themes, and is indeed an integral part of such things. I analyse aspects such as the choice of words and images, the verse forms, rhetorical heightening, and characteristic syntax of each tale.

In addition, I provide separate discussions of the linking passages or prologues. One characteristic of the links is the quantity of critical or theoretical comment they contain, and I have tried to bring out this emphasis.

Such a division into separate areas of discussion is a matter of convenience, and the most frustrated or sceptical reader will still not be as conscious as I am of the artificiality of some of these boundaries. How Chaucer treats a source is inseparable from what he wants to say; we seldom read the tales as isolated units, without being aware of the Reeve's breathing fire at the Miller, or the Merchant's glancing over his shoulder at the Wife of Bath. I have tried to arrange the material so that it is possible to find the discussion of a specific point where it would most reasonably be expected, but the sections, like the tales, are not watertight units, and there are plenty of spills and leaks.

I have not attempted to give a complete survey of critical viewpoints on the tales, though the annotated bibliographies at the end of each section record some of the lines of battle. My own approach shares in the recent critical stress on Chaucer's literary and stylistic awareness, his sheer multifariousness, rather than in readings that see the tales as dramatic speeches by their tellers, or as allegories of orthodox Christian teaching, though I have learnt much from such interpretations. But there are as many interpretations of Chaucer as there are readers; he is supremely skilled at providing material for an almost infinite variety of readings (though he would be startled at some of the interpretations he has produced). It is impossible, therefore, to write a definitive study of the *Tales*, and I am very much aware of how far this book falls short. The scholarship on the work is vast; I have had to make a large number of omissions in the course of selecting material, and there will inevitably be other accidental ones. But more importantly, Chaucer is not the kind of author on whom it is possible to be definitive. The *Tales* itself is unfinished; its possibilities are endless. I have tried to keep the sense of the work's open-endedness, even where it has led me down some unexpected paths. I do not expect that every reader will follow me along all of them: to try to claim the Clerk's Tale for feminism is perhaps a lost cause before it starts.

Bibliographical Note

The Riverside Chaucer, edited by Larry D. Benson—alias 'Robinson 3'—came out when I was half-way through the writing of this book. I have adjusted all quotations by reference to its text, and profited greatly from its scholarship. I have also kept alongside me its predecessor, the second edition of F. N. Robinson's *Works of Geoffrey Chaucer*; the eight volumes of Manly and Rickert; Skeat's magnificent edition; and those volumes of the Variorum Chaucer that have so far appeared. As no edition of a work such as the *Canterbury Tales* can replace the manuscripts, I have also relied heavily on manuscript facsimiles, especially that of Hengwrt; and I have frequently consulted the Chaucer Society prints of other manuscripts and occasionally the manuscripts themselves. Full details of the printed editions I have used are given below.

Each section of the discussion of the tales is followed, wherever appropriate, by its own brief annotated bibliography, which records works I have used in compiling the section and areas of further reading. I am most deeply indebted for factual material; the interpretations I give are usually my own.

I have profited from reading many excellent critical works on the *Tales* as a whole, and these are listed in the General Bibliography. I give abbreviated references to them in the section bibliographies only when I owe them a specific debt, or where their discussion is of particular importance.

Editions

Benson, Larry D. (general ed.), *The Riverside Chaucer* (Boston, 1987, Oxford, 1988 (paperback)); 3rd edn. of Robinson (see below). This is the most recent standard student edition of Chaucer, and is the text used in this book.

Donaldson, E. T. (ed.), *Chaucer's Poetry: An Anthology for the Modern Reader* (2nd edn., New York, 1975). This edition omits the prose tales and slightly modernizes the spelling, but contains excellent critical material.

Fisher, John H. (ed.), *The Complete Poetry and Prose of Geoffrey Chaucer* (2nd edn., New York, 1989). A useful comprehensive edition.

Manly, John M. (ed.), *The Canterbury Tales* (New York, 1928). Although in many respects superseded, some of the critical material is still of value.

Manly, John M., and Rickert, Edith (eds.), *The Text of the Canterbury Tales* (8 vols., Chicago, 1940). This describes the manuscripts and records all textual variants.

Robinson, F. N. (ed.), *The Works of Geoffrey Chaucer* (2nd edn., Boston and Oxford, 1957).

Skeat, W. W. (ed.), *The Works of Geoffrey Chaucer* (7 vols., Oxford, 1894–1900). Although his scholarship is often outdated, Skeat is still a lucid and valuable source of essential information.

A Variorum Edition of the Works of Geoffrey Chaucer (Norman, Okla.) is a multi-volume edition, currently in progress, under the general editorship of Paul G. Ruggiers. Volumes on individual tales that appeared before this book was completed are listed in the appropriate bibliographies.

Manuscript facsimiles and transcripts

Ellesmere: *The Ellesmere Manuscript Reproduced in Facsimile* (2 vols., Manchester, 1911), reprinted as *The Ellesmere Manuscript of Chaucer's Canterbury Tales: A Working Facsimile*, with introduction by Ralph Hanna III (Cambridge, 1989).

Gg.4.27: *The Poetical Works of Geoffrey Chaucer: A Facsimile of Cambridge University Library MS Gg.4.27*, with introductions by M. B. Parkes and Richard Beadle (3 vols., Cambridge, 1979–80).

Hengwrt: *The Canterbury Tales: A Facsimile and Transcription of the Hengwrt Manuscript*, ed. Paul G. Ruggiers (Variorum I, Norman, Okla. 1979).

Chaucer Society transcripts edited by Frederick J. Furnivall:

Cambridge MS Dd.4.24 (1901–2).
Corpus MS (1868–77).
Harleian MS 7334 (1885).
Lansdowne MS (1868–77).
Petworth MS (1868–77).

The Canterbury Tales

Date

The writing of the *Canterbury Tales* occupied the last dozen or so years of Chaucer's life. He probably started work on it in the late 1380s; he died in 1400, and it is not known whether he continued working on it until his death. Within this period, all dates are conjectural, and are discussed separately for each tale in the course of the book. Two of the tales, the Knight's and Second Nun's, were written at some earlier date, and from time to time early composition has been suggested for a number of the others. Many were probably written before a specific place in the sequence was assigned to them, or a specific teller; the General Prologue need not have been written first, nor need the articulating device of the pilgrimage have given Chaucer the idea of writing a story-collection.

The year 1387 is the traditional date of the pilgrimage. This particular pilgrimage, however, is fictional, and Chaucer himself does not date it. It could be any sweet April of the later fourteenth century, or of the Middle Ages. The work's placing between contemporaneity and timelessness is peculiarly ambivalent. It contains a handful of references to such specific matters as the nefarious financial activities of the hospital of St Mary Rouncesval, and the Peasants' Revolt; but one would never guess from reading it just how troubled were the years in which it was composed. They were years of social and political unrest that led to the execution of several of Chaucer's close associates and culminated in the deposition of Richard II. Wyclif and his followers were challenging the institutions and the beliefs of Christendom; and the whole idea of feudal hierarchy was under pressure from the peasants' demands for rights, the demographic collapse following on the Black Death, and the continuing rise in the importance of money rather than land or rank in the social machinery. Yet the *Tales* does belong to this era. It is reflected in the impatience of both the 'cherles' and the moneyed bourgeoisie of the *Tales* to accept any humble place assigned to them, in the satire on the corruption rife within the Church, in the ability to ask questions of a kind disallowed by the official faith as to the nature of the providential ordering of the world, in the stress on the qualities of the good ruler. The work is more concerned with ethics than with politics; but the ethical questions it considers are both the timeless ones of fallible human beings living in an unstable world, and those raised by the frightening breakdown of hierarchy and stability in late fourteenth-century England.

W. W. Skeat (*Works of Chaucer* (p. 4 above), iii. 373) calculated the 1387 date out of the need to find a year when a pilgrimage that started on 17 April (see II(B¹)5) would not include a Sunday; but the whole argument rests on an anachronistic notion of realism.

Barbara W. Tuchman, *A Distant Mirror: The Calamitous Fourteenth Century* (New York, 1978), is the most telling study of late fourteenth-century Western Europe.

Anthony Tuck, *Richard II and the English Nobility* (London, 1973), gives a detailed account of the political events of the period.

Paul Strohm, *Social Chaucer* (Cambridge, Mass., 1989), analyses Chaucer's social and political affiliations, and the *Tales* as a model of contemporary social diversity.

Text

There are fifty-five surviving manuscripts that appear once to have contained the complete *Tales*, though some of them are now damaged. A further twenty-eight contain one or more individual tales, or survive in such fragmentary form that it is impossible to tell whether the remaining leaves once belonged to a manuscript of the whole work or to a copy of a single tale.

The texts vary in multitudinous small details and some major ones, and attempts to reconstruct Chaucer's original, or the copy of his work that served as archetype for the earliest manuscripts, have met with only partial success. Some variants are due to miscopying, but the nature of others suggests that Chaucer himself was still in the process of making alterations, additions, and excisions to his work. Furthermore, it is not known whether he had a final arrangement in mind for the order of the tales, and so whether any of the extant manuscripts preserve an order that has any authorial justification. There is however more consistency among the manuscripts than this might suggest. They all start with the General Prologue and end with the Parson, and most of the tales move around in constant groups, or 'Fragments'. There are two widespread orders for them, differentiated only by the different places assigned to Fragment VIII(G). The one most widely adopted in modern editions, and which I use in this book, is as follows:

Fragment I(A)	General Prologue, Knight, Miller, Reeve, Cook
Fragment II(B¹)	Man of Law
Fragment III(D)	Wife, Friar, Summoner
Fragment IV(E)	Clerk, Merchant
Fragment V(F)	Squire, Franklin
Fragment VI(C)	Physician, Pardoner
Fragment VII(B²)	Shipman, Prioress, *Sir Thopas*, *Melibee*, Monk, Nun's Priest
Fragment VIII(G)	Second Nun, Canon's Yeoman
Fragment IX(H)	Manciple
Fragment X(I)	Parson

In the alternative manuscript ordering, Fragment VIII(G) appears before VI(C), to give an order Second Nun–Canon's Yeoman–Physician–Pardoner. Fragments I and II (A and B¹) appear together in almost all manuscripts; Fragments VI and VII (C and B²) and IX and X (H and I) also consistently follow each other. By contrast, Fragments IV and V (E and F), of Clerk–Merchant–Squire–Franklin, are frequently broken up, and the four tales are often separated. The positions of these four tales and of the wandering fragments are discussed in more detail in the course of this book. There is no manuscript justification for the Victorian partiality, preserved in some more recent editions, for moving Fragment VII (B²) forward to follow the Man of Law's Tale.

The earliest extant manuscript is preserved in the National Library of Wales, MS Peniarth 392 D, known as 'Hengwrt'. This was copied at about the time of Chaucer's death, and it contains the best text—the nearest, that is, to what Chaucer apparently wrote. The scribe, however, appears to have received his copy in bits and pieces; his attempts to order it are very much an *ad hoc* affair, and they have been rendered still worse by later misbinding. The order in which the tales appear is therefore disjointed to an unusual degree. Some of the copy for the *Tales* appears never to have reached his hands at all: most notably, the Merchant's Prologue and the entire episode of the Canon's Yeoman are both lacking. Even here, however, most of the constant groups appear—Fragment I(A), III(D), VI–VII(C–B²), IX–X(H–I).

It was probably the same scribe who not long afterwards wrote the most beautiful of the extant manuscripts, the Ellesmere (Ellesmere 26.C.9 in the Huntington Library, San Marino, California). This is so finished and elegant a work that later editors were naturally inclined to use it as a base text, although some of its readings are inferior to those of the battered Hengwrt. It is the earliest manuscript to contain the tales in the order listed above, which may well not be Chaucer's own but which does make good sense.

I have tried not to complicate this book by too many manuscript sigla: scholars of Chaucer's text will in any case require far more detail than I can give here. I therefore refer only to a few manuscripts apart from Hengwrt and Ellesmere: two from the Cambridge University Library, Dd.4.24, whose scribe had some intriguingly eccentric moments, and Gg.4.27, the earliest 'complete works' of Chaucer; and one from Corpus Christi College Oxford, MS 198, known as Corpus. All belong to the early years of the fifteenth century.

A bibliography of editions and facsimiles of the *Tales* that I have used is given on pp. 3–4 above. Manly and Rickert's *The Text of the Canterbury Tales* remains the indispensable work of reference on textual variants, although its conclusions are increasingly called into question (see in particular George Kane's critique in Paul G. Ruggiers (ed.), *Editing Chaucer: The Great Tradition* (Norman, Okla., 1984), ch. 11) Ralph Hanna III summarizes the present state of scholarship in his textual notes to Benson's 'Robinson 3'.

The 'Paleographical Introduction' by A. I. Doyle and M. B. Parkes to Ruggiers's facsimile of
   Hengwrt is essential reading on the problems of establishing the text of the *Tales*.
N. F. Blake has argued on a number of occasions for Hengwrt as the sole authority for
   Chaucer's text: see in particular *The Textual Tradition of the Canterbury Tales* (London,
   1985). This book is a useful source of information on the earliest manuscripts, but his main
   argument has not stood up to detailed criticism.
Larry D. Benson, 'The Order of the Canterbury Tales', *SAC* 3 (1981), 77–120, argues that
   both the principal orders for the *Tales* found in the manuscripts are Chaucer's, and that
   Ellesmere represents his final arrangement.

Genre

The *Canterbury Tales* is a collection of stories—and if that seems too loose a
term to serve as a generic category, the number of other story-collections
known in the fourteenth century, and the forms they took, suggest that it
was sufficiently familiar as a literary kind to raise certain audience
expectations in the same way as any other genre. It is therefore an
instructive definition, for Chaucer's work is extensively and precisely
different from the other collections.

   The differences lie in three principal areas: the kind of frame narrative he
uses, with multiple tellers of different outlook and social class; connected
with that, the variety of the stories told; and the lack of any clear moral
framework. The simplest story-collections were ragbags of exempla for use
by preachers, relentlessly moral, with no inherent ordering principle
(though they sometimes arranged their stories alphabetically by moral point
made), and no variation of genre or voice. Others collected stories of a
particular genre, such as saints' lives, or beast-fables; Chaucer's own *Legend
of Good Women* and Monk's Tale are of this sort, and demonstrate clearly
the limitations of such a kind. Even the most highly developed frame
narratives of the Middle Ages, such as Boccaccio's *Decameron*, show little of
Chaucer's rigorous generic and stylistic variation; and in the *Decameron*
itself, each day's tales are confined (at least in theory) to a single theme. The
primary expectations of story-collections were that they would be moral,
and that they would be reasonable homogeneous. Chaucer provides no
moral pattern or framework, and the individual tales are often strongly
resistant to providing one. He also exploits a generic and poetic range for the
individual tales that is unparalleled in any other collection. It comes close to
offering a *distinctio*, a normative array, of all the literary forms current in the
late Middle Ages.

   Such variety makes unprecedentedly high demands for any method of
articulating the stories. Chaucer's answer takes two forms, both again
without parallel: the pilgrims, and the competition. The frame story of the
pilgrimage allows him to assemble a mixture of people to match the variety

of the tales. The setting of the competition encourages the reader to compare the tales, regardless of their differences, and so invites recognition of subtler details of association. It also insists on the importance of aesthetic as well as exemplary or didactic values—'tales of best sentence and moost solaas' (I(A) 798). The competition element and the variety of the tales go together: Chaucer can prove his poetic mastery by writing the best romance, the best beast-fable, the best saint's life.

On story-collections, see Piero Boitani, *English Medieval Narrative in the Thirteenth and Fourteenth Centuries*, trans. Joan Krakover Hall (Cambridge, 1982), ch. 5, and Helen Cooper, *The Structure of the Canterbury Tales* (London and Athens, Ga., 1983), ch. 1.
On the *Tales* as *distinctio*, see Judson Boyce Allen and Theresa Anne Moritz, *A Distinction of Stories: The Medieval Unity of Chaucer's Fair Chain of Narratives for Canterbury* (Columbus, Ohio, 1981).

Sources and Analogues

That Chaucer's scheme for the *Tales* is unprecedented qualifies what one can hope to find in the way of sources and analogues for the work as a whole. He had many models to draw on if he had wished, from the Classical, in the shape of Ovid's *Metamorphoses* (another unusually structured collection, where the tales lead into each other without any formal framing device), to the contemporary, in John Gower's *Confessio amantis*. He does indeed borrow material from these, but he does not copy the form of either. Similarly, he borrows individual tales from collections of saints' lives, Miracles of the Virgin, and beast-fables, but his own total scheme is very different. Boccaccio's *Decameron*, written some forty years before Chaucer started on the *Tales*, provides the closest parallel, and a quarter of the tales in Chaucer's collection have analogues in Boccaccio's work. Most of these, however, have closer analogues, or known sources, elsewhere. If Chaucer knew the *Decameron* at all, it was probably through reading or hearing some of it while he was visiting Italy; there is no evidence that he had access to it while he was writing, and even a memorial knowledge falls short of proof. There is no known model for the setting of a story-collection within a pilgrimage, nor need there be. That Chaucer did so often rework existing stories—as all writers did from Homer to Milton and beyond—can encourage too much of a belief that he never made anything up. It was a familiar literary convention, probably reflecting fact, that pilgrims did tell stories on the road. It was Chaucer who saw the potential in the idea.

Each tale has its own individual sources or analogues, and these are discussed separately in the course of this book. There was in addition an assortment of works, ranging from the Bible to the *Roman de la rose*, to which he had frequent recourse in the writing of the *Tales*, and which are described in the *Bibliography of recurrent sources and analogues* given below. These works provide him with a store of exemplary tales, plots, aphorisms, miscellaneous information, ways of presenting character, arguments, and allusions, and on occasion some sublime poetry.

A major problem in source studies of the *Tales* is how much Chaucer could have read. By the most conservative estimates, the quantities were impressive. Manuscripts are not however easy reading; and he was occupied at court or in demanding administrative posts throughout much or all his adult life. Reading late into the evenings, as he describes himself doing in the *House of Fame*, could not have enabled him to cover a fraction of the works he has been credited with knowing; nor, in many cases, did he have any obvious means of access to manuscripts of them. Some of his knowledge of more obscure authors may have come by way of *florilegia*, anthologies of famous or worthy extracts from authoritative works. He almost certainly worked like any modern scholar or writer, asking friends with more specialized information about matters of immediate interest to him (I suspect—it is by nature unprovable—that the golden nets used by Nero for fishing, VII. 2475/B². 3665, came to him at second hand from some such source). Many *sententiae*, and many biblical quotations, came to him by way of other works that cited them; more may have been culled from sermons. Establishing a written source is therefore not the same as claiming that Chaucer had read the work in question. Even less does it mean that he had the book open in front of him as he wrote: he will have worked with a copytext when producing a translation, but he clearly also had an exceptional memory for words—for phrases, cadences, maxims, and stories. This in turn raises a further problem, because of the frequency with which medieval works, and especially moral and didactic ones, repeat the same adages and use the same examples. It is often difficult to be sure from which of various works Chaucer might have derived an idea, or whether he is conflating several similar formulations.

I have tried to tackle these problems by citing, wherever possible, works that can be proved to have been known to Chaucer. This has meant treating the whole scholarly literature on his sources with some scepticism. I could not have written this book without it; but a not inconsiderable proportion of all the works written before 1400, and a handful written later, have been proposed at one time or another as his sources. I have in the course of writing drawn up a mental list of books that Chaucer need not have read: a list that includes the entire works of St Augustine, a generous number of the works of Boccaccio and Ovid, all but one of the moralizations of the *Metamorphoses*, Deschamps's *Miroir de mariage*, the *Lamentations* of Matheolus, and several other staple favourites of source scholars, amounting in all to some thousands of pages of prose and over a hundred thousand lines of poetry. I may well be wrong: it is, after all, almost impossible to prove a lack of knowledge. Given the present state of scholarship, however, they seem to me to be unnecessary hypotheses.

Thomas R. Lounsbury was concerned as long ago as 1892 at the amount of learning credited to Chaucer—that 'he not only knew everything, but he also knew it very well'. His survey of the 'The Learning of Chaucer' remains a very useful introduction to the whole subject (in his *Studies in Chaucer* (repr. New York, 1962), ii. 169–426).

Chaucer Source and Analogue Criticism: A Cross-referenced Guide, compiled by Lynn King Morris (New York and London, 1985), provides the scholarly bibliography on the universal knowledge attributed to Chaucer.

Anthologies of Sources

W. F. Bryan and Germaine Dempster (eds.), *Sources and Analogues of Chaucer's Canterbury Tales* (1941, repr. New York, 1958) (henceforth *Sources and Analogues*), is the standard collection of source material for individual tales. It is however outdated in some instances, most notably in its opening section on 'The Literary Framework of the Canterbury Tales' by R. A. Pratt and Karl Young. Their advocacy of the *Novelle* of Giovanni Sercambi as Chaucer's model for the *Tales* is certainly wrong, as Sercambi's work was not completed until about the time of Chaucer's death: see Luciano Rossi (ed.), *Giovanni Sercambi: Il novelliere* (Rome, 1976), i. xix–xx.

F. J. Furnivall, Edmund Brock, and W. A. Clouston (eds.), *Originals and Analogues of Some of Chaucer's Canterbury Tales* (London: Chaucer Society, 1872–7), has been largely superseded by *Sources and Analogues* but contains some useful additional material.

Larry D. Benson and Theodore M. Andersson (eds.), *The Literary Context of Chaucer's Fabliaux* (Indianapolis and New York, 1971), is a useful anthology of analogues to Chaucer's fabliaux, with translations.

Robert P. Miller (ed.), *Chaucer: Sources and Backgrounds* (New York, 1977), collects together medieval writings on a generous range of subjects related to the *Tales* and Chaucer's other works.

Bibliography of recurrent sources and analogues

Bersuire: Pierre Bersuire (died *c*.1362) wrote a prose Latin commentary on Ovid's *Metamorphoses*, the *Ovidius moralizatus*, as the fifteenth book of his encyclopaedic *Reductium morale*. The first chapter of this, the *De formis figurisque deorum*, on the iconography of the pagan gods, was used by Chaucer in the Knight's and Manciple's, and probably also the Merchant's, Tales. The version he knew was the revision made in the 1350s; it is edited by J. Engels as *Werkmateriaal* 3 of the Instituut voor Laat Latijn der Rijksuniversiteit Utrecht (1966) under the title of *Petrus Berchorius, Reductium morale Liber XV: Ovidius moralizatus cap. i, De formis figurisque deorum*.

Bible: There is scarcely a single tale that does not make some reference to the Bible. Among the most significant or extensive allusions are those of the Miller's and Man of Law's Tales, the Wife of Bath's Prologue, the Friar's, Summoner's, Clerk's, and Merchant's Tales, the Pardoner's Prologue and Tale, the Prioress's Tale, *Melibee*, and the Monk's, Nun's Priest's, and Parson's Tales. The extent of Chaucer's direct debt to the Vulgate is however a matter of debate. Most of his undisputed biblical references came to him embedded in other texts, and he takes especial care in translating those.

Of the many editions of the Vulgate, the *Biblia sacra iuxta vulgatam versionem*, ed. Robertus Weber and others (2 vols., 2nd edn., Stuttgart, 1975), is especially useful in containing some variants, Jerome's prologues, and the Apocrypha. I have used the Douai translation.

On Chaucer's use of the Bible, see in particular W. Meredith Thompson, 'Chaucer's Translation of the Bible', in Norman Davis and C. L. Wrenn (eds.), *English and Medieval Studies presented to J. R. R. Tolkien* (London, 1962), pp. 183–99; and three essays in David Lyle Jeffrey (ed.), *Chaucer and Scriptural Tradition* (Ottawa, 1984): Chauncey Wood, 'Artistic Intention and Chaucer's Use of Scriptural Allusion' (pp. 35–46); Edmund Reiss, 'Biblical Parody: Chaucer's "Distortions" of Scripture' (pp. 47–61); and Lawrence Besserman, '*Glosynge is a Glorious Thyng*: Chaucer's Biblical Exegesis' (pp. 65–73). All such essays are in part a response to D. W. Robertson, jun., *A Preface to Chaucer: Studies in Medieval Perspectives* (Princeton, 1962). A full bibliography is given by Lawrence Besserman, *Chaucer and the Bible* (New York, 1988).

Boccaccio, Dante, and Petrarch: Chaucer was the first English poet to profit from the writings of the great fourteenth-century Italians. A useful collection of essays on their influence is Piero Boitani (ed.), *Chaucer and the Italian Trecento* (Cambridge, 1983). See also Mario Praz, 'Chaucer and the Great Italian Writers of the Trecento', *Monthly Criterion*, 6 (1927), 18–39, 131–57, 238–42.

Boccaccio: The *Decameron* is a possible model for the whole *Canterbury Tales*, and in addition provides analogues to a number of Chaucer's stories (the Reeve's, Clerk's, Merchant's, Franklin's, and Shipman's; it also contains more distant analogues to the Man of Law's Tale and the Pardoner's Prologue, and motifs similar to the Miller's Tale).

I have used the edition by Enrico Bianchi, Carlo Salinari, and Natalino Sapegno, *Decamerone, Filocolo, Ameto, Fiammetta* (La letteratura italiana 8, Milan, 1952); and the translation by G. H. McWilliam, *Decameron* (Harmondsworth, 1972).

For a discussion of Chaucer's knowledge of the work, see Donald McGrady, 'Chaucer and the *Decameron* Reconsidered', *ChR* 12 (1977–8), 1–26.

Chaucer also used the *Teseida* in the Knight's Tale; the *De claris mulieribus* and, almost certainly, the *De casibus* in the Monk's Tale; and possibly the *Filocolo* in the Franklin's Tale. He must have known either the *Decameron* or the *Filocolo*, but not necessarily both, and the evidence for the *Decameron* is stronger (parallels claimed between the *Filocolo* and other works of Chaucer's tend to be of minor significance).

Boethius: The *Consolation of Philosophy* of Boethius (d. 524), the 'Boece' whom Chaucer translated, is the philosophical work used most extensively in the *Tales*, most notably in the Knight's, Franklin's, and Monk's Tales. There are further possible allusions in the Manciple's and Squire's Tales.

It is edited by H. F. Stewart, *The Theological Tractates and the Consolation of Philosophy* (Loeb Classical Library, London and Cambridge, Mass., 1918, and reprints to 1968), with the delightful 1609 translation of 'I.T.'; the new edition of 1973 substitutes a modern translation by S. J. Tester.

Bromyard: The English Dominican John Bromyard composed his encyclopaedic handbook for preachers, the *Summa praedicantium*, some time before 1354, and its material was widely used in sermons in the later part of the century. It provides a close analogue, possibly a source, for the story of the cock and the fox in the Nun's Priest's Tale. The nearest other similarities to the *Summa* shown in the *Tales*—the affinity between the rapacious and the devil that is developed in the Friar's Tale, material on the damnation of unjust judges that bears on the Physician's Tale—occur just before and after the fable. It is therefore possible that Chaucer had looked at a couple of consecutive pages of a manuscript, or that he had heard sermons that drew on adjacent passages from this section. Material from other sermon handbooks appears in the Manciple's Tale.

The *Summa* was frequently printed in the sixteenth and seventeenth centuries. I have used the edition printed in Venice in 1585; the numbering system for the work is consistent through all editions.

Dante: The *Divine Comedy* provided the Monk's tragedy of Ugolino, inspired the Prioress's and Second Nun's Prologues, and occasionally contributes to phrasing elsewhere, notably in the Knight's Tale, and possibly in the Nun's Priest's.

A useful edition, with generous notes and a parallel translation, is that of Charles S. Singleton, *The Divine Comedy of Dante Alighieri* (3 vols., Princeton, 1970–5). Howard H. Schless, *Chaucer and Dante: A Revaluation* (Norman, Okla., 1984), is a collection and critique of all the passages in Chaucer proposed as showing influence from Dante.

Chaucer also used the Fourth Tractate of the *Convivio* in the Wife of Bath's Tale, and possibly in the Knight's Tale and elsewhere.

Distichs of Cato: This collection of metrical aphorisms was probably compiled (not by Cato) *c*. AD 200. It was widely known through its use as a school textbook, and a handful of other works came to be associated with it. Chaucer borrows from this group of writings on numerous occasions, including the Miller's Prologue and Tale, the Wife's Prologue, the Merchant's, Canon's Yeoman's and Manciple's Tales, and at second hand in *Melibee*. The nature of the work made omission and augmentation particularly easy, and the work also acquired a series of glosses; the precise form in which Chaucer knew it is not known.

A convenient edition with parallel translation is in *Minor Latin Poets*, ed. and trans. J. Wight Duff and Arnold M. Duff (Loeb Classical Library, rev. edn., London and Cambridge, Mass., 1935). A fuller edition is that of Marcus Boas and Henricus Johannes Botschuyver, *Disticha Catonis* (Amsterdam, 1952).

The parallels with the *Tales* are collected and discussed by Richard Hazelton, 'Chaucer and Cato', *Speculum*, 35 (1960), 357–80. Hazelton also points out striking similarities of phrasing between some of Chaucer's aphorisms and a Middle English translation of the work.

Gower: John Gower was an older contemporary of Chaucer's, and his friend; but the apparent allusions to him in the *Tales*, in the Man of Law's Prologue and the Manciple's Tale, are more teasing than the warm respect shown in the dedication to him of *Troilus and Criseyde*. Chaucer shows some signs of acquaintance with his works in Latin (the *Vox clamantis*, largely about the Peasants' Revolt) and French (the *Mirour de l'omme*), as well as the English *Confessio amantis*. The *Vox* and the *Mirour* both contain passages describing the estates of society, which may have contributed to the General Prologue; the *Vox* may also lie behind a thought association in the Nun's Priest's Tale and an aphorism in the Manciple's. Four of Gower's stories from the *Confessio* also appear in the *Tales*, as the tales of the Man of Law, the Wife of Bath, the Physician, and the Manciple; but the question of which poet is sometimes indebted to the other, or how far they worked independently, is probably unanswerable.

For the *Confessio*, see *The English Works of John Gower*, ed. G. C. Macaulay (2 vols., EETS ES 81–2, 1900–1); the *Mirour* and the *Vox clamantis* appear in vols. i and iv of his *Complete Works of John Gower* (Oxford, 1899–1902). The *Vox* is translated by Eric W. Stockton, *The Major Latin Works of John Gower* (Seattle, 1962).

Innocent III: According to the Prologue to the *Legend of Good Women* (G. 414–15), Chaucer translated the *De miseria* of the future pope Innocent III (d. 1216) as 'Of the Wreched Engendrynge of Mankynde'. His translation is lost, but he draws on the treatise in the Man of Law's Prologue and Tale, the Pardoner's Tale, and possibly also the Monk's and Nun's Priest's Tales.

It is edited and translated by Robert E. Lewis, *Lotario dei Segni (Pope Innocent III): De miseria condicionis humane* (Chaucer Library, Athens, Ga., 1987).

Jerome: Jerome (d. *c*.420) wrote his polemic *Adversus Jovinianum* in response to an opponent who had dared to suggest that chastity and marriage were of equal value. It is in fact less theological than antifeminist— as is demonstrated by his inclusion of a vivid description of the bad habits of wives translated from the pagan Greek author Theophrastus, and preserved only here. The work was also used by Jean de Meun in his continuation of the *Roman de la rose*. Jerome and Theophrastus between them furnish Chaucer with much of the material for the Wife of Bath's Prologue, with a handful of *sententiae* in the other tales of Fragments III–V(D–F), notably the Friar's, Summoner's, and Franklin's, and with some details of the Nun's Priest's.

The Latin text is in vol. xxiii of the *Patrologia latina*, ed. J. P. Migne (Paris, 1845), cols. 211 ff,; there is a translation in the *Library of the Nicene and Post-Nicene Christian Fathers*, 2nd ser., vol. vi (Oxford and New York, 1893).

John of Salisbury: The magisterial *Policraticus* of John of Salisbury (d. 1180) is used in the Pardoner's Tale, the Wife of Bath's Prologue, and possibly for the description of the Clerk. It is edited by Clemens C. I. Webb, *Ioannis Saresberiensis episcopi Carnotensis Policratici* (2 vols., London, 1909). There are complementary translations of different parts of the work by John Dickinson, *The Statesman's Book of John of Salisbury* (New York, 1927, repr. 1963), and Joseph B. Pike, *Frivolities of Courtiers and Footprints of Philosophers* (Minneapolis and London, 1938).

Liturgy: Chaucer's debt to the liturgy is apparent in a number of tales, most often in religious contexts (in the Man of Law's, Prioress's and Second Nun's Tales) but occasionally elsewhere (such as in the Merchant's). Liturgical uses were not uniform in fourteenth-century England, though the use of the Sarum Missal was probably familiar to Chaucer. The most extensive modern study is Beverley Boyd's *Chaucer and the Liturgy* (Philadelphia, 1967); this is supplemented by a number of source analyses listed separately for the various tales.

For an edition of the Sarum Use based on early printed texts, see A. Jefferies Collins (ed.), *Manuale ad usum percelebris ecclesie Sarisburiensis* (Henry Bradshaw Soc. xci, Chichester, 1960).

Ovid: The *Metamorphoses* is given a mention by name in the Introduction to the Man of Law's Tale, in a context that indicates its significance as a model for the whole story-collection. The work supplies the plot of the Manciple's Tale, the basic story of Midas for the Wife of Bath, some material for the Monk's tragedies, and some of the details of the gods in the Knight's Tale; and it is a constant source for mythological allusion. A convenient modern edition with translation is that by Frank Justus Miller (2 vols., Loeb Classical Library, London and Cambridge, Mass., 1916). Of Ovid's other works, Chaucer may have known only the *Heroides* at first hand.

The *Metamorphoses* received the attention of a number of commentators and glossators in the Middle Ages. The extent of Chaucer's debt to these has probably been overestimated, but his debt to one of them, Pierre Bersuire, is evident in the *Tales* (see the entry for Bersuire above).

The evidence for Chaucer's use of the *Metamorphoses* and other Ovidian works is set out by Richard L. Hoffman, *Ovid and the Canterbury Tales* (Philadelphia, 1966). Allen and Moritz, in *Distinction*, further argue that the tales reflect the four divisions made by medieval commentators of the stories in the *Metamorphoses*. A more general study, which also argues against Chaucer's knowledge of the French octosyllabic *Ovide moralisé*, is Helen Cooper's 'Chaucer and Ovid: A Question of Authority', in C. A. Martindale (ed.), *Ovid Renewed* (Cambridge, 1988), pp. 71–81 and 264.

Roman de la rose: Whether or not Chaucer ever translated the entire *Roman de la rose*, as his comments appear to suggest (see *Legend of Good Women* G 254–60), he certainly knew it very thoroughly indeed, and its influence is apparent in almost every one of the tales. The first section, written by Guillaume de Lorris c. 1230, survives in part in Chaucer's translation (Fragment A of the Middle English *Romaunt of the Rose* being fairly certainly his); its influence is apparent in various ways in the General Prologue, the Knight's and Merchant's Tales, and possibly the Second Nun's Prologue. The poem was continued, at great length, some fifty years later by Jean de Meun, and the borrowings from this section in the *Tales* are still more extensive. The Wife of Bath would be an impossibility in her present form without Jean de Meun, and the Friar and Pardoner might have turned out somewhat differently. Two further sections contribute especially generously: the Lover's Friend's speech on wives is ransacked for the Wife's Prologue, the Merchant's Tale, probably the Shipman's and Manciple's, and, from a different part of it, the Franklin's;

and Reason's speech to the Lover provides the plot of the Physician's Tale, the idea and some of the material for the Monk's, a suggestion for the end of the Pardoner's, and possibly something for the Manciple's. Various images and aphorisms in the *Tales* also derive from the *Roman*.

I quote from the convenient edition by Daniel Poirion (Paris, 1974), which preserves the numbering of the scholarly edition by Ernest Langlois (5 vols., SATF, Paris, 1914–24; repr. New York, 1965). There are complete translations by Charles Dahlberg (Princeton, 1971) and, in a freer version, by Harry W. Robbins (New York, 1962).

Valerius Maximus: The 'nine books of memorable deeds and sayings', the *Factorum et dictorum memorabilium libri novem*, was put together by the Roman Valerius Maximus *c.* AD 35. It is a collection of short exemplary stories, grouped by theme, with each theme illustrated by examples drawn from within Rome and from outside it. The reading of the Wife of Bath's fifth husband includes Valerius Maximus; Chaucer may have misattributed Walter Map's *Epistola Valerii* to the same author. The work probably also contributes to the Monk's and Nun's Priest's Tales.

Editions are scarce; I have used that of Carolus Kempf, *Valerii Maximi factorum et dictorum memorabilium libri novem* (Bibliotheca Teubeneriana, Leipzig, 1888; repr. Stuttgart, 1966).

Vincent of Beauvais: One way to solve the problem presented by the apparent width of Chaucer's reading would be to find an encyclopaedia that included most of his knowledge. The three-part *Speculum maius* of Vincent of Beauvais has been proposed as such a work, principally by Pauline Aiken in a series of articles on the learning of the Knight's, Friar's, Monk's, Nun's Priest's, and Canon's Yeoman's Tales; the more important of these articles are cited in the source bibliographies for individual tales. Although Chaucer used the historical section of Vincent's work in the *Legend of Good Women*, and mentions it by name in the Prologue (G. 307), the arguments fall short of decisive proof so far as the *Tales* are concerned.

The *Speculum* is printed as the *Speculum quadruplex, sive speculum maius: Naturale, doctrinale, morale, historiale* (Douai, 1624; facsimile reprint, Graz, 1964–5). The 'Speculum morale' is in fact probably a later compilation, and did not form part of manuscript copies of Vincent's own work.

Structure

The basic structure of the *Canterbury Tales* is linear, like the road to Canterbury itself: one story succeeds another. There is, however, a great deal more going on in the work than a mere succession of tales. The care with which Chaucer arranged them, the evidence for revisions of the arrangement, and the more extensive evidence of final decisions as to arrangement still having to be made show how much the order matters. When Chaucer places tales together, he does so for more than casual reasons. The ideas of the pilgrimage and the story-competition provide a logic for one story to succeed another, but not for the arrangement of particular tales. The variety of the stories means that the collection runs a greater risk than most of flying apart.

Chaucer overcomes this in various ways. In contrast to the prologues to most collections, the General Prologue does not directly introduce the kind of stories to be told, but the people who will tell them: people who are again defined by variety, to constitute something like a professional and moral cross-section of society, from the gentry to the peasants, the ideal Parson to the blackguard Summoner. The Host seems at the start to have some hopes of imposing a hierarchical order on the tale-telling—'were it by aventure, or sort, or cas' he manages to arrange for the Knight to begin. But Harry Bailly's plans, and any expectations raised in the audience by opening with the highest ranking of the pilgrims, are rapidly foiled by Chaucer. The Miller's interruption substitutes a very different principle from hierarchy for articulating the tales: dramatic interplay between characters who are not going to stay humbly in their social place, and literary interplay between adjacent tales. As the tales accumulate, a further principle develops, whereby similar themes, ideas, and plot motifs can be taken up by tales at some distance from each other. Chaucer both selects and adapts stories to fit with these larger concerns; a collection of the tales' sources would show few of the centripetal qualities that his own versions acquire. The variety of the tales is turned to advantage in the process of integration, as recurring themes and motifs appear in new and unexpected lights and patterns.

The effect is kaleidoscopic, both in the continued defamiliarization of familiar elements, and in the absence of any consistent line of development. One tale may follow from its predecessor and cue its sequel, as the Miller's Tale connects the Knight's and the Reeve's, but it does not provide an otherwise 'missing link' in the evolutionary sense. The lack of a fixed order for the tales of the middle of the work indicates Chaucer's reluctance to impose any single scheme for arranging the stories, including the pilgrimage itself. He mentions few place names, gives no details of stopping-places on the way, and generally shows little interest in giving the journey any fictional development. The links between the stories are used much more to comment on the tales—or for the related phenomenon of the pilgrims' comments on each other—than to give any topographical or physical background. The emphasis again falls on the literary nature of the work, not on its verisimilitude as an account of a journey to Canterbury.

The scribes themselves devised various methods of imposing an ordonnance lacking in Chaucer's text, or of explaining its lack. A number of manuscripts, including Ellesmere, describe Chaucer as the compiler of the work, as if it were an anthology or a miscellany. Corpus numbers the tales, as if they were chapters (capituli) of a single, more unified work. Others treat the links rigorously as prologues, to the point where the General Prologue itself can be described as the Prologue to the Knight's Tale; the function of some of the links in looking as much backwards as forwards is rationalized into a more familiar structural form.

Charles A. Owen, *Pilgrimage and Storytelling in the Canterbury Tales: The Dialectic of 'Ernest' and 'Game'* (Norman, Okla., 1977), argues that the existing tales should be organized into the framework of an outward and return journey.

Samuel Schuman, 'The Link Mechanism in the *Canterbury Tales*', ChR 20 (1985–6), 200–6, notes Chaucer's tendency to use a middle term—whether a unit of syntax, or a portrait, or a tale—to co-ordinate the otherwise unrelated terms on each side of it.

A. I. Doyle and M. B. Parkes, 'The Production of Copies of the *Canterbury Tales* and the *Confessio amantis* in the Early Fifteenth Century' (in M. B. Parkes and Andrew G. Watson (eds.), *Medieval Scribes, Manuscripts and Libraries: Essays Presented to N. R. Ker* (London, 1978), pp. 163–210), discuss scribal attempts to organize the *Tales* and the significance of the *compilatio* interpretation.

Themes

The themes, motifs, and ideas that hold the *Tales* together take abundant forms. Many of them are first announced in the story that heads the series, the Knight's: questions about Fortune and Providence; the suffering of the innocent; what men or women most desire; the choices they make, and the *entente* behind those choices; the nature of friendship, love, the good ruler, and good living. The most famous of the themes that run across several tales, women's role in marriage, is introduced later; but it is a part of a larger theme of sexual love and the role of women in the world that is sounded in one way or another in most of the stories and many of the links.

That the Knight's Tale is followed by the Miller's, in disregard of social hierarchy or poetic consistency, announces one of the key themes and methods of the *Tales*: that the work will encompass not only official ideals, the acknowledged patterns by which people were supposed to guide their lives and which poets supposedly existed to urge and celebrate, but also the joyful rebellion against such conventional pieties and orthodox rules of behaviour. The contrast is that which critics such as Mikhail Bakhtin and Derek Brewer have spoken of in terms of the ordered and the grotesque, Lent and Carnival, officially approved culture and its unofficial, riotous, and high-spirited underside. The *Canterbury Tales* is by no means the only medieval work to bring contrasting ideologies into sharp juxtaposition. A work such as the *Dialogue of Solomon and Marcolphus*, known throughout medieval Europe in Latin and a number of vernacular translations, is a pithy encapsulation of such contrasts, in a series of one-liners from the wise king and a down-to-earth churl. Its method can be illustrated from a single exchange—of particular relevance to the *Tales* since Chaucer so often quotes Solomon's remarks on women—in the fifteenth-century English translation:

SOLOMON. A good wyf and a fayre is to hir hosbande a pleasure.
MARCOLPHUS. A potfull of mylke must be kept wele from the katte.

The drop in both tone and overt subject in the response—from abstraction to physical availability, from virtuousness to animals—is typical of Chaucer's method in the *Tales*. There is no direct evidence that he knew the *Dialogue* (though it is mentioned by several English writers, including

Lydgate); he was certainly in sympathy with its principles. It is a very short step from Marcolphus'

What thanne shulde [a man] do wyth vij wyves: it is aboven any mannys myght or power. It were bettyr ordeyned that oon woman shulde have vij husbondes,

to the Wife of Bath's

Welcome the sixte, whan that evere he shal,   (III(D) 45)

or to Chauntecleer's difficulties in managing the chief wife of his seven.

The storytelling in Chaucer's work is set up as a competition—a game: and as such, it places itself outside the order of the physical or the moral world to impose its own rules, its own aesthetic. Their participation in the game gives the medley of pilgrims a common interest and purpose alongside that of the pilgrimage. Game and play are closely associated with festivals and feasts; the sense given by the opening of the General Prologue that pilgrimage is a way of celebrating the spring, and the promise of a supper to conclude the competition, become part of this taking time off from the ordinary world. That the *Tales* defines itself as play gives Chaucer a vantage-point outside any of the official readings of human experience. His excuse for taking time off from such orthodoxy is inseparable from the basic conception of the work: 'whoso shal telle a tale after a man' has to be true to his own fiction, to portray the attitudes appropriate to the assorted pilgrims who serve as surrogate poets. He can therefore record impartially the secular idealism of courtesy and chivalry, the ineradicable human addiction to the physical facts of living, and the religious imperative to turn from things of this world to God.

This element of carnival, of play, coexists with a more serious reading of the work, and the world. The *Canterbury Tales* is a work about living, about the choices made in the course of life and their consequences. Every medieval theory of literature stressed such a connection between literature and life. The method of the *Tales* works to distance it from moral concerns; the content of the stories repeatedly insists on the centrality of moral choice. There is no way, however, that such concerns can be directly mediated through language. The word is at best 'cosyn to the werkyng' (IX(H) 210), a relationship at some removes; and the only truth Chaucer claims for the words of the *Tales* is that they accord with the 'dede' of storytelling (I(A) 742), of fictions within a fiction.

The *House of Fame* is a poem about the untrustworthiness of literary authority, of the great authors of the past, which ends by substituting as poetic material the tidings 'of fals and soth compouned' (2108) told by shipmen and pilgrims. The *Canterbury Tales* goes further, to question the stability of language. Medieval linguistic theory was as conscious as our own of the distance between words and what they represent. Discourse is a symbolic representation of reality; but there may be a large gap between the two—the gap indicated by Marcolphus' rewording of Solomon's aphorism on beautiful wives into a cat-and-milk adage that conveys a very different message. Chaucer possesses an acute consciousness of the slipperiness of these processes of representation, and the difficulty of establishing the nature of 'reality' when verbal means of expressing it are so untrustworthy. It is a problem he addresses directly on occasion, most notably in the discussion in the Manciple's Tale on how the choice of words prescribes moral reactions. The whole matter is implicit too in the very nature of the *Tales*. Different genres give different readings of the world: the fabliau scarcely notices the operations of God, the saint's life focuses on those at the expense of physical reality, tracts and sermons insist on prudential or orthodox morality, romances privilege human emotion. Each genre defines its own vocabulary and imagery, its own area of experience, and its way of signifying that experience. The links between the stories build into the work the fact that each listener will interpret the signs offered in different ways. They call attention to the impossibility of writing, or interpreting, with any final authority. The Host and many of the pilgrims take the application of the stories to their own lives very literally indeed: the Host wants his wife to hear about Prudence, the Reeve will take a tale about carpenters as a personal insult. Chaucer is pressing for an interpretation of the *Tales* that is altogether larger—a questioning of the nature of fiction, the nature of language, the relation between the act and the sign.

It is of crucial importance that for Chaucer 'reality' does exist. He is writing within a Christian culture, and he shares its beliefs; the indeterminacy of the *Tales* works within clear limits. A key word for him is *trouthe*, which he uses in a range of senses from human integrity to God (as in his *Balade de bon conseil*). The *Canterbury Tales* may be set up as play, and spend much of its time urging the relative; even the Parson, with his unsparing religious orthodoxy, is still one voice among many. But the relativism is not absolute: the *Tales* never finally advocates moral anarchy. Play takes time out from the ordinary world, it does not abolish it. The relation between words and the world they describe is contingent, and Chaucer is fascinated by the area of uncertainty; he is acutely conscious of areas of experience that the Christian vocabulary and reading of the world do not or will not explain. But he has too that belief in a *trouthe* that ensures an ultimate stability, however little it may be apparent to human eyes. It is the inaccessibility of such an order that gives depth and urgency to his questioning; but the certainty of its existence allows the joy with which he can write of mankind's habit of ignoring it.

On the double culture of the Middle Ages see: Mikhail Bakhtin, *Rabelais and his World*, trans. Hélène Iswolsky (Cambridge, Mass., and London, 1968).

Derek Brewer, *Towards a Chaucerian Poetic* (Sir Israel Gollancz Memorial Lecture, British Academy: London, 1974), repr. in *Chaucer: The Poet as Storyteller* (London, 1984), pp. 54–79.

The Dialogue or Communing between the Wise King Solomon and Marcolphus, ed. E. Gordon Duff (facsimile reprint of 1492 edn., London, 1892); quotations from fos. 4^a, 16^b. The Latin text is edited by W. Benary, *Salomon et Marcolfus* (Heidelberg, 1914). For a discussion, see Maria Corti, 'Models and Antimodels in Medieval Culture', *NLH* 10 (1979), 339–66.

On the significance of play, see Johan Huizinga, *Homo ludens: A Study of the Play Element in Culture* (London, 1949). Although he does not talk specifically about the *Tales*, he stresses the particular importance of play in medieval culture, and much of what he says illuminates many aspects of the work. See also R. A. Lanham, 'Game, Play and High Seriousness in Chaucer's Poetry', *ES* 48 (1967), 1–24.

On language theory in the Middle Ages, see Marcia Colish, *The Mirror of Language: A Study on the Medieval Theory of Knowledge* (rev. edn., Lincoln, Nebr. and London, 1983), and P. B. Taylor, 'Chaucer's *Cosyn to the Dede*', *Speculum*, 57 (1982), 315–27.

Most of the works listed in the General Bibliography, p. 428, contain thematic studies of the *Tales*. A summary of critical approaches is given by Alcuin Blamires, *The Canterbury Tales* (The Critics Debate, London and Atlantic Highlands, NJ, 1987). The following list, arranged in chronological order, is selected to give some indication of the major lines of interpretation offered over the past few decades.

Robert M. Lumiansky, *Of Sondry Folk: The Dramatic Principle in the Canterbury Tales* (Austin, Tex., 1955), treats the pilgrims as real characters (in the manner of Bradley on Shakespeare) and explains the work in terms of their psychologies and past lives.

Ralph Baldwin, *The Unity of the Canterbury Tales* (Anglistica 5, Copenhagen, 1955), argues that the metaphor of man's earthly pilgrimage underlies the work, but he has little to say on the individual tales. (Extracts are reprinted in Richard Schoeck and Jerome Taylor (eds.), *Chaucer Criticism*, i: *The Canterbury Tales* (Notre Dame and London, 1960).)

Charles Muscatine, *Chaucer and the French Tradition* (Berkeley and Los Angeles, 1957), insists on the inseparability of style and meaning, and studies a number of the tales in terms of their stylistic variation.

D. W. Robertson, jun., *A Preface to Chaucer: Studies in Medieval Perspectives* (Princeton, 1962), argues forcefully—and controversially—that all medieval poetry, including Chaucer's, expresses the orthodox truths of Christianity, by way of allegory if not overtly.

Gabriel Josipovici, *The World and the Book* (London, 1971; 2nd edn., 1979) contains a notable section on the *Tales* that stresses the significance of their tonal interplay and the importance of the elements of fictionality and game.

Donald R. Howard, *The Idea of the Canterbury Tales* (Berkeley, Los Angeles, and London, 1976), is currently one of the most influential books on the *Tales*. It treats the work on its own terms rather than as evidence for something else (such as characters or Christian orthodoxy), and so gives generous attention to the multifariousness of the work.

V. A. Kolve, *Chaucer and the Imagery of Narrative: The First Five Canterbury Tales* (Stanford and London, 1984) looks at the iconographic patterns in and behind the tales as a key to their inner meanings.

Carolyn Dinshaw, *Chaucer's Sexual Poetics* (Madison, 1989) offers a powerful feminist reading of selected tales.

Works that offer tale-by-tale studies include the following:

Paul G. Ruggiers, *The Art of the Canterbury Tales* (Madison, and London, 1965).

Trevor Whittock, *A Reading of the Canterbury Tales* (Cambridge, 1968).

Derek Pearsall, *The Canterbury Tales* (London, 1985) (this summarizes current criticism as well as offering new readings).

Works that concentrate on thematic connections between the tales include:
P. M. Kean, *Chaucer and the Making of English Poetry*, ii: *The Art of Narrative* (London and Boston, 1972).
Traugott Lawler, *The One and the Many in the Canterbury Tales* (Hamden, Conn., 1980).
Helen Cooper, *The Structure of the Canterbury Tales* (London and Athens, Ga., 1983).

Style: Language, Rhetoric, and Prosody

It follows from the argument given above that language is of key importance in the *Tales*, not just because Chaucer chooses the medium of words rather than music or painting, but because the work constitutes a critique of language and its functions—in particular, of style. Chaucer's linguistic awareness is remarkable. It shows itself in overt comments on language, in puns and loaded choice of words, in rhetorical figures, and above all in stylistic variety.

Many of the earliest recorded comments on Chaucer's work, from the fifteenth and sixteenth centuries, select his use of language and style for particular praise. It is symptomatic of his varied exploitation of English that many of these comments should contradict each other. In Lydgate's phrase, echoed many times by other writers, Chaucer was 'the first that euer enlumined our language with floures of Rhetorique and Eloquence'. Skelton pointed out a different quality, of simplicity rather than elaboration: the young girl in *Phillip Sparrow* approves of Chaucer because

> His termes were not darke,
> But pleasaunt, easy and playne;
> No worde he wrote in vayne.

Plainness and 'sugarit eloquence' might seem unlikely companions, but both terms are true, and true, moreover, of the same poems. *Troilus and Criseyde* had broken the known limits of what could be accomplished in the English language and definitively established Chaucer's reputation for rhetorical skill; the *Canterbury Tales* consolidated and extended this achievement.

Chaucer was working against the background of an understanding of language that encouraged such diversity of approach. Medieval rhetorical theories recognized and encouraged a range of styles. One scheme, derived from commentaries on Virgil, divided literature into three styles, high, middle, and low, distinguished from each other by density of rhetorical figures, by vocabulary, and by imagery. St Augustine, in the *De doctrina christiana*, describes a different three-style scheme: the majestic persuades, the temperate pleases, and the subdued teaches. A more flexible system for adapting style to the requirements of the moment is summarized in the mnemonic hexameter,

> Quis, quid, cui dicas; cur, quomodo, quando requiras

—style, in other words, should take into account the speaker, subject, audience, purpose, manner, and occasion. All such schemes emphasize the separation of language as a semantic system from the world it describes.

Chaucer does not follow these or any other rhetorical theories with any consistency; his handling of style has much in common with all three. The last of them, the six-point consideration of all the circumstances of speech, would appear to cover most eventualities, but Chaucer's use of fictional narrators and a fictional audience within the *Tales* builds ambiguities into his work from the start: a tale like *Sir Thopas* signifies different things to the pilgrims and to his literal audience; the tale of the three rioters shifts in meaning according to whether it is told by the Pardoner or a more orthodox preacher, and again according to the occasion on which the Pardoner himself tells it, to a congregation in church or as part of his description to the pilgrims of such money-grabbing activities. Throughout the work, Chaucer exploits levels of style with remarkable subtlety, either to reflect the subject, as the Virgilian three-part scheme suggests, or to manipulate audience response, as the Augustinian theory advocates.

The basic principle underlying Chaucer's attitude to style is decorum, appropriateness—what is fitting for narrator, subject, genre, and most of the points mentioned in the hexameter. Some of these, however, are complicated by his use of surrogate (and fallible) speakers; others he manages to sidestep altogether. He avoids any need to fit the *Tales* to a specific audience—the decorum the Host refers to when he speaks of 'heigh style, as whan that men to kynges write' (VI(E) 18)—as the social mixture of the pilgrim audience justifies a stylistic 'hotchpot', to use one of his own terms (VII. 1257/B². 2447). He doubles the need to adapt style to subject and genre by assigning certain literary kinds to different kinds of people: 'cherles tales' for the churls, romances or pious tales for the *gentils*. Each form establishes its own stylistic level. The fitting of style to genre is advocated in a number of rhetorical textbooks including one known of by Chaucer (he parodies it in the Nun's Priest's Tale), the *Poetria nova* of Geoffrey of Vinsauf. What Chaucer practises in the *Tales*, however, goes far beyond the scope of any medieval theory.

The distinctions between stylistic levels in the *Tales* generally depend less on the density of rhetorical figures, though that can be important, than on selection—of figures, of vocabulary, and imagery. Even the fabliaux put into the mouths of the unlearned churls can be stylistic and rhetorical masterpieces. The higher-style tales use a different range of tropes, most notably those that call attention to the methods and processes of narration: rhetorical questions, apostrophes ('O firste moevyng! cruell firmament . . .', II(B¹) 295), *occupationes* ('. . . shal nat be toold for me' introducing a lengthy account, I(A) 2924), and all kinds of first-person comments on the structure, action, or import of a story. The stylistic level of the various tales is defined equally by different ranges of imagery and similitude. The images of the higher-style tales tend to the exalted or exotic or symbolic—angels or lions or figurative lambs. The imagery of the fabliaux draws on the commonplace or domestic or subhuman—mice or ducks or leeks. Morning is heralded in the romances by the lark, in the fabliaux by the cock. The local and contemporary settings of the fabliaux encourage such differentiation, and Chaucer exploits it to the full: neither the leopard in the Knight's Tale nor the cat that is shoved off a bench in the Summoner's Tale is essential to the story, but they help to define the tonal level.

Differences in vocabulary can be equally marked. High-style vocabulary has a larger proportion of Romance-derived words, often polysyllabic, which may be required for the greater philosophic reach of many of these tales. Low-style tales make more use of Germanic words and concentrate on the immediate facts of the narrative. The same concept may therefore take different verbal forms according to the speaker: to the *gentils*, the pilgrims form a 'compaignye', to the lower-class characters, a 'route'. The Manciple is given an excursus on the moral identity of 'lady' and 'wenche' (IX(H) 205–22); Chaucer never uses 'wenche' in a courtly context, nor 'lady' in any of the churls' tales. A more subtle effect can come from contrasting uses of the same word, where what in the high style is an abstract concept—*pitee* or *trouthe*—is given a low-style pragmatic sense. In the Merchant's Tale, 'pitee' to May means sex with Damian; in the Canon's Yeoman's, 'trouthe' is a cash contract.

Differences of this kind are very marked in the *Tales*, but they do not follow rank or speaker or literary genre in any schematic way. There is only one tale where the lexical register is completely consistent, and that is *Sir Thopas*, where a specialized vocabulary is used as parody, to devalue the concepts it expresses. Chaucer is much more likely to vary style within the tales, sometimes with dazzling or deeply unsettling effect: the Merchant's and Nun's Priest's Tales are the most striking examples. The Knight's Tale likewise interweaves its spacious rhetoric with passages of unsparing directness.

In the *Tales*, Chaucer pushes to new limits all the linguistic and many of the prosodic resources available to him. The line he uses for the *Tales* is assimilable to the French or Italian decasyllable, and so is the direct ancestor of the iambic pentameter. A detailed analysis of the metrics of *Troilus* has shown just how close his verse already is to the pentameter, though

Chaucerian riding rhyme still lays more emphasis on stress patterns. One frequent effect of this is that many of his lines contain a mid-line caesura, often (though inconsistently) indicated by a slash in the manuscripts. Its distinction from the alliterative line with its medial pause is therefore not absolute; one of the earliest descendants of Chaucer's line was the 'heroic' or (less euphemistically) 'broken-backed' prosodic line of the late fifteenth and early sixteenth centuries.

Chaucer consistently keeps to this metrical form of the line throughout the *Tales*, *Sir Thopas* and the prose tales excepted. The mixture of verse forms in the *Tales*, however, and its mingling of verse and prose, again make the work unique among story-collections. His use of riding rhyme throughout Fragment I(A) both establishes it as the norm for the *Tales* and shows how supple a medium it can be. Chaucer opens the General Prologue with a single sentence ranging easily over eighteen lines. In the portraits, the single line is often the most telling medium. Rhythm and syntax show constant variation, and the couplet structure of the rhyme is never allowed to dominate. In addition, different tales handle syntax in different ways: the high style of the Knight's Tale tends to long verse paragraphs with anything up to forty lines in a single sentence, while the fabliaux and the links generally work with simpler syntactic units and rarely run a sentence across more than four lines. The differences between the handling of rhyme royal in different tales are less marked, but all four tales that use the form—the Man of Law's, Clerk's, Prioress's, and Second Nun's—are concerned to move the audience through pathos, and the length of the stanza unit aids such affective treatment. There is more contrast between the rhyme royal tales in their range of vocabulary and imagery. The prose tales are again differentiated from each other stylistically; and *Sir Thopas* and the Monk's Tale use stanza forms unique in the *Tales*.

Early comments on Chaucer are assembled by Derek Brewer in *Chaucer: The Critical Heritage*, i: *1385–1837* (London, 1978); quotations from pp. 49, 85. Almost all the fifteenth-century comments on Chaucer single out his use of language for praise.

The three rhetorical theories summarized here are from *The Parisiana poetria of John of Garland*, ed. and trans. Traugott Lawler (New Haven and London, 1974), pp. 40–1 (*c.*1234, but developing an idea current since the earliest Virgilian commentaries); St Augustine, *De doctrina christiana*, iv. caps. 17–26 (trans. J. F. Shaw, in *Nicene and Post-Nicene Fathers of the Christian Church*, ser. I, vol. ii: *The City of God and Christian Doctrine* (1886, repr. Grand Rapids, Michigan, 1979)) (elaborating on Cicero, *De oratore*); and Albertanus of Brescia's *Ars loquendi et tacendi*, on which see the entry to item 43 in *Sixty Bokes Olde and Newe*, ed. David Anderson (Knoxville, Tenn., 1986).

The *Poetria nova* of Geoffrey of Vinsauf (written *c.*1200–15) is edited by Edmond Faral in *Les Arts poétiques du XIIe et du XIIIe siècle* (Paris, 1924), and translated by Margaret F. Nims (Toronto, 1967).

Works that concentrate on the style of the *Tales* include Muscatine, *Chaucer and the French Tradition*, and his 'The *Canterbury Tales*: Style of the Man and Style of the Work', in D. S. Brewer (ed.), *Chaucer and Chaucerians: Critical Studies in Middle English Literature*

(London, 1966), pp. 88–113; and C. David Benson, *Chaucer's Drama of Style: Poetic Variety and Contrast in the Canterbury Tales* (Chapel Hill and London, 1986).

David Burnley, *A Guide to Chaucer's Language* (London, 1983), is an excellent introduction both to Chaucer's language and to his manipulations of it.

Joseph Mersand, *Chaucer's Romance Vocabulary* (2nd edn., New York, 1939), provides tables of the percentages of Romance and Germanic words in each of the tales.

B. A. Windeatt (ed.), *Geoffrey Chaucer: Troilus and Criseyde* (London and New York, 1984), establishes the closeness of Chaucer's line to the Italian decasyllable (pp. 55–64).

The General Prologue

Date and Text

Although the General Prologue was probably written fairly early in the course of Chaucer's work on the *Tales*, it was not necessarily the first item to be composed, nor need it all have been written at one time. There is at least a possibility that some parts were written or adapted when the writing of the tales was well advanced; the Wife of Bath's deafness, for instance, acquires its significance only retrospectively, and the last five pilgrims, the Miller, Manciple, Reeve, Summoner, and Pardoner, are fitted into the scheme a little oddly, being both briefly listed and described in detail. There is however no evidence for extensive revision in the manuscripts, where the text is unusually consistent—a consistency that can itself be problematic, as the 'preestes thre' universally assigned to the Prioress result in the wrong number of pilgrims. Two couplets are omitted in some manuscripts; the second of these (on the Summoner's speaking Latin when drunk, 637–8, missing from Hengwrt and apparently the cause of trouble to some other scribes) is required by the sense; the first, found in only five manuscripts including Hengwrt, notes the Friar's territorial jealousy:

> And yaf a certeyn ferme for the graunt;
> Noon of his bretheren cam ther in his haunt. (252*a–b*)

The lines certainly sound Chaucerian: he may have queried them for possible excision without actually deleting them. In addition, fifteen manuscripts, including Gg.4.27, read 'aryve' for 'armee' at line 60; the word is not attested elsewhere, but its likely meaning of 'incursion' does not significantly change the sense of the line.

The title 'General Prologue' is a modern one. Many manuscripts provide no opening rubric; a few describe it as the prologue to the whole book, as 'prologus libri' or some such phrase; Hengwrt announces simply, 'Here bygynneth the Book of the tales of Caunterbury'.

Many manuscripts note the name of each pilgrim in the margin, but there are no other glosses of any significance. The few surviving manuscripts that provide miniatures of the pilgrims—Ellesmere is the most famous—give them not in the Prologue but at the start of each tale.

Genre

Many story-collections open with prologues that announce the nature of the tales to follow, or, for those with more developed fictional frames, the circumstances under which the tales are told. The General Prologue does not reveal such a purpose until the end; the bulk of it is designed, not simply as an introduction to the real business of the work, but on the model of an independent genre—that of estates satire.

Estates satires, which aim to give an analysis of society in terms of hierarchy, social function, and morality, were widespread throughout medieval Western Europe. They work by enumerating the various 'estates', the classes or professions of society, with the object of showing how far each falls short of the ideal to which it should conform. Chaucer's Parson, despite himself being an ideal, comes close to illustrating the conventional methods of the genre, since much of his portrait is taken up with describing the abuses that he avoids.

The simplest division of society was into three estates, those who fight, those who pray, and those who labour, typified by the knight, the priest, and the ploughman. Estates satires generally give a more elaborate classification in terms of hierarchy and specialization: they often start at the top, with the pope or emperor or king, and work down through different examples of lay or ecclesiastical life, including burgesses, to peasants. Women were often treated as an estate to themselves—a fact that goes a long way towards accounting for the Wife of Bath, who is quite capable of single-handedly counterbalancing some twenty-seven men.

The General Prologue differs from the standard pattern of estates satire in a number of significant ways, but the model none the less remains crucial. The basic tripartite division of society, for instance, is reflected in Chaucer's making his Knight, Parson and Ploughman the three ideal characters on the pilgrimage—along with the Clerk, to stand for those who learn and teach.

One of the most obvious differences is that the pilgrims are single individuals, not plural groups—a Friar, not friars in general. Every pilgrim is still known primarily by his profession, not by name (most of them remain anonymous, or have their names mentioned only casually later in the work), so Chaucer is able to move freely between group characteristics and individual eccentricity: the Monk's reluctance to stay within his cloister, for instance, against his bald head. Purely individualizing details are, however, rare: most are in some way connected with what any particular pilgrim ought, and usually fails, to be or to do. They come over as individuals, but much of the force of the portraits comes from the knowledge shared between author and audience of what is expected of the group or profession to which the individual belongs.

The sense that the pilgrims are not a formal collection of estates, but a chance collection of individuals from a real society, is further enhanced by Chaucer's choice of professions from those one might actually find on a pilgrimage in fourteenth-century England, whether they were conventional figures in estates satire or not. Kings and cardinals are out; franklins, dyers, shipmen, manciples, and summoners come in. He still keeps one representative of each estate (if one excludes the Prioress's 'prestes thre' and the overlap between the Carpenter and the Reeve-carpenter), but he combines this with a powerful illusion of historical authenticity.

Chaucer also avoids conforming in any simple sense with the 'satire' model. Estates satires tended to take the form of invective; Chaucer is the master of irony by way of the superlative. All the pilgrims are the best of their kind; sometimes it is true, but there is no critical unanimity as to just when. The irony furthermore is sometimes much more subtle than an attack on a failure to live up to an ideal. That the Friar is the 'beste beggere in his hous' (252) clearly shows that charity and poverty have gone amiss, but since friars are beggars, there is a certain logic in equating the best beggar with the best friar. The language of the text demands approval; knowledge of the fraternal ideal demands condemnation. The pilgrims are often in part defined by what Chaucer does not say about them, when he writes all around a convention of praise or blame, but leaves an appropriately shaped hole in the middle.

It follows that the area in which moral judgement has to be established shifts between the factual and the textual, and from the author's presentation of abuses to the reader's reaction. Irony appeared in medieval rhetorical arts as a subsection of allegory: the surface narrative states something different from what the author means. But medieval allegories also consistently spell out what they do mean; Chaucer, as ironist, does not. Judgement depends on the reader's picking up cues in the text, and some of them are deeply ambiguous. Moral certainty tends to be replaced by a semiological slither. 'Amor vincit omnia', reads the Prioress's brooch, and it would be a foolhardy critic who could say definitively what the words refer to, or what the pilgrim Chaucer who records them thinks they mean, or what the poet Chaucer wants us to think the Prioress thinks they mean.

Jill Mann, *Chaucer and Medieval Estates Satire: The Literature of Social Classes and the General Prologue to the Canterbury Tales* (Cambridge, 1973), is the standard work on the subject. She gives accounts of Chaucer's similarities to and differences from other works of the genre, and stresses his shift of ground from the factual to the linguistic.
Gerald Morgan, 'The Universality of the Portraits in the *General Prologue* to the *Canterbury Tales*', *ES* 58 (1977), 481–93, stresses the importance of reading the pilgrims as 'concrete universals', not individuals.
On the Prioress's brooch, see John Livingston Lowes, *Convention and Revolt in Poetry* (2nd edn., London, 1930), p. 45.

Sources and Analogues

Descriptions of spring appear in a multitude of medieval works, lyric, history, romance, and dream vision, but almost all secular. One of the most famous of such descriptions, and one that Chaucer knew best, provides the setting for the dream in the *Roman de la rose*. He had already drawn on this in his inductions to the *Parliament of Fowls* and the *Legend of Good Women*; and although there is little close correspondence of detail in the General Prologue, the *Roman* is likely to be among the works that helped shape it. Such dream poems often use the spring opening as a prelude to a debate (such as is set up across the various tales), illustrated or conducted by personifications presented in pageant style (as are the pilgrims), and where the first-person narrator is taken through the dream experience by a figure of authority (as the pilgrim Chaucer delegates his authority as *auctor* to Harry Bailly as director of the storytelling).

The personifications of the *Roman*, and the emblematic detail of their portrayal, may have had some influence on the presentation of the pilgrims, but their principal models lie neither here nor in real life but in estates satires. Paradoxically, this serves to make them more lifelike. The estates types became typical because they reflected fact: like all conventions, they become conventional precisely because they are true. The interchange between the literary type, the lifelike fiction, and the historical is thus all the easier. But half the point of art, and not least of the General Prologue, is to show more than a photograph could do, and Chaucer achieves that brilliantly. A search for historical prototypes can only be reductive. When Chaucer offers such models, as he does for the Cook and the Host, he mentions them only after the characters have been well established on other terms.

It is difficult to pin down precisely which estates satires Chaucer knew, for most of them work with much the same material, and the General Prologue is radically different from all of them. He may well have know the Latin and French satires included by his friend John Gower in his *Vox clamantis* and *Mirour de l'omme*; the French *Roman de carité* probably provided some lines for the Parson's portrait. The work that has the strongest claim to being his direct model is written in English: the early version, known as the A-text, of William Langland's *Vision of Piers the Plowman*. This opens with a prologue that contains a spring setting followed by an estates satire, of the people working (or not) in the 'field of folk' that is an epitome of late fourteenth-century England. They include ideal ploughmen, merchants who appear to be thriving, priests who run off to London chantries to sing for silver, friars who dress in fine copes and give absolution in return for cash, a venal pardoner, rich sergeants-at-law, and a group of assorted burgesses, mostly clothworkers, ending, as does Chaucer's list of guildsmen, with cooks. The prologue and the other sections of the A-text that offer estates portraits provide analogues to some sixteen of Chaucer's pilgrims, including such unusual inhabitants of estates satire as cooks and pardoners, and there is a generous coincidence of detail between the works.

Even without these similarities, it would be likely that Chaucer knew Langland's work. It was probably written on Cornhill, within a mile of the house on Aldgate where Chaucer wrote many of his own poems; and it was widely disseminated in the South-east well before Chaucer began work on the *Tales*, as is attested by John Ball's use of it in his propaganda for the Peasants' Revolt of 1381. Take out the superficial differences between the two prologues, such as Langland's plurals—ploughmen, friars—against Chaucer's singulars, and the similarities are striking. Langland's prologue, moreover, supplies not only estates details, but a hint as to how such an opening could generate a story-collection, for among the inhabitants of his field of folk are storytelling pilgrims.

Individual portraits sometimes draw on sources beyond those of the Prologue as a whole, and these are discussed in connection with the various pilgrims. While many details of the portraits owe something to generic models, their handling is remarkably free of stereotyping: the pilgrims have none of the predictability of their literary ancestors. It is of key importance, none the less, that such literary ancestors exist—that the pilgrims are not merely individuals—for much of the depth of the Prologue lies in the interplay between the type and the individual, between the ideal monk, or the stereotypical corrupt monk, and the particular eccentricity of Chaucer's Monk. It is the familiarity of such established models that shows up how rich and strange are the transformations that Chaucer works on them.

J. V. Cunningham, 'The Literary Form of the Prologue to the *Canterbury Tales*', *MP* 49 (1952), 172–81, argues for the opening section of the *Roman de la rose* as the model for the *General Prologue*.

Muriel Bowden, *A Preface to the Canterbury Tales* (2nd edn., New York and London, 1967), surveys the historical background for pilgrimages and the pilgrims, and gives selected literary parallels. She also includes the springtime description from Book IV of Guido delle Colonne's *History of the Destruction of Troy*, a work used by Chaucer in composing *Troilus*, and which contains some of the closest verbal resemblances to the opening of the General Prologue.

Mann, *Chaucer and Estates Satire* (p. 29 above), establishes the literary background for each pilgrim by generous quotation from analogous estates satires. Her principal object is to identify the general type rather than specific sources, but she discusses the particular connections with Gower and Langland.

The possibility of Langland's influence on the General Prologue has been noted by a number of scholars: for a full argument in favour of the A-text and for further bibliography, see Helen Cooper, 'Langland's and Chaucer's Prologues', *Yearbook of Langland Studies*, 1 (1987), 71–81. To allow comparison with the B and C texts, I cite the parallel-text edition of W. W. Skeat, *The Vision of William Concerning Piers the Plowman* (Oxford, 1886, repr. 1965).

Structure

The General Prologue fulfils two functions: it tells the story of how the tales came to be told, and it introduces the tellers. The portraits make up the bulk of the Prologue, but in its structure they figure almost as a digression or a parenthesis: in April, there assembled at the Tabard twenty-nine pilgrims—the Knight, etc.—who at the Host's suggestion agreed to tell tales. By the end, the expected story of a pilgrimage has been redefined as a story about storytelling. The final section is less important for getting the pilgrims started on their journey than for initiating the tales, so that its function as a General Prologue to the whole work shades into its being a prologue to the Knight's Tale.

Chaucer apologizes that he does not 'set folk in hir degree' (744), but his organization of the pilgrims is not altogether arbitrary. He starts with the highest-ranking layman, the Knight, with his entourage, and continues with the highest-ranking ecclesiastics, the Prioress and the Monk, keeper of a daughter 'celle' (172). The Friar seems to owe his place here more to his ability to be 'lyk a maister or a pope' (261) than to his own rank, though other satires also frequently placed friars after monks. The Merchant, Clerk, Sergeant of Law, and Franklin who follow were regarded more or less as social equals, and various other representatives of the middle classes, most of them keen to push themselves up the social ladder, follow in somewhat haphazard order. The Parson provides the transition in the direction of the peasants and artisans; by the rules of precedence he belongs with the Clerk and Franklin, but his origins are comparatively humble—he is the Ploughman's brother—and to be a parish priest, then as now, was not the obvious point from which to rise in the Church hierarchy. His placing reflects his moral humility as well as his rank. The Manciple, described between the Miller and Reeve, might have some claim to be ranked above them; the whole of this final group may have been an afterthought. The Summoner and Pardoner who complete the company are social and moral misfits in almost every sense, with no obvious place either in a class hierarchy or in the 'common weal', society as a system of mutual support.

The basic organization, then, is by rank, but with some telling exceptions and some haphazardness: society is not an ordered hierarchy, not least because the people who compose it are reluctant to stay in their places. The forces that make for cohesion or disruption are sometimes suggested by the juxtaposition of portraits, or by the telling variation of details in different contexts. The Knight and Squire represent very different types, and functions, of chivalry. The Monk is described in terms that make him a different kind of antitype to the Knight, and the attributes that might be expected of each are exchanged: it is the Monk who hunts and loves good food and clothes, while the Knight is the ascetic who has devoted his life to the service of Christ. The Friar, who has no 'thredbare cope, as is a povre scoler' (260), and the pompous Merchant are followed by the very threadbare Clerk with his modesty and restraint of speech. The ideal priest is accompanied by the ideal labourer; the Summoner and Pardoner are associates, presumably in villainy.

If there is a certain logic in the order of the pilgrims, however, the content of the individual portraits shows a constant variation. The stress can fall on appearance, past life, the pilgrim's own voice or self-image, moral probity (or its lack), or tastes and priorities. The estates structure suggests that the pilgrims will be defined by their work, but while many of the portraits adopt an appropriate language, only a few show their subject doing what his or her office requires.

Gerald Morgan, 'The Design of the *General Prologue* to the *Canterbury Tales*', *ES* 59 (1978), 481–98, discusses the logic of the order of portraits.
On the social equality of various estates, see John Russell's *Boke of Nurture*, in *The Babees Boke*, ed. F. J. Furnivall (EETS OS 32, 1868) especially pp. 188–9. This dates from the early fifteenth century, but may be based on an earlier work; and such protocol had not changed since Chaucer's time.

Themes and Style: A Guided Tour of the General Prologue

The magnificent eighteen-line sentence that opens the General Prologue serves as a paradigm for responses to the *Tales*. Its surface clarity covers layers of irony and suggestion that never quite stay still long enough to be pinned down. It is often the most innocuous-looking words in Chaucer that can be the most loaded: *when* spring arrives, the season of mating and new growth, *then* 'longen folk to goon on pilgrimages'. It is not just the temporal statement it claims to be, but it does not state anything about motive either, however mischievous the rhyme of 'pilgrimages' with the sexual 'corages'. The motive, when it does come, is entirely proper:

> The hooly blisful martir for to seke,
> That hem hath holpen whan that they were seeke.   (17–18)

The recovery from sickness matches the regeneration of the earth; the pious impulse may seem denied by the holiday urge, but it is also in keeping with the order of nature. It is not simply wrong for regeneration and recovery to be celebrated together. Piety and natural impulse are not here entirely at odds, as they will be in the Parson's Tale; and that natural regeneration is described in terms of sexual activity sounds a theme that will recur throughout the *Tales*.

The movement from sickness to health, winter to spring, death to life, is the movement of both secular romance and Christian belief. Chaucer is here setting up both a tension and an equivalence between the two orders that continue throughout the *Tales*. The sacred does not stand in any simple relation to the secular; of the four ideal pilgrims, two, the Knight and the Ploughman, are laymen, and the Clerk is a devotee not of theology but of its secular sister, philosophy. The tales similarly refuse to divide into 'good' religious stories and 'bad' worldly ones. The presence of ideal characters among the pilgrims none the less indicates that Chaucer participates in the concern of so much medieval literature with perfectibility. Both the courtly romance and the penitential manual—forms represented in the *Tales* by the first and last, the Knight's and Parson's Tales—make the issue central, in very different ways: one positively, by showing its heroes' growth from weakness towards perfection; the other negatively, by showing the prevalence of sin. The opening lines of the General Prologue demonstrate that love and penitence, fallibility and the seeking of perfection, the order of nature and the order of the spirit, cannot in practice be disentangled.

Arthur W. Hoffman, 'Chaucer's Prologue to Pilgrimage: The Two Voices', *ELH* 21 (1954), 1–16 (repr. in J. J. Anderson (ed.), *Chaucer: The Canterbury Tales: A Casebook* (London, 1974), pp. 105–20, and Edward Wagenknecht (ed.), *Chaucer: Modern Essays in Criticism* (New York, London, and Oxford, 1959), pp. 30–45), discusses procreative love and *amor dei* in the opening of the General Prologue and a selection of portraits.

The Knight

The function of a knight was to fight; but throughout Christian history, and increasingly in the late fourteenth century, there was a profound unease at the thought of Christian fighting Christian. This did not generally affect the chauvinism attendant on all wars—one of the reasons for the unpopularity of Richard II was that he sought peace with the French, instead of knocking them into smithereens as his father and grandfather had done—but the wars that were held in the highest esteem were those fought in the cause of God, against the infidel. The Knight is not only a fighter: he is that most honoured of warriors, a Crusader.

He has fought, moreover, in every crusading theatre of Chaucer's lifetime: against the Muslims in Spain, North Africa, and the Near East; and with the Teutonic knights against the pagans around the Baltic. It is generally assumed that the Baltic campaigns would be the most recent of these: Henry Bolingbroke, the future Henry IV, went there on crusading expeditions, *reysen* (cf. 54), in 1390 and 1392. Englishmen had however been fighting alongside the Teutonic order for much of the century; in 1349 a group of forty English knights decided to build a castle and chapel on the frontier of Lithuania (Chaucer's 'Lettow') to further the war against the heathen on both the military and spiritual fronts. There had been no fighting in Russia, 'Ruce', since the same year, though Urban VI, the pope supported by England, authorized a further crusade in 1378, against the schismatics of the Russian Orthodox Church.

Hard factual information is not Chaucer's primary concern here, but he shows some knowledge of these various crusades. Supply lines from the home base to the eastern Mediterranean were impossible to maintain, so it was essential for the Christians to make alliances with well-disposed pagans; the Knight accordingly fights for the pagan 'lord of Palatye' against his heathen enemies (65–6). His beginning the board (52) records the Prussian custom of the *Eretisch*, the table of honour, a feast occasionally given for crusading contingents at the beginning or end of a *reysa*. Chaucer seems however to have been more concerned to associate his Knight with every possible crusading movement than to give him a plausible historical career. It can be roughly paralleled by amalgamating the crusading activities of a number of fourteenth-century Englishmen—or of various members of a family known to Chaucer, the Scropes—but English knights are not known to have participated in all the campaigns Chaucer mentions, and some of them (such as the combat at Tramyssene, Tlemcen in Algeria) may never have happened at all. The ones that did take place were less glorious than the portrait makes them sound; battles fought in the name of God can be particularly bloody. The sack of Alexandria was certainly no exception, whatever Chaucer may imply about it both here and in his account of Pierre de Lusignan, Peter of Cyprus, in the Monk's Tale (VII. 2392/B². 3582). For the purposes of the portrait, it is the Miltonic roll-call of the names that matters: many of them familiar as great victories fought in the name of God, others equally resonant for being exotic.

The Knight's portrait differs from those of most of the other pilgrims in several respects. We are told of his life history more than of his present state. He is described rather in terms of moral attributes than physical appearance—and when that does come, with his coarse rust-stained gipon (the surcoat usually worn over armour), it reinforces the sense of his asceticism, his devotion more to God than to things of the world. He is also described, uniquely, in terms of what other people think of him: he is 'evere honoured for his worthynesse', set 'aboven alle nacions' at the table of honour, 'everemoore he hadde a sovereyn prys' (50, 53, 67). It is a portrait of ideal Christian knighthood: Chaucer knows all about human fallibility, but within his culture, and within his fiction, he can portray 'a verray, parfit, gentil knyght' without irony. The irony is reserved for all those who fall

short of the standard of perfection he sets. Almost every pilgrim has some
particular object of desire: that the Knight's should be

chivalrie,
Trouthe and honour, fredom and curteisie,   (45–6)

is no bad thing, in an age that knew that virtue existed, however rare it might
be.

Maurice Keen, 'Chaucer's Knight, the English Aristocracy and the Crusade' (in V. J.
Scattergood and J. W. Sherborne (eds.), *English Court Culture in the Later Middle Ages*
(London, 1983), pp. 45–62), sets out the historical evidence for the high regard in which
crusades were held in the late fourteenth century. In doing so he disproves the argument
that the portrait is ironic, put forward in the tendentious—and seductive—*Chaucer's
Knight: The Portrait of a Medieval Mercenary* by Terry Jones (London, 1980).
Eric Christiansen, *The Northern Crusades: The Baltic and the Catholic Frontier 1100–1525*
(London, 1980), mentions the knights of 1349, p. 153, and describes the various Baltic
campaigns.

The Squire

The Knight loves 'chivalrie'; the first item of information about his son is
that he is a 'lovyere' in a different sense. He is young—twenty—the age at
which love naturally and properly 'upgroweth with your age' (*Troilus* v.
1836), according to the medieval definitions of the various Ages of Man. He
has all the other proper attributes to go with his being a young lover: a fine
figure; a dashing military career (in the campaigns nearer home, of the
Hundred Years War, a French *chyvachie* rather than his father's Germanic
reysa); and all the courtly accomplishments described in the *Roman de la
rose* as being appropriate for winning one's lady (*Roman* 2195–210; cf. the
Middle English *Romaunt* 2311–18). He is the one poet of the pilgrimage
besides Chaucer, and a musician too; but probably not an artist—'purtreye
and write' is most likely to mean 'mentally conceive and put down on paper'.
'Purtreye' is a common Chaucerian verb for the activity of the imagination,
and a courtier-artist would be so unconventional as to break the brilliant
surface of the portrait.

   The conventionality matters: the Squire fulfils a recognized and familiar
model. This is acknowledged again later when the young and lovesick squire
of the Franklin's Tale turns out to be his double (V(F) 926–34). He is also
recognizably the iconographic image of young love and its month of May
(92), for the month was often presented as a fashionable and gaily dressed
youth on horseback. Chaucer does not quite offer us the Squire at his own
valuation—a total failure to sleep on account of love has an affectionate
touch of the ridiculous about it, as well as of the hyperbolic—but the
'fresshe floures' embroidered on his clothes, and his associations with the

spring and with sleepless birds, all recall the opening lines of the General
Prologue. A lifetime, like the year, has its spring, and the Squire is the
courtly version of it. The closing couplet draws him back into his function as
a squire: carving at table is the distinguishing detail of his rank and office.
He is not only young, strong, and in love; he is courteous, eager to serve, and
in all respects perfect of his type, however different a type that may be from
his father's.

The Yeoman

A knight held a position in society that had to be visibly maintained, by the
presence of at least a minimal retinue. The Yeoman is the one servant he
brings apart from the Squire, a modesty of display that Chaucer comments
on (100–1). One would expect a Yeoman in the company of such a Knight to
be a military figure, a longbowman; by the addition of green clothes and the
hunting-horn, Chaucer defines him more closely, as a forester. A forester
could be anything from a senior administrative official (one of Chaucer's
own posts was as deputy forester of a royal forest in Somerset) to a
gamekeeper: the Yeoman's knowledge of 'wodecraft' shows him to be one of
the more practical kind.

The Yeoman is not a standard figure in estates literature, but Chaucer
creates an iconography for him as effectively as he recreates the conventional
images of the Squire. Whether the Yeoman really needs his bow, peacock
arrows, and horn on a pilgrimage is less important than the way they serve to
define him. The portrait is almost entirely external. Any further qualities are
implied only through the adjectives and adverbs applied to his gear: his
'myghty' bow, the efficiency ('thrift') with which he carries his equipment,
'bright' peacock feathers on his arrows, his 'gay' bracer and dagger, the
'silver sheene' of his St Christopher medal. His excellence as a yeoman is
summed up in the neologism Chaucer creates for him, 'yemanly'.

The Prioress

The portrait of the Yeoman gives the audience a false sense of security. We
have had a knightly Knight, a 'lusty bacheler' (in the chivalric sense), and a
'yemanly' Yeoman; but the 'Nonne' is not in any simple sense nunly. She
shows, in Lowes's famous phrase, 'the engagingly imperfect submergence
of the feminine in the ecclesiastical'; but the degree of satire Chaucer offers
has been the subject of intense debate.

Part of the problem of interpretation lies in the fact that the evidence for
satire can be the same as the evidence for dramatic realism: we know that
prioresses did frequently go on pilgrimage, because of the frequency of the
injunctions against their doing so. Another difficulty is the correctness of
some of her attributes: one would not want her to be a messy eater, or sing

the divine office in other than seemly fashion. The nasal intonation was itself a recognized technique for easing the vocal strain of the many services. Yet the balance and substance of the portrait are clearly amiss for a nun, with their concentration on her imitation of 'cheere of court', her table manners, her pet dogs, and the attractiveness of her appearance. The opening two lines of a portrait often establish not only the identity but the actual nature of the pilgrim: here, we have,

> That of hir smylyng was ful symple and coy.   (119)

The phrase 'simple and coy' is a formula of approval, but for courtly heroines; and the 'smylyng' does not altogether suggest the near-Islamic modesty required of a nun. That she has the romance name 'Eglentyne', with all its associations of the white-and-red roses to which poetic heroines are so often compared, confirms the duality of the portrait. She, like the Squire, has the *Roman de la rose* as a resonance behind her, in her meticulous (and, in the original context, sexually attractive) table manners. But the Prioress is not only an imperfect prioress (her extravagance towards her lapdogs, and her pleated wimple that displays her forehead, are sins of commission by any religious rule); she is not quite right as a courtly lady either. Her French is the provincial convent-school variety; her courtly behaviour is not quite the genuine article (hence 'countrefete', 139). The final detail of her appearance is also flawed:

> Sikerly she hadde a fair forheed;
> It was almoost a spanne brood, I trowe;
> For hardily, she was nat undergrowe.   (154–6)

A wide forehead was an attribute of beauty, but eight inches is too much— and the third line insists that it is not just poetic licence. 'Nat undergrowe' cannot, in this context, mean 'well-proportioned': it is a litotes, like Rome being no mean city or death no small thing. The Prioress is a *large* woman.

Chaucer does not pause on this: he moves on rapidly to her clothing and her jewellery, thinly disguised as devotional objects. His method throughout is to treat as positive virtues all the things that the satirists usually regarded as topics for condemnation. It is what remains unsaid—the image of what a nun ought to be—that gives the portrait much of its edge; but Chaucer, as reporter, keeps his air of innocent admiration. The Prioress is described not, like the Knight, in terms of the respect accorded by the world at large, nor, like the Yeoman, as a collection of proper physical attributes, but in terms of how she tries to present herself in society, and of the impression she succeeds in making on at least one onlooker.

Like the Knight, the Prioress rides with attendants, and despite their anonymity here both the 'Second Nun' and her Priest will be given tales.

See Eileen Power, 'Madam Eglentyne: Chaucer's Prioress in Real Life', *Medieval People*
(rev. ed., London, 1963), pp. 73–95; Mann, *Chaucer and Estates Satire* (p. 29 above),
pp. 128–37; and Lowes, *Convention*, pp. 40–5 (quotation from p. 45).

There have been various defences of the Prioress; one of the more recent is Hardy Long
Frank's demonstration that some of the courtly imagery Chaucer uses for her was also
applied to the Virgin ('Chaucer's Prioress and the Blessed Virgin', *ChR* 13 (1979),
346–62).

The Monk

If the Prioress displays the distance between the woman and her office, the
Monk is similarly, to misapply the traditional image he himself quotes, a fish
out of water—'a manly man' in a thoroughly inappropriate profession. The
Knight is a secular figure who has devoted his life to God and had no
concern with worldly luxury. The Monk's portrait is that of a country
gentleman.

That the Knight's portrait can serve as a foil to the Monk's sharpens the
satiric implications that Chaucer disguises with superlatives and apparent
approval. The Knight rides out for love of chivalry; the Monk is 'an
outridere, that lovede venerie'—the echo of the rhyme brings home the
contrast between them. The Knight's 'good' horses give way to the Monk's
abundance of 'deyntee' and gaily apparelled steeds, fustian to expensive fur
and gold ornaments, the maiden-like demeanour of the warrior to the
aggressive manliness of the hunter of hares. The voice in this portrait
rapidly establishes itself as the Monk's own, in a way that in retrospect
colours the opening suggestion that he is fit for high office, 'to been an abbot
able'. There is no nonsense about humility here, and the reporter takes him
at his own valuation, as a 'fair prelaat' (204).

Like the Wife of Bath in her Prologue, the Monk has a technique for
dealing with satires on his kind: he takes the offensive by appropriating their
arguments for his own case. The rules of St Benedict and St Augustine—the
rules that governed two of the main monastic orders—are old-fashioned and
can be scornfully dismissed:

> Lat Austyn have his swynk to hym reserved!   (188)

The next line is introduced by one of Chaucer's most damning uses of an
apparently innocuous conjunction:

> *Therefore* he was a prikasour aright.   (189)

The materials of antimonastic satire are all here: the good living, his failure
to keep within the cloister, his approval of secular offices for religious (187),
his hunting. But it is he himself, not a satirist, who relays all the standard
texts and aphorisms on the ills of such a life; and he then dismisses them by
reference to those items of food—oysters (a cheap dish), plucked hens—that
fall well below his favourite diet of roast swan.

The Monk clearly breaks his vows of poverty, obedience to his rule (and perhaps to his superiors, given his high opinion of himself as a candidate for promotion), and 'stability', staying within his monastery. Whether the venery and the love-knot suggest a breaking of chastity too is more open. The only attested meaning of *venerie* in fourteenth-century English, and its near-universal meaning in French, was hunting. The Host's later speculations about his love-life (VII. 1945–62/B². 3135–52) apparently fail to take hold. The satirical image of the lustful monk is held over until Daun John of the Shipman's Tale. There is more conventional material of estates satire present here than in almost any other portrait, but Chaucer avoids any simple conformity to the stereotype, and what conformity there is takes a highly individualistic bent.

Mann, *Chaucer and Estates Satire* (p. 29 above), pp. 17–37.
R. E. Kaske, 'The Knight's Interruption of the Monk's Tale', *ELH* 24 (1957), 249–68, discusses the antityping of Knight and Monk.
Robert B. White, 'Chaucer's Daun Piers and the Rule of St Benedict: The Failure of an Ideal', *JEGP* 70 (1971), 13–30, analyses the ways in which the Monk falls short of his rule.

The Friar

The three pilgrims in religious orders show a steady decline in standards. The Prioress may pay more attention to her manners than to the substance of her calling, but at least that results in the seemly singing of divine office. The Monk cares nothing for his rule, the bells on his bridle drown out the chapel bell at least in his own consciousness, but he is not directly harming anyone. The Friar's betrayal of his calling is altogether more radical.

Chaucer's method is again far from the invective customary in antimendicant satire. The Friar, like the Prioress, comes with a set of epithets and attributes that in other circumstances might be complimentary; he is 'worthy', like the Knight, and 'curteis' and 'lowely of servyse' like the Squire (99, 250). But his worthiness—and it is his own voice we hear—shows itself in his refusal to fulfil the basic function of his calling, the relief of the diseased and the outcast.

> For unto swich a worthy man as he
> Acorded nat, as by his facultee,
> To have with sike lazars aqueyntaunce.
> It is nat honest; it may nat avaunce,
> For to deelen with no swich poraille. (243–7)

Given his inflated ideas of his social importance—his hobnobbing with the local franklins, his overgoing of the Monk in being not just like a 'prelaat' but like a pope (261)—it is not surprising that his courtesy and lowliness should be limited to the occasions 'ther as profit sholde arise' (249).

Langland, in the Prologue to *Piers Plowman* (A. 55), brings in 'freres, all the foure ordres' for mass condemnation. Chaucer manages to make his satire equally inclusive in the single figure of Friar Huberd:

> *In alle the ordres foure* is noon that kan
> So muchel of daliaunce.   (210–11)

Coming so early in the portrait, the words have the effect of making this Friar the epitome of all the mendicant abuses—or, as the style suggests, their virtues:

> Ful swetely herde he confessioun,
> And plesaunt was his absolucioun.
> He was an esy man to yeve penaunce,
> Ther as he wiste to have a good pitaunce.   (221–4)

The friars' undermining of confession and penance was one of the most serious of the many charges against them, for it attacked the whole penitential scheme whereby the soul might achieve salvation. The Friar is the first of the pilgrims who explicitly sets money above God. Destitute widows are the objects not of his charity but of his greed. Over twenty lines of his portrait are devoted to his skill in extracting money; seven more go to his dubious relationships with young women, fair wives, and barmaids (the *tappesteres* of 241). The detail of the portrait is elaborated later in the activities of his double, friar John of the Summoner's Tale.

Few of the superlatives of the portrait, or the qualities that at first sight look attractive, are innocent. If a man such as this is a 'noble post' to his order, the whole order is condemned along with him. His skill in 'yeddynges', popular songs and ballads, is a sign of spiritual sloth in those whose professional duty is the praise of God—a point emphasized by writers on both the sins and ecclesiastical corruption, Langland included (A. v. 401–3). The whiteness of his neck—a whiteness compared to the courtly French fleur-de-lys—contrasts with the filth attendant on saintly mortification of the flesh, as practised by (among others) St Francis and St Thomas of Canterbury. Yet there is no doubt that all such things make the Friar socially attractive: the whole emphasis of the portrait falls on the busyness of his social life, on taverns and love-days, on all the people with whom he is on good terms (as well as on those he despises). It is the most densely populated of all the portraits. The closing detail of his eyes twinkling 'as doon the sterres in the frosty nyght' pulls the description further into the mode where sign dominates over moral substance, where physical and poetic attractiveness threaten to substitute for or outweigh morality. It is no accident that among the Friar's literary antecedents is Faux-Semblant, 'False Seeming', from the *Roman de la rose*, the personification of hypocrisy, who finishes by taking the shape, among the many he (or she) can assume, of a pilgrim friar

(*Roman* 12042, 12082–4: *Romaunt* 7362, 7406–8). The style of the Friar's portrait puts the same principle of false seeming, of privileging appearances, into practice; one can know what Huberd really represents only by knowing what the fraternal ideal was, and how far he falls short. It is potentially the most damning of the portraits (the Summoner and Pardoner perhaps excepted), and Chaucer provides the evidence for such a reading; but the verdict given on the surface of the text is more the Friar's own, by which he is a social success, than that passed by his victims.

Mann, *Chaucer and Estates Satire* (p. 29 above), pp. 37–54; Arnold Williams, 'Chaucer and the Friars', *Speculum*, 28 (1953), 499–513.
Penn R. Szittya, *The Antifraternal Tradition in Medieval Literature* (Princeton, NJ, 1986), stresses the symbolic quality of such satire.
Miller, *Sources and Backgrounds*, pp. 235–68, contains a group of translations of some of the many antifraternal writings of the Middle Ages.

The Merchant

The Merchant is anonymous, not only at the end—'I noot how men hym calle' (284)—but at the start: the forked beard, figured cloth of his clothing (possibly the livery of one of the great merchant companies), and beaver hat reveal nothing except a certain level of wealth. He talks about the things that merchants do talk about—how well he is doing, and the risks attendant upon doing it—as does the merchant of the Shipman's Tale. The smooth and self-important ('solempne', 'estatly') surface is broken by a single line:

> Ther wiste no wight that he was in dette.   (280)

This does not quite say outright that he was in financial trouble, and the following lines maintain the ambiguity: either no one guesses his difficulties because of the *estatly* front of financial expertise he assumes (the *bargaynes* and *chevyssaunce*, 282, though the words have overtones of sharp dealing); or else his skill has kept him out of debt. Chaucer's style will not allow a clear perception of any reality behind the lines, only the ambiguity of signs. The comment on debt is placed between two descriptions of the Merchant as a 'worthy man', an epithet thoroughly debased in the course of the preceding portrait of the Friar. The hollowness of the repetition underscores the refusal of the description to accept the Merchant at his own valuation.

The portrait compensates for its anonymity by its topicality, in the reference to the passage between Middleburg and Orwell, the Netherlands and East Anglia, through which much of the English trade in wool and cloth passed from the 1380s onwards. The Merchant, like the Knight and Squire, has his own areas of contemporary campaign. The reference also connects him with the great companies of the Merchants of the Staple and the Merchant Adventurers. The mention of Middelburg would have been appropriate for either company in different years, and it is no more possible to connect the Merchant with one or the other than to link the Monk or Friar to specific orders.

The Clerk

The Clerk's defining characteristics, as mentioned in the opening lines, are his devotion to logic, and his, and his horse's, leanness. Not every pilgrim has his horse or manner of riding mentioned, but the comments are always telling. The Clerk's horse is so thin that all its ribs show ('as leene . . . as is a rake', 287), to match his own hollow looks.

The Friar would never appear at love-days with a threadbare cope; the Clerk seems to have no clothes that are not threadbare. He is the archetypal impoverished student—or perhaps even a three-dimensional copy of the personification of Logic, for the study of philosophy notoriously never made anyone rich, and traditionally made one thin as well. The word 'philosophre' (297) doubled as the word for an alchemist; Chaucer waits until the Canon's Yeoman's tale to show that that sort of philosophy likewise fails to make one rich.

Logic was both part of the elementary bachelor's degree, and a major branch of study in itself—the pursuit of wisdom. The Clerk is not a theologian, but he is no less pious for having chosen the more secular branch of learning: he will not serve the world, in the Monk's phrase, by taking up a secular office (187, 292), and he prays 'bisily' for the souls of those who have provided him with the means to study. As a subtext to his portrait, there runs a concurrent description of less ideal clerks: the kind who were quite worldly enough to treat education as a pathway to worldly office, who would prefer expensive clothes and music-making to the books for which the Clerk longs. Nicholas, the Oxford student of the Miller's Tale, manages to have both books and a 'gay sautrie' (I(A) 3208–13). Chaucer does not adopt the Clerk's own voice in the portrait, though much of its vocabulary belongs to the world of learning. In striking contrast to the previous three pilgrims, he is reluctant to speak at all, and when he does it is of 'moral vertu'. This is the proper end of philosophy, and it once more shows the Clerk fulfilling the highest aims of his calling. It is logic, too, according to St Augustine (quoted by John of Salisbury), that 'teaches both how to teach and how to learn'. The Clerk, who would gladly learn and teach, has learned his lessons well.

John A. Alford, 'The Wife of Bath versus the Clerk of Oxford: What their Rivalry Means', *ChR* 21 (1986–7), 108–32, discusses the similarity of the Clerk to earlier personifications of Logic (though the medieval examples are female). The St Augustine–John of Salisbury citation is given on p. 120.

Bowden, *Preface* (p. 31 above), pp. 155–64, gives information on the late medieval curriculum at Oxford.

Mann, *Chaucer and Estates Satire* (p. 29 above) pp. 74–85, includes an analysis of the language of the portrait.

The Sergeant of Law

If 'moral vertu' is the end of philosophy, the object of law, so far as one can tell from the portrait of the Sergeant, is to make money. Langland's lawyers refuse to open their mouths unless they are paid (A. Prol. 84–7); one gets no sense of the Sergeant's doing anything for anyone except himself. His skill in 'purchasyng' land is apparently used primarily for himself as purchaser.

The portrait starts without apparent irony: there were only about twenty lawyers of sergeant rank in the country, and for this one to be 'war and wys' and experienced sounds appropriate enough. But the certainty of the language soon begins to become unfixed. He is

<blockquote>
ful riche of excellence.
Discreet he was and of greet reverence—
He semed swich, his wordes weren so wise.   (311–3)
</blockquote>

For a lawyer to be 'riche' suggests something more than an abundance of good qualities, in the fourteenth century as now. 'Reverence' has here a social meaning, of dignity, distinctly at odds with its last usage seven lines earlier, where it described the respect with which the Clerk spoke: it is the difference between showing humility, and requiring it in others. The verb 'semed' is more obviously suspicious: his 'wordes', his manner of speaking, are used to suggest a different character from the front he projects. The suspicions are confirmed later with the narrator's statement that he is less busy than he likes to seem (322).

The portrait concentrates, however, on the Sergeant's professional expertise: the impression, once again, is of the superlative, whatever qualifications Chaucer may imply. The impression is clearly the one the lawyer is keen to foster. That his legal knowledge might have any aim apart from making money never seems to occur to him, nor to the narrator in spite of his degree of privileged vision. The portrait thus holds back from being satirical in the ways one would expect: the irony is ostensibly aimed at what the Sergeant conceals from the world, not at what he fails to do at all. His acquisition of wealth has come, we are given to understand, from skill alone. He may be rich, but he is not ostentatious. The vocabulary of the portrait is appropriate to his profession—there are some dozen legal terms in its twenty-two lines—but the word 'justice' is never used, except as the title of one of his offices.

Bowden, *Preface* (p. 31 above), pp. 165–72, stresses the Sergeant's high rank, and discusses the possible model of Thomas Pynchbeck—conceivably a source of the verb 'pynche' in line 326. It is however unlikely, as always, that Chaucer was drawing so directly from life.
Mann, *Chaucer and Estates Satire* (p. 29 above), pp. 86–91, discusses the Sergeant under the telling heading 'The Omission of the Victim'.

The Franklin

The apparently innocuous Franklin has come to be the centre of the fiercest debate over any of the pilgrims. There is no question that the Pardoner is evil, or the Prioress less than perfect, though one can argue over how much less; the Franklin can be made to seem either the backbone of the social fabric or a man in the grip of deadly sin, a glutton, proud, and uncharitable.

One matter can be resolved: the Franklin is not inherently a social climber, or a *nouveau riche*. The evidence is strongly that franklins were landed members of the minor gentry, with a long-standing stake in land ownership. This Franklin also accepts the responsibilities that go with such a position: he has held the offices of knight of the shire (i.e. parliamentary representative), sheriff, auditor, and justice of the peace—offices that overlap with those undertaken at various times by Chaucer himself. There is no criticism of the way he fulfils these roles, nor approval beyond the fact that he is the only pilgrim to be involved in the running of society. As justice of the peace, he shares with the Sergeant a concern for the administration of the law; that they ride 'in compaignye' is therefore fitting without its necessarily indicating that they are partners in graft. The Franklin is, in Chaucer's conclusion, a 'worthy vavasour': an old-fashioned word even at the time, with resonances about it of chivalric romance, hospitality, and assistance to knights errant.

The first items of information provided about him are a greater mixture than for any other pilgrim:

> Whit was his berd as is the dayesye;
> Of his complexioun he was sangwyn.
> Wel loved he by the morwe a sop in wyn.   (332–4)

The white beard is one of the rare details that appear to be purely individualizing, with no further implications. The sanguinity indicates an open and generous temperament with a good stomach and digestion (but not gluttony, a feature associated with other complexions). The object of the Franklin's love, his morning snack of bread in wine, is very different from the Knight's chivalry, the Squire's lady, or the Merchant's winnings, either as a principle of life or as the defining characteristic of his social type. It does, however, sound the key for much of the rest of the portrait: where the vocabulary associated with the Merchant is financial, and with the Sergeant legal, for the Franklin it is gastronomic.

Such characteristics make the Franklin the test case for how far Chaucer divides the literal attribute from the symbolic indicator. The Parson condemns as gluttonous an excess and luxury of eating, but a detailed knowledge of the preparation of fine food was an essential part of running a good household; John Russell's *Boke of Nurture* attests abundantly to that, and it includes details for 'A Fest for a Franklin'. Such an attitude was not incompatible with homiletics: a certain householder of Paris, for instance, who at about this time was writing a handbook for his young bride on how to be a model wife (which includes the highly moral stories of Griselda and of Melibee and Prudence), gives plentiful instructions for menus and recipes without any sense of incongruity. The Franklin, moreover, shares his food: the comparison of him to a saint—St Julian, patron saint of hospitality— may be hyperbolic, but there is no suggestion that it is purely ironic. Moreover, the careful adjustment of diet to season, and the need to serve 'poynaunt and sharp' sauces to accompany fish—the hot and dry elements balancing the cold and moist—reflect medieval beliefs about wholesome eating. The Franklin has some claim to be a fourteenth-century health-food addict.

The lines that have been taken to justify a less sympathetic interpretation come earlier:

> To lyven in delit was evere his wone,
> For he was Epicurus owene sone,
> That heeld opinioun that pleyn delit
> Was verray felicitee parfit.   (335–8)

It is explicitly an unchristian view to hold; but the 'opinioun' is, in the first instance, Epicurus'—it avoids saying distinctly that the Franklin identifies 'felicitee' with pleasure. When Philosophy describes the same theory in Boethius' *Consolation*, in a passage that probably provided Chaucer with his information on the subject, she seems to think it natural enough, though inadequate (iii. pr. 2). The nature of true 'felicitee' is to be one of the great debating points of the *Tales*, and Chaucer does not resolve it here. Once again, his voice refuses to be assimilated in any simple way to that of the moralist. It reports, it comments; it avoids any interpretation beyond that of appearance.

Henrick Specht, *Chaucer's Franklin in the Canterbury Tales: The Social and Literary Background of a Chaucerian Character* (Copenhagen: Publications of the Department of English, University of Copenhagen, 10, 1981), is the most detailed study of the status of franklins and of the implications of the portrait.

For Russell, see p. 33 above. For the handbook for the ideal wife, see *Le Ménagier de Paris*, ed. Georgine E. Brereton and Janet M. Ferrier (Oxford, 1981), trans. Eileen Power as *The Goodman of Paris* (London, 1928).

Roy J. Pearcy, 'Chaucer's Franklin and the Literary Vavasour', *ChR* 8 (1973–4), 33–59, suggests the implications behind 'vavasour'.

The strongest opposition to the Franklin is expressed by D. W. Robertson, jun., 'Chaucer's Franklin and his Tale', *Essays in Medieval Culture* (Princeton, 1980), pp. 273–90 (repr. from *Costerus*, NS 1 (1974), 1–26). Mann, *Chaucer and Estates Satire* (p. 29 above), pp. 152–9, stresses the distance of the portrait from moralistic or satiric treatment (though the franklin does not appear elsewhere in estates literature).

On the relation of diet and cookery to health, see in particular Terence Scully, 'The *Opusculum de saporibus* of Magninus Mediolanensis', *MÆ* 54 (1985), 178–207.

The Guildsmen

The four clothworkers Chaucer lists could all belong to a single craft guild, but the inclusion of the Carpenter makes it more likely that Chaucer had in mind a parish guild: an organization in which the members associated for acts of piety and mutual welfare. At least one of the London parish guilds had a special connection with St Thomas of Canterbury. It was the craft guilds, however, that wielded political power in the city, and Chaucer may be combining features from both.

The portrait of the Guildsmen is largely devoted to expressing the conviction, whether their own or the pilgrim Chaucer's, that they are suitable for advancement, 'shaply for to been an alderman'. All the content of the group portrait is devoted to their anxiety to impress others by social climbing. Within the craft guilds, the word 'fraternity' by this date was coming to denote the more powerful and exclusive inner core of guild members. Their fraternity moreover is 'solempne', and the adjective brings with it from the portrait of the Merchant overtones of 'self-important'. The silver chasing on their knives is illegal, such ornament being the prerogative of the gentry. Their wives wish to be accorded the superior title of 'madame'. Their desire for aggrandizement is expressed with less and less euphemism as the portrait proceeds. Any pretence that sitting on a dais in a guildhall is just part of their professional obligations, or that their true qualification for aldermanhood is wisdom, is dropped when their wives' motives are introduced. Even here, however, Chaucer keeps up the front of approval, as with his endorsement of the Monk:

> And elles certeyn were they to blame.   (375)

The commonest accusation brought against such burgesses in estates literature was not of pride but of avarice: of fraudulent trading practices and so on. The Guildsmen are the first of several lay townsmen and craftsmen and, in particular, women, in the course of the *Tales*, who want to set themselves up as superior to their fellows: the Wife of Bath and Simkin's wife are two of the most obvious. The description of the Guildsmen includes a concurrent description of their wives, and it shows them not as they are but as they would like to be. To be able to behave 'roialliche' is the final accolade of social success in a society that had a few million peasants and craftsmen and only one king.

George Unwin, *The Gilds and Companies of London* (London, 1908), chs. 6–11, describes the guild system in the city in the fourteenth century; ch. 9 describes the parish guilds. See also Mann, *Chaucer and Estates Satire* (p. 29 above), pp. 103–5.

The Cook

The Cook, whose presence in the Guildsmen's service may be a further sign of their wish to distinguish themselves from the ordinary run of pilgrims who ate whatever they could find, has no literary stereotype behind him, though Langland ends his own survey of the estates of England with the cooks. In the Prologue of his own Tale, Chaucer gives him the name of a figure somewhat notorious around London, Hodge, or Roger, of Ware (I(A) 4336, 4345). For the moment he is defined only by his professional skill—much of what purports to be the description of him reads more like the index to a cookery book—and by the notorious running sore on his shin, a symptom in medieval diagnosis of self-indulgence or venereal disease. The ulcer is dropped into the portrait between the pies and the savoury mousses, and rather qualifies one's reaction to his being among 'the beste' of cooks. Penitential literature on gluttony sometimes makes its point by associating gourmandise with excretion and vomiting to introduce a sense of disgust; the Pardoner gives a good example, VI(C) 526–43. Here, the food becomes nauseating for reasons to do more with hygiene than sin.

The Shipman

The Shipman, like the Cook, is an exceptional figure in estates literature. Chaucer may have included him in his cross-section of society as he had come across so many, not only as a traveller but also as Controller of Customs. He is the first of the 'good felawes' of the *Tales*, an epithet also applied to the Summoner and his partners in crime (648, 650, 653). The Shipman seems to have earned the appellation by his habits of thievery, piracy, and mass murder, a set of practices disguised by either strictly factual description (drawing wine, 396) or euphemistic metaphor (sending defeated crews home by water, 400). The Prioress's 'conscience' led her to weep over trapped mice; the Shipman's lack of 'nyce conscience' leaves him devoid not only of sentimentality but of any moral sense at all.

The Shipman is not only a 'good felawe' but a fine seaman, and Chaucer implies more affinity than contrast between the two. He knows every haven along the Atlantic and North Sea coasts of Europe, and perhaps has an acquaintance with the Baltic and the Mediterranean as well (depending on the identification of 'Gootlond' and the literalness of Carthage). Such a skill requires not only geographical knowledge but a detailed mass of information about currents and the times, directions, and levels of tides, with all their myriad variations along such a coastline—variations he has to know without the benefit of tide tables, and that are potentially fatal to anyone who gets them wrong. A highly sophisticated system existed to schematize such knowledge, and the Shipman is an expert.

After the information about the Shipman's port of origin, the next item Chaucer mentions is his horse, a 'rouncy': a beast that, in the understanding of the Ellesmere miniaturist, is about as appropriate for riding as a carthorse. It is also, like a carthorse, hard to fall off. The Shipman is less of an expert on horseback than shipboard (390), so the choice may have been wise.

On the Shipman's navigational skills, see E. G. R. Taylor, *The Haven-finding Art: A History of Navigation from Odysseus to Captain Cook* (London, 1971), ch. 6, and Charles O. Frake, 'Cognitive Maps of Time and Tide among Medieval Seafarers', *Man*, 20 (1985), 254–70. On the Shipman's 'conscience', see Mann, *Chaucer and Estates Satire* (p. 29 above), p. 171.

The Doctor of Physic

The Physician's portrait opens with an ambiguity:

> In al this world ne was ther noon hym lik,
> To speke of phisik and of surgerye.   (412–3)

Does 'to speke' mean 'when one speaks'—which would endorse his superiority to all other practitioners—or 'for talking about', which would mean that his supreme skill lay in talk? There is little implied speech from him in the portrait, but even by General Prologue standards the proportion of the description that is phrased in his own professional jargon is high. His methods of diagnosis (by reference to the planets, in accordance with accepted practice) and the remarkable collection of medical authorities he knows (few libraries in Britain came near to possessing all of them) get rather more stress than any results he achieves. The one line that sounds promising turns out to mean something else:

> Anon he yaf the sike man his boote.
> Ful redy hadde he his apothecaries
> To sende hym drogges and his letuaries,
> For ech of hem made oother for to wynne.   (424–7)

'Boote' means 'remedy', but not in the sense of 'cure' that one assumes on first reading of the line: it turns out to mean merely 'medication'. The end result is not the recovery of the patient (which is never mentioned) but the mutual profit of physician and pharmacist. The end of medicine, it appears, is rich pickings. He may not have found the philosophers' stone, which bred not only gold but a health-giving elixir; but he is doing almost as well without it:

> Gold in phisik is a cordial,
> Therefore he lovede gold in special.   (443–4)

His learning has taught him the importance of 'mesurable' diet, so that he can keep out of the hands of doctors himself. His earthly food is coupled with a mention of his lack of spiritual food (438), perhaps another of

Chaucer's covert biblical allusions (on the need for the Word of God as well
as bread, Matth. 4:4); the charge was a common one against physicians. His
clothes are as excessive for his rank as the Monk's are for a religious. They
may be designed as advertisement, to show how successful a physician he is;
his clients, like the admiring reporter, may not ask what sort of success they
represent.

The Doctor is one of the few pilgrims who seem to be somewhat
misplaced, in terms of rank, within the sequence. Physicians were
customarily associated with lawyers, merchants, and burgesses in estates
satire, and he is not far away from them here; but, as a learned professional,
one would expect him to be placed with the group around the Sergeant of
Law. One is reluctant to claim that Chaucer placed him after the Shipman to
suggest that he is even more lethal; there is more clearly a relationship
between the two portraits in terms of the practical and theoretical
applications of the study of the heavens—the Shipman using the moon and
stars for tides and navigation (*lodemenage*, 403), the Doctor for astrological
inference.

The Wife of Bath

There is no single motif that dominates the Wife's portrait, as various kinds
of professional jargon so often figure in the men's. The first detail appears
purely arbitrary:

> But she was somdel deef, and that was scathe.   (445)

How she came to be deaf only emerges much later. At this point it is solely an
individualizing touch, devoid of any cues that might suggest spiritual
deafness; the rest of the portrait encourages one to infer that she has a loud
voice, and that she would rather listen to herself than to other people.

A homiletic analysis of the Wife of Bath would include pride, wrath,
envy, immodesty, lust, and *curiositas*—her 'wandrynge by the weye'. What
Chaucer chooses to stress is an account of her professional pre-eminence,
her conduct in church, her clothes, her marital status, her travels, her riding
outfit, and her sociability. Where the moral reading would imply a
monochrome world, everything about the Wife is larger, and more highly
coloured, than life: scarlet stockings and red face, five husbands, ten-pound
Sunday headdress, buckler-sized hat, three visits to Jerusalem. Everything
is a bit too much, or too many. She herself is of a size to match to her clothes
(472). Only the Knight and Shipman can lay any claim to have travelled
further than she has; but her motives may be less pure than theirs, as wives
proverbially used pilgrimages as a cover for other activities, and she herself
later quotes the proverb in question (III(D) 655–8, 555–9).

'Women' were often treated as an estate to themselves in estates literature (if they were treated at all), and are sometimes held over to the end. The Wife is certainly no appendage, and women in her person are given a sufficiently high profile to equal all the male pilgrims put together. She owes her place among the middle-class group most obviously to her skill in cloth-making. This may mean weaving; or it could suggest a more entrepreneurial role between the artisans who processed the wool and the merchant companies that exported the finished cloths. Chaucer, as so often, qualifies his comment on her skill: it is not that she is a better weaver than the renowned craftsmen of Ypres and Ghent, but that she has that reputation; the possibility remains open that she is the one to put it about, just as the Monk's voice is behind his suitability for promotion. It appears, in any case, that such a reputation for any west-country weaver would have been lacking in credibility. She is first introduced, however, not as a cloth-maker—there have already been a Webbe and a Tapycer, weavers of cloth and of hangings and rugs, among the Guildsmen—but as a wife; and matrimony is clearly her main profession. Her five husbands (not to mention the unenumerated 'oother compaignye') are given a place in the middle of the portrait, though the centrality scarcely registers: they become another set of attributes, on a par with her Sunday coverchiefs, her florid complexion, and her checklist of famous pilgrimages. It is not until her Prologue that they come into their own. Her particular art—the one that exceeds even her cloth-making—is related to this, but it is held back until the end: she is an expert in 'the olde daunce' of love. This is not the *fin amor* of the Squire, but the tricks and conquests of sexual pursuit. She herself is clearly well prepared for battle, with her sharp spurs and a hat that could double as a shield; the term *virago* would scarcely be metaphorical for the Wife.

Various other more specialized readings have on occasion been suggested for her. The exegetical school equates her with the much-married Samaritan woman met by Christ beside a well, 'Bath' being equivalent to 'well': the principle seems to be that if one cannot find salmons in both the Bible and Chaucer, but salmon in one and minnows in the other, at least both are fish; or, in the case of salmon and old boots, allegory or irony will explain away the difference. One can say with some safety that no medieval author ever expected his audience to pick up such a distant connection without a very clear cue. Chaucer has the Wife herself make the link with the Samaritan woman in her Prologue, but not on the basis of baths and wells. More recently, her florid face, bright clothes, implied loud talk, and metaphorical armour have been compared to personifications of Rhetoric, to set her up as a countertype to the Clerk's Logic. There is indeed to be a very special relationship between the Wife and the Clerk; if Chaucer has it in mind at this point, however, it remains unstressed.

Mann, *Chaucer and Estates Satire* (p. 29 above), pp. 121–7, is excellent on Chaucer's
variations on the estates background.
Mary Carruthers, 'The Wife of Bath and the Painting of Lions', *PMLA* 94 (1979), 209–22,
discusses the Wife's cloth-making.
Robertson, *Preface*, p. 320, suggests that Chaucer hints at the Bath–well connection, and the
hint has become established fact in the work of his followers.
See Alford, 'The Wife of Bath' (p. 43 above), for the identification with Rhetoric.

The Parson

After the highly coloured mosaic of the life experiences of the 'good Wif' of
Bath, comes the portrayal of the principles by which the 'good man . . . of
religioun' lives. Chaucer gives no facts about the Parson as pilgrim, about
his clothing or his horse. His voice makes itself clearly heard in the portrait,
but it is a voice that belongs as much, or more, to the world of his parish as to
the Canterbury road:

> This noble ensample to his sheep he yaf,
> That first he wroghte, and afterward he taughte.
> Out of the gospel he tho wordes caughte,
> And this figure he added eek therto,
> That if gold ruste, what shal iren do?   (496–500)

The Parson, like the Monk, appropriates the arguments of estates satire for
himself, but to endorse the ideal of his vocation, not to reject it: to set
himself a standard to live by, not to justify his failure. As a secular priest he is
not under obedience, but whereas the Monk scorns his monastic rule, the
Parson lives by the rule of the Gospels. The Ellesmere miniature, set before
his tale, portrays him with the crossed arms symbolic of humility.

The portrait is a double one, of the good parson, and of the bad.
Contemporary criticism of bad priests can be reconstructed from the
description simply by omitting the negatives: they readily excommunicate for
non-payment of tithes, they expect a high standard of living, they leave their
pastoral duties undone, they rent out their benefices in exchange for the easy
life of a chantry priest in London ('for seluer is swete', as Langland explains,
A. Prol. 83), they flatter their social superiors where they ought to rebuke
them. The Parson himself keeps this anti-model before his eyes as an
incentive to do better: he will not be a 'shiten shepherde', nor a mercenary, the
'hireling', *mercenarius*, of John 10: 12. That the Bible should be the work to
which the Parson reaches for his allusions is entirely right, and he lives by the
standards set in the Gospel texts he refers to. Chaucer himself has other
sources in mind as well—both the filthy shepherd and the rusting gold are
images found elsewhere, notably in the French estates satire the *Roman de
carité*—but the Parson needs only the Gospels and his own conscience.

Mann, *Chaucer and Estates Satire* (p. 29 above), pp. 55–67.

The Ploughman

The portrait of the Ploughman is a miniature, not only of the life of a ploughman, with its muck-spreading, threshing, and digging, but of the life of the good Christian:

> God loved he best with al his hoole herte
> At alle tymes, thogh him gamed or smerte,
> And thanne his neighebor right as hymselve.   (533–5)

The lines ought, in theory, to be applicable to any of the pilgrims, or to anyone in a Christian society; that Chaucer chooses a ploughman to exemplify them may be due to the influence of Langland. It is not just Piers who is ideal: the first people mentioned in the field of folk are the hard-working ploughmen whose labour provides the means of livelihood for all mankind. Langland's vision of a society where every man should be 'pilgrim at the plough for pore menis sake' (A. vii. 94) is mirrored in the Ploughman's readiness to labour

> For Cristes sake, for every povre wight,   (537)

and, moreover, 'withouten hire'—a marked contrast to the ploughmen of Chaucer's England as represented in the landowners' complaints about relentless demands for high wages, or to the lazy labourers of estates satire or Piers's half-acre.

The Ploughman pays his dues to God and his neighbour, in 'parfit charitee'; he also pays his dues to the Church, in the form of tithes. Unlike most of the pilgrims, he is content with his position in society, wearing the humble tabard appropriate for his rank, riding a socially unacceptable mare, and never trying to be anything other than he is. He is 'brother' to the Parson spiritually as well as (presumably) by birth: the metaphorical sense of the word was stronger in the Middle Ages than now, and its appearance as the first item of information about the Ploughman links the two by more than blood.

Nevil Coghill, 'Two Notes on *Piers Plowman*: ii: Chaucer's Debt to Langland', *MÆ* 4 (1935), 89–94.

The Miller

Chaucer reveals nothing of the Parson's appearance, next to nothing of the Ploughman's; his range of reference for them was to the Bible or to the Christian life lived in the world of rainstorms and manure. The Miller is decisively different: within seven lines we learn that he is large, strong, a prize wrestler, and given to breaking down doors with his head if he can't heave them off their hinges. Chaucer mentions this detail as an illustration, a rhetorical *amplificatio*, of the Miller's strength, and leaves the audience to speculate on the circumstances in which he may practise such brute hooliganism.

The animal imagery used for the Miller, of sows and foxes, is typical of the stylistic register Chaucer uses for his *cherles*; the sparrow and jay in the description of the Summoner belong to the same level.

The Miller is also seen, as none of the other pilgrims has been, in somewhat revolting close-up:

> Upon the cop right of his nose he hade
> A werte, and theron stood a toft of herys,
> Reed as the brustles of a sowes erys;
> His nosethirles blake were and wyde.   (554–7)

It is an effect used by Chaucer only to repel—January on his wedding night is a later example of the technique. His mouth, open like a huge furnace, suggests in such a close-up an intensity of smell to add to the sharpness of visual impression; and the next line adds noise—he is a 'janglere', a loudmouth. The description also encodes a good deal of further information as to his character. According to physiognomic writings, red hair and large nostrils both denote anger, and possibly also folly and lechery; and a large mouth gluttony and boldness.

The account of the Miller's work, more blatantly even than for the Sergeant of Law and the Physician, is an account of how well he does out of it. Their profit was at least combined with professional expertise; the Miller's professional expertise is defined solely in terms of thievery:

> Wel koude he stelen corn and tollen thries.   (562)

A proverb recorded only later, but probably current by this time, describes honest millers as having golden thumbs—the whole concept, in other words, is an impossibility. This Miller's thumb is golden for reasons that have little to do with honesty. There are, so far as I know, no honest millers in medieval English literature. Langland's Miller is introduced, along with his Reeve, in the service of Meed, dishonest money-making.

The bagpipe was a distinctively rustic instrument, and its noise is not inappropriate for the Miller. It is occasionally given symbolic connotations of lechery and loose living, but Chaucer lays no emphasis on this: it seems to have been the commonest musical instrument of the English countryside, and the literal meaning dominates. Its music does not help to make the pilgrimage any more pious; but when a couple of decades later the Lollard William Thorpe objected to bagpipe-playing on pilgrimages, the Archbishop of Canterbury defended the practice.

Physiognomic treatises are notoriously contradictory, but the treatment of red hair and wide
nostrils is more consistent than most: see the various translations of the *Secreta secretorum*,
ed. M. A. Manzalaoui (EETS 276, 1977), e.g. pp. 11, 12, 105, and R. Steele (EETS ES 74,
1898), e.g. p. 222.
For William Thorpe on bagpipes, see Douglas Gray (ed.), *The Oxford Book of Late Medieval
Verse and Prose* (Oxford, 1985), pp. 15–16.

The Manciple

The Manciple appears somewhat out of place in the final group of
countryfolk and rascals, even if one does not take his epithet of 'gentil' at its
face value. He may be placed at this point because his work is in many
respects parallel to that of the Reeve: both are responsible for management
and accounts, one as domestic bursar of an Inn of Court, the other on the
land. His financial acumen is outstanding: he is better than the best—able to
run rings around the legal experts who themselves manage the financial
affairs of 'any lord that is in Engelond'. The continued relocation of
pecuniary skill and wisdom—from the Manciple to his thirty legal masters,
to the most expert dozen of those, to the financial credit of their conjectual
lords—avoids any need for the description ever to commit itself as to how
the Manciple's skill shows itself. If it is by profiting on the side, Chaucer
never says so; the air of wide-eyed innocence is even more marked here than
usual:

> Now is nat that of God a ful fair grace
> That swich a lewed mannes wit shal pace
> The wisdom of an heep of lerned men?   (573–5)

The whole portrait, in fact, is characterized by its failure to impart any
firm information at all beyond the number of the Manciple's employers. It
says nothing of his looks, his horse, his temperament, his conversation, his
desires, his morality or lack of it, or, apart from the obvious definition of
'byynge of vitaille', what his work consists of. That he regrets his one speech
in the course of the pilgrimage, and tells a story against ever opening one's
mouth, is of a piece with this inscrutability.

The Reeve

The Reeve, by contrast, is clearly visualized. The first six lines are devoted
to his thinness, six of the last eight to his horse and accoutrements. Most of
the middle is taken up with his skill at overseeing and managing his lord's
lands, where he can outclass any auditor. He has made himself rich
'pryvely', but as with the Manciple, Chaucer avoids any outright
accusations of dishonesty. Financial skill need not be used only in the service
of one's master; but the stress falls so much on his clever management of
accounts (594, 600, 602), and on his familiarity with all the tricks other

people might try (603–4), that the reader is steadily pushed towards a conclusion from which the portrait holds back. The Reeve himself gives nothing away: his voice is never heard in the course of the portrait, he rides in the last place, and even his clothes, haircut, and shave are kept close to his body.

The kind of detail given about the Reeve is in many respects unique in the General Prologue. For no other pilgrim do we learn the situation of his house, his place of origin, or the name of his horse. That he comes from Norfolk is more than a piece of authenticating realism, however; Norfolk men were stereotyped as covetous. 'Scot' was apparently especially popular as a horse name in East Anglia, though the word also meant 'tax' or 'rent'.

The Reeve is also the only pilgrim, apart from the ambiguous cases of the Yeoman and the Wife, to have a second occupation. His carpentry is mentioned just after his wealth; but one seldom got rich by being a carpenter. The reference is made in a single couplet (613–14), unrelated to the rest of the portrait, which could perhaps have been added to give grounding for the later quarrel between himself and the Miller over the tale of a carpenter. There is already another Carpenter among the pilgrims, but the Miller, who is out to cheat all comers, and the Reeve, whose job is to outwit fraud, are inherent enemies.

That he is 'choleric' by complexion goes with his leanness. Other associations, of lechery and vengeance, are held over until the Prologue of his tale.

On a reeve's duties, see D. W. Robertson, jun., 'Some Disputed Chaucerian Terminology', *Essays*, pp. 291–301 (repr. from *Speculum*, 52 (1977), 571–8).
Alan Fletcher, 'Chaucer's Norfolk Reeve', *MÆ* 52 (1983), 100–3, notes the associations of Norfolk with covetousness.

The Summoner

The Summoner and his 'compeer' the Pardoner are the most unashamed rascals of the whole pilgrimage—the lack of shame being implied by the openness with which their rascality is described. Both invert the true function of their offices: the Summoner, whose job it is to summon offenders to archidiaconal courts, finds the post ideal for colluding with, and profiting from, the sexual offences the courts existed to suppress; the Pardoner, who should be helping people towards salvation and the God who is Truth, is concerned only with fraud.

The account of the Summoner's work consists entirely of a list of malpractices. His substitution of worldly and pragmatic for spiritual values is adopted by the narrating Chaucer even as he claims to reject it. The Summoner advises keeping clear of the archdeacon because of his powers of fining rather than those of excommunication; Chaucer has a proper fear of hell, and therefore equally advises keeping on the right side of the archdeacon—but for both, the object is not to avoid guilt, but to avoid being summoned. The narration also takes on the Summoner's own idiolect, both in his parrot-Latin and in his thieves' slang of pulling finches and 'good felawes'—though the distinction between being a good man and a 'good felawe' is at its sharpest here:

> He was a gentil harlot and a kynde;
> A bettre felawe sholde men noght fynde. (647–8)

He is, like all the pilgrims, outstanding, but for more suspect reasons than most. He is decisively the most hideous in appearance: the symptoms Chaucer describes were associated with a form of leprosy, linked to unclean living, for which the corrosives he lists were the approved medicines. Both the disease and its resistance to the more violent remedies suggest inner corruption. If he terrifies children, he is less aggressive in one respect than many of the pilgrims: no mention is made of any weapons except the shield he has made himself out of a cake.

One line may carry a more far-reaching innuendo. The garlic, onions, and leeks of 634 were thought to aggravate diseases such as his; they were considered aphrodisiac, appropriately enough for his lechery; they suggest violent tastes to go with his liking for strong wine; and they make his breath as noxious as his appearance. It has been further suggested that they are meant to recall the cucumbers, leeks, onions, and garlic of Egypt that the Jews preferred to manna (Num. 11:5), and so to indicate his rejection of the grace of God. The text was quoted occasionally by satirists writing in Latin, and Gower uses it in the *Vox clamantis* to characterize a worldly churchman; but it is doubtful whether an allusion to the *porri, et caepe, et allia* of the Vulgate would have been picked up across the language shift by a medieval audience, especially when the naturalistic meaning is so strongly endorsed by the context. Half the fun of such an allusion, in any case, would lie in removing the symbolic element, in replacing the allegorical with the vegetable. It is one of many points in the *Tales* where a naturalistic detail could have a figurative resonance, but where the dividing line between intention and coincidence is very hard to draw.

Thomas Hahn and Richard A. Kaeuper, 'Text and Context in Chaucer's *Friars' Tale*', *SAC* 5 (1983), 67–101, give a fascinating account of summoners' recorded malpractices.

R. E. Kaske, 'The Summoner's Garleek, Oynons, and eek Lekes', *MLN* 74 (1959), 481–4, and Chauncey Wood, 'The Sources of Chaucer's Summoner's "Garleek, Oynons, and eek Leeks"', *ChR* 5 (1971), 240–4.

The Pardoner

The Summoner comes embedded in the system of archidiaconal courts that produced him, with their jargon and the range of vices they were supposed to punish. The Pardoner, 'of Rouncivale', is set with greater particularity into the late fourteenth-century world, for the abuses attendant on the attempts made by the Hospital of St Mary Rouncesval to raise money through the sale of indulgences had twice resulted in open scandal, in 1379 and again in 1387. Chaucer defines the Pardoner as a rascal almost as much by associating him with such a place as by associating him with the Summoner.

The theory behind indulgences was that Christ and the saints had laid up an infinite treasury of merit under the guardianship of the pope, on which Christians could in effect draw cheques in return for a cash payment—a payment that supposedly demonstrated their penitence, and so fulfilled the punishment, *poena*, required as satisfaction or reparation for sin. The indulgence did not normally absolve guilt, which required confession and contrition; but the system was wide open to abuse, and the Pardoner is quite ready to claim powers of absolution (VI(C) 387, 939). Other common complaints against pardoners included the forgery of supposedly papal indulgences: the Pardoner's own are advertised as coming 'from Rome al hoot' (687). If he has himself been there (671), we may be intended to believe in the authenticity of his pardons, but Chaucer clearly has a low opinion even of 'genuine' indulgences. Another complaint concerned pardoners' preaching and taking part in church services without being in orders. The Pardoner is a 'noble ecclesiaste' in such matters, and he boasts of being able to behave 'lyk a clerk' (VI(C) 391); but neither in looks nor in lifestyle—he talks later of planning to get married (III(D) 166)—does he ever show any sign of being the real thing. Pardoners were supposed to be authorized by the religious house for which they were collecting, to be licensed by the bishop, and to hand over most of the money they collected; that this one can get as much money himself in a day as a poor parson in two months suggests that he is not over-scrupulous in such matters. Much of this income, however, comes from his sideline—even more profitable, since he does not have to share the pickings at all—of selling relics. The narrative makes no attempt to disguise the fact that his professional skills consist entirely of fraud:

> Thus, with feyned flaterye and japes,
> He made the person and the peple his apes.   (705–6)

His aim in life is undisguised: it is 'to wynne silver'.

It is his skill in such matters that renders him unique:

> fro Berwyk into Ware,
> Ne was ther swich another pardoner.   (692–3)

The context for the remark is however far from complimentary, for it refers as much to his person as to his practices. His looks are effeminate, and suggest sexual deviancy of some kind—what kind has been the subject of an impressive quantity of scholarship. One theory, based on dubious physiognomic data, is that he is a congenital eunuch, a state that can be read metaphorically as spiritual sterility such as excludes him from salvation (Deut. 23:1). Another interpretation, developing possible hints in the opening lines (the love song he sings with the Summoner, the latter's rousing bass chorus taken through a double series of puns—'burdoun' meaning not only chorus but staff, staff being a phallic image), has seen him as homosexual. The hare to which he is compared (684) was supposedly hermaphrodite. Effeminacy could indicate any of these; its most immediate associations, however, both in physiognomic theory and generally in satire, were with womanizing. That is how the Pardoner himself behaves, with his talk of having a 'joly wenche' in every town (VI(C) 453); and that is how the author of the fifteenth-century *Tale of Beryn* understood him, when he gave the Pardoner a sexual adventure with a barmaid in Canterbury that is unsuccessful for reasons that have nothing to do with his physique. Chaucer himself implies abnormality or perversion but refuses to predicate any specific 'reality' behind it:

> I trowe he were a geldyng or a mare. (691)

The real joke here is simply that the other pilgrims *ride* their horses; and even as a horse, the Pardoner would be an unprepossessing specimen.

For Langland's pardoner, see A. Prol. 65–79.

On the theory of pardons and the abuses of pardoners see: Bowden, *Preface* (p. 31 above), pp. 274–90; Alfred L. Kellogg, 'Chaucer's Satire of the Pardoner', in his *Chaucer, Langland, Arthur: Essays in Middle English Literature* (New Jersey, 1972), pp. 212–44 (repr. from *PMLA* 66 (1951), 251–77, written with Louis A. Haselmeyer); and the editions of *The Pardoner's Tale* by A. C. Spearing (Cambridge, 1965) and by C. W. R. D. Moseley (Penguin Masterstudies, Harmondsworth, 1987).

On the Pardoner's sexual condition: the eunuchry proposed by W. C. Curry is given its classical exegetical interpretation by Robert P. Miller, 'Chaucer's Pardoner, the Scriptual Eunuch, and the Pardoner's Tale', in Richard J. Schoeck and Jerome Taylor (eds.), *Chaucer Criticism*, i: *The Canterbury Tales* (Notre Dame, 1960), pp. 221–44 (repr. from *Speculum*, 30 (1955), 180–99). On his homosexuality, see Mann, *Chaucer and Estates Satire* (p. 29 above), pp. 145–8, and Monica McAlpine, 'The Pardoner's Homosexuality and How it Matters', *PMLA* 95 (1980), 8–22; for general sexual deviancy, see Howard, *Idea*, pp. 338–45. For a general critique, not least of the physiognomic evidence, see the articles by C. David Benson and Richard Firth Green in *Mediaevalia*, 8 (1985 for 1982), 'Chaucer's Pardoner: His Sexuality and Modern Critics' (pp. 337–49) and 'The Sexual Normality of Chaucer's Pardoner' (pp. 351–8). Both conclude that the Pardoner's effeminacy is intended to indicate womanizing. For the *Tale of Beryn*, see pp. 415–17 below.

The Tabard

Before he recounts how the storytelling contest is set up, Chaucer pauses for an apology—an apology that presupposes what follows: 'whoso shal telle a tale after a man' must do it 'proprely', no matter how improper it may be. It is the first of a number of such disingenuous passages in the *Tales* where Chaucer apologizes for the wrong thing, or for the right thing for the wrong reason. The reason he gives here, that avoiding blunt speech would mean he had to 'feyne thing', fictionalize, conveniently overlooks the fact that the circumstances of the tale-telling are as fictional as the tales themselves. It is a brilliant authenticating device, to strengthen the illusion that he is indeed reporting fact; it also calls attention to one of the most important elements in the tales, their use of language. Chaucer justifies his broad speech by a quick appeal to Christ and Plato—so quick as not to allow time for reasoned protest—but the main point he is making is a different one: that different tellers, different tales, use different registers. As an argument, the passage collapses: if one 'moot as wel seye o word as another' (738), the word cannot be 'cosyn to the dede' (742), for the words are interchangeable while the deed stays the same. The General Prologue has already demonstrated a further principle: that deeds cannot necessarily be identified at all when they are shifted into the medium of language.

The introduction of the Host returns narrative to the forefront. He is named only later, by the Cook, as Harry Bailly (I(A) 4358): there was in Southwark in the early 1380s a 'Henri Bayliff, ostyler', probably the same man who represented the borough in Parliament in 1378–9 and acted as tax collector. For the moment, however, Chaucer gives him no historical prototype; what matters is that he sets the key for the storytelling, of 'myrthe'. He himself is a 'myrie' man; and the two words are echoed through the description of him and his speeches. His plans for the contest cover the serious as well as the mirthful aspects of story—the tales are to be of the 'best sentence and moost solaas' the pilgrims can manage—but the whole scheme is festive, with its aim of 'disport' (775) and its promise of a supper back in the Tabard at the end. The Knight reflects the sense of the occasion when he tells his tale 'with right a myrie cheere' (857).

The Host's declared plan is for four tales from each pilgrim. It is not clear whether Chaucer envisaged this as a possibility, and changed his mind only later; certainly the Host is a born optimist. A number of later references in the course of the work indicate that a single tale is reckoned to fulfil each pilgrim's obligation (most notably in the Parson's Prologue, 'Every man, save thou, has told his tale', X(I) 25). The Host has the pilgrims draw cuts as to who shall speak first: 'were it by aventure, or sort, or cas', or because Harry Bailly fixes it, or because Chaucer wants the epic romance of Palamon and Arcite to open the storytelling, the cut falls to the Knight.

The Knight's Tale

Date

The Knight's Tale was originally written as a separate work, apparently before Chaucer conceived the idea of the *Canterbury Tales*. The evidence for this lies in the reference to it in both versions of the Prologue to the *Legend of Good Women*, where Alceste lists it among Chaucer's works as 'al the love of Palamon and Arcite|Of Thebes' (F. 420–1, G. 408–9). The dates of the two versions of the Prologue are themselves uncertain, but the earlier was probably written about 1386.

The placing of the composition of the early 'Palamon and Arcite' in relation to Chaucer's other works depends on his use of material from the *Teseida*. He presumably got to know Boccaccio's poem on one of his visits to Italy in 1372–3 or 1378. He made one abortive attempt to use it in the unfinished *Anelida and Arcite*, which almost certainly predates the writing of 'Palamon and Arcite'. He also used the *Teseida* in the *Parliament of Fowls*, for the description of the temple of Venus; and in *Troilus and Criseyde*, for Troilus' ascent to the heavens. As he has to supply new material for the description of Venus' temple in the Knight's Tale, it would seem likely that the *Parliament* was written first. The death of Arcite is more problematic. The laconic dismissal of Arcite's soul in the Knight's Tale could be partly due to the ascent of his spirit already having been used in the *Troilus*, but Chaucer certainly adapts the *Teseida* freely, and the change is very much in line with his reshaping of the meaning of the story. It is equally possible that the episode was overmatter from the Knight's Tale, and therefore available for use in *Troilus*. That the two were written in close proximity, whichever came first, is further suggested by the extensive use of Boethius in both. On all counts, a date in the early 1380s is likely.

The question remains as to whether the original 'Palamon' was substantially rewritten for its inclusion in the *Canterbury Tales*. There is very little that specifically relates the poem to its new context: essentially four lines near the beginning (889–92) with their reference to the storytelling and the supper, and the concluding blessing on 'this faire compaignye', which is paralleled abundantly in the *Tales* but in no individual works of Chaucer's. There are a number of references to *telling* the story, such as would suit an oral narration, but these are found also in works such as *Troilus*; and there are also some references to 'endyting' or 'writing' the tale (1201, 1209, 1380, 2741). All Chaucer's works have a first-person narrator, and after the opening there is little to link the 'I' of the tale specifically with the Knight. The apology for inadequate skill in 'ryming' sounds distinctly Chaucerian (1459–60). The concern with chivalry and the right ordering of tournaments belong in the first instance to the story, whoever is telling it; and the appeal to 'yow loveres' (1347) to answer the *question d'amour* of whether Arcite in exile or Palamon in prison is the worse off is much more appropriate for a recitation of a courtly poem to a courtly audience than to the conditions of the Canterbury pilgrimage. There is, in fact, no clear evidence for any revision except at the very beginning and end.

Text

The most significant difference between the various manuscripts of the Tale lies not in the words but in the structure. The four-part division adopted by all modern editions is found only in Ellesmere (and possibly one other damaged manuscript). Most manuscripts do not divide the Tale at all; those that do provide anything from two to five sections. Only one point of division is common to all these, that at 1880 (the end of Ellesmere's Part II, where the lovers return to Thebes to prepare for the tournament). Hengwrt offers an introduction and three main parts; the divisions given there and in Ellesmere are set out in diagram form on p. 74 below. The Hengwrt introduction ends at line 892, at the end of the Knight's reference to his role in the story competition, and so covers the possible replacement opening of the original 'Palamon and Arcite'; its first part, headed 'Incipit narratio', runs from the start of the story proper, 'This duc . . .', to the end of Ellesmere's Part II. The second part in Hengwrt covers not only the temples and prayers but also the tournament, and ends with the transition formula from the battle to the lovers at 2742; the third part opens with the account of Arcite's death.

The principal textual variant in the manuscripts lies in the omission from several of the most authoritative, including Hengwrt, Ellesmere, and Gg, of the antifeminist couplet on Emily's looking kindly at the victorious Arcite:

> For wommen, as to speken in comune,
> Thei folwen alle the favour of Fortune.   (2681–2)

There is no reason to doubt that it is genuine—there is a hint for it in the *Teseida*—but it is impossible to say whether its occasional omission is merely scribal or indicates that Chaucer marked it in as a late addition or queried it for cancellation. Hengwrt also omits two couplets from Arcite's dying speech (2779–82). There are a handful of other minor variants: whether Theseus 'slough' or 'wan' the Minotaur (980); whether he restores the bodies of the widows' 'freendes' or 'housbondes' (992; the difference in sense is minimal); whether Emily is 'fyner' or 'fayrer' than roses (1039);

whether she knows less of the lovers' intentions than a cuckoo or a hare, or than a cuckoo of (about) a hare (1810).

Only two glosses appear with any regularity. A line and a half from Statius' *Thebaid* announcing Theseus' triumphal return from Scythia head the Tale in some manuscripts, including Hengwrt and Ellesmere, and could well go back to Chaucer; the same words are quoted in *Anelida and Arcite*. The Boethian original of 'who shal yeve a lovere any lawe?' is frequently quoted at 1164. Other marginalia are explanatory (including 'mania' for Arcite's *manye*, 1374), or mark points in the text.

In addition to its appearance in complete manuscripts of the *Tales*, the Knight's Tale survives in two copies, once with the Man of Law's, Wife of Bath's, Clerk's, and Franklin's Tales, once with the Clerk's alone.

Genre

Of all the generic varieties available to the Middle Ages, the romance was one of the most widespread but least clearly designated. By etymology 'romance' means merely a work in the vernacular, and the medieval semantic range of the word was greater than ours. Chaucer never uses the word 'romance' to describe his own original works (though he associates *Sir Thopas* with the term); the pilgrims speak of the Knight's Tale as a 'noble storie' (3111), and it is a useful phrase for a genre more easily recognized than defined, or, rather, definable only in terms of its characteristics. Romances are substantial narratives about high-born people, set far away or long ago (or both); their plots are concerned with love or chivalry, or both; the vast majority have happy endings (though the exceptions are some of the most famous—the stories of Arthur, Lancelot, and Tristan, of Troilus, and arguably *Sir Gawain and the Green Knight*); they are not allegorical, but the more courtly ones, or those with any pretensions to poetic quality, are concerned to express some kind of inner meaning, the *sentence*, often related to the highest courtly or human ideals. These ideals are likely to be compatible with Christianity, but most romances are primarily secular in focus.

Within this very general set of characteristics—and by no means every romance fits all of them—there is abundant room for variation, and Chaucer exploits this variety to the full. He includes five romances in the *Canterbury Tales*, all of very different kinds: the Knight's, Wife of Bath's, Squire's, and Franklin's Tales, and the *Tale of Sir Thopas*. The Man of Law's, Clerk's, and Merchant's Tales also have significant affinities with the form.

The Knight's Tale, as is appropriate for the opening tale of the series, represents the most serious and weighty end of the spectrum—the point where romance is furthest from fantasy and shades into history or epic. The relationship is explicit in the work Chaucer used as his main source,

Boccaccio's *Teseida*—the 'Theseid', the story of Theseus, to match the *Aeneid* and the *Thebaid*. Statius' *Thebaid* is indeed the work that provides Boccaccio with the background story of Thebes (though not with the story of Palemone and Arcita, the source of which is unknown). Boccaccio announces that his work is the first to sing of arms, the epic subject, in the vernacular (*Tes.* xii. 84): he divides it into twelve books, like the *Aeneid*, and it contains almost exactly the same number of lines. He also provided a series of glosses after the manner of a Classical text. Despite all this, the main plot is not of war, heroism, and the fate of nations, but a love-story; the full title of the work is the *Teseida di nozze d'Emilia*, the 'Theseid of the marriage of Emily'.

The Knight's Tale, like *Troilus and Criseyde*, is thus a poem written in the highest poetic traditions: it too can kiss the footsteps of 'Virgile, Ovide, Omer, Lucan and Stace' (*Troilus* v. 1792). Moreover, material of the Virgilian or Statian kind was considered essentially historical, and therefore in a different category from the more fantastic or fairy-tale romances (such as are represented in the *Tales* by the Wife of Bath's and *Sir Thopas*). The term 'storie' likewise suggests the historical rather than the fabular.

If the *Teseida* is primarily a love-story, however, Chaucer's version is even more exclusively so. The martial sections of Boccaccio's poem are drastically cut back: the central issue of the plot is more firmly love rather than war. Such an emphasis brings it closer into line with medieval romance than with Classical epic. Two features, however, make it distinctly atypical of romance. One is the philosophical reach, the concern with issues of fate, fortune, and the conditions of mortal life. The second is that the characteristic happy ending of romance in marriage happens to only one of the two protagonists. The other is killed—the ending that belongs to one of the antitypes of romance, tragedy. *Tragedie* in the Chaucerian sense (as derived from Boethius) is a non-dramatic form showing the fall of a great man from Fortune's wheel, from high to low. Romance makes the circle complete: through downfall and real or apparent death to recovery and renewed life. Chaucer superimposes the two movements: Palamon's happy ending, his recovery from despair, is only possible because of Arcite's death.

Robert S. Heller, 'The *Knight's Tale* and the Epic Tradition', *ChR* 1 (1966–7), 67–84, discusses the distance of the tale from Classical epic.

C. David Benson, 'The Knight's Tale as History', *ChR* 3 (1968–9), 107–23, argues against the definition of the tale as fictional romance.

Paul Strohm, 'Some Generic Distinctions in the *Canterbury Tales*' *MP* 68 (1971), 321–8, analyses Chaucer's usage of 'storie'.

Sources and Analogues

The General Prologue exemplifies one kind of difficulty in talking about Chaucer's sources, the problem of identifying where and how he draws on analogues of various kinds. The Knight's Tale presents a different but even more intractable set of problems. Here there are two major sources, both long recognized: the story comes from Boccaccio's *Teseida*, but this subject-matter (the *mateere*) is shaped by a new inner meaning (the *sentence*) derived from the *Consolation of Philosophy* of Boethius. The difficulties arise, first when one tries to spell out just what Chaucer takes over and how he uses it, and then when one tries to establish minor sources for particular ideas. For the tale is in no sense a translation: Chaucer summarizes, alters, transforms, adds, omits; even when groups of lines are directly translated from Boccaccio, they frequently appear in different contexts that make a profound difference to their meaning. This can result in some scholars citing as strikingly close to Boccaccio the very same passages that others will identify as being original to Chaucer; and his use of Boethius presents similar problems. Identifying the sources of specific themes or lines not found in either of these authors is a minefield. One can be sure that the *Roman de la rose* influenced certain passages, and almost equally certain that Statius' *Thebaid* (also extensively used by Boccaccio), Dante's *Divine Comedy*, and the *Metamorphoses* lie behind others (all being texts that Chaucer read and used elsewhere). In addition, however, some one hundred and fifty other works, ranging from Latin encyclopaedias to vernacular romances, have been suggested as sources or close analogues of various passages. Some of these conjectures are no doubt correct; many more, simply on grounds of probability, will be wrong, but it is by no means easy to know which is which. Chaucer seems to have had an exceptionally capacious memory, even by medieval standards, but this in turn presents problems of interpretation. A poet does not write with half a dozen books open in front of him for reference (and certainly not over a hundred); even Chaucer's use of the *Teseida* seems more likely, from its very freedom, to be based on a finely intimate knowledge of the text rather than any process of picking out lines from the manuscript for use in his own poem. I attempt no more here than to indicate the kind of shaping that Chaucer gave to the *Teseida*, the *Consolation*, and some other sources, to produce his own poem.

1. Boccaccio: The Teseida

Boccaccio wrote the *Teseida* c.1340–1; he may have invented its central story of the love of Palemone and Arcita for Emilia, though he claims a written source for it. As is appropriate for a work that lays claim to epic status, it is long—almost 10,000 lines. The Knight's Tale tells the same story at less than a quarter the length, in 2,250 lines; of these, less than a hundred are close translations, and a further four hundred show verbal resemblances. Even these lines, however, frequently appear in different contexts in Chaucer's poem from in Boccaccio's.

Boccaccio also wrote a series of glosses on the text which are found in about half the surviving manuscripts, and it is possible, though not certain, that the manuscript known to Chaucer contained these. The evidence is slight, as the strongest apparent resemblances could well have other explanations: Boccaccio's explication of Classical allusions, for instance, generally draws on the *Metamorphoses*, which Chaucer himself knew well on his own account. The glosses in any case could serve Chaucer's purposes only poorly. They tend to the explicatory and rationalizing, frequently offering Christian or euhemerizing interpretations of the poem's references to the gods. The *sentence* of Chaucer's own work is concerned with the metaphysical problems of human existence, of fate and fortune and free will, in a pagan world where the orthodox Christian answers are not available; Boccaccio's glosses tame such questions and direct them back into the Christian fold.

Many of Chaucer's changes to Boccaccio's story have the effect of stressing such difficulties: Arcite in particular is given a number of Boethian laments, discussed in more detail below. The gods in the *Teseida* are clearly based on Classical epic machinery; Chaucer by contrast stresses their quality as astrological influence, so that they cannot be dismissed as mere pagan error—they are continuing influences within his own universe. The malevolent and hostile aspects of the gods are stressed more than in the *Teseida*, and the accounts of the effects of Saturn (the nastiest of all) and Diana are added. Chaucer also adds the appearance of Mercury in Arcite's dream to utter the fallacious promise of an end of his woe if he returns to Athens; the Italian Arcita has no dream, and makes the same determination for himself. It is only Chaucer's Arcite, too, who makes the tragically ironic plea 'Yif me victorie; I aske thee namoore' (2420). On the positive side, Chaucer introduces from Boethius (and perhaps Aquinas and Dante) ideas of a providential 'first moevere' whom Theseus identifies with Jupiter; Teseo's final speech in Boccaccio is concerned only with the common mortality of man and the need for mourning to be superseded by joy. The most platitudinous lines that Boccaccio gives him, on every man who dies having previously lived and every man who lives eventually dying (KT 2843–6; *Tes.* xii. 6), are transferred by Chaucer to Egeus: in the *Teseida*, Egeo attempts to comfort the mourners, but his words are not specified and nobody listens to him anyway. Egeus' famous lines on life as a pilgrimage (2847–8) have no parallel in Boccaccio. Chaucer's poem emerges from all of this as a much more profound work than the *Teseida*: it is a poem that raises issues of ultimate significance for human life, both in the unfolding of the plot and in Theseus' final speech.

Chaucer makes a number of other changes, and adds some new episodes. The Knight's Tale emphasizes the month of May, when Emily appears, for the scene in the forest, and before the tournament. Chaucer's Arcite in disguise calls himself not Penteo but Philostrate, 'il filostrato', the epithet that provided the title for Boccaccio's poem on Troilus and which he took to mean 'the one stricken down by love'. Theseus' threat to execute the lovers when he finds them in combat and the ladies' pleading for them are both original to Chaucer; so is the intensity of the lovers' jealous rivalry when Palamon reveals Arcite's identity and asks for death for them both, but preferably Arcite first (1723–9). It is Chaucer who describes the building of the amphitheatre for the tournament, and who makes the temples part of the structure. The rules of the tournament are brought closer into line with contemporary practice, and are announced by a herald, not by Teseo in person (2543–7).

The main difference between the two works, however, lies in Chaucer's conciseness and tightness of structure. He summarizes Boccaccio's first book, on Teseo's war against the Amazons, in the opening twenty-five lines of the Knight's Tale, part of it in an *occupatio*—'I wolde have toold yow . . .' (876). He omits the narrative of events in Thebes that serves as background to the widows' complaints. Emilia's numerous visits to the garden are reduced to a single one, and the whole process of Palemone and Arcita's falling in love, and her response, are differently handled: in the *Teseida* the lovers offer each other mutual sympathy, where Chaucer turns them into bitter rivals; and Emily is unaware of their presence, where in Boccaccio she is something of a deliberate coquette. Chaucer extensively cuts Books IV–V, on Arcita's travels after his release and Palemone's escape; various subsidiary characters disappear (including Emilia's original fiancé), and Arcita's visits to the grove are reduced in the Tale to a single occasion, when his laments are overheard by Palamon. Boccaccio has a servant overhear the laments and report to the still imprisoned Palemone, who escapes and comes to the grove armed ready for the combat; Chaucer's version, with Arcite finding armour for Palamon and their arming of each other, is considerably more powerful. Of the list of legendary figures who come to participate in the tournament, which occupies most of Boccaccio's Book VI, Chaucer retains only one, Lygurge (who in Boccaccio supports Arcita, not Palemone), but he invents another, Emetreus, to balance him on Arcite's side. Book VII, on the temples and prayers, is the section most extensively mined by Chaucer, though with a good deal of rearrangement; in the *Teseida* the prayers are personified and seek out Mars and Venus in their own dwellings. The tournament is much more concisely handled than in the *Teseida*, as are the long-drawn-out scenes of Arcita's decline and death, which in Boccaccio included a formal marriage to Emilia. The ascent of Arcita's soul to the eighth sphere also disappears (into *Troilus and Criseyde*), and his fate remains dismissively and disturbingly uncertain. The long *occupatio* describing the felling of the trees, the pyre, and the funeral rites

(2919–65) summarizes most of Book XI. Palemone's objections to marrying Emilia, the long description of her, and the accounts of the marriage and the wedding night are replaced by seventeen lines that give a comment from Theseus that Palamon will need little persuasion, and an announcement that they were married 'with alle blisse'.

Despite this drastic reduction of Boccaccio's text, Chaucer's revision is in one way more expansive, for he greatly increases the time span of the love-story. Time passes 'yeer by yeer' for Palamon and Arcite in prison before they see Emily; in the *Teseida* it is less than a year. Palamon spends seven years in prison after Arcite's release, while Arcite spends 'a yeer or two' at Thebes and again as a page, then three years in Theseus' service; Boccaccio leaves this period unspecified. 'Certeyn yeeres' pass between Arcite's funeral and Theseus' command to Palamon to marry Emily, rather than a few days. Boccaccio's Emilia is too young for 'amore intero' when she is first seen (iii. 18), and barely fifteen at her marriage.

These changes affect not only the meaning of the story but its structure: both are discussed in more detail below. Chaucer makes of Boccaccio's rambling and unfocused romance-epic a perfectly balanced and tightly symmetrical work of deep human significance.

The *Teseida* and a version of Boccaccio's commentary are edited by Alberto Limentani in *Tutte le opere di Giovanni Boccaccio*, ed. Vittore Branca, vol. ii (Verona, 1964). The most relevant sections are translated by Nicholas Haveley, *Chaucer's Boccaccio* (Chaucer Studies 5, Cambridge and Totowa, NJ, 1980).

Piero Boitani, *Chaucer and Boccaccio* (Medium Ævum Monographs NS 8, Oxford, 1977) is the most detailed source study. His table of corresponding lines is rather different from that of Skeat, which is adopted in *Sources and Analogues*, p. 91, and in 'Robinson 3', p. 826. Boitani's tentative conclusion that Chaucer knew the glosses is questioned by William E. Coleman's more recent work: see 'Chaucer's MS and Boccaccio's Commentaries on *Il Teseida*', *Chaucer Newsletter*, 9:2 (1987).

Elizabeth Salter, 'Chaucer and Boccaccio: *The Knight's Tale*', *Fourteenth-century English Poetry: Contexts and Readings* (Oxford, 1983), pp. 141–81, contains a stimulating account of Chaucer's changes of emphasis.

2. Boethius

Boethius' *Consolation of Philosophy* was composed, early in the sixth century, in the form of a dialogue between a first-person narrator, the prisoner 'Boethius', and Philosophia, who offers him comfort by demonstrating that the highest good consists of internal virtue alone and by asserting the providential ordering of the universe. The prisoner's complaints and objections are each refuted in turn. It is therefore a handy rule of thumb that if a Chaucerian character uses the words of the prisoner, or of Philosophy's listing of men's errors, he or she is probably missing something; if it is Philosophy's explanations that are quoted, they are probably right.

Boethius himself was a Christian, but the *Consolation* is not a specifically Christian work. It is Philosophy and not Theology or Faith that offers instruction; the book sets out to provide the highest answers attainable by the exercise of reason. It therefore suits Chaucer's purposes particularly well in the Knight's Tale, with its pagan setting. The ultimate Christian answers are not available; the problems are all too present. The passages from Boethius that Chaucer uses most extensively are moreover set out almost in debate fashion: the two complaints from the lovers against Fortune and destiny are followed up by the opening part of Theseus' concluding speech, in which not fate but Providence is seen as the ruling principle.

Even apart from these passages, examples of Fortune and fate pervade the tale: in the Theban widows' laments (925–6); in the destiny, the executive power of Providence, that brings Theseus to the grove where the lovers are fighting (1663–5, Boethius IV. pr. 6); in the sword hanging by a single thread over the head of Conquest in Mars' temple (2029–30, Boethius, III. pr. 5). Arcite's citation of 'olde clerkes' in support of his notion that lovers are subject only to the laws of love, not of man, is also a covert reference to Boethius (1164–6, Boethius III. m. 12).

The first extensive Boethian complaint is Arcite's, when he hears he is to be released and exiled (1235–74), and it draws together a number of themes widely scattered in the *Consolation*. He discovers that exile and home, heaven and hell, depend on one's state of mind and the cast of Fortune (Boethius II. pr. 4); and he cries out against apparent goods, riches or release from prison, that are in fact evils (Boethius II. pr. 4, 5). Man's blindness in seeking wrong ways to felicity, the sovereign good, echoes Chaucer's translation of Boethius particularly closely:

> We faren as he that dronke is as a mous.
> A dronke man woot wel he hath an hous,
> But he noot which the righte wey is thider,
> And to a dronke man the wey is slider.
> And certes, in this world so faren we;
> We seken faste after felicitee,
> But we goon wrong ful often, trewely.   (1261–7)

The corage alwey reherceth and seketh the sovereyne good, al be it so that it be with a dyrkyd memorie; but he not by whiche path, ryght as a dronke man not nat by whiche path he may retourne hom to his hous. (Boece III. pr. 2. 83–8)

Philosophy is criticizing the blindness of men, from her vantage-point of detached wisdom; Arcite is speaking from the other side of the great divide, as a man desperately seeking happiness and failing to find it.

Arcite's complaint is balanced by the lament from Palamon that follows it, in the insistent symmetrical structure of the work (1303–33). The first part of this is derived from a single passage of the *Consolation*, the prisoner's complaint that the wicked prosper while the good suffer:

O thou governour, governynge alle thynges by certein ende, whi refusestow oonly to governe the werkes of men by duwe manere? Why suffrestow that slydynge Fortune turneth so grete enterchaungynges of thynges? so that anoyous peyne, that scholde duweliche punysche felons, punysscheth innocentz? (Boece I. m. 5. 31–7)

> O crueel goddes that governe
> This world with byndyng of youre word eterne . . .
> What governance is in this prescience
> That giltelees tormenteth innocence?   (1303–4, 1313–4)

The change from 'governour' to 'crueel goddes', and Palamon's extended unfavourable contrast of men to beasts, strengthens the sense of malevolent forces at work in the world.

The speech of Theseus at the end of the work is very different. The opening thirty lines (2987–3016) are made up of an amalgam of Boethian passages, all spoken by Philosophy, on the ordering of the cosmos (in particular, II. m. 8, III. m. 9, III. pr. 10, IV. pr. 6, and IV. m. 6). The most important concept Theseus announces is that of *purveiaunce*, providence, which is introduced to contrast with and override the lovers' consciousness of destiny. In Book IV. pr. 6, Philosophy explains that Fate is in effect a man's-eye view of Providence: what in the simplicity of God's mind is Providence, is perceived by men as destiny, which unfolds 'by tymes', in the temporal order. Theseus' speech is about coming to terms with mutability, mortality, death: to do so, he reaches beyond the corruptible order of earth to the stable and eternal First Mover.

The attitudes embodied in the complaints of the Theban widows and the lovers and in Theseus' speech reflect the combination of genres of the Tale. Boethius' definition of tragedy, as the 'unwaar strookes' of Fortune, is precisely applicable to the widows and to Arcite. Theseus, in asserting a providential ordering of the universe, is insisting on the happy ending as the ultimate guiding principle. One change in plot that Chaucer makes is probably connected with this: the immediate incentive for the wedding of Palamon and Emily is the prospect of an alliance between Athens and Thebes. The verses of Philosophy that close Book II of the *Consolation* are devoted to asserting the stability that underlies the inconstancy of Fortune. Their opening section is quarried for Theseus' speech, but the ending becomes part of the plot, as both alliances between nations, 'peples', and matrimony are seen as aspects of the same chain of love that binds the universe.

That the world with stable feyth varieth accordable chaungynges; that the contrarious qualites of elementz holden among hemself allyaunce perdurable; . . . al this accordaunce and ordenaunce of thynges is bounde with love, that governeth erthe and see, and hath also comandement to the hevene. . . . This love halt togidres peples joyned with an holy boond, and knytteth sacrement of mariages of chaste loves; and love enditeth lawes to trewe felawes. (Boece II. m. 8. 1–4, 13–15, 21–5)

The opening war with Thebes and the cousins' broken friendship are cancelled out in the ending.

There is however one striking omission from Chaucer's selection of Boethian passages on the harmony of the natural world. He leaves out the section of IV. m. 6 where the orderliness of the courses of the planets is seen as an indication of their closeness to divine Providence: 'and thus is discordable bataille yput out of the contre of the sterres'. Providence may ultimately put the rivalry of the planetary gods to an end, but the substance of the Knight's Tale is devoted to man's bitter experience of their effects.

On the *Consolation* see p. 12 above. The edition of *The Knight's Tale* by J. A. W. Bennett (2nd edn., London, 1957) is very useful on this and many other aspects of the work.

3. Minor Sources: Statius, the Ovidian Tradition, the Roman de la rose, *Dante, English Romance*

Statius was Boccaccio's source for the story of Thebes, but the interesting thing for the Knight's Tale is how little use Chaucer makes of the *Thebaid*. The Statian epic elements of the *Teseida* are drastically cut back for a concentration on the central love-story, and he brings in only a few details directly from Statius: Theseus' night march (970); his use of the Minotaur as his emblem (980); some details of the temple of Mars; the nakedness of the wrestlers at Arcite's funeral games (2961; Boccaccio suggests that they wore leather suits); the epigraph, if it is authorial and not scribal. The one explicit mention of Statius in the Knight's Tale, where he is cited as a reference for the rites of Diana (2294), is, as so often in Chaucer, a blind.

Much of the ease and richness with which Chaucer handles the material of Classical legend and myth is due to his thorough familiarity with Ovid's *Metamorphoses*. Many of the Classical allusions found in the Tale are already present in Boccaccio, but Chaucer's expansions and additions show a wide debt to Ovid. The major additions include the description of Mercury and, most notably, the figures portrayed in Diana's temple. The only metamorphoses of men into beasts in the whole of Chaucer's works are found in this passage: it is a topic he avoids everywhere else, even in retelling stories from the *Metamorphoses*.

The Ovidian elements of the Tale are supplemented by Bersuire's work on the iconography of the gods, the *De formis figurisque deorum*, for the descriptions of Venus and Mars. Venus' 'citole in hir right hand' (1959) is found only in this source; the man-devouring wolf in the temple of Mars (2048) is probably based on Bersuire's etymology of Mars as deriving from *mares vorans*, i.e. 'devouring males'.

Some details in the Tale which at first glance look Ovidian, or at least Classical, in fact go back to the *Roman de la rose*. These include the presence of Narcissus in the temple of Venus, especially as he is mentioned alongside 'the porter Ydelnesse' (1940–1), and the unusual version of the story of the descent into hell of Theseus and Pirithous (Chaucer's Perotheus, 1199–200). The influence of the work is however wider than individual lines or passages: it has much to do with the whole conception of love in the tale.

Chaucer's use of Dante is fascinating, though less for what it contributes to the Tale than for what it shows of his methods of working. He can move with ease from one authority to another, synthesizing their ideas and phrasing seamlessly so that the destiny that brings Theseus to the grove in a strongly Boethian passage is described in a phrase from the *Inferno* as 'ministre general' (1663, *Inf.* vii. 78). As with destiny, so also with Providence, which is identified with the 'Firste Moevere' in a phrase that may go back to Dante's 'colui, che tutto move' (*Par.* i. 1) and through him to Aquinas and ultimately to Aristotle. Even more striking is the description of the dawn when Arcite comes to the grove:

> Firy Phebus riseth up so bright
> That al the orient laugheth of the light.   (1493–4)

Boccaccio at the same point has the heavens laughing for Venus, the morning-star, in lines which are themselves derived from Dante's

> Lo bel pianeta che ad amar conforta
> faceva tutto rider l'oriente.   (*Purg.* i. 19–20)

Chaucer appears to have recollected Dante's lines behind Boccaccio's and imitated them; this usage of 'orient' to mean the eastern sky is indeed the first in Middle English.

One line of the Knight's Tale deserves particular mention, as it was Chaucer's favourite, and he used it four times in all—'Pitee renneth soone in gentil herte' (1761; cf. IV(E) 1986, V(C) 479, *Legend* F503). The line represents a recurrent problem in Chaucer studies, of having too many possible sources. Dante has an equivalent line, which substitutes love for pity, in the episode of Paolo and Francesca: 'Amor, che al cor gentil ratto s'apprende' (*Inf.* v. 100). He also quotes a similar line by Guido Guinicelli, 'Al cor gentil ripara sempre Amore', in the *Convivio* (iv. 20), and it could have been picked up from there by Chaucer: his knowledge of the work is attested by the Wife of Bath's Tale. Another suggested source, in Ovid's

Tristia, is less likely, as Chaucer did not know the work in any complete form.

The possible influence of English vernacular traditions appears in a number of ways. The alliteration of the tournament scene and the use of familiar proverbs are discussed in more detail under 'Style', but there is in addition one section that reflects the content of English metrical romance. This is the passage where Arcite returns to Athens as a 'povre laborer' (1409), a considerably lower position than Arcita's in the *Teseida*, but one strongly reminiscent of Havelok and some other English romance heroes. The phraseology as well as the situation recalls these romances:

> Wel koude he hewen wode, and water bere,
> For he was yong and myghty for the nones,
> And thereto he was long and big of bones.   (1422-4)

Chaucer's longest excursion into the world of the metrical romances was for *Sir Thopas*; the Knight's Tale shows that they could serve him to serious purpose as well, alongside the most renowned Classical and European authorities.

Statius, *Thebaid*: ed. and trans. J. H. Mozley, *Statius* (Loeb Classical Library, London and New York, 1928).

Bersuire: see p. 11 above; and on the iconography of Venus, Meg Twycross, *The Medieval Anadyomene* (Medium Ævum Monographs NS 1, Oxford, 1972).

Dante: see J. A. W. Bennett, 'Chaucer, Dante and Boccaccio', in Boitani, *Chaucer and the Trecento*, pp. 89-113.

Structure

The structure of the Knight's Tale is one of the most remarkable things about it. There is nothing comparable anywhere else in Chaucer's work, and in the whole corpus of Middle English literature it is only matched, or overgone, by *Sir Gawain and the Green Knight*. The two poems are in fact remarkably similar in structure: both are symmetrical, with parallel episodes working in from the beginning and end to centre on a set of paired threes—in *Gawain*, the hunt and the bedroom scenes; in the *Knight's Tale*, the three temples and prayers (treated consecutively, not, as in *Gawain*, interlaced). The patterning is distinctive and unusual enough to open the question of direct influence. Furthermore, the Ellesmere text of the Knight's Tale, like *Gawain*, is divided into four sections, the third of which contains the triple motifs. The *Teseida* shows none of the same precision and balance of structure, and Chaucer moves around, or invents, a number of episodes to shape his work.

The symmetry of the Knight's Tale can be outlined as follows, with the events of the story working in order down the left-hand column and up the right. The part divisions of Ellesmere are indicated by continuous lines, and of Hengwrt by broken lines.

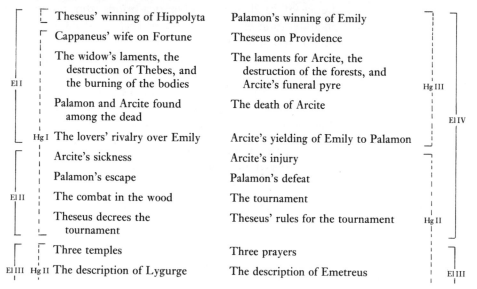

	Theseus' winning of Hippolyta	Palamon's winning of Emily	
	Cappaneus' wife on Fortune	Theseus on Providence	
El I	The widow's laments, the destruction of Thebes, and the burning of the bodies	The laments for Arcite, the destruction of the forests, and Arcite's funeral pyre	Hg III
	Palamon and Arcite found among the dead	The death of Arcite	
	Hg I The lovers' rivalry over Emily	Arcite's yielding of Emily to Palamon	El IV
	Arcite's sickness	Arcite's injury	
El II	Palamon's escape	Palamon's defeat	
	The combat in the wood	The tournament	Hg II
	Theseus decrees the tournament	Theseus' rules for the tournament	
	Three temples	Three prayers	
El III Hg II	The description of Lygurge	The description of Emetreus	El III

Hengwrt's arrangement emphasizes the centrality of the temples and prayers, but some other effects are lost, notably the structural symmetry within the Ellesmere Parts II and III. Ellesmere Part II opens with Arcite's sorrowful return to Thebes,

> Whan that Arcite to Thebes comen was,
> Ful ofte a day he swelte and seyde 'Allas!'   (1355–6)

and ends with the joyful return of both lovers:

> And thus with good hope and with herte blithe
> They taken hir leve, and homward gonne they ride
> To Thebes with his olde walles wyde.   (1878–80)

(One might compare the Troy references in the first and last lines of *Gawain*.) The Ellesmere Part III contains little apart from the three contrasted temples, the two opposing kings, and the three irreconcilable prayers.

The symmetry is not there merely for the sake of the pattern: many of the episodes of the right-hand column provide a commentary on their counterparts, sometimes ironic, sometimes tragic, sometimes comic in the widest sense. The greatest controlling structural movement in the poem is indeed of this kind, as Palamon's romance is balanced by Arcite's tragedy, death against renewed life.

The balance of the work is further emphasized by the frequent pairings of sequences, characters, and episodes independently of the symmetrical structure. The intercession of the kneeling ladies in the forest for Palamon and Arcite is a scene original to Chaucer that recalls the scene of the kneeling widows asking for mercy; the first initiates the battle at Thebes and the rites for the husbands, the second leads to the tournament and so ultimately to Arcite's funeral pyre and beyond that to the alliance with Thebes. Chaucer's heroes are more closely twinned than Boccaccio's: they are found side by side, bearing the same coat of arms; they are much more similar in character. They are given parallel speeches—on falling in love, on their mutual jealousy, on the changeability and injustice of Fortune, their prayers to the gods. Arcite is twice compared to a tiger, Palamon to a lion (1655–7, 2626–33). Chaucer provides a god to parallel each of his main characters: to Boccaccio's Mars, Venus, and Diana he adds the controlling Saturn, and ultimately Jupiter, to occupy the position in the heavens corresponding to Theseus on earth. Theseus' father Egeus may be retained in the poem partly in order to provide the correspondence with Saturn, father of Jupiter, so that Theseus can be identified with the highest of the gods. Episodes that echo each other include Mercury's misleading promise to Arcite of an end to his woe and Mars' equally deceptive promise of victory. Arcite's exile and his realization that heaven, hell, and purgatory depend on one's state of mind may be ironically recalled in the departure of his soul from the earth 'I kan nat tellen wher' (2810).

The plot of the Knight's Tale requires a complex form of narration even without these structural parallels, for there are occasions when it diverges into separate stories. The main events are told in chronological order, known in medieval rhetoric as *ordo naturalis*, natural order (as distinct from *ordo artificialis*); but there are occasions when Chaucer needs to recount earlier or concurrent events, and he employs various methods to deal with these. The story of Creon's past outrages at Thebes is put into the mouth of Cappaneus' widow. Concurrent activities, such as those of the prisoner Palamon and the liberated Arcite, of the lovers and Perotheus, or of gods and men, are handled by transition formulae of the kind extensively used in French interlaced romance: 'Now wol I stynte of . . .', 'I wol yow telle of . . .', 'Now wol I turne to . . .', 'to th'effect . . .'. Rhetorical questions are also sometimes used for transitions: 'Why sholde I noght as wel eek telle yow . . . ?' (1967), 'What kan now faire Venus doon?' (2663). They are also useful for abbreviation: 'What nedeth wordes mo?' (1029), 'What sholde I al day of his wo endite?' (1380). The method of narration is in fact to concentrate on single scenes and to give minimal linking information between them. The lovers' first sight of Emily in the garden and their ritual speeches, for instance, are set between four lines describing the lovers' lengthy imprisonment and a single one describing their 'great and long' strife over her before Arcite is released (1030–3, 1187).

This same section of Emily in the garden illustrates another distinctive feature of the Tale, that is, how large a proportion of it is taken up by formal descriptions and set speeches. Action is at a discount, and is often summarized briefly or dealt with through *occupatio*, the pretence of a refusal to describe some episode. Only the section that runs from Arcite's return to Thebes after his release to both lovers' return there to plan for the tournament (Part II in most editions) is at all consistently concerned with event and action.

Themes

The Knight's Tale has elicited a wide range of responses over the centuries. Lydgate admired it enough to add a parallel Theban tale of his own, the *Siege of Thebes*, to the end of the Canterbury sequence. Wyatt selected it as the finest example of Chaucer's work. Shakespeare drew on it in *A Midsummer Night's Dream* and, with Fletcher, dramatized it in *The Two Noble Kinsmen*. Dryden regarded it as 'not much inferior to the *Ilias* or the *Æneis*'. Its fortunes this century have been less successful. Initially it was ignored in favour of the 'marriage group'; more recently a number of critics have seen it as deliberately ironic, as showing up the inadequacies of Theseus or the Knight or both, and others have tried to interpret it as a variation on an astrological textbook. It must be axiomatic in any interpretation, however, that the Tale is a major work in its own right. It is, after all, Chaucer's longest single poem after *Troilus and Criseyde*, and the one which he chose to head the tales of his master work.

The variety of reactions is itself an indicator of the tale's complexity. It refuses to be limited by generic expectations; the very fact that it combines the opposing movements of romance and tragedy ensures that the poem will be full of tensions—that it will, to a large degree, be *about* those tensions. Two almost indistinguishable young men fall in love on first sight with the same woman; apart from the fact that one has a moment's priority, their claims are exactly equal. Up to this point their life histories and their moral states are, for the purposes of the poem, identical. There can be no moral or metaphysical justice in the different fates that befall them; yet one dies wretchedly wounded, while the other lives out his life with Emily 'with alle blisse'.

If this account of the poem is accepted, then a number of its distinctive features become explicable. The characterization, which by comparison with the pilgrims of the General Prologue can seem flat, must necessarily not be too highly individualized, or there will be personal and psychological reasons for one or other of the lovers to win Emily, or for her to choose one. There are some distinctions made between them—Palamon has the higher devotion, thinking of her as goddess as much as woman; he looks to ends where Arcite looks to means—but these do not amount to providing any justification as to why he should win her. Both cousins fall in love absolutely and finally, and Emily is presented in terms that make such a reaction to her entirely explicable. The very element of convention in her portrayal emphasizes this, for it recalls every other courtly lady who had been associated with May, spring, lilies, roses, angels; and through these associations, the description is given a resonance that a more original set of images could never achieve. All that the tale requires of her is that she should be seen to be worthy of the lovers' devotion, and she is all the more desirable for being inaccessible.

The emphasis of the Knight's Tale is less on what happens than on why it happens, in metaphysical, not psychological, terms. The *sentence*, the meaning of the poem that controls structure and treatment, is focused in Palamon's demand,

> What governance is in this prescience
> That giltelees tormenteth innocence? (1313–14)

The question is all the more significant since, despite the setting in legendary Athens, the human events of the tale are not at all unrealistic. Two prisoners fall in love with the first woman they have seen in years; they quarrel over her; the victor in the tournament is fatally injured when his horse unexpectedly rears. But this is only one side of the story; and Palamon's question is made urgent by the presence in the poem, alongside the humans, of the gods, and the planetary influences they represent.

If the questions are to be asked seriously, then the gods must be seen in their planetary roles, otherwise they would be mere pagan fictions; as it is, they are continuing influences in the contemporary world of writer and audience. Astrology and its related mythography were highly sophisticated branches of learning in the fourteenth century—they were to modern horoscopes what biochemistry is to a bestiary. The Knight's Tale incorporates some of this learning in remarkable, and sometimes puzzling, detail, which I discuss in a separate note at the end of this section.

The main configurations, however, are clear. Each lover puts himself under the protection of a particular god, or, to put it another way, declares his association with a particular set of astrological influences. Palamon aligns himself with Venus, goddess of love, but love is far from being purely good: it destroys the friendship of the lovers and reduces Arcite to a melancholic wreck (1369–76); and the description of Venus's temple contains personifications of rape, lies, jealousy, and pimping, along with pervasive sighs and laments. Arcite commits himself to Mars, an 'unfortunate' planet, and finally suffers death from the same kind of irrational violence that is portrayed in his temple. A number of the images there illustrate the instability of Fortune: Conquest with a sword hanging over him 'by a soutil twynes threed' (2030), the violent deaths of great emperors, and an image reminiscent of Fortune's wheel that shows that the humble are spared no more than the great,

> The cartere overryden with his carte—
> Under the wheel ful lowe he lay adoun.   (2022–3)

Also shown is 'who shal be slayn or elles deed for love' (2038), a category that could include Arcite himself. Emily's chosen deity is Diana, goddess of chastity, who in her planetary form as the moon stands for change— 'wexynge it was and sholde wanye soone' (2078); and Emily's own change of state is implicit in the iconography of the temple, not least in the presence of the goddess in one of her threefold aspects as Lucina, goddess of childbirth. Diana herself here appears as hostile as Venus and Mars: Chaucer describes her metamorphoses of men into beasts (a subject he generally goes to some lengths to avoid), and the woman in travail is given no assurance of help.

Of the other gods who play key roles in the Tale, Saturn is the most malevolent of all planets, the 'greater infortune'. Arcite imagines the lovers' initial imprisonment as being due to his influence—'som wikke aspect or disposicioun|Of Saturne, by some constellacioun' has written this fate in the stars from the moment of their nativity (1087–90). This may at the time appear to the reader as Arcite's rationalization of events; but the tale endorses his judgement when the planetary gods become participants in the action, not just ideas in the minds of the characters. (The only deity mentioned who is not also presented in action is Juno, who has no astrological function and therefore no 'real' existence in the Christian world.) Saturn's malevolence is emphasized rhetorically by the fact that the horrors he controls are described not iconographically but in his own words:

> Myn is the drenchyng in the see so wan;
> Myn is the prison in the derke cote;
> Myn is the stranglyng and hangyng by the throte.   (2456–8)

Jupiter, by contrast, is the most fortunate of the planets, opposed to the workings of Saturn; his sphere of influence is especially concerned with justice and the bringing of peace—attributes both highly appropriate for his association with Theseus. The one time Jupiter is dramatized, however, he is seen as ineffectual in his astrological function of mediating between Mars and Venus (2442). That the influence of the stars is by itself insufficient is further implied in the speech of Saturn, the most evil: the one specific instance he cites of his action is that he slew Samson (2466), an allusion that must immediately recall its larger context in the scheme of God's Providence. Theseus' final speech looks beyond astrology to Providence, as his conception of Jupiter moves beyond the spheres of the planets to the First Mover, God.

The point of all this, then, is not simply to show men as the stars' tennis-balls, although things seem that way to the cousins. It is given only to God, not to men, to see things otherwise: Providence, according to Boethius, is God's view of what men can perceive only as destiny or blind chance. Arcite's deathbed questioning of the meaning of life has all the pain of desperate involvement:

> What is this world? What asketh men to have?
> Now with his love, now in his colde grave,
> Allone, withouten any compaignye. (2777–9)

By contrast with that, Theseus' speech can look like an exercise in patching grief with proverbs. His answers are curiously oblique to the main thrust of the poem: to the question of why Arcite should die, he can respond only with generalizations—that all things die, that there are advantages in dying at the height of one's fame and powers. The poem as a whole, however, does offer a wider view than Arcite's. It ends not with death but marriage; the bliss does not cancel out the suffering, but Palamon's joy is none the less contingent upon Arcite's mortality. The world is made up of good and ill together, but in the structure of this tale the cycle reaches completion with the good. Although the poem is so insistently pagan, therefore, it offers itself as an instance of the providential model of the universe such as Theseus asserts and that was an essential part of Christian doctrine. In *Troilus and Criseyde* the Christian ending was pushed beyond the action of the poem, into the closing words of the narrator. In the Knight's Tale, it is incorporated within the action.

In spite of the pagan limitation of vision that leads Theseus to identify the First Mover with Jupiter, his speech is far from being a repetition of the astral determinism of the cousins' perception of the gods. Men are not mere victims, but can make 'virtue of necessity', just as it is possible to make 'o parfit joye, lastynge everemo' out of the double sorrow of Arcite's death and his friends' mourning. Unlike the mischances of the story, the happy ending is brought about not by the planets, but through human decision and action. That the marriage is used as a means of confirming the proposed alliance with Thebes is a detail of plot original to Chaucer that underlines the shift from determinism to Boethian cosmic order, for in Boethius the 'faire cheyne of love' not only binds the cosmos and the elements but also expresses itself in treaties between nations, in matrimony, and in true friendship. Philosophy ends her verses on the subject with the exclamation, 'O weleful were mankynde, yif thilke love that governeth hevene governede yowr corages' (Boece II. m. 8. 25–7). The ending of the tale is designed to put just such a programme into action, to govern earth with a reflection of the same love that governs heaven.

Such an ending makes its point by contrast with what has gone before. The earlier parts of the tale are concerned with the opposite of all this: with the wars against Scythia and Thebes, the destructive passion of unfulfilled love, the breaking of friendship. The prisoners' first sight of Emily destroys their sworn brotherhood; Palamon's appeal to their oaths is countered by Arcite's response that love and law-breaking go together,

> And therefore, at the kynges court, my brother,
> Ech man for hymself, ther is noon oother.   (1181–2)

That 'brother' is echoed again, but with more poignant irony, in the preparations for the combat in the forest:

> Ther nas no good day, ne no saluyng,
> But streight, withouten word or rehersyng,
> Everich of hem heelp for to armen oother
> As freendly as he were his owene brother.   (1649–52)

The right relationship between 'felawes' is exemplified in the poem by Theseus and Perotheus, and the legend of Theseus' support for Pirithous' attempt to carry off Persephone from the underworld is given in an unusual version that stresses their mutual friendship beyond death:

> So wel they lovede, as olde bookes sayn,
> That whan that oon was deed, soothly to telle,
> His felawe wente and soughte hym down in helle.   (1198–200)

The restoration of *felaweship* between the lovers is marked in the tale by Arcite's dying words commending Palamon to Emily, by Palamon's mourning of the man he had hoped to kill, and by Theseus' insistence that the wedding is no betrayal of the cousin's friendship.

In other ways too Theseus can reflect in ideal form traits that are found only imperfectly in the other characters, but this does not happen all at once. In the conventional division of man's life into separate ages, he represents the prime of maturity between the cousins' emotional youth and Egeus' wise but inactive old age (1812–14, 2449, 2850–3). He is associated with each of the lovers' gods in turn. Mars is portrayed on his banner when he rides against Thebes; when he goes hunting, 'after Mars he serveth now Dyane' (1682); in his time he has himself been a servant of love (1814). He can, moreover, act like destiny itself in executing the Providence of God (1663–73), and he appears at the tournament 'as he were a god in trone'

(2529). His decrees appear to have absolute power, as in his condemnation of the cousins to perpetual imprisonment, but he can be moved to mercy by prayer: by the prayers of the widows for assistance, of Perotheus for the release of Arcite, of the ladies to spare the lovers. When he has power over life and death, he chooses life; he does not execute the cousins, he modifies the rules of the tournament to reduce serious injury. His provision for resolving the lovers' dispute is described as not *destinee* but *grace* (1874). When he builds the lists in the wood (Chaucer's own variant on the *Teseida*), he is both literally and metaphorically imposing order on chaos. He substitutes a combat fought under rule and judgement for the lovers' fight; and he replaces the *silva*, the philosophical term used by Bernardus Silvestris and others for primeval unformed and ungoverned matter, with the perfect circle of the lists with its quadrants marked by the temples and his own seat of judgement. The vocabulary used for him stresses his function as ideal ruler: he possesses *wysdom, chivalrie, pitee*; he is *gentil*, worthy, mighty, and, above all, noble (865, 952–3, 998, 1742, 2536, etc.). He tempers his anger with mercy, discretion, and humility (1773–81). He is an upright judge and hopes to deserve the same himself at Judgement (1863–4), so fulfilling the first requirement that Langland and every other medieval political thinker demanded of a ruler. Creon, by contrast, is a tyrant, 'fulfild of ire and of iniquitee' (940), and prepared to act ignobly, with 'vileynye', in refusing burial to his enemies (942). Although Theseus starts off as Creon's opponent, however, the means he employs are war and destruction, and no reason is given for his exceptionally harsh treatment of the cousins, treatment that falls well outside the limits of acceptable chivalric behaviour. These things are of course required by the story, but Chaucer develops a pattern from them of change and growth even within Theseus, so that he ends the tale not under the banner of Mars but as the follower of Providence in the guise of Jupiter, bringing joy rather than death and accord in place of conflict. After the tournament, Saturn thwarts his schemes; at the end, he can plan and act with consequences that are entirely good.

Following the curve of the story in this way can none the less lead to falsification. The happy ending is an assertion of faith in the providential ordering of the universe; but it is still an assertion made to some degree in the teeth of the evidence. The Knight's Tale derives much of its power from the force with which the questioning is undertaken. This may be why Chaucer chooses a pagan story as the setting for such questions: an overtly religious tale would have pre-empted the answers, denied the human suffering that underlies the questioning. Religious narrative forms in the Middle Ages tended to solve all such problems through miracle (as a glance at the later Canterbury tales will illustrate—Custance surviving years at sea in an open boat, Cecilia sitting comfortably in a bath of flame). For the question of cosmic injustice even to be posed, such pious naïvety had to be distanced. Boethius perhaps made a similar decision when he turned to philosophy rather than theology to argue the case for Providence.

It is not, however, quite the story one would expect the Knight to tell. At the level of literary decorum, appropriateness, it suits him exactly: approximating to epic, it is the highest generic form of the whole sequence, and so entirely fitting for the highest-ranking pilgrim; its range and grandeur and its concern with martial events match his own epic career. It is a noble tale told by a man who loves 'chivalry,|Trouthe and honour, fredom and curteisie'. The Knight, however, has devoted his life to the service of Christ—he is a Crusader; so the lack of any explicit Christian content might appear odd. Apart from the very beginning and end, there is little one can relate directly to the Knight as teller, and what there is is either trivial or inappropriate: the comments on the tournament, for instance, that 'every lusty knyght | That loveth paramours' (2111–12) would long to be there if such an event were to take place in England, would suit the lovesick Squire much better than his ascetic father. One does not need to have fought in Prussia to refer to a Prussian shield (2122), or to have been placed at the head of the table to refer to precedence in seating (2200).

The reasons for all this probably lie in the history of the writing of the Tale, though they apply more widely in the Canterbury sequence as well, for many tales may have been written without a specific teller in mind and few bear any close psychological relationship to their tellers. Given the lack of firm evidence for any substantial revision of the original 'Palamon and Arcite' for inclusion in the *Tales*, to deduce the character of the Knight from the story he tells is likely to be a hollow exercise. Chaucer assigns him the story for reasons that have more to do with style and genre than with novelistic psychology. There may however be a dramatic reason too, if I may be allowed a counter-factual (those dangerous arguments based on a missing premiss). If Harry Bailly were ever to give judgement on the tales, it would be unthinkable that the prize should be given to anyone but the Knight. The Host is too class-conscious to do otherwise (Chaucer's listing of three synonyms for chance, as the reason why the Knight is drawn first, encourages the inference that the draw was rigged), and the other pilgrims generally have too little respect for anyone else to make any other outcome acceptable; it is only the Knight who can stay a quarrel when Harry Bailly fails, after the Pardoner's Tale. It is therefore essential that he should be given a story that is worthy of the supper. The Knight's Tale, with its brilliant poetry, its epic reach, and deep *sentence*, would be entirely fitting.

Useful general studies of the Tale include those of Muscatine, *Chaucer and the French Tradition*, pp. 173–90; Kean, *Art of Narrative*, ch. 1; Peter Elbow, *Oppositions in Chaucer*

(Middletown, Conn., 1975), ch. 3; Howard, *Idea*, pp. 227–37; Joerg O. Fichte, *Chaucer's 'Art Poetical': A Study in Chaucerian Poetics* (Studies and Texts in English 1, Tübingen, 1980), pp. 81–96; Pearsall, *Canterbury Tales*, pp. 115–38; William Frost, 'An Interpretation of Chaucer's Knight's Tale', *RES* 25 (1949), 289–304 (repr. in Schoeck and Taylor, *Chaucer Criticism*, pp. 98–116); and Elizabeth Salter, *Chaucer: The Knight's Tale and the Clerk's Tale* (London, 1962), and *Fourteenth Century English Poetry: Contexts and Readings* (Oxford, 1983), ch. 5. Kolve, *Chaucer and Imagery*, ch. 3, studies the Tale's themes in relation to its key images of prison and garden (related, in his view) and the amphitheatre.

A. J. Minnis, *Chaucer and Pagan Antiquity* (Chaucer Studies 8, Cambridge and Dover, NH, 1982), discusses the sources and significance of the non-Christian elements in the Tale.

John P. McCall, *Chaucer among the Gods: The Poetics of Classical Myth* (Pennsylvania and London, 1979), includes a discussion of the effects of Chaucer's development of the gods.

T. McAlindon, 'Cosmology, Contrariety, and *The Knight's Tale*', *MÆ* 55 (1986), 41–57, studies the opposing elements in the tale, including *silva* as chaos.

J. A. Burrow, 'Chaucer's *Knight's Tale* and the Three Ages of Man', in *Essays on Medieval Literature* (Oxford, 1984), pp. 27–48, discusses the characters' ages.

J. D. Burnley, *Chaucer's Language and the Philosophers' Tradition* (Chaucer Studies 2, Cambridge and Totowa, NJ, 1979), pp. 11–28, examines the semantics associated with the good ruler.

A Note on Astrology

The earth was believed to be influenced, hour by hour, by the particular configuration of the planets. Each planet had especial influence at certain times, over certain kinds of events, certain emotions or casts of character, and particular kinds of people.

Each planet presides over the first hour after sunrise on its own day (the Sun on Sunday and so on), and the other planets follow in sequence through the twelve 'unequal' hours of daylight and darkness (their length depending on the season). The prayers of Emily and the cousins are all made at the correct astrological hour: Palamon prays to Venus at the twenty-third hour of Sunday, that is, two hours before sunrise on Monday (2209–11); Emily's prayer follows in the first hour after sunrise on Monday, which is the day devoted to Diana, the moon (2271–4); Arcite's prayer is made in 'the nexte houre of Mars folwynge this' (2367), which would be the fourth hour. The rest of the day is spent in feasting, dancing, and jousting. The next day, the day of the tournament, is Mars' day, when Arcite, who has put himself under the protection of Mars, has his prayer for victory answered. Palamon is overcome just before sundown; the first hour of Tuesday night is Saturn's. The text does not specify the precise hour of the appearance of the Fury, but Saturn had a general influence over all the third quarter of the day, from 3 p.m. to 9 p.m.

The time of year as well as the days of the week are chosen so that this astrological scheme can be developed. It is early May, a year after the meeting in the forest, and Chaucer makes use of this in the design of the amphitheatre. Scorpio, which was a domicile of Mars, is then on the western horizon at sunrise, in the position of Mars' temple; the location of Venus' temple, to the east, is matched by Taurus, a domicile of Venus; and Cancer, a domicile of Luna, lies to the north, corresponding to the temple of Diana. As with the ordering of the prayers, the order of the planets means that once again Emily is in effect placed between the two lovers. On the southern horizon is Capricorn, a domicile of Saturn, the fourth planetary god to take part in the day's action. The sending of the Fury thwarts Theseus' plans for allotting Emily to the victor in the tournament; it is in fact Saturn, not Theseus, who is in control at this point, and human will is at a discount against planetary operation. Mars is an unfortunate planet, the 'lesser infortune'; Saturn is the most malevolent, the 'greater infortune'.

The planets have particular influence not only over hours and days and within certain zodiacal signs, but also over certain types of people, their 'children', and over physiognomic features and 'complexions', the balance of humours within the body. This affects such matters as the listing of the barber, butcher, smith, carter, and cook as the 'children' of Mars in the account of his temple (2020–5); the description of Lygurge and Emetreus; and Arcite's final illness, where again Saturn dominates. He dies because the Saturnian 'retentive virtue' prevents the 'expulsive virtue' from expelling the corrupt matter from his blood and lungs. The four planets of the work represent the four complexions—Mars, hot and dry; Venus, warm and moist; Diana, cold and moist; and Saturn, cold and dry.

Emetreus, who assists Arcite in the tournament, is described in terms that establish him, fittingly enough, as a Martian figure. He rides 'lyk the god of armes, Mars' (2159); he has some Martian physiognomic features, such as yellow eyes, and appropriate attributes such as the eagle and leopard. He also, however, displays certain features that make him almost as much a Solar as a Martian figure, and the result of this is to alter the emphasis from astrological association to physical complexion, since both Mars and the Sun are hot and dry (choleric). Lygurge, who aids Palamon, is not, as one might expect, Venerean, but Saturnian, in keeping with the god who turns out to be Arcite's most decisive enemy. His black beard, rough hair, and large size all mark him as Saturnian; the size of Saturn's orbit, and therefore the slowness of the planet's movement, resulted in the mythographic image of his chariot being pulled by bulls, as is Lygurge's (2139). The simile of the gryphon (2133) may also have Saturnian associations. Dogs and ravens (2148, 2144) were both associated with melancholy, the Saturnian complexion.

I have relied in this section largely on J. D. North, 'Kalenderes Enlumyned Ben They', *RES* 20 (1969), 129–54, which includes a useful glossary of astrological terms; and Douglas Brooks and Alastair Fowler, 'The Meaning of Chaucer's Knight's Tale', *MÆ* 39 (1970), 123–46. I have however disagreed with some of their conclusions where the Tale does not appear to provide sufficient evidence. The fullest account of Chaucer's astronomical knowledge is J. D. North's *Chaucer's Universe* (Oxford, 1988).

The Tale in Context

The placing of the Knight's Tale at the head of the whole Canterbury sequence means that its function in the work is rather different from that of the later tales. There are as yet no other tales for it to reflect, either directly or in a distorting mirror. It can have a place in the web of interlinking ideas and motifs and images only retrospectively. It does, however, serve to introduce a great many of these: there are very few significant motifs in the later tales that have not already had a place in the Knight's. In many instances, too, the usage of a motif in the Knight's Tale seems to serve as normative: that is, it can provide a kind of standard by which others can be evaluated, or the tune on which other tales provide variations. The description of Emily will serve as an example. She is recalled, for better or worse, by a number of other heroines of the *Canterbury Tales*, most particularly by the Alison of the Miller's Tale, May in the Merchant's, and Cecilia in the Second Nun's. The description of Alison, attractive and accessible, is one of Chaucer's masterpieces in its own right, but it also serves to define Emily by contrast, and it gains much of its point from the contrast. May is a sham courtly heroine, and the existence of Emily, who has been so closely associated with the month, serves to show up how hollow the imitation is. Cecilia is the religious heroine, whose standards are defined by their difference from all earthly conceptions: the lilies and roses of her garland are unfading, and invisible except to the eye of faith. Again, the description gains its point from the height of earthly perfection expressed in Emily.

The motifs taken up in later tales are of all sizes and varieties, from skeleton plots to abstract ideas, principles of style to single lines. I shall give only a summary here, since the effects of the later usages are most telling in the tales where they occur, and are best discussed there.

Of plot motifs, the most striking is the love-triangle, the girl with two lovers. The Miller's, Merchant's, and Franklin's Tales resolve this in very different ways, not least because the heroine is married, and generally much more accessible than Emily. The Second Nun's Tale is a variant on this, where it is the lover who is jealous of the husband, not the other way around, and that lover is God. The Manciple's Tale uses the same motif, and there it is not, as in the Knight's Tale, one of the lovers who is killed, but the wife.

The use of a level beyond the human to resolve the action of the plot, as the gods do in the Knight's Tale, is found again in many other tales. In the Merchant's Tale, where the introduction of Classical gods is unparalleled in the sources and analogues, the change seems to have been made with the Knight's Tale in mind. The element of miracle in the Man of Law's Tale is also probably designed to link specifically with the pagan chance of the

Knight's Tale; and in the Second Nun's, there is no room for anything but the shaping will of Providence. The world of the Monk's tragedies is controlled equally tightly by Fortune. The marked absence in the Miller's Tale of God's promised intervention in the form of a flood underscores the insistently secular focus on action alone, where teleology is identified with the mechanics of sex. In the Franklin's Tale, too, the gods significantly fail to act. Ideas of Providence or Fortune pervade many of the tales even when they do not shape the plot: the Nun's Priest's Tale is an outstanding instance.

Questions of Providence are closely linked to the idea of the sovereign good, felicity, of what men, or more particularly women, most desire. Arcite dies still wondering; the Wife of Bath knows exactly, and the hero of her tale has the specific job of finding out. The question is of key concern too in tales such as the Merchant's, in January's notions of paradisal matrimony, and the Pardoner's, where the rioters complete their quest for death only when they have seemingly been diverted by their desire for gold. The notion of men's inability to see what they truly want, what the nature of felicity is (1260–7), is made literal in the blinding of January and in Chantecleer's 'winking'. Only in the religious tales, most particularly the Second Nun's, do the characters achieve an explicit clearness of sight.

Dreams, whether false, true, or—as most often happens—deceptive, figure in a number of tales, and again the Knight's introduces the motif. The human limits on interpretation are a parallel to the limitation of sight. Arcite's dream of an end to his woe prefigures Absolon's equally fallacious dream of a feast or Croesus' dream in the Monk's Tale of being tended by the gods. Sir Thopas's dream of his elf-queen is, like so much else in that poem, beyond hope of classification.

Conceptions of virtue in the *Tales* are often embodied in a small number of words—*pitee*, *trouthe*, *gentillesse*. The Knight's Tale has little specific to say on *gentillesse*, a good deal more on the other two. *Trouthe* is seen most often in terms of inner integrity expressed as a relationship between people, and especially in the keeping of an oath. Palamon and Arcite break their sworn brotherhood; the devil and the summoner of the Friar's Tale, and the rioters of the Pardoner's Tale, swear similar oaths to each other with even more disastrous results. Theseus' *pitee* is ironically recalled by May's (1761, IV(E) 1986), his instinct for compassion against her instinct for adultery.

Love is, of course, one of the key themes of the Knight's Tale, and more than half the others play variations on it. The Wife of Bath redirects the discussion along the lines of the nature of marriage, and especially the woman's role; it is probably no accident that Theseus' first action in the poem is to conquer 'al the regne of Femenye'. He is prepared to listen to women's pleas, but he always acts on his own judgement; the Wife's King Arthur comes out of a similar scene very differently.

   All this is made possible by the fact that the Knight's Tale is more than just a noble tale about noble life. It includes the carter of the temple of Mars as well as the godlike Theseus, death as well as love, the principle of providence as well as random events. Love itself is given a multiple interpretation in the temple of Venus, and the events of the tale show its destructive as well as its positive aspects. Emily may at one moment be the angelic nonpareil, but then in one version of the text she can elicit the comment,

> Wommen, as to speken in comune,
> Thei folwen alle the favour of Fortune.   (2681–2)

The bluntness of the statement matches the crudeness of the sentiment, and in this too the Knight's Tale prefigures the rest of the *Tales*, for its stylistic range embraces almost every other possible register of poetry. Time and again, it opens up possibilities that the later tales explore.

Most studies of the *Tales* include some consideration of the grouping of the tales in Fragment I(A); see in particular Owen, *Pilgrimage and Storytelling*, ch. 4, and Allen and Moritz, *Distinction*, ch. 4. On the wider implications of the Knight's Tale for the whole work, see Cooper, *Structure*, ch. 4, and Kean, *Art of Narrative*, pp. 110–39, 165–85.

Style

The Knight's Tale opens the Canterbury series not only by coming first but by containing within itself much of the stylistic and thematic range of the tales that follow. Its stylistic and rhetorical elevation is as high as anything in the *Tales*, but that is varied by a readiness to use simple, colloquial, sometimes even bathetic, language, that reflects its concern with the whole range of human experience. The juxtaposition of different stylistic registers can be sharp and unsettling. 'The temple of Mars armypotente' is a formal description of place, a *topographia* seething with personifications, technical astrological and mythographic references, Classical allusions, elevated vocabulary, and figures of parallel syntax, but what is actually being said is anything but ordered or ornamental:

> The sowe freten the child right in the cradel;
> The cook yscalded, for al his longe ladel.   (2019–20)

The magnificent spectacle of the tournament and the elaborate ritual of Arcite's funeral hinge on his wounding, where none of the physiological ugliness is spared:

> Blak he lay as any cole or crowe.   (2692)

The image is dehumanizing, without any of the nobility that characterizes many of the other animal images of the poem.

An analysis of this animal imagery illustrates the care with which Chaucer aligns style and theme. The high, middle, and low styles of medieval Latin rhetoric were defined partly in terms of attributes—the appropriate kinds of animal, tree, weapon or tool, name, and so on—and although Chaucer's interpretation of propriety of style is wider than this, most commonly the Knight's Tale conforms with the high style. The similes of the lion and tiger for Palamon and Arcite (1655–9, 2626–34) are of this kind, as are the eagle, lions, and leopards that accompany Emetreus: these are all 'noble' beasts and measure the high chivalry of the combats, although it is their destructive and aggressive energy that is most stressed. Arcite's crow, in the line quoted above, is very different: there is nothing noble about pain. The speech of the characters is also scattered with low-style animal similes that serve to belittle their subjects. Arcite sees himself and Palamon arguing over Emily as dogs fighting for a bone (1177) in a miniature animal fable, a genre far removed from courtly romance. When Theseus castigates the folly inspired by love, he points out that Emily

> woot namoore of al this hoote fare,
> By God, than woot a cokkow or an hare!   (1809–10)

The commonplaceness of the animals reinforces the brusque colloquial tone of the lines; but cuckoos and hares also had sexual connotations, so the choice of image underlines how far the lovers are from achieving, or even envisaging, any practical end. Of deeper metaphysical significance is the belittlement of humankind suggested by both lovers. Man should occupy a place between animals and gods; instead, the cousins see mankind as thrust down to the level of the most un-elevated of animals, the sheep huddled in the fold ready for slaughter (1308–9), or a drunk mouse (1261)—mice having had a habit of falling into beer-vats.

One of the most interesting things about all this is how seldom the point of likeness between object and image relates to anything physical or visual. 'As black as coal or crow' is exceptional; the other similes depend on some moral or abstract or metaphysical attribute (or its lack: the irrationality and moral blindness of beasts, for instance). The *effictio*, the formal description, of Emily shows the positive side of this:

> Emelye, that fairer was to sene
> Than is the lylie upon his stalke grene . . .   (1035–6)

could conceivably indicate that she is wearing green, but the real point of the comparison is one of beauty in general, not particular appearance; and the lily brings with it other associations, of purity and virginity. She is 'fressher than the May', in a long process of association that runs throughout the passage: she and the month are mentioned alternately four times each in fifteen lines (1034–48), in a way that makes the qualities of the two seem almost interchangeable. A similar effect of association is achieved later when 'Up roos the sonne, and up roos Emelye' (2273). Moreover, she sings like an angel—a simile that not only describes her song, but has the wider effect of elevating her above the common run of mortals, just as the image of the drunk mouse reduces the status of mankind. Similes can also be used to describe a state of mind, as Palamon and Arcite before their combat are compared to Thracian hunters awaiting the charging lion (1638–47). This is also the one full epic simile of the poem, and its presence is a measure of the conscious epic element of the Tale.

There are only three lines of narrative for the combat itself: Palamon and Arcite thrust at each other with spears, and fight up to the ankles in blood. All the rest is simile. The effect, as so often in the Tale, is to shift the emphasis from action to spectacle, or to something more like pure meaning or symbol. In the descriptions of the temples, spectacle takes over the functions of both action and meaning. In the temple of Mars, violence as a principle of human life and particular acts of violence are turned into wall-paintings—though the visual impression is often illusory:

> Ther saugh I first the derke ymaginying
> Of Felonye, and al the compassying ...   (1995–6)

Jorge Luis Borges wrote that the line 'The smylere with the knyf under the cloke' marked the point of transition from allegory to novel. The tournament is unique in the poem in being a set piece of concentrated action, and even that is a tightly controlled rhetorical passage that shows to the full the balance of syntax and vocabulary that pervades the Tale, in a miniature version of its structural balance:

> West and est
> In goon the speres full sadly in arrest;
> In gooth the sharpe spore into the syde.
> Ther seen men who kan juste and who kan ryde.   (2601–4)

That this is the most densely alliterative passage in Chaucer's entire works is not accidental; many alliterative poems contain fine battle scenes. The lines follow only the loosest set of rules for alliterative poetry, but they do frequently alliterate across a half-line break:

> Out goon the swerdes / as the silver brighte,   (2608)

or on each side of the break, or throughout the line:

> Out brest the blood / with stierne stremes rede;
> With myghty maces / the bones they tobreste.
> He thurgh the thikkeste of the throng gan threste.   (2610–12)

Chaucer is one of the first poets in English to use alliteration specifically for local and rhetorical effect rather than as a literary medium or a set of formulae.

The balancing of syntax is often most marked when the two lovers are the subject, and again it has thematic implications. It can be done through repetition, often the syntactical parallelism known as *compar*:

> Who looketh lightly now but Palamoun?
> Who spryngeth up for joye but Arcite?   (1870–1)

More often it is done through *commutatio*, where the expected pattern is rearranged:

> Of whiche two Arcita highte that oon,
> And that oother knyght highte Palamon.   (1013–14)

The similes used for them also tend to come in pairs, as do their speeches. Just occasionally this syntactic repetition will serve a very different purpose, as in Palamon's appeal to Theseus after they have been discovered fighting:

> But sle me first, for seinte charitee!
> But sle my felawe eek as wel as me;
> Or sle hym first.   (1721–3)

The parallelism of phrase here is used to ironic ends, for while Chaucer sees the equivalence of the lovers' situations, Palamon in the last line is aware primarily of having a new and brilliant idea.

This speech of Palamon's is unusual in that he is actually using it for purposes of communication. Almost all the dialogue of the Tale comes in the Ellesmere Part II; the great majority of the speeches elsewhere are soliloquies, apostrophes, or prayers to the gods. The two complaints of the lovers against Fortune that begin 'O deere cosyn Palamon' and 'Arcita, cosyn myn' are in fact spoken to empty air. Arcite's dying speech is addressed to Emily, but it includes the line, 'What is this world? What asketh men to have?', and a reply from her, either to these questions or to the speech as a whole, would be unthinkable. Similarly, Theseus' final speech, which in the *Teseida* leads into a debate with Palamon, is here absolute and unchallenged.

The effect of all this is to make episodes that one would expect to be an integral part of the action seem like comments on it. Chaucer tells his audience what is there to be seen, not what his characters see. Even Emily in the garden is seen through the narrator's eyes (he does not know whether her colour or the roses' is finer); the temples are introduced by the formulae 'ther maystow se' or 'ther saugh I'. The whole manner of presenting the tale is equally self-conscious. A high proportion of the rhetorical figures belong to the process of narration, not to the story itself. There are abundant *sententiae*: 'May wole have no slogardie anyght' (1042), 'It is ful faire a man to bere hym evene,│For al day meeteth men at unset stevene' (1523–4), 'Men may the olde atrenne, and noght atrede' (2449). The proverbial nature of these is sometimes explicit: 'Sooth is seyd, go sithen many yeres,│That "feeld hath eyen and the wode hath eres"' (1521–2). There are comments addressed more or less to the participants: 'Let hym be war!' (1218). There are overt devices for abbreviation, from *occupatio*—'I wolde have toold yow . . .' (876)—to a mere 'shortly' (1480). Time and again one is made aware of the techniques of narration: in the transition formulae of 'Now wol I turne to . . .'; in the refusal to tell what is actually described at length (the great *occupatio* covering Arcite's funeral rites); in numerous comments addressed to the audience on the progress of the story or the narrator's inadequacy (1459–60). These culminate in the question inviting the audience to debate the issue of 'who hath the worse, Arcite or Palamoun?' (1348). One is never allowed to forget that the story is a story, told by a narrator to an audience, and not a series of events. The effect is found again in most of the more serious of the Canterbury tales; only in some of the *cherles tales* is the action allowed the illusion of autonomy.

Rhetoric has acquired a bad name for itself, and two or three generations ago the overtness of some of the stylistic devices of the Knight's Tale was seen as a fault. In fact, every one of them has its own function in the larger scheme of the Tale; and Chaucer makes equally conscious rhetorical choices when the style points away from order or balance or elegance. The vigorous, jeering tone of an individualized voice marks the breaking of harmonious friendship:

> And therefore, at the kynges court, my brother,
> Ech man for hymself, ther is noon oother. (1181–2)

Likewise, the erratic viciousness of the gods, the clinical processes of corruption in Arcite's body, and the flippancy with which his soul is dismissed are a necessary counterpoint to the formality and control with which much of the tale is told and an essential part of its meaning.

Stephen Knight, *Rymyng Craftily: Meaning in Chaucer's Poetry* (Sydney and London, 1973), contains a long analysis of the rhetoric in the Knight's Tale.
Jorge Luis Borges, 'From Allegories to Novels', in *Other Inquisitions 1937–52*, trans. Ruth L. Simmons (Austin, 1964); quotation from p. 157.

The Miller's Tale

Most manuscripts designate the links between the tales as 'prologues' to the following tales, and it seems likely that the terminology is in most instances Chaucer's own, but it can on occasion be misleading. Many of the links function as epilogues as much as prologues: they both sign off the preceding tale and introduce the next, and in the process they often serve to indicate a relationship between the two.

The links also carry the frame story within which all the other stories are inset: but they do not tell the story of the pilgrimage to Canterbury. References to places are rare and notoriously confusing. There are few mentions of any events, nor do the pilgrims ever eat or pass a night. Instead, Chaucer provides their voices. The fictive medium of the *Canterbury Tales* is speech—the telling of tales—and this is underlined by the handling of the links. They provide variation from the storytelling, but not distraction, for the pilgrims' voices continue throughout, and what they talk about is the tales themselves. The links constitute a running commentary on the tales, on their tones, themes, and genres, on the range of responses offered by a fictional audience, on the nature of fiction and authorship. Even quarrels between the pilgrims serve less as roadside drama than as elements in this larger debate.

The Miller's Prologue is particularly important as establishing this range of functions. It opens by looking back at the Knight's Tale by recording the approval that that receives from both young and old (and, in view of the significance of the theme of youth and age in both the Knight's and Miller's Tales, the choice of the formula is pointed). Like so many pseudo-historical poems of the Middle Ages, the story of the Theban lovers is seen as worthy of memory; literature exists in part to keep famous deeds in mind. It is defined as a 'noble storie', and admired especially by the 'gentils': the stress on its courtliness makes the Host's colloquialisms and the Miller's highly uncourtly interruption all the more telling.

The Host invites the Monk to follow on—the highest ranking of the ecclesiastics, at least in his own estimation, to follow the highest ranking layman. Hierarchical ordering, however, is not to be allowed to control the world of the pilgrimage, any more than divine justice rules the Knight's Athens or the Miller's Oxford. The drunken Miller interrupts, offering a 'noble tale' of his own to 'quite' the Knight's (3126–7). Both phrases call attention to the paralleling of the tales, but the context in which this 'noble tale' is introduced, with a vigorous oath, makes it quite clear that the words have changed their meaning. The plot elements of the Miller's Tale are likewise similar to the Knight's, but they are just as subversive of the normal expectations of a 'noble tale'. The Miller declares that his story will be 'a legende and a lyf|Bothe of a carpenter and of his wyf' (3141–2). The implications of this highly ambiguous generic formula—'legende' meant primarily a saint's life—are developed in the Tale itself; for the moment, the words serve to annoy the Reeve, the professional enemy of dishonest millers, and himself a carpenter as well. He objects on three grounds: that the Miller is talking 'harlotrye' (a charge of which he will in turn be guilty); that the tale will be slanderous; and that it will be insulting to wives. The matter of whether one can find a good woman will be raised later by the Wife of Bath, in the Clerk's Envoy, by Proserpina in the Merchant's Tale, and by Prudence in *Melibee*. Here, the Miller gives a particularly optimistic answer (in a couplet omitted by Hengwrt and some other manuscripts, 3155–6), but adds a more dubious rider: there are a thousand good wives to every bad one, and it helps to keep the statistics favourable if one does not enquire too fully into the *pryvetee* of one's wife. Women, like God, have secrets it is rash to scrutinize too closely (3164–5): the collocation is a mischievous elaboration of one of 'Cato's' more complacent aphorisms. The discussion introduces some of the main themes of the Tale, and the quarrel with the Reeve lays the groundwork for the story to follow.

The Prologue concludes with Chaucer's apology for reporting 'harlotrie'—an apology already prepared for in the Miller's own excusing of his tale on the grounds of his drunkenness (3139–40). There is no ironic euphemism here about 'noble' tales; the story to come will be a 'cherles tale', not only a tale told by a churl, but a churlish tale, with all its associations of content, vocabulary, and style. Any sense of dramatic naturalism is however illusory. Drunken millers do not really tell tales to this standard, and Chaucer is apologizing for the wrong thing—he is not reporting someone else's story but creating one of his own, however hard he may declare his innocence:

> I moot reherce
> Hir tales alle, be they bettre or werse,
> Or elles falsen som of my mateere.   (3173–5)

Boccaccio had defended the improper tales of the *Decameron* along similarly disingenuous lines. It is the literal author who chooses to write the tale; but since it is possible to 'turne over the leef', it can be presented as the reader's fault, not the author's, if the tale is found objectionable:

> Blameth nat *me* if that *ye* chese amys.   (3181)

Furthermore, the tale is told in 'game', not 'ernest', and so serious moral objections are out of place; so long as the rules of the game are observed, play lies ouside ethics. The rules that apply here are simply those of the storytelling compact.

The Miller's Tale is, in the modern sense, indecorous; but it keeps rhetorical decorum in being appropriate for its teller. Its placing on the moral and rhetorical spectrum as a churl's tale means that it is not pornographic—as it would be if it were told by, say, the Prioress. Such placing means that the apology itself becomes somewhat paradoxical, for its effect is to show that no apology is needed. The truth of fiction is not absolute, nor does an author need to give sincere moral endorsement to every word he writes: since the world contains both *gentils* and *cherles*, fiction can encompass both noble tales and *cherles tales*, *moralitee* and *hoolynesse*. The Miller's Prologue serves to introduce the relativity, the all-encompassing reach, of the whole *Canterbury Tales*. It was implicit in the social and moral variety of the pilgrims of the General Prologue; here, it is given a specifically literary range of reference and defines the method of the entire work.

For the *Distichs of Cato*, see p. 13 above.

Date and Text

There is no certain date for the Miller's Tale, but it was clearly written when Chaucer's poetic skill was at its most developed. The closeness of its relationship with the adjacent tales suggests that it was written specifically to follow the Knight's and to pair with the Reeve's. It would have been written, in other words, not only after Chaucer had decided to compose a story-collection, but when he realized how the sequence of tales could be articulated internally, through the parallelism of adjacent stories, and externally, through dramatic exchanges between the pilgrims. The coherence of Fragment I(A) in all the manuscripts may also suggest that Chaucer never had the tale copied independently of its place in the sequence.

Textual variants are mostly minor. The couplet 3721–2 is omitted by Hengwrt and a number of other manuscripts. The word that most often appears as *verye* in John's charm (3485) may be a rationalization of an unfamiliar survival such as *nerye*, 'protect'.

There is a single gloss, 'Unde Ovidus: Ictibus agrestis' ('Hence Ovid: the boorish with blows'), by 3382, on women being won 'for strokes', in Hengwrt, Ellesmere, and some other manuscripts; one manuscript extends the phrase. It is not in fact Ovidian, and its source is unknown. Scribes occasionally added other headings or comments, notable among them being

Hengwrt's 'Nota malum quid' to call attention to the naughtiness of Absolon's kissing Alison's backside.

E. Talbot Donaldson argues for the 'nerye' reading in 'The Miller's Tale A 3483–6', in his *Speaking of Chaucer* (London, 1970), pp. 131–3.
Textual and critical issues are capably surveyed by Thomas W. Ross (ed.), *The Miller's Tale* (Variorum II 3, Norman, Okla., 1983).

Genre

The Miller's Tale is a fabliau—the first of five in the Canterbury Tales (the others being the Reeve's, Cook's, Summoner's, and Shipman's). While it is probably chance that there are also five romances, it is no chance that this most brilliant of fabliaux is juxtaposed with the epic-romance of the Knight. The characteristics of the two forms are in diametric opposition to each other, and Chaucer exploits the contrasts to the full. There seems to have been no English equivalent of the word 'fabliau', but Chaucer's phrase 'cherles tale' places it perfectly in contradistinction to the courtly romance. The fabliau is set in the contemporary everyday world, not the far away and long ago; its characters are bourgeois, peasants, or clerks, not aristocrats; it generally concerns humankind's most basic functions, mostly sex, sometimes excretion, whereas romance looks to ideals and idealized love; it is concerned more with cunning and folly than virtue and evil; it opposes all pretensions to authority; it often contains an element of burlesque or parody of courtly values or language; above all, it is funny.

Despite all this, the fabliau is not a bourgeois phenomenon. The French examples are commonly found in manuscripts alongside romances, and fabliaux were written by poets notable for more courtly forms. It seems, indeed, to have been at least in part an aristocratic form that mocked middle- or low-class pretensions, or the lack of them. The Miller's Tale itself confirms such a view: it is written by the same poet who wrote, and for the same audience that read, the Knight's Tale, and the element of burlesque becomes very specific from the detail with which the two works are paralleled. What distinguishes the Miller's Tale from other examples of the genre is the sheer detailed brilliance of its handling—of style, character, narrative structure. It is in no way typical of the form; as befits its place in a story-competition, it is the best.

The fabliau was predominantly a French form; the earliest examples date from about 1200. The commonest plot is the love-triangle, on which the story of Alison and her lovers is a variation. There is only one surviving English example before Chaucer, the late thirteenth-century *Dame Siriz*, but it is likely that others have been lost. The genre stands in a problematic relation to exemplum and fable; fabliaux can be used for exemplary

purposes in homiletic collections, and independent examples also frequently end with a moral, though it may be a spoof. In essence, however, the
point of the form is its amorality: the fabliau is the expression of the non-
official culture of carnal irreverence, of all those feelings suppressed by
courtly politeness or religious asceticism that break into joyous burlesque.

On fabliaux, see Per Nykrog, *Les Fabliaux* (1957; repr. Publications romanes et françaises
123, Geneva, 1973).

Sources and Analogues

The sources for the Miller's Tale are of four kinds. The first two categories
are the familiar ones—works that may have provided the plot, and works
that contribute aphorisms and allusions. The second two are not often
discussed as sources, but are at least as important in the shaping, detail, and
final impression made by the tale. One is the story that precedes it in the
Canterbury sequence, the Knight's. This contributes (most often by
specific contrast) to the treatment and language of the tale, and probably
dictated the choice and handling of the plot. The last source category is not
literature but life: contemporary Oxford, reproduced with remarkable
accuracy to provide the setting and many details of the work.

A direct source for the plot of the Miller's Tale has never been found, but
close analogues exist in Flemish, Italian, and German; there is a remote
analogue in the *Decameron*, 3, 4. Chaucer is generally assumed to have found
the story in a French fabliau, now lost; the only direct trace of it in the text
may be in the remark on John's finding no bread to sell in his fall (3821–2),
apparently a translation of a French colloquialism. The plot is made up of a
number of separable motifs—the flood, the misdirected kiss, the branding—that are found in combination in the analogues. The earliest of these,
and the only one that could predate the Miller's Tale, is a Flemish fabliau
called the *Dits van Heilen van Beersele*. This tells of a woman of easy virtue
whose favours are sought by a miller, a priest, and a smith, who come to her
in succession one night. The first lover to arrive, the miller, hides in a trough
hung from the rafters to avoid the priest, and overhears him prophesy a
flood. The third to arrive, the smith, kisses the priest's arse in a trick like that
practised by Alison on Absolon, and returns to repay him with an iron
heated in his smithy. The priest's cry for water makes the miller cut the rope
of his trough, and he breaks an arm and a leg.

Though this may not represent the form in which Chaucer came to know
the story, it still serves to indicate the lines along which he modelled his own
version. His heroine is married, and to an older husband—motifs that will
re-emerge many times in the course of the *Tales*. She is also more implicated
in the practical joke on the last lover—it is her arse that Absolon kisses

first—although she still comes off unpunished at the end. The three lovers become (as in some other versions) a husband and rival suitors. The miller is now not participant but narrator; the priest and smith become the rival clerks, and Chaucer's smith Gerveys is added as an extra character. The rivals for the wife's favours are sharply differentiated from each other. The differences between all the analogues and Chaucer's text are however primarily a matter of transformation rather than alteration. The wonderful verisimilitude of setting that becomes crucial for the working out of the plot, the development of characterization that makes Nicholas's gulling of the carpenter plausible and gives Alison and her husband and lovers a degree of vitality rare in any of the stories of the Canterbury sequence, the richness of stylistic development, emphasize how inadequate any notion of plot source alone must be.

The tale is markedly non-sententious, in keeping with its cheerful amorality. Its few maxims paradoxically contribute to the lack of coherent surface morality. Cato is heavy-handedly, and incorrectly, called in as witness to the platitude of the desirability of equality in marriage (3227–9); both that and John's account of the astronomer who falls in a marl-pit (3457–61) may be from Walter Burley's *Liber de vita et moribus philosophorum*, though other sources are possible. The lack of cited authority for the marl-pit story gives it the force more of folk wisdom than of learning. The Bible, as always, contributes a good deal, though rather backhandedly. The clerk Nicholas is the only character who can quote it all accurately (3530), and then in the service of his adultery. The Song of Songs is a resonance behind Absolon's love-language (3698–706); his biblical prototype was genuinely beautiful, where Absolon is primarily merely vain. The general background for the story of Noah's Flood is of course from the Bible, but Nicholas's version of it (and John's understanding of it) are strongly coloured by the version current in the cycle plays, where Noah's wife is an unwelcome liability (3538–43). Many of the cycle play versions of 'a legende and a lyf | Bothe of a carpenter and of his wyf' (3141–2) develop Joseph as the husband who believes himself to have been cuckolded. Nicholas's singing of the 'Angelus ad virginem', a hymn on the Annunciation, may add a latently blasphemous touch in this context. The play references start early in the Miller's Prologue, when he speaks 'in Pilates voys' (3124), and become most literal in Absolon's acting of Herod. The Tale, in fact, sets no value on traditional learning for the sake of its moral or philosophical value, and its strongest range of literary reference is towards the vernacular.

Such an emphasis is in marked contrast to the Knight's Tale—as indeed is everything about this story. The choice of this plot for this point in the sequence, much of the shaping and selection of detail, and even some of the words depend on the Tale's relationship to the Knight's. The correlations are occasionally positive, most often very precisely negative. The plot appears in context as almost a parody of the tale of Palamon and Arcite. The reduction in the number of rival lovers from the three of the analogues to two (plus husband) may be due to the Knight's Tale; the close paralleling of the cousins is reflected in Chaucer's turning the rivals into two sorts of clerks. The portrait of Alison is a countertype to that of Emily, and its style and imagery, and those of the tale are large, are drawn from registers precisely opposite to those of the Knight's. Nicholas has his chamber to himself 'allone, withouten any compaignye' (3204), like Arcite's vision of mankind in the grave (2779): the repetition serves to encapsulate the different worlds of the tales. The morality of the tales is also in precise contrast: one seeks endlessly for meaning in the world; the notion that there might be any meaning never enters the other. The Knight's Tale celebrates the wisdom of age, the Miller's Tale points out its folly. Palamon and Arcite tend to sublimate their love, and aim at marriage; the Miller's Tale opens with marriage, and never considers love in any but the most earthy physical terms.

The contrast is also clear in the setting of the tales—ancient Athens versus contemporary Oxford. This setting provides an abundance of details drawn not from literary sources but from life in the city itself. It was conventional for fabliaux to have a contemporary bourgeois or peasant setting, in contrast to the exotic settings of romance; Chaucer is however unique in the fullness of local detail that he provides. It is a tale that relies on particularities, and almost every one can be given a firm Oxford context. Nicholas needs to have lodgings in the carpenter's house, since few students lived in halls. It is John's involvement in the great building works at Oseney Abbey that takes him away from home on the day Nicholas first makes a pass at Alison. The care for local detail extends to the use of proper names: Absolon is recorded as a town name, but not within the university, in the fourteenth century; St Nicholas was the patron saint of scholars. The saints who are called on all have local reference—St Frideswide (3449), the most notable local saint; St Neot (3771), who according to tradition encouraged King Alfred to found the university (New College was founded on the site of St Neot's Hall); even St Thomas of Kent (3291, 3425, 3461), as there was a parish church, a fraternity, a hall, and an annual feast bearing his name. Some holy days were kept specifically by women, as Alison goes to church with the other wives on the day that Absolon falls for her. Professional details are also accurate. Absolon's multiple occupations of parish clerk, barber, and land conveyor fit the Oxford context well (one Oxford scrivener of the period taught conveyancing), and would bring in enough to finance his fine clothes and his presents to Alison. The carpenter makes the ladders in preparation for the Flood, but he acquires the tubs, which would have been joiner's work. Smiths often worked at night or in the early mornings, just as Gerveys is busy preparing 'plough harneys' for the next day's work.

The tendency of most fabliaux is to combine an unlikely plot with plausible detail. The Miller's Tale is as unlikely a story as any in the whole Canterbury collection (except perhaps for the Wife of Bath's): the story of the Knight's Tale is a model of plausibility compared with a lover's disposal of a jealous husband by persuading him to string himself up in a tub in the roof for fear of a repeat of Noah's Flood. What comes over in a reading of the two tales, however, is much more the contrast of noble epic distance, where little is detailed except for the paintings in the temples, with the bustling everyday life of a university town. The plot may come from a lost fabliau, but one of the things that makes the Miller's Tale unique is its firm grounding in fourteenth-century Oxford.

Stith Thompson, 'The Miller's Tale', in *Sources and Analogues*, gives the texts of four analogues, including the *Dits van Heilen* (with a translation). Texts and translations of eleven analogues are provided by Benson and Andersson, *Literary Context*.

R. E. Kaske, 'The *Canticum canticorum* in the *Miller's Tale*', *SP* 59 (1962), 479–500, argues for the significance of the Song of Songs.

J. A. W. Bennett, *Chaucer at Oxford and at Cambridge* (Oxford, 1974), chs. 1–2, gives a fascinating analysis of the local detail of the Tale.

Structure

It says much about the narrative method of the Miller's Tale that an account of the structure is almost identical to an account of the plot: both work to the model of the all too predictable surprise. The red-hot coulter is waiting for Nicholas's fart, and the carpenter, who has his moment at the centre of the stage in the middle of the tale and has been forgotten up in the ceiling while the narrative concentrates on the three lovers, is brought back into the story decisively and inevitably by the cry for water.

In one sense it is indeed, as the Miller claims, the tale of a carpenter, with the wife second. He is, in theory, the 'authority figure' of the tale, and it therefore opens with him; his gulling occupies the central section; and it closes with his literal and metaphorical downfall. One thinks of him none the less as a peripheral character. Neither he nor Alison is named when they are first introduced, as the young men are: we hear their names first from each other, when they are in bed together (3366–9). The moment of naming is frequently important: it may not be altogether irrelevant that in the *Divine Comedy* we first hear Dante's name spoken by Beatrice. The three opening lines of the tale are devoted to the carpenter, but then the focus shifts to his lodger Nicholas, who occupies the next thirty; and most of the following fifty are devoted to the still unnamed 'yonge wif'. By the time the introductory descriptions are complete, we know that Nicholas is interested in everything except his studies, but especially (for it is mentioned first) 'deerne love'; that the carpenter fears being cuckolded; and that Alison is young, wild, full of animal vitality, and that thoughts of bedding her precede thoughts of wedding her (3269–70). The plot, when it finally gets under way eighty lines into the tale, follows the pattern one might expect. The narrative pace is fast, but never at the expense of telling detail, and Absolon, the third most important character, is described on his first appearance in as much detail as the earlier two—including his squeamishness over farting.

After the opening descriptions, the tale is divided into a series of scenes: Nicholas's accosting of Alison; Alison's visit to church, which serves principally as an excuse for the introduction of Absolon, the one main character from outside the household; his serenading of her; the plan to dispose of the carpenter, and how John falls for it; the night when all three climb into the kneading-tubs and Alison and Nicholas climb out again; Absolon's discovery that the carpenter may be away, and his wooing; the misdirected kiss; Absolon and the smith; the branding; and the carpenter's fall. Transitions are kept to a minimum: there is none of the 'Now wol I stynte . . . forth I wol yow telle' of the Knight's Tale. Here, the next event simply happens, so that Absolon at church and his serenade succeed each other without any narrative discontinuity. There is a brief comment on the progress of the story to mark the next break—'This passeth forth; what wol ye bet than weel?' (3370)—but the only transition to be handled with any degree of elaboration is at 3611–13, when the carpenter's laments are linked to his acquisition of the troughs and making of ladders by way of a comment on 'ymaginacioun'—a passage that stands out by reason of its uncharacteristically abstract vocabulary.

The end of the tale is signalled first by the coming together of all the plot strands—Absolon, Nicholas, and Alison in interaction as they never have been before, the climax of the Flood motif—then by a distancing from the main characters, as Chaucer withdraws his sharp focus on events to the 'folk' who comment on the carpenter's folly. Where one might expect a final summing up by way of moral, Chaucer gives a four-line plot summary; and the final line of blessing provides as startling a juxtaposition as any in the whole *Tales*.

> And Nicholas is scalded in the towte.
> This tale is doon, and God save al the rowte!

Themes

The main purpose of literature in the Middle Ages was ethical and didactic; almost all works pointed beyond or outside themselves, to exemplary or allegorical functions. The Miller's Tale is a triumphant exception. Harry Bailly had suggested that the tales could be of *sentence* and *solaas*, and the Miller opts decisively for the latter. The story can none the less be given a somewhat paradoxical meaning, even within the *Canterbury Tales*—or especially within the *Tales*, for, as with every story in the work, it is altered by its context. Its juxtaposition to the Knight's Tale makes its very lack of significance significant: where that raises questions about the providential ordering of the universe, the Miller's Tale refuses to look beyond the individual's immediate interests.

The tale works not in abstracts but action: it has a plot, not themes. What one might describe as its themes are often the absence or the parody of something else. One such is the burlesque of the courtly that pervades both the narrative and the direct speech: it shows in the stylistic elaboration of the portraits of the city wife and the parish clerk, in Nicholas's threats to die for love (the *double entendre* of 'die' is only established from the sixteenth century: evidence from the fourteenth relies entirely on passages such as this, so falls short of proof), Absolon's aping of courtly manners, and his linguistic extravaganzas in his serenades. The cure for his lover's malady, in discovering some unsavoury aspects of his lady, is ludicrously close to recommended medical remedies. The ideals of religion come in for as severe a knocking as the ideals of love. Absolon refuses the wives' offerings out of 'curteisie' (3351); Christ's works and the business of sex are closely interlinked (3303–8, 3654–6); motifs of the Flood and the 'legende' of a carpenter and his wife are secularized to a point of near-blasphemy. God as controller of human events never gets a look in, and His place is taken by Nicholas until Absolon decides that vengeance is his. One of the most pervasive motifs of the tale is the idea of *privetee*, whether God's or woman's, and from the initial reference to both in one breath in the Prologue (3164) the two are easily confused with one another: the carpenter's insistence on the value of not knowing 'Goddes pryvetee' (3454) indicates nothing so much as that he knows little of his wife's, and Nicholas appeals to the same principle to hide his true motive of sleeping with Alison (3555–8). When John tells her of his own 'pryvetee' (3603), by contrast, she already 'knew it bet than he'.

The world of the tale is circumscribed by the limits of Oxford and Oseney, or by the walls of the carpenter's house and the street outside. Ethical issues are never raised; the story is not immoral so much as cheerfully amoral. It does not even mete out justice within the terms of its own plot. Nicholas and Absolon may get their deserts, but the tale is grossly unfair, by any normal standards, to both Alison and John—to Alison because she gets away with everything, to John because he suffers a broken arm and general ridicule in return for mere gullibility. It is, of course, in the nature of comedy (including fabliau) to deal in cleverness and folly rather than moral categories, and it is worse to be a fool than a knave; the very lack of reflection with which such principles are accepted itself serves to define the vision of the world, the reading of life, implied by this fabliau. Many fabliaux do present a moral at the end (though not necessarily a serious one); here there is only a brief and vivid plot summary.

Defences of the morality of the Miller's Tale have followed two lines, neither wholly convincing. The traditional defence of comedy is that it teaches what to avoid: the very lack of expressed morality is itself ironic, as pointing towards known standards of correct behaviour. It is however almost impossible to read the Miller's Tale in quite these terms, and Alison's escape is hardly conducive to such an interpretation. The second defence would assert that such apparently unethical works could be seen as recreational and therefore healthful—ethics thus being allowed to re-enter by the back door. One cannot, however, imagine any writer composing a fabliau in order to promote the general health of his audience: the justification comes after the event.

The amorality of the tale is underscored, not only by its relationship to the Knight's, but by its being given to the Miller. It is a 'cherles tale' in content and also style, with its constant reference to popular poetics, but it also belongs to this particular churl. The Miller, with his thumb of gold, has no great concern for morality, and is given to talking of 'synne and harlotries' (561); and, as often happens in the *Tales*, there is a miniature portrait of him within the tale itself. Here it is John's servant, likewise called Robin (3129, 3466); both are described as a 'stout' or 'strong carl for the nones' (545, 3469), and both are given to heaving doors off their hinges. Further attempts to read off the psychology of the Miller from the tale Chaucer gives him are more likely to point to qualities in the tale than in the teller. The fact that Chaucer ascribes *this* tale to a character like the Miller itself makes a statement about the nature of the story: it makes no claim to being a sufficient reading of the world, or even a particularly admirable one. The effect is remarkably liberating. One can enjoy the tale on its own terms all the more for the presence of counter-examples close to hand. Moral strictures are undercut by Chaucer's disarming acknowledgement in the Prologue that they would be entirely appropriate.

Among the many interesting general studies of the Tale are Alfred David, *The Strumpet Muse: Art and Morals in Chaucer's Poetry* (Bloomington, Ind., and London, 1976), ch. 6; Kolve, *Chaucer and Imagery*, ch. 4; Paul E. Beichner, 'Characterization in *The Miller's Tale*', in Schoeck and Taylor, *Chaucer Criticism*, pp. 117–29.

Morton W. Bloomfield, 'The Miller's Tale—an UnBoethian Interpretation', in Jerome Mandel and Bruce A. Rosenberg (eds.), *Medieval Literature and Folklore Studies: Essays in Honor of Francis Lee Utley* (New Jersey, 1970), pp. 205–12, argues for the significance of the absence of moral order in the tale.

Edward C. Schweitzer, 'The Misdirected Kiss and the Lover's Malady in Chaucer's *Miller's*

Tale', in Julian N. Wasserman and Robert J. Blanch (eds.), *Chaucer in the Eighties* (Syracuse, NY, 1986), pp. 223–33, notes the appropriateness of Absolon's cure.

Glending Olson, *Literature as Recreation in the Later Middle Ages* (Ithaca, NY, 1982), describes the medieval medical justification of literature.

The Tale in Context

If the Miller's Tale in isolation would be a tale without a meaning, its context in the Canterbury sequence works dynamically to suggest more. Its elements of burlesque of the courtly are highlighted by its following the Knight's. The description of Alison establishes her as the accessible and sensuous antitype to the distant and spiritualized Emily; she is more animal than goddess. Love is reinterpreted as sex, and the rivalry of Palamon and Arcite, with its formal speeches, the fight in the wood, the magnificent tournament, is reduced finally to the business of Nicholas's arse. Even the Knight's high themes of man's ignorance of his own destiny and of the ambiguous or misleading promises of the gods are parochialized, in John's folly and in Absolon's rash optimism that the itching of his lips signifies kissing. He even manages a comically unprophetic dream.

It is a process not only of reduction, however, but of transformation. The Miller's Tale is not primarily—or not only—*less* than the Knight's: it is *different*. They share an almost identical plot—the rival loves of two young men for the same girl (with John the carpenter thrown in for good measure, for the 'caging' of Alison is an added complication comparable with the knights' imprisonment)—but they operate in different worlds. Ancient Athens and modern Oxford are divided by more than time and space, just as the Knight and Miller are divided by more than class and character. The tales offer contrasting readings of human experience, of the world in which choices are made and actions are taken. The readings are radically different, but not in terms of right and wrong. The Knight's and Miller's Tales coexist: one does not cancel out the other. It is no accident that Chaucer decided to set these two at the head of his story-collection. The Knight's Tale had opened up possibilities beyond the courtly, the moral, the providential; the Miller's Tale reads the world not for meaning but for fact. The rest of the stories explore the range between.

The Miller's Tale serves as the hinge between its enclosing stories, connecting tales that otherwise would have nothing in common. The Knight's Tale provides the impetus for the Miller's and suggests many of its themes; the Miller's in turn cues the Reeve's—both dramatically, in the quarrel between the two pilgrims, and in terms of plot and motif. It is likely that Chaucer altered his sources to cast the lovers as clerks because he already had the Reeve's Tale in mind as its pair.

Many other themes that recur throughout the work figure as motifs in the Miller's Tale: ideas of marriage, of old husbands and young wives, of wifely obedience (or the lack of it), and adultery; notions of wisdom or folly, especially as associated with age. The very choice of the name Alison draws an equation between the young sex-loving wife and the older one, Alison of Bath; each finds her most congenial mate in the form of an Oxford student. Before marrying the Wife, Jankin has lodgings with yet another Alison, who was the Wife's 'gossib' and who knew her 'privetee' better than her parish priest—a group of themes strongly reminiscent of the Miller's Tale. The relationship of clerks and women is one on which the Clerk of Oxenford will also have something to say. The various answers in the Wife of Bath's Tale as to what women most desire are foreshadowed in the Miller's suggestions as to how women are best won, by riches, *gentillesse*, or a beating (3381–2). If the Wife's list does not include the third, her fight with Jankin suggests that there may be some truth in it.

On the contrast of this Tale with the Knight's, see Cooper, *Structure*, pp. 110–16, 227–30; Benson, *Chaucer's Drama of Style*, ch. 4; and the studies of David, Bloomfield, and Schweitzer listed on p. 102 above.

Style

The style of the Miller's Tale can perhaps best be illustrated from one of its most famous lines:

'Tehee!' quod she, and clapte the wyndow to.   (3740)

The narrative pace is fast—a speech and an action in a single line; the words are short, with a high proportion of Germanic to Romance vocabulary; there is plentiful recourse to direct speech and its most unsophisticated idioms; and the syntax is spare and uncomplicated, with minimal subordination. The effects of all this are much more striking in an oral delivery than on the printed (or manuscript) page. Line for line, the Miller's Tale reads aloud at almost twice the rate of the Knight's—an astonishingly large differential, and an indication of the extraordinary narrative pace of the tale.

Simplicity of syntax and vocabulary alone does not begin to account for the poetic brilliance of the work. There is an abundance of rhetoric, though not of the kind that calls attention to itself, and the detail of its use is often very specific to this tale. There is, for instance, no shortage of imagery, especially simile, but its range of reference is strictly circumscribed. The animal predominates: not the noble beasts of the Knight's Tale, but farmyard animals, and especially young ones (the kid, calf, and colt of the description of Alison, 3260–3). Alison is also like a weasel, or like a mouse to Absolon's cat (3346–7). John will swim as merrily as a duck after the drake

(3575–6). The tendency of all this imagery is emphatically low style; it works as a counterpoint to the high register of reference of the Knight's Tale, it equates the sexual appetites of the various characters with the natural world (and the tone consistently stresses more the naturalness than the beastliness), and it offsets the courtly level of imagery that the Tale seems to keep reaching out for and signally failing to achieve. Absolon may (correctly, in poetic terms) sing like a nightingale, but his eyes are 'greye as goos' (3377, 3317), and Alison's song is like a swallow's. Absolon's comparison of himself to a turtle-dove has good associations with true love from both courtly literature and the Song of Songs, but his mourning 'as dooth a lamb after the tete' is ludicrously non-symbolic (3706, 3704). That he later weeps like a beaten child does little to restore any sense of manhood about him (3759). Other kinds of image in the Tale are equally insistent on their reference to the circumscribed contemporary world. There are cultivated plants: the herbs *lycorys* and *cetewale* (3207), sufficiently commonplace for them to reappear with the kitchen-garden collection in *Sir Thopas*; the sloe, or the pear-jonette to which Alison is compared, and which had bawdy connotations in the Middle Ages—witness the pear-tree of the Merchant's Tale, or the fifteenth-century lyric 'I have a newe gardin' that uses grafting pears as a euphemism for the sex act. Her face is shinier than gold, not in its pure and therefore potentially symbolic form, but the gold of hard cash (3256). Absolon's shoes are carved like the tracery windows of St Paul's (3318). In the more courtly tales, the lark announces the day; here, as in all the lower-style tales, it is the cock.

The vocabulary of the Tale is similarly homely in register. Polysyllabic words tend to occur in clusters, only to be identified as jargon and pushed aside—as are Nicholas's conclusions and interrogations, 'I may nat rekene hem alle' (3193–8), or his almagest and astrolabe that lie unused in his bedroom. A word such as 'cynamome' is deflated by rhyming with 'speketh to me' (3699–700). There are remarkably few abstract nouns: the story does not require them. The sensitivity of register to context is shown most strikingly in direct speech. Nicholas, as a clerk, is allowed greater articulateness than John the carpenter: he can run a spoken sentence over several lines, and his vocabulary easily takes in words such as *suffisaunt* and *purveiaunce*. By contrast, two of John's longest speeches are charms, and his attempts at words such as *Noah* and, probably, *astronomy* are sad failures (3477–9; 3483–6; 3818; 3457). Absolon's speech is equally distinctive by reason of its cloying imagery, often wonderfully contrasted with Alison's directness (3698–717). His style of speech changes completely after the first kiss: his exchange with the smith is the first businesslike thing he has said in the whole poem. Even the minor characters, the Oseney cloisterer and Gerveys the smith, are given distinctive ways of speaking, one taking seven

lines to say he doesn't know where John is (3664–70), the other fitting into
five lines three religious exclamations, three nonce-words ('what', 'ey', the
problematic 'viritoot'), and a verbal dig in the ribs (3767–71).

  The vocabulary of the narrative passages is less idiomatic; its main
function is always to further the story. The most notable exceptions to the
purely functional are some of the adjectives and adverbs: when the
carpenter 'broghte of myghty ale a large quart' (3497) for his and Nicholas's
consumption, we are told generously more than is required by the plot
alone. The most notorious aspect of the Tale's low-style diction is the use of
basic words for basic concepts: *ers, swyve, fart*—words that reappear only in
the other fabliaux. 'Queynte' may well, however, be a euphemism,
equivalent to the Wife of Bath's 'bele chose'; it does of course recall the
absent word *cunt*, but does not strictly mean the same thing—so all the puns
on the word that critics have found may well be illusory.

  The homeliness of the vocabulary and imagery is matched in the use of
poetic devices. There is a single rhetorical question, not now on the meaning
of the universe, but on more practical concerns:

> Who rubbeth now, who froteth now his lippes
> With dust, with sond, with straw, with clooth,
>   with chippes
> But Absolon . . . ?   (3747–9)

The elaborate amplification devices of the Knight's Tale have largely gone,
though Alison and Absolon are each given a formal description, an *effictio*;
the potential high-style effect of these is however decisively thwarted by the
homeliness of detail. The correct ordering of a description was to start at the
head and work downwards; Alison's, by contrast, starts around her middle,
and keeps returning compulsively to that region, even finishing by working
up her legs (3267). The description of Emily is done in terms of sight and
hearing, the spiritual senses; Alison is perceived as much in terms of the
baser physical senses, of smell and taste (sweet and intoxicating, 3261), and
touch ('softer than the wolle is of a wether', 3249—how would one know
without poking her?). A phrase in the description of Absolon points to a
different poetic device: his surplice is 'as whit as is the blosme upon the rys'.
The image is most familiar in vernacular lyric and romance, and other
phrases—especially alliterating pairs—similarly evoke a traditional vernacular frame of poetic reference: *morne milk, stille as stoon, wilde and wood,
clepe ne crye*, and numerous others (3236, 3472, 3517, 3587). Certain words,
notably *hende* and *lemman*, belong to the same vernacular tradition, but had
become downgraded in a way that makes them distinctly uncourtly. 'Hende'
is regularly used for Nicholas (somewhat ambiguously, since it means both
'nice' and 'ready at hand') in a way that recalls the attachment of epithet to

noun of oral tradition; the carpenter is customarily 'sely' and Absolon 'joly',
until he too takes over the carpenter's epithet at the end (3744)—'sely
Absolon'. The term covers the meanings 'innocent', 'simple-minded' and
'wretched', or any combination of them.

One other stylistic feature is especially characteristic of the Miller's Tale:
the exploitation of incongruity. This can emerge in individual words, most
strikingly rhyme words (*kiss/piss* is the most notorious example, 3797–8).
Similar juxtapositions on a larger scale often play off the idealistic against
the pragmatic or the religious against the lustful:

> 'For deerne love of thee, lemman, I spille,'
> And heeld hire harde by the haunchebones,
> And seyde, 'Lemman, love me al atones,
> Or I wol dyen, also God me save!'   (3278–81)

The episode is followed immediately by Alison going off to church, 'Cristes
owene werkes for to wirche' (3308). Later, the 'melody' that Nicholas and
Alison make in bed concludes with the bell ringing for lauds and friars
singing in the chancel (3655–6). Sometimes the incongruity is a matter of
overlay rather than juxtaposition, as in Absolon's misplaced 'curteisye'
(3351), or as phrases from the Song of Songs keep not quite breaking surface
in his love-language.

On the vocabulary of the Tale, see Larry D. Benson, 'The Queynte Punnings of Chaucer's
   Critics', *SAC* Proceedings, 1 (1984), 23–47 (*queynte*), and Donaldson, 'The Idiom of
   Popular Poetry in the Miller's Tale', repr. in *Speaking of Chaucer*, pp. 13–29 (*hende, derne,
   joly, gent, ore*).
On the description of Alison, see Kevin S. Kiernan, 'The Art of the Descending Catalogue,
   and a Fresh Look at Alison', *ChR* 10 (1975–6), 1–16. 'I have a newe gardin' is no. 21 in
   Rossell Hope Robbins's *Secular Lyrics of the XIVth and XVth Centuries* (2nd edn.,
   Oxford, 1955).
On imagery in the tale, see Janette Richardson, *Blameth Nat Me: A Study of Imagery in
   Chaucer's Fabliaux* (Mouton Studies in English Literature 58, The Hague, 1970), ch. 9.
On the style of the Tale as contrasted with the Knight's, see Benson, *Chaucer's Drama of
   Style*, ch. 4, and Christopher Dean, 'Imagery in the *Knight's Tale* and the *Miller's Tale*',
   MS 31 (1969), 149–63.

The Reeve's Tale

Prologue

The Miller's Tale is greeted by most of the pilgrims with laughter: Chaucer disarms potential moral objections by refusing to let it be taken too seriously. The only pilgrim who raises particular objections does so for entirely the wrong reasons. The Reeve, himself a carpenter, takes it as a personal insult, and determines to 'quite' the Miller in his own 'cherles termes' (3916–17). The relationship of the two tales is thus grounded in the dramatic quarrel of the tellers; but the quarrel itself makes a literary point, for it is itself a churlish way of behaving, and the distance of the fabliaux from any notions of courtesy or *gentillesse* is emphasized by that fact. Ill will motivates the telling of the Reeve's Tale as later it inspires the Friar's and Summoner's; the goodwill of the *gentils* gives rise to the Franklin's romance as a response to the Squire's.

The Reeve's Prologue serves to do more than just introduce his tale, however. It is specifically in line with the 'choleric' complexion mentioned in his portrait (587), quick in anger and eager for revenge; and his dialect ('so theek', 3864) and his covetousness were both conventional characteristics of Norfolk men. It is the first of the 'confessional' prologues, like the Merchant's, the Pardoner's, or the Wife of Bath's. He is old and cynical and hates himself; his lust is as great as ever, but to have 'an hoor heed and a grene tayl' (3878) is impossible—the desire and the folly are still there, but not the ability. He is limited to four sins he associates specifically with the old: boasting, lying, anger, and covetousness. His philosophy of life is indistinguishable from a philosophy of death:

> For sikerly, whan I was bore, anon
> Deeth drough the tappe of lyf and leet it gon. (3891–2)

Proverb here gives way to a metaphorical mode of impressive imaginative power. Much of his imagery, like that of the Miller, is everyday, low style, but the effect is very different. The empty tun, the fruit that rots before it is ripe, the glowing embers of sin among the ash, that 'gras tyme is doon', deny the energy, vitality and freshness of the Miller's Tale. 'Deeth' is a living presence such as is not encountered again until the Pardoner's Tale.

'Whan we may nat doon, than wol we speke' (3881): if the Reeve is past sexual performance, he can at least still tell obscene stories. The Parson will in due course condemn such entrenched lechery, as he will condemn the ire that motivates the Reeve (X(I) 535, 548–50, 857–8); for the moment, Chaucer gives Oswald a tale that, while not so sombre as the Prologue might suggest, is still in keeping with such an outlook. Although it is outwardly similar to the Miller's in genre, it is very different in tone.

Date and Text

The close relationship of the Reeve's Tale to the Miller's suggests that it may have been composed immediately afterwards; it is the second half of a closely integrated pair.

The scribes seem to have had some difficulty with the students' northern dialect, and sometimes attempt to regularize such forms as *boes* (4027) and *howgates* (4037). Other variants make little substantive difference—whether Simkin's tippet is 'wounde' or 'bounden' round his head (3953), whether 'revelrye' or 'reverye' (in the sense of wantonness) is intended at 4005, whether the couple's snoring carries for a furlong or for two (4166). At 4098, Simkin's comment on the horse, 'Lo, wher he gooth!', sometimes appears as a comment on the clerks, 'Lo, wher they goon!'. One further variant, which may be correct though it is attested only by a handful of late manuscripts, is the name 'Scoler Halle' for 'Soler Halle' (3990); the 'scoler' form is closer to the alternative names for the King's Hall, which Chaucer seems to have in mind.

Glosses are sparse. Ellesmere and others gloss line 3912, on driving out force with force, with the Latin legal maxim from which it derives; and another such maxim sometimes appears beside 4181–2, on compensation for being 'agreved'.

On 'Scoler Halle', see '*The Reeve's Tale* and the King's Hall, Cambridge', in Derek Brewer, *Tradition and Innovation in Chaucer* (London, 1982), pp. 73–9 (repr. from *ChR* 5 (1971), 311–17).

Genre

The Reeve's Tale, like the Miller's, is a fabliau, with its staple content of sex and practical jokes designed for laughter. The tale does not, however, have the same gaiety as the Miller's, as the emphasis on sex is replaced by an emphasis on revenge. The quarrel between the two pilgrims in which the Reeve's Tale is given its dramatic grounding highlights another quality in the fabliau: its customary cast of low- or middle-class characters can be employed by Chaucer's pilgrims for direct insult, since the tellers and the characters belong to the same world.

On the fabliaux, see pp. 95–6 above.

Sources and Analogues

There are three main source categories for the Reeve's Tale: analogues for
the plot; the Miller's Tale itself; and details drawn from contemporary
life—in this case Cambridge rather than Oxford. The other source category
relevant for most tales, of authorities who contribute aphorisms or exempla,
is scarcely applicable here, for almost the whole range of such reference is
proverbial, to oral or folk tradition. Even when Latin parallels are known,
Chaucer insists on a homeliness of connotation. The most striking instance
is the lines

> 'The gretteste clerkes been noght wisest men,'
> As whilom to the wolf thus spak the mare.   (4054–5)

The reference is to the widely known tale of the wolf who wanted to buy the
mare's foal; she told him the price was written on her rear hoof, and kicked
him when he bent to look. Such a use of fable is of a piece with Chaucer's
whole treatment of the tale: it is low style, and its range of language and
imagery is appropriate to its restricted world and to its teller. The one
possible exception, Aleyn's legal maxim on being 'releved' in return for
being 'agreved' (4181–2), comes over sounding more like an English
proverb.

A number of analogues to the tale are known, in several languages, and it
may have been current in oral tradition. Two versions earlier than Chaucer's
survive in French, one in Italian (*Decameron* 9, 6), and two in German. The
one that is closest to the Reeve's Tale is the thirteenth-century French *Le
Meunier et les II clers*. This exists in two manuscripts, each with unique
passages; Chaucer's tale contains some features from each, and others that
are found only in different analogues. Among these are the wife's belief at
the end that it is the clerks that are fighting, and the moral, given in Chaucer
by the Cook, of being careful whom you lodge. A similar motif, on the
preferability of lodging people you know, appears at the beginning of the
Decameron story. It is possible that Chaucer extracted this moral from the
story independently, as he seems to have done for the other maxims with
which the tale ends; both the Reeve and the Cook have a taste for proverbial
wisdom.

Le Meunier et les II clers contains the basic story of the Reeve's Tale. Two
poor clerks take their wheat to a mill to be ground, but the miller steals their
horse and wheat. They spend so long searching that they have to lodge at his
house. During the night one clerk transfers to the bed of the miller's
daughter, the other moves the baby's cradle when the wife gets up so that
she mistakes his bed for her own. The first student, wishing to return to his
own bed, is misled by the crib and gets in with the miller, to whom he boasts

of his success. From this point the Reeve's Tale parts company from the French. In *Le Meunier*, the fight between the miller and the student ends when the miller makes a light and sees his wife in bed with the other clerk. He calls her a whore; she calls him a thief; and the students beat up the miller, recover their grain and go elsewhere to have it ground. None of the analogues has the daughter reveal that the stolen flour has been made into a cake; it is a detail that gives an unexpected depth of characterization to Malyne. That it is the wife who delivers the decisive blow of the battle is also a detail unique to Chaucer that adds considerably to the final mayhem.

The whole Reeve's Tale is given a vividness found nowhere else. The opening descriptions of the dishonest, violent, and bald miller and his proud wife have no parallels in the analogues, and their daughter is rather less attractive than she is elsewhere. Chaucer's version is clearly not a simple translation of any source; and the immediate stimulus to many of the changes he makes is the Miller's Tale itself. It is the potential for parallelism in the two plots that makes him put this story here, so that the Reeve can 'quite' the Miller with his tale. That the location is Cambridge, and that the Miller's name for the cuckolded carpenter, John, now belongs to the man who cuckolds the miller, are both inspired by the Miller's Tale. The description of Simkin, with his dishonesty, his wrestling skills, his weapons kept handy (he has four, from a sword to a knife), his broad nose, and his ability to play the pipes, are all reminiscent of the pilgrim Miller as described in the General Prologue (and a good many of them recall the stereotype of millers in general, not least the dishonesty).

The Cambridge setting is developed as carefully as the Oxford of the preceding tale. Soler Hall, or Scoler Hall, is probably a name for King's Hall, which was the institution in medieval Cambridge most nearly approximating to a modern college, containing both undergraduates and masters; Chaucer refers to Soler Hall as a 'collegge' (3989), the earliest English use of the term. King's Hall took the highest proportion of its scholars from Norfolk, the Reeve's county, and many more from the North, as are Aleyn and John. Its head was entitled *magister* or *custos*, master or warden; Chaucer calls him the warden. The head of a house was allowed to keep a horse at the college's expense, while scholars were not allowed them, so it is the warden's beast that the clerks borrow to carry their corn. Both wheat and malt for the college are ground at the mill, to provide the essentials for bread and ale. The sluggishness of the Cam meant that it could not drive a sufficient number of mills within the city to fill the requirements of both town and university, hence the need to use the Trumpington mill. Horses were indeed kept in the fen nearby, where the mares of the tale are running free. Simkin's wife is the daughter of the parson of Trumpington; an historical Trumpington parson was succeeded by his son in 1343—

though such clerical misconduct needed no particular local instance as a source. As in the Miller's Tale, however, the local detail serves to transform the sparse narrative of the fabliau into something infinitely richer, and to give an illusion of realism to an outrageously implausible story.

Walter Morris Hart, in *Sources and Analogues*, gives the two texts of *Le Meunier et les II clers*; Benson and Andersson (*Literary Context*) give translations and, in most cases, texts of six analogues, including *Le Meunier*, and also (pp. 80–3) a comparative chart of episodes. On the Cambridge setting, see Bennett, *Chaucer at Oxford* (p. 99 above), ch. 4.

Structure

The opening line of the tale serves to establish its relationship to the Miller's: not now Oxenford, but Cantebrigge. The descriptions of the inhabitants of the carpenter's household are balanced by those of Simkin's—the miller himself, his wife and daughter, and, in a single couplet, the baby in the cradle that is to play such a key role in the plot. As in the Miller's Tale, many other innocuous-looking details of the portrait turn out to be highly significant: Simkin is bald, with a keen sense of social standing, and of course he is a skilled thief of the corn brought to him. The plot of the Reeve's Tale gets under way only later, when the clerks establish their need to go to the mill—the point at which all the analogues begin.

The Trumpington opening necessitates a shift to the town before the story can get started, and Chaucer makes the transition by surveying the mill's 'sokene' (3987), its area of business, including Soler Hall. From that point on the story moves rapidly and with no structural diversions, from the manciple's illness that necessitates the clerks' trip and their determination not to be robbed, to their arrival at the mill and the loosing of their horse; then comes the chase, into which is inset, in correct chronological progression, the miller's stealing of their wheat (4090–100). By the time the horse has been recaptured it is night, and after a detailed account of the sleeping arrangements they all go to bed. Aleyn determines on his revenge, and from that moment on—from line 4193 to the end of the tale, little over a hundred lines later—all is action, told in rapid consecutive order: Aleyn's success with Malyne, John's removal of the cradle and its results, Aleyn's parting with Malyne (with information on the cake), his getting into bed with the miller, the fight (of a general chaos unique to this version, in that it involves everyone in the house except Malyne and the baby), and the wonderful final irony of the wife's braining her own husband. The clerks make their exit with their horse, meal, and cake, and, as the closing lines point out, with justice nicely satisfied. The Reeve ends his tale with the customary blessing on the company, and a parting shot aimed at the Miller.

Themes

The main theme of the Reeve's Tale is not, as one might expect, sex, but revenge. Aleyn shows no interest in Simkin's daughter, except for a perfunctory enquiry as to the health of the family, until he decides to get his own back on the miller by sleeping with her; and John's only expressed motive for making love to the wife is to stay even with his fellow clerk. She has no function in the story except as Simkin's wife; she is not even named. The tale thus has an extra appropriateness to its dramatic function, as the Reeve's revenge on the Miller.

Revenge is hardly an admirable motive for telling a story, and neither getting one's own back nor illicit sex can lay any claim to virtue, yet the tale is more moralistic in its manner of narration than the Miller's. There is overt condemnation of Simkin's pride, violence, and thievery, of his wife's social snobbery and malice, and of her father the parson's betrayal of Holy Church. There is a spattering of proverbs throughout the tale, though they are more concerned with pragmatic wisdom than moral virtue. It ends with a double proverb, on evil not resulting in good and the guiler being beguiled; the morality of even such platitudes is however undermined by their context in the rivalry of Reeve and Miller, for the Reeve's application of them is more local than their nature might suggest. They are his *quod erat demonstrandum*, and the last line of his recital is not his prayer for the company but the triumphant

> Thus have I quyt the Millere in my tale.

The tale is the first in the Canterbury sequence to have so close a relationship to its teller: its sterility, coarseness, and fascination with dishonesty and sharp practice are predicted in the initial description of the Reeve and, in particular, in his own Prologue. As always, however, the tale goes far beyond mere psychological or physiological projection, and takes on a life that is directly under Chaucer's control. The Reeve's impotent voyeurism would hardly produce the moment of tenderness between Aleyn and Malyne, when we hear her name for the first time from her lover's mouth (4236)—a naming that effectively makes a person out of her, not a mere instrument of vengeance; though the effect is somewhat lessened by the fact that the name, like 'Moll', could be a type name for a loose woman, most often in its form 'Malkin'. Malyne, however, almost weeps as she prays for the man who has (presumably) taken her virginity: it is the one emotional moment of the tale, and so has the effect of pointing for a brief instant to the heartlessness of the rest.

The cruelty of the tale is qualified by the fact that the worst physical damage is inflicted where it is most deserved, on the dishonest miller.

Simkin's fury, moreover, comes not from care for his daughter nor outraged morality, but from the affront to his social standing:

> Who dorste be so boold to disparage
> My doghter, that is come of swich lynage?   (4271–2)

The clerks have got satisfaction, but their revenge does not swamp the tale. Simkin does not discover what has happened to his wife; his injuries are the result of accident in the shape of his wife stepping in to take the role one might expect to be accorded to his outraged victims or to a just providence. Everybody except Simkin, it would seem, has had a good time, and there is no reversion to the one other person who might suffer from the episode, the daughter. The plot is complete, and there is no 'real life' to carry on afterwards.

One curiosity that demands some mention is that the tale should be given to the Reeve at all. The excuse is, of course, that he is a carpenter; but if the rivalry of a miller and a carpenter were all that were required, the Carpenter among the Guildsmen could presumably have filled the bill. Millers and reeves, however, were professional enemies—one devoted to dishonesty, the other to maximizing his lord's (and his own) income—so their quarrel gains an added edge; and the tale's concern with balancing debts, with the precise requital of sex for theft, one tale by another, fits well with a reeve's function of accountant. His carpentry may have been invented simply to provide the hinge between the plots of the two tales—a miller on the subject of a cuckolded carpenter, an affronted carpenter on a cuckolded miller. And why should he be given the name Osewold (3151), if not for the rhyme with 'cukewold'?

Kolve, *Chaucer and Imagery*, ch. 5, discusses the sombreness of the Tale as revealed by the presentation of the Reeve and the images he sees as crucial, the Prologue image of Death as a tapster and the runaway horse.
Paul A. Olson, 'The *Reeve's Tale*: Chaucer's *Measure for Measure*', *SP* 59 (1962), 1–17, discusses the revenge theme of the Tale and its telling.

The Tale in Context

The Reeve promises to speak in the Miller's own 'cherles termes', and to 'quite' him—not just to repay him but to pay him back, to avenge himself. Such an introduction ensures that the tales are read initially in a specified relation to each other, and Chaucer constantly adds or adapts details to bring the two together. The Miller told of one Oxford student who slept with a carpenter's wife; the carpenter Reeve will tell of two Cambridge students who sleep with a miller's wife and daughter. In this particular competition, the Reeve achieves double his opponent's score. The Tale is, so far as I know, the earliest literary expression of the rivalry of Oxford and Cambridge. The Miller's cuckolded carpenter is named John; the carpenter-Reeve gives the name to the student who gets his revenge on the miller. Nicholas will 'rage and pleye' with Alison, but no one dares do the same with Simkin's wife for fear of his array of weapons (3273, 3958). While John snores in his tub, Alison and Nicholas keep 'revel and melodye' through the night until lauds, the earliest morning service; the snoring of the miller's family is compared to compline (4171), the night service with its opening prayer for quiet rest, which ironically keeps the clerks awake for their own revelling.

The Tale glances at a number of themes that will recur later, but here they are always limited to their particular plot function. Drunkenness is made an issue many times elsewhere; so, more notably, are a husband's attempts to keep control over his wife. The linked ideas of illusion, understanding, and blindness are touched on in Simkin's determination that he will 'blere' the clerks' eyes 'for al the sleighte in hir philosophye' (4050), and in his mock that their academic training will enable them

> by argumentes make a place
> A myle brood of twenty foot of space.   (4123–4)

This notion, that you believe what you want to believe, is to be given its fullest treatment in the Merchant's Tale, and there are significant variations on it in the Franklin's, Second Nun's, and Canon's Yeoman's Tales. Such references in the Reeve's Tale are slight, and do not become significant themes (except as part of the 'biter bit' idea, of the man who applauds himself on his cleverness being himself outwitted—another recurrent motif of the *Tales*), but Chaucer seems to have added them to his source, and they serve to introduce the later and fuller treatments of the ideas.

Style

The style of the Reeve's Tale stands in marked contrast to the metaphorical resonance of his long speech in the Prologue. The Tale stresses narrative speed, with few pauses for syntactic elaboration, similitude, or, after the opening section, anything too far from the strictly functional. The closing lines of the action are particularly compressed but give the idea of much of the narrative:

> Thise clerkes beete hym weel and lete hym lye,
> And greythen hem, and tooke hir hors anon,
> And eek hire mele, and on hir way they gon.
> And at the mille yet they tooke hir cake
> Of half a busshel flour, ful wel ybake.   (4308–12)

'And' is by far the commonest conjunction in the Tale, varied primarily by 'for', 'whom', and 'til', the barest statements of cause and succession; and there is little syntactic subordination. Bare narrative, however, is always enlivened by the telling detail—in this passage, the note on the excellence of the cake. The effects of even such a plain style can be superb:

> Wery and weet, as beest is in the reyn,
> Comth sely John, and with him comth Aleyn.   (4107–8)

'Plain' is indeed a misleading term for such lines: the simplicity of the language is belied by the playing with word order, the telling image of misery, the repeated verb, the adjective 'sely' (last used of John the carpenter and the hapless Absolon). The vocabulary, however, here as throughout the Tale, is very simple: it is largely monosyllabic except for inflectional endings: it avoids the abstract; and it contains decisively the lowest proportion of Romance-derived words of all the tales, using only those that were fully absorbed into English—*gay*, *rage*, *clerk*, and so on. Word such as the rhyming pair *amendement/esement* (4185–6) are rare in the Tale, and those are spoken by one of the scholars; two more, *philosophy* and *argumentes* (in the technical sense of 'syllogisms', 4123) are used by Simkin in mockery of the clerks, and the contrast of register underlines the fact that he regards such words as pedantic jargon. It is a vocabulary that, as in the Miller's Tale, extends to the *cherles termes* for bodily functions, and that prefers words such as *lemman* and *wenche* to anything more idealized. Colloquialisms intrude even into the narrative, as Aleyn mistakes the beds 'a twenty devel way' (4257).

The style of the Tale is sparer than that of the Miller's: it takes little over half of the number of lines to tell just as complicated a story. The character descriptions are briefer, there is much less direct speech, and there is none of the skilful use of imagery and allusion that turns the Miller's Tale from being merely a bawdy story into something full of energy and life. The Reeve's Tale does indeed share with the Miller's a predilection for animal imagery, but the animals chosen differ from the Miller's almost as much as the Miller's do from the Knight's. Where the animals of the Knight's Tale were noble and fierce and those of the Miller's young and skittish, the Reeve's Tale tends to select animals that have connotations of sin. Simkin is as proud as a peacock (3926); heavy drinking is associated with swine (4262); the horse to which the snoring miller is compared, as he 'took no keep' of his tail (4163–4), recalls the association of the horse with lechery or unbridled passion, a link already made by the Reeve in his Prologue (3888) and amply demonstrated by the chase of the clerks' own horse after the wild mares. The ape to which Simkin's bald head is compared (3935) also has associations of sin, though its main connotation here is physical repulsiveness—very different from the skipping kid or soft woolly wether of Alison. His wife is made equally repulsive by the comparison of her to ditchwater (3964), where the satire turns into open condemnation.

Satire is the point behind the one passage of the Tale that calls attention to itself rhetorically, on the parson's wish to make his granddaughter his heir:

> For hooly chirches good moot been despended
> On hooly chirches blood, that is descended.
> Therfore he wolde his hooly blood honoure,
> Though that he hooly chirche sholde devoure.   (3983–6)

The lines sound at first like the priest's own views, just as the pilgrims' voices in the General Prologue are allowed to take over from the narrator's; but it is impossible to tell where the indirect speech ends and the voice merges back into commentary. The third line could be an expression of the parson's ignorant hypocrisy—a priest's 'blood', in the shape of offspring, could scarcely be holy, and the very existence of offspring denies his own sanctity; it could be a satiric cut from the narrator; it could be both at once. The last line, by contrast, is absolutely serious—the most serious line in the whole tale, and one that belongs more to Chaucer than the Reeve.

The care Chaucer devotes to reproducing the idiom of direct speech is seen most clearly in a striking linguistic peculiarity of the tale, the clerks' dialect. Their speech is full of forms instantly recognizable to a contemporary audience as northern, from the moment of Aleyn's opening 'Al hayl'. The vocabulary (*boes, lathe, hethyng,* and so on), the meanings ascribed to words (*hope* for 'think'), inflections (such as the plural verb ending in *-s*), vowel sounds (especially *a* for southern *o*, in *swa, ga, bathe,* and many others) and consonants (especially *-k* for *-ch,* as in *whilk* and *slik,* and *s-* for *sh-,* as in *sal*), are all distinctively northern. Chaucer is not totally consistent in their dialect, nor does he particularize it to any one area, but the effect recurs throughout their speech, though it is most marked at the start. The content as well as the manner of their speech is also distinguished from that of Simkin and his family: they are allowed most of the few abstract nouns in the Tale and the few sophisticated allusions, and Aleyn's justification of his seduction of Malyne is the nearest anyone ever gets to constructing an argument (4179–86). Even he, however, seems unaware of the incongruity of swearing to his sexual prowess by reference to Christ and St James (4263–4).

See also Benson, *Chaucer's Drama of Style,* pp. 90–103 (on the style compared with that of the Miller's Tale); 'The Poetry of Chaucer's Fabliaux', in Brewer, *Chaucer: The Poet* pp. 107–19; and Richardson, *Blameth Nat Me,* ch. 5. For the exceptionally low incidence of Romance vocabulary, see Mersand, *Chaucer's Romance Vocabulary,* pp. 76–7.

The Cook's Tale

Prologue

The Cook enters the action of the pilgrimage, not through being called on for a story, but through the vigour of his response to the Reeve's Tale. He picks out two aspects, both of which will colour his own tale: the 'jape', and the moral. The Reeve told of a 'jape of malice'; he himself will tell of a 'litel jape'. His addition of a third moral to the two the Reeve has already given (4320–1) demonstrates the taste for aphorisms that is to characterize his tale: 'Ne bryng nat every man into thyn hous' (4331). He cites Solomon as the source for the maxim (Ecclus. 11:29), though the dangers of *herberwynge* are pointed out in some of the analogues to the Reeve's Tale; but the immediate stimulus to his comment is the 'conclusion', sexual rather than philosophical, that the clerks have brought to Simkin's 'argument of herbergage' (4329, cf. 4122–6). There may be a punning comment on the tale's genre here, for *argumentum* was the rhetorical term for a palpably fictional story— a category that includes most, if not all, fabliaux.

Tavernkeepers and cooks, like millers and reeves, were professional enemies. There may be a topical allusion to something of the kind when Chaucer gives the Host and the Cook, alone of all the pilgrims, the names of historical prototypes. The Host accuses Roger of Ware of all kinds of nasty culinary practices tending to food poisoning, though with a more subtle malice than the Reeve establishes in his Prologue—he assures 'gentil Roger' that his insults are only playful, even if they are true. The Cook in turn promises to tell a tale of a 'hostileer', in the manner of the Reeve speaking against millers or the Summoner against friars.

He does not in fact do so. He decides,

> I wol nat telle it yit;
> But er we parte, ywis, thou shalt be quit.   (4361–2)

It does not sound as if he means that his present tale is going to turn into a story against a tavernkeeper; Chaucer, or the Cook, apparently has a future tale in mind—the Host has, after all, suggested four from each pilgrim. The Cook does not in fact finish even one tale; and when, in the Manciple's Prologue, Harry Bailly turns to him to demand a story, there seems to be no consciousness that he has started one before. The discrepancy cannot be solved within the *Tales* as we have them; it is presumably one of the many indications of their unfinished and only partially revised state.

Date and Text

The coherence of the Cook's Prologue with the Reeve's Tale suggests that it was written soon, or immediately, afterwards, and their consistent appearance at the end of Fragment I(A) suggests that they circulated together without a break. The tale's opening reference to 'our citee' picks up from the 'Londoun' of the opening line of the Prologue: a tale of London will follow the tales of Oxford and Cambridge. Its incompleteness is possibly also an indication of continuous composition: Chaucer seems to have intended to follow the pattern of the 'quiting' of tale by tale set up in the rest of the Fragment, but he perhaps found the material intractable— whatever that material might have been.

Almost every manuscript witnesses in some way to the incompleteness of the tale. The scribe of Hengwrt and Ellesmere left a gap for the rest to be added; a number of other manuscripts add a couplet in which the Cook deliberately breaks off the tale and substitutes the non-Chaucerian *Gamelyn*. It is conceivable that Chaucer did indeed write more, but it was lost before being copied, perhaps because a new, separate, quire began at this point. This would account for the anomaly of the incompleteness in what is otherwise the most carefully 'finished' of the fragments. The scribe of Hengwrt and Ellesmere appears to have believed the rest existed at the time of copying; but he returned to add in the margin of Hengwrt, 'Of this Cokes tale maked Chaucer na moore', and there is finally no reason to doubt his word.

Two attempts were made in the fifteenth century to finish off the tale, one by adding two final couplets, the other by rewriting it in 98 lines. These are described in more detail in the final chapter (pp. 413–14 below); both despatch Perkin Revelour to a speedy sticky end.

Genre

The Cook promises to tell 'a litel jape' to match the 'jape of malice' told by the Reeve. The term would suggest synonymity with fabliau; and this is supported by such characteristics as the contemporary London setting, the bourgeois characters, the revelling and dicing and prostitution. The manner of the telling, however, casts doubt on this classification, for after the description of Perkin the tone turns pervasively moral. Of the last thirty-two lines of the piece (4391–422), fifteen are proverbs or similar generalizations of practical or moral wisdom. If this were to be a fabliau, it would scarcely be a typical one. It is interesting as a measure of medieval reaction to the tale that the two endings invented for it later pick up from the didacticism rather than the 'jape'.

Sources and Analogues

The plot of the Cook's Tale has not got sufficiently under way for any identification of source to be possible. The first part of his story—the London location, the description of Perkin Revelour—could be modelled structurally on the openings of the Miller's and Reeve's Tales. The rest is devoted to his master's throwing him out, generously amplified with sententious material, and his moving in with a comrade with a prostitute wife. The plot could go almost any way from this point, and it is conceivable that Chaucer himself had no idea what direction it was to take—that, perhaps, the Cook's Tale is unfinished partly because there is no source.

Structure, Themes, and Style

The Cook's Tale appears to promise a continuation and intensification of the revelry and sexual licence of the preceding two tales, but the sententiousness of its second half belies this. Like the earlier fabliaux, it starts with a description of the central character, then moves on to the plot. Since so little of the potential action happens, the result is a split down the middle; and this division is emphasized by the stylistic contrast of the two sections. The portrait of Perkin Revelour is done with the panache and gaiety of the Miller's Tale: he is compared to things from the natural world—merry as a goldfinch, brown as a berry, as full of love as a hive is full of honey. As with the formulae of approval in the General Prologue, the very absence of any moral framework makes itself forcefully felt by the end of the portrait: what does it mean that no other prentice could dice more beautifully (4385–7)? The moral void does not remain for long, however, as Perkin's master, who is robbed to pay for the gaming, enters the tale, and with him the tone of moral generalization. The vocabulary accordingly becomes more abstract, even philosophical ('convertible' (4395) is the technical term for a proposition whose subject and predicate are interchangeable: theft is riot: riot is theft). Even apples now are metaphorical and moral (4406). The style reverts to the concrete and particular (and impolite) only when Perkin takes over the action at the end.

Although there is no identifiable source, some clue as to the way the tale might go is provided by the Cook in his Prologue. He spends several lines on analysing the Reeve's theme of the dangers of *herbergage* (4328–34), and the fragment of his tale suggests that he might have developed the idea. Perkin's master throws him out before he can infect the rest of the household, however; and it is hard to see what further harm could come to the companion with whom he moves in, since he is already both dissolute and a thief (4395), and his wife is safely beyond dishonour.

Kolve, *Chaucer and Imagery*, ch. 6, attempts a rehabilitation of the Cook, and gives a useful commentary on the sententiousness of the tale.

E. G. Stanley, 'Of This Cokes Tale Maked Chaucer Na Moore', *Poetica*, 5 (1976), 36–59, suggests that the tale is in fact complete as it stands, forming a conclusion to the 'argument of herbergage' running through the three earlier tales of the Fragment by showing how no honour can be lost by a host who has none to lose.

The Tale in Context

After Oxford and Cambridge, London; after the assorted amorous clerks, Perkin Revelour; after the seducible women, a professional whore. The Athens of the Knight's Tale had been a distant and exotic setting, its heroes idealized, its heroine inaccessible, kept separate by the walls of the prison; the next women were guarded by jealous husbands or fathers, but were accessible to those with sufficient cunning and prepared to take the risks; the wife of Perkin's comrade is accessible to all comers. If the Reeve had 'quitted' the Miller by doubling the number of couplings, the Cook threatens to overgo the Reeve by further multiplication. It is perhaps no wonder that the tale diverges into moralism and breaks off.

The theme of *herbergage*, of taking people into your house and the attendant dangers, is picked up by the Cook from the Reeve's Tale, but it reaches back through all the tales of the Fragment. John the carpenter is tricked into enabling his lodger to sleep with his wife; Arcite enters Theseus' household under false pretences in order to win Emily. The honourableness of Arcite's intentions might seem to make a considerable difference, but not in Palamon's eyes: he twice accuses his rival of 'japing' Theseus (1585, 1729), the same word that is used about the adventures of the other three tales (3799, 3842; 4201, 4207; and the Cook's comments on the Reeve's and his own tales, 4338, 4343). Arcite's jape, by contrast with the fabliaux, ends in tragedy.

The Knight's Tale is the only other story of Fragment I(A) that has the same tendency to draw moral generalizations from particular actions, though there, of course, it is done on a much larger and more serious scale; the Cook reduces the process to the commonplace. The only later tales to have as high a proportion of *sententiae* as the Cook's are the prose tales, *Melibee* and the Parson's.

The Man of Law's Tale

Introduction

The Introduction covers two distinct sections, the Proem, or, as the Ellesmere manuscript calls it, 'the wordes of the Hoost to the compaignye', and the Man of Law's rhyme royal Prologue to his tale. Together they raise a multitude of unanswered questions, and few lines are altogether unproblematic.

The main subject of the Proem is storytelling and story-collections. When the Host calls on the Man of Law to fulfil his part in the pact, he responds with a survey of tales told elsewhere by Chaucer, most particularly his other story-collection, the *Legend of Good Women*; and he looks back through them to Ovid's *Heroides* (54–5), the *Metamorphoses* (91–3), and apparently also Gower's *Confessio amantis* (77–85). Chaucer emerges from all this as more prolific a poet than Ovid (53–5, though the list of 'Chaucer's' works that follows is entirely Ovidian and includes some stories that Chaucer never did write), and more moral than Gower (in his reluctance to write about incest, 86–8), but also as a poet who is less than perfect at such matters as language, rhyme, and scansion (47–9). The Man of Law then introduces a comparison of himself with Chaucer by declaring his reluctance to be likened

> To Muses that men clepe Pierides—
> *Methamorphosios* woot what I mene. (92–3)

The allusion seems to be to the daughters of King Pierus who challenged the Muses to a singing-contest (not altogether different from the story-competition in which the Man of Law finds himself) and were changed into chattering magpies on their defeat (*Met.* v. 295–307, 669–78). They, at least, are the only Pierides appropriate for the context, and the only ones in the *Metamorphoses*; but 'Pierides' was also a name for the true Muses. It seems to be an irony not lost on Chaucer that Muse and magpie share the same name, just as the true poet is the ventriloquist for the Man of Law as he declares himself capable of producing only the most miserable fare. Chaucer, as master of the surrogate narrator, can choose whatever voice he will, but it will still always be the poet's voice. The whole section combines a surface commentary on Chaucer's inadequacies as a writer with an equally pervasive underlying insistence that he is a poet in the highest traditions.

Above all, the Introduction emphasizes the quality of story as story—as something told, rather than as something that happened: as text rather than 'life'. The Man of Law, indeed, seems to think of story material as a limited commodity, which Chaucer has already largely exhausted, and, as with any other commodity, he is reliant for his on a merchant (131–3). That merchants, travellers, should be 'fadres of tidynges | And tales' (129–30) recalls the theme of travellers' and pilgrims' *tidynges*, truth and lies together, of the end of the *House of Fame* (2121–31). The effect of all this, surprising in the introduction to a pious tale, is to weaken any claim that the Tale might have either to historical truth—what happened—or to moral truth, as an exemplum of God's Providence. It becomes simply one more story to set alongside the rest.

In spite of its width of reference, the Introduction does have a particular relevance to the tale of Custance that follows. The Man of Law spends a long time listing the stories he is *not* going to tell, either because Chaucer has told them already, or because, in the case of the stories of Canace and Apollonius of Tyre, the topic of incest is too *wikke*. The list serves to some degree to define the area left free for his own tale: it is a story of female faithfulness and suffering, like those of Ceys and Alcyone (in the *Book of the Duchess*) and of the *Legend of Good Women* (57–76), but without the incest motif that characterizes the majority of the analogues of the Constance story (excluding Gower's version, although he is guilty of the stories of Canace and Apollonius). The lines serve as a reminder that the telling of stories involves a series of choices, of one tale rather than another, and between different ways of telling any particular story.

In other respects, the Introduction is less appropriate to the tale that follows, in ways that raise questions over Chaucer's processes of composition.

Many features of the Proem, notably the Host's injunctions against wasting time and the listing of Chaucer's works, suggest that the piece may originally have been intended to introduce the whole of the storytelling. If Chaucer did once have such a scheme in mind, he must have abandoned it at a fairly early stage, as it has left no trace in any manuscript ordering of the tales, where this fragment consistently follows Fragment I(A). The date of composition of the Introduction relative to the other parts of the *Tales* remains uncertain. The fictional date on which the story is told likewise presents problems, since 18 April (5) does not square with the estimations of date given in the General Prologue or the Parson's Prologue. The various calculations of the time of day (1–14) are also inconsistent.

A further puzzle is that the Man of Law announces that he is going to speak in prose (96). The obvious explanation for this would seem to be that Chaucer did once intend him to tell a prose tale, such as would balance the

Parson's prose treatise at the end. The most likely candidates are the *Melibee*, which Chaucer eventually assigned to himself (a nice irony, if the tale had once been so specifically contrasted with Chaucer's 'rymes'); or the translation, now lost, of Pope Innocent III's *De miseria condicionis humanae*. Most of the short rhyme royal Prologue immediately preceding the Man of Law's Tale is taken from this work; but the passages used in the Prologue are also quoted in both the Latin and French versions of the *Melibee*, and there are a number of allusions to it in the course of the tale of Custance as well. The use of rhyme royal suggests that the Prologue was designed specifically for the Custance story, as Chaucer's other rhyme royal prologues introduce tales in the same form. It is, however, curiously disproportionate to its apparent point, on the Man of Law's shortage of stories, and it is possible that Chaucer altered the original ending of some verses designed for something else to provide a rather perfunctory lead in to the tale.

The fullest discussions of the original placing of the Introduction are by Carleton Brown, 'The Man of Law's Head-link and the Prologue of the Canterbury Tales', *SP* 34 (1937), 8–35, and Owen, *Pilgrimage and Storytelling*, esp. pp. 25–31.
On the calculation of date and time, see *The Kalendarium of Nicholas of Lynn*, ed. Sigmund Eisner (The Chaucer Library, Athens, Ga., 1980), pp. 29–31.

Date and Text

Although it has been suggested that the Man of Law's Tale may have been written as an independent piece before the *Canterbury Tales* was conceived, it seems most likely to have been written about 1390. This date would fit its use of Innocent's *De miseria* (Chaucer's translation probably having been made between the two versions of the Prologue to the *Legend of Good Women*, conjecturally 1386–94), and its subject of female suffering, which clearly occupied Chaucer's mind in the 1380s when he was working on the *Legend*. It also seems slightly more likely that Chaucer used Gower's version of the story than the other way around, again suggesting a later date. The calculation of time in the Introduction is based on Nicholas of Lynn's *Kalendarium*, of 1386; this would indicate a similar date, though Introduction and Tale need not have been written together. Composition or revision specifically for the Canterbury scheme is suggested by lines 1116–17, when the narrator recognizes the need to hurry his tale to an end, and by the blessing in the final line.

The Tale contains some motifs on the ordering of the universe and on matrimony that connect with the Knight's and Wife of Bath's Tales, and which could suggest that Chaucer already had in mind for his story-collection a structure of interrelated themes. Its lack of explicit linking to other tales suggests that it was not written for any specific point in the sequence, though its consistent placing in the manuscripts after Fragment I(A), and its possible thematic connections, may indicate that the ordering is Chaucer's own. The Tale appears at a later point in Hengwrt only because the intervening sections were misplaced.

Most manuscripts signal the Tale as beginning at line 99, where modern editions start the Prologue, and they present Prologue and Tale as a single rhyme royal unit; only eleven, including Hengwrt and Ellesmere, separate the 'wordes of the Hoost', the Prologue, and the Tale into distinct sections. Still fewer manuscripts divide the Tale itself into three, Ellesmere being the most notable; this tripartite division may well not be Chaucer's. Other textual variants in both Introduction and Tale are minor, and do not significantly affect the sense.

The most interesting feature of the presentation of the Tale is its abundance of Latin glosses, which appear in more manuscripts than those of any other tale. These give the originals of some of the learning and *sententiae* of the Tale. Four come from the *De miseria* (at 421, 771, 925, 1135); one is from the Bible (Ecclus. 18: 26, at 1132); three elaborate on astrological references (from the *Megacosmos* of Bernardus Silvestris at 197, from Ptolemy's *Almagest* at 295, and from the *De electionibus* of the Jewish astrologer Zahel at 309). There is one further explanatory gloss that defines Europe as a third of the world (161). The persistent inclusion of these glosses and their range of reference make it a distinct possibility that they originate with Chaucer.

There are two surviving copies of the Tale made independently of the complete work, though one of them is part of an anthology of five of the tales; and there is also a two-leaf fragment.

Genre

The Man of Law's Tale inhabits the undefined border area between romance and saint's life. Its principal analogues belong with romance or folktale; its source claims it as history; its repeated motifs of the sufferings of the high-ranking suggest *tragedie* in its non-dramatic Chaucerian form. Some of its earliest antecedents may lie in Greek romance, with its typical motifs of loss, sea voyages, and recognition scenes; such a source has been tentatively proposed for one of its more distant analogues, Boccaccio's tale of Gostanza (*Decameron* 5, 2). Chaucer's treatment of his material shows some awareness of the story's potential in these various directions, but he is concerned principally to treat it as pious legend, as an extended exemplum of faith, endurance, and the dispensations of Providence. This is emphasized by the numerous exclamations on such things as God's ordinances, the Virgin, and the Passion from both the narrator and Custance herself; and by the way the rhetoric avoids dwelling on the happy ending, to stress instead the transitoriness of earthly life.

Paul M. Clogan, 'The Narrative Style of *The Man of Law's Tale*', *M&H* NS 8 (1977), 217–33, discusses the tale as hagiographic romance.

Sources and Analogues

The immediate source for the tale is in Nicholas Trevet's Anglo-Norman Chronicle, which was written in the early fourteenth century for a daughter of Edward I, Marie, who was a nun at Almesbury. He was the first to give the story such a full historical context. His own sources were probably the *Vitae duorum Offarum*, a pseudo-historical work attributed to Matthew Paris, and a French romance, *La Belle Hélène de Constantinople*, both of which start with an incest motif; and he added further details from various hagiographical works. His story contains a substantial element of the marvellous or the miraculous, but although its import is strongly Christian, it is much less overtly religious than Chaucer's version. It contains nothing on destiny and the stars, such as Chaucer has at the beginning, and only bare suggestions for the Man of Law's numerous exclamations on the workings of Providence. Trevet allows his Constance one brief remark on God's mercy, as she is put to sea for the second time; Chaucer's Custance is given five such speeches, one before each of her first two sea voyages, two when she is exiled from Northumberland, and one when she is accused of murder.

Chaucer follows Trevet's story outline closely, though with abundant expansion of comment and exclamation and reduction in peripheral detail. He cuts out many of the names supplied by Trevet, for Constance's father and her dead mother, the constable of Northumberland, the rapist, the senator and his wife, and two popes. Some of Trevet's characters also go, notably Bishop Lucius of Bangor. Chaucer's more restricted use of names serves to focus the story on a few individuals—Custance, Hermengild, Alla, Donegild, Maurice—while the other characters are limited to more stereotyped roles: father, pagan husband, mother-in-law, villain, and so on. The change of name, from Trevet's Constance (derived from her father Tiberius Constantine) to Custance, may be designed to stress individuality above personified virtue. Gower's version (*Confessio* ii. 587–1598) has Constance adopt the name Couste when she wishes to stay anonymous, and Chaucer could have taken a hint from him—or Gower from Chaucer.

The relationship of Gower's and Chaucer's tales remains unsettled, though it is clear from many coincidences of treatment and phrasing that one knew the other: both heroines, for instance, are given a much more moving scene than in Trevet when they are cast out to sea for the second time. The balance of probabilities is that Chaucer knew Gower's version, not least because of the apparent references to the *Confessio* in the Introduction to the Tale. Chaucer seems to be at pains to cover his tracks as regards his sources; the Man of Law declares he heard the story from a merchant. There is one point in the tale where Chaucer explicitly parts company with what 'som men wolde seyn' (1009), where in both Trevet and Gower the senator sends Maurice to invite King Alla to a feast, while Chaucer has the senator go in person. Gower's version is throughout closer to Trevet's than Chaucer's, with fewer apostrophes and digressions and more of the original detail. Gower's story, however, is told by Genius to the lover as a warning against the dangers in love of backbiting and envy: the Sultan's mother is motivated by jealousy, not, as in Trevet and Chaucer, concern for her pagan religion. This is a very different kind of moral from the one Chaucer accords the tale.

There are numerous analogues to the story in romance and folktale, but one more distant analogue is of particular interest: the story of Gostanza in the *Decameron* 5, 2. The plot here is very different—Gostanza casts herself to sea in an open boat when she hears a mistaken report of the death of the man she loves—but there are two details that could link the tale with Chaucer's. It opens with a poverty-and-riches motif; and when she comes ashore in Barbary, she is able to speak in 'latino' (probably meaning Italian) with a native woman who has learnt the language from Christian fishermen. Chaucer's Custance manages to converse in 'a maner Latyn corrupt' (519). Trevet's Constance, by contrast, has learnt numerous languages and can speak Saxon. The coincidence of names—Gostanza, Custance—remains unexplained.

A large proportion of the Man of Law's Tale is devoted not to story but to comment, exclamation, and rhetorical question. The principal works quarried are the Bible, including the Apocrypha and the Apocryphal Gospels; and the *De miseria*, to which the glosses call attention, and which is itself packed with biblical allusions. In addition to the Prologue, Innocent's treatise lies behind the two stanzas on the evils of drunkenness and lechery (771 ff., 925 ff.), and is the primary influence on the Tale's stress on the instability of earthly joy (particularly lines 421 ff., 1135 ff.). The three cosmographic works quoted in the glosses are adapted in the Tale to give much gloomier applications than their originals suggest, and the reworking raises unsettling questions about the final thematic import of the Tale. More orthodox readings are suggested both by the use of biblical exempla, and by Custance's use of the liturgy for her prayer to the Cross at 456–62; the passage may reflect the votive Mass that invoked the protection of the Cross for travellers.

Margaret Schlauch, in *Sources and Analogues*, gives the versions of Trevet and Gower (*Confessio amantis* ii. 587–1589); they are discussed by Roger Ellis, *Patterns of Religious Narrative in the Canterbury Tales* (London and Sydney, 1986), ch. 6. Translations of Trevet into modern and Middle English are given in Furnivall *et al.*, *Originals and Analogues of Some of Chaucer's Canterbury Tales* (London: Chaucer Society, 1872–7), pp. 2–84 (with other ME analogues), 223–50; a text closer to Chaucer's is being prepared by Robert M. Correale for the Chaucer Library.

For the *De miseria* of Innocent III, see p. 13.

On the liturgical associations of Custance's prayer, see Mary-Virginia Rosenfeld, 'Chaucer and the Liturgy', *MLN* 55 (1940), 357–60.

Structure

In the three sections of the Tale found in the Ellesmere manuscript and most modern editions, the first section covers the narrative surrounding the first sea voyage of the Christians from Rome to Syria; the second part gives the circumstances surrounding the second voyage, from Syria to Northumberland, when Custance is set adrift alone, and her life until she is put to sea yet again; and the third part gives an account of the third voyage, from Northumberland by way of a heathen castle back to Rome. The first part contains Custance's parting from her father and the machinations of the first mother-in-law; the second, the false accusation of murder, her marriage, and the jealousy of her second mother-in-law; the third the attempted rape and the reunions of mother and child with husband and father.

Whether or not the formal divisions of the text go back to Chaucer, they serve to emphasize the most striking characteristic of the structure of the Tale, its method of repetition with variation. The same method is found within the substantial commentary that accompanies the bare narrative of event, in the repeated motifs of Custance's prayers, the narrator's apostrophes to the hostile elements of the story (the firmament, the Sultaness, Satan, 'sodeyn wo', Donegild, drunkenness, and lust, among others), and his rhetorical questions on God's Providence—'Who kepte Jonas in the fisshes mawe?' (486), 'Who yaf Judith corage or hardynesse?' (939), and so on. The pattern of structural repetition may account for the elaboration of Custance's grief when she first leaves her home (264–94). Narrative takes up little over half the tale, while comment of various kinds occupies the rest, most of it in the form of interjections by the narrator, some from Custance. The narrator comments on the progress of the tale from the outside, as one who knows the course of the plot, who deplores the grievous and applauds the miraculous; Custance's comments take the form of prayers, for she, as a character within the story, does not know what will happen, and within the fiction only God can influence the course of events. Both commentaries, from inside and outside the story, are designed above all to call attention to the intervention of the divine in the world.

It is this element of the divine that underlies the romance structure of the tale, its movement through suffering and endurance to final joy, with a strong resurrection motif (as is found in many more secular romances—*Sir Orfeo, Sir Gawain and the Green Knight, Amis and Amiloun,* and others; most famously in Shakespeare's last plays). Where most romances follow a single cycle, from joy, through suffering and trial and often apparent death, to a renewed equilibrium of happiness, the Man of Law's Tale gives the cycle twice: Custance with her father at Rome, the massacre and the first rudderless boat, leading to the joy of her marriage with Alla; then the next exile, and the final reunions with both husband and father, the two figures at the high points of the cycles from whom she has been reluctantly separated. The second cycle doubles as Alla's romance, as his happy marriage yields to loss and matricide, and only through penance does he win his wife back (again the penitential movement is found in more secular romances, from *Perceval* to *Guy of Warwick*). The tale ends, however, not with the protagonists living happily ever after, but with a reminder of the brevity of bliss, and their deaths. The structure appears to promise a return to a state of stable joy, but Chaucer holds back from completing the pattern.

Themes

The controlling ideas of the Man of Law's Tale are implicit in the structure, in the double movement from joy through suffering and trial under divine protection to renewed joy. The exemplary quality of the story demands that the audience should apply it to their own lives to increase their piety, in lines such as

> God liste to shewe his wonderful myracle
> In hire, for *we sholde seen his myghty werkis* . . . (477–8)
>
> *Wel may men seen,* it nas but Goddes grace. (938)

There are also abundant appeals to the audience's pity, and unequivocal condemnations of sin, Satan, and fiendish women. The oddest series of exclamations, however, comes in the first part of the tale, and is hard to reconcile with the themes of Providence; for the dominant force here is seen not as God nor principally the devil, but as fate and the stars, and they bring not good but ill. 'The deeth of every man' is written in the stars (190–203), including the Sultan's death for love. The day Custance leaves Rome is 'the woful day fatal' (261); and the configuration of the planets is desperately unfavourable for the whole undertaking (295–315). This first marriage is seen as being not under the control of a divine First Mover, but merely of the 'firste moevyng, crueel firmament' (295)—the *primum mobile,* the outermost sphere whose movement affects all the other planetary motions.

The whole undertaking of converting Syria to Christianity is presented as being doomed by fate.

It is not until the second part, when Custance is put to sea, that 'He that is lord of Fortune' takes over (448); Providence in this tale takes the form of personal providences, of a series of miracles surrounding Custance herself—her double preservation at sea; Hermengild's healing of the blind man under her direction; the hand that strikes the false accuser dead; God, Christ, and the Virgin helping her to push the rapist overboard. Nineteen lines are devoted to this last intervention (920–4, 932–45); by contrast, the final movement towards joy is credited to the Virgin in a distinctly perfunctory three (950–2). The final series of rescues and reunions, where the motivations and actions are not supernatural but human, proceeds without reference to God; and the themes of Fortune and death re-emerge forcefully at the end, in Alla's death:

> Litel while in joye or in plesance
> Lasteth the blisse of Alla with Custance.
>
> For Deeth, that taketh of heigh and logh his rente . . . (1140–2)

At this juncture, rather disconcertingly, Custance is described as joyfully returning to her father having 'scaped al hire aventure' (1151), as if the only blissful life were living with one's father 'in vertu and in hooly almus-dede'. Presumably her qualities of sanctity make married life a less desirable condition, as when she has to 'leye a lite hir hoolynesse aside' (713) to sleep with her husband, though it is Christ that devises the marriage and so makes her a queen (693). The final formula of blessing is carefully chosen to fit with the alternations of grief and happiness throughout the tale:

> Now Jhesu Crist, that of his myght may sende
> Joye after wo, governe us in his grace!   (1160–1)

It is not at all easy to find any coherent pattern in all this. There is a general shift from astral determinism to providential ordering such as is entirely in keeping with Christian orthodoxy, which insisted that the influences of the planets were always subject to the exercise of free will under the dispensation of God; and most recent readings of the tale have seen it as a Christian answer to the problems of fate and Fortune. It is hard to credit so serious a thinker as Chaucer, however, with believing that the naïve folk piety of the tale, with its miracles provided to order, answered any serious questions; nor would such an attitude explain the blanket appeal to determinism in the first part, or the reversion to patterns of an unstable fortune at the end. The lines on the transience of joy (1132–8) are indistinguishable from similar statements in poems with pagan settings such as *Troilus* or the Knight's Tale. One way out of the problem is to ascribe such instabilities to the failings of the Man of Law. Assigning the weakness of a tale to the weakness of the teller is a widespread, and comfortable, critical practice, but raises the awkward question of how many bad tales the complete work can hold; there is no question here of downright parody, as there is with *Sir Thopas*.

It would seem reasonable to give a poet of Chaucer's status the benefit of the doubt as to knowing what he was doing, without having to resort either to naïvety or to a plea of deliberate bad writing for the narrator's sake such as avoids facing the actual issues raised. Those issues—destiny and Providence—are the same as in the Knight's Tale, only this time the story is Christian, not pagan. The world, however, is the same world of disasters and suffering—the world in which 'the strif of Thebes' and the death of Samson are written in the stars (200–1, cf. I(A) 1087–90, 1329–31, 2466), and in which the innocent suffer as much as or more than the guilty (813–16). This vision of the world, the vision of tragedy, is set in sharp juxtaposition with the conventions of hagiography, with their insistence on miracle and unmediated divine intervention, and on a simple triumph of God over Satan. Either genre, either reading of life, is valid on its own terms, but the contrast between them is jarring when they are put side by side in the same story. What Chaucer seems to be doing in this poem is similar to what he does over the whole *Canterbury Tales*: to set up generically incompatible views of the world and let a pattern of relativity, and therefore of fullness of vision, emerge from the juxtaposition. The Man of Law's Tale, with its unsettling and unexplained mixture of blind fate and providential miracle, takes account of a fuller range of human experience, and of the literary forms that offer different ways of making sense of experience, than if it were tragedy, romance, or hagiography alone. In the Knight's Tale, however, the conflict is central to the story, and some kind of resolution is suggested; here, the narrating voice seems unaware of the contradictions, and they remain unresolved. The abundance of rhetorical questions in the text, with their assumed answers—'Who saved Danyel?' (473) and the rest—never takes account of the deeper questions that other parts of the Tale go to such lengths to raise. If the miracles and allusions to miracles assert that *tragedie* is not enough, there is also a quiet but insistent suggestion that neither is hagiography.

The presence of the narrator is pervasive in the Tale; there is scarcely a stanza that does not have some kind of interjection that insists on the fact that the story is being *told*. The rhetorical elaboration and the seriousness of the subject make it appropriate for the Man of Law, but it in no way provides an intimate psychological portrait. The tale is told with all the armchair complacency of a man who has never himself suffered (e.g. 1065–72), and it displays a keen respect for rank (652–5, 693); but both characteristics are more generic than personal. The genre they suggest is however less religious exemplum than secular *tragedie* of the Monk's Tale type, where the highest ranking become patterns of fortune and misfortune. The style of narration therefore points more to qualities in the story than to characteristics of the Man of Law.

Recent criticism has tended to see the tale as a less equivocal demonstration of Providence than I suggest here: Kolve, *Chaucer and Imagery*, ch. 7, is the fullest argument, based on a symbolic reading of ships as the Church and the sea as the world. Neither Chaucer nor Trevet nor Gower signals such a comprehensive scheme of symbolism, however. See also Howard, *Idea*, p. 215, and Kean, *Art of Narrative*, pp. 114–22.
Dinshaw, *Sexual Poetics*, ch. 3, gives an interesting feminist analysis.

The Tale in Context

Although the Man of Law's Tale stands as a Fragment to itself, it contains a number of issues and themes that recur throughout the Canterbury sequence. Some of the clearest of these connections are with Fragment I(A), a fact which tends to confirm its manuscript placing. The issues of fate and God that figure so largely in the Knight's Tale and recur again here have already been discussed, but it is perhaps worth emphasizing the closeness of the relationship. Palamon's demand, for instance,

> What governance is in this prescience,
> That gilteless tormenteth innocence?,   (I. 1313–14)

is closely echoed in the Constable's

> Sith thou art rightful juge, how may it be
> That thou wolt suffren innocentz to spille,
> And wikked folk regne in prosperitee?   (814–15)

Saturn's control over 'the drenchyng in the see so wan' (I(A) 2456) is turned inside out in God's keeping Custance 'fro the drenchyng in the see' (485). The drowning motif indeed partly answers Palamon's question, since here ultimately the guilty do suffer, and the rapist is drowned 'for vengeance' (923), presumably on God's part. Custance's innocence is vindicated by a series of miracles, but not without extreme suffering.

   The Tale has less in common with the fabliaux that immediately precede it; here the relationship is one of contrast rather than parallel. The four tales of Fragment I show women of increasingly easy accessibility, from Emily in the garden to the whore of the Cook's Tale. Custance reverses the process with a vengeance. Her would-be seducer and would-be rapist are both killed; so is her first husband. We are only ever told of her sleeping with her second husband, and that is by dispensation of Christ (690–3, 708–14); and even this marriage leads to Alla's killing his mother and having to do penance. The heroine of this tale is not only sexually inaccessible but dangerous.

The poem also has wider references to the themes of women and marriage in the *Tales* at large. There are a few lines, for which there are no hints in the source, that appear to look forward to the Wife of Bath and the discussion on marriage that she institutes: it is certainly appropriate that the story of Custance is followed by the Wife in the tale orders that appear most authoritative. Custance's lament on first leaving Rome,

> Wommen are born to thraldom and penance,
> And to been under mannes governance,   (286–7)

is barely relevant in the context, but places her in the spectrum of heroines that includes Grisilde, Cecilia, May, Pertelote, the hag of the Wife of Bath's Tale, and above all the Wife herself. The incompatibility of sex and holiness (708–14) becomes a major theme in the Second Nun's Tale, and, rather differently, in the Wife of Bath's Prologue and the Merchant's Tale. Many of the women of the *Tales*, not least Cecilia and May, are partly defined by reference to the female archetypes of Eve and the Virgin, and both are strongly present as standards by which to judge the women of the Man of Law's Tale. The Sultaness is described as 'serpent under femynynytee' (360), recalling the iconographic tradition of presenting the serpent of the Temptation of Eve with a woman's head, and in the following stanza Satan's perversion of her is directly compared to his seduction of Eve (365–8). Custance is aware of both archetypes:

> 'Mooder', quod she, 'and mayde bright, Marie,
> Sooth is that thurgh wommanes eggement
> Mankynde was lorn, and damned ay to dye . . .   (841–3)

> 'Thow glorie of wommanhede, thow faire may,
> Thow haven of refut, brighte sterre of day.'   (851–2)

She also appeals to the Virgin's 'gentillesse' (853), a quality that is to undergo extensive examination and definition in tales such as the Wife's, Franklin's, and Parson's; it is crucial for this process that the concept includes the religious dimension expressed here.

One other major theme makes an appearance in the tale: that of the contrast of physical and spiritual blindness. It has been sounded already in the Knight's and Miller's Tales, in such passages as John's remarks on the astronomer who falls into the marl-pit (I(A) 3457–61); it becomes of key importance in the Merchant's, Second Nun's, and Canon's Yeoman's Tales. Here it occurs in the episode of the blind Christian man who can see only 'with thilke eyen of his mynde' (552), and whose miraculous cure leads to the conversion of the constable.

David, *Strumpet muse*, ch. 8, gives a sharp account of the Tale and its function in the work. Kolve, *Chaucer and Imagery*, ch. 7, argues for Fragments I–II (A–B¹) forming a unit.

Style

The most distinctive stylistic feature of the Tale is its generous proportion of comment to narrative. The use of rhyme royal makes this particularly easy: the verse form breaks up the action, allowing for exclamations and apostrophes that come in multiples of seven lines, while smoothly continuous action is harder to achieve. Frequently an opening line of a stanza that looks as if it is going to advance the action turns out to introduce something very different:

> The day is comen of hir departynge;
> I seye, the woful day fatal is come . . .(260–1)

and it is over fifty lines before Custance actually steps on board ship. The poetry is rhetorically ambitious in a way that constantly calls attention to itself. There is the most epic of epic similes, on the falls of Troy and Thebes and the Punic Wars (288–94). The text is liberally scattered with apostrophes, often for two or three stanzas in succession (295–315, 358–71, etc.), sometimes addressed to characters within the text, sometimes to the more or less abstract forces at work behind the action (stars, sultanesses, Satan, and sins, but never God: that is left to Custance in her prayers), sometimes to the audience. The audience can itself be something of a rhetorical fiction:

> O queenes, lyvynge in prosperitee,
> Duchesses, and ye ladyes everichone,
> Haveth som routhe on hire adversitee!   (652–4)

Even Chaucer's courtly audience would not often have included a plurality of queens, and the fictional audience of the pilgrimage has been left far behind. The rhetorical questions on God's miracles, on the other hand, are more directly addressed to an audience of all believers. The effect of all these devices is aimed at heightening both the pathos of the tale and its appeal to piety, to inspire horror of sin and admiration of the divine. The narrator's avoidance of any direct address to God stresses both the wonder and the pathos, by leaving a proper distance of awe between himself and the author of the miracles he cites, and by allowing Custance a unique area of experience within the tale where she can appeal not to God's power but to the sufferings of Christ and the Virgin (449–62, 841–54).

Audience reaction to Custance herself is directed not only by such overt rhetorical means but also by incorporating a fictional audience response within the action of the story. Onlookers and bystanders are present at almost every turn. Her virtues and beauty are first described through 'the commune voys of every man' (155); there is abundant weeping when she departs for Syria (288–93), and again when she is cast out to sea from Northumberland; and even when it is not known *who* she is, *what* she is can still speak for itself:

> Alle hir loven that looken in hir face.   (532)

Such effects are occasionally reinforced by symbolism, as when she is compared to a lamb ready for slaughter (617): she herself has already recalled the Passion of the Lamb of God (459). The Sultaness, by contrast, is a serpent, 'lik to the serpent depe in helle ybounde' (360–1). Even when the action is in full swing, characters are often morally placed by comments from the narrator—'this sely innocent' (Custance, 682), 'this false knyght' (the false accuser, 619), 'the mooder of the Sowdan, welle of vices' (323). The effect throughout is to prescribe audience response at every opportunity.

Occasionally rhetorical comment will usurp the function of narrative. That Custance spends three years at sea is mentioned in the course of a rhetorical question (499). The lines on Custance's prophetic dream of evil do not make it clear whether she actually had one or not:

> O my Custance, wel may thy goost have feere,
> And, slepynge, in thy dreem been in penance,
> Whan Donegild cast al this ordinance.   (803–5)

Alla's death is enclosed within an aphorism on universal mortality (1142–4). Very few stanzas (apart from those in direct speech) escape without some comment from the narrator that calls attention to the fact that the tale is a story being told and not the events of Custance's life, whether those comments are on the moral to be drawn, the shortcomings of the source (905, 1086–92), audience expectations (246, 470), or his own views on the progress of the tale and his role as storyteller (411, 428, 881, 965, etc.).

Epilogue: A Textual Note

The Epilogue is not found in some of the most authoritative early manuscripts, including Ellesmere and Hengwrt; in the great majority of the manuscripts that do contain it, the next pilgrim to speak is identified as the Squire (1179), and the Squire's Tale does in fact follow on. The lines are however entirely inappropriate for the Squire, in the strict process of matching level of language with speaker that Chaucer follows. Whoever Chaucer had in mind, it is not one of the *gentils*. Some manuscripts name the

Summoner but still follow the speech with the Squire's Tale; Hengwrt omits the Epilogue, leaves a blank leaf, and again follows with the Squire's Tale. There is negligible manuscript support for naming the Shipman as speaker, or for placing his tale next.

That the Epilogue is missing in Hengwrt and an important group of manuscripts is a strong indication that Chaucer had not found a place for it in the latest revision he made. Although in the manuscripts where it appears it universally follows the Man of Law's Tale, there is nothing in the text to make the link necessary: the word 'thrifty' is repeated before and afterwards (46, 1165), but on its first occurrence the Man of Law is denying that he can tell a 'thrifty tale'. The next pilgrim's refusal to speak of philosophy or in 'termes queinte of lawe' (1188–9) sounds like a reference to the Man of Law but scarcely to the tale of Custance; the comment would be more appropriate if he had told the *Melibee*.

There are plenty of hypothetical solutions to the puzzles, but no way to arbitrate between them. The absence of the Epilogue from the early manuscripts suggests that it was originally written on a separate sheet, not continuously with the end of the Man of Law's, or any other, tale; so it could be moved around and fitted in wherever it proved to be appropriate. Every author will be familiar with the phenomenon of having a good passage lying around waiting to find a new home. It may not therefore have been cancelled in the sense of being decisively deleted; it is more likely that Chaucer saved it from deletion in the course of a rearrangement, but never finally gave it a place.

The substance of the link is especially interesting for containing Chaucer's only explicit reference to Lollardy. One wonders indeed if the mention of the topic were a cause of the passages being dropped, especially as the anti-Lollard position is presented so satirically. Of the heretical symptoms perceived in the Parson, preaching and opposition to swearing scarcely ought to carry the stigma of heterodoxy, and 'glosing' the gospel was a practice of the Church strongly opposed by the Lollards. When the Parson does eventually present his Tale, its doctrine is entirely orthodox.

The Wife of Bath's Prologue

Date and Text

The Wife of Bath's Prologue is one of the high points of Chaucer's writing specifically for the *Tales*. It may have been written quite late, probably after the Shipman's Tale, which seems once to have been Chaucer's choice of story for the Wife: the prologue deals at more length and discursively with some of the issues raised in the narrative of that tale.

There are four passages between lines 575 and 720 that are not found in Hengwrt and some other manuscripts, and that may represent revisions. These are 575–84, on the Wife's recounting invented dreams to Jankin; 609–12, on her being Venerian in feeling and Martian in heart; 619–26, on Mars' mark on her face and her appetite for every sort of man; and 717–20, where the reference to the Passion gives the Wife an unusual touch of serious piety.

A further six lines, customarily numbered as 44*a-f*, are found in only three manuscripts, of which Dd.4.24 is the most important. These have the Wife picking out the best men in terms of both sex and wealth, and describing herself as being an expert scholar of husbands just as a clerk becomes perfect by varied study. The lines cannot be proved genuine, but they are at worst an admirable imitation both of the Wife's style and of the themes Chaucer is pursuing through her.

The arrangement of the Prologue is not completely consistent across all manuscripts. A few indicate a break before 193, where the Wife promises to 'telle forth my tale'. Some mark the end of the Prologue at 878, 'now wol I seye my tale', so separating off the interchange between the Summoner and the Friar; two omit this section altogether.

Verbal variants include such things as whether the Wife 'truly' (*sothe*) does not intend to keep chaste, or will remarry 'because' (*sith*) she does not so wish (46); whether she is addressing the singular Pardoner or the plural company in line 193; whether 'I' or 'it'—the Wife or her husband's belief in her love—tickled his heart (395); how much of an exclamation she gives at 457; and whether the alternative to ambling, trotting, and sitting down is 'pees' (rest), 'pace' (walk: an editorial conjecture), or 'piss' (838). Line 117 appears in numerous different forms, from 'And for what profit was a wyf ywroght?' (Gg.4.27) to 'And of so parfit wys a wight ywroght'. The second version, but reading 'wright'—God—for 'wight', is arguably correct.

In some manuscripts, notably Ellesmere, the Wife's Prologue is the most heavily glossed section of the *Tales*. Some of the glosses, which mostly quote the originals of the Wife's remarks, may go back to Chaucer himself, whether as source notes for his own or the reader's information, as his own working notes, or as guides to interpretation. Most of the glosses quote from Jerome and his own citations from Scripture, rarely directly from the Bible. The Wife's comments on astrological disposition (609–19, 697–705) are glossed from a Ptolemaic work, the *Almansoris propositiones* from the *Astrologia aphoristica Ptolomoei*; the quotations she ascribes to Ptolemy's *Almagest* are in fact from a section of maxims appended to Gerard of Cremona's translation of that, and again the Latin is quoted as a gloss (by Dd.4.24 at 180–1, by Ellesmere at 326–7). There are also a few more rueful or indignant comments in the margins that register the scribes' reactions to the material they were copying. The two kinds of glosses reinforce the double sense of the Prologue both as literary text with authoritative sources and as an outrageous instance of female domination.

There is one separate manuscript of all Fragment III (plus the Clerk's Tale), but, surprisingly, none of the Prologue alone.

Robert A. Pratt, 'The Development of the Wife of Bath', in MacEdward Leach (ed.), *Studies in Medieval Literature in Honor of Albert Croll Baugh* (Philadelphia and London, 1961), pp. 45–79, argues that the Prologue was composed in several stages; it is an interesting hypothetical study of Chaucer's development of the Wife, but falls well short of proof.
Donaldson, '*Canterbury Tales*, D 117: a Critical Edition' (*Speaking of Chaucer*, pp. 119–30, repr. from *Speculum*, 40 (1965), 262–33), argues for the 'wright' reading.
On the glosses, see Graham D. Caie, 'The Significance of the Early Chaucer Manuscript Glosses (with Special Reference to the *Wife of Bath's Prologue*)', *ChR* 10 (1975–6), 350–60, and Daniel S. Silvia, 'Glosses to the *Canterbury Tales* from St. Jerome's *Epistola adversus Jovinianum*', *SP* 62 (1965), 28–39.

Genre

It may seem odd to question the genre of the Prologue at all: it is, after all, a prologue. But there is no other prologue like it either in the *Tales* or in medieval literature at large. Its materials are principally derived from antifeminist tracts, but it is certainly not a tract. The medieval version of autobiography was closely linked to the idea of *confessio*, but although the Wife freely admits her past misliving, and in that sense it can be described as 'confessional', its tone and purpose take it far away from any recognizable theological form of confession: it does not conclude with any submission to the will of God, or even of her husband, and she has not the slightest intention of changing her way of life. Several of Chaucer's discursive sources had allowed the woman's voice to be heard to reinforce their misogynist messages: Chaucer allows it to take over completely. Authority is reprocessed as experience; text is glossed from one meaning into its opposite with an ease rarely equalled until Freud. The very impossibility of assigning the piece to the safe pigeonhole of a recognized genre is typical of everything Chaucer does with the Wife.

Sources and Analogues

The first thing to stress about the Wife of Bath's Prologue is that she, and Chaucer, are dealing in commonplaces; the second, that she turns them inside out. Her materials are part of the vast medieval stock of antifeminism, but she uses them as a triumphant vindication of herself and her way of life, at least to her own satisfaction.

The Prologue draws on an exceptionally large range of sources, both covert and explicit. The explicit sources are cited by the Wife herself; they are Latin, authoritative, and listed at some length, and we are even told how she comes to know them—they were the favourite reading of her fifth husband, the Oxford scholar Jankin. The most important is St Jerome's treatise *Adversus Jovinianum*, written to refute the proposition put forward by one Jovinianus that virginity and marriage were of equal worth. This provides the Wife with most of her polemical arguments and a good many of her exempla, though the saint would have wept at her mishandling of them. It has to be admitted, though, that both the book and Jerome's relationships with women were something of a scandal in his lifetime. He included in his treatise a long extract from a work he describes as the 'liber aureolus de nuptiis', 'a book on marriage worth its weight in gold', which he ascribes to the Greek philosopher Theophrastus (author of the *Characters*); known only from Jerome, this passage was often extracted from the treatise and given independent manuscript circulation. Jankin's book, tautologously, includes both Jerome and 'Theofraste'. Chaucer's covert sources are largely French; they provide material for what the Wife herself *is*, and for what (dramatically speaking) she believes she is saying on her own account. The most important of these, and of even greater significance than Jerome in creating the character of the Wife, are two passages from Jean de Meun's continuation of the *Roman de la rose*. The first of these is where Ami, the Friend, recounts a husband's denunciation of marriage (8455–9999); in the second an old woman, La Vieille, describes her own past life and women's tricks (12740–4546). Jean de Meun incorporates much material from Jerome–Theophrastus into his own work, and so for a number of passages one can be faced with a choice of sources.

The problem of too many possible sources becomes yet more acute when one looks outside these major works. On the Latin side, it is possible to pin down a few and eliminate others. Allusions to the Bible, and especially the Epistles, are often but not always mediated through Jerome. Of the works listed as being in Jankin's anthology, 'Valerie' is Walter Map's *Dissuasio Valerii de uxore non ducenda* ('On Not Getting Married'), which Map included in his *De nugis curialium* but which also had a separate manuscript circulation, often in conjunction with Jerome–Theophrastus. This provides some illustrative material, notably the story of the tree on which a man's three wives hanged themselves (745–64); more instances are taken from the Classical collection of exemplary stories compiled by Valerius Maximus, the *Factorum et dictorum memorabilium libri novem* (460–3, 642–9), and it is possible that Chaucer took Valerius Maximus and Map's pseudonymous Valerius to be the same person. Of the other authors in Jankin's book, most are blinds: 'Ovides Art' and Héloïse were probably known to Chaucer only through the *Roman de la rose* (all the Prologue's apparent quotations from the *Ars amatoria* are mediated through the *Roman*, and Héloïse's arguments to Abelard against their marrying are included there); 'Crisippus' is merely the name of an offended male cited by Jerome. One work that does not appear on Jankin's list but that ought to, to judge from the exempla that follow, is the *Policraticus* of John of Salisbury, certainly used by Chaucer in the Pardoner's Tale, which repeats a good deal of Jerome but also adds the group of instances at 765–71.

The 'Parables of Solomon' is more interesting. The reference is presumably to Proverbs, which provided Chaucer with more of his scriptural quotations than any other book in the Bible. It also includes the description of the perfect wife (31: 10–31), itself a perfect antitype of Alison of Bath.

Minor French sources are harder to pin down, in particular because so many deal with the same materials as Jerome–Theophrastus and Jean de Meun. Two have been persistently advocated: the *Miroir de mariage* of Eustache Deschamps; and Jehan le Fèvre's translation of the *Lamentations* of the thirteenth-century poet Matheolus, a supposedly autobiographical work that describes the agonies inflicted on a husband by his wife. There is however considerable doubt as to whether either work could have been known in England in time for Chaucer to have used it—Deschamps was still working on the *Miroir* in the late 1380s; Le Fèvre's translation was completed *c*.1371, but the only manuscripts now in England are both apparently fifteenth-century. Both offer numerous parallels to the Prologue, but nearly all of these are also found in the standard Latin antifeminist works and the *Roman*; those that are not amount to only a handful of lines from poems of a good many thousand, and are frequently trivial. The one significant parallel not in the *Roman*, of the singed cat (348–84), occurs in both Deschamps and Le Fèvre, but the idea seems to have been proverbial, and Chaucer's application of the image is different from theirs. Le Fèvre also uses the euphemisms 'quoniam' and 'beauls instrumens' (cf. 608 and

132, 'sely instrument'); but these may well have been current as slang—
'quoniam' sounds like a students' variation on 'con'.

● The three sections of the Wife's Prologue draw on different source areas.
The first, Alison's defence of marriage, is largely based on Jerome. The
second, in which she describes her life with her various husbands, draws
extensively on Theophrastus, often by way of, and supplemented by, the
Roman de la rose. The sources for the third, Jankin's antifeminist reading,
are listed in his book's contents and the Wife's own footnoting. ●

If the Wife herself has any single literary model, it is unquestionably La
Vieille from the *Roman*, but the differences between them are instructive.
La Vieille is little better than a raddled elderly whore; Alison is, as her title
indicates, a *wife*, by both profession and vocation. La Vieille, like the Wife,
is by turns aggressive, defensive, regretful, and determined to make the best
of what is left; but the Wife has far more left, and she is altogether a more
vital and optimistic figure than her prototype. Chaucer draws in most detail
on just those lines where La Vieille's vitality does emerge: on the
advisability of a second hole for every mouse, for instance (572–3, *Roman*
13150–2), or the recollection of times past—a section worth quoting in full:

> Par Dieu, si me plest il encores
> Quant je me sui bien porpensee;
> Mout me delite en ma pensee
> Et me resbaudissent li membre
> Quant de mon bon temps me remembre
> Et de la jolivete vie
> Dont mon cuer a si grant envie;
> Touz me rejovenist li cors
> Quant y pense et quant le recors;
> Touz les biens du monde me fait
> Quant me sovient de tout le fait,
> Au mains ai je ma joie eüe. (12932–43)

God, how much it pleases me now when I remember all that! It thrills my mind and
tickles me all over when I remember the good times and the gay life I led, which my
heart longs for. It makes me quite young again to think about all that. It does me all
the good in the world to remember all I got up to. At least I've had my fun.

> But—Lord Crist!—whan that it remembreth me
> Upon my yowthe, and on my jolitee,
> It tikleth me aboute myn herte roote.
> Unto this day it dooth myn herte boote
> That I have had my world as in my tyme. (469–73)

La Vieille, like the Wife, had a lover who mistreated her but who could
always win her over by his sexual skill, as Jankin can Alison. The old

woman, however, rarely manages to transcend her antifeminist origins to become as fully a three-dimensional character as the Wife.

The more one looks at Chaucer's sources, the harder it becomes to pin down just how he manages this. The answer does not lie in real life, whatever the opening lines of the Prologue may claim:

> Experience, though noon auctoritee
> Were in this world, is right ynogh for me
> To speke of wo that is in mariage.   (1–3)

This very assertion of independence from textual authority is modelled on La Vieille's insistence that she has acquired all her own knowledge not from theory but from 'experiment' and practicals (*Roman* 12801–5). The Wife, moreover, goes on to cite more authorities than anyone else in the *Tales* apart from Dame Prudence in *Melibee*, and almost everything she fails to footnote would still be thoroughly familiar from the conventional body of antifeminist propaganda. Her account of her life with her husbands draws its inspiration and much of its detail from Theophrastus and Jean de Meun's development of that; in Theophrastus, for instance, are found the wives' false accusations of their husbands' misbehaviour such as the Wife plagues her own husbands with; all the demands made by wives that she accuses her husbands of accusing her of (293 ff.), such as wanting to be praised, to have her birthday remembered, and to have him honour a host of her relatives and hangers-on; the fact that a wife is the only commodity one buys untried (285–92); and that rich, poor, beautiful, and ugly wives all have disadvantages (248 ff., and of course the Wife's Tale). The conversion of such materials into her own speeches and actions makes Alison into the point of reference for every conventional accusation and aphorism. Native proverbial wisdom is added to the French and Latin materials:

> Whoso that buyldeth his hous al of salwes,
> And priketh his blynde hors over the falwes,
> And suffreth his wyf to go seken halwes,
> Is worthy to been hanged on the galwes.   (655–8)

But the Wife dominates all such material; just as the Monk of the General Prologue appropriates satire for his own purposes, she flaunts the fact that she is guilty of every charge that could be brought against women.

If she embodies the Theophrastian view of wives, she mangles St Jerome sadly, and the Bible with him. Scripture, like all the authorities she cites, is made to serve her own inclinations, by wilful misinterpretation or selection if necessary. She conveniently overlooks, for instance, the fact that St Paul allows for two sides in matrimony: his

Let the husband render unto the wife due benevolence: and likewise also the wife unto the husband. The wife hath not power of her own body, but the husband: and likewise also the husband hath not power of his own body, but the wife. (1 Cor. 7: 3–4; compare also Eph. 5: 22–5) ✳

becomes the Wife's

> I have the power durynge al my lyf
> Upon his propre body, and noght he.
> Right thus the Apostel tolde it unto me;
> And bad oure housbondes for to love us weel.   (158–61) ✗

Some manuscripts quote the verses from Corinthians as a marginal gloss, but the Wife's reference to 'the Apostle' invites the completion of her citation even without that. It is, however, a tit-for-tat process, for male homilists persistently put the stress on the other side. The Parson is as guilty as any: he devotes only a few phrases to a husband's love out of two lengthy passages on a wife's subjection (634*b* from X(I) 631–4, 929 and 937*a* from 922–37).

Jerome suffers equally badly at the Wife's hands, and it is equally well deserved: he too is quite prepared to wrench Scripture to his own purposes. She shares none of his reservations as to the relevance of the matrimonial habits of the patriarchs; she explicitly does not care that 'folk seye vileynye' of the bigamist Lamech (a murderer to boot in Jerome, as is quoted in a manuscript gloss) (35–58). She may not be sure whether Christ's words to the Samaritan woman meant that five husbands were more than enough, but she will take the benefit of the doubt (15–25). Jerome admits that virginity was advised but not commanded, but he has no doubt as to what the norm of behaviour ought to be; the Wife, also noting the absence of command, is equally sure of her different norm. The root quotation behind Jerome's comparison of golden and wooden vessels (2 Tim. 2: 20, quoted as a gloss by Egerton 2864) associates the wooden ones with *contumelia* and *juvenilia desideria*, dishonour and youthful lusts to be eschewed; the Wife reduces the contrast to a matter of domestic economy (99–101). Her comparison of wheat and barley bread (143–4) also comes from Jerome, though she omits the inconvenient fact that the most Jerome will allow is that barley bread is preferable to dung. Her argument that marriage is necessary as a source for the next generation of virgins (71–2) is one of Jovinian's arguments rejected by Jerome. His allowance of octogamy (33) is heavily ironic, and his discussion of the uses for which the genitals were created (115 ff.) is, in marked contrast to the Wife's, hedged around with apologies and reluctance. Only the sections of the tract quoted at her by her husband come over unperverted: the aphorism that women put off their shame with their smocks (782–3; Jerome quotes it from Herodotus, Jankin as a proverb), and the exempla of Socrates' wives, Pasiphae, Clytemnestra, and Eriphyle

(727–46, though Chaucer supplements the last with details from Statius' *Thebaid*).

The misuse the Wife makes of the raw materials of antifeminism and scriptural quotation is palpable, and is frequently emphasized by the glosses. More problematic is Chaucer's possible use of biblical allusions of which the Wife is unaware. With these, as with the Summoner's onions, garlic, and leeks in the General Prologue, it is perhaps finally impossible to know whether one is looking at allusion or coincidence. The problem is exemplifed by the Wife's lines on her gay clothing:

> Thise wormes, ne thise motthes, ne thise mytes,
> Upon my peril, frete hem never a deel;
> And wostow why? for they were used weel.   (560–2)

That fine clothing is subject to corruption by moths is used by Christ to point to the need to store up treasure in heaven (Matt. 6: 14–20); veiled allusion appears to be made to the passage in both *Pearl* (731) and *Piers Plowman* (B. xiv. 22–4) in scarcely more explicit language than Chaucer's, though in these at least the context is overtly biblical. It would be typical of the Wife's treatment of Scripture to get hold of the wrong end of the stick, but when a constant battle against moths was one of the everlasting problems of medieval domestic economy, one cannot be sure how far to push the allusion. The lines remain unglossed in the manuscripts, and the immediate context is not such as to encourage an ironic reading; but the allusion would fit admirably, and especially for a woman whose greatest desire is her 'will' rather than treasure in heaven.

Bartlett J. Whiting, in *Sources and Analogues*, gives extracts from Jerome–Theophrastus, Walter Map, the *Roman*, and Deschamps's *Miroir*. For full texts and translations of Jerome and the *Roman*, see pp. 13, 14; for Map, *Walter Map: De Nugis Curialium: Courtiers' Trifles*, ed. and trans. M. R. James, rev. C. N. L. Brooke and R. A. B. Mynors (Oxford, 1983).

On Chaucer and Deschamps, see John Livingston Lowes, 'Chaucer and the *Miroir de mariage*', *MP* 8 (1910–11), 165–86, 305–34; his case is rejected in favour of Matheolus–Le Fèvre by Zacharias P. Thundy, 'Matheolus, Chaucer and the Wife of Bath' (Edward Vasta and Zacharias P. Thundy (eds.), *Chaucerian Problems and Perspectives: Essays Presented to Paul E. Beichner* (Notre Dame, 1979), pp. 24–58), which in turn overstates Chaucer's debt. Full texts are edited by A. G. van Hamel, *Les Lamentations de Matheolus et le Livre de leesce de Jehan le Fèvre* (2 vols., Bibliothèque des hautes études 95–6, Paris, 1892–1905).

Robert A. Pratt, 'Jankyn's Book of Wikked Wyves: Medieval Antimatrimonial Propaganda in the Universities', *Annuale medievale*, 3 (1962), 5–27, looks at the history of the works that compose Jankin's book. A reconstruction of the book is being prepared for the Chaucer Library by Pratt, Ralph Hanna, and Traugott Lawler.

David Hugh Farmer, in *The Oxford Dictionary of Saints* (Oxford, 1978), describes Jerome as 'cantankerous', but notes that the scandalous gossip connected with his relationships with women was 'largely unjust'.

See also Robert A. Pratt, 'A Note on Chaucer and the *Policraticus* of John of Salisbury', *MLN* 65 (1950), 243–6; James L. Boren, 'Alysoun of Bath and the Vulgate "Perfect Wife"', *NM* 76 (1975), 247–56; and p. 15 above for Valerius Maximus.

Structure

The surface impression given by the Prologue is of an accurate imitation of rambling garrulity, jumping from one idea to another and occasionally losing itself:

> But now, sire, lat me se, what I shal seyn.
> A ha! by God, I have my tale ageyn.   (585–6)

Chaucer has caught perfectly the inveterate talker's trick of starting on the next subject before completing the previous one, so that interruption becomes almost impossible: the Pardoner has to break into the middle of the Wife's flow of opinion. Behind her apparent free association of ideas, however, Chaucer provides a distinct structure for her speech that moves from the general to the increasingly particular, and from her own appropriation of antifeminist arguments to her attack on them by force when they insist on appearing in their own colours.

The opening six lines outline the Wife's 'experience' in a summary biography of herself and her five husbands. At this point, however, she is distracted from detailing her life by a thought

> —If I so ofte myghte have ywedded bee—   (7)

which leads into the first major section, her summary of arguments in favour of marriage in general and multiple marriages in particular. Her determination to be her husband's 'tribulacion' (156) is the cue for the Pardoner's interruption regretting his imminent marriage. This leads to her undertaking to recount her own experiences, though before she embarks on her life story she pauses for an apology:

> If that I speke after my fantasye,
> As taketh not agrief of that I seye;
> For myn entente nys but for to pleye.   (190–2)

As with the Miller's apology, one can sense behind this Chaucer covering his own tracks. It is also excellent advertising copy.

The second section, on the history of her marriages, starts with her account of her first three husbands, treated as a conglomerate. 'The thre were goode men, and riche, and olde' (197), and she had them just where she wanted them. She is especially adept at seizing the initiative, in accusing them of accusing her of all the standard antifeminist charges: she reports to the pilgrims her own speeches in which she takes out of her husbands' mouths the words they never spoke. One of the charges she denies is suspiciously particularized (though it still goes back to Theophrastus):

> And yet of oure apprentice Janekyn,
> For his crispe heer, shynynge as gold so fyn,

> And for he squiereth me bothe up and doun,
> Yet hastow caught a fals suspecioun.
> I wol hym noght, thogh thou were deed tomorwe!   (303–7)

This is the first we have heard of Jankin, and it is some time before we hear of him again, but it is already clear that the Wife is protesting too much.

A further hundred and fifty lines of accusation and misbehaviour are sufficient to finish off her first three husbands. Her account of her fourth husband proceeds by even greater indirection than usual, and becomes hopelessly tangled with the story of her wooing of Jankin. The entanglement is not accidental: she despises the mouse that has only one hole (572–3). She already has her Oxford clerk lined up before her fourth husband's funeral, both in her life and in her narration.

In the third major division of the Prologue, the tables are turned: it is now Jankin who takes the antifeminist initiative. His unceasing misogynist propaganda wears down her patience rather than her convictions, and she attacks the source of his authority in its most concrete form, the book. The debate on men vs. women turns into a battle of man vs. woman, but the winner in the scrap is not the winner of the matrimonial battle. The scene is set for the following story of marital 'sovereynetee'—except for the brief quarrel of the Friar and the Summoner that promises more fireworks to come in the tales that follow the Wife's.

Themes

The Wife's Prologue confirms what her portrait in the General Prologue has indicated: that she is a professional wife, and pursues husbands with the same devotion that the Knight pursues chivalry or the Parson God. She focuses the question of the nature of women, dealt with at large in the *Tales*, into a more restricted theme, of the nature of the woman's role in marriage, and of her own in particular. In theory, the opening section of her harangue (as in its source in Jerome) ought to be discussing the relative merits of matrimony and virginity in general, for men and women alike; she turns it into a justification, first of sex, then of multiple marriages, and swings the balance of the whole argument towards the female of the species: 'men may conseille a womman' to be a virgin (66), her husband must leave father and mother and cleave to her (30–1).

Above all, she is concerned to justify her own way of life; not in any defensive way, nor by insisting that others ought to do as she does, but to remove the theological ground from under the feet of potential critics. The central point of her argument throughout the Prologue is her own will:

> I wol bistowe the flour of al myn age
> In the actes and in fruyt of mariage.   (113–14)

To that not only her five husbands but all the misogynist authors from the Greeks onwards must buckle.

The Wife of Bath is every antifeminist's nightmare come true; Chaucer's triumph is to make her irresistibly attractive. She may devour men whole, but she has captivated every reader of the *Canterbury Tales* since Chaucer's own lifetime (from the evidence of *Lenvoy de Chaucer a Bukton*), and she dominates the pilgrimage on the road as on the page: she alone of all the pilgrims makes her way into other people's tales (IV(E) 1170 (Clerk), 1685 (Merchant)). Her sixth victim is not going to have a chance against her. Her defence of her way of life comes from simply admitting all the charges but refusing to see anything bad in them; and in any case, the worst charges against women are as nothing compared with what could be said about men 'if wommen hadde writen stories' (693). Her own Prologue is a misogynist male text rewritten from the female point of view, where the men deserve all they get.

Three themes emerge distinctly from this: sexuality, behaviour in marriage, and dominance—of women in general, but mostly her own. The 'jolitee' she remembers from her youth has a wider reference than the pleasure she got from her earlier husbands; her inability to

> withdrawe
> My chambre of Venus from a good felawe   (617–18)

is not a remark about continence within marriage. There is no question about why she loved Jankin, for all his rough treatment of her:

> In oure bed he was so fressh and gay.   (508)

For all his antifeminist reading and his (biblically justified) habit of chastising his wife, Jankin cannot be taken as any principle of correct Christian marriage. Even he, however, when it comes to the point, is not tough enough for her, and whether in the shock of thinking he has fatally injured her, whether from the force of her return blow, or whether simply by the process of attrition, 'atte laste, with muchel care and wo' he agrees to hand over to her the governance of himself and his possessions. She acquires, like the loathly lady of her tale, 'maistrie' and 'soveraynetee'. But that is not quite the end.

> After that day we hadden never debaat.
> God helpe me so, I was to hym as kynde
> As any wyf from Denmark unto Ynde,
> And also trewe, and so was him to me.   (822–5)

We have only the Wife's word for it, but the lines still represent a remarkable turn-around, and one that prefigures the similar volte-face at the very end of her story of the knight and the ex-loathly lady.

The Wife, obviously, does not represent official Christian values, despite her generous use—or abuse—of biblical texts. A major recent line of criticism, led by D. W. Robertson, jun., has seen her as a representative of the unredeemed Old Law. Her aligning of herself with Solomon and the patriarchs, and her preference for the instruction to increase and multiply over the commendation of perfection and virginity, are called in evidence for such a reading, and the distance is stressed between the Wife's notion of what constitutes marriage and the Christian concept that regards matrimony as a figure for the relationship between Christ and His Church. The Prologue would thus become a damning indictment of the Wife and the religious failure she can be taken to represent.

It is a possible reading; the Wife, and Chaucer through her, and many of the manuscript glosses, call attention to a pattern of approved doctrine that she signally fails to obey. But the immediate context for the Wife is not the Bible but Jerome, through whom most of the scriptural references are filtered; and his work is about not the Old and New Law but marriage versus virginity. By the time he gets on to quoting the pagan Theophrastus, his lurking antifeminism has ceased to carry any doctrinal validation at all. Whether the biblical glosses go back to Chaucer or to early editors or scribes, they do not support such a generalized doctrinal reading. It would be ironic indeed if the glosses were to carry the meaning, in a group of tales that treat 'glosing' with consistent cynicism. Other glosses that are certainly scribal suggest a much more literal contemporary understanding of the Prologue: the scribe of Dd 4.24 adds a cynical 'Verum est' beside

> Kan ther no man
> Swere and lyen, as a womman kan;   (227–8)

and the Ellesmere scribe jumps to the defence of the first round of husbands:

Bihoold how this goode wyf served hir iij first housbondes whiche were goode olde men.

He, like the Clerk and Merchant within the *Tales*, clearly takes the Wife literally. It was standard practice in medieval works both fictional and theological to spell out allegorical meanings if they were not obvious—hence the need to gloss the Bible; and similarly, *Pearl* explicates the Parable of the Vineyard, and Ovid is given elaborate moralizations. Robertson has to provide such a commentary precisely because the meanings he sees are not apparent in the text.

A narrowly religious interpretation of the Prologue is however clearly not an exercise parallel to moralizing Ovid: Ovid could not have intended the religious meanings read into him, Chaucer is at pains to keep the scriptural context of the Wife's arguments in the foreground. The reason need not, however, be to point the reader through irony to her moral ignorance. The reader is indeed invited to ponder on the antifeminists' equal readiness to bend truth for their own purposes: the picture of a lion being killed by a peasant was, as the Wife notes (692), painted by a man, not a lion. Her outspoken support of non-official values is a reminder that the lion's point of view has its own legitimacy. She appeals to the whole area of festive liberation, of the Rabelaisian cocked snook, of which mockery of the rational and the proper and the ascetic is an integral part. The Wife's assertion of bodily fact—of the various functions of the genitals, for instance—is an appeal to the half of human experience that cannot be disallowed by official doctrines on the greater importance of the spirit over the flesh. The Wife is Carnival to Jerome's Lent; and that is why it is so important that Jerome should be so strongly present. Parody and mockery are of the essence of this counter-official reading of the world, and for those to exist there must be both a text to parody and an object to mock. Above all, carnival denies the official culture's claim to represent the whole truth and nothing but the truth—not countering it with any equal claim to absoluteness, but by insisting on the relative, the irreverent, the earthy. Her very insistence on the detail of life in the world is a reminder of the limitations of abstract scholasticism; and if tearing Jankin's book is not a rebuttal of the arguments it contains, the ensuing physical scrap results in an entirely non-Jeromian victory for her own views on the place of women, meaning herself, in marriage and the world. Even if the Wife's 'experience' is, in terms of sources, no more than applied authority, in the final fight it is the clenched fist of experience that wins.

Notable studies of the Wife include Muscatine, *Chaucer and the French Tradition*, pp. 204–13; Dinshaw, *Sexual Poetics*, ch. 4; David, *Strumpet Muse*, ch. 9; Pearsall, *Canterbury Tales*, pp. 71–91; and Carruthers, 'The Wife of Bath' (p. 52 above).
E. Talbot Donaldson's 'Designing a Camel: or Generalizing the Middle Ages' is the wittiest and most convincing support of the Wife against Jerome and his modern descendants (in *Tennessee Studies in Literature*, 22 (1977), 1–16).
Robertson, *Preface*, pp. 317–31, discusses the Wife's heterodoxy; for a contrasting reading, see Alcuin Blamires, 'The Wife of Bath and Lollardy', *MÆ* 58 (1989), 224–42.

The Prologue in Context

Chaucer's construction of the Fragment opened by the Wife implies a connection between her tale and those that follow, of the Friar and Summoner, rather than with the other tales on marriage or women, but it is these that have been given the most critical attention. The notion of a 'marriage debate' has at times threatened to overwhelm everything else of interest in the *Canterbury Tales*. The question of sovereignty in marriage first raised in the Wife's Prologue is continued in her Tale and taken up later by others including the Clerk, Merchant, and Franklin, sometimes with explicit reference back to her; but this theme is only one of many raised by the Prologue, and it is itself part of a bigger question—are women a Good Thing, or not?—raised in a much wider range of tales. The most specific prolepsis in her Prologue is accordingly her accusation, picked up later by the Clerk, that

> it is an impossible
> That any clerk wol speke good of wyves,
> But if it be of hooly seintes lyves.   (688–90)

The Clerk manages to do just that, though scarcely in a way that would endear him to the Wife of Bath.

The opposition of the Wife and the Clerk goes back to their portraits in the General Prologue, which, it will be recalled, bear some resemblance to the personifications of Logic and Rhetoric. The Wife's harangue, with its submergence of strict logic under her wealth of words, continues the contrast. In addition, Chaucer gives Wife and Clerk a relationship a little like that of Miller and Reeve, where the Reeve-carpenter revenges his fictional persona on a fictional miller. The Wife's clerk is not even (within the fiction of the *Tales*) a character in a story, but a character from her past life, the 'clerk of Oxenford' Jankin, who was her most special victim. It is true that Jankin sounds as if he had more in common with that other Oxford student, Nicholas, than with the Clerk of the General Prologue—he has had lodgings with yet another Alison, who sounds exactly like what the Alison of the Miller's Tale would turn out to be twenty years on—but although the Clerk himself makes no response as yet, Chaucer is preparing the ground for the defence.

The Clerk's Tale will take up the issue of sovereignty; many others take up the issue of sexuality. It is carried by women across the whole of the *Canterbury Tales*: by the increasingly accessible women of Fragment I(A); by Custance, who has to lay aside her holiness to sleep with her husband; by Cecilia, whose virginity, even within marriage, is guarded by an angel. There is, of course, one key difference between them and the Wife: they are presented as fictional—they belong within the tales, not on the Canterbury road—and specifically (since even the tale told by the Second Nun is a translation 'after the legende') as men's fictions. It is true that the Wife is just as much Chaucer's fiction as any of the others, but by giving her the illusion of autonomy he also gives her a claim to her own existence and her own voice such as is never made for the others. In point of fact, as her literary antecedents show, her ancestry lies more specifically in men's views of women than any of the rest; but by having her openly cite his sources, Chaucer allows her to appropriate all such views on behalf of her own sex. If the Wife proves the misogynists were right all along, she also reduces them to mere appendages of her own dominant self.

The Wife's contribution to the views on women expressed in the *Tales* is relevant to the work at large; a rather different issue raised in her Prologue is picked up in the tales that are directly linked to hers, the Friar's and Summoner's. This is the question of text versus gloss, of literal meaning as against the interpretation it can be twisted to fit. The Wife is herself an expert glossator, but it is her literal readings that threaten to be most subversive: of the patriarchs' polygamy, for instance, and of a scatter of Old Testament texts that were customarily sanitized by being read only in the light of their New Testament counterparts. The Wife's use of glossing to make her texts serve her own sexual inclinations intrudes in metaphor into the sex act itself:

> In oure bed he was so fressh and gay,
> And therewithal *so well koude he me glose*
> Whan that he wolde han my bele chose,
> That thogh he hadde me bete on every bon,
> He koude wynne agayn my love anon.   (508–12)

Jankin's 'glosing' foreplay can convert the Wife's original intentions to the service of his own desires. The Friar's distinction between the letter and the intention, and the Summoner's friar's skill at perverting Scripture to serve his own graft, will pick up and extend the theme.

The classic study of the 'marriage group' is George Lyman Kittredge's 'Chaucer's Discussion of Marriage', *MP* 9 (1911–12), 435–67 (repr. Schoeck and Taylor, *Chaucer Criticism*, pp. 130–59, which also contains a bibliography for further discussions, p. 158). Of more recent studies, see Kean, *Art of Narrative*, pp. 139–64; R. E. Kaske, 'Chaucer's Marriage Group', in Jerome Mitchell and William Proust (eds.), *Chaucer the Love Poet* (Athens, Ga., 1973), pp. 45–65; and for a wider view, Allen and Moritz, *Distinction*, ch. 6, and David Aers, *Chaucer, Langland and the Creative Imagination* (London, 1980), ch. 6. Lawler, *The One and the Many*, ch. 3, analyses Chaucer's generalizations about women as against the few about men.

W. G. East, ' "By preeve which that is demonstratif" ', *ChR* 12 (1977–8), 78–82, argues that Fragment III(D) is 'a disputation about academic disputations'.

Style

The vividness of the Wife's Prologue is the effect of style. Its materials, assembled from various authorities and often with their sources named, have the potential for turning it into another *Melibee*; as it is written, it could scarcely be more different. Chaucer's ear for the colloquial is here shown at its best; the speech rhythms, idioms, interjections, choice of words, all convey the sense of a distinct character, more fully dramatized than any other figure in the *Tales*, and of a speaking voice quite distinct from a narrating voice. The Wife's tone—highly personalized, digressive, observing just those pieties that suit her—is established at the very start:

> Experience, though noon auctoritee
> Were in this world, is right ynogh for me
> To speke of wo that is in mariage;
> For, lordynges, sith I twelve yeer was of age,
> Thonked be God that is eterne on lyve,
> Housbondes at chirche dore I have had fyve—
> If I so ofte myghte have ywedded bee—
> And alle were worthy men in hir degree.   (1–8)

Once the voice has been so decisively established, variations towards the formal become possible, as the Wife develops her arguments against virginity; but such formality never lasts for more than a few lines before the general principle of the argument is brought back to its real centre, herself. Even the Bible is personalized:

> Right thus the Apostel tolde it unto me,
> And bad oure housbondes for to love us weel.
> Al this sentence me liketh every deel.   (160–2)

First-person pronouns are her favourite words. That she is speaking to her fellow-pilgrims is established early, in her addresses to them as 'lordynges' or the rhetorical questions to which she demands answers,

> Wher can ye seye, in any manere age,
> That hye God defended mariage
> By expres word? I pray yow, telleth me.   (59–61)

Her appeals to an imaginary audience of 'ye wise wyves' (225) can thus come over as a rhetorical ploy without jarring.

The colloquialism is rarely developed purely for its own sake: it becomes, in ways beyond her fictional consciousness, a part of her larger argument. The epithets by which she addresses her husbands—'sire olde kaynard' (235), 'lorel' (273), 'olde barel-ful of lyes' (302), 'false theef' (800)—are all an integral part of Chaucer's portrait of the archwife. The shrill tongue and the garrulity that the misogynist tracts present as a disagreeable inconvenience to the husband are here an expression of her vitality: she, not her almost invisible spouses, becomes the norm. Her syllogisms make up in determination what they lack in logic:

> Oon of us two moste bowen, doutelees;
> And sith a man is moore resonable
> Than womman is, ye moste been suffrable.   (440–2)

Her vocabulary of reason and learning is similarly played off against a more spontaneous vocabulary of her own experiences, of appetite, of the parochial or the domestic:

> Yet in bacon hadd I nevere delit.   (418)
>
> My gossib, dwellynge in oure toun;
> God have hir soule! hir name was Alisoun.
> She knew myn herte, and eek my privetee,
> Bet than our parisshe preest, so moot I thee!   (529–32)
>
> I holde a mouses herte nat worth a leek
> That hath but oon hole for to sterte to.   (572–3)

The real delight of her Prologue lies in the way that the apostles and the patriarchs and planetary influences can share the same mental compartment as 'Wilkyn, oure sheep', and her 'bele chose', and come out decidedly second in significance.

See also Muscatine, *Chaucer and the French Tradition*, pp. 204–13; and Lee Patterson, ' "For the Wyves Love of Bathe": Feminine Rhetoric and Poetic Resolution in the *Roman de la rose* and the *Canterbury Tales*', *Speculum*, 58 (1983), 656–95.

The Wife of Bath's Tale

Date and Text

The Wife's Tale was probably written specifically for her, displacing the tale now told by the Shipman, which seems to have been originally assigned to her. If it was written all at once, including the digression on friars, it is likely to be close in date both to the Prologue and to the Friar's and Summoner's Tales that follow it; the Friar's interjection at the end of the Prologue and the Wife's response in her Tale link the two together unusually closely.

Verbal variants are trivial. There is disagreement over God's 'prowesse' or 'goodnesse' (1129), but 'prowesse' scarcely makes sense in the context. Poverty cannot be 'sinne' (1191), as some manuscripts say; the alternatives are 'an high joye' or 'syngeth', the latter reading being explained by the following lines and confirmed by a gloss quoting Juvenal. This and four other glosses on the sources of the hag's speech are given by Ellesmere and a small number of other manuscripts (Seneca's Epistles at 1182, Rev. 3: 7 at 1186, 'Philosophus Secundus'—probably by way of Vincent of Beauvais— at 1195, Jerome's *Adversus Jovinianum* at 1202). Another manuscript (Egerton 2864) gives three further biblical glosses. Marginal notes of the subject in hand include 'De generositate', 'on *gentillesse*', at the start of the hag's speech, and 'Verum est' from the scribe of Dd.4.24 beside the comment on women's love of flattery (930).

Genre

The story told by the Wife belongs in the borders between folktale—even fairy-tale—and romance. The choice is something of a stroke of genius on Chaucer's part. The genre does not have the obvious appropriateness of romance for the Squire, nor the satiric inappropriateness of fabliau for the Summoner, both of which make statements about the professional type represented by the teller. The Wife's choice is appropriate for her profession as a practitioner of matrimony, but not in the ways one would have expected. The fabliau of the Shipman's Tale that was apparently once intended for her, with its venal wife getting the better of her unsuspecting husband, would have been a more obvious fit. By giving her a romance, Chaucer adds another side to her character: she is an incurable romantic, a secret Mills and Boon addict. The tale may overtly be about women's love of sovereignty, but it ends with marital—and especially sexual—bliss. It offers a fulfilment not only of the Wife's conscious desires for mastery and a young and virile husband, but of the desire she can express only as regret, for the restoring of her lost youth and beauty. This is the one tale of the entire Canterbury sequence where this kind of intimate psychology plays a role alongside the more generalized matching of literary kind to character (and even here, of course, there is plenty going on in addition to, or in opposition to, dramatic character development). Romance typically includes a return from some kind of threatened or symbolic death, and the figure so saved in the Wife's Tale is overtly the knight; but in so far as the hag, with her desire for sovereignty, is a figure for herself, the Wife is offering herself an image of restoration.

It is appropriate in more general terms too that the romance should be of the kind it is—Arthurian in setting (Chaucer seems to have had a low opinion of Arthurian material), abounding in magic, with analogues possibly in vernacular oral tradition. This marks it as being after *Sir Thopas* the closest to popular literature of the five romances of the *Tales*, at the far extreme of the spectrum of romance from the Knight's epic with its Classical and continental sources. The Wife is the only character to tell a romance who has no claim to *gentil* status or to connections with the court. It is also, therefore, despite its closeness to folktale, in keeping with her pretensions to social superiority over the lesser wives of her parish.

The placing of the Tale as a follow-on from her 'long preamble' points to another generic function it bears, as a narrative exemplum to illustrate the argument developed discursively in her Prologue. That it will not quite work as such is again an indication of the psychological depth envisaged for the Wife.

Sources and Analogues

All the significant analogues of the Wife of Bath's Tale are in English—a distinction it shares only with *Sir Thopas*. The principal analogues are Gower's tale of Florent from the *Confessio amantis* (i. 1407–864); the romance of *The Weddynge of Sir Gawen and Dame Ragnell*, probably of the fifteenth century, though the manuscript in which it appears also contains some fourteenth-century material (including the Clerk's and Prioress's Tales); and the ballad *The Marriage of Sir Gawaine*, recorded in the mid-seventeenth century. If, as this suggests, the story was familiar as a folktale, Chaucer's audience could well have been aware of the perversions to which the Wife subjects the original story. His precise source is unknown, but its outline is probably indicated by the plot of the romance and the ballad.

The basic story, of the hag who promises to tell what women most desire in return for marriage and who ends up by becoming beautiful, is common to Chaucer and all the analogues. Gower's Florent is however set the riddle as a way of avoiding a death sentence passed for an accidental killing, not for a crime. In the romance and the ballad, Gawain takes on marriage with the loathly lady voluntarily to save Arthur's honour, when it is Arthur's own life that is at stake for the lack of an answer to the riddle. Chaucer keeps the Arthurian setting, but alters the details of the story to make it more coherent, and more responsive to the purposes he has in mind for the Wife.

All of Chaucer's major variations show these tendencies. The knight and hag are never named: they remain embodiments of a male and female principle—not in any abstract sense, but the lack of particularity underlines their quality as paradigms in the battle between the sexes. The tale opens with the knight's crime of rape, the ultimate assertion of male *maistrie* over woman, and therefore closely integrated with the ending. It is the ladies of the court, led by the queen, who take over judgement on him (in Gower's version the test is set by an old woman, grandmother of the knight that Florent has killed, in pursuit of the family's revenge for the death; in the *Wedding* poems the tester is a knight who is brother to the hag, and who has overcome Arthur in battle). Chaucer's loathly lady demands the knight's agreement to do whatever she asks him without telling him that her request is marriage; in the analogues, the potential bridegrooms are told the condition in advance. Chaucer gives no explanation of why his hag is ugly, least of all one that places her under someone else's control through enchantment: the possibility remains open that she is the 'elf-queene' of 860. Most significant of all, the choice offered to the knight at the end is changed from her being fair by day or by night to her being foul and chaste or beautiful and let him take the consequences. The issue becomes, in fact, one of women's virtue rather than beauty—an issue much more in keeping with both the Wife's Prologue and the many other Canterbury tales that are concerned with women or the nature of marriage.

Verbal parallels exist between the Wife's story and both Gower and the romance, but they are not so marked as to prove direct debt. The most striking is the assemblage of answers to the riddle in the romance:

> Somme sayd they lovyd to be welle arayd,
> Somme sayd they lovyd to be fayre prayed;
> Somme sayd they lovyd a lusty man,
> That in theyr armys can clyppe and kysse them than

—compare Chaucer's (or, in the last line, indisputably the Wife's)

> Some seyde wommen loven best richesse,
> Somme seyde honour, somme seyde jolynesse,
> Somme riche array, somme seyden lust abedde,
> And oftetyme to be wydwe and wedde.   (925–8)

The closeness could well come from coincidence of subject, however—or indeed from Chaucerian influence on the *Weddynge*. Both Chaucer's knight and Florent hide away like owls from the light on the day of their marriage (1081, *Confessio*, i. 1727). Chaucer fails to tell of the joy at the wedding feast because there was none (1073–8): if the lines are more than a rhetorical ploy, they could refer to a source episode such as that in the *Weddynge* where the hag insists on the most public and splendid wedding possible. Both the *Weddynge* and Gower use the terms 'soverein' or 'sovereynte' in the answer to the riddle, as Chaucer does—though he holds back the answer until the knight has to produce it at court, and we never hear it from the hag's lips. Only Chaucer adds 'maistrie' to 'sovereyntee' to underline the Wife's point (1038–40, cf. 1236). In the *Confessio*, the whole tale is told to illustrate the virtue of obedience in love.

The rape that opens the tale has no parallels in these other English versions, though similar adventures are on occasion credited (or discredited) to Gawain in some French romances. The most likely series of analogues for this, however, if literary sources are required at all, would be French *pastourelles* and similar poems in which passing knights, sometimes, like the Wife's, out hawking, rape or attempt to rape girls found by the wayside. The girls are most often peasants or shepherdesses, but not necessarily: crossing a forest seems especially to have invited disaster for women of all kinds. The classlessness of the Wife's 'mayde', like the anonymity of her hero, keeps the story as a battle not between social ranks but between the sexes.

Chaucer does have one episode not found in the analogues that would seem to be extraneous to the main theme: the dance of the twenty-four ladies and their sudden disappearance. It is a superb passage, and works admirably to create an atmosphere of wonder for the first appearance of the hag, but any further indications as to its function within the movement of the story remain unspoken. It could be taken to prefigure the hag's reverse change from loathesomeness to beauty, or suggest that her appearance is under her own control—she is never rationalized into any mere enchanted princess. The dance of the beautiful and supernatural women who cannot be caught by the hero is a common folktale motif even though it does not appear in the analogues; Walter Map's *De nugis curialium*, for instance, provides a number of medieval examples derived from oral tradition.

As in most of the *Tales*, more goes on than story alone, and there are two major passages that have their sources elsewhere: the digression on Midas, and the hag's speech on *gentillesse*. The Wife mangles the story of the telling of the secret of Midas' ass's ears as much as she does that of the loathly lady. It comes, as she says, from Ovid; but she insists on retelling it with her invariable bias that puts women at the centre of everything. The original bearer of the secret was Midas' barber, not his wife, so it is she herself who is turning it into an exemplum of women's inability to keep a secret—an inability she describes with comfortable complacency. Her omission of the ending, in which it is the reeds that tell the secret to the world, helps to keep the responsibility for tattling firmly on the women. As with most of Chaucer's borrowings from the *Metamorphoses*, the alterations seem to be original to him, and owe nothing to the moralizing commentaries.

The hag's disquisition on *gentillesse*, like the Wife's Prologue, has almost too many possible sources, for the distinction between virtue and birth was as much a medieval commonplace as the wickedness of women. It was a favourite theme of Chaucer's, both elsewhere in the *Tales* and in his *balade* of *Gentillesse*, which is based primarily on Boethius (iii. pr. 6, m. 6; the hag recommends Boethius as further reading, 1168). The *Roman de la rose* also devotes several hundred lines to the subject (18561–896), and 'the wise poete of Florence | That highte Dant', cited with magnificent anachronism by the Arthurian loathly lady, discusses the issue at length in the Fourth Tractate of the *Convivio* and its introductory *canzone*, though there are no lines precisely corresponding to those she ascribes to him. 'Valerius' (1165) is the exempla anthology of Valerius Maximus beloved of the Wife's fifth husband; and if a naturalistic source is required for Alison's learning as projected on to the hag, Jankin can be called on to provide it. It has been suggested, indeed, that he is responsible for the perversion of the story of Midas; and if that is going too far into the realms of extra-textual speculation, Chaucer's whole presentation of the Wife and her biography invites such an approach.

Bartlett J. Whiting, 'The Wife of Bath's Tale', in *Sources and Analogues*, gives the texts of Gower, the ballad, and the romance, and also extracts from the *Metamorphoses* (xi. 180–93, on Midas), the *Convivio*, and the *Roman de la rose*. On the *Convivio*, see Boitani, 'What Dante Meant to Chaucer', in his *Chaucer and the Trecento*, pp. 130–3.

Sigmund Eisner's attempt to derive the tale from Irish legends that personify the sovereignty of Ireland is unconvincing (*A Tale of Wonder: A Source Study of 'The Wife of Bath's Tale'* (Wexford, 1957)).

Structure

From what we can speculate of Chaucer's sources, it appears that he altered the story he received to focus on the main theme of sovereignty. He adds, however, three digressions that have little to do with either the story or the theme. The first of these is the passage of satire on friars, who have replaced elves and incubuses in their habit of dishonouring women as they roam about the countryside. The second is the story of Midas, adapted as an exemplum of how women cannot keep a secret. The third, occupying a full quarter of the tale, is the loathly lady's discourse on *gentillesse*. Each bears a different structural function in the tale.

The purpose of the first digression is primarily a cue for the following tale, the Friar's. The immediate excuse for introducing it lies solely in the parallel drawn between friars and the fairies who do belong in the tale. The second digression, the story of Midas, is digression for its own sake, a match for the ramblings of the Wife's Prologue, as her own voice takes over from the impersonal voice of the storyteller. Both her voice and the story recall the antifeminist propaganda of the Prologue. The excuse for its introduction is again tenuous: if 'somme seyn' that women like to be thought good keepers of secrets, the Wife will tell the tale as an exemplum to show the nonsense of any such idea. The third passage, the *gentillesse* speech, is not strictly a digression since it is given as part of the main narrative, as the hag's attempt to win over her bridegroom. Its presence does some startling things to the final meaning of the story, and its sheer length shifts the balance of the tale markedly from story for its own sake towards story for the sake of a moral.

So far as the narrative itself is concerned, the structural tightness can best be appreciated by the differences between Chaucer's version and its analogues: his grounding of the test in punishment for rape, his excision of extraneous testers and surrogate victims. He introduces a greater sense of suspense and climax by holding back until the knight's return to court the answer to the riddle and the hag's demand of marriage. Another striking feature of the Tale, also present to some degree in the *Weddynge*, is the high proportion of direct, or occasionally indirect, speech. From the knight's first meeting with the hag until her turning beautiful (997–1249), there are only some twenty-seven lines that are not speech of some kind. Even the non-description of the wedding feast is done in the form of 'Now wolden som men seye . . . I seye ther nas . . .'.

Themes

The central theme of both the matter and the *sentence* of the tale is the answer to the question of what women most desire:

> Wommen desiren to have sovereynetee
> As wel over hir housbond as hir love,
> And for to been in maistrie hym above.   (1038–40)

This is what the Wife's Prologue has led us to expect, and why the riddle was the appropriate condition for pardon for the male violence of the initial rape. The hag's pressing of sexual attentions on the unwilling knight, and his final handing over of free choice to her, are the comic aspects of the same theme:

> 'Thanne have I gete of yow maistrie,' quod she,
> 'Syn I may chese and governe as me lest?'   (1236–7)

But this, although so important, is not all that happens in the *sentence* of the tale, and some of the other things are distinctly surprising.

The disquisition on *gentillesse* is the most astonishing of these. Nothing has led us to expect that either the Wife of Bath, with her social snobbery and her readiness to subordinate scriptural interpretation to her own sexual inclinations, or the Arthurian fairy shape-shifter, would be capable of the high idealism of

> Crist wole we clayme of hym oure gentillesse.   (1117)

Least of all do we expect a discourse on vice and virtue rather than men versus women. Neither Chaucer nor the hag has available the locution 'persons', but it is still startling, after the Wife's insistent feminizing of speech, to hear

> Therefore sholden ye be gentil men . . .   (1111)
>
> Taak hym for the grettest gentil man . . .   (1116)
>
> Ful selde up riseth by his branches smale
> Prowesse of man . . .   (1128–9)

The loathly lady is out to teach *gentillesse* to her husband, but most of all to assert her own claim to the *gentillesse* of virtue. The means by which she does so assert a human ideal transcending sexual difference just as it transcends distinction of rank or wealth. The brutal male substitution of violence for rationality in the rape gives way to a model of reasoned persuasion, put into the mouth of a woman but applicable to both sexes.

The Wife has, I think, been left behind by this point. She might have access to Valerius Maximus (1165), but it is Chaucer who knows Dante and Boethius (1126, 1168), named sources who for once are not a blind. The reasons for introducing the passage, and at such length, reflect Chaucer's convictions rather than the Wife's psychology; and we can, for once, be fairly sure of Chaucer's own views since he returns to the theme so often and so consistently, not only through the fallible narrators of the *Tales* but in his *balade* of *Gentillesse*. The effect within this tale is to alter the nature, not only of the story, but specifically of the ending. The change from his sources that Chaucer introduces here (from fair by day or by night, to ugly, humble, and faithful or beautiful with all its risks) has an obvious congruence with the Wife's Prologue and its discussion of the demerits of every possible kind of wife; but the resolution, that the lady will be both fair and faithful, is already implicit in her long speech.

> Yet maye the hye God, and so hope I,
> Grante me grace to lyven vertuously.   (1173–4)

The emphasis shifts from the magic of *fayerye* to inner virtue. The story may be fanciful to a degree unmatched in Chaucer's works outside *Sir Thopas*—fairies are not, for him, the stuff of which serious literature is made—but he gives it an inner core of human idealism that asserts its right to be read with seriousness.

This new stress on virtue has a congruence with the very end of the tale. It concludes not with the woman's being boss, but with the romance achievement of 'blisse' and, most surprisingly, with obedience.

> For joye he hente hire in his armes two,
> His herte bathed in a bath of blisse.
> A thousand tyme a-rewe he gan hire kisse,
> And she obeyed hym in every thyng
> That myghte doon hym plesance or likyng.   (1252–6)

The context may suggest female obedience in a sexual situation, but it is still in marked contrast to the male submission to female sexuality desired by the Wife in her concluding prayer for 'housbondes meeke, yoonge, and fressh abedde' (1259). She may reassert the familiar theme of wifely domination in her final lines, but it is not exactly the moral expressed by the story.

The Tale in Context

The nature of the Wife of Bath's contribution to the *Canterbury Tales* is thoroughly familiar. She sets up the nature of marriage and of marital sovereignty as a dominant theme, though not in such simple ways as might at first appear: the ending of her tale in mutual bliss, and the bride's doubling of *maistrie* with obedience, presents a view of marriage that is not, when it comes to the point, very different from that propounded by the Franklin's Tale or established at the end of the Clerk's after Walter's aberrant appetite for testing Grisilde is sated. The independence of virtue and *gentillesse* from rank or riches is also a leading theme of both the Clerk's and Franklin's Tales, and so is the granting and keeping of *trouthe*. The knight's pledging his word to the hag and keeping to it through all that follows is re-enacted by Grisilde, just as it is by Dorigen, and vicariously on her behalf by Arveragus. The extended debate in the *Tales* on female chastity versus sexuality, or the contrasting images of woman as Eve or the Virgin, owe much more to the Wife's Prologue than to her Tale.

The tale that follows, the Friar's, is most obviously paired with the Summoner's, but it is also connected to the Wife's dramatically and in plot. The connection is cued both by his comments on her Prologue and by her attack on friars at the start of her Tale. The 'quityng' is carried through in the parallelism of plot motifs in the two tales, of the forest meeting with a supernatural shape-shifter, the plighting of troth and so on. The Wife's loathly lady, in a projection of her own desires, can turn young: she is the Wife's *alter ego*. The Friar has his shape-shifter turn out to be a fiend, so producing an insult parallel to the Miller's and Reeve's turning their fictional counterparts into cuckolds. The transformation of shape-shifter into fiend could also indicate retrospectively that the loathly lady is herself a *succuba*, the female equivalent of the incubus replaced by the friar (873–81). She would therefore be leading the knight to damnation as surely as the fiend leads the summoner. But such an interpretation may load more on to the parallelism of the stories than it will bear. The tales of the Canterbury sequence may be given alternative readings from their place in the series, but in the first instance every tale carries its meaning as an independent work.

Penn R. Szittya, 'The Green Yeoman as Loathly Lady: The Friar's Parody of the Wife of Bath's Tale', *PMLA* 90 (1975), 386–94, points out the connections of the tales.

Style

There are two principal styles in the Wife's Tale: there is the personal voice familiar from her Prologue, assertive, colloquial, packed with first-person pronouns and gender words; and there is the voice of the Chaucerian narrator, which can be indistinguishable from Chaucer's own voice as poet. There is no stylistic means by which it is possible to differentiate the loathly lady's

> Crist wole we clayme of hym oure gentillesse,
> Nat of oure eldres for hire old richesse.
> For thogh they yeve us al hir heritage,
> For which we clayme to been of heigh parage,
> Yet may they nat biquethe, for no thyng,
> To noon of us hir vertuous lyvyng   (1117–22)

from the impersonal voice of the *balade* of *Gentillesse*:

> Vyce may wel be heir to old richesse;
> But ther may be no man, as men may wel see,
> Bequethe his heir his vertuous noblesse.   (15–17)

The lady's speech uses 'man' for the whole human race as the Wife never does; even its 'we' and 'us' have become universalized, where the Wife's usages are always explicitly female.

The style of most of the narrative likewise concentrates on the action rather than on the individuality of the speaker. Simplicity in this tale can seize the imagination more than rhetorical elaboration in others:

> But hoom he gooth; he myghte nat sojourne;
> The day was come that homward moste he tourne.
> And in his wey it happed hym to ryde,
> In al this care, under a forest syde,
> Wher as he saugh upon a daunce go
> Of ladyes foure and twenty, and yet mo;
> Toward the whiche daunce he drow ful yerne,
> In hope that som wysdom sholde he lerne.
> But certeinly, er he cam fully there,
> Vanysshed was this daunce, he nyste where.
> No creature saugh he that bar lyf,
> Save on the grene he saugh sittynge a wyf—
> A fouler wight ther may no man devyse.   (987–99)

The passage is a unique demonstration of Chaucer's ability to evoke a sense of the fairy supernatural. The drab movement of the opening lines highlights the marvel that follows, which becomes all the more credible for the commonplace way it is introduced. The lines do not, however, share the anonymity of fabliau narration: they are told from a point of view within the story, the knight's, whose thoughts and feelings mediate the events, and whose puzzlement at the end allows the dance and its vanishing all the more power for being unexplained. Elsewhere, what looks at first glance like familiar Chaucerian apology turns out to make a point about the action:

> Now wolden som men seye, paraventure,
> That for my necligence I do no cure
> To tellen yow the joye . . .   (1073–5)

One expects the lines to introduce an *occupatio*, as a variant on 'I will not tell you how . . .'. On this occasion there is in fact nothing to recount:

> I seye ther nas no joye ne feeste at al.   (1078)

This is a rhetorical strategy turned inside out, and all the more effective for that. The most formal use of rhetoric comes, as one would expect, in the hag's speech on *gentillesse*; but Chaucer can also combine rhetorical elaboration with convincing colloquialism, as in her first speech in bed, with its parallelism of syntax coinciding with line unit and couplet form:

> Is this the lawe of kyng Arthures hous?
> Is every knyght of his so dangerous?
> I am youre owene love and youre wyf;
> I am she which that saved hath youre lyf.   (1089–92)

The lines constitute a stylistic change of key, of register, between the broad comedy of her opening 'O deere housbonde, *benedicitee*!', and the moral seriousness and abstract diction of the discourse that follows.

There are moments none the less where the Wife's own characteristic voice breaks through the folktale anonymity. The impersonality of the various answers to the riddle the knight is given, 'somme seyde . . .', is disrupted by a sudden spate of first-person pronouns, 'we', 'us', referring to women in general but most of all to herself. The language suddenly becomes much more idiomatic:

> For trewely ther is noon of us alle,
> If any wight wol clawe us on the galle,
> That we nel kike.   (939–41)

Her 'Wol ye heere the tale?' (951) introducing the story of Midas is also much more direct, much more identifiably her own voice; and even when the action of the main tale is in full swing, there are still characteristic moments when we are forcibly reminded who is speaking:

> Oftetyme to be wydwe and wedde   (928)
>
> Ful many a noble wyf, and many a mayde,
> And many a wydwe, for that they been wise— (1026–7)
>
> In al the court ne was ther wyf, ne mayde
> Ne wydwe—   (1043–4)

The 'wife, maid, and widow' formula may be conventional (though Chaucer only uses it once elsewhere, I(A) 1171; and cf. IV(E) 836–8), but there is nothing formulaic about its uses here: we are not going to be allowed to forget whose story this is.

The Friar's Tale

Prologue

Like so many links, the Friar's Prologue starts by looking backwards, but in this instance it looks beyond the preceding tale to the Wife's Prologue. It is there that 'scole-mateere' of 'greet difficultee' is found, packed with 'auctoritees' (1272–6). His own tale, he promises, will be very different.

The 'louryng chiere' cast by the Friar on the Summoner also goes back to the Wife's Prologue, where the Summoner's insult to the Friar had led to their mutual threat to tell stories against each other. The Friar now accordingly undertakes to tell a 'game' of a summoner, adding that it is impossible to say anything good about the whole profession. The Host responds that 'a man of youre estaat' should be 'hende and curteys'—a curiously secular pair of adjectives to use about members of a religious order, but entirely appropriate to the ingratiating Friar of the General Prologue. The Host's aim is to avoid 'debaat', quarrelling, among the company, but the Summoner promises to 'quiten every grot' of what the Friar can say in his own story, which thus promises to be, like the Reeve's, a reprisal for the preceding tale. This Prologue thus serves to introduce not just the Friar's Tale but the Summoner's as well.

Date and Text

The text of the Friar's Tale shows no significant variants in the major manuscripts, and there is no evidence that Chaucer ever had any intentions for the tale other than those indicated by its present context. It is likely that this and the Summoner's Tale were written as a pair.

The text is unglossed in the manuscripts except for a single line at the end, 1657 (on the lion lying in wait), for which biblical parallels are sometimes cited (Ps. 10: 8 in Ellesmere, elsewhere also 1 Pet. 5: 8).

Genre

The terms in which the Friar speaks of his tale make it sound as if it will be a fabliau: it will be a 'game' of a summoner whose job it is to be 'a rennere up and doun | With mandementz for fornicacioun' (1279, 1283–4), and its object is insult of a fellow-pilgrim. The concentration on narrative, with very little of the generalizing digression that characterizes so many of the Canterbury tales, is most commonly a feature of fabliau; and the tale's insistent contemporaneity (stressed by the reference to 'my contree' in the

opening line), and the dependence of its plot on trickery and the out-
manœuvring of stupidity, also recall fabliau methods.

In fact it is something very different from fabliau, as its analogues
confirm: it is an extended exemplum, an exemplary tale about rapacity and
intent, whose moral is not an appendage, but structurally integral. To be
precise, it is a set of contradictory exempla. In his last address to the fiend,
the summoner speaks of himself being an *ensample* to his companion of skill
in extortion (1580), the very opposite moral pattern from that offered by the
exemplum of the tale. The Friar intends his story as a different kind of
exemplum again, against summoners. His blindness to the moral inherent in
the tale is indicated by his inclusion of an extra moral at the end, distinctly at
odds with the plot, where the audience is invited to consider how the devil
lies in wait to entrap the *innocent*—scarcely the point of this story.

Sources and Analogues

Although the central story of the Friar's Tale can be traced back to two early
thirteenth-century versions (one in a Latin compilation of exempla by the
monk Cesarius of Heisterbach, one in German couplet verse by the Austrian
poet Der Stricker), Chaucer seems to have known a distinctively English
version. His immediate source is unknown, but its likely shape can be
reconstructed from two Latin sermon exempla more or less contemporary
with him that survive in manuscripts now in the British Library (Harley
4894, a version by Robert Rypon; and Cotton Cleopatra D.viii). Chaucer
shares with each of these features not found in continental analogues. In
Rypon's version, the central character is a *ballivus*, a bailiff, such as the devil
first mistakes the summoner for—a proposition to which the summoner, for
'shame', agrees (1392–3). The animals that receive the first curse are, like
Chaucer's, draught animals, in this case oxen, where other versions use an
assortment of animals being driven to market. The Cotton analogue has as
its main character a man who collects fines for ecclesiastical offences
(*senescallus et placitator*), and who shares the summoner's obtuseness as to
the dangers of his position. It also stresses the *likeness* between devil and
placitator—'Ego tui similis sum', the devil tells him. It is perhaps from such
a hint that Chaucer develops the sense that his devil is the summoner's
demonic second self.

Medieval homiletic literature abounds with looser parallels to the tale. In
his encyclopaedic handbook for preachers, the *Summa praedicantium*, John
Bromyard notes that 'evil acquisitors are the devil's companions', 'Mali
acquisitores sunt socii demonum' (cf. 1521–2). That bailiffs were among the
worst offenders appears in Bromyard and widely elsewhere. Peraldus'
treatise on the vices and virtues, which in some form probably underlies the

Parson's Tale, contains similar maxims, and notes further (under the heading of Avarice) that the curses of the widows and children who are the victims of *raptores* will rebound on the wrongdoers. The closest analogues to the list of the summoner's malpractices are however to be found not in homilies but in historical records. Both Church and State had already been trying for over two centuries to combat the abuses associated with the summoning to archdeacons' courts, without, as the tale indicates, producing much in the way of results.

Allusion to other texts is largely limited to the fiend's speeches on the nature of devils (1482–520). It is intriguing that he does not refer to the Bible as such, merely to certain episodes in it, such as Job and Samuel and the Witch of Endor ('Phitonissa', 1510, from Vulgate 1 Chr. 10: 13 and 1 Sam. 28: 7). Biblical material for the fiend thus represents not authority but experience, personal history, and he doesn't need to bother about theology (1512). By contrast, he recommends that the summoner read Dante for further information on hell; he couples his name with that of Virgil, presumably less because of the account of Aeneas' visit to the Underworld than because Dante's Virgil acted as tour guide for the infernal regions. The fiend no more needs a source for his demonology than he does for his past experience, but Chaucer may have used here the *Speculum maius* of Vincent of Beauvais.

The Friar's concluding words carry an explicit level of biblical reference, and may also echo that pervasive source for Fragment III(D), Jerome's *Adversus Jovinianum*. Two of the allusions to the Bible in the tale carry particular significance. One is that the fiend claims his habitation to be 'in the north contree', as Lucifer's is in Isaiah 14: 13. His last words to the summoner—'Thou shalt with me to helle yet tonyght' (1636)—sound suspiciously like an inversion of Christ's words to the penitent thief (Luke 23:43). A similar inversion comes in the Friar's words at the end, where he comments that 'no tonge may devyse' the pains of hell (1650): it recalls the formula customarily used about the joys of heaven, and confirms the Friar's unbroken vision of evil.

Peter Nicholson, 'The Analogues of Chaucer's *Friar's Tale*', ELN 17 (1979), 93–5, supplements and corrects Archer Taylor's section in *Sources and Analogues*. Taylor gives texts of the versions by Cesarius and Der Stricker, and that in the Cotton MS; Benson and Andersson, in *Literary Context*, give a translation of Cesarius. For Bromyard, see p. 12; the same section of the *Summa*, J.xiii, might also provide the cue for the moral drawn by the Friar on the ensnaring of the innocent.
Przemyslaw Mroczkowski, 'The "Friar's Tale" and its Pulpit Background', *English Studies Today*, 2nd ser. (1961), 107—20.
Pauline Aiken, 'Vincent of Beauvais and the Green Yeoman's Lecture on Demonology', *SP* 35 (1938), 1–9.
See also Hahn and Kaeuper's article on summoners cited on p. 57.

Structure

I have already glanced at the Chinese-box structure of the *moralitees* of the Friar's Tale. That the Friar tells the story at all serves as a satire on him; he means it to satirize summoners; the story itself damns extortioners; the summoner within the tale sees himself as a model of successful extortion.

The central story of the Tale, once the Friar gets down to it, is unusually unified, with very little of the digression that characterizes Chaucer's other moral or pseudo-moral tales. It is one of the few tales where an important part is played by suspense, and the strong forward thrust of the action gives the story an impressive power. It is not the kind of exemplary tale that needs a separate exposition; the main plot is enclosed, however, between opening and concluding sections in which the Friar is given his own voice. The tenor of these pulls away from the generalizing moral against avarice and grinding the faces of the poor, such as the analogues stress, to give a much more particular and personal attack on summoners in general and the pilgrim Summoner in particular. At both beginning and end, the Friar moves from speaking of 'a' summoner to 'this' summoner, and although in Middle English the locution could refer to a fictional subject or to a man actually present, the tone suggests that the Friar has moved from story to pilgrimage. The shift is confirmed by the pilgrim Summoner, who interrupts to link art with the 'real life' of the Canterbury pilgrimage by turning one of the Friar's remarks back on him as an insult—that friaries, like brothels, are exempt from summoners' jurisdiction.

The story opens, like so many of the Tales, with character descriptions, with that of the nominal authority figure, the archdeacon, first. Once the summoner and the fiend have met, the tale moves into dialogue, and after this point remarkably little narrative occurs outside speech and its accompanying directives: six lines for the cart's getting stuck (1536–41), three lines for the fiend's carrying the summoner off to hell (1639–41).

The first part of the action, in which 'yeman' and summoner meet and agree to keep company in extortion, reaches its climax in the revelation to both summoner and audience, 'I am a feend' (1448). From this point on, the reader's understanding of the events of the narrative parts company from the summoner's, who is incapable of seeing the logic of the narrative movement; and so a strong element of dramatic irony enters, and with it suspense—though the conclusion is delayed by the devil's exposition of demonology. Although this is not strictly necessary to the story (and is not found in the analogues), it is absorbed into the main action by being shaped as a prophecy that is fulfilled at the end: the summoner is to learn such things by his 'owene experience' (1517), and he ends up on his way to do just that (1636–8).

Themes

Like the Pardoner's Tale, the Friar's Tale contains two different and even contradictory sets of of themes, one inherent in the story, the other arising from the context in which it is told. The orthodox morality of the story proper picks up widespread homiletic and confessional themes, on the association of avarice and the devil, and on the importance of intention in speech—the fiend will carry off the summoner when the widow commits him to the devil, but not the carter's horses. The stress on *entente*, however, rebounds on the Friar himself, for his intention in telling the tale is clearly not homiletic or didactic or to promote virtue, but to insult the Summoner. As in the Pardoner's Tale, the theme of avarice also turns and bites the teller, for Friar Huberd in the General Prologue has been portrayed as thoroughly rapacious, even if he manages his extortions with rather more elegance and urbanity than his summoner, working by smooth talking rather than by threats. He can talk a widow out of her last farthing (I(A) 253–5), without having to resort to his summoner's methods with the widow within the tale; alarmingly, his own techniques of acquisition have more in common with the devil's.

While the substance of the tale, then, suggests an impersonal and stable morality, the circumstances of its telling dig holes underneath the very concepts of moral stability or literary disinterestedness. Not that Chaucer is promoting total moral relativism: the Friar may be satirizing summoners, but his method of doing so turns into a Chaucerian satire with rather different targets, recognition of which depends on accepted moral norms and ideals—that avarice is sinful, that both the Friar's words and the summoner's actions represent a perversion of ecclesiastical office and social function, and that fiction ought, by all medieval literary theory, to operate as a branch of ethics. The Friar's Tale may yet achieve that last aim, but not in the way the Friar intends. Its vision scarcely allows for a glimpse of anything resembling virtue or common human decency—a limitation that is itself a comment on the Friar.

After his introductory remarks (signalled by the intrusion of 'quod the Frere' at 1338, and again at 1645), the story advances by its own logic and develops its ideas independently of its context. The nature of those ideas is made clear by the repetition of certain words or groups of words. One of the most persistent is the set of verbs connected with extortion and profit: *geten*, *taken*, *wynnen*, *pilen*. Both summoner and fiend are described as pursuing their *pray*, perhaps in the manner of wolves in disguise, though the plot turns the hunter into the hunted as the summoner turns out to be the devil's quarry. The two swear brotherhood, and address each other in almost every speech as *brother*: the fiend is the summoner's diabolic moral twin.

The notion of *entente* also takes its place in the narrative from an early point, the primary 'intention' in the Tale being the summoner's *entente* to extract some money (1389, 1402, 1452). The fiend diverts him away from talk to active extortion equally intentionally (1478–9), but he lets slip in the course of his account of Job that devils' intentions (in contrast with the summoner's) are subordinate to God's (1484–5, 1499), or even the saints' (1501–3). In the event, it is the widow's heartfelt curse, contrasted with the carter's lack of any such *entente*, that delivers the summoner into the fiend's power, and the summoner confirms his own damnation by insisting that he has no intention of repenting.

This refusal links the tale back to its homiletic origins. The summoner is not a fool or a gull, as John the carpenter is. He puts profit way above conscience, and explicitly refuses confession and absolution (1422, 1437–42). That the chance for repentance is offered him at the end underlines the deliberateness of his choice of sin (1629–32)—in theological terms, his contumaciousness. The Tale has sometimes been criticized for implausibility on the grounds that the summoner is not troubled by discovering that his companion is a devil and takes no steps to avoid his fate. The exemplary qualities of the story make it clear that the narrative form is giving expression to what is already true: that the summoner is the devil's creature, and they could be separated only by the summoner's deliberate choice (1521–2). Chaucer treats the fiction as literal, not allegorical, but the motivation within it and the shape of the plot owe more to moral allegory than to psychological drama. The anonymity of all the characters (the widow alone being a possible exception) underlines its breadth of reference.

Chaucer's drawing out of the potential ironies of his material is explored by Earle Birney, ' "After his ymage": The Central Ironies of the Friar's Tale', *Essays on Chaucerian Irony*, ed. Beryl Rowland (Toronto, 1985), pp. 85–108 (repr. from *MS* 21 (1959), 17–35); and R. T. Lenaghan, 'The Irony of the *Friar's Tale*', *ChR* 7 (1972–3), 281–94.
V. A. Kolve, ' "Man in the Middle": Art and Religion in Chaucer's *Friar's Tale*', *SAC* 12 (1990), 5–46, stresses the importance of the carter as Everyman figure.

The Tale in Context

As the central story of a three-tale fragment, the Friar's Tale serves a structural function analogous to that of the Miller's parodying the plot of the preceding tale and developing a dramatic context that cues the tale to come. Its more abstract themes—sworn brotherhood, the pledging of *trouthe*, the centrality of experience, and the short road from avarice to hell—look more widely across the *Tales*, to such others as the Knight's, Clerk's, Franklin's, Pardoner's, and Canon's Yeoman's, and to the Wife's Prologue.

In the Wife's Tale, an unnamed knight meets a shape-shifting hag as he rides 'under a forest syde' (990), and pledges his troth to her to give her what she asks—in the event, to become her husband. The summoner meets a shape-shifting devil, likewise 'under a forest syde', and with an equally strong implication that the 'syde' marks the boundary of this world with another; and he pledges his troth to him to be his sworn brother. Whether or not the Friar is returning the Wife's insult to friars by recasting her double as a fiend, it is clear that Chaucer paired the tales deliberately: the echoes of plot are confirmed both by similarities of phrasing and by such details as that both hag and devil cite Dante (1126, 1520). That the hag refers to him as an authority on the nature of true virtue and the fiend cites him for further reading on hell nicely encapsulates the contrasting movement of the tales. The compromise enacted at the end of the Wife's Tale, whereby female *maistrie* is made compatible with a two-way human relationship, allows for an ending in *blisse*; the summoner's persistent refusal to allow anything to get in the way of his own insatiable desire for profit ensures his ending in hell.

'Trouthe is the hyeste thyng that man may kepe', Arveragus observes in the Franklin's Tale, and, with rather more duplicity in mind, the Canon's Yeoman's alchemist says much the same thing (V(F) 1479, VIII(G) 1044). The knight in the Wife's tale, Grisilde in the Clerk's, and the Friar's summoner all give their word and hold to it come what may; but where Grisilde commits herself to the official virtue of wifely obedience, the summoner, Faust-like, makes a pact with the devil. His pledging of *trouthe* underlines the full commitment of his will to continuance in sin (1527–34). He and the fiend become brothers in crime; the partnership of the Pardoner's rioters likewise leads down the short road to damnation, while the Christians of the Second Nun's Tale are able to form a holy fellowship, a community of the saints that will continue in heaven. It is again a reflection of the underlying structure of moral allegory in the Friar's Tale that the summoner, unlike Palamon and Arcite or the Pardoner's rioters, actually maintains the brotherhood he has sworn—though by the end of the tale he does not have much choice in the matter.

See Szittya, 'The Green Yeoman', p. 164 above.

Style

Three characteristics dominate the style of the Friar's Tale. One is the high proportion of direct speech, which allows for the differentiation of the idiolects of summoner and fiend. The second is the pervasive use of a vocabulary of sin in general, and acquisition and extortion in particular, that welds plot and meaning into a single unit. The third is the weight given at the start to authenticating detail, which, as in the fabliaux, serves to lend an illusion of realism to an implausible or impossible story. By the time the supposed yeoman 'gan a litel for to smyle' (1446), disbelief would be aesthetic heresy.

Visual particularity, in this tale, is none the less rare: it is effectively limited to the description of the yeoman-fiend. His green tunic and black-fringed hat may at one level be reminiscent of colour symbolism of the devil, but his description recalls most strongly the gear of the Yeoman of the General Prologue—hence the impenetrability of his disguise until he confesses to his true identity. Apart from this, narrative particularity is devoted to lists of sins—those the archdeacon punishes (fornication, witchcraft, and so on), and those practices, described in more detail, that the summoner commits, and with which he is interchangeably identified:

A theef, and eek a somnour, and a baude. (1354)

The method of description contrasts with that used, for instance, about the Friar in the General Prologue (whose practices are less distasteful only by virtue of being more polished), by the fact that superlatives here are used directly to emphasize badness—he is like Judas, knows of more 'briberyes' than could be recounted in two years, can sniff out lechery better than any hunting-dog in the world can track a wounded deer. To give added point to this emphasis, the voice is identified at the start of the passage specifically as the Friar's own (1338).

The speech of each of the figures within the tale is precisely differentiated. The summoner's speech is coarse, full of exclamations and oaths, and incapable of conscious irony; the fiend is urbane, even elegant, soft-spoken, and consistently gives the impression of knowing more than he cares to say, as in his bribing of the summoner into brotherhood by the offer of gold and silver (1398–402), or his carefully mundane account of his hard master (1426–8). The ten lines allotted to the carter, appropriately for his role in the plot, consist entirely of oaths and ejaculations, of execration or approval. The old woman shifts her rhetorical ground from the fawning ('God save you, sire, what is youre sweete wille?', 1585) and the use of 'good' oaths—God, Christ Jesu, St Mary—to the sharp vituperation of 'Thou lixt!' and her appeal to the devil. The careful differentiation of polite and familiar (or insulting) forms of *you* and *thou* is observed in her speech and throughout the tale. The fiend always addresses the summoner as *thou*, with the suggestion both of *felaweship* and of his own superiority; the summoner's response to the fiend is more uncertain, moving to the polite form after the yeoman's mention of his abundant gold and silver and again after his announcement that he is a devil, slipping into the more personal form as familiarity breeds false security. The control the fiend has over the summoner is indicated again by his greater control of language. The summoner scarcely manages to spread a sentence over more than two lines, and his vocabulary can be much cruder than the devil's—'olde virytrate', 'olde stot'. The devil can encompass a range of styles from the most direct ('I am a feend') to the highly conceptual, as in his account of the freedom given to devils, with its theological vocabulary and its more elaborate syntactic subordination. He also has a notably smooth tongue: his speech abounds with phrases such as 'brother deere', 'leeve sire summoner', 'myn owne mooder deere'. These get all the more emphasis from the scarcity of adjectives in the whole Tale: it is a story about speech and action, not (except for the devil's disguise) appearance.

Simile and metaphor are likewise sparely used, but those that appear are significant: images of animals and hunting. The summoner can call up bawds as a hawk comes to the lure; he is as sharp-nosed as a hunting-dog; and both he and the devil are out for prey (1376, 1455). The rhetorical focus of the tale is kept firmly on those ideas of getting whatever you can that are the summoner's prime interest in life, and that finally lead him to fall prey to the fiend.

Richardson, *Blameth Nat Me*, ch. 4, analyses the 'prey' imagery of the Tale.

The Summoner's Tale

Prologue

The Summoner's Prologue binds firmly together the tales that it links: it continues the quarrel between himself and the Friar, and so prepares the dramatic ground for his Tale. The particular example of antifraternal satire given here, that friars are lodged in the devil's arse, may possibly be a motif invented for the Summoner. The lines are closely cued by the ending of the Friar's Tale, where Huberd dispatches his villain 'where as that somonours han hir heritage'—which is very painful—and adds a prayer that Christ may keep 'us' (all the pilgrims, that is, except the Summoner) from hell and 'the temptour Sathanas'. The Summoner's response shows Satan equally to be the destination of friars.

The story of the friars in hell is a parody of one told about the Cistercians (found, among other sources, in Cesarius of Heisterbach, who also tells one analogue of the Friar's Tale), who could not be discovered among the blessed in heaven until the Virgin lifted her cloak to reveal them there under her special protection. The degeneration of the story in the Summoner's mouth prefigures the possible elements of religious parody at the end of his tale.

Date and Text

The Summoner's and Friar's Tales seem likely to have been written as a pair. As with the Friar's Tale, there are no significant variants in the major manuscripts, but in Ellesmere and some related manuscripts this Tale contains a number of brief glosses. Three are marginal notes of the content of the text, on prayer at 1884 and for the story of the 'irous potestat' at 2017 (both in Latin), and for the squire's solution at 2243 (in English). In addition, short Latin originals or analogues (mostly biblical, one proverbial, one from Jerome) are provided for some of friar John's choicer allusions (lines 1794, 1880, 1881, 1968, 1973, 1989).

Genre

The Summoner's Tale is a fabliau: a comic story in verse with an everyday, middle-class setting, more concerned with folly than evil, in which the con-man gets his come-uppance. The term Chaucer uses for the Miller's fabliau, 'cherles tale', is echoed here in the 'cherles dede' (2206) on which the story hinges. The Summoner also defines himself as churlish by using his tale as an expression of ill will against his personal and professional enemy. Alone of the five fabliaux of the *Canterbury Tales*, its obscenity contains no sexual element, and so the quality of parody found elsewhere in Chaucer's fabliaux (especially the Miller's and Merchant's Tales) cannot here be turned against amatory ideals. Instead, it is ecclesiastical and spiritual elements that are parodied, even satirized: friar John's sermons on the poor in spirit and against anger (which themselves serve as counter-genres, tales within tales); and, probably, the arranging of the convent of twelve friars around the wheel, for which there are possible religious analogues. The satire of literary form is however trivial compared with the unsparing thrust of the Tale as satire against friars.

Sources and Analogues

No precise source has been discovered for the Summoner's story of the scatological bequest to the friars. The closest known analogue is the French fabliau 'The Tale of the Priest's Bladder' (*Li Dis de le vescie a prestre*), written by a poet otherwise known for more courtly writings, Jacques de Baisieux. He was probably writing early in the fourteenth century, but he claims to be translating his tale from a Flemish source. The closest analogue to the Miller's Tale is also Flemish; but there is no evidence as to the form or language—French, Flemish, English, or something else—in which this story became known to Chaucer. In Jacques de Baisieux's version, the dying man is a virtuous priest, and he bequeaths the Jacobin friars a 'jewel' that he loves too much to part with in his lifetime: the friars feast in expectation of the bequest, but it turns out to be his bladder, which he suggests they put their pepper in.

There is no equivalent in Jacques's version to the 'ars-metrike' that arranges twelve friars around a wheel with friar John in the centre, but two parallels from religious iconography have been proposed. One is the portrayal of Pentecost, where the descent of the Holy Spirit to the twelve apostles was sometimes drawn as a wheel, with a dove in the centre—the inspiration, 'inbreathing', of the mighty wind of the Holy Spirit in this iconography being equivalent to the fart. The second is more immediately relevant to the Tale and was more widely disseminated: a twelfth-century tract on the religious life, Hugo de Folieto's *De rota verae et falsae religionis*, presented the monastic vices and virtues in diagram form as a twelve-spoked wheel, with the influence of the head of the house, for good or ill, at the hub—the place friar John has to take at the end of the tale. Half the surviving manuscripts have four religious drawn around the circumference; they are there, somewhat in the manner of a Wheel of Fortune, to indicate the abbot's reluctant, or over-eager, rise to power, but the effect is not unlike the scenario envisaged for the division of the fart, and the downfall theme implicit in the image of Fortune fits the tale well.

There are two main sources for supporting matter within the tale, almost all of it relating to friar John's speeches. His three exempla on the dangers of anger all come from Seneca's *De ira*; the rest of his conversation is abundantly sprinkled with scriptural quotation and allusion, invariably perverted to his own ends, if necessary by the process of 'glosing' the original out of existence. He also mentions Jovinian (1929), and the selection of biblical material in his long speech to Thomas and his wife (1877 ff.) also owes something to Jerome's treatise, as is confirmed by the quotation from it in Ellesmere's gloss to line 1880.

Walter Morris Hart, in *Sources and Analogues*, gives the texts of the *Dis de le vescie* and the relevant extracts from Seneca. Benson and Andersson, *Literary Context*, give a text and translation of the *Dis*, and a sixteenth-century translation of a later analogue.

Alan Levitan, 'The Parody of Pentecost in Chaucer's *Summoner's Tale*', *UTQ* 40 (1970–1), 236–46, notes the Pentecost parallel; but there is no clear evidence for its being known in England.

V. A. Kolve proposed the parallel from the *Rota* of Hugo de Folieto in a paper entitled 'Chaucer's Wheel of False Religion: The Logic of Obscenity in *The Summoner's Tale*', given at the New Chaucer Society Conference in York, 1984; a full account will be published in the volume to follow his *Chaucer and the Imagery of Narrative: The First Five Canterbury Tales*. The *Rota* was known in England, but there is no obvious way to demonstrate the line of dissemination by which Chaucer or his audience could have been likely to come across it. Of the three surviving manuscripts of English provenance, only one (now MS Bodley 188) illustrates its diagram of the *rota* with monastic figures, and that belonged to Haughmond Abbey, in Shropshire. The text is edited by Carlo de Clerq, 'Le "Liber de rota verae Religionis" d'Hugues de Fouilloi', *Bulletin du Cange*, 29 (1959), 219–28, 30 (1960) 15–37.

Structure

Where the Friar's Tale drives steadily towards its climax, the Summoner's Tale proceeds by diversion and indirection. If the story was already familiar in outline to any of Chaucer's audience, they would hardly have been able to identify the particular plot he is using until the first decisive action of the story, the gift of the fart, four hundred lines into the tale. That too is handled without the building up of suspense found in the French analogue, where the friars are promised a gift one day and return to receive it the next; here, promise and payment are made within twenty lines. Nor is this presented as the climax of the tale: a third of it is still to come, and that is devoted to the question of how the friar can fulfil his oath to share the fart equally among his fellow friars.

The indirection in the tale before the gift is made is devoted largely to building up the portrait of the friar (who is named only later (2171), by the lord of the village, as friar John). His concerns with eliciting gifts in general and Thomas's in particular are separated from each other by a series of long speeches from him, all tending to promote himself at others' expense. Direct speech is, indeed, as in the Friar's Tale, the primary medium of the story; after the usual introduction of setting and characters, the only passage of narrative, apart from very occasional 'stage directions', has friar John receiving the fart, being thrown out of the house, and rushing off to complain to the lord (2145–67). The two halves of the story are in effect two conversations, between the friar, Thomas, and his wife, and the lord, his wife, and his squire. Friar John hogs most of the first conversation for himself; by the second, he has been rendered speechless (2168).

Themes

Some of the themes that run throughout the tale—graft, antifraternal satire—are predictable enough from the story outline. They are however only two aspects of a larger theme that is also expressed in other, more innovative ways: the theme of the reduction of spiritual ideals to their deformed earthly, or earthy, counterparts. Just as the friar's appeals for charity are blatant self-love, and the professed poverty of his calling a cover for avarice, so in his preaching he converts the text of the Word of God to self-interested gloss; and, if the arguments from iconography are right, the harmonious balance of fraternal virtues becomes the equal sharing of a nasty smell, and the Pentecostal inspiration of the Holy Spirit the breathing in of the most crudely physical stink. Nothing in this tale is given its potential religious value: even in plot terms, the insult to Holy Church (2193) is treated simply as a problem in physics, or in 'ars-metrike'.

The pun is typical of the Tale: language is as slippery here as anywhere in the Canterbury sequence. Friar John's own readiness to pervert the Word of God is itself parodied by a series of puns appropriate to the nature of Thomas's gift. Some of these are put into the friar's own mouth: he uses the quotation 'cor meum eructavit' in its more literal sense ('belched', 1934; in the Douai translation (Ps. 44: 1), 'My heart hath uttered'), and he endorses it with the onomatopoeic 'buf', which seems to have been the conventional litteralization for a belch (compare our conventions of ugh, zap, etc.). His question, 'What is a ferthyng worth parted in twelve?', and his complaint of an 'odious meschief' done to his order (1967, 2190) bear an obvious punning relation to the end of the tale, and it is tempting to read a similar pun into *fundement* (2103). He claims to be 'as just as is a squyre', a carpenter's square (2090); but the mathematically fair solution to the problem offered by the squire again suggests a punning irony, especially since this technical use of 'squyre' is unique in Chaucer's works. 'Grope', likewise a rare word for Chaucer, is used by friar John to refer to his finding out sin in the confessional, and also for his searching under Thomas's buttocks. The friar's readiness to twist words to serve his own ends becomes a ground of dramatic irony, as his words acquire meanings beyond his conscious control. The final episode ignores the gloss of blasphemy he wants to apply to Thomas's gift and insists on its most literal meaning, with the problem as one of arithmetic rather than an affront to the Church. Fart and speech are explicitly seen as parallel, as broken air (2233–4).

The earthiness of this story, emphasized by the shift from the Friar's exemplum to fabliau, is rhetorically in keeping with the portrayal of the Summoner, but as always the tale goes beyond its dramatic function alone. Its psychological link with the Summoner is minimal once its coarseness and its antifraternalism have been acknowledged: the style of telling, its procedure by indirection, the skill with which the damning portrait of the unctuous friar John is developed, are qualities of the tale, not the teller. Characteristics of the tale that were for long attributed to the Summoner make more sense as part of an independent story: friar John's losing the didactic thread of his exempla against anger, for instance, so that he starts advising flattery to lords instead (2074–8), is entirely in keeping with what he shows of his priorities in the rest of the tale. The character of friar John is indeed of far more importance than the character of the Summoner, though it is no accident that he is Friar Huberd's double (as the pilgrim Friar confirms when he interrupts to object to only one of the many malpractices ascribed to friars in the opening section of the tale). Both John and Huberd are *limitours*, though the orders to which they belong are never specified; both are smooth talkers, out for what they can get, unconcerned with their own or anyone else's spiritual welfare, and keen on the company of women.

The tale allows plenty of space for friar John to condemn himself, and every detail shows him doing so. The obvious larger motifs in the catalogue of his abuses—his preaching in favour of those virtues (poverty of spirit) he does not possess, and against those sins (gluttony and anger) that he does—are reinforced by Chaucer's meticulous attention to tones of voice and shades of hypocrisy. A summary of his vices would be in effect a summary of the tale: one of the more subtle examples must suffice, of his readiness to butter up his social superiors. Thomas and his wife both address him as 'maister' unrebuked; when the lord does the same, John pulls himself together for the one speech in his own preferred style that he manages in the final part of the tale:

> 'No maister, sire,' quod he, 'but servitour,
> Thogh I have had in scole that honour.
> God liketh nat that "Raby" men us calle.' (2185–7)

The lines show a brilliant combination of hypocrisy, servility, and self-advertisement.

Birney, 'Structural Irony within the *Summoner's Tale*', *Essays*, pp. 109–23 (repr. from *Anglia*, 78 (1960), 204–18).

John V. Fleming, 'The Antifraternalism of the Summoner's Tale', *JEGP* 65 (1966), 688–700, studies the elements that make the Tale 'a work of some intellectual pretensions and achievements'. On the satire, see also pp. 40–2 above.

The Tale in Context

The degeneration of the storytelling contest into downright quarrelling, into doing down your fellow-pilgrim on personal and professional grounds rather than striving to overgo him in literary skill, is generously illustrated by the Friar's and Summoner's rival tales, but again the connections between the stories go beyond the dramatic. The shift in the nature and significance of the vengeance wreaked on the protagonists of the tales is one example of this. The Friar's summoner is damned, the Summoner's friar is humiliated by a practical joke (and twelve of his fellows with him); but in *literary* terms, there is little to choose between the two different sorts of come-uppance. If the first tale invites meditation on the nature of damnation, and the second appreciation of the squire's 'subtiltee and heigh wit' (2290–1), the gulf between the two moral levels is bridged by their common context. As so often in the Canterbury sequence, the ability of fiction to express 'truth', even anagogical truth, is called into question.

The Friar's story picked up plot motifs from the Wife's Tale; the Summoner's looks further back, to her Prologue. She too is an expert glossator of texts, with a neat line in converting them into what she would like them to mean, though she professes scorn for the kind of 'glosying' that men go in for (III(D) 26, 119, etc.). Both the Wife's Prologue and the Summoner's Tale also parody the processes of scholastic debate. The Wife has a fondness for settling arguments by way of a proof that is more physical than logical, as in her fight with Jankin; the squire of the Summoner's Tale, also called Jankin, similarly finds a 'preeve which that is demonstratif' (2272) that everyone takes as settling the quarrel between friar John and Thomas. The battle between authority and experience fought between the Wife and her fifth husband, and discussed further by the Friar's fiend, is reduced in this tale to experience alone: Thomas's gift refutes the claims of verbal authority as decisively as Samuel Johnson's kicking of a stone refuted Berkeley. The whole medieval cosmos of the Word—text, gloss, narrative, moral, authority, and the rest—are reduced to the semantics-free broken air of Thomas's gift.

Mary Carruthers, 'Letter and Gloss in the Friar's and Summoner's Tales', *Journal of Narrative Technique*, 2 (1972), 208–14, sees the Friar as seeking to deny the letter and the Summoner the gloss. See also East's article, p. 153 above.

Style

Friar John himself speaks a good proportion of the Summoner's Tale, and his style of speech—unctuous, hypocritical, peppered with scriptural allusion, designed for the moral improvement of everyone but himself—is so much hot air, all the more ready to go flat when his self-esteem is punctured by Thomas's gift. After that he says little, and only briefly manages to recapture his earlier idiom of self-satisfaction: events have deprived him of his loquaciousness (2168), and the lord of the village, whom one would expect to call out all his oiliness, is addressed in a much more down-to-earth fashion than Thomas and his wife. All his elegant little phrases of court French are expended on the couple who will be impressed by them, not on the higher-class couple who might be expected to use them—though lord and wife and squire all speak with a directness that shows up friar John's attempted touch of linguistic class for the sham it is.

If friar John has his own idioms, so does the Tale, and in one respect at least, that of punning, its idiom encroaches on that of the characters. In addition, speech and narrative are set in stylistic counterpoint. Friar John talks in generalizations and abstractions—his speech is full of words such as *resonable, diligence, suffisaunce, effectueel, rightwisness, confusioun.* The accompanying narrative may be brief, but it has a lively particularity that serves as a contradictory commentary on everything he says—a nice example of the opposition of text and *glose.* Even his famous removal of the cat from the bench before he sits down shows that he—and perhaps all friars, like all cats—is choosing the most comfortable spot. Adverbs and images can fatally slant what might otherwise be a perfectly conventional greeting:

> The frere ariseth up ful curteisly,
> And hire embraceth in his armes narwe,
> And kiste hire sweete, and chirketh as a sparwe
> With his lyppes.   (1802–5)

The courtesy he shows is certainly not the religious sort (compare *Pearl*), and how far the tightness of his embrace and sweetness of the kiss go beyond polite form is indicated by the simile of the proverbially lecherous sparrow. The typical 'and . . . and' syntax sets off the narrative sections from the speeches. It also serves to show up friar John's weakness for rhetorical elaboration, illustrated not least in his alternating use of repeated and strikingly varied syntax patterns:

> A, yif that covent half a quarter otes!
> A, yif that covent foure and twenty grotes!
> A, yif that frere a peny, and lat hym go!

Nay, nay, Thomas, it may no thyng be so!
What is a ferthyng worth parted in twelve?
Lo, ech thyng that is oned in himselve
Is moore strong than whan it is toscatered.   (1963-9)

Such linguistic pretentiousness is offset in the narrative by the use of the
animal imagery common to all the fabliaux. Besides the literal cat and the
proverbial sparrow, there are similes of a carthorse (2150) and a wild boar
(2160). All are associated in one way or another with friar John, and serve
once again as a commentary on his self-glorification.

The Clerk's Tale

Prologue

This passage functions very much as a prologue rather than a link. It offers no connection with any preceding tale, and by the time it finishes, the Clerk is already paraphrasing from the 'prohemye' to Petrarch's tale of Griseldis. Even the Host's plea to him not to talk in 'heigh style' may show Chaucer already at work on Petrarch, as his manuscript seems to have contained a reference to the *stilo alto* in which the work is written (as the Clerk notes at 41; Petrarch in fact wrote 'stilo alio', meaning a different language, Latin rather than Italian). The Host's opening comparison of the Clerk to a new bride both recalls the commonplace comparison of the ideal clerk with a maiden, and glances forward to the content of the tale to come. So too does the Clerk's response to the reminder that he has agreed to take part in the 'play' of the storytelling:

> I am under youre yerde;
> Ye han of us as now the governance,
> And therefore wol I do yow obeisance,
> As fer as resoun axeth, hardily.   (22–5)

He speaks, moreover, 'benignely'—a favourite term of Chaucer's for Grisilde. As so often, the prologue serves as a thematic as well as a dramatic introduction to the tale that follows. Its further implications for relationships between the pilgrims—in this case, Clerk versus Wife of Bath—are reserved for the end.

The Host, as usual, is demanding mirth, action ('aventures'), and simplicity rather than homiletics and rhetoric. He defines high style, as many rhetorical treatises did, in terms of its suitability for its audience ('as whan that men to kynges write') rather than for its subject-matter; plainness will allow the pilgrims to understand. Despite the closeness of his paraphrase in the Tale, Chaucer does indeed lower the style from Petrarch's Latin, using a simpler vocabulary and syntax.

It is entirely appropriate for a scholar to footnote his sources, and the Clerk does so with unique care. In his homage to Petrarch he no doubt speaks for Chaucer, but Chaucer does not let him become a mere mouthpiece: as befits a scholar who has studied at Padua (as many English students did), the Clerk is concerned with philosophy and law as well as rhetoric. It is Chaucer, however, through the Clerk, who implies that he can follow this 'lauriat poete' on his own terms, as he has the Man of Law compare him with Ovid and (by implication) Gower, or as he attaches himself to the list of Virgil, Ovid, Homer, Lucan, and Statius at the end of *Troilus and Criseyde*. Chaucer may indicate (29) that he knew how soon Petrarch had died after completing his revision of his tale of Griseldis. The fictional Clerk describes himself as receiving the story direct from Petrarch; it is the literal Chaucer who is more truly Petrarch's heir.

Petrarch's 'prohemye' is summarized by the Clerk in accordance with his principle of speaking no more than is necessary (I(A) 304): the whole of Petrarch's proem would be beside the point ('impertinent', 54). Chaucer none the less gives the substance of it in the form of an *occupatio*—this is what the Clerk is not going to tell. The Tale also accords with his manner of speaking, 'souning in moral vertu'. Any more dramatic application it might have is held back until the end.

Date and Text

The appropriateness of the tale of Grisilde for the Canterbury sequence, as a counterbalance or *quityng* to the Wife of Bath in particular, has led to the assumption that it was written for the place it now holds in the *Tales*, although the only references to its context come at the very end after the story is completed. The Tale is in fact well able to stand on its own, as is indicated by the frequency with which it was copied independently—more often than any other individual Canterbury tale, if the number of surviving manuscripts (six and a possible, fragmentary, seventh) is anything to go by. Its position in the sequence of the whole *Canterbury Tales* is less clear than modern editions, or critical fondness for the 'marriage group', make it seem: its prologue offers no connection to any earlier tale, and although it follows the Wife–Friar–Summoner group almost universally, the scribe of Hengwrt apparently copied it after the Franklin's Tale and placed it after the Second Nun's Tale; he clearly received his copy for it separately from that for Fragment III(D). Its concluding stanzas and the Envoy that lock it into the Canterbury scheme as a response to the Wife of Bath may have been added as an afterthought after the rest of the Prologue and Tale were complete, perhaps as a consequence of the revision of the Wife's own function in the *Tales* (as shown by her change of story); this in turn may have prompted the composition of the Merchant's Prologue and entailed additional revision of the Clerk's ending. The evidence lies in the omission or rearrangement of the concluding stanzas in some manuscripts, and is far from decisive. The appearance in one group of manuscripts of the verse beginning 'Ye archewyves—' (1195–1200) at the end of the Envoy is demonstrably incorrect on grounds of sense. The stanza of the Host's comments on his own wife (1212*a–g*) is sometimes omitted, perhaps because it interrupts the repetition of 'weeping and wailing' at the end of the Envoy and the first line of the Merchant's Prologue; part of its subject-matter appears again after *Melibee* (VII. 1893–4/B². 3083–4). Its rhyme royal form might also suggest that it once followed on from the end of the Tale, taking the place of the Envoy (which, together with the preceding stanza on the Wife of Bath, does not appear in some manuscripts). Any coherent hypotheses on the processes of textual development are foiled by the refusal of the manuscripts to support them. The Host stanza, if it is present, always follows the Envoy; Hengwrt ends the Envoy with the 'weeping and wailing' as if to introduce the Merchant's Prologue, but follows it with the Host stanza, and does not contain the next Prologue at all.

The division of the Tale into parts is unusually consistent (in contrast to the divisions of the Knight's Tale), though the 'Part VI' division at line 939 has little manuscript support and is not Chaucer's: its appearance in most printed editions goes back to Caxton. The Tale is occasionally copied undivided, but elsewhere the breaks always appear at the same points, and reflect divisions in the French source, so are clearly authorial.

A few verbal variants are of interest. At 867–8, Grisilde sometimes gives 'your' clothing and wedding ring to Walter, sometimes 'my' clothing and ring, sometimes 'your' clothing and 'my' ring. This last reading makes a neat distinction between the passing attributes of Fortune (the clothes) and her own indissoluble change of state from maiden to wife (the ring as emblem of marriage). At 916, the more authoritative manuscripts suggest that her old clothes are unwearable because she, not they, is older—'she moore of age'—indicating her growth into mature womanhood. At 429, Chaucer may have written 'humblenesse', not 'hoomlinesse', so keeping a sharp focus on the central group of Grisilde's virtues.

The tale is generously glossed with quotations from Petrarch's Latin original. These may well go back to Chaucer, both because of the assortment of manuscripts that contain them (including both Hengwrt and Ellesmere) and because they preserve corrupt readings that are followed in Chaucer's translation. Most serve as markers for new points in the action; one, 'suspecta viri fama, suspecta facies, suspecta hora, suspecta erat oratio', points up Chaucer's imitation of the same rhetorical pattern (540–2).

J. Burke Severs, 'Did Chaucer Rearrange the Clerk's Envoy?', *MLN* 69 (1954), 472–8, argues for the correctness of Ellesmere's arrangement (that adopted in modern editions, and including the Host stanza).

Genre

Earlier versions of the tale of Griselda show a consistency of story line but not of generic shaping. Its original form was almost certainly a folktale (medieval evidence is lacking, but a story with similar motifs is current in the Eastern Mediterranean); certain folktale elements—the impossibility of full psychological realism, the motifs of promise and of testing (last met in the *Tales* in the shape of encounters between a mortal and a fairy or a devil)—are inseparable from the plot and remain through all redactions. Boccaccio treated the story in the *Decameron* with a greater degree of dramatic realism and an aura of historical plausibility, though for him it remains very much a tale, a *novella*: if it has any moral, it is that one should avoid behaving like Walter. Admiration for Griselda is indicated, but not imitation. Petrarch was the first to turn it into an exemplum, and a specifically religious one—since Griseldis is scarcely imitable as a model of behaviour for wives, men should read the tale as an incitement to constancy in the face of temptation.

There are strong elements of potential contradiction in these various generic shapings of the material, and Chaucer's treatment tends to sharpen these. He emphasizes that the story comes to a 'blisful ende', like a romance, and the return of the children from apparent death, with its promise of renewal through the younger generation, is a romance motif; but his stress both on the details of Grisilde's poverty and on her saint-like virtue puts her outside romance boundaries. Even the Host recognizes this double emphasis, as he describes it at the end both as a 'legende', with its primary meaning of saint's life, and a 'gentil tale', the romance opposite of the 'cherles tale'. Chaucer also heightens both the dramatic plausibility and the irrationality of the tale. Religious symbolism is enhanced; narratorial comment on the action is strengthened; the concluding moral interpretation is at once stressed and made overtly problematic, and a second ending, the Envoy, is added, which both comments on the tale and ties it firmly back into the setting of its telling on the pilgrimage. This reminder of its context adds yet another element to its generic possibilities, for, as the Envoy makes explicit, the tale functions as the anti-thesis to the Wife of Bath in a debate on the nature of women and of marriage. The Wife denies that clerks can speak good of wives: the Clerk tells the story of a fictional good wife. The Envoy makes the syllogism complete in a parody of formal debate, by concluding that good wives do not exist outside fiction.

Francis Lee Utley, 'Five Genres in the *Clerk's Tale*', *Ch:R* 6 (1971–2), 198–228, discusses the Tale as drama, as exemplum, as fairy-tale, as *novella*, and as religious allegory.
William Edwin Bettridge and Francis Lee Utley note the folktale parallel, 'New Light on the Origin of the Griselda Story', *Texas Studies in Literature and Language* 13 (1971–2), 153–208.

Sources and Analogues

The literary history of Griselda begins with the final story of Boccaccio's *Decameron*. Chaucer's telling of the tale shows enough similarities of treatment—most notably the sharp condemnation of Walter—to leave open the possibility that he had come across this version, but it was not his immediate source. This was in fact twofold: Petrarch's Latin adaptation of Boccaccio's tale, revised in 1374 and included in his *Epistolae seniles*, and a close French translation of that, the anonymous *Livre Griseldis*. The care with which Chaucer follows Petrarch is indicated by his meticulous noting of his *auctour*, 'Fraunceys Petrak, the lauriat poete'; his version is indeed considerably closer to Petrarch's than Petrarch's to Boccaccio. It was Petrarch who turned the story into an exemplum, both of the faithful soul and of wifely obedience and loyalty—he gives his redaction the heading, 'De insigni obedientia et fide uxoris'.

The evidence that Chaucer uses both the Latin and French versions is unequivocal, despite their closeness. The proem on the geography of Saluzzo, summarized by the Clerk in his Prologue, appears only in the Latin text. The *Livre* provided the division of the tale into parts (the Clerk's Parts I, II, III, and V correspond precisely to divisions in the French, though Petrarch's Latin is sometimes also divided), a few additional narrative details, and some phrasing.

The closeness of Chaucer's paraphrase excludes moral or philosophical digression such as he gives elsewhere; but his departures from his source—mostly additions or expansions, from a few words to a stanza in length, only rarely more—have little to do with narrative and everything to do with interpretation. Exclamations on the needlessness of Walter's testing are consistently elaborated and sharpened (e.g. 459–62, 621–3). The pathos of Grisilde's situation is heightened, in the first place through fuller characterization—her eagerness to see Walter's new bride is more developed in Chaucer—then through a greater concentration on her reactions at key moments of the tale: her leavetaking from her first child (554–67), her contrast of Walter at the time of their marriage and when he turns her away (851–61), and the intensity of her joy on recovering her children. Chaucer is alone in his suggestions of anguish in the joy: only here does she maintain her embrace of her children in her faint. Reactions from the bystanders are also elaborated—here, their *pitee*; elsewhere, their instability (995–1008).

The alteration or addition of small details can also be telling. The French version occasionally provides such variations on Petrarch, and Chaucer picks them up when they can enhance the thematic thrust of his version. The contrast of Grisilde's states of poverty and riches, for instance, is reinforced by his adopting from the *Livre* such details as the 'wortes or other herbes' that she and her father eat (226), or that her old robe in which her father attempts to clothe her is unwearable (915–17; Chaucer strengthens the point made in the *Livre* by spelling out that Janicula could only wrap, 'cover', her in it, not 'bring it on her body'). Chaucer himself adds the detail

of the 'clooth of gold' and jewelled crown in which she is clothed at the end
(1117). A more startling alteration occurs in the course of the final
moralization, when Petrarch denies that the tale is addressed to married
women since Griseldis' example is scarcely imitable, *vix imitabilis* (*a peine
ensuivable*): in Chaucer's version, Grisilde's example is *inportable* (1144),
unbearable. It means 'impossible to maintain'; it may also mean
'intolerable', to the onlooker or reader; it is a clear reminder of the division
between exemplum and life. The impossibility of imitating Grisilde leads
into the sarcasm of the last two stanzas of the Tale and the Envoy on the state
of contemporary womanhood.

    Of particular importance in guiding audience response to the tale, and to
Grisilde, is Chaucer's development of biblical allusion. Petrarch's Griseldis,
like Job, had spoken of coming naked from her father's house and returning
naked (871–2); Chaucer adds an entire stanza comparing women's humility
to Job's, and his Janicula also echoes Job's cursing of the time he was born
(902–3). Parallels between Grisilde and the Virgin or Christ are
strengthened or added. Petrarch's Griseldis seems sent down from heaven
for the public good; Grisilde

> from hevene sent was, as men wende,
> Peple to save and every wrong t'amende.   (440–1)

That God's grace can descend to poor cottages becomes

> Hye God somtyme senden kan
> His grace into a litel oxes stalle,   (206–7)

and the 'oxes stalle' is recalled later too (291, 398). Echoes of the
Annunciation and the Magnificat, which would perhaps tend to focus too
much attention on Walter as God, are treated more quietly. Where
Petrarch's Griseldis, for instance, describes herself as Valterius' handmaid,
ancilla, rather than wife, Chaucer uses 'chamberere . . . servant' (819, 824),
echoing the 'chamberiere et servente' of the *Livre*. The Passion, by contrast,
is brought to the fore in a scene reminiscent of those lyrics in which the
Virgin lulls her infant son and laments His death to come. Grisilde's speech
to her daughter, which has no parallel in the sources, is largely made up of
echoes of the Passion:

> 'Sith I thee have marked with the croys
> Of thilke Fader—blessed moote he be!—
> That for us deyde upon a croys of tree,
> Thy soule, litel child, I hym bitake,
> For this nyght shaltow dyen for my sake.'   (556–60)

The Passion is again a level of allusion behind the similes of Grisilde as lamb
(538) and as worm (880; cf. Ps. 22: 6, generally interpreted as prefiguring

the Passion). Such allusions are however never allowed to become allegory, and they are ignored—except in so far as Christ and the Virgin are implicitly models of obedience to God's will—in the concluding moral on temptation, which is defined, as Petrarch and Chaucer both note, in terms of the Epistle of James. Here Griseldis is seen as a figure for the individual Christian, but where Petrarch twice draws a parallel between Walter and God, Chaucer generalizes the application of the tale and makes Walter less an analogy for God than a contrast to Him:

> Sith a womman was so pacient
> Unto a mortal man, wel moore us oghte
> Receyven al in gree that God us sent.   (1149–51)

The point is of particular interest since analogues to the tale occasionally appear as parables or allegories specifically designed to illustrate God's treatment of the soul. The early thirteenth-century English treatise for anchoresses, the *Ancrene Riwle*, describes God's wooing and disciplining of the soul in terms of a husband's behaviour towards his bride; and a century later the French mystic Marguerite Porete imagined analogies for her total submission to the will of God in terms of the harshest treatment a lover could possibly deal out to test her obedience, including his claiming to love another more than herself. Marguerite's treatise, 'Le Miroir des simples ames', 'The mirror of simple souls', was translated into both Italian and Middle English in the fourteenth century. There is no evidence that either Petrarch or Chaucer knew it, but it does indicate how motifs of wifely submission could be carried to Grisilde-like extremes as a form of spiritual exercise.

J. Burke Severs, 'The Clerk's Tale', in *Sources and Analogues*, gives transcriptions of the texts closest to Chaucer's of the story section of Petrarch's *Epistola* and the *Livre Griseldis*. The full text of the *Epistola* (*Seniles* xvii. 3), including the reception accorded the story by Petrarch's friends, is given in Furnivall *et al.*, *Originals and Analogues*, pp. 151–72 (see p. 11 above). For more distant analogues, see Bettridge and Utley, 'New Light' (p. 188 above).

Discussions of the relationships of the Tale to Boccaccio, Petrarch, and the Bible include Elizabeth Salter, *Chaucer: The Knight's Tale and the Clerk's Tale* (London, 1962); Ellis, *Patterns*, ch. 2; and Kellogg, 'The Evolution of the "Clerk's Tale": A Study in Connotation', in his *Chaucer, Langland, Arthur*, pp. 276–329.

Marguerite Porete is edited by Romana Guarnieri, 'Il "Miroir des simples ames" di Margherita Porete', *Archivo italiana per la storia della pietà*, 4 (1965): see in particular ch. cxxvi, pp. 628–30. The Middle English version is in 5 (1968), 247–355, ed. Marilyn Doiron; see pp. 350–1.

Structure

Chaucer took considerable care over structuring the Clerk's Tale. The evidence lies both in his adoption and adjustment of the division into parts offered by the *Livre Griseldis*, and in the structural changes he made to his sources in handling the story.

Following the *Livre*, he divided the Tale into five parts (the sixth part is a scribal addition), which can be summarized as follows:

Part I—The introduction of Walter and his agreement to marry.

Part II—The introduction of Grisilde, her pledging of obedience, her wedding, and the birth of her daughter.

Part III—The taking of the child (Walter's first testing of Grisilde).

Part IV—The birth of her son and his removal (the second testing); Walter's pretence that he is to remarry.

Part V—The casting off of Grisilde (the third test), her preparation of the household for the wedding (arguably a fourth test), and the restoration of her husband and children.

Chaucer moves the start of his own Part IV to divide the tale at the four-year interval between the taking of Grisilde's daughter and the birth of her son; this is a more logical point to make the break than Walter's second sending of the sergeant, where the *Livre* has its division. That occurs in mid-stanza and mid-line of the tale (667), as if Chaucer were concerned to emphasize the continuity of the narrative at this point.

There are numerous structural parallels between these sections, and others that provide symmetry across the Tale. Each of the three parts that contain the tests (III–V) opens with a condemnation of Walter by the narrator. This is followed by a similar patterning of the speeches in each section, where a demand from Walter for patient submission to his will is followed by a speech of acceptance from Grisilde; only after that does the action reveal what his will is to be. Part I follows a somewhat similar pattern, with Walter's requiring that his people will 'neither grucche ne stryve' against his choice. For the three tests, Walter's words always follow the same form, reminding Grisilde of her lowly birth and making the palpably false claim that he only acts at the will of his people (cf. 445, 615–16, 722–31). Grisilde's replies, added or developed by Chaucer from his sources, all stress her unwavering love and her determination to have no will separate from his. Her speeches are followed each time by a report of Walter's double reaction, of feigned 'drery contenance' but actual pleasure, or, eventually, *pitee* (893).

Part V is at once the culmination of the story, the climax of the testing, and a double replay, backwards and then forwards, of all that has gone before. The people's appeal to Walter to marry and their promise of acceptance are inverted in his pretence that they wish him to remarry and their final faithlessness to Grisilde. His taking of her in marriage and his clothing of her is undone in his casting her off and her stripping off her clothes. The taking of the children is balanced by their return. Walter's final reacceptance and reclothing of Grisilde complete the symmetry, with the same words repeated to reinforce the pattern:

> 'This is ynogh, Grisilde myn,' quod he.   (365,1051)

The line originally referred to her promise; the second time it refers to its fulfilment. Grisilde's constancy is the structural and thematic constant of the tale.

The whole movement of the story, which takes Grisilde through 'the adversitee of Fortune' (756, cf. 812), testing, and grief, to a happy ending, gives the Tale a structure closely similar to that of romance. A romance's 'blisful ende' (1121) happens in this world, that of a saint's life in the next; the concluding religious moral, however, never takes up the possibility offered by the tale that the one might be a figure for the other. Instead, it turns back to the world of the pilgrimage:

> But o word, lordynges, herkneth er I go—   (1163)

The last two rhyme royal stanzas and the Envoy move decisively away from the world of the story: 'Grisilde is deed, and eek hire pacience', and we have the Wife of Bath and the tribe of 'archewyves' in her place. The 'envoy' to a *balade* was the final stanza in which the content of the preceding verses was linked to the world of the audience through direct address. The religious moral offers something similar, with its shift into the first person plural— what 'moore us oghte' to do. The Envoy offers a world where women are as caricatured as Grisilde was idealized, and mischievously pretends it to be real.

Themes

The Clerk's Tale is not a poem to which one can remain neutral. The strength of reactions to the story of Griselda go back to its earliest retellings: its narrator in the *Decameron*, Dioneo, expresses his horror at Walter's behaviour; Petrarch describes two friends as reacting in markedly different ways to his version of the story, one by weeping in sympathy with Griseldis, one more soberly on the grounds that he did not believe it really happened— that he took it as fable, not history. Chaucer's version invites heightened forms of all three responses. Walter is vigorously condemned; both Grisilde's pathos and her narrative and psychological plausibility are strengthened; and the pointers towards a symbolic or exemplary reading are enhanced through intensified religious reference.

The Tale is not, however, an allegory. Grisilde is at the centre of any exemplary reading, as she is at the centre of the story, but the interpretations offered at the end limit its moral significance to her and do not spread to include the whole tale. Chaucer lessens the parallelism between Walter and God offered in Petrarch's moral application, and stresses discrepancy instead. The text from St James that both authors cite (1153–4, Jas. 1: 13) insists that God does not tempt, but that is precisely the verb Chaucer uses for each of Walter's three tests (458, 620, 786). Walter's behaviour is presented as stupidity, wickedness, psychological aberration, or monomania (455–62, 621–3, 701–7, 785, etc.)—certainly as an example of how one should *not* behave. The Epistle of James indeed offers a moral scenario according to which Walter would be the man who falls prey to internal temptations, while Grisilde resists temptations imposed from without. If she is compared to Job, it was Satan (as the fiend in the Friar's Tale noted) who tempted him, though Chaucer does not take up the possibility of such an identification for Walter. The only associations of Walter with God within the Tale are put into the mouth of Grisilde, in her insistence that her will is his, that he can do what he wishes with his own, he can give or take away, she is not worthy to be his servant (502–4, 509, 652–3, 814–26). His actions are self-justifying in her eyes, as God's are by definition good. On two unlikely occasions, she even ascribes to Walter her own quality of 'benignitee' (827, 1097), the second time coupling it with God's mercy. The Tale as a whole, however, holds back from endorsing her reading of him; if his larger plans, beyond the scope of Grisilde's vision, can be seen as 'providential', the narration insists on calling attention to their immediate cruelty. He is associated on several occasions with Fortune (69, 756, 812), a comparison that stresses his own instability in contrast to Grisilde's steadfastness. By the Parson's definition of patience, it is she herself who is most 'lyk to God' (X(I) 661). If Walter is too fallibly human to be an analogy for God, Grisilde is too perfect to be an analogy for Everyman, just as she is impossible as a model for wives.

That the story is given to the Clerk may be a recognition of this paradox, for the Clerk's close association with logic is continued from the General Prologue into the Tale. The Host, in calling on the Clerk to speak, suggests he is pondering some 'sophyme' (25), a logical problem whose terms are limited only by imagination, not possibility: the Envoy to the Tale suggests that the model of a patient wife might be just such an imaginable impossibility. His tale functions as a form of 'proof' on a proposition about patience. Its language also frequently recalls philosophical terminology, most particularly in its discussion of Grisilde as *patiens*, that which suffers the effect of an action: her steadfastness, for instance, is seen in terms of her resistance to movement, change, and variance (498, 510–11, 601–8, 709–11, 754–7, 1047, etc.). It has further been suggested that the tale supports Occamist principles of theology such as were current in late fourteenth-century Oxford (and, it must be added, commonplace in similar forms through much of Christian history), in particular the widely held tenet that God does not withhold His grace from those who do what is in them ('facientibus quod in se est Deus non denegat gratiam'), that He will remain faithful to those who are faithful to Him. Grisilde, who loves Walter for his sake alone and not for any benefits or rewards, acts out on an earthly level the paradigm of the spiritual. The tale ends, however, with a reminder that the spiritual meaning overgoes the human story: we ought joyfully to accept God's will 'wel moore' than Grisilde did Walter's, not least because Walter and God are not commensurable.

It is important both for a religious and a literal reading of the tale that Grisilde is not an unwilling victim. Her promise of obedience is freely given and fully intended. Walter acts high-handedly, and as feudal master, over her marriage: his request for her hand from Janicula is preceded by a reminder that his 'feithful lige man' can only want what his lord does (310), and although he says he is going to ask Grisilde if she is willing to be his wife, his actual words to her are,

> It liketh to youre fader and to me
> That I yow wedde, and eek it may so stonde,
> As I suppose, ye wol that it so be.   (345–7)

Her acceptance of his conditions, however is both deliberate and unequivocal:

> Heere I swere that nevere willyngly
> In werk ne thoght, I nyl yow disobeye,
> For to be deed, though me were looth to deye.   (362–4)

Her submission will be absolute, but she recognizes that it may entail a real emotional cost.

Walter's demand is not, as it would be in fairy-tales, completely unmotivated: it follows from his reluctance to sacrifice his liberty to the 'servage' of marriage. It is one of the ironies of the tale, however, that his obsession with testing Grisilde deprives him of his freedom far more effectively than marriage alone could have done—his inability to break free of his cycle of cruelty leaves him as if 'bounden to a stake' (704; the simile is Chaucer's addition). By contrast, Grisilde's unwavering commitment of her integrity to maintaining her vow turns her suffering and endurance into a very positive virtue. *Suffrance*, according to the Parson, is the sure way to victory (X(I) 661). She is, ultimately, the rock on which Walter breaks.

In both narrative and theme, the tale is worked out between sets of oppositions: testing and endurance, cruelty and benignity, poverty and riches. The contrasts are consistently enforced through vocabulary and, more sparingly, through imagery and concrete detail: Grisilde as lamb, the poverty of her own clothes compared with the rich robes, jewels, and crowns that Walter bestows on her. The emphasis of the telling, however, falls not on to external details of this kind but on to Grisilde's own feelings. We are given, overtly, more insight into Walter's unspoken thoughts than into Grisilde's (239–45, 451–4, 512–13, 687–95, 892–3); by contrast, his wife's thoughts and feelings appear to be one with her speeches and actions. The story is, none the less, told from her point of view, and the narrator expresses the anguish that she will not—on her loss of her daughter,

> I trowe that to a norice in this cas
> It had been hard this reuthe for to se;
> Wel myghte a mooder thanne han cryd 'allas!'   (561–3)

or, on her hearing the rumours of her impending rejection,

> I deeme that hire herte was ful wo.   (753)

Grisilde is consistently described in generalizing terms, with epithets derived from the virtues, or by comparison with any mother or with humble women at large, but her individual suffering comes over all the more strongly for this. Frequently the analogies between herself and the Virgin work similarly, for they associate her not with a theological paradigm but with an affective tradition that invites identification with sorrow.

The tale carries three clear 'morals', one all-pervasive but implicit, the other two stated at the end. The first of these, and in some ways the most important, is the familiar Chaucerian theme of true *gentillesse*, the independence of virtue from social rank. The Wife of Bath's and Franklin's Tales make more of it in overt comment, but the Clerk's Tale is the one that most fully realizes it. Walter chooses Grisilde for her *wommanhede*, *vertu*, and *bountee*, visible through her abject poverty. Moreover—and in this the story is almost unique in Western literature before the rise of the novel— Grisilde is a real peasant, not a long-lost princess: she is no Perdita or Pastorella, whose virtue is explained and justified by noble birth. Grisilde's goodness is unchanging throughout the transformations of her outward appearance, from her initial poverty, dirt, and uncombed hair (375–80), to jewelled glory, the stripping to her smock, and her final reclothing. Walter is a lout despite his high birth (Boccaccio notes that he deserved to keep pigs); Grisilde shows innate nobility.

By being shown rather than expounded, this theme of inherent *gentillesse* works rather more forcefully than the moral application of the tale as inciting obedience to God; but it also strengthens that moral, since it insists that such virtuous obedience is independent of the accidents of birth or fortune. It is also rather less problematic than the spiritual reading offered for the tale. At the end, the potential equation between Walter and God, which Chaucer has been at such pains to play down, reasserts itself, for

God's motivation, like Walter's, is left without any justification. God 'preeveth' mankind, but for no very obvious reason—'nat for to knowe oure wyl', for instance (1155, 1159). One can still apply the moral to one's own life—

Wel moore us oghte
Receyven al in gree that God us sent   (1150–1)

—but one has to leave the story behind to do so.

The final application offered for the tale is a very different one, but it has tended to dominate interpretation. Grisilde is presented at the end not as suffering individual nor as the potentially obedient soul, but as a counter-model of wifehood to the Wife of Bath. And for that, it is time to move on to the next section.

General studies of the Tale include Salter, *Chaucer: The Knight's Tale* (p. 197 above); Muscatine, *Chaucer and the French Tradition*, pp. 190–7; David, *Strumpet Muse*, ch. 10; Pearsall, *Canterbury Tales*, pp. 265–77; and Dinshaw, *Sexual Poetics*, ch. 5.

Mary J. Carruthers, 'The Lady, the Swineherd, and Chaucer's Clerk', *ChR* 17 (1982–3), discusses the comparative *gentillesse* of the characters in the light of early attitudes to the Griselda story.

Jill Mann, 'Satisfaction and Payment in Middle English Literature', *SAC* 5 (1983), 17–48, studies the thematic significance of the vocabulary associated with Grisilde.

James R. Sledd, 'The *Clerk's Tale*: The Monsters and the Critics', in Schoeck and Taylor, *Chaucer Criticism*, pp. 160–74 (repr. from *MP* 51 (1953–4), 73–82), summarizes earlier critical views on the Tale.

David C. Steinmetz, 'Late Medieval Nominalism and the *Clerk's Tale*', *ChR* 12 (1977–8), 38–54, studies the philosophical possibilities of the Tale.

The Tale in Context

The opposition of Clerk and Wife goes back to the General Prologue, where they are given opposite sets of attributes. By the time the Wife has finished her Prologue, the dramatic ground has been prepared for a *quityng* at least as vigorous as that of the Miller by the carpenter-Reeve or the Friar by the Summoner. She has claimed to have fought out some very literal battles with another clerk of Oxenford, not least over his addiction to antifeminist reading, and she has thrown down a challenge for the Clerk to pick up:

It is an impossible
That any clerk wol speke good of wyves,
But if it be of hooly seintes lyves.   (III(D) 688–90)

Grisilde is not, quite, a saint, and Chaucer, or the Clerk, goes so far as to praise women in general for their virtue of humility while conceding that 'clerkes preise wommen but a lite' (935); but in speaking 'good' of such a very different kind of wife, the Clerk also manages to deliver a mighty insult to Alison of Bath herself. The mock-encomium of the Envoy is a second, more direct insult; and for those readers or listeners who find Grisilde less than persuasive as a role model, his loud-talking, combative 'archewyves' may do the task of conversion that she has failed to achieve.

Yet the Envoy is also a tribute to the Wife. She is the only pilgrim who spills over from the frame into the stories, here and within the fiction of the Merchant's Tale. Grisilde is as much a product of male fantasy as Alison of Bath, one of dream, the other of nightmare; but neither will stay merely subservient, either in ideology or narrative. Walter finally capitulates to Grisilde's greater strength; generations of listeners (beginning with the pilgrim audience) have been as captivated by the Wife as she was by Jankin's legs.

To a curious degree, the tales are not finally opposed. A quarter of the Wife's Tale is devoted to expounding the principle that

> Crist wol we clayme of hym oure gentillesse,
> Nat of oure eldres for hire old richesse;   (III(D) 1117–18)

Grisilde embodies the same idea as Walter summarizes it,

> Bountee comth al of God, nat of the streen
> Of which they been engendred and ybore.   (157–8)

The hag takes up what (in the analogues at least) is her 'true' form, of virtuous beauty; Walter abandons his own moral monstrousness, or his pretence of it. The Wife's knight allows his bride 'soveraynetee', at least the power to decide her own future, and they appear to end the tale in a state of mutual obedience and 'blisse'; Walter ends the tale by honouring Grisilde rather than humiliating her (belatedly, he even gives houseroom to Janicula, 1133), and they live in mutual 'heigh prosperitee . . . in concord and in reste'. Both tales end by advocating a way of moderation and balance at odds with the professed motives of their telling.

The tales of the Merchant and Franklin, as is almost too well known, pick up the questions of wifely obedience and the nature of a good marriage from the Wife's Prologue and the Clerk's Tale. The Franklin's Tale, in its opening excursus on human relationships, contains a few lines that, despite their attribution to 'clerkes' in the plural, closely recall the Clerk's own story in which Grisilde's constancy has broken Walter's power to hurt her:

> Pacience is a heigh vertu, certeyn,
> For it venquysseth, as thise clerkes seyn,
> Thynges that rigour sholde nevere atteyne.   (773–5)

The traditional view of the 'marriage group' is as a dramatic debate; more recently it has been seen as a series of glosses on the description of the good wife, the 'mulier fortis' of Proverbs 31: 10–31; but Chaucer rarely alludes specifically to that, and his accounts of good and bad wives generally get their inspiration from rather nearer home. Generalized virtue apart, the similarities between Grisilde and Solomon's good woman are minimal.

The tales recalled most directly by the Clerk's, as parallels rather than contrasts, are those of female suffering, most particularly the Man of Law's. A comparison of the two shows up particularly clearly the narrative realism of the Clerk's Tale—no satanic mothers-in law, no years in open boats, no hands of God chopping down enemies—and also its psychological realism, the cost of suffering. The easy moralizing of the Man of Law's Tale is rendered impossible by Chaucer's handling of the Clerk's. Yet the same female archetypes operate in these as in all the *Canterbury Tales*: the heroines are aligned either with the antifeminist, disobedient model of Eve (May, the Wife herself, even Pertelote), or with the Virgin (Custance, Grisilde, Cecilia).

Despite all this, the Clerk's Tale does not provide easy support for clerical antifeminism. It presupposes a patriarchal society in which husbands have power over their wives, but it does not take it for granted. Overtly, it is a tale about the abuses of male power, but the handling suggests something more far-reaching. Grisilde may be obedient, and therefore conform with oppressive social, political, and religious norms, but the tale functions as a critique of those ideologies in ways she never dreams of. It is not just that she can do Walter's job rather better than he can (430–41; compare 75–82): it is rather that the tale offers the possibility of a reading in which the literal application of those ideas is so ludicrous as to call the ideologies themselves into question. Chaucer specifically denies that the moral of the tale is that wives should follow Grisilde's example (1142–4). The Wife of Bath mounts an open attack on the whole scheme of antifeminism that allowed Chaucer to create her as he does; Grisilde is more quietly subversive of such male ideologies. Patriarchal boundaries are harder to transgress even than social ones. The tale does not blench at a marquis's marrying a destitute peasant, however revolutionary it would have been in practice (and it is rare enough even in fiction); it does, I think, call into question the subjection of women that makes Walter's mindless cruelty possible. In the *Decameron*, the libertine Dioneo comments that Walter deserved that Griselda should have looked for her fun and her nice clothes elsewhere; Chaucer's attack goes rather deeper, to produce a medieval equivalent to *The Wrongs of Woman*.

The Host, as usual, hears in the tale only what he wants to hear. He overlooks the devotional application to himself and he misses any sense of the Tale's attack on its own ideological foundations; he wants to use the story as a put-down for his own wife (1212*b–f*). His 'purpos' is pure male chauvinism. But stories, especially in Chaucer's hands, are individual, not merely exemplary. The Clerk's Tale and other contrasting stories look at relationships in practice, not at ideological theory: at the human, not the conceptual. And in the Clerk's Tale, the human and the conceptual remain at odds.

On the Tale as part of the 'marriage group', see the bibliography on p. 153; on the Tale's relationships with Fragment III(D) and with the theme of needless suffering, see Whittock, *Reading*, ch. 7.

Style

The Clerk's Tale, like those other religious or semi-religious tales of pathos, the Man of Law's, the Prioress's, and the Second Nun's, is in rhyme royal. The possibilities offered for stanza-length interruptions by the narrator are rarely used in this tale; instead, the verse serves to focus on a series of particular moments. The five stanzas of 351–85, for instance, contain in turn Walter's request for Grisilde's submission, her vow, his presentation of her to the people, her stripping, and her reclothing. The stanza serves as the unit of action, of thought, and effectively of syntax—in a lightly punctuated manuscript text, the stanza stands out as the unit of sense, even though modern punctuation may need to supply full stops. The syntax is more complex than in the preceding tales of Fragment III(D): this allows for a reflection of Petrarch's Latin (though Chaucer reduces its syntactic complexity), and also for the expression of motive and emotion as well as action.

   The detail of the writing is of a piece with its meaning. In narrative development and circumstantial detail the style is restrained, even ascetic; the emphasis falls on a group of words associated with Grisilde's qualities of virtue and of poverty, set against a vocabulary of cruelty, instability, and magnificence for Walter, his court, and his people. Grisilde indeed comes close to exhausting the synonyms for her virtues: *benigne*, *pacient*, *sadde* (in the sense of 'serious', 'steady', 'consistently true to one's self'), *humble*, and *discreet* are persistently used to characterize her; she shows *obeisaunce*, *diligence*, *bountee*, *wommanhede*, *innocence*, *wyfhood*, and increasingly in the second half of the tale—since it is only through process of time that it can be shown—*stedefastnesse*. Of her outward appearance we are told only briefly of 'vertuous beautee', and of the wretched and rich clothes of which she is stripped and reclothed; aside from all this, the only word repeatedly used about her is *povre*, a word appropriately devoid of elaborating synonyms. This vocabulary, fittingly for its semantic focus on steady endurance, surrounds her throughout; Walter, by contrast, starts 'ful of honour and of curteisye; | Discreet ynogh', but he is increasingly associated with cruelty, even wickedness (74–5, 723, 785). Grisilde's virtue is opposed too to the 'suspecious', 'suspect', and 'ugly' sergeant, and to the instability of the people ('unsad', 'untrewe', 'indiscreet', 'chaungynge', inconstant, and untrustworthy, 995–1001). All the other characters in the tale are thus defined by contrast to Grisilde—including her children, who are described in terms of physical fairness and beauty alone. Even riches acquire something of this comparative quality against a stable norm of poverty, when Grisilde warns her husband that a 'povre fostered creature' can endure adversity—remain steadfast, stable, through changing circumstance—as one 'tendrely' fostered could not (1040–3).

Narrative detail is always subordinated to this scheme. Grisilde's diet of chopped boiled greenstuff (226–7) and the decrepitude of her old robe contrast morally as well as visually with the gowns, jewels, and cloth of gold of her wedding and reinstatement. The 'oxes stalle' has more function as symbol than as a detail from a genre painting. Similes are rare—Grisilde as lamb or as worm, Walter as one bound to a stake—and again are moral or symbolic in import rather than visual.

The tale's steady focus on the issues of endurance and submission emerges both in the details of speech and in the larger plot structures. Even in Part I, before there has been any mention of Grisilde, Walter is talking of marriage in terms of *servage* for himself, and demanding assent without complaint from his people (147, 169–75). Grisilde's changing status is expressed within his speeches to her by such small but significant details as the variations in his use of *you* and *thou*. He asks her for her agreement to his terms of marriage as *you*, honouring her virtue, while her vassal father has been merely *thou*. During their marriage, she is *you* to him until he talks of his people's disparagement of her low birth, which he echoes in referring to her as *thou* (481–5); when he has cast her off, he addresses her directly with the subordinate *thou*, both when he gives her permission to keep her smock and when he orders her to prepare the house for his new bride. He does not revert to the formal usage at the end, but the 'thou' itself changes to denote not subordination but intimacy and equality.

Brewer, 'Some Metonymic Relationships in Chaucer's Poetry', in his *Chaucer: The Poet*, pp. 37–53 (repr. from *Poetica*, 1 (1974), 1–20).
Colin Wilcockson, ' "Thou" and "Ye" in Chaucer's Clerk's Tale', *Use of English*, 31.3 (1980), 37–43, discusses the use of personal pronouns in the Tale.

The Merchant's Tale

Prologue

The omission of the Merchant's Prologue from Hengwrt and some other manuscripts, together with the signs of revision at the end of the Clerk's Tale, suggest that it was composed at a late stage and written on a separate leaf. The Tale may originally have been written for a different narrator; the addition of the Prologue both specifies the Merchant as teller, and gives him an appropriate motive in his own personal experience for warning against women and marriage. To extend this motivation into the realm of the psychological, or to try to unfold layers of irony in reading January as a figure for the Merchant, is to go beyond the text, though in changing narrators Chaucer opens up the possibilities for such interpretations.

The Clerk's Prologue had spoken of the sources for his Tale, his authority; the Merchant speaks of his experience. In his *Envoy*, the Clerk reruns the Wife of Bath's Prologue in miniature; the Merchant picks up the victim-husband's viewpoint of 'wepyng and waylyng'. The Host invites him to tell more of what he knows of the 'art' of the sorrow of marriage, as if there were no significant distance between the experience of women's 'cursed-nesse' and tale-telling. The Merchant agrees, but with the proviso that what he says should not be taken personally:

> Of myn owene soore,
> For soory herte, I telle may namoore.   (1243–4)

Many such comments from the pilgrims are there precisely to be discounted, and there is a general critical assumption that the Merchant is protesting too much; but there is no simple equation to be made between himself and January. His 'art' will be fiction, with none of the claim to direct experience made in the Wife's Prologue.

Date and Text

The Merchant's Tale was unquestionably written for the Canterbury collection, but apparently for a different teller. That the narrator twice appears to contrast himself to 'folk in seculer estaat' (1322; cf. 1251, 1390) suggests that it was originally intended for an ecclesiastic. Of the various possibilities, the nicest suggestion is that of J. M. Manly, that the tale was once intended to be told by the Monk to 'quite' the Wife's original telling of the Shipman's Tale, in which a monk plays something resembling the villain's role. As with Miller and Reeve or Friar and Summoner, the Wife's tale of a monk would be answered by the Monk's tale of a wife. This is of course pure hypothesis, though an attractive one; what does seem clear is that the composition of the Tale preceded its present placing in the sequence.

The one major set of verbal variants occurs in the couplet 1305–6, where the exemplar seems to have stopped short after 'And if thou take a wyf—'. Assorted scribes completed it in widely varying ways, the Hengwrt copyist coming back later to do so. Lines 2230 and 2240 also seem to have had words missing or miswritten in the exemplar, and the bland filler 'that sit in Trinitee' is often substituted in 2290 for 'but neither he nor she'. The manuscript reading of line 2133 runs 'er the month of Juil'; the date must in fact be early June (2222–4).

There is extensive glossing of the section on marriage (1311–85) in some of the earliest manuscripts, which may go back to Chaucer. It consists largely of the Latin originals of the text's paraphrases from Albertanus of Brescia, which themselves include quotations from the Bible; Fulgentius (wrongly identified in both text and gloss as Seneca, 1376); and the Distichs of Cato.

J. M. Manly (ed.) *The Canterbury Tales* (New York, 1928), p. 624, suggests the Monk as original teller.

Genre

The tale of January and May, like all its analogues, is a fabliau, with the standard ingredients of adultery and the tricking of authority. As so often, however, Chaucer complicates matters by his treatment. The tale opens with a long section that resembles homily, and which takes the form of a mock-encomium—or an encomium: the two are at times barely distinguishable—on marriage; and this is followed by something resembling a debate on the same subject, which retreads some of the ground familiar from the Wife of Bath. After this elaborate and largely satiric prefatory matter comes the story proper; but if in subject it is all fabliau, the literary treatment it is given suggests something very different. The discursive opening suggests the story should be read as an exemplum; the paraphrase of the Song of Songs suggests a mystical work; the explanation of why women always have a ready answer suggests a just-so story, a folktale *pourquoi*. Above all, the characters of knight, lady, and amorous squire, the trappings of gardens and gods, the courtly vocabulary, and the parody of a happy ending all suggest that what one is reading is really a romance. The disparity between the generic expectations aroused by the plot and its handling is the source of much of the power of the tale, and makes it one of the most startling, in literary and poetic terms, of the whole Canterbury sequence.

Sources and Analogues

Chaucer's precise source for his pear-tree story is not known, though analogues are found across Europe. The one closest to Chaucer's version comes from Italy (in the late thirteenth-century *Novellino*), and similar tales appear in Germany in the fifteenth century; it has been conjectured that Chaucer's source was a lost French fabliau. The story was probably also current in oral tradition. The husband's blindness and jealousy are common to all these close analogues, and the tree is specified as a pear-tree in almost all, but St Peter and Christ play the parts Chaucer allots to Pluto and Proserpina. January's building of the garden is unique to Chaucer, as are his use of the gods of the underworld and his definition of the characters as knight, lady, and squire. There are numerous other analogues that tell the story slightly differently: in some, the husband is suspicious and himself prays for his sight to be restored; in others (including the *Decameron* 7, 9) the husband is deceived although he is not literally blind at all.

The materials for the earlier parts of the tale are largely drawn from Chaucer's familiar reading, the *Roman de la rose*, Jerome–Theophrastus, and the Bible. Two further texts are of some importance, and are frequently quoted in the glosses on the narrator's speech on marriage (1311–85): these are the *Liber consolationis et consilii*, which Chaucer translated as the *Tale of Melibee*, and the *De amore Dei*, both by Albertanus of Brescia. The borrowings from the *De amore* consist largely of commonplaces, but that it was his source is confirmed by verbal details common to Chaucer's text and the glosses that quote it.

Apart from the Claudian and Martianus Capella that Chaucer mentions in passing (2232, 1732), three other texts have been suggested as sources for parts of the tale. Boccaccio's *Ameto* includes an account of an old husband's love-making, but there are no close verbal similarities, and Chaucer was quite as capable of writing such a piece for himself as Boccaccio was. The other two are closely related to each other: the *Lamentations* of Matheolus in Jehan le Fèvre's French translation, and Deschamps's *Miroir de mariage*. As I have discussed with reference to the Wife of Bath's Prologue, it is unlikely on grounds of date that Chaucer would have known either work, and they are themselves made up of the standard materials of antifeminism familiar to him from elsewhere. The *Miroir* contains a long debate in which four different allegorical characteristics of Franc Vouloir (Free Will, the potential husband) put the case in favour of marriage, and Repertoire de Science (Collective Wisdom) puts the case against; but the debate bears only slight resemblances to the non-debate between Placebo and Justinus, and all the closest verbal resemblances between the works are found again in Chaucer's other sources for the tale, sometimes in a form closer to Chaucer than Deschamps offers (as with the list of Old Testament heroines, 1362–74, from Albertanus, supplemented probably by the Bible itself). Other similarities to both Deschamps and Le Fèvre may well be due simply to coincidence in treating the same arguments on the basis of much the same material: when both French authors pursue their purpose so exhaustively over so many thousand lines, it would be surprising if Chaucer did not come up with ideas in common.

Of much more importance than these ghosts are texts that are deliberately recalled for purposes of allusion and resonance. The first of these is the marriage service, which figures not only at the wedding itself but in the opening encomium on marriage (1702–5, 1287–91), where wives are envisaged as being 'buxom', 'trewe', and concerned to love and serve their husbands in sickness and in health, for richer or poorer ('wele or wo'), in terms closely reminiscent of the marriage vows in their Middle English vernacular form. The first of the Biblical exempla, Rebecca, is also named in the marriage service, as January's own wedding illustrates (1704).

The second work to provide a resonance behind Chaucer's text is the *Roman de la rose*, cited by name at 2032 in connection with January's love garden. In the *Roman*, the garden is the idealized place of courtly 'mirth' and the elaborate rituals of courtship (even if, by the end of Jean de Meun's section, courtship is redefined as seduction); in the Merchant's Tale, the garden exists solely for sex. The antifeminist sections of the *Roman* are not explicitly cited, but among the more suggestive parallels is a passage by Jean de Meun on how Venus and all other women could argue their way out of the most compromising of situations regardless of what their husbands might believe they had seen. The context for the passage is a discussion of distorting-mirrors, which may lend poignancy to the simile of January's mental mirror; and it ends with the saying of Solomon that is squabbled over by Chaucer's Pluto and Proserpina (among others), on the difficulty of finding a good woman (*Roman*, 18061–152).

The third work behind the Tale would have been almost as well known to Chaucer's audience as the marriage service, and the effect of its appearance in this context is decidedly more subversive: this is the Song of Songs, closely paraphrased by January for his appeal to May to enter the garden (2138–48). Medieval interpretation of the work insisted on its figurative meanings, as expressing the love of Christ for the Church or for the individual soul, or as describing the immaculate purity of the Virgin. To have put some of the greatest erotic poetry ever written into the mouth of a disgusting old lecher addressing his adulterous wife would be horrible enough; when that poetry is traditionally used in the service of the highest mystical or spiritual traditions, the effect is dizzying.

One other poem, from considerably closer to home, serves as a key resonance behind the Tale and influences its shaping: the Knight's Tale. This too offers images of the courtly garden, the lady 'fressher than the May', gods who stand in structural parallel to the earthly characters (as January and May are reflected in Pluto and Proserpina) and who intervene to hasten the plot crisis. That the Merchant's Tale offers such a different reading of the same motifs underlines the perversion of its reading of the world.

Germaine Dempster, 'The Merchant's Tale', in *Sources and Analogues*, gives extracts from Deschamps's *Miroir* and Boccaccio's *Ameto*, and a wide geographical range of analogues. Benson and Andersson, *Literary Context*, give texts and translations of seven analogues.
J. D. Burnley, 'The Morality of *The Merchant's Tale*', *Yearbook of English Studies*, 6 (1976), 16–25, includes a discussion of the use of the marriage service. Miller gives a full text in *Sources and Backgrounds*, pp. 373–84.
D. W. Robertson, jun., 'The Doctrine of Charity in Medieval Literary Gardens: A Topical Approach through Symbolism and Allegory', *Essays*, pp. 21–50 (repr. from *Speculum*, 26 (1951), 24–49), studies January's garden in contrast to its analogues.

Structure

The sordid tale of a wife whose ready answer tricks her blind husband into accepting her adultery is transformed in Chaucer's handling both by the poetic richness of his treatment and by his restructuring of the story. Almost the entire action of the analogues is contained within Chaucer's last eighty lines—barely a twelfth of the whole tale. The rest provides a context that transforms one's reading of this final section. The opening discourses on marriage serve to generalize the story, to make it seem an illustrative rather than an individual piece of action. May's adultery, by contrast, is given a personal motivation: she is unfaithful not, or not only, because that is the nature of wives, but because of the nature of her husband. Most importantly, from the very first lines of the tale onwards, January's wilful refusal to see clearly is made to seem inevitable.

Every structural block of the Tale serves to demonstrate his powers of self-delusion. The lengthy prefatory material on the nature of matrimony describes both its joys (as foreseen by January) and its horrors (as paraphrased from Theophrastus). Placebo and Justinus are brought in ostensibly to conduct a 'disputisoun' on the advantages (or otherwise) of marriage (1474), but the debate never happens, Placebo's speech being devoted merely to his refusal to disagree with January. A second non-debate follows after a brief narrative interlude in which January chooses his bride (1580–606). He asks his friends to advise him on whether it is possible to have bliss both on earth and in heaven; the outcome is pre-empted by his demand that they should

> none argumentes make
> Agayn the purpos which that he hath take.
>
> (1619–20)

Placebo accordingly says nothing; and January is already expert at not taking any notice of Justinus.

The narrative effectively starts with the wedding and the wedding night. It opens with sections on the sacramental and mythological dimensions of marriage, in the church service and in the feast. There follow in stark contrast accounts of January's sexual fantasies of his bedding his bride, and the anti-erotic crudity of the actuality; but between these comes the introduction of the young and virile squire Damian and his passion for May. That the plot will turn out to be one of adultery is already clear even before May has endured her wedding night. By the time she has completed her four days' seclusion and a day back in the household, she has determined to reciprocate Damian's passion. He is a man of action, not words; his only speech consists of two lines whispered to May to request her silence (1942–3). While others debate general patterns of human behaviour, his role is limited to the practicalities by which those generalizations are tested.

Again, the substance of the plot, the pear-tree episode, is delayed, by the description of the garden January builds, by the excursus on his blindness, and the exchange between January and May on wifehood; but even in the course of this, events are moving forward, as Damian gets the key duplicated and himself into the tree. As in the wedding scene, the transference of narrative attention, however brief, to Damian, serves as a persistent ironic commentary on January's speeches and behaviour, and May's declaration of loyalty is likewise undermined by her accompanying gestures to her lover. Even now, however, with Damian in the tree, Chaucer delays the moment of narrative (and sexual) climax, with the further debate of Pluto and Proserpina. The final section serves not only to give the bulk of the plot: it also, like the last act of a Mozart opera, presents all the characters for the first time in interaction, the married human and fairy couples and the lover. They do not, however, all speak: the focus is entirely on January and May (even if she is supposedly prompted by Proserpina) in what is practically the only conversation of the tale—the only time speech serves the function of communication. Typically, it is used to convey a falsehood that makes January's self-deception complete.

Themes

That the Merchant's Tale will be about marriage is self-evident from the moment he promises to tell about wives' 'cursednesse' in his Prologue. The theme is carried through in the Tale in such things as the varied views of marriage as paradise or purgatory, the reference to the Wife of Bath, the discussion between Pluto and Proserpina on biblical views of women, and the ready answer that Proserpina gives to May 'and alle wommen after, for hir sake' even when they are caught *in flagrante delicto* (2266–71). Less immediately obvious, but ultimately at least as important, is the continuous pressure behind all this of January's self-deception, his *fantasye*. It is his own power of self-delusion, not anything in the nature of women, that makes him believe he can have paradise for the asking, discount both Justinus' sober advice and his sarcasm, regard himself as sexually equal to the best of heroic lovers, and, eventually, refuse to believe the evidence of his own eyes. He has opted for moral blindness from the start, and the recovery of his physical sight at the end only confirms the loss.

From the opening lines, marriage is talked about in terms of self-deception. That January has 'folwed ay his bodily delyt | On wommen' (1249–50) indicates a lack of self-knowledge in both spiritual and secular terms: Chaucer regards faithfulness in love as a measure of human goodness as consistently as the Church regards lechery as a sin. That he wishes to marry 'for hoolynesse or for dotage' (1252) confirms his inability to know himself: the narrator, it is implied, reads as dotage what January chooses to read as holiness. The encomium on marriage that follows expands on both the holiness and the dotage. It pretends to take seriously January's declaration that marriage is a 'paradys', but insistently carries its arguments to logical absurdity: man and wife are one flesh and therefore have one 'herte'; a wife cannot want anything different from her husband, so will be instantly obedient; wives are so wise that their advice should always be followed. Stories are half told: that God created Eve is taken to show that a wife is man's 'paradys terrestre', with the Fall omitted. The Old Testament heroines cited as exempla do not readily bear out the moral point they are supposed to prove, of the trustworthiness of one's wife's advice, since Rebecca deceived her old blind husband to further her son's interests; the widow Judith saved her people by murdering her would-be seducer; Abigail could scarcely wait to remarry; and Esther was a determined promoter of her relative's interests, a point held against women in the Wife's Prologue and its antifeminist sources. They were all expounded with approval in biblical exegesis, and by Albertanus of Brescia and his creation Dame Prudence in *Melibee* (VII. 1098–101/B². 2288–91); but here the context of insistent hatred of women undermines their exemplary function, and all the other ideals apparently offered. The lines where the cynicism becomes open suggest that the images of perfection contained in the passage—of Christ's love for His Church as an analogy of marital love, for instance—are mere wishful thinking.

The effect, however, is not simply destructive, for the biblical subtext also serves to show up the imperfection of the narrator's own sight. He may criticize January's wilful blindness, but Chaucer makes it clear that there are other visions that the tale refuses to see. He makes its ideology explicit in Justinus, whose views may, in accordance with his name, be right within the tale, but who is far from representing any final truth. Justinus plays the Jerome to January's Jovinian, and his polemic has the same specious plausibility. His first speech, advising caution in the choice of a wife, is in part no worse than common sense, though he regards wives on much the same level as horses (1537–43); it never occurs to him, though it does to Chaucer, that May is given no option in the choice of her 'coltissh' husband (1847). He seems none the less to regard a happy marriage as an impossibility—a conclusion based, like the Merchant's, on his own experience (1544–53). The Merchant would no doubt identify himself with Justinus rather than January, if Chaucer allowed him to do so—and something of the kind does indeed happen when Justinus cites the Wife of Bath to prove his point (1685). The antifeminism of his second speech is 'japerye' motivated by hatred of January's 'folye' (1655–6); it is a speech as much against January as against women. If May in the event proves him right, it is her husband's folly that is in part responsible. Justinus is so called, not because the tale endorses his antifeminism, but because he represents the truth that January rejects. Placebo's name likewise has nothing to do with women, and everything to do with his being a side-kick to January's self-deception.

The two men are described as January's brothers (1475, 1478, 1653); whether the term is literal or idiomatic matters less than the fact that it is symbolic. Their names, like those of January and May—'stouping age' and 'tendre youth'—suggest an abstract moral patterning of a kind Chaucer usually rejects; hence, in all likelihood, his renaming of Constance to avoid the allegorical. Such a generalizing reading is disrupted by the refusal of both January and May to conform to any simple type. May is chosen for her outward looks (as if seen in a mirror); and from her 'myddel smal' January infers 'wyse governance' and a Grisilde-like 'sadnesse' (1582, 1599–604). The folly is too particularized to be comfortable; the degree to which January wants, needs, to be deluded is built up through the tale to the point where it becomes pitiable. His initial fantasies about his sexual powers cannot survive his blindness, but although he is forced to admit his age and jealousy he still clings to the idea that May reciprocates his love. He needs her love and will buy it if necessary (2160–84), and by the end he is a willing accomplice in his own deception.

The reader's perception of May is pushed in the opposite direction. Pity is invited for her, in the way she is bought with 'scrit and bond' (1697), or as her 'so benygne a chier' at the wedding feast is juxtaposed with January's eagerness to 'offenden hire'. Yet one's pity is jolted at the very moment it should be most intense:

> She preyseth nat his pleyyng worth a bene.   (1854)

Chaucer's good wives would never indulge in such implied comparisons, or cash valuation, of sexual experience; the line associates May too clearly for comfort with an interest in sexual gratification. When Damian is reintroduced a few lines later, all attempts at inviting pity for her are abandoned. She is much too capable of looking after her own interests, on the excuse of 'pitee' for others (1979, 1986), to require any more from the reader.

   The detail of the narration, the choice of words and images, insists again that January is responsible for his own downfall, as everything that happens is ironically prophesied in his own words and actions. He regards May as a sex object (1599–602, 1752–4, 1828–30, 1958–61); she makes herself into one. He believes that a young woman can be plied like warm wax (1430); May does the plying to provide Damian with a duplicate key (with its obvious sexual connotations). He wants children to carry on his line; May's pretence of a craving for pears is designed to suggest to him that she is pregnant, though it is too good to be accidental that almost her last word is 'mysconceyveth'. His own authoritative judgement, his 'auctoritee', is linked to the proverb

> Love is blynd alday, and may nat see,   (1598)

and his fantasies (what he 'purtreyed in his herte', 1600), his literal blindness, and his wilful stupidity at the end all follow.

   None the less, the tale is not content with the message that it is all January's folly. May stands in for all women in being given a quick answer by Proserpina; and the paradigm for all marriages in Adam and Eve results in the replay of the Fall in the garden, with the blame insistently laid on Eve. Even before Damian has declared his love, May appears to be a woman looking for a way to fall; and she assists the serpent, the 'naddre' (1786), to enter the marital paradise. The elements of garden, couple, tempter, and tree never become allegorical, however; they insist rather that the story of January and May has happened before and is going to happen throughout time.

   The female archetypes of Eve and the Virgin are themselves counter-types—man both fell and was redeemed through the agency of a woman. May functions both as a replay of Eve and as the negative of the Virgin. Her name recalls Mary's month. The words from the Song of Songs that January addresses to her were often used to refer to the Virgin: 'a garden enclosed is my sister, my spouse' (Cant. 4:12, cf. 2143–4); 'there is no spot in thee' (4:7, cf. 2146). She also, of course, reverses all those qualities of the good wife that have been expounded at the start of the tale. She has often recently been regarded as the antitype of the 'mulier fortis', the good wife of Proverbs 31; but the liveliness of the narrative context would necessitate clearer cues if Chaucer wished his audience to make the association.

The imagery of winter and spring contained in the names would seem to offer a more clearly signalled line of approach, but again it is not a simple one. In the other tale about the marriage of an old man with a young wife, the Miller's, Alison is associated with the vitality of spring and youth, in a way that deflects moral comment towards a reading of her as part of the natural resurgence of the world. May's name gives her a similar potential, but Chaucer constantly frustrates it. His standard epithet for her, 'fresshe', becomes staler with each recurrence. If January and May are part of the natural cycle, the story embodies a thoroughly cynical view of nature. Proserpina likewise, for all her gathering of flowers when she was ravished (2230–1), is not here a harbinger of new life or of romance-style resurrection. The gods' associations with winter and spring give them a congruence with January and May that perhaps obviates the need to find other reasons for their appearance; but one of Chaucer's leading sources on the iconography of the gods, Bersuire's *De formis figurisque*, offers Diana-Proserpina-Hecate as (among other things) a type both of the Virgin and of the wicked woman, the 'mala mulier'. Yet the roles they are given within the tale get in the way of an allegorical or religious reading; their main function is a moderating one, as they are seemingly happily settled in their own bickering marriage. Proserpina counters Pluto's automatic male condemnation of women by reminding him of virtuous female pagans and saints, and she firmly deflates the claims to moral superiority of the Canterbury pilgrims' favourite authority on women, Solomon.

If the tale stopped at this point, the high moral ground might yet be held by the women. The last hundred lines make it clear there is no moral ground at all. The ideals offered by the tale—of romantic love; of marriage as reflected in Christ and His Church, the Song of Songs, or an old man's fantasizing; of the harmonious ending of romance—all prove to be mere delusions, not for January alone, but because in the world presented in the tale ideals can have no reality.

See also Robert M. Jordan, *Chaucer and the Shape of Creation: the Aesthetic Possibilities of Inorganic Structure* (Cambridge, Mass., 1967), ch. 6; David, *Strumpet Muse*, ch. 11; Pearsall, *Canterbury Tales*, pp. 193–209; J. A. Burrow, 'Irony in the *Merchant's Tale*', *Essays on Medieval Literature* (Oxford, 1984), pp. 49–59 (repr. from *Anglia*, 75 (1959), 199–208); and Karl P. Wentersdorf, 'Theme and Structure in the Merchant's Tale: The Function of the Pluto Episode', *PMLA* 80 (1965), 522–7.

Morton W. Bloomfield, '*The Merchant's Tale*: A Tragicomedy of the Neglect of Counsel—the Limits of Art', in Siegfried Wenzel (ed.), *Medieval and Renaissance Studies 1975* (Medieval and Renaissance Series 7, Chapel Hill, 1978), pp. 37–50, discusses the difficulties of categorization, seeing it as 'a tale of limits and their transgression'.
On Proserpina and Hecate as aspects of Diana, see Bersuire, pp. 28–30 (full reference on p. 11).

The Tale in Context

The pilgrims' understanding of the Tale is, as so often, misleading, or at best partial. Its Prologue and Epilogue insist on a single theme within it, of woman's 'cursednesse'—as exemplified in turn by the Merchant's own wife, by May, and by the spouse of Harry Bailly; and for good measure the Merchant has Justinus throw in the Wife of Bath. The counter-type of woman is the Clerk's Grisilde (1224). Every discussion of wives and marriage in the *Tales* enlarges to encompass the question of whether women in general are good or bad, are modelled on the Virgin or Eve. The Bible itself authorizes the conflation of thoughts on women and marriage—Eve was Adam's spouse, Solomon's most famous remarks about women included both the impossibility of finding a good woman and the description of the ideal wife (Eccles. 7: 28, Prov. 31: 10–31). The Host, inevitably, reads the battle between sexes personally and partially—'wommen' versus 'us sely men' (2422–3); but if one enlarging context is offered by the Bible, another rather different one is offered by the *Tales* themselves. For there are not only sinful women and virtuous women; there are courtly ladies like Emily, and fabliau heroines like Alison; and the Wife of Bath, Proserpina, and Dame Prudence join forces in a vigorous defence of women against all the antifeminist platitudes. There are also good and bad husbands, about whom the Bible may make fewer pronouncements, but on whom Chaucer has plenty to say. It is striking, however, that Chaucer almost never generalizes about men except to use them as a contrast in his frequent sweeping generalizations about women.

Chaucer does not isolate the four tales of the 'marriage group', as the dramatic school of criticism tended to do; and although he reminds us of the Wife of Bath (in Justinus' speech) and Grisilde (in the Prologue, and through images of the fantasy wife's instant obedience, 1344–6), the connections of the Merchant's Tale with other stories are of major importance. The Knight's Tale is perhaps the most significant of these. It may in effect serve as a source for the tale, in particular for Chaucer's decision to introduce pagan gods to match the characters. It contains in ideal form many of the courtly attributes and motifs that are debased in the Merchant's Tale: the beautiful garden, in which the lady is inaccessible; Emily's reluctance to yield up her chastity even in marriage to a young warrior; the awesome power of the gods. Emily is closely associated with the month of May, without May's own staleness creeping in. Pluto and Proserpina are gods of the underworld, not the heavens, and are further reduced to bickering fairies. According to Bersuire, Proserpina, May's goddess, is Emily's Diana is a different form. Even the basic plot situation of the tales, the love-triangle, is similar. May, however, is never in any doubt as to where her preferences lie. In this respect the other tales of married women offer a closer comparison: the Miller's, where Alison has two lovers to choose from; the Franklin's, where the woman's love is undeviatingly set on her husband; and even the Second Nun's, where God has an absolute right to the woman's sexuality over the claims of the husband.

The Second Nun's Tale contains a further implied commentary on the story of January, in its insistence on the importance of spiritual clear-sightedness. The Parson's Tale, with its analysis of human behaviour and misbehaviour, contains some particularly devastating comment. January's skill at self-deception is made explicit enough within the tale; the Parson unequivocally condemns excessive sexual love of one's wife (X(I).375), 'olde dotardes holours' (lechers) whose desire outlasts performance (857), and the fallacy that a man cannot sin through 'likerousnesse that he dooth with his wyf', for 'God woot, a man may sleen hymself with his owene knyf' (859). January may have uttered the proper pieties on the function of sex (1448–52), but he does not adhere to them in practice, and he is ludicrously sure that his own knife will not hurt him (1840).

The clashing styles in which the Merchant's Tale is written also derive additional resonance from being used elsewhere in the Canterbury sequence to enforce rather than undermine the readings of the world offered by the various stories. This wider context serves as a reminder that all styles, all genres, all human visions of what life is, are relative. The Merchant's Tale encapsulates the process in miniature: the crudity of the sexual scenes shows up as hollow the courtly pretensions of the garden, but the mystic and symbolic resonances of the garden also indicate the inadequacy of the merely physical. It is the same Solomon-and-Marcolphus process as has been enacted in the Knight's and Miller's Tales, and in one form or another throughout the sequence; but here the conflicting elements are out of balance. For all its technical virtuosity, the Tale will not stand for the *Canterbury Tales* in little.

On the Tale as part of the 'marriage group', and for Chaucer's generalizations on gender, see the bibliography on p. 153. For its parodying of the Knight's Tale and its contribution to other major themes of the *Tales*, see Cooper, *Structure*, pp. 66–8, 214–30.

Style

The generic contradiction that characterizes the Tale, and its insistence that the ideal is no more than a cosmetic sham, is conveyed principally through sharp disruptions of style. The plot may be pure fabliau, but its literary treatment continually pulls it towards other modes, of homily or romance. The tension between the three kinds pervades everything from the larger plot structures to the finest verbal detail. Conflict in the tale becomes less a matter of dramatic interaction of characters than of unresolved clashes of literary expectations.

The low style typical of fabliau, with its concentration on authenticating narrative particulars and its tendency to call a man an ape, is adopted for the passages describing those favourite subjects of the genre, trickery and sex. It shows itself in the mean domestic and animal similes of January's wedding night: the bristles of his beard

> Lyk to the skyn of houndfyssh, sharp as brere,   (1825)

that he is 'ful of jargon as a flekked pye'. The kind of close-up Chaucer gives of the slack skin of January's neck resembles the details elsewhere given about 'cherles', such as the Miller's black nostrils or the broad buttocks of Simkin's daughter. The fabliau's concentration on action unmediated by rhetorical elaboration is taken here to extremes:

> This Damyan
> Gan pullen up the smok, and in he throng.   (2352–3)

In the other fabliaux, sex is 'myrie'; here it is at best merely physical. The only linguistic elaboration lies in the Merchant's apology that prefaces these lines, and that serves to emphasize the brutality of the language.

This fabliau style is largely confined to passages about sex, though given the plot structure this means that it appears at the key moments. The homiletic style, with its fondness for apophthegm, generalization, and authority, is largely confined to the first few hundred lines of the tale, before the fabliau narrative gets under way. The most significant thing about its use is not its predictability of sentiment and expression—

> Mariage is a ful greet sacrement   (1319)

—but the way such platitudes are undermined. This can be done by juxtaposition, for instance by countering the sacraments with Theophrastus; by overt sarcasm—that if all other gifts of God pass away,

> A wyf wol laste, and in thyn hous endure,
> Wel lenger than thee list, paraventure;   (1317–18)

by misreading a narrative (with its paratactic 'and then' construction) as a logical argument ('and therefore') in the best fashion of sermon exempla:

> Thanne he made him Eve.
> Heere may ye see, and heerby may ye preve,
> That wyf is mannes helpe and his confort,
> His paradys terrestre;   (1329–32)

and by downright misrepresentation of experience:

> 'Do this,' seith he; 'Al redy, sire,' seith she.   (1346)

Some of this might be acceptable in a straight homily, but the lack of discrimination between the truism and the distortion dissolves all possibility of didacticism: one is never quite sure on which side the voice is arguing, and the worst arguments have the best justifications.

The gear change from the homiletic style, with its assembling of maxims and generalities, to the romance style of courtly vocabulary and attributes occurs when January gets down to the business of selecting his wife:

> Heigh fantasye and curious bisynesse
> Fro day to day gan in the soule impresse
> Of Januarie aboute his mariage.   (1577–9)

There is a new spaciousness here in the vocabulary and the syntax that sounds very impressive: a closer look indicates that both 'fantasye' and 'curious bisynesse' are rather suspect qualities. January is looking for a woman with the best attributes of an Emily, a Criseyde, and a Grisilde rolled into one:

> Hir fresshe beautee and hir age tendre,
> Hir myddel smal, hir armes longe and sklendre,
> Hir wise governaunce, hir gentillesse,
> Hir wommanly berynge, and hire sadnesse   (1601–4)

The description of May at the wedding feast confirms the picture of her as an ideal courtly lady:

> She was lyk the brighte morwe of May,
> Fulfild of alle beautee and plesaunce.   (1748–9)

The description of the feast, with its vocabulary of 'joye and blisse', its superlatives, its learned similitudes, and its attendant pagan gods, moves into a height of style not heard in the *Tales* since the Knight's. This part of the tale proceeds not, as the fabliaux do, by description and action, but by association and indirection (it is almost impossible to derive any factual information from the thirty lines describing the feast, except that there was music and wine); and the forward movement of the action is held up by abundant comment and by apostrophes fired off in all directions.

> O perilous fyr, that in the bedstraw bredeth!
> O famulier foo . . .
> O servant traytour . . .
> God . . .
> O Januarie . . .   (1783–8)

The abrupt change of key back to fabliau directness comes after a five-line
periphrasis for nightfall, as January gets down to the business of his
wedding night. The brutality of the language is stressed by the interruption
even here of details from other registers: the learned reference to 'daun
Constantyn', authority on aphrodisiacs, or lyricism that collapses into
bathos:

> Januarie hath faste in armes take
> His fresshe May, his paradys, his make.
> He lulleth hire; he kisseth hire ful ofte,
> With thikke brustles of his berd unsofte.   (1821–4)

These disorienting shifts of register continue throughout the tale.
Damian's whispered plea for 'Mercy!' is followed by May's tearing up his
letter into the privy. Her capitulation to his advances is preceded by a
passage on destiny and planetary influence, though the sequence of events
suggests that the interposed detail of January's love-making has more to do
with her decision (1955–67). Her acceptance of adultery is conveyed
through an excursus on womanly *franchise* and *pitee*. January's garden is
explicitly compared to the ideal courtly garden of young love in the *Roman
de la rose*, though he uses it as an aid to his failing sexual powers (2051–2).
The superlatives and similitudes look like the purest romance aesthetic:

> Ne Priapus ne myghte nat suffise,
> Though he be god of gardyns, for to telle
> The beautee of the gardyn and the welle.   (2034–6)

The inexpressibility topos ('nat suffise to telle') is stylistically *de rigueur*, but
Priapus brings with him associations that have nothing to do with gardens.
The neat handiwork with the key alternates with apostrophes to Ovid and
with the superb erotic poetry—described as 'swiche olde lewed wordes'—
from the Song of Songs, put into January's mouth. May never lets slip the
proprieties in her speeches, but she is gesturing to Damian even while her
declarations of womanly virtue are flowing. The machinery of gods and
fairies belongs to romance, but the plot in which they are involved is pure
fabliau.

See also Benson, *Chaucer's Drama of Style*, pp. 116–30, and Muscatine, *Chaucer and the
French Tradition*, pp. 230–7.

FRAGMENT V(F)

The Squire's Tale

Prologue

The Squire's Prologue, as Ellesmere and other manuscripts call it, is found as a unit in all the manuscripts that contain it; division into Epilogue and Introduction is editorial. Although Hengwrt and some other manuscripts use it to link the Merchant's Tale to the Franklin's, with appropriate changes in the names, the content of the lines strongly suggests that Chaucer wrote it with the Merchant and Squire in mind: it refers back to women's deceits and it specifies the next teller as an expert on love. The logic of the progression of the link is disguised by its splitting in half. The Host avoids giving details of his own wife's vices because he is sure his tale-telling would get back to her, so he invites instead a tale of love—that is, one that will offer a contrasting positive view of women. The Squire, as befits both his courtesy and his youth, has to be called on to speak: he does not, in contrast to the *cherles*, volunteer his services.

The movement of the passage around the *Tales* is presumably due to its having been originally written on a separate leaf. The organization of Fragments IV and V (E and F) apparently took place at a late stage, when the tales that compose it were already complete and copied in separate quires—hence the ease with which they could appear at different places in the sequence, and the links between them be adapted to connect other tales.

Date and Text

There has been much debate as to the date of the Squire's Tale, between those who believe that it must be an early work of Chaucer's because its poor quality suggests immaturity; those who believe these characteristics to be a brilliant imitation of how the Squire himself would compose; and those who regard it as a work of the 1370s or early 1380s on the grounds of its similarities to the unfinished *Anelida and Arcite*. The *Anelida* was probably the first work of Chaucer's to use Boccaccio's *Teseida*, and its abandonment could have freed Chaucer to use its material in the stories both of the jilted falcon and of Palamon and Arcite.

The argument for immaturity is logically shaky: Chaucer's earliest known poetry is already of high quality, and in any case poets do not progress simply from a worst to a best. The use of riding rhyme in the Tale would also tend to eliminate a very early date. The argument might be stronger for senility, but happily nobody seems to have suggested that. Objective internal evidence for dating is inconclusive. It is clear that the second part at least was written after he had become familiar with Boethius, who does not appear as an influence in his early poetry. The most direct quotation ('alle thyng, repeirynge to his kynde | Gladeth hymself', 608–9) has its Boethian original as a gloss in the early manuscripts; the lines following, on caged birds, come from the same section of the *Consolation*, though they were also used in the *Roman de la rose*. There are a few indications that the work was written in the course of the main period of composition of the *Canterbury Tales*, although none is decisive. The reference to the time of day (73) indicates either composition or revision for the Canterbury sequence. It shares with its neighbouring tales an explicit interest in rhetorical method: here and in the Clerk's Prologue, Chaucer talks about levels of style; and in those two and the Franklin's Prologue, he mentions 'colours' of rhetoric—the only references to either in the whole canon, apart from a passing mention of rhetorical colours from the eagle in the *House of Fame*. The Wife of Bath's, Nun's Priest's, and Squire's Tales contain his only allusions to Arthurian romance.

The position of the Tale in the Canterbury sequence is also problematic. In many manuscripts it appears after the Man of Law's Tale and is followed either by the Merchant's (as in Hengwrt and others) or by the Wife of Bath's. Its placing in the sequence Clerk–Merchant–Squire–Franklin is found in comparatively few manuscripts, though they include Ellesmere and the early Harley 7334. The internal evidence of the links before and after the Squire's Tale in this ordering suggests clearly that it is Chaucer's own, but the tales of Fragments IV–V do not appear to have been written as a group, and he may have experimented with different orders.

The Tale is consistently divided at line 346, between Parts I and II. The final couplet, the beginning of Part III, is omitted in some manuscripts. Textual variants are trivial. Three glosses are found in both Hengwrt and Ellesmere and some other manuscripts: the quotation from Boethius alongside 'thilke text' at 608–9 (from the *Consolation*, iii. m. 2), and two brief explanatory glosses—'centre' (22) is glossed as 'centrum circuli', 'Pegasee' (297) as 'equus Pegaseus'.

There is no clue in the state of the manuscripts as to whether the tale was left unfinished or deliberately broken short, or indeed whether it simply lost the later pages of its original exemplar.

Genre

The Squire's Tale is a romance; just what sort has been the subject of more debate. The closing lines of plot summary indicate a story to come on a vast scale, far too long for the Canterbury sequence; they suggest that the Tale as we have it is the opening of an interlaced romance of the sort most commonly found in French but of which there are also some fourteenth-century English examples, where various plot threads and the adventures of different characters are pursued in turn across a lengthy narrative. The size and scope of the existing examples, and the spaciousness of the material summarized at the end of the tale, may suggest that Chaucer wrote just enough of the Squire's Tale to indicate its nature as an interlaced romance, and that its unfinished state is deliberate. The emphasis on magic and marvel is again a characteristic of these romances, though exceptional for Chaucer.

It has been argued, with some plausibility, that the tale is less a romance than a parody of one. If there is an element of parody, and if it is aimed at the genre rather than the Squire—both propositions that are open to question—then there is not a great difference between the original romances and the parody offered here. Worse examples were written with a straight face, and Chaucer's story is faithful to its kind. It may indeed be his literary sophistication that enables him to see and record the potential weaknesses of the genre, though they are weaknesses that can become strengths: the development of the interlaced romance in the sixteenth century in Ariosto's hands combines high chivalry, high sophistication, and artistic mockery, and Chaucer may be moving towards a similar effect.

As so often in the *Tales*, the main story contains a contrasting inset genre, in the form of the complaint uttered by the falcon. This in turn is used to tell another story, this time a kind of anti-romance of unfaithful love. To devote so much space in a romance to the adventures of a bird is without parallel elsewhere.

David Lawton, *Chaucer's Narrators* (Chaucer Studies 13, Cambridge and Dover, NH, 1985), pp. 106–29, discusses the parallel with Ariosto in the course of an interesting study of all aspects of the Tale, including a conjectural outline of the final plot.

Sources and Analogues

Chaucer does not seem to have had any single source for the Squire's Tale. There are a number of analogues and possible sources, at varying distances from him, but all distant from each other. He apparently exercised more freedom than usual in assembling its various parts, and perhaps more imagination in creating some of it. Two mutually exclusive accounts can be given of the tale's origins, one Oriental, the other based on French and English sources. The second option is empirically more likely, but the multiplicity of Oriental elements seems too great to be mere coincidence. The French romances in question were themselves based on Eastern stories probably transmitted through Castile in the late thirteenth century, but they show few overt traces of their origins.

Many medieval romances of course abound in Oriental settings and marvels, but such elements in the Squire's Tale go beyond incidental motifs. There is a close analogue to the tale of the magic gifts in the *Thousand and one Nights*, itself unknown in the medieval West. There are some more distant analogues of the story of the lovesick bird in Eastern tradition, and one at least made its way to the West to appear in the work of Alexander Nequam; none of these, however, bears much resemblance to Chaucer's story. In Nequam's tale a caged bird (a parrot, therefore able to talk) gets a traveller to take a message to its mate; in the *Thousand and One Nights* a princess is warned against love by dreaming of a pair of pigeons captured by fowlers, where the female helps the male but the male fails to reciprocate. Chaucer's own works offer more likely analogues.

Oriental sources for the setting of the tale are likewise possible but problematic. It is set in the Mongol Empire, a detail original to Chaucer's version, though one of his possible French sources places its action in Armenia. The names he chooses are also Oriental: 'Cambyuskan' is probably based on the Latin form of Genghis Khan, Cambiuscan; 'Theodora' and 'Canacee' are Byzantine; 'Elpheta' and 'Algarsyf' are apparently derived from star names of Arabic origin; 'Cambalo' may be derived from Cambaluc (the Westernized form of the Mongol name for Peking) or from a similar personal name.

It has been suggested that the setting was also influenced by a work purporting to be a letter from Prester John describing the marvels of his Eastern kingdom, but resemblances are either negligible or have alternative sources elsewhere: the magic mirror, for instance, figures in the French version of the story of the gifts, and a dry tree seems to have been the conventional place for bereaved Western birds to perch in. Chaucer does not attempt to carry authenticity of setting throughout the tale, nor to adapt such things as range of reference to an Eastern culture. The 'lewed peple' and the falcon both refer to standard Classical and biblical examples; the one Arabic scholar mentioned, Alocen, comes by way of the *Roman de la rose*. The falcon's long simile of caged birds comes from Boethius, but is unattributed in the text—presumably, like the Friar's fiend on biblical history, it is regarded as part of a falcon's natural range of reference.

In view of all this, there must be a strong possibility that Chaucer was aware of the Oriental origins of the various elements of the tale and assembled them deliberately. An assemblage of the more immediate French and English sources and analogues fails to provide any other thread to justify their connection. Most strikingly of all, the means by which the two main plots are connected, with one story starting off an apparently unrelated one in a series of accumulating narratives, is much more typical of Oriental than Western story-collections or interlaced romances.

Two thirteenth-century French romances based on the Oriental story of the magic horse, the *Cleomadès* of Adenet le Roi and the *Meliacin* of Girard d'Amiens, contain the greatest number of parallels to the first part of the tale, and Chaucer could have been working with a free hand from either. *Meliacin* has an Armenian setting; in other respects the romances are so similar in outline that one manuscript starts off with 1,500 lines of *Cleomadès* with the names changed and switches to *Meliacin* for the rest. Both authors seem to have spent some time in England, at the court of Edward I. Froissart, Chaucer's contemporary at the English court, refers to *Cleomadès*, so it may still have been available in England.

In *Cleomadès*, the king of Sartaigne, apparently synonymous with Spain, has one son, Cleomadès, and three beautiful daughters (as against the two sons and one daughter of the Tartar king in the Squire's Tale). Three kings come to woo the daughters bringing magic gifts, one of which is a flying ebony horse operated by metal pegs. There follows a discussion of the way people wonder at such marvels, in the course of which Adenet cites the magic mirror made by Virgil which revealed treason plotted against Rome. The gifts are presented at the king's birthday feast. (Chaucer has a messenger from the 'King of Arabe and of Inde' present four gifts at Cambyuskan's birthday feast, including a flying peg-operated brass horse for the king and a magic mirror for Canacee; the people wonder at them, and the mirror at Rome is mentioned (231) as a comparison.) So much occupies the first 2,000 lines of Adenet's poem; the remaining 16,000 are concerned with the adventures of Cleomadès after he has been tricked into flying off on the horse without knowing how to bring it down, and with his wooing and (eventual) winning of the lady he finds when he does discover how to land it. This section could offer a parallel for the plot thread concerning Cambyuskan's son Algarsif and his winning of a lady by the help of the horse, which Chaucer summarizes in four lines at the end. The rest of the summary (Cambyuskan's military exploits, and Cambalo's winning of his sister Canacee in a fight against two brothers) bears no relation to the French romances.

Chaucer's own writings offer the most immediate analogues for the second part of the tale. The serious treatment of birds of prey as lovers finds a close parallel in the *Parliament of Fowls*. The falcon's complaint is closely similar in situation and phrasing to his unfinished *Anelida and Arcite*, in which Anelida laments her lover's unfaithfulness; it seems likely that he raided the poem for the contrast of true and feigned love (especially *Anelida* 86–112, 127–33, Squire's Tale 505–7, 523–42, 562–71; both also cite Lamech as a bigamist, *Anelida* 150–3, Squire's Tale 550–1). The whole falcon episode could be described as being by the *Parliament* out of *Anelida*. The problem remains, however, as to why Chaucer should have linked an Anelida-style bird story with *Cleomadès–Meliacin*, and linked them in the way he does, if he had only such Western analogues in mind.

One other source has been proposed: the silence that falls when the stranger knight rides into the hall on horseback, with its accompanying reference to 'Gawayn, with his olde curteisye' (95), is reminiscent of *Sir Gawain and the Green Knight*. The entry of mounted knights into feasts is a widespread occurrence in romances and history, however, and Chaucer's association of Gawain with 'Fairye' suggests his own consistent marginalization of Arthurian material rather than the Gawain-poet's serious engagement.

H. V. Jones, in *Sources and Analogues*, gives the relevant sections of *Cleomadès* and Prester John's letter, and discusses some Oriental parallels for both halves of the tale. These are further discussed by Haldeen Braddy, 'The Genre of Chaucer's *Squire's Tale*', *JEGP* 41 (1942), 279–90. Selections from *Meliacin* are edited by Paul Aebischer, *Girard d'Amiens: Le Roman du cheval de fust, ou de Meliacin* (Textes littéraires français, Geneva, 1974).

Thomas W. Best, *Reynard the Fox* (Boston, 1983), p. 123, notes a Dutch analogue to the magic gifts.

Albert C. Friend, 'The Tale of the Captive Bird and the Traveller: Nequam, Berechiah, and Chaucer's *Squire's Tale*', *M&H* NS 1 (1970), 57–65, gives the only known analogues to the bird episode told in the West. The habit of bereaved turtle-doves of perching in dry trees is described in e.g. the fifteenth-century *Regnault et Jehanneton*, *Œuvres complètes du Roi René*, ed. Comte de Quatrebarbes (Angers, 1845), ii. 127.

Dorothee Metlitzki, *The Matter of Araby in Medieval England* (New Haven and London, 1977), gives a full account of the names in the tale, and of the Oriental story groups that offer similarities to it.

Salter, *Fourteenth Century*, ch. 3, argues for Chaucer's knowledge of the Gawain-poet.

Jennifer Goodman, 'Chaucer's *Squire's Tale* and the Rise of Chivalry', *SAC* 5 (1983), 127–36, looks at parallels in 'composite' romances such as *Generides*.

Structure

The structure of the tale is not as simple as it looks, and is puzzling on several counts. Part I introduces Cambyuskan and his family, especially Canacee, describes his birthday feast, and has the four magic gifts presented. Part II despatches the guests to bed with hangovers, so that Canacee, the only person not to be suffering, can get up in the dawn for a quiet walk, and, thanks to her ring, overhear and understand the falcon's complaint. One major difficulty lies in the sheer incongruity between the two parts: the first a chapter from a novel by Jules Verne, the second by Henry James. The opening gives descriptions and actions—of feasts, of marvels. The second half has the potential for moving to the more familiar Chaucerian ground of human motivation and emotion, but this time it turns out to be not human but avian. If there was ever to be a structural logic that would have justified the two parts as we have them, it lies in the unwritten or missing portion of the tale.

There is a further difference between the two parts, no less puzzling but in some ways more intriguing: the first half tells a story, the second tells of a story being told. The tales of the Canterbury sequence often contain inset stories—the Wife of Bath on Midas, Chaunticleer recounting tales of dreams—but their function is usually moral, and they have clear borders as fictional exempla within the main tale. The falcon's tale serves rather as narrative flashback, the-story-so-far. If the Squire's Tale were complete, this story would presumably have finished in the form of direct narrative, interwoven with the plot set in action in Part I. Such a structure, of one story opening into another apparently unrelated one, is closer to Oriental story-collections than to the related plots of French interlaced romances, and it is unique in Chaucer's work. All Chaucer's stories apart from that of the falcon begin at the beginning, as the Squire's Tale itself starts with the setting in which the magic gifts are presented; but the only use to which these marvels are put is to open up another story, and one that is already part-way through.

The design therefore offers yet another way of linking tales, a further possibility to set beside the thematically interlinked sequence of the *Canterbury Tales* itself, the repeated pattern of the Monk's Tale, or the tales within tales within tales of the Nun's Priest's. The opening out of one tale into another in an accumulating series of narratives itself has the potential of infiniteness—which may be another reason for the unfinished state of the Squire's Tale.

Themes

There is no disagreement over what the Squire's Tale is about: its major themes are clear—marvels, faithfulness in love, *gentillesse*. It is concerned with virtuous characters, and the criteria for virtue are again explicit. Cambyuskan may be heathen, but he is a good pagan on the model acknowledged in the fourteenth century, in that he keeps 'his lay, to which that he was sworn' (18); the adjectives describing him are a roll-call of all the secular virtues. Canacee is beautiful, temperate, and capable of *pitee* and *routhe*. Even the birds are described in terms of the moral criteria Chaucer uses elsewhere in full seriousness for humans, of faithfulness (or its lack), *trouthe*, *gentillesse* in its sense of virtue rather than high birth. There is none of the destructive irony of the Merchant's Tale in these expressions of what should be ideals, even though the story proves some of them wrong:

> Pitee renneth soone in gentil herte . . .   (479)
>
> Gentil herte kitheth gentillesse . . .   (483)
>
> His manere was an hevene for to see . . .   (558)

And I so loved hym for his obeisaunce,
and for the trouthe I demed in his herte.   (562–3)

The counterpoint to all this is not the incongruity of having the lines spoken by a bird (as happens in the Nun's Priest's Tale), but the moral condemnation of, and grief at, the tercel's hypocrisy, his failure to accord with the courtly ideal.

Controversy starts when one tries to make sense of all this. One fifteenth-century scribe, copying the *Tales* for Jean d'Angoulême, who had spent many years in England as a prisoner after Henry V's French campaigns, cut the tale short, presumably on instructions, with the comment that it was too silly, *valde absurda* (though Jean seems to have been given to extreme reactions: the Monk's Tale is abbreviated for being too sad). Renaissance readers, however, including Spenser, clearly found the tale imaginatively powerful, and Milton singled it out for special mention. Modern criticism has found problems in such matters as the tale's frequent and excessive calling of attention to its own rhetoric; the lack of any inner logic to its succession of events (for which *Sir Thopas* would offer the nearest analogy in Chaucer's works); the fact that the only emotional focus of the Tale as we have it, its only human interest, is displaced on to birds; and its occasional apparent ludicrousness of action, as when the magnificent courtly feast dissolves into hangovers (347–60), or when Canacee, carefully holding out her skirt to receive the falcon on its next swoon, fails to catch it (441–3, 472–5). The concluding summary also seems to predict incest in Cambalo's winning of his sister Canacee, but the lines are too brief to allow of any certain elaboration.

The argument that all this adds up to an exposition of the Squire's poetic inadequacy is much overstated, though Chaucer's customary concern with decorum, appropriateness, in allotting tale to teller is relevant here. That it is fitting for this young lover to tell a story of love is obvious even to the Host; if his tale stops short, he himself can still have 'continuance' in virtue (680), as the Franklin wishes him. Many characteristics of the Tale make good sense if it was written specifically for him. The concern with style is appropriate for the one practising poet (Chaucer excepted) among the pilgrims—'he koude songes make and wel endite' (I(A) 95)—though his references to style are distinguished from those of other narrators only by reason of their frequency. The greater interest shown in the first part of the tale in exciting marvels than in human psychology is appropriate for a young teller. Even the 'self-portrait' of the requirements of the poet capable of describing the revels—

He moste han knowen love and his servyse,
And been a feestlych man as fressh as May   (280–1)

—is typical of Chaucer's frequent practice of inserting miniatures of the narrating pilgrims within the tales, such as John the carpenter's door-breaking servant Robin in the Miller's Tale, or the food-conscious host in the Franklin's Tale. Such things do not prove composition especially for the Squire, however: the similarity between the lines quoted, the description of the Squire in the General Prologue, and that other courtly squire of the Franklin's Tale, Aurelius, may all simply reflect a formulaic repetition of qualities recognized as the best. The use of superlatives throughout the Squire's Tale indeed overgoes even that of the General Prologue, though here they are used for direct rhetorical effect and not for irony.

The effect is important: within the Tale, they give a sense primarily of proper romance perfection and wonderment rather than of youthful over-enthusiasm. The subject-matter, of Eastern exoticism and marvels, makes appropriate the comparisons with that other body of exotic and marvellous romance, the Arthurian. Yet the Tale treats its material as more than an assemblage of exciting plot motifs. Possible explanations of the magic gifts are offered, mechanical, scientific, or astrological; the magic of the ring works not in the context of *event*, as one would expect, but to open up a new area of story and emotion in the falcon's lament—a new area both in the tale and (perhaps more importantly, though the curtailment of the story prevents our knowing) in Canacee's understanding of experience. The falcon tells her own story 'to maken othere be war by me' (490): her story perhaps offers itself as an analogy to the mirror that will reveal lovers' treachery. Such shifting of magic and marvel along the spectrum from plot, action, and technology towards emotion and meaning would be consistent with the practice of many of the greatest medieval romances, including the Knight's Tale, with its careful integration of the gods into the human action, and the Franklin's, where the disappearance of the rocks is primarily of interest in so far as it serves as a catalyst for human response.

To read the tale either as a parody of romance or as an imitation of callow immaturity may be too simple. Much modern discomfort with the tale arises, I suspect, from a characteristic found widely in romance: its insistence on treating all its elements with the same degree of seriousness—in this case, its hyperboles and its hangovers, its princesses and its passing kites, the deathly swoon of the abandoned lover and a bird falling out of a tree. This is too different from Chaucer's normal practice to be accidental. If each of the Canterbury tales is offered as a model of its kind, such literary self-consciousness allows for a demonstration of the weaknesses as well as the potential of each form, as the Prioress's Tale reveals the sentimentality of Miracles of the Virgin, or the Man of Law's the implausibility of pious romance. The stylistic flattening of the Squire's Tale and its lack of clear logical, moral, or narrative direction are accurate enough as a reflection of typical practice in interlaced romances of marvels and adventures; Chaucer calls attention to them just enough to mark them as limitations. The very stress on the rhetorical processes of storytelling in the Tale may be a backhanded way of reminding the reader of the element of literary convention in so much of what is being narrated—a convention that here has a more obvious potential for becoming cliché, than for taking on the kind of resonance that makes the telling of the Knight's Tale so powerful. Such a flattening, such attention to convention for its own sake, is the source of many of the strengths of the Tale; its supremely kingly king, its beautiful princess, its magic gifts, even the pathos of the falcon's lament, could not exist without them. But the setting of the story in the wider context of the *Canterbury Tales* allows for a rival reading to be set up in addition and contrast to what the tale contains in itself: a reading in which such a story and such a style can be appraised by their being put into the mouth of the youngest pilgrim present, an amorous squire with a taste for chivalrous exploits and courtly pastimes, and in which story and style can be contrasted with other varieties of romance, other methods of narration, and interpretations of the world in which marvels and adventures are not the only considerations.

On Jean d'Angoulême's manuscript (now Paris, fonds anglais 39) see Manly and Rickert, *Text* i. 403 (p. 3 above).
Gardiner Stillwell, 'Chaucer in Tartary', *RES* 24 (1948), 177–88, is the seminal study of the tone of the Tale.
D. A. Pearsall, 'The Squire as Story-teller', *UTQ* 34 (1964–5), 82–92, gives the most persuasive dramatic reading.
John P. McCall, 'The Squire in Wonderland', *ChR* 1 (1966–7), 103–9, analyses the ludicrousness of the Tale.

The Tale in Context

The Squire's Tale has particular affinities with the other Canterbury romances, notably the Knight's and Franklin's Tales. Its placing between Merchant and Franklin makes good sense in thematic and dramatic terms, and is likely to be Chaucer's own.

The Knight's Tale is of especial relevance not only because it stands at the head of the storytelling and sets standards for all that follow, but because of the Knight's own relationship to the Squire. The story of Palamon and Arcite has a philosophical depth and a structural perfection that the tale of Cambyuskan does not begin to imitate. At one level, this marks the difference between the neo-Classical epic and the fashionable tale of the marvellous; but it is also appropriate for the older man to be given a story that questions the rationale underlying the order of things, and the twenty-year-old to tell a tale in which logic and motivation take decidedly second place to the physical properties of the adventure story. The distinction is a matter more of literary appropriateness than of individual psychology, but as so often in the *Tales* the distinction is a fine one.

The contrast of the Squire's and Merchant's Tales is primarily literary, though stylistic, generic, and personal readings of the world once more overlap. The attitudes of the two tales to women are diametric opposites. The Merchant's Tale refuses to give credence to any of the ideals and hyperboles offered by romance; their function is purely cosmetic, and the cosmetic skill that of the mortician. It never occurs to the Squire's Tale to question its hyperboles: every superlative is taken at face value.

The most telling contrast, however, and the one that gives the Squire's Tale its full *raison d'être*, is with the Franklin's Tale. The Franklin's words to the Squire, whether they constitute an interruption or not, pick up a key theme from the tale, that of *gentillesse*, and the concept becomes the basis of the Franklin's own story. Where the Squire's Tale deals with ideals of unfaithfulness and virtue in relation to birds, the Franklin's Tale treats such ideas with a human depth unparalleled elsewhere in the *Tales*. Plot motifs likewise reappear in different guises: the marvels of the Squire's Tale and their possible explanations as astrology or illusion are repeated in the disappearing rocks; the noble lover who leaves his lady to maintain his honour, as the tercelet does, is replayed in Arveragus. The Squire's sequential plots of magic apparatus and of threatened love are welded in the Franklin's Tale into a single structure. The long and rambling form of the interlaced romance is replaced by the tightest and most concentrated kind of romance, the Breton lai.

One other feature of the tale takes on a particular weight from its placing in sequence, and that is its generalizations about women—all favourable, but all largely gratuitous. Canacee 'was ful mesurable, as wommen be' (362); her 'maistresse' is aligned with 'thise olde wommen that been gladly wyse' (376); blue symbolizes 'trouthe that is in wommen sene' (645). The very fact that women are so persistently generalized itself betrays a presupposition that they are a separate species within the human race, but the insistence on their goodness is appropriate for a lady-worshipper trying to make up for the battering the sex has received in preceding speakers' generalizations. It also marks out the professed ideology of secular romance in opposition to the general clerical failure to 'speken good of wyves'.

Style

More than any other of the tales—more even than the Knight's—the Squire's Tale concentrates on the processes of telling rather than on the advancement of the story. Rhetorical elaboration is at a premium, and frequently calls attention to itself through comments on the teller's own inability to express fittingly all the superlatives required by his material. Many other tales used the medium of direct speech almost from start to finish, but here the narrating voice dominates the whole of the first part. The only other voices heard there are the strange knight's, and, very briefly, those of the 'lewed peple'. The second part is largely taken up by the falcon's voice, with a further speech from Canacee.

· A markedly different style is used for each of the voices. Despite the elaborate introduction of the strange knight's skills in the 'art of speche', what he actually says is more succinct than anything else in the tale: he describes the workings of the marvels with the efficiency of a user's manual, not the flummery of the advertising brochure. He sums it all up with,

> This is a verray sooth, withouten glose,   (166)

and the line could be the epigraph for the whole speech. Yet even this speech is offered by the narrator as something greater than is given: it is, he claims, not a verbatim report but a paraphrase, since he 'kan nat sowne his stile' (105–8).

The knight's speeches concentrate on things in the physical world— weather, pegs, thumbs, purses, the flat surfaces of swords. The two short speeches from the onlookers are about interpretation: 'I trowe', 'He lieth' (213, 217). Canacee's speech to the falcon uses a vocabulary of emotion and passion: *sorwe, wo, ire, drede, compassioun*. The falcon herself tells the story of her betrayed love less as a sequence of events than as an opposition of moral qualities. Vice and virtue are contrasted, either in the tercelet and herself or in his appearance and reality: he

> semed welle of alle gentillesse;
> All were he ful of treson and falsnesse,
> It was so wrapped under humble cheere,
> And under hewe of trouthe . . .   (505–8)

What all three main speakers within the Tale have in common, and what is largely missing from the intervening narration, is a sense of cause and effect—whether mechanical, in the knight's instructions, or emotional, in Canacee's promise to help and the falcon's account of her relationship with the tercelet. By contrast, the main narrative tends to concentrate on the moment in hand at the expense of the logic of the story. Canacee's spreading out her skirt to catch the falcon and its fall to the ground thirty lines later are each, independently, valid moments in describing the bird's agony, but the rhetorical concentration on the extremity of the sorrow overlooks the lack of narrative connection. The Boethian image of caged birds in one sense matches image to speaker, but disregards emotional logic in the process. Canacee has an unspecified vision connected in some unspecified way with her mirror, and it is this that makes her want to get up early (372–3), but if her learning of the treachery of the falcon's lover is supposed to be connected with the mirror, the text does not say so. Similarly, her gathering of healing herbs at the end remains unconnected with the properties of the ring: bird speech excepted, the gulf between the two parts of the story is absolute. Within the first part, the knight's entry into the hall constitutes almost the only purposive movement. The teller himself notes the need to get on to the 'knotte' of the story (whatever that may be) and avoid boring the listeners with 'fulsomnesse of his prolixitee' (405)—a phrase that comes dangerously close to being a performative utterance. 'Fulsomnesse' bears a strong resemblance to rhetorical *amplificatio*, and that constitutes a temptation the narrator can rarely resist. Every reference to the time of year or day comes in the form of astronomical periphrasis; the horse is not only the perfection of nature and art, it is 'horsly', unsurpassable from tail to ear, like a Lombardy or Apulian steed or one 'of Fairye', comparable to others from 'olde poetries', and the occasion for some strictures on 'lewed peple'.

The direction of all this is towards the superlative, and that is the dominant mode of the romance throughout. There can be no comparisons for Cambyuskan or his feast; Gawain could not improve on the strange knight's speech; there has been no such wondering at a horse since Troy; Canacee's compassion brings her to the verge of death. The frequent declarations of rhetorical inadequacy are connected with this: only Lancelot could tell of the dances; the teller himself cannot describe Canacee's beauty. Yet there is often something just slightly wrong with all this. The dances that only Lancelot could describe are the setting for intrigue, 'subtil lookyng and dissymulynges' (285). There is no tiger so cruel that it would not have wept at the falcon's grief, except that tigers cannot weep (419–22). The contagious yawns of a personified Sleep are backed up by a medical platitude (347–53). It is not that Canacee's beauty is beyond description, but that it would require a 'rethor excellent' to describe it (38). The rhetorical expression of modesty is appropriate for the context, but it does signal a tale that, although often striking in local effect, frequently delivers less than it promises. There is nothing resembling the lovingly detailed awfulness of *Sir Thopas*; with all its hyperboles and its inconsistencies, it is an imitation, not a parody, of a certain romance style. The difference from its model lies in the literary sophistication that enables Chaucer to see the inadequacies, and the implications, of such a style. Hyperbole works by distancing the verbal surface of the text from normal experience. The incongruities in the Tale are not so concentrated or so marked as in the Nun's Priest's, but marvels and magic and grief-stricken birds are denied substance by the Tale's concentration on manner at the expense of matter.

The Franklin's Tale

The Ending of the Squire's Tale: The Squire–Franklin Link

In a number of manuscripts, including Hengwrt, the Merchant–Squire link is used as the Franklin's Prologue, and the words that follow the unfinished Squire's Tale are given, not to the Franklin, but to the Merchant, to introduce his tale. This is, for once, demonstrably wrong: both the awkward substitution of 'quod the Merchaunt certeyn' for 'quod the Frankeleyn' in 699, and the concern of both the link and the following tale with *gentillesse*, confirm that Chaucer wrote the lines for the Franklin. It is Chaucer's standard practice to introduce a tale's theme in its preceding link. The prologues to the *cherles tales* demonstrate churlishness; the link between the romances demonstrates courtesy and good will.

The key question raised by the Franklin's words is whether they constitute an interruption, or were meant to follow a complete tale that Chaucer in fact never finished. The question cannot be altogether separated from the matter of whether the summary at the end of the Squire's Tale substitutes for an ending. Opponents of the theory of interruption cite its difference in tone from the other such interjections, the 'Namoore of this!' of the Host after *Sir Thopas* or the Knight after the Monk's Tale. But the Franklin is one of the *gentils* on the pilgrimage, speaking to another *gentil*: the tone needs to be different. The dramatic circumstances of the interruption require tact and courtesy, and these are supplied. The Squire's performance is praised as if it were complete, but the very fulsomeness of the praise of the storyteller (as distinct from the pilgrims' usual practice of praising the story) could be designed to counter the inherent rudeness of interrupting. That the Squire's performance has been so admirable 'considerynge thy yowthe', and that no one shall surpass him in eloquence if he lives long enough, suggest a quality of praise tinged with faint damns such as his story invites. The Franklin comes across indeed as having paid more attention to the Squire than to his tale: on other occasions the pilgrims make connections between the characters in a tale and the world outside— witness the Host's many invidious remarks about his wife—but here it is the storyteller himself who is contrasted with the Franklin's son.

Two words echo throughout the Franklin's speech: *gentil* and *vertu* in their various forms, three times each in twenty lines. The stress on *gentillesse* has often recently been interpreted cynically, as showing the Franklin's concern with social climbing: an interpretation that in turn allows the idealism of his tale to be summarily dismissed. But franklins were in fact long-established *gentils*; the valuing of 'vertu' above wealth (686–7) is a recurrent Chaucerian theme; and the Franklin's Tale insists that *gentillesse* can be found lower in the social scale as readily as among those gently born. He does indeed go on rather too long about it in the link, and at some cost in discourtesy to his absent son; Harry Bailly's impatient interjection is not undeserved. The Franklin's reply, however, is a model of courtesy. Individuals may not live up to their ideals, but they may be all the better for trying.

The three-part division into 'wordes', 'prologe', and tale goes back to Ellesmere—the 'wordes' being the Franklin's address to the Squire and his exchange with the Host, the 'prologue' giving his introductory remarks on the genre and style of his story. Hengwrt copies the Prologue and Tale as an undivided unit, though there is a marginal note 'narrat' and a large capital at 729, where Ellesmere starts the Tale.

Date and Text

The Franklin's Tale fairly certainly dates from the high period of Chaucer's work on the *Tales*. Its thematic concerns (*gentillesse*, patience, marriage) and its use of Jerome's *Adversus Jovinianum* would tend to associate its composition with the tales of Fragments III and IV (D and E), from the Wife's Prologue through to the Merchant's Tale. A further clue as to date may be given by the G Prologue to the *Legend of Good Women*, if the supposition is correct that this represents a revision made after the death of Anne of Bohemia in 1394, for Chaucer included in this version a long passage on virtuous women, 'an hundred on a rewe', summarized from Jerome (281–301), which is very similar to Dorigen's list of chaste and renowned maidens and wives.

A few manuscripts show some variations in line order, though these are unlikely to be Chaucerian. The exchange between Aurelius and Dorigen (999–1000) is occasionally placed after his sigh in 1006, so that his 'wo' 'whan that he this herde' relates to her flat denial; and the warning to wives to beware of their promises (1541–4) sometimes follows the narrator's interjection at 1550. There are also two passages that appear only in Ellesmere and one other manuscript: the final couplet of Dorigen's complaint (1455–6), and the plea to the audience to withhold judgement on Arveragus (1493–8). These may be scribal additions, but they are not obviously spurious on stylistic grounds, and their limited dissemination is the only reason to doubt their authenticity.

Glosses in the tale are almost entirely limited to Dorigen's complaint, where the relevant passages of Jerome are quoted in abundance. Hengwrt contains only a couple of glosses at the beginning of the complaint, but the whole series may well go back to Chaucer. A further batch of exempla listed

in the margin at the end of her speech might explain the abruptness of the
final couplet, as they could in effect constitute working notes. There is also a
handful of explanatory glosses; and one manuscript adds the Latin form of
the proverb at 773–6, 'Pacience . . . venquysseth', as 'Pacientes vincunt'.

Genre

In declaring his tale to be a Breton lai, the Franklin gives it almost the only
definitive characteristic of the genre, in French or English: that is, that it
identifies itself as such. He describes the genre in terms found in other
Middle English examples and in the Anglo-Norman lais of Marie de
France: such lais, he says, were composed by Breton minstrels about
'diverse aventures' that are worthy of bearing 'in remembraunce'. Chaucer
backs up his classification of the tale by setting it 'in Armoryk, that called is
Britayne', and giving his characters names that have British-Celtic
associations from the legendary history of Britain.

The Breton lai is in effect a mini-romance—short both in length and in
scope. It is more likely to recount a single episode or group of related
episodes than a series of adventures that covers several generations and
countries. It also tends to focus much more on emotion than on event: its
primary interest is in the internal lives of its characters. The Franklin's Tale
illustrates all these qualities, and they are highlighted by its juxtaposition
with the wide-ranging romance of the Squire's Tale.

One thing Chaucer's Breton lai does not share with the rest is a Breton or
Celtic origin. It contains certain folktale motifs that appear there, but its
closest analogues are found in Boccaccio. In one of these, the story is used as
an extended *demande d'amour*, a matter of love inviting debate, and Chaucer
puts his own story to a similar use. Like the Clerk's Tale, and for similar
reasons, it threatens to become ludicrous or abhorrent if it is read as if it were
a novel; both tales set up extreme cases in the form of implausible situations,
and Chaucer is no more advocating that husbands should dispatch their
wives to commit adultery than that wives should acquiesce cheerfully in the
apparent murder of their children. It is the generic stylization that makes the
stories tolerable, and the psychological realism with which the implausibili-
ties of plot are treated that makes them moving. The Clerk's Tale ends by
admitting its improbability; the definition of the Franklin's Tale as a Breton
lai helps to disarm criticism by associating it with a form where magic is
commonplace and where the characters frequently act by an ethic oblique to
the norms of Christianity.

Kathryn Hume, 'Why Chaucer Calls the *Franklin's Tale* a Breton Lai', *Philological Quarterly*
(1972), 365–79, discusses the popularity of the Breton lai in England and Chaucer's use of
its conventions.

Sources and Analogues

The closest analogues to the Franklin's Tale are two versions of a single story by Boccaccio, one in the *Filocolo*, one in the *Decameron* (10, 5). It is widely assumed that the *Filocolo* was Chaucer's immediate source, but his own tale is radically different from either.

In both Boccaccio's stories, a knight persists in pressing his attentions on another knight's wife until she decides to get rid of him by demanding of him that he produce a blossoming garden in January. With the help of a magician, the lover accomplishes this, and the lady comes to visit it. Unable to hide her distress from her husband, she tells him everything, and he commands her to fulfil her promise. The lover is so moved by the husband's reaction that he releases her, and the magician in turn refuses payment.

The version in the *Filocolo* is considerably longer than that in the *Decameron*, and includes a lot of extra matter on the magician and how the garden was made, complete with a ride throughout the known world in a dragon-drawn chariot and some alarming rituals. It has generally been preferred to the *Decameron* as a source, because the point of the telling lies in just such a question as the Franklin asks about the comparative liberality of the three men, and because of a few slighter similarities—the wife, for instance, makes a somewhat perfunctory attempt to kill herself. It is also widely held that Chaucer's knowledge of the *Filocolo* is attested elsewhere in his works, while his familiarity with the *Decameron* remains unproven; but the case for the *Filocolo* is not decisive. The similarities to it identified in *Troilus and Criseyde* are either trivial or conventional, and fall short of definite proof of acquaintance. The *Decameron* also offers some closer parallels to the Franklin's Tale. The story there is followed by a debate over the men's liberality, and, unlike in the *Filocolo*, no answer is given. The wife in the *Filocolo* goes to her lover with a large company, in the *Decameron* with only two (compare Chaucer's 'squier and a mayde', 1487). The differences between the two versions are not sufficient to identify either finally as Chaucer's source, especially since he changed the story so much; but the case for a memorial recollection of the *Decameron* on Chaucer's part cannot be ruled out.

The differences are many and varied. The setting is moved to Brittany; the love of Arveragus and Dorigen is firmly established; Dorigen's desperate concern for her husband's life is provided as a motive for her impossible demand of the removal of the rocks. The knight–lady–squire pattern mirrors the Merchant's Tale, and allows for a difference in rank that meshes with the concern for *gentil* behaviour independent of birth. The garden becomes the setting for Aurelius' courtship, on the model of the *Roman de la rose*. Arveragus' concern for his wife's *trouthe* is unmatched in the Italian, where the husband of the *Filocolo* reckons that the lover deserves his reward for all his labours, and in the *Decameron* he is afraid of what the magician might do to them if he forbids his wife to fulfil her part of the bargain. Only Chaucer's lover is going to be left destitute, and is prepared to be so, if he is to pay the debt. Chaucer's plotting, in fact, is much tighter, much more focused on the wife's love for her husband, and much more interested in emotional responses and morality.

Three passages in the Tale have other clearly established sources. The discourse on the need for marriage to be an equal partnership is influenced by the *Roman de la rose*, where Ami, the Friend, argues that the servant-lover should not turn into the tyrant-husband, and that the woman must be free if love is to stay alive (*Roman* 9425–54). Dorigen's questioning of God's Providence in His creation of the rocks is based on Boethius (iv. pr. 6), a clerk who does indeed prove 'by argumentz, that al is for the beste' (886). Her complaint, with its long list of women who preferred death to dishonour, is drawn, as the marginal glosses indicate, from Jerome's mighty blast against sexual activity in general and women in particular, the *Adversus Jovinianum*. Jerome's only good women are dead ones, who have removed themselves from the world as soon as opportunity offered; but it is right that Dorigen should align herself with those she can see as victims, and not with the wicked wives with whom the Wife of Bath identifies herself. There is a clear logic to the selection and arrangement of her exempla, indicated in her introductory lines,

> Yet have I levere to lese
> My lif than of my body to have a shame,
> Or knowe myselven fals, or lese my name.   (1360–2)

The list of women is accordingly arranged in terms of virgins who preferred death to loss of maidenhead (1367–94); then of wives who, even more than maidens (1395–8), ought to kill themselves rather than be false to their husbands (1399–441 or 1442: Dorigen seems to associate Alcestis with the true wives, the marginal gloss would associate her with the next group); and wives who have won fame through their chastity (1442/3–56).

Germaine Dempster and J. S. P. Tatlock, in *Sources and Analogues*, give the *Filocolo* version of the story, some brief extracts from Geoffrey of Monmouth on British legends, and others from Breton lais. An attractive Elizabethan translation of the Boccaccio is H. G.'s *Thirteene Most Pleasaunt and Delectable Questions* (1566; ed. Edward Hutton, London, 1927), 'The fourth question'. For the *Decameron*, see p. 12 above.

Gerald Morgan (ed.), *Geoffrey Chaucer: The Franklin's Tale from the Canterbury Tales* (London, 1980), contains an excellent discussion of all aspects of the Tale, including the structure of Dorigen's complaint.

Structure

The basic plot of both the Franklin's Tale and Boccaccio's stories is inherently symmetrical, of a rash promise and its fulfilment. Chaucer's treatment elaborates on this symmetrical patterning to produce a structure not unlike that of the Knight's Tale, where the progress of the story falls into two halves that mirror each other around a mid-point. Whether Chaucer fully intended this scheme or whether it developed as an adjunct to his reworking of the story, the pattern is intriguing, and illuminating. It is given below on the same model as that used for the Knight's Tale, where the events of the tale and the accompanying excursus follow in sequence down the left hand column and up the right.

Marriage in 'blisse'	Arveragus and Dorigen in 'sover-eyn blisse'
The importance of liberty in love	'Fredom' in relationships
'Patience is an heigh vertu'	'Trouthe is the hyeste thing'
Averagus' departure	Arveragus' return
Dorigen on Providence	Dorigen's lament
Dorigen swears by the rocks	The disappearance of the rocks; reminder of the vow
Aurelius' prayers to the gods	'Magik natureel'

The clerk and his 'illusiouns'; winter

Maybe the most interesting point to emerge from such a layout is the central place occupied by 'illusioun'. It suggests a structure that moves from happiness and virtue, through increasing uncertainty—Dorigen's questioning of Providence, her rash promise, Aurelius' prayers to the pagan gods to disrupt the order of nature—to a point where truth is no longer distinguishable. The astrological activities of the clerk are similarly disruptive, obscuring truth—'it semed that alle the rokkes were aweye'—and threatening the happiness of the initial marriage all the more intensely. Dorigen's plans for suicide likewise offer no way forward; it is only Arveragus' insistence on *trouthe* and the contagiousness of his *gentillesse* that enable the final return to equilibrium, or to a 'sovereyn blisse' that surpasses the opening.

Such a pattern follows closely the mythic cycle of romance, from spring, through winter, hardship, and threatened death to a renewal of life. Winter is also placed at the centre point of the tale, whether for reasons to do with such a cycle or simply as a leftover from Boccaccio's midwinter garden; that Chaucer both keeps and elaborates the seasonal reference indicates that its presence is not mere chance. His winter, moreover, looks both ways.

> The bittre frostes, with the sleet and reyn,
> Destroyed hath the grene in every yerd.
> Janus sit by the fyr, with double berd,
> And drynketh of his bugle horn the wyn:
> Biforn him stant brawen of the tusken swyn,
> And 'Nowel' crieth every lusty man.   (1250–5)

The green of the garden where Aurelius danced is dead, but Janus, the god of the old and new year, is revelling, and the revels are specifically those of Christmas—'Nowel'—with its reminder, however briefly touched, of the renewal of the Incarnation. There is no further reference to the season in the tale; but the clerk has to wait for the right moment to work his illusions (1263), and by the time Dorigen sets off to fulfil her tryst in the garden there is perhaps an assumption that the year has started its own process of renewal.

Themes

The Franklin's has in recent years been one of the more controversial of the Tales. The least sympathetic readings see a middle-class man trying to assert his membership of the gentry by mouthing empty platitudes about *gentillesse* and honour that his story refuses to support, and that in any case are mere grand words to disguise the collapse of late medieval chivalry. In addition, the upholding by 'Epicurus owene sone' (I(A) 336) of casuistic secular values including equality in marriage has been read as an ironic inversion of divine truth, a model to be avoided, not admired.

Such interpretations are, I think, too extreme. The first privileges twentieth-century cynicism as truth, and disregards both historical perspective and historical fact. By all evidence, Chaucer, in common with most writers of the Middle Ages and Renaissance, couples a profound sense of human fallibility and the mutability of the world with a passionate belief in the possibility of virtue. His own *balade* of *Gentillesse* shows how seriously he regarded the concept, and there is no reason to think he is parodying those ideas through the Franklin—franklins themselves being *gentils*, landed gentry, not *nouveaux riches*. The second interpretation, by contrast, tries to impose on the story a supposedly medieval view that denies the validity of any reading of the world that violates patristic Christian orthodoxy. Secular values, by this reading, are a contradiction in terms, and Chaucer's apparent secularity is really a cover to lead men back to the divine.

Both readings approach the tale from sets of assumptions derived from outside it, and both deny validity to the expressed meaning of the text. It is not at all clear, however, that such a denial is justified. Arveragus may take the revolutionary step of voluntarily renouncing *maistrie* in marriage where his wife so wishes (747–8), but the comments that follow insist on the compatibility of such a renunciation with the natural order: mutual respect between husband and wife is associated with *humblesse, gentillesse, trouthe,* love, liberty, patience, temperance, suffrance—virtues that require to be taken seriously, and are so taken across the whole range of the *Canterbury Tales.* There is nothing in this to suggest an ironic indictment of inadequate worldly values, or of a narrator straining up the social ladder. The changes Chaucer made to the story confirm its seriousness of purpose on its own terms. The wife's vow is now not just a device to get rid of an unwanted lover; its conditions link it intimately to her fear for her husband, and so with her love for him. The folktale motif of the rash promise therefore becomes both a way to set the plot in motion and a genuine moral dilemma—a dilemma not just as to what Dorigen should do, but as to how one can reconcile intentions and actions in a world where clear foresight is impossible. Furthermore, the rather crass reasons given by the husbands in Boccaccio's versions for sending the wife to her lover—that he has earned her, or that the magician might turn nasty—are replaced by a deep moral concern, in particular with *trouthe.*

The most frequent objection to the seriousness of the surface meaning of the tale is that the promise was unlawful in the first place, so Dorigen had no right to give it nor any obligation to fulfil it once given. This is true, and the story takes account of it. In the *Filocolo* indeed it is made a matter for explicit statement, in the discussion following the judgement, that a wife is bound by her prior vow to her husband. Chaucer makes the point, not by insisting on the special quality of the marriage vows, but by insisting on Dorigen's swearing of *trouthe* to her husband:

> Sire, I wol be youre humble trewe wyf—
> Have heer my trouthe—till that myn herte breste.   (758–9)

The sops to conventional morality come later: every wife should 'be war of hire biheeste', and avoid getting into the mess that Dorigen did (1541–2); Arveragus looks too much like a 'lewed man . . . that he wol putte his wyf in jupartie' (1494–5). The second of these passages is found only in two manuscripts, whether because a scribe felt impelled to answer the plain man's objections, or because Chaucer failed to make the status of the apologia clear—possibly its inclusion or exclusion was still an open question in his own mind.

The tale flies in the face of conventional morality, to assert something different and rather more difficult. The story is set up precisely as a test case: what if—? Without that, there would be no story: just as there would be no *Hamlet* without the ghost's demand for revenge, no Clerk's Tale if Grisilde had decided enough was enough, no *Gawain and the Green Knight* if Gawain had followed the opinion of the court that it was silly to go out and risk getting his head chopped off. These last two are of particular relevance, for both turn on the question of a promise made in opposition to common sense, and on the paramountcy of *trouthe*.

The question is not, then, whether it was sensible or right of Dorigen to make her vow, or of Arveragus to send her to fulfil it. The rash promise is a condition of the story, and it is moreover given a clear and sympathetic psychological motivation in Dorigen's fears for her husband. She may never have intended to grant Aurelius her sexual favours, but Aurelius reads her promise in that way, and so her *trouthe*, her integrity, even her identity (as Gawain's identity is coupled with his *trouthe*), is linked to the fulfilling of her vow. Arveragus may have the right as her husband to order her to break it, but he has foregone *maistrie* (747) in favour of a mutual respect, a recognition of precisely that integrity and individual identity she has pledged to Aurelius. A promise, like a debt, can rightly be set aside only by the person to whom it is owed, not by the person who makes or incurs it. Arveragus therefore gives up his own share in Dorigen's vow of *trouthe* to him, just as Aurelius gives up his claim to her, and the clerk his right to payment. The final question for debate, 'Which was the mooste fre?', focuses on this virtue of generosity precisely because in order for the ending to be happy the men have to give up what they could rightfully claim as theirs.

The same division between convention or common sense and a different imperative underlies another controversial feature of the tale, Arveragus' concern for his honour. He seems more occupied with appearance than with substance: he wants to look like Dorigen's lord 'for shame of his degree' (752), he leaves her alone in order 'to seke in armes worshipe and honour' (811), and he is prepared to send her off to commit adultery just so long as no one knows about it. But his concern with reputation is a proper one in the chivalric world; his departure in the cause of honour is familiar enough as a romance motif to show that his love for and deference to Dorigen have not become uxoriousness—it is the knight that stays at home who is criticized. His love for Dorigen extends to a care for her good name, and it is her reputation, as well as his own, that he is trying to protect in his one act of *maistrie* in the tale, when he forbids her to speak of what has happened lest 'folk of yow may demen harm or gesse' (1486). Care for one's reputation, as Dame Prudence notes, is an essential quality of the *gentil* man, and she quotes Solomon and St Augustine as authorities (VII. 1636–47/B². 2826–37). A concern for appearance is not the same as hypocrisy, any more than Arveragus' 'glad chiere' is hypocritical before he breaks down weeping. Appearance and reality are much more complex in the moral world than in the physical, where the clerk's illusions take place. In a profound sense, the reputation Arveragus is so concerned to preserve is more fully justified than if he followed more conventional ways of keeping it. His insistence on marriage as companionship rather than lordship is more honourable than the customary male dominance; Dorigen's promise was an expression of her deep and admirable love for her husband, her keeping it is an expression of his concern for her *trouthe*.

That reality and its interpretation or appearance are key themes of the tale is confirmed by the centrality of *illusioun* in its structuring, and in the plot. 'It semed that alle the rokkes were aweye', but it is not stated whether they were or not, and nobody within the tale so much as goes to look: the interest is not in what 'really' happened, but in how it makes people behave. (The text does not support the argument that the clerk just picked a high tide; high tides do not last 'a wyke or tweye' any more than they last the two years Aurelius had requested.) Dorigen had identified the existence of the rocks as the main threat to her marriage, and had questioned the ordering of the world for good on their account. The course of the tale turns their disappearance into the greater threat; only their continued existence will guarantee the stability of her love. Her questioning of Providence is shown to be wrong within the terms of the story, not because there is an absolute opposition between such questioning and proper Christian faith, but because it misleads her into inviting an upset of the natural created order. Her conviction that it can never happen reflects a deeper faith that represents the stability apparently denied by *illusioun*.

The universe of the Franklin's Tale is a Christian one, but the characters are not allowed a full participation in that: Aurelius prays to the pagan planetary gods, the clerk manipulates the workings of the natural world through astrological knowledge 'as hethen folk useden in thilke dayes' (1293). The characters have to act by their own highest principles, not by Christian law. The Church's ban on suicide cannot be relevant to Dorigen (and it was at best half-hearted where sexual purity was at issue), nor the Ten Commandments to Aurelius, nor the sacramental nature of marriage to Arveragus. The semi-pagan setting disallows certain kinds of judgement while giving the characters a broader space in which to exercise their natural virtue.

The virtue is genuine, but the world is not stable; it is subject to parting and sorrow, shipwreck, pain, lack of foresight, the gap between intention and outcome. The later part of the tale is in effect an exemplum of how the virtues that have created the 'blisse' of the marriage of Arveragus and Dorigen can enable it to survive all this. He bids her go to Aurelius, not as an order, but by supporting her in what she has done:

> Ye shul youre trouthe holden, by my fay! (1474)

None the less, Dorigen looks to her husband to sort things out for her: that is appropriate for the kind of character Chaucer makes of her, and if it further suggests that a husband's refusal of *soveraynetee* may not be final, and that in the natural order of things he will be the leader and head, it would be anachronistic to demand otherwise. By basing Dorigen's reliance on her husband on individual characterization rather than ideological principle, Chaucer does at least substitute a potential freedom of action for a universal repressive law.

The two great principles on which the tale operates are relevant to society's treatment of women but also larger than that: *patience* and *gentillesse*. The discourse on patience, whether one thinks of it as the Franklin's or Chaucer's, is a clear programme for all human dealings and relationships, using marriage as a model. The independence of noble action from noble birth that is the quintessential idea in Chaucer's concept of *gentillesse* is appropriate enough in the mouth of a franklin, a representative of the lower ranks of the gentry, and therefore the man in the middle, able to acknowledge and approve generous action in both knights and clerks. It is virtue, in this romance, rather than plot, that brings about the happy ending: the complications in the action bring it to the edge of catastrophe, and it is only the example of Arveragus' nobility that can give the tale a new direction. The general form of romance is itself providential, with events working out for good, but the characters have to act in ignorance of the outcome. 'It may be wel, paraventure,' Averagus comforts his wife, and then bursts into tears. He and the other men make their choices for good without privileged knowledge and out of free will: a free will that reflects the liberty given to Dorigen within her marriage. A happy ending requires not that God should unmake the rocks, but that a series of individuals should opt to yield up and to give rather than take.

A sinful, ambitious, or patriarchal Franklin is regarded as justifying an ironic reading of the tale by critics as diverse as Robertson, 'Chaucer's Franklin' (*Essays*, pp. 273–90); Alan T. Gaylord, 'The Promises in *The Franklin's Tale*', *ELH* 31 (1964), 321–45; A. C. Spearing in his edition of the tale (1966); and Aers, *Chaucer, Langland*, pp. 160–9, through a study of the language. David, *Strumpet Muse*, ch. 12, varies the pattern by arguing that the Franklin has too optimistic a view of the world.

For arguments closer to that given here, see Pearsall, *Canterbury Tales*, pp. 144–60; Gerald Morgan's edition cited p. 234 above, and his 'Boccaccio's *Filocolo* and the Moral Argument of the Franklin's Tale', *ChR* 20 (1985–6), 285–306; and Kathryn Jacobs, 'The Marriage Contract of the *Franklin's Tale*: The Remaking of Society', *ChR* 20 (1985–6), 132–43.

For a discussion of the kind of calculations Chaucer might have envisaged for the clerk, see North, *Chaucer's Universe*, ch. 13.

The Tale in Context

For most of this century, criticism of the Franklin's Tale has concentrated on one element in it: the argument against *maistrie* in marriage, and its function as a complement, and an answer, to the rival views of marriage presented in the Wife's Prologue and the tales of the Clerk and Merchant. The length of the excursus on marriage at the start is scarcely required by the story: it is important for the plot that Dorigen should pledge her *trouthe* to Arveragus, but the debate on obedience has more to do with establishing the nature of this marriage in clear contrast to those of the Wife, Grisilde, and May.

The tale is about far more than who rules the household, however, and its thematic connections spread much wider than the 'marriage group' alone. The Franklin first interrupts his tale to stress that it is a model for all human relationships:

> Freendes everych oother moot obeye,
> If they wol longe holden compaignye,   (762–3)

and from 'freendes', the generalization spreads, to 'wommen', 'men' in the masculine sense (770), 'men' in the general sense (776), and finally to direct address:

> Lerneth to suffre, or elles, so moot I goon
> Ye shul it lerne, wher so ye wole or noon;
> For in this world, certein, ther no wight is
> That he ne dooth or seith somtyme amys.   (777–80)

The pilgrim audience, the literal audience, every person in the world, needs to show tolerance because at some point they will themselves need to be shown it. The tale gives an exemplum of such a relationship in practice; the *Tales* at large show how far such an ideal is from achievement. The sharp practices, deceits, and downright villainy found in most of the stories are extreme forms of the abuses, squabbles, and ill will portrayed in the General Prologue and links. The Franklin himself is presented as not sustaining the tolerance he advocates—his cook falls foul of him for inadequate seasoning of his sauces, his son for gambling and preferring low company—but he does manage one rare piece of courtesy on the pilgrimage: where the fabliaux tend to be told as examples of churlishness, of mutual insult, the Franklin's romance reciprocates the Squire's in a rivalry of good will. His tale contains, not a vicious parody of a professional rival on the pilgrimage, but a model image of a handsome, attractive, and accomplished squire.

The Tale bears particular affinities with the Squire's, the Knight's, and the Merchant's, working in each case by contrast. It takes the concentrated form of the Breton lai as against the Squire's infinitely expandable interlaced romance; it deals with many of the same themes as the Squire's—magic and illusion, love and *gentillesse*—but treats them not as exciting story motifs or blank walls on which to paint rhetorical murals, but as matters of real human import. Like the Knight's Tale, it questions the providential ordering of the world, in Dorigen's soliloquy on the rocks; but although Aurelius prays to the planetary gods, they do not intervene in the plot. Theseus has to assert a faith in a benevolent Providence in the teeth of the natural order; the Franklin's Tale has it expressed through the stability of the natural order. The programme of forbearance between friends that the Franklin offers at the start is in marked contrast to the cousins' quick enmity; and Arcite learns the virtue of yielding up only when he has no life left to enjoy his rightful prize.

The most precise series of contrasts is with the Merchant's Tale, at the level of plot as much as meaning. The two sets of characters are identical, of knight, lady, and amorous squire, but the stories take opposite courses. The moral blindness of the Merchant's Tale is replaced by physical illusion. The paradisal garden is the scene for Aurelius' declaration of love, and should be the setting for its consummation; but, unlike in January's enclosed garden, the Fall never happens. The fairy gods who precipitate the final climax of the Merchant's Tale, in which adultery, brazenness, and wilful folly compete for attention, are replaced here by the free choice of human goodness.

The wider context of the *Tales* emphasizes how seriously the virtues propounded by the Franklin's Tale are to be taken. *Patience* is advocated in tale after tale, and endorsed by the Parson as making one 'lyk to God' (X(I) 661). *Fredom*, the readiness to give to others, is the opposite of the desire to 'wynne' that embodies Chaucer's vision of evil in the Friar's, Summoner's and Pardoner's Tales. *Gentillesse* in the Man of Law's Tale is an attribute of the Virgin; to the Wife of Bath's loathly lady, it is a quality derived not from ancestry but from Christ; to the Parson, it substitutes being 'Cristes child' for high lineage (X(I) 462). *Trouthe*, in the sense of a promise supported by the whole of one's moral being, is a key element in the run of tales preceding the Franklin's, from the knight's oath to the hag and Grisilde's to Walter, to the summoner's commitment of himself to the devil. In the Second Nun's Tale, the word takes on a wider connotation, of the stable truth of God against the illusoriness of the world. It is a definition not irrelevant to the disappearing rocks.

Style

That the Franklin's disclaimer of rhetorical skill in his Prologue is itself a rhetorical ploy is demonstrated by the terms in which it is couched: word-play, metonymy, learned allusion, and Classical reference flicker and play across its surface. Once the Tale itself starts, however, the virtuosity rarely calls attention to itself. One is kept aware of the process of narration and comment—of the tale's being *told*; but it does not keep up a running commentary, as the Squire's Tale does, on its own procedures. The sense of a speaking voice and the comments it makes are devoted rather to bringing out the significance of the matter in hand and controlling the hearer's response to that.

The main result of this is that the style is constantly and subtly modulated in accordance with the immediate subject. Each of the major characters is allotted a specific idiom or stylistic mode that operates both when they are the subject of the narrative and in direct or reported speech. These idioms can accompany or override other specialized vocabularies: Aurelius' on the motions of the sun, for instance, or the philosophical terminology of Dorigen's monologue on Providence. Similar stylistic modulations are associated with objects and visual images. There is another mode again for moralizing or generalizing commentary—a style that can mix the colloquial with the abstract, that is at once authoritative, persuasive, and intimate, and where there is no sense of distance between the import of the words and the intention of the teller.

Not everything in the tale, however, is taken so seriously. Aurelius' stylistic mode, for instance, is exaggeration (which belittles, whereas hyperbole, its apparently close relation, enhances). There is almost always a slight distancing between statement and tone when he is the subject, a refusal to endorse wholly either his words or his actions. It shows in the histrionics of his threats of 'sodeyn deth horrible' (1010), the way references to his suffering keep breaking through his instructions to Apollo on how to organize the mechanics of a two-year high tide, his 'blisful' 'Fy on a thousand pound!' to the magician (1226–7). It pervades both the reported facts (endless words about keeping silent) and the indirect speech of his

> many layes,
> Songes, compleintes, roundels, virelayes,
> How that he dorste nat his sorwe telle,
> But langwissheth as a furye dooth in helle.   (947–50)

The same idiom is used about him as he uses himself:

> In langour and in torment furyus
> Two yeer and moore lay wrecche Aurelyus.   (1101–2)

It is all very emotional, but the emotion is much more Aurelius' than the reader's. By contrast, the legal language he uses to release Dorigen from her contract (1533–5) shows an impersonality associated with a new maturity: he can also, for the first time, speak of Arveragus and Dorigen without regarding them as adjuncts of himself. Earlier, Dorigen had been 'my sovereyn lady deere' (1072), and Arveragus' absence simply a marker for his own despair (969–71).

Arveragus, by contrast, is always treated seriously, in both narrative and speech, and the stylistic mode associated with him is one more of understatement than of exaggeration. His one line of response to the news that his wife has sworn adultery—'Is ther oght elles, Dorigen, but this?'— shows absolute restraint both of emotion and language. His reaction, when it does come, takes the form of a mere five words of factual statement—'he brast anon to wepe'—that conveys far more than all Aurelius' years of languishing. The idiom for Dorigen lies somewhere between the two. She can be shocked into directness, as in her initial downright rejection of Aurelius; but her monologues, supposedly impersonal arguments, are tempered by her emotional involvement. Her questioning of the nature of Providence is disrupted by the personal appeals and exaggeration of

> Se ye nat, Lord, how mankynde it destroyeth?
> An hundred thousand bodyes of mankynde
> Han rokkes slayn, al be they nat in mynde.   (876–8)

Her aggregation of exempla of chaste women actually gets in the way of her doing anything about the proposition they are supposed to support, that she should kill herself, as the narrator implies at the end:

> Thus pleyned Dorigen a day or tweye,
> Purposynge evere that she wolde deye.   (1457–8)

Both Aurelius and Dorigen are treated with an affection that refuses to take them altogether seriously; the presentation of Dorigen adds a touch of sympathy. Arveragus is the only character to be treated with consistent respect.

The narratorial voice, then, is not a single or stable one; it responds closely to subject, whether that subject is personal or descriptive. The clerk in effect *becomes* his astrological skill through the sheer technical virtuosity of the poetry describing his practices. The garden is described less in terms of what it looks like than of the effect it makes—a passage worth quoting at length, both because the spaciousness of the syntax and verse rhythms require it, and because the ideal conventions of courtly garden description that stir 'any herte' modulate so finely into the idea of suffering, into 'Dorigen allone', and finally into the absence at the centre of her perception:

> May hadde peynted with his softe shoures
> This gardyn ful of leves and of floures;
> And craft of mannes hand so curiously
> Arrayed hadde this gardyn, trewely,
> That nevere was ther gardyn of swich prys
> But if it were the verray paradys.

The odour of floures and the fresshe sighte
Wolde han maked any herte lighte
That evere was born, but if to greet siknesse
Or to greet sorwe helde it in distresse,
So ful it was of beautee with plesaunce.
At after-dyner gonne they to daunce,
And synge also, save Dorigen allone,
Which made alwey hir compleint and hir moone,
For she ne saugh hym on the daunce go
That was hir housbonde and hir love also.   (907–22)

Its effect in context adds to the power of the passage. It offers a strong image of paradisal beauty and fertility to contrast with the demonic image—as Dorigen sees it—of the 'grisly rokkes blake', to which she adds the word 'feendly'. But the dangers of illusion are implicit even at this stage of the tale. The rocks are in fact part of the natural order; the garden will have its greenness destroyed by winter (1251). Nor is the paradise safe: among the dancers mentioned at the end of the passage quoted is Aurelius. The springtime garden is the appropriate setting, by romance convention, for him to make his declaration of love, but the self-centredness of his passion leaves him oblivious to the irony of offering himself to a lady who has eyes only for what is not there.

Arveragus' absence from the dance is genuine; when Aurelius sees himself and his lady dancing, it is illusory (1200–1). By a nice paradox, the brother's account of illusions and those they see in the clerk's house are presented as a list of *things*, of a physical density unparalleled elsewhere in the tale—a barge, a lion, flowers, a vine with grapes, 'a castel, al of lym and stoon' (1144–9); a hunt, the bleeding deer, hawking, jousting (1190–8). Each account is structured by anaphoric formulae, 'somtyme—' in the brother's speech, 'he saugh—' in the clerk's house; and both end the same way, in nothingness. It is a tale in which 'things' are unstable: the illusions, the beauty of the garden, the rocks. The absolutes of the tale are moral qualities: patience, *fredom* or generosity, *gentillesse*, *trouthe*.

FRAGMENT VI(C)

The Placing of the Fragment

There is no headlink to the Physician's Tale to indicate its placing in the Canterbury sequence, and the Pardoner's exchange with the Host at the end of his tale finishes without the next storyteller being named. In the manuscripts, they are consistently placed before Fragment VII(B²), so the Pardoner's Tale is always followed by the Shipman's; such an arrangement may be Chaucer's, but one would expect him to have written a linking passage if the placing were final. There is a division of evidence among the manuscripts as to what tale the Fragment should follow. Ellesmere and some others place it after the Franklin's; elsewhere the Franklin's Tale is followed by the tales of the Second Nun and Canon's Yeoman (Fragment VIII(G)), and the Physician's and Pardoner's Tales follow those. The Hengwrt scribe, who seems to have received his copy in sections at different times, and who omits the Canon's Yeoman's altogether, gives the order Franklin–Second Nun–Clerk–Physician–Pardoner–Shipman. In critical terms, the Physician's Tale follows well from the Franklin's—it tells at length a story similar to those cited by Dorigen in her list of maidens who preferred death to shame—but it may well be that Chaucer had not decided on a final position for the Fragment.

Helen Storm Corsa (ed.), *The Physician's Tale* (Variorum II 17, Norman, Okla., 1987), reviews the arguments for the placing of the Fragment, pp. 53–61.

The Physician's Tale

Date and Text

The story of the girl killed by her father to save her from the sexual attentions of an unjust judge bears some resemblances to Chaucer's collection of stories of distressed, abandoned, and damaged women, the *Legend of Good Women*. It is possible that this Tale dates from the same period, the 1380s, and therefore may antedate the conception of the *Canterbury Tales*. There is, however, no independent evidence to support or disprove such a dating. Since Chaucer's sister-in-law was both the mistress of John of Gaunt and the governess to his daughters, it is hard to believe that the lines on guardianship at the start of the Tale were written entirely ingenuously; but if Chaucer wrote them with any more specific topical reference in mind, the sentiments are too generalized to enable it to be recovered.

One group of manuscripts, including Corpus, contains a number of textual variants, including 'will and thought' rather than 'wyn and youthe' as promoting lechery (59), and a different warning at 82—'kepeth wel tho that ye undertake'. A few spurious lines appear in other manuscripts. Glosses found in both Hengwrt and Ellesmere and some other manuscripts identify a handful of sources: the Book of Judges for Jephtha (240); the *Metamorphoses* for Pygmalion (14), the *Alexandreis* for 'Zanzis' (Zeuxis), and Cicero for Apelles (16), though Chaucer in fact took these last three references from the *Roman de la rose*. The note 'Augustinus' by the line 'The doctor maketh this descripcioun' (117) may be there either for source identification or to avoid confusion with the Doctor of Physic himself.

Corsa's Variorum edition cited above discusses the status of the textual variants.

Genre

The Physician's Tale ends in the manner of a cautionary exemplum, with ten lines of *moralitee* that start

> Heere may men seen how synne hath his merite.
> Beth war, for no man woot whom God wol smyte
> In no degree . . .   (277–9)

The central interest of the tale, however, focuses not on Apius and the various ways in which judges can be unjust, but on Virginia, whose chastity and temperance are clearly offered as models to be followed:

> In hir lyvyng maydens myghten rede,
> As in a book, every good word or dede
> That longeth to a mayden vertuous.   (107–9)

Further direct moralizing is addressed to 'maistresses' who look after lords' daughters, and 'ye fadres and ye moodres eek', who need to set their children a good 'ensample' and chastise them as necessary.

The mode of the tale, then, is exemplary; but much of this moralizing is so hard to square with the story as to set the two at odds. Virginia's virtue does not profit her—if she were less an embodiment of virtue, indeed, there would be less reason to kill her; and it has no such positive function as a saint's life would provide. The advice to parents and guardians is explicitly irrelevant: Virginia 'neded no maistresse' (106), and when her father does turn his hand against her it is for her goodness, not for wickedness. His action may, in the terms of the story, be noble, but any attempt to claim that it invites imitation would be appalling. Even the final moralization on the downfall of the sinful loses touch with Apius, whose wickedness was certainly not 'privee'. If the tale as a whole is an exemplum, it is very hard to see what it exemplifies.

Two other ways of approaching the tale are offered in the text itself. One is the insistence that the story is not fiction but history,

> no fable,
> But knowen for historial thyng notable.   (155–6)

Chaucer's category of the historical was broader than ours (it included, for instance, the stories of both Troy and Thebes), but this is the only time in the *Tales* that such a claim is made. Moreover, 'the sentence of it sooth is' (157): the factual accuracy, *sooth*, of history, makes it a genre to itself, whose facts may not accord with hagiographic or exemplary readings. The lines occur as a parenthesis in the middle of the tale; generic pointers are more frequently given in the links, and it is interesting that one manuscript provides a spurious prologue in which the 'historial' quality of the tale is emphasized. Here the Host invites, and the Physician promises, a story drawn from chronicle history, 'in cronyke'—presumably in anticipation of the opening reference to Livy. Chaucer himself offers a different generic interpretation in the end link, where the Host describes it as a 'pitous tale'. 'Pitous tales' scarcely constitute a recognized genre, but Chaucer's exploitation of pathos here and in a number of other tales—the Man of Law's, Clerk's, Prioress's—does set a similar horizon of expectation. A 'historial' tale would suggest a chronicle style of treatment, which Chaucer does indeed accord much of the narrative, and to which the spurious prologue calls attention: but his greatest alteration in the story as he received it is to increase its quality as a 'pitous tale'. The Host, for once, may have got things just about right.

The 'cronyke' prologue is found in British Library MS Lansdowne 851; see J. M. Manly and Edith Rickert (eds.), *The Text of the Canterbury Tales* (Chicago, 1940), vii. 3–4, Corsa, *The Physician's Tale* (p. 247 above), pp. 44–5.

Sources and Analogues

> Ther was, as telleth Titus Livius,
> A knyght that called was Virginius,   (1–2)

but Chaucer in fact took the story from the *Roman de la rose* (5589–658), where Livy is also cited—no doubt truthfully—as the source. There is negligible evidence that Chaucer used Livy's account; similarities that have been claimed (such as Virginius' absence from the court when Claudius first makes his demand) in fact make better sense as a development of the story in the *Roman* than as an adaptation of Livy, where Virginius is away from the city altogether. There is no trace of influence from other versions of the story, such as those in the *Confessio amantis* (vii. 5131–306) or in Boccaccio's *De claris mulieribus* (chapter 56). Jean de Meun had already cut down Livy's story to the spare outline Chaucer follows, eliminating, for instance, the many extra characters who populate the original. The father, the daughter, the unjust judge, and the suborned witness are all that is necessary, and the crowd scenes are held back until the very end.

Chaucer adapts Jean de Meun's narrative fairly freely in many areas, but the *Roman* is responsible for some of the best and worst lines in the tale. That Virginius kills his daughter 'for love, and nat for hate' (225), comes from that; so does the gratuitous couplet on the execution of the 'remenant' of the conspirators (275–6), gratuitous both because they have not previously been mentioned and because the worse villain, Claudius, has been reprieved through Virginius' intercession.

Of the changes Chaucer makes to the *Roman* the most significant concerns the manner of Virginia's death. In Livy, the killing is a public act carried out in support of Roman honour, and done to preserve her liberty as much as her virginity—Claudius is claiming her as a slave. Both there and in the *Roman*, Virginia herself is present in the court when she is ordered to be handed over; her father at once cuts off her head and presents it to Apius, all within a single scene. Chaucer divides the action into public and private scenes: Virginius returns home and summons his daughter to tell her of his intentions and lament her fate, and she is allowed a few lines of mourning before Virginius kills her.

The prefatory matter to the story—the long description of Virginia's beauty and virtues, the advice to parents—requires no direct sources, though Chaucer derived the triple reference to Pygmalion, Appelles, and Zeuxis from a later section of the *Roman*. The creation of the courtly heroine as a perfect work of Nature has parallels both there and more widely in French romance. Virginia's virtues encapsulate those expounded at enormously greater length in such treatises as St Ambrose's *De virginibus*, Vincent of Beauvais's *De eruditione filiorum nobilium*, and a Spanish reworking of Aegidius Romanus' *De regimine principum* made by Fray Juan García de Castrojeriz. This last work brings together many of the commonplaces repeated by Chaucer on maidenly virtues, and also alludes to the story of Virginia. Castrojeriz was confessor to the mother of Pedro of Castile (of the Monk's Tale), and the work was written as a guide to his education. Pedro's daughter Constance became John of Gaunt's second wife, and in view of Chaucer's connections with her household through his own wife, his knowledge of the work is not altogether implausible. The overlap of the Tale with all these works may however be testimony less of direct borrowing than of the wide currency of such ideas.

Edgar F. Shannon, 'The Physician's Tale', in *Sources and Analogues*, gives the relevant extracts from the *Roman de la rose*, Livy, and St Ambrose.

Karl Young, 'The Maidenly Virtues of Chaucer's Virginia', *Speculum*, 16 (1941), 340–9, presents the case for Vincent's *De eruditione*; it looks more convincing when, as here, the needle is extracted from the haystack for perusal. On Castrojeriz, see Martha S. Waller, '*The Physician's Tale*: Geoffrey Chaucer and Fray Juan García de Castrojeriz', *Speculum*, 51 (1976), 292–306. Not all the parallels to the tale appear in Aegidius' original, but the most striking figure in other sources; see Glending Olson, 'Juan García de Castrojeriz and John of Wales: A Note on Chaucer's Reading', *Speculum*, 64 (1989), 106–10.

Structure

As in many of the Canterbury tales, Chaucer provides a large amount of prefatory matter before letting the plot get under way. The opening section follows his favourite structural model: he introduces the authority figure of the story, in this case Virginius, and follows that up with a description of the central character, his daughter, as yet unnamed. The shift into moralizing is also paralleled elsewhere, in the Pardoner's diatribe against gluttony, or friar John's, in the Summoner's Tale, against anger, though there is no apparent element of irony in this instance.

By the time this introductory matter is complete, over a third of the way through the tale, anyone unacquainted with the *Roman de la rose* or Livy would still have no idea of the course the plot will take or the kind of tale it might be. The heroine endowed with such beauty and virtue should, on the balance of probabilities, finish up either as an object of courtship or as a Christian martyr; Virginia comes close to being both at once. The first indication that something may go wrong comes with the mention of Envy

(114); and within a few lines the judge has seen and desired her. From this point the story moves fast through his machinations to obtain possession of her, and pauses again for the pathos of the account of the sorrow of both father and daughter. The beheading, the presentation of the head to Apius, the people's uprising, and the disposing of the various conspirators to death or exile are accomplished in a summary twenty-two lines. The final lines of moralization draw on a single element of the tale, of how evil comes to grief.

   The still centre of the story is the scene, original to Chaucer, between Virginius and his daughter, here named for the first time:

   'Doghter,' quod he, 'Virginia, by thy name—'   (213)

Before this, speech is used only to advance the plot: Claudius' accusations, Apius' exercise of false judgement. In the exchange between parent and child, speech expresses emotion, and the events of the tale, which in the *Roman* proceed at a steady pace throughout, are held up for their lamentations. The passage constitutes in effect a commentary on the action, and it concentrates in itself all the pathos that the spare narrative refrains from expressing.

Themes

Historial as the tale of Virginia was believed to be, in the Physician's Tale it is presented as something more than or other than a sequence of facts. It is not easy, however, to find a satisfactory meaning for it, or even a set of themes that make consistent sense; nor, given the story, is it easy to imagine what such a meaning might be. Faced with similar plot elements of an unjust judge, sex, and death, Shakespeare notoriously came up with a drama categorized by default as a 'problem play', *Measure for Measure.*

   The first problem lies simply in establishing the cultural basis of the tale. Its setting is, strictly speaking, pagan, but this is barely indicated by Chaucer, in the opening reference to Livy and a single mention of a 'temple' (119). Instead, a Christian reading is repeatedly postulated: in Nature's discourse on God, whose 'vicaire general' she is; by Virginia's frequent references to God, and her comparison of herself to Jephtha's daughter; and in the emphasis on virginity and other virtues associated with medieval Catholicism. Virginia's fiancé, who figures in Livy's version of the story, accordingly disappears from Jean de Meun's and Chaucer's. Female sexual honour, in a broader sense than virginity, was also of supreme importance in Roman culture, and, as the stories of Lucretia and all those other women cited by Dorigen indicate, its loss was literally a fate worse than death. St Augustine had made clear the theological distinction—which is also an anthropological one—between guilt, shame, and pollution, and this interpretation would render both Lucretia's suicide and the killing of Virginia gratuitous and sinful. St Jerome, however, had thoroughly confused the categories, and the early Church had canonized some women who had killed themselves to preserve their chastity. As late as the twelfth century, Gratian, in his compendium of canon law, concluded that the avoidance of rape was the only justification for suicide. The Middle Ages combined many features of a shame culture, which sets the highest value on honour and reputation, with a guilt culture, which operates on the principles of an inner conscience. Stories such as those of Lucretia, Virginia, and the virgin martyrs could therefore be given peculiarly schizophrenic readings. Popular piety did not tend to make nice Augustinian distinctions where female sexuality was at issue. Virginius' act of murder, however, is more problematic: by most human as well as theological principles, he is wrong, and Chaucer removes the element of urgent impulse that explains his action in the sources. Jephtha's killing of his daughter, recalled by Virginia, is condemned at the level of historical fact by medieval biblical commentators. Yet if Virginius' action is justifiable only in terms of a pagan shame culture, the status of perfection accorded to virginity by the Church is alone sufficient to make the story comprehensible in medieval cultural terms (and even after the Reformation, Shakespeare endorsed the value of virginity to Isabella by making her a postulant nun). The tale seems to offer, and require, admiration both for inward virtue and for an outward honour that can express itself in murder.

The explicit moralization offered can be equally contradictory, or baffling. That 'no man woot whom God wol smyte' (278) is safe as a platitude, but its particular relation to the story is unclear. Virginia's virtue ensures an early death: the survivors are those who know 'the olde daunce' (79), poachers turned gamekeepers. The advice to parents to chastise their children lest they perish is deeply ironic in the light of what follows, but it is an irony of which the tale seems unaware.

Occasional efforts have been made to justify this muddled morality by fathering it on the Physician; the Tale would thus become a sophisticated literary exposure of a morally inadequate narrator. This will not do, for several reasons: because the muddle over the value of unblemished sexuality was so widespread even within the Church; because the portrait of the Physician cannot justify such an interpretation—it is too big a jump to go from the fact that his vast medical scholarship left him little time or inclination for biblical reading (I(A) 429–38) to blaming him for subtle changes in a story that has its outlines already established in Latin and French texts; and because there is no evidence that the story was written with him in mind. Even if it was composed specifically for the *Canterbury Tales* and not earlier, many tales seem to have been written before their ascription to particular tellers. The only lines that link the tale to the Physician come after it is finished, so there is no prologue, such as Chaucer supplies for the Pardoner, to cue an ironic interpretation. The ascription is appropriate enough in rhetorical terms: the Physician is a professional man with pretensions to learning and status, but without the social rank that would call for a romance; nor does he have the low rank or downright rascality that would associate him with *cherles tales*, or the ecclesiatical connections that would suggest something overtly pious. Chaucer does not have so many pilgrims left who would be appropriate for a story of this particular kind. The Man of Law, Merchant, and perhaps the Clerk and Manciple would be almost the only alternatives to the Physician; and on the basis of their portraits in the General Prologue (disregarding, that is, any extra development allotted to them in relation to the tales they do in fact tell), any of them would have been suitable.

If one cannot explain away the tale by reference to its teller, its relationship to its source does indicate one line of thematic development that Chaucer takes up. The context for the story in the *Roman* is the debate between Reason and the Lover, and Reason is arguing that love—not sexual love but good love, *bonne amor* (*Roman* 5489)—is superior to justice because universal charity would render justice unnecessary. The story of Apius is told as an exemplum of the corruption of justice without love. The Physician's Tale insists that injustice can make even good love, a father's paternal care, dance to its tune:

> For love, and nat for hate, thou most be deed.   (225)

The line appears in the *Roman* as a comment from the narrator; here, Virginius is given full awareness of the paradoxes of his own actions.

> O deere doghter, endere of my lyf . . .   (218)
>
> O doghter, which that art my laste wo,
> An in my lyf my laste joye also . . .   (221–2)
>
> My pitous hand moot smyten of thyn heed. (226)

His sentencing her, seated in his hall and summoning her before him to pronounce her death for love, mirrors Apius' sentence uttered for 'lecherie' in open court to the father he has summoned.

The story presents an extreme instance of that pervasive concern of the *Tales*, innocent suffering. Virginia is cast more completely in the role of passive victim than any other leading character. The world of the tale is one where moral hierarchy is in chaos. In Livy, the public killing sparks off an uprising by the Roman people that restores rightful order; in Chaucer, the private killing is largely separated in the train of cause and effect from the revolt, and a popular uprising in any case is by the fourteenth century antihierarchical, a paradoxical way of reasserting order. It is a world where sexual maturation (only Chaucer specifies Virginia's age, as fourteen) is closely associated with death, where love expresses itself in murder, and unblemished virtue can avoid corruption only by destruction. The ending claims to offer a moral, but it fails to meet many of the issues raised. *Measure for Measure* deals with similar issues, but it is written with a far greater sense of the difficulties involved: I doubt if any future generations of readers will accord the Physician's Tale as high a ranking among Chaucer's works as the play has recently been accorded among Shakespeare's. The potential is there, but the tale deflects audience response away from a questioning of moral values or even the horror of the facts, the *historial sooth*, into *pitee* and a bland admiration for virtue. What makes the story so problematic is that Virginia can express, and the narration apparently endorse, an unquestioning conformity to patterns of conventional sexuality, filial obedience, and piety, in circumstances that cry out for a sense of moral difficulty:

> Blissed be God that I shal dye a mayde! (248)

The conventionality, whether modern readers like it or not, is the point of the tale. But it is not the final point: once again, the meaning the tale would have in isolation is modified by its context in the whole *Canterbury Tales*.

Ian Donaldson, *The Rapes of Lucretia* (Oxford, 1982) discusses the cultural problems raised by stories of the Lucretia–Virginia variety. For Gratian on suicide, see the *Decretum*, pt. ii c. 23 q. 5 ch. 11 (ed. A. Friedberg, *Corpus juris canonici*, vol. i (Leipzig, 1879)).
Ellis, *Patterns*, ch. 8, gives a useful analysis of the Tale, including the parallels between the two 'trial' scenes.
Anne Middleton, 'The *Physician's Tale* and Love's Martyrs: "ensaumples mo than ten" as a Method in the Canterbury Tales', *ChR* 8 (1973–4), 9–32, is an interesting and extensive study of all aspects of the Tale.

The Tale in Context

Whether Chaucer intended the Physician's Tale to follow the Franklin's or not, the two offer very precisely different readings of the problem of female sexuality. The similarity of the story of Virginia to the exempla summarized by Dorigen, of women who preferred death to rape, is obvious. Yet, where Virginius chooses to preserve his daughter's physical integrity and honour at the cost of destroying her, and despite the innocence of her will and conscience, Arveragus is prepared to take the opposite course. Dorigen's will is likewise innocent: she has never had any intention of committing adultery. Arveragus places that purity of intention above physical shame, inward virtue above outward pollution. The Franklin's Tale thus operates more by the values of a guilt culture (though it is not, of course, presented as fully Christian), even while it recognizes, in Arveragus' order to his wife never to speak of it, that both they and society at large care about reputation and honour. The tales work by different sets of ideals; and those of the Physician's Tale, of virginity and shame, are much more formulaic than the patience, *trouthe*, and *gentillesse* of the Franklin's. The comparison does not help to make the Physician's Tale any more acceptable.

The tale acquires other significance too from its setting in the wider context of the *Tales*. It is one of the most striking examples (the deaths of Ugolino's children in the Monk's Tale being the nearest equivalent) of the suffering of the innocent, the problem that Palamon sees as threatening the moral order of the universe. Other tales—the Prioress's, the Second Nun's—offer a justification and recompense for such suffering in terms of Christian martyrdom; but although the Physician's Tale suggests a similar pattern, the pagan setting holds it back from any endorsement, either by statement from the narrator or by miracle within the narrative. Virginia's death remains gratuitous, a witness to the destructive power of evil.

The one tale with which the Physician's is certainly linked, the Pardoner's, takes up precisely this point. The Host's comments between the two tales introduces the idea: Virginia may enjoy the gifts of Nature and the Pardoner's rioters the gifts of Fortune, but both sets of gifts are equally 'cause of deeth' (296). The rioters may be destroyed by their own evil, but Virginia is not saved by her innocence.

The two tales are in many ways antitypes: certainly the main characters are. Virginia is an embodiment of virtue, the rioters embody sin; and the two states are defined in terms precisely opposite to each other. She is temperate, and avoids wine and its associated lechery (58–9) and anything resembling a revel; the rioters, as their designation indicates, are identified with such things, drink and 'luxurie' included (481–7). Yet both stories show violent and unnatural death striking when it is least looked for.

There are two lines in the tale that run against this presentation of Virginia as a model of virtue, and that serve as a reminder of how far she is from being a mere personification. These are the lines that connect the tale not with the Pardoner's but with the wider dramatic context of the debate on the nature of women. Virginia's purity can be preserved from corruption only by death, for without that, time and full womanhood may do their work:

> For al to soone may she lerne loore
> Of booldnesse, whan she woxen is a wyf. (70–1)

They are the only openly cynical lines in the whole tale, and peculiarly gratuitous. Mary may be the pattern for all virgins, but Alison of Bath is the model for wives, and by this reading it is a short step from one to the other.

For a further discussion of the connection between the Physician's and Pardoner's Tales, see Cooper, *Structure*, pp. 154–60.

Style

If the tale recalls the *Legend of Good Women* in length and subject, its style is very different. It cuts the invocations, apostrophes, and rhetorical questions that characterize the legends, and omits the comments on the process of the story or its telling that pervade them and most of the non-fabliau tales of the Canterbury series. Even the addresses to fictional audiences are restrained: 'Ye maistresses, in youre olde lyf', 'Ye fadres and ye moodres eek also', are very different from such things as the Man of Law's 'O queenes, lyvynge in prosperitee . . .'. There are no overt appeals to the listener for pity or compassion, no scattering of the text with 'Alas!' Affective words are related to the characters' own emotions rather than being the author's or narrator's directions to the audience, and they are used to indicate fact rather than interpretation: Apius is 'fals', even 'cursed' (since he has been taken over by the fiend, 130), Virginius does have 'fadres pitee stikynge thurgh his herte', the 'routhe and pitee' felt by the people take practical expression in their uprising. The mode of the tale is towards factual statement, in keeping with the description of it as 'historial thyng'. Even the expression of emotion, when it does come, takes factual form, in the reporting of direct speech from father and daughter. Virginia's passivity is demonstrated linguistically through her effective limitation to being the object of verbs, of other people's actions.

The style of the tale is however more varied than this might suggest. The description of Virginia at the beginning is something of a rhetorical *tour de force*: the imagined speech of a personified Nature—'thus semeth me that Nature wolde seye' (29)—is a world away from the sober narration of the main plot. The limitations of art compared with Nature are not only stated, but reflected in the language: the greatest artists can only 'forge and bete, | Or grave, or peynte', 'grave, or peynte, or forge, or bete' in an endless round of repeated process (14–17), while Nature's creation has a freedom and an authority lacking in them:

> He that is the formere principal
> Hath maked me his vicaire general,
> To forme and peynten erthely creaturis
> Right as me list.   (19–22)

Virginia's looks are described through association with established images of courtly perfection—the lily and rose of Emily and so many other romance heroines—and by reference to the gods who embody her qualities: Phoebus for the sunshine of her hair, Pallas for wisdom. Her virtues call on further rhetorical resources: hyperbole ('a thousand foold moore vertuous was she', 40), repeated syntax patterns, epanalepsis, polyptoton:

> Shamefast she was in maydens shamefastnesse.   (55)

The tone throughout demands audience acceptance of such beauty and virtue, so the sudden drop into cynicism in the comment on the boldness of wives is all the more disruptive. The courtly mode makes only a brief return later in the tale, when Apius sees Virginia going to the temple in a brief scene reminiscent of Troilus' first sight of Criseyde:

> Anon his herte chaunged and his mood,
> So was he caught with beautee of this mayde.   (126–7)

But this is no secular ideal: 'the feend' enters his heart at once, and it is not love that is in question.

The section of advice to guardians and parents contains the main similitudes of the tale: the 'theef of venysoun', the shepherd and wolf. As is appropriate for such a didactic passage, the expression tends towards apophthegm and *sententia*:

> Of alle tresons sovereyn pestilence
> Is whan a wight bitrayseth innocence.   (91–2)

The syntax here proceeds through a series of complex causal relationships, balances, and generalizations: 'lest . . . for whoso . . . though . . . whil . . . for . . . if'. The syntax of the main narrative proceeds much more paratactically: 'and . . . for . . . that'. The spareness of the main narration allows the events of the story to speak for themselves: further comment could only reduce their power. It is no accident that, alone among the tales of pathos in the Canterbury series, this one is told not in rhyme royal, with its encouragement of apostrophe and emotional commentary, but in riding rhyme.

The devices that Chaucer uses elsewhere to elicit emotional response are here concentrated in Virginius' speech: interjections—'allas . . . allas!'— and apostrophes: 'O deere doghter . . . o gemme of chastitee'. Virginia's request for leisure to lament her death is something of a tear-jerker, but there is no lament given to distract from the pity of the fact of her death. This is the climax of the tale, and the rest of the action is disposed of in very summary fashion.

The Physician–Pardoner Link

'The words of the Hoost to the Phisician and the Pardoner' form a skilful transition from one tale to the next, at the thematic level as well as the dramatic. The Host is sufficiently moved by the story of Virginia to swear, curse the judge, and utter a few platitudes on how the gifts of Nature—here specifically 'beautee'—are as fatal as the gifts of Fortune: these are to be the subject of the next tale. The Host's emotions are uncomplicated by any questioning of the morality of the previous story, either as regards Virginius' killing of his daughter or the suffering of the innocent. He claims, however, that his heart is so affected by the story that it requires some medicine— either from the Physician, or some 'moyste and corny ale', or a 'myrie tale'. There is some critical theory—or a parody of it—even in this: one of the medieval justifications for fiction, and for the apparently irreligious pastime of storytelling, was the therapeutic qualities of stories in raising sick men's spirits and keeping the well cheerful and healthy. The Host's notion that ale will do the same job hardly endorses the seriousness of the justification.

Harry Bailly calls on the Pardoner for 'myrthe or japes'; the *gentils*, forseeing some 'ribaudye', demand a moral story instead. But there is an alehouse to hand to assist the Host's recovery, and the Pardoner will think up 'som honest thyng' while he indulges in a bout of two of those very sins he is about to preach against, drinking and gluttony. (The third sin, blasphemy, has been nicely exemplified by Harry Bailly at the start.) The contrast between the vicious teller and the honest tale is already set up in these lines.

The pause for a drink has led to some fine novelistic flights of fancy describing Chaucer's scene-setting of the pilgrims sitting around in the tavern listening to the Pardoner. If anything, the passage indicates his lack of interest in the pilgrimage as such: neither here nor at the end of the tale is it clear whether the story is told in the tavern or on the road. The emphasis is all on the substance of the tales, not the physical accidents of their telling.

A number of manuscripts contain only the first twelve lines of the link, giving the conclusion to the Physician's Tale but not the introduction to the Pardoner's. This may represent an early draft, but clear evidence is as usual lacking. One couplet (291–1) is different in this abbreviated version; a second couplet (297–8, which reworks the sentiments of 292–3 on Virginia's beauty) is found only in the short form of the link, and probably has no rightful place in the full text.

On the medieval medicinal justification for fiction, see Olson, *Literature as Recreation* (p. 103 above).

The Pardoner's Prologue and Tale

Date and Text

The Pardoner's Tale belongs to the great period of the writing of the *Canterbury Tales*—not only on grounds of art, but because of its use of such sources as Innocent III's *De miseria* and Jerome's *Adversus Jovinianum* that were at hand for the writing of the Man of Law's Prologue and most of the tales of Fragments III, IV, and V. There is no proof that the Tale was composed with the Prologue in mind; they work together brilliantly, but the tale has a grim power of its own independent of its speaker. Some of the pecularities of the opening homiletic material, however, and the transition back to the frame at the end of the tale, confirm that the conception of Prologue, Tale, and dramatic ending probably developed as a unit.

The texts of the Prologue and Tale show many minor variants, but most are clearly scribal. Hengwrt, Ellesmere, and a number of other manuscripts give eleven short glosses to the tale, indicating sources in the Bible, Jerome, and (once) John of Salisbury's *Policraticus*.

The Prologue: Sources and Analogues

Treatises, sermons, and statutes all bear witness to the abuses of pardoners' methods of collecting money. Their practices were condemned by moralists and satirists within and without the Church, and were the subject of endless clerical diatribes. The invectives were mostly aimed against the selling of pardons for cash, and not against the sale of false relics; but if that practice was not generally associated with pardoners, it was similarly subject to satire, the best-known instance being Boccaccio's gem of a tale of Fra Cipolla. There are plenty of stories too of pardoners overcoming the resistance of potential donors by declaring that adulteresses or similar categories of sinner would not be able to give. How much Chaucer was drawing on written sources, or a kind of pardoner folklore, and how much on observed practice, is impossible to say. Certainly there is nothing in the Pardoner's Prologue, except the wit and the cheek, that would come as a surprise to Chaucer's audience.

The Prologue takes confessional form, but it is not confession in any theological sense: the Pardoner is talking, or boasting, to his companions. To have a character declare his own practices and motives is a standard method of displaying vice in moral allegory; Langland's Sins and Jean de Meun's personified vices or typical characters all expound their true nature in a way that shows more of self-congratulation and advertisement than abhorrence. One figure from the *Roman* is of particular relevance to the Pardoner: Faux-Semblant, 'False Seeming'. There is less of a match between the figures than between La Vieille and the Wife of Bath, but the hypocrite Pardoner's open declaration of his hidden wickedness and a few of his lines and phrases closely recall Jean de Meun's figure. Faux-Semblant, however, can take any form—clerical or lay, male or female—and has a particular fondness for the shape of a friar. One curiosity of Chaucer's borrowing is that the closest similarities in phrasing are not to the French text but to the English, pseudo-Chaucerian, translation of this section of the *Roman* (Prologue 403 and *Romaunt of the Rose* C 6837; 407–8 and *Romaunt* B 5763–4; 443–4 and *Romaunt* C 6845–6). The third of these has no parallel in the French; and Chaucer takes the second not from Faux-Semblant's 'confession' but from Reason's exposé of corrupt preachers six thousand lines earlier (*Roman* 5113–14; the three passages occur close together in the *Romaunt* only because of the omission of a long section of the original).

The gullibility of the Pardoner's congregation can appear so caricatured as to be implausible; modern analogues to his false relics provide abundant testimony to the contrary. The kind of newspapers currently sold in supermarkets in the United States, in which British advertising standards no more apply than they do to the Pardoner, are stuffed with advertisements that make a similar double appeal to the superstition and the graft of their readers. To take just two of the miracle-working talismans offered (with certificates of authenticity) in a single issue of *Weekly World News*: a gold cross containing some Holy Earth of Fatima promises not only instant success in the casinos but also unquestioning love ('all those you adore are faithful to you always') in return for a mere ten dollars; a 'Fast Money-drawing Soap', the secrets of which 'are all in the Bible', comes with an assurance that there will be 'lots of money drawn to you like a magnet when you wash, shower or bathe with this soap'. Beside this, the sales talk of the Pardoner to an uneducated and illiterate congregation begins to sound positively restrained. Such advertising also demonstrates very clearly another quality it shares with the Pardoner: an utter contempt for the people who can fall for such nonsense—a contempt the Pardoner extends to the fate of their souls.

Germaine Dempster, *Sources and Analogues*, pp. 409–14, gives part of the speech of Faux-Semblant selected from the *Roman*, 11065–974, and some analogues to the 'gaude' of getting women to give. Boccaccio's tale of Fra Cipolla is *Decameron* 6, 10.

On the connection of the Pardoner with Faux-Semblant, see Kean, *Art of Narrative*, pp. 96–109, and for a more sweeping view, Lawton, *Chaucer's Narrators*, ch. 2.

The number of *Weekly World News* used here was that for 14 May 1985 (vol. 6: 31), but any issue will serve to make the point.

The Prologue: Structure, Themes, and Style

The structure and the main theme of the Pardoner's Prologue are indicated by his triple allusion to his text:

> My theme is alwey oon, and evere was—
> *Radix malorum est Cupiditas.*
>
> (333–4; cf. 400–1, 425–6)

It is his own personal theme as well as the text of his sermon—the vice that he both preaches against and practises (427–8). The first section of his 'confession' is devoted to expounding his techniques (335–99); the second, to making quite clear what his 'entente' is in preaching—to make money, or if the going gets rough, to 'spitte out venym', but certainly not to save souls (400–34); the third section extends his avarice to cover his whole way of life, and also relates his vice to the processes of storytelling (435–62).

There is a superficial similarity of imagery throughout the Prologue that at once masks and expresses a deeper perversion. Part of the Pardoner's success lies in the fact that he deals in the everyday concerns of rural life: cows and oxen, cocks crowing, wheat, oats, wells, soup, mittens. It is a world of material fact, not religious doctrine; but he never moves beyond the material to the spiritual. His relics are likewise mere physical objects, bones and rags. He uses Latin 'to saffron with my predicacioun', an image drawn from gourmet food; he looks like a dove as he addresses people, stretching out his neck to look around—brilliant as a visual comparison, but, in the context of preaching the Word of God, a ludicrously animalistic downgrading of the dove of the Holy Ghost. Damnation is similarly trivialized into the commonplace in the image of souls going blackberrying. He rejects in so many words the apostolic life of labour and poverty, preferring the solid gains of 'moneie, wolle, chese and whete', wine and wenches. If doves are a normal part of the life of every village or great household, the serpent that stings with the venom of its tongue is biblical (Jas. 3:8). The speech that starts, in fact, with a concern for the merely physical, turns into an overt rejection of religious values.

The Pardoner's high regard for storytelling is of a piece with his skill as a preacher. That 'lewed peple loven tales olde' was a fact acknowledged in all handbooks on the art of preaching, and there were numerous collections of such *ensamples* made for preachers' use. The Pardoner may even, as a side-effect, bring people to repentance through his sermons. His main concern, however, is to line his own pockets. Stories in sermons—fiction in general— were supposed to be morally profitable; the Pardoner has discovered that they can also be financially profitable. It is yet another instance of his determined conversion of the spiritually valuable into material wealth, of

God into Mammon. His Tale can thus both be morally abhorrent, as a cynical exploitation of religion for his own financial advantage, and yet draw men away from evil. It is at once an image of how one should not live, and how he himself does.

> Though myself be a ful vicious man,
> A moral tale yet I yow telle can.   (459–60)

Knowledge of evil in the Pardoner works to enable him not to choose the good but to exploit it.

The line of argument that declares the Pardoner to be a congenital eunuch and, by interpretation, spiritually sterile, has also seen in the Prologue an image of utter evil on the Augustinian model, of sin feeding upon sin in a tortured agony of despair. Such a reading can only, however, be imposed when one starts from Augustine. The text of the Prologue as Chaucer wrote it shows no signs whatever of despair or torture on the part of its speaker. Its self-congratulatory complacency is indeed one of the most horrific things about it—and the source of much of its comedy: it is an anti-authoritarian flouting of Christian principle that has touches of carnival licence in it as well as plenty of the devil. Like most Chaucerian satire, it condemns by wit and sheer outrageousness rather than by invective. It is in any case an absurdity to argue that the Pardoner ought to show the Augustinian pattern of tortured sinfulness; the point of the Prologue is that he ought not to be behaving like this at all.

Dewey R. Faulkner (ed.), *Twentieth Century Interpretations of the Pardoner's Tale* (Englewood Cliffs, NJ, 1973), is a very useful collection of essays on the Prologue and Tale. C. W. R. D. Moseley's capable edition of the Prologue and Tale notes the biblical parallel at 413; A. C. Spearing's edition is also useful (see p. 59 above).

Alastair Minnis, 'Chaucer's Pardoner and the Office of Preacher', in Piero Boitani and Anna Torti (eds.), *Intellectuals and Writers in Fourteenth-century Europe: The J. A. W. Bennett Memorial Lectures 1984* ('Tübingen and Cambridge, 1986), pp. 88–119, is the fullest discussion of the implications of a vicious man's telling a moral tale.

Kellogg, 'An Augustinian Interpretation of Chaucer's Pardoner', in his *Chaucer, Langland, Arthur*, pp. 245–68 (repr. from *Speculum*, 26 (1951), 465–81), and Miller, 'Chaucer's Pardoner', in Schoeck and Taylor, *Chaucer Criticism*, pp. 221–44, are the classic exegetical studies of the Pardoner. For a critique, see the articles by Benson and Green cited on p. 59, and Gabriel Josipovici, 'Fiction and Game in *The Canterbury Tales*', excerpted in Faulkner (above) from *Critical Quarterly*, 7 (1965), 193–7.

The Tale: Genre

'Lo, sires, thus I preche', declares the Pardoner at the end of his tale (915), and it does indeed have a good deal in common with a sermon—a biblical text; an indictment of sin; the main story as illustrative exemplum; the application of the story to the congregation; and a concluding prayer. These elements do not altogether fit the formula for sermon construction, however, and a number of other features fail to match such a generic model. The biblical text precedes the Prologue, not the sermon; the exemplum dominates over everything else; the application has more to do with the Pardoner's acquisitiveness than with the substance of the tale; the prayer appears to fall outside the sermon and into the frame. None the less, given that vernacular sermons were often more loosely constructed than Latin ones, and given the particular requirements here of the context—that the Pardoner has been asked for a story, and so the extent of the exemplum is justified by the *Tales* rather than the genre—the category of sermon is elastic enough to serve.

Chaucer may have thought of it in the looser terms of homily: when the Pardoner has run through the opening didactic sections with their short exemplary anecdotes, he announces,

> But sires, now wol I telle forth my tale.   (660)

This line could simply mark the next section of the address, but the dominant impression is not of the structural unity of a single sermon, but of homiletic prefatory matter leading up to a story that fulfils both a function within the sermon and also the Pardoner's obligation in the storytelling competition.

Robert P. Merrix, 'Sermon Structure in the *Pardoner's Tale*', *ChR* 17 (1982–3), 235–49,
    contains a useful critique of attempts to fit the Tale into the sermon mould.

Sources and Analogues

The tale of the men who find death in the shape of treasure is widespread in both East and West, and Chaucer's precise source is not known. The versions current in the late Middle Ages, in Latin, Italian, and German, show many points in common with Chaucer's version, but some major differences. They all start, not with the rioters seeking death, but with a philosopher or holy man—sometimes even Christ—finding the treasure and directing the thieves to it. The malefactors are usually three in number: the one sent to town for food often brings specifically bread and wine. In one Italian saint's play, probably of the fifteenth century, he asks for poison to kill rats, like Chaucer's youngest rioter who claims to be troubled by rats and a polecat.

Most of the analogues are much shorter and sparer than Chaucer's version: they are *novelle* or exemplary tales. The widespread appearance of some of the tale's motifs should none the less be a warning against over-interpretation of Chaucer's version, despite his greater elaboration of the story. Readings that regard the old man as evil, or see Chaucer writing demonic allegories of the Trinity and the Eucharist (as distinct from alluding to them), have to contend with Chaucer's apparent lack of concern about changing the substance or emphasis of the analogues in these matters.

The tale of the rioters contains few allusions; most of those that do appear cluster round the old man. His knocking on the ground to ask his mother the earth to let him in comes from the first elegy of Maximian, widely read as a school text and also translated into Middle English; and he quotes the Bible to the rioters (743–4, from Lev. 19: 32, quoted in a gloss). Attempts have been made to read exegetical parallels into the oak, but they soon get lost in a forest of sacred groves, terebinths, and other dissimilar phenomena. A more certain biblical allusion is the rioters' threat that 'Deeth shal be deed' (710), from Hosea 13: 14—a text taken as a prophecy of the Redemption, and so doubly ironic here.

The homiletic material at the start of the tale draws on a variety of sources. The sins of gluttony and drunkenness, gambling ('hazardrye'), and blasphemy, collectively known as the 'tavern sins', were favourite subjects of preachers and moralists. Chaucer draws a number of ideas from two authorities, Innocent's *De miseria* and Jerome's *Adversus Jovinianum*. Many of his biblical references are already collected in these texts. He also draws briefly on Seneca's *Epistles* (493–7). The stories of 'Stilbon' (correctly Chilon—there is some confusion with a character from Seneca) and Demetrius are found in John of Salisbury's *Policraticus*, which also supplies some of Jankin's examples of wicked wives.

Most of this learning is kept hidden: it is Chaucer's, not the Pardoner's. The impression given by the text of the poem—and therefore by the sermon to its hearers—is of a preacher with a good fund of exemplary stories, a smattering of learned references to flavour his preaching, and, above all, an extensive knowledge of the Bible—which apparently includes, in the Pardoner's eyes, the story of Attila the Hun (574–86).

One other work deserves a mention, though less as a source than as an inspiration to a train of thought. In the course of Reason's speech to the Lover in the *Roman de la rose* (the same speech that contains the source story of the Physician's tale of Virginia), she uses the word 'coillons', testicles. The lover objects that the word is improper. Reason replies, among other arguments, that no word can be improper, for words are a purely arbitrary means of signification, and *coillons* might just as well be called *reliques* (7108–9). It may be this that lies behind the association of the two that Chaucer puts into the mouth of Harry Bailly at the end.

Frederick Tupper, 'The Pardoner's Tale', in *Sources and Analogues*, gives Latin and Italian prose and German and Italian dramatic analogues, and also excerpts from the First Elegy of Maximian and from English homiletic material on the tavern sins. For Innocent, Jerome, John of Salisbury, and the *Roman*, see pp. 13–14.

Structure

The Pardoner's Tale shows less similarity in structure to the sermon it has been claimed to be than to other tales in the Canterbury sequence, notably the Merchant's and Manciple's, where a brief narrative introduction (here, of the 'compaignye' of rioters) is followed by a long moralistic digression before the story gets properly under way. Many tales (the Summoner's, the Nun's Priest's) put these digressions into the mouth of a character; here, they are presented as part of the Pardoner's address to his congregation—he himself is a character within his own tale.

The structure of the Tale cannot finally be separated from the Prologue. It is not just that the text for the sermon precedes the Prologue and that the theme of avarice and evil is expounded there in the Pardoner's own practices: the Prologue also acts as frame for the Tale. Once again, Chaucer is offering different ways of articulating successive stories so that their connection is something other than linear. Here, the Pardoner tells about himself preaching, and the sermon is inset within that as part of the story of his own life; and inset within the sermon is the story of the rioters. The structure is emphasized by repetitions of *tell* and *tale*. He declares at the start, 'I kan al by rote that I telle' (332), and proceeds to expound what he tells to his congregation. After describing his abuses, he announces,

> A moral tale yet I yow telle kan,
> Which I am wont to preche for to wynne.
> Now hoold youre pees! My tale I wol bigynne.   (460–2)

It is a story, in fact, of himself telling a tale. When the moralizing on the tavern sins is over, he signals the start of the main story:

> But, sires, now wol I telle forth my tale.   (660)

It scarcely matters by this time whether the 'sires' are his congregation or the pilgrim audience.

It does matter, however, at the end. 'Lo sires, thus I preche' (915) must be addressed to the pilgrims: but the lines that follow sound like the closing formula of a sermon—of this sermon, since he has ended by offering pardons:

> And Jhesu Crist, that is oure soules leche,
> So graunte yow his pardoun to receyve,
> For that is best; I wol yow nat deceyve.   (916–18)

The lines need not spoil his sales pitch: they add to his illusion of sincerity ('I wol yow nat deceyve', for once palpably true, but no doubt for the wrong reasons), and in any case Christ's pardon seems to be offered as an extra to his own rather than an alternative. The formula is certainly powerful, but it is none the less a formula, and it lacks the compelling particularity of

> Cometh up, ye wyves, offreth of youre wolle!
> Youre names I entre heer in my rolle anon;
> Into the blisse of hevene shul ye gon. (910–12)

Christ's pardon can at best be prayed for in the subjunctive; the Pardoner can give salvation for the medieval equivalent of cash down and a certificate of authenticity.

There follows, however, the oddest line of the whole performance:

> But sires, o word forgat I in my tale— (919)

and he proceeds to offer the pilgrims the relics and pardons he has already declared to be spurious. The much-debated reasons for the con-man's overreaching himself may lie not in the psychological complexity of the Pardoner, but in the phrasing of that particular line. The sermon should be finishcd by now; the Pardoner has returned to the autobiographical frame ('thus I preche'). But in the single overwhelming *entente* of avarice, the two have got mixed up. The interlocking of tale and frame is visible even in the story layout: all the manuscripts divide off the 'Host's words' from the Prologue, and the Prologue from the Tale, but there is no single point at the end where such a separation can be made. The sermon is addressed through the congregation to the pilgrim audience, and the two sets of hearers will interpret it in opposite ways. But the Pardoner is accustomed to listeners he can treat with contempt. Here, I think, he has confused the two audiences, 'forgat' that he has in fact moved outside his 'tale' to the point where the fiction has broken down. He is trying to get back in to that fiction of sincerity, to reach an audience who will serve his overriding desire for acquisition.

Within this larger structure, the 'moral thyng' that he tells has a structural logic of its own. As befits an oral delivery, its stages are clearly announced—except for the first, where the transition from the narrative setting of the 'compaignye|Of yonge folk' to the invective against drunkenness is elided so smoothly that the audience is given no opportunity to switch off their attention. After that, the shifts of subject from gluttony to gambling (589–90), to blasphemy (629–30), and to the main story (660) are all clearly signalled.

One difference of this tale from all the others of the *Canterbury Tales* is that the characters introduced in the first few lines are not particularized. The Pardoner later appears to recall 'thise riotoures thre of whiche I telle' (661), but this is in fact the first time they have been distinguished from the 'compaignye'. The revellers mentioned at the beginning are there to introduce not so much the story as the preaching against the tavern sins. The effect is to reinforce the exemplary and the sinister qualities of the story when it does get under way: almost every one of the rioters' speeches and actions has been exposed in advance as damnable.

The exemplum of the rioters manages to combine a high proportion of direct speech with a strong sense of narrative speed, especially up to the buying of the poison. The rioters start up from their places in the tavern to search for death, they run to the treasure when they are directed to it. This literal speed of movement halts only for the eerie quietness of the old man's speech, and for their contemplation of the gold. The deaths are accomplished almost in parenthesis—'what nedeth it to sermone of it moore?' (879). Most of the space in this later part of the story is devoted not to events but to the rioters' plans for their own destruction.

The move back to the congregation is accomplished smoothly. First comes the rhetorical climax—

O cursed synne of alle cursednesse!   (895)

—then the transition to the listeners' need to avoid avarice and to seek forgiveness. The offer of pardon follows easily and with spurious logic. It is in the next transition, from imagined congregation to the immediate audience of the pilgrims, that the Pardoner's smooth talk turns into a banana-skin.

Themes

The Pardoner's Tale embodies two contradictory sets of meanings. In itself, it is a powerful moral tale against avarice and the tavern sins. Spoken by the Pardoner, it becomes deeply immoral—not only as a revelation of his own vice, but as a means to advance his own love of money; and moreover he chooses this tale while drinking in the tavern setting he so fiercely condemns. Its two sets of significances are in direct opposition; but they reinforce each other rather than cancelling each other out. The Pardoner's vices become all the more unpardonable for being laid bare in the tale, and the message of the tale is all the clearer by virtue of the perversion of its purpose.

The themes of the story itself are clear enough, as befits the moral purpose of a sermon. The condemnation of the tavern sins is resounding, and, in the case of gluttony, revolting. The tale of the rioters emphasizes the power of evil to bring about its own destruction: only in Chaucer's version do the malefactors set out to seek death, the treasure being no more than a catalyst for the forces of destruction already within them. Their swearing by 'Cristes blessed body al torente' that 'death shal be deed' constitutes a blasphemy in the substance as well as the uttering of the oaths: they are arrogating to themselves a power shown only by God in the Redemption.

The threat is also a powerful example of a pervasive motif of the tale—the reduction of the spiritual to the physical, such as has been shown already by the Pardoner in his Prologue. The destruction of Death is taken as a material quest. The condemnation of the tavern sins likewise allows the Pardoner to concentrate on the physical. Gluttony is the sin that has most to do with the body, and the physiological processes of eating, defecating, and letting off wind are described with horrible relish. Cooking becomes the material obverse of transubstantiation, in which the substance of the eucharistic elements of bread and wine are transformed, while the outward appearance, the accidents, remain the same; cooks, by contrast, 'turnen substaunce into accident' (539). The Fall is described in terms of gluttony alone, physical abuse, rather than as a spiritual rejection of God. The physical effects of drunkenness are brilliantly evoked. Blasphemy consists of the tearing to pieces of 'oure blissed Lordes body' (474, cf. 651–4, 692, 695). Even the dice are 'bones' (656). Bread and wine are potentially the redemptive elements of the Eucharist; when the youngest rioter—the Son of this unholy Trinity, though that is unstressed in the text—fetches them from the town, it is to turn them into the vehicle of bodily death. Even the treasure of the traditional tale becomes, in the mouth of the Pardoner, an ironic transmutation into the material of the *infinitum thesaurum*, the infinite treasury of grace stored up by Christ and the saints on which pardoners were supposedly able to draw cheques in the form of indulgences.

The one figure in the tale who can see beyond this materialism to God is the old man. He envisages death, it is true, in corporeal terms—the death of the body rather than the salvation of the soul—but he can pray for the rioters' salvation by the Redemption (766).

What is the old man? His equivalent in the analogues is a wise man or philosopher, even Christ: here he keeps the wisdom, now associated also with old age, and the virtue—a reading of him as evil has to ignore the way Chaucer presents him. He cannot be Death, since death is his greatest desire, and part of the point of the tale, paradoxically, is that death is not a material thing that can be found—the gold is death to the rioters, but only by metonymy for the self-destruction they bring with them. He is not the Wandering Jew, though he has something of the same compelling mythic power. Nor is he *vetus homo*, unredeemed or sinful man, since he knows all about the Redemption, quotes Holy Writ, and sees himself as following 'Goddes wille' (726). He is what the text says he is: an old man seeking death. The implications of that, however, are extensive.

In the first place, he is a familiar medieval type, though more familiar in visual than literary art. Allegorical pictures of the universality of death invariably show Death leading away the young, the beautiful, the rich, the carefree, and leaving behind cripples, beggars, and the aged, who reach towards him with outstretched hands. The theme had gained extra poignancy at the time of the Black Death, when the plague struck most viciously at the young and healthy—and it is 'pestilence' that is Death's weapon in this story (679). At one level, the tale is giving verbal form to the pictorial allegory of death. The particular power associated with the old man, however, which has prompted so many attempts to explain him, comes in part at least from his most literal meaning. He is the truth of what the rioters are seeking: life without death. He is not immortal (725–6), but like the Wandering Jew or Swift's Struldbrugs, he is cursed with that most terrible of human myths, an infinitely prolonged old age. He has learnt that earthly treasure is valueless compared with a pauper's shroud (734–6); the rioters chase off after the gold and find in the gift of Fortune the death they had scorned.

The rioters are 'exemplary' characters: the point of their appearance in a sermon is to warn the congregation off similar vices. They are accordingly never given individual names, and are often referred to by their degree of sinfulness—'the proudeste', 'the worste'. The figure outside the Tale who most nearly resembles them is however the Pardoner himself. He too is on a quest for treasure, and the quest becomes explicit at the end of the tale, in his double appeal to his congregation and to his pilgrim audience. The Pardoner makes it quite clear why he has come on the pilgrimage: he has only one *entente*, of acquisition (403), and when he turns to the pilgrims he is aiming to put it into practice. Just as his spurious pardons are a corruption and perversion of penance, so the penitential aim of pilgrimage is corrupted to pecuniary ends. The morality of his tale is similarly perverted for his own unethical purposes.

The rioters find Death at the end of their quest; the Pardoner finds a threat of castration—'Lat kutte hem of!'. It is at this point, if anywhere, that the image of the Pardoner as spiritual eunuch is suggested: his Prologue and Tale have insistently deprived things of their potential spiritual meanings, and the Host's threat would show in physical form his lack of spiritual fruitfulness. But the passage is not allegory, nor is the threat given literal expression. All that happens is that the Pardoner's quest for income is guaranteed unfruitful, and he has to perform his one act of charity and reconciliation in the entire work, in exchanging a kiss with Harry Bailly. The two elder rioters had killed the third 'as in game' (829, 880–1); the Knight turns aside the violence that threatens their own 'pleye'. That the Pardoner is so angry, however (957), adds the final sin of wrath to complete the list: pride, in his contempt for God and his fellow-men; gluttony, in his fondness for wine, and which he himself has associated with the Fall; lechery, in his boasting about wenches, and his other more doubtful sexual practices; envy, in backbiting and defamation (415); sloth, in his spiritual deadness; and above all, avarice—the sin that was seen as the most threatening of the later Middle Ages by many moralists, including the Parson, who repeats the Pardoner's own text: 'The roote of alle harmes is Coveitise' (X(I) 739).

There is one last irony in the tale, in Harry Bailly's outburst,

> 'Thou woldest make me kisse thyn olde breech,
> And swere it were a relyk of a seint,
> Though it were with thy fundement depeint!'   (948–50)

It is the last, and potentially the most damaging, reduction of the spiritual to the earthly, for one of the most prized relics of the shrine of St Thomas at Canterbury, to which the pilgrims were making their way, was the saint's filthy breeches, unchanged over the years as part of the process of his mortification of the flesh. A little over a century later another Catholic pilgrim, Erasmus, was appalled by both the unspirituality of the relics and the avarice of their custodians. Chaucer almost certainly knew Langland's valuing of spiritual pilgrimage, the search for truth in the heart, above geographical pilgrimage, and the thought was by no means original with Langland. Chaucer's Pardoner is a forerunner of the Reformation, not only as an instance of corruption within the Church and as a peddler of false pardons, but because he opens the way to questioning the connections between outward forms and spiritual meaning. He threatens the harmony of this pilgrimage: what he stands for will destroy the whole basis of pilgrimage, and any possibility of the harmony of a universal church.

Faulkner's *Twentieth Century Interpretations* (p. 263 above) assembles many of the notable studies.

Good general studies include Janet Aldman, 'That We May Leere Som Wit', in Faulkner, *Twentieth Century Interpretations*, pp. 96–106; and Ian Bishop, 'The Narrative Art of the Pardoner's Tale', *MÆ* 36 (1967), 15–24.

On the old man, I have developed the line indicated by John M. Steadman, 'Old Age and *Contemptus mundi* in *The Pardoner's Tale*', reprinted in Faulkner, *Twentieth Century Interpretations*, from *MÆ* 33 (1964), 121–30, and, more particularly, Elizabeth R. Hatcher, 'Life without Death: The Old Man in Chaucer's *Pardoner's Tale*', *ChR* 9 (1974–5), 248–52.

John M. Steadman, 'Chaucer's Pardoner and the *Thesaurus meritorum*', *ELN* 3 (1965–6), 4–7, notes the connection of the Pardoner's office with the rioters' treasure.

Daniel Knapp, 'The Relyk of a Seint: A Gloss on Chaucer's Pilgrimage', *ELH* 39 (1972), 1–27, discusses the possible allusion to the relics of St Thomas in the Host's words.

John Halverson, 'Chaucer's Pardoner and the Progress of Criticism', *ChR* 4 (1970), 184–202, contains a useful survey of criticism.

The Tale in Context

The immediate context for the Pardoner's Tale, and the one that transforms it most, is the Prologue; but the significance of the two together is itself enlarged by their wider context in the *Tales*.

The contrasts between the two stories of Fragment VI have been discussed in connection with the Physician's Tale. The tellers as well as the tales are implicitly compared by the juxtaposition. The Physician should be a healer of bodies, but he tells a tale in which death is inflicted by a father on the young and healthy. Pardons should be a way to spiritual health, but the Pardoner's Tale tells of death cutting off sinners in their pride of life.

Many of the tales, from the Knight's forward, concern themselves with people's various choices of their sovereign good, their felicity or (more often) false felicity. Wealth, the choice of material over spiritual good, has been the commonest desire, just as it is among the pilgrims themselves. The Friar's summoner finished in hell for it; the Canon's Yeoman will describe alchemists pursuing the same infernal highroad. Of all the forms of secular good valued in the various tales—one's lady, sexual gratification, 'soveraynetee', marital paradise on earth—money is the one consistently, and insistently, presented as antithetical to God. The 'heigh felicitee' envisaged by the 'worste' rioter turns into grisly death from poison, and the avarice of Pardoner and rioters alike prevents their having any vision of the spiritual.

In a number of manuscripts the tales of the Physician and Pardoner are preceded by the other two-tale floating fragment of Second Nun and Canon's Yeoman. Whether or not Chaucer ever considered such a position for them, the pairing of the fragments is suggestive. Fragment VI(C) consists of Virginia's secular martyrdom after the threat of rape from an unjust judge, followed by a tale in which gold is metaphorically transmuted into death. Fragment VIII(G) consists of a saint's life in which a virgin, determined to preserve her virginity even through lawful marriage, is martyred by a spiritually blind governor likewise described as a judge (463); and following that, a tale in which the attempts to transmute base metals into gold result in spiritual death. The unholy brotherhood of the three rioters is replaced in the Second Nun's Tale by the holy company of those converted to God's true way, Valerian, Tiburce, and Maximus. Cecilia's 'bisynesse' is spiritual, that of the Canon's Yeoman and the Pardoner (399) self-seeking.

Chaucer does not insist on such cross-patterns of allusion; it is enough that the tales have a double existence, as independent stories and as elements in a larger whole. He does not insist either on the ultimate destination of his pilgrims; there is no moralizing voice damning the Pardoner as he inveighs against the rioters, and Harry Bailly's objections are raised against the Pardoner's attempt to con him rather than against his salvational status. The frame story preserves an unbroken level of the literal, of a group of people on a holiday outing, without moving to the anagogical, their final status before God's judgement. Yet just as the tales by implication comment on each other, they also comment on the pilgrims. It is the Pardoner himself who confuses his sermon exemplum with his address to the pilgrims, and in so doing he invites condemnation not only by the standards of the secular dramatic frame but also by the more rigorous standards of the stories.

There is one other tale of crucial importance to the Pardoner's: the Parson's. The Parson too tells a homily to condemn sin; but he is concerned not only with sin but with reformation and virtue. He calls his audience, not to receive pardon for cash, but to penitence. He rejects art altogether, and the comparison with the Pardoner's Tale shows why: however moral the Pardoner's material may be in itself, his rhetorical skill enables him to pervert it to evil ends. The Parson's Tale condemns the hollowness of both the substance of the Pardoner's preaching and the art with which it is presented.

On the Pardoner and the Parson, see Howard, *Idea*, ch. 6.

Style

The Pardoner can put on and off different styles with all the slickness of the quick-change artist. The Prologue is in two related styles: one for his address to the congregation, full of false assertions spuriously authenticated by physical objects; the other for addressing the pilgrims directly, where his favourite word is 'I'. The effect, appropriately enough for a figure with False-Seeming in his ancestry, is at odds with the substance: the verbal method is superb art, the effect one of colloquialism, of a distinctive speaking voice.

The Tale again has two styles, sharply differentiated from each other and from the styles of the Prologue. One is used for the overtly homiletic material, and contains some of the most high-flown rhetoric found anywhere in the *Tales*:

> O glotonye, ful of cursednesse!
> O cause first of oure confusioun!
> O original of oure dampnacioun,
> Til Crist hadde boght us with his blood agayn!
> Lo, how deere, shortly for to sayn,
> Aboght was thilke cursed vileynye! (498–503)

This is the kind of art that shamelessly calls attention to itself, and as such is profoundly inappropriate for preaching. St Augustine had stressed the need for preachers to use a plain style, and strictures against rhetorical excess had been constantly repeated throughout the Middle Ages; the Pardoner's very skill in handling words points to the lack of real substance behind them. It is a lack specifically of spiritual substance: the spin-offs from his litany of bodily evils include a recipe for extracting the marrow from bones, instructions on where not to buy wine, and a phrase-book for potential blasphemers. The dangers of the tavern sins are expressed consistently in physical or worldly terms: the stinking breath of the drunk (552), the effects of self-indulgence and of wind (513–14, 536), the bad name attached to the gambler (594–6).

The homiletic sections could almost serve as an *ars poetica* of rhetorical figures: apostrophe and *sententia*; *enumeratio*, polysyndeton and asyndeton ('est and west and north and south, | In earthe, in eir, in water', 518–19); metaphor ('dronkenesse is verry sepulture | Of mannes wit', 558–9); simile ('as . . . a styked swyn', 556); transferred epithet ('a lecherous thyng is wyn', 549); exclamation ('O, wiste a man . . .', 513); synecdoche ('the tendre mouth', 517); anaphora and parison (498–500, quoted above); periphrasis ('white and rede', 526); synonymy ('his glorie or his renoun', 625); antanaclasis (the two meanings of 'Sampsoun!', 554–5); anastrophe (the distorted word order of 530–3); diazeugma ('thise cookes how they stampe, and streyne, and grynde, | And turnen . . .', 538–9); amplification (the cooks' activities, 541–6); the use of philosophical *termes* (substance and accident, 539); exempla and hyperbole in plenty; and the list could be extended generously. The Pardoner reverts to a similar style at the end of his outburst against the 'cursed synne of alle cursedness' (895–903).

In these sections of the tale we are listening to a sophisticated and self-conscious verbal artist; and serious as much of the material is (it does slip occasionally, as with the confusion over avoiding wine and avoiding adulterated wine, 562–6), one is much more conscious of the artistry of the speaker than of the moral import of what he is saying. The Pardoner is a man who by his own account makes a rich living from corrupt preaching. The voice we are presented with here does not belong to a psychologically three-dimensional individual, but to the vicious preacher.

The story of the rioters, when it finally comes, is completely different. One almost ceases here to be aware of a voice at all; even the designations of the rioters, 'the proudeste', 'the worste', belong to the story rather than to a judgemental narrator. There are no intrusions from the teller into the narrative, to comment either on the story, as the Man of Law and the Clerk do, or on the manner of its telling, as the Knight and Squire do: here we are given the voices of the boy, the taverner, the old man, and the rioters, with minimal linking passages of essential action. Verbs and nouns, with all their directness and energy, dominate the writing. The narrative only pauses to linger on the gold, and that is a lingering that reflects the rioters' own:

> Ther they founde
> Of floryns fyne of gold ycoyned rounde

Wel ny an eighte busshels, as hem thoughte.
No lenger thanne after Deeth they soughte,
But ech of hem so glad was of that sighte,
For that the floryns been so faire and brighte,
That doun they sette hem by this precious hoord.   (769–75)

Throughout the story, stylistic detail, as here, confirms the larger thematic issues. The rioters' mode of speech is strongly contrasted with that of the old man. The sense of mystery and power about him derives in part from the fact that he talks in metaphors: exchanging youth for age, knocking on his mother's gate, the crooked way, finding Death. To these he adds biblical allusions and the formulae of prayer. The rioters talk in short phrases with an abundance of oaths, and mostly about practicalities. When they do use abstract words, it is in their most reductive senses: 'myrthe' is simply a life of dissipation, 'grace' good luck, 'felicitee' having a good time, and 'trouthe' a pledge of mutual self-interest preserved no longer than expediency dictates. This reduction of everything, including language, to material fact includes the metaphor of a personified Death—the 'privee theef', understood by them literally: they set out to kill him, they run to find him under the tree.

It is crucial for the homiletic function of the story, its status as a 'moral thyng', that it should condemn a whole way of life rather than three individuals. The avoidance of particularity is a crucial part of this. After the mention of Flanders in the first line, the story is effectively locationless: its scenes are given moral as much as topographical setting—the tavern, the crooked way, perhaps (in view of the sinister associations of the 'forest syde' in the Wife of Bath's and Friar's Tales) also the tree. Descriptive adjectives are rare, except when the gold is mentioned. The rioters, the boy, and the old man are none of them named; only one name is heard in the whole story, and that is a name that implies not individuality but universality—

Ther cam a privee theef men clepeth Deeth.   (675)

The pursuit of Death is suggestive of allegory, but outside the old man's speeches the language keeps the tale solidly in the physical world—both a world of material objects, and a world that cannot admit any element of spiritual life.

Benson, *Chaucer's Drama of Style*, ch. 3, and Ralph W. V. Elliott, 'The Pardoner's Sermon and its Exemplum' (reprinted by Faulkner (see p. 263) from *The Nun's Priest's Tale and the Pardoner's Tale* (Oxford, 1965)), are both interesting studies of the style of the Tale.

FRAGMENT VII(B²)

The Placing of the Fragment

Fragment VII(B²) is the longest in the *Canterbury Tales*, and consists of six tales—those of the Shipman and Prioress, two from the pilgrim Chaucer, and the Monk's and Nun's Priest's. Virtually all manuscripts place the group after the Pardoner's Tale, though Chaucer did not provide any link to connect them; nineteen manuscripts supply a rather uninspired one to fill the gap. Only one late and unauthoritative manuscript places the Fragment after the Man of Law's Tale (Fragment II(B¹)). The earlier editorial fondness for following this arrangement was due to a belief that such an order gave a correct sequence for two topographical hints for the journey given in the links. There is however no logical reason why the Summoner's remark indicating that Sittingbourne is still a considerable distance ahead (III(D) 847) needs to follow the mention of Rochester (VII. 1926/B². 3116)); and there is negligible evidence that Chaucer was so interested in the geographical detail of the journey, or had revised the work sufficiently, to make such references a reliable indication of tale order.

It is unlikely that he wrote the tales of the Fragment as a group. *Melibee* and the Monk's Tale may have been composed before the *Canterbury Tales* was conceived, and Chaucer appears originally to have had different intentions for the Shipman's Tale. The Nun's Priest's Tale, by contrast, was probably written to complete the sequence once the rest of the Fragment was assembled.

The Shipman's Tale

Date, Attribution, and Text

The use of 'we' and 'us', and the oral delivery assumed by the narrator—
'but herkneth to my tale' (23/1213)—indicate clearly that the Tale was
written specifically for the *Canterbury Tales*, but the attribution of the story
to the Shipman almost certainly represents second thoughts on Chaucer's
part. He seems originally to have intended it for the Wife of Bath: the
opening twenty lines and the final couplet contain several first-person
pronouns referring to wives in general, very much in the manner of those
found in the present Wife's Tale (III(D) 929–50) and Prologue. There is no
parallel to a purely dramatic usage of a female 'us' from a man anywhere else
in the *Tales*, nor in medieval English literature outside the specialized case
of the theatre (where the imitation of a female speaker by a man can be
unambiguously indicated by the context). The list given by the wife in the
tale of the six qualities most desirable in a husband (173–7/1363–7) is also
found in slightly different form in the present Wife's Tale.

The tale of the monk and the merchant's wife may once have been told by
the Wife in rivalry with the Monk's telling the tale of January and May: a
wife's story of a monk's misbehaviour answering, or being answered by, a
monk's story against wives. Chaucer may have taken it away from the Wife
because it was too similar to her Prologue, or because he conceived the idea
of writing the Prologue instead, or because he found the tale of women's
sovereignty more appropriate for her. The attribution to the Shipman seems
to be an *ad hoc* arrangement; he is a sufficiently dubious character—'a good
felawe' (I(A) 395) in Chaucer's ironic idiom—for a fabliau to be
appropriate, and the French setting of the tale and its interest in foreign
exchange have a marginal relevance to him, but teller and tale have less
connection here than in any other of the *Canterbury Tales*.

Textual variants are never of sufficient significance to affect the sense,
though it is sometimes difficult to be sure of Chaucer's original. The
proportion of successful merchants (228/1418) varies between two out of
twelve, ten out of twelve (certainly incorrect), and twelve out of a hundred.
The merchant sometimes asks 'Quy la?' in French with an English gloss,
sometimes the other way round 214/1404); the French phrase is presumably
correct. There is little other glossing, none of it likely to be authorial.

Genre, Sources, and Analogues

The Shipman's Tale is a fabliau, with its usual contents of sex and trickery.
It has an urbanity of surface unique among similar tales of the Canterbury

serics, but its unquestioning acceptance of the interchangeability of money and sex gives it an unpleasant edge, and the amorality typical of the genre leaves judgement unspoken.

The tale may be based on a French fabliau, especially in view of its location in France and the accompanying circumstantial detail, but the existing French analogues are very different from Chaucer's story. The outline of the plot was widely familiar as a folktale motif ('the lover's gift regained'). One of the shortest versions of the story is preserved in Latin verse in a thirteenth-century English manuscript. This, and a number of other analogues, have the lover claim that the gift he has given the wife was actually surety for a loan of some object—a pepper-mill in the Latin, elsewhere a mortar and pestle—that allows for some sexual punning at the end similar to that in the tale.

The version closest to Chaucer's is the first story of the eighth day in Boccaccio's *Decameron*. This was in turn retold by Giovanni Sercambi, but too late for Chaucer to have known it. That the *Decameron* supplies the closest analogue must strengthen the case for Chaucer's knowledge of the work, though if it was his direct source the freedom with which he treats the story suggests a memorial adaptation.

The stories of the eighth day take trickery as their theme. The first story tells of the wife of a rich merchant who is desired by a German soldier of fortune, a man of upright character named Gulfardo. When Gulfardo asks Madonna, the lady, to grant him her favour, she agrees on condition of a payment of two hundred gold florins. Disgusted by her rapacity, Gulfardo decides to play the trick used by Chaucer's monk: he borrows the money off her husband, and later tells him that he has repaid it to the wife. The woman's readiness to sell her body is condemned both within the tale and beforehand by the narrator.

The most obvious change in Chaucer's version is the substitution of a monk for the soldier. He may have found the different character in an alternative source; but he was quite capable of making the change himself, whether for sheer mischief, to add to the recurrent satire of religious orders in the *Tale*, or possibly in order to cue the Monk's telling of the tale of January and May. A further possible source for the idea lies in the following tale in the *Decameron*, which tells a rural version of a somewhat similar story in which the lover is the village priest. This is one of the stories that ends with some mortar-and-pestle puns. Both Boccaccio's tales end with the wife's having to hand over her gifts; only Chaucer's version allows the wife to deceive her husband in turn and keep the money.

Some circumstances of Chaucer's story may have been prompted by the *Roman de la rose*. In a passage that Chaucer drew on extensively for the Wife of Bath's Prologue, the Lover's Friend imagines a jealous husband accusing his wife of taking advantage of his absence on business trips and of claiming that she has to dress extravagantly for his sake (8475–84, cf. Shipman's Tale, 179/1369 and 418–21/1608–11). The husband in the speech also swears to the scarcity of honest women by St Denis (8687), who gives his name to the town in which the tale is set, and by whom Daun John also swears (151/1341); and earlier the Friend recalls the story of Ganelon (7866, cf. Shipman, 194/1384, though it is a legend Chaucer refers to on several occasions). The expense of wives, their fondness for revelling, and their inability to keep secrets are all themes found in the *Roman* and widely elsewhere in antifeminist literature.

The fullest account of the analogues is given by Benson and Andersson, *Literary Context*, though they provide only summaries of *Decameron* 8, 1 and 2. The text of 8, 1 is given by John W. Spargo in *Sources and Analogues*.
On the dating of Sercambi's version, see his *Novelliere*, ed. Luciano Rossi (p. 11 above).
Murray Copland, '*The Shipman's Tale*: Chaucer and Boccaccio', *MÆ* 35 (1966), 11–28, compares the tales in the *Decameron* with Chaucer's version.

Structure

The Shipman's Tale shares with the fabliaux of the Miller and Reeve a concern with the story alone. The only digression is the short passage at the beginning on the expense of wives. As so often, the authority figure, this time the husband, is introduced in the first line; the wife follows at once, and the monk after the digression. The three are characterized on their first introduction just enough for the purposes of the tale, with none of the elaboration of the figures of the fabliaux of Fragment I: the merchant is rich, 'for which men held him wys'; the wife beautiful, with expensive tastes; the monk handsome, young, and bold.

The narrative is divided into three main parts. In the first, the wife asks the monk for a hundred francs and he arranges to borrow it off her husband; the second section summarizes the consummation of the affair; and the matter of the repayment occupies the third. Much of the first and third sections consists of speeches, all of which are to do with business arrangements, though these sometimes double as sexual arrangements.

The transitions from one section to another are handled through colloquial versions of the formula of 'Now wol I stynte—I wol yow telle—'. The first transition is signalled by

Na moore of this as now, for it suffiseth, (52/1242)

for the shift from the introductory matter to the point where the plot gets under way with the merchant's decision to travel away from home; the second, by 'there I lette hym dwelle' (306/1496), for the move from the merchant's stay in Bruges to what is going on in his absence; the third, by 'namoore of hym I seye' (324/1514), when the monk rides back to his abbey after his night with the wife and the merchant returns home. These formulae also mark the major shifts of time and place, though the husband's second set of travels (366–9/1556–9) is dealt with very summarily.

Themes

The Tale comes as close as any in the Canterbury series to the simple telling of a story. It has nothing in the way of digression on moral, philosophical, or religious considerations; unlike the other fabliaux, it does not stand in any precise dramatic or thematic relationship to other tales. The story is none the less developed around a theme inherent in the plot—that of money; and it is a leading example of Chaucer's wider concern in the *Tales* with the nature of language.

The subject of money is sounded in the course of the opening lines, in the one diversion from the narrative, on the expensiveness of wives. The various relationships in the tale are all defined, at least in part, in terms of finance: the monk is careful 'to doon pleasaunce, and also greet costage' (by distributing gifts) around the merchant's household (45/1235); the wife defines her relationship with her husband at the beginning in terms of his niggardliness, and offers her body at the end in repayment of the hundred francs; she offers herself to Daun John in return for money. The merchant himself appears not to trade in commodities, but to be a financier, dealing in international exchange. Although usury was forbidden by the Church, dealings of this sort were within the law; but the breeding of money was none the less regarded as a form of sin, even as fornication. The merchant's thousand-franc profit may have appeared to Chaucer's audience as a kind of adultery paralleling the wife's hundred-franc selling of her body. The merchant himself unwittingly implies something of the sort—though without the suggestion of sin—when he speaks of merchants' money being their plough (288/1478): in this tale of *doubles entendres*, the image strongly suggests a sexual meaning behind the metaphor of agricultural fertility.

The merchant is never presented as sinful, however, or even as a bad husband. He is not jealous; he gives his wife liberty; he at least is of the opinion that she has sufficient clothing, livelihood, and silver in her purse, even if he expects her to run a 'thrifty houshold' (243–8/1433–8). Her complaints about his sexual inadequacy to Daun John look suspiciously like an invitation, in view of his amorous activity at the end—unless this is one more instance of the equation of sex with money that runs throughout the tale, with his financial success being reflected in renewed potency (375–9/1565–9). The terms used about him, after the satiric second line—'that riche was, for which men helde hym wys'—are approving. His fear of bad luck, 'hap and fortune in oure chapmanhede' (238/1428), is treated by the narrator not as a criticism of his failure to lay up treasure in heaven but with admiration for the professional skills that can avoid misfortune; the line also shows the customary pessimism of the successful. He is honest and open in his financial dealings, and he alone speaks without any deliberate second meanings. His rebuke of his wife at the end is a very mild one in what he believes to be the circumstances, and he sees that further complaint 'nere but folie' (428/1618). His wife's adultery for cash should appear all the more shocking for his forebearance, but moral judgement on any of the characters is entirely lacking, overtly or indirectly. The gulled husbands in the other fabliaux are presented as those standard butts of comedy, the foolish. If the merchant of St Denis is a fool at all, it is not because he mistrusts his wife, but because he trusts her.

His first quality, however, is that he is rich. He is shut up in his counting-house reckoning his books while his wife is in the garden making arrangements to borrow money off the monk and pay him later—and since the monk's response is a promise to deliver her 'out of this care' when her husband is safely in Flanders, followed by a hard embrace and lots of kisses, it is clear enough that they both understand what that payment will involve. Her complaint that her husband

> is noght worth at al
> In no degree the value of a flye   (170–1/1360–1)

seems to apply equally to niggardliness and sexual inadequacy: 'value' is interchangeably erotic and financial. The story is full of such *doubles entendres*, some, as here, more or less deliberate on the speaker's part, some operating as the idiom of the tale rather than of a particular speaker. The wife's final invitation to her husband to score his debt upon her 'taille' is the most explicit; the pun on *tail*, in its sexual meaning, and *tally*, the method of recording accounts, is associated with another on *dette*, in both its financial sense and the sense used by the Bible (and by the Wife of Bath and the Parson, III(D) 130, X(I) 940), for sexual activity owed between husband and wife. Her promise

> Ye shal my joly body have to wedde   (423/1613)

continues the series of equations of sex and finance, 'wedde' being a pledge or a guarantee for a loan.

Everything in the tale is subordinated to this dominant theme. People are attracted to the merchant's house 'for his largesse, and for his wyf was fair' (22/1212): expense and an implied promise of sexual spending. The plighting of troth between wife and monk has nothing to do with love or fidelity and everything to do with sex and money and confidentiality

(130–42/1320–32, 198–202/1388–92). The fulfilling of the 'acord' between the two of them is described in even-handed terms of money and sex:

> For thise hundred frankes he shoulde al nyght
> Have hire in his armes bolt upright;
> And this acord parfourned was in dede.   (315–17/1505–7)

In these circumstances, even the nonce-phrase 'in dede' suggests a pun on a written contract.

Gerhard Joseph, 'Chaucer's Coinage: Foreign Exchange and the Puns of the Shipman's Tale', *ChR* 17 (1982–3), 341–57, and Thomas Hahn, 'Money, Sexuality, Wordplay and Context in the *Shipman's Tale*', in Wasserman and Blanch, *Chaucer in the Eighties*, pp. 235–49, discuss the connection between the merchant's financial dealings and the Tale's language.

V. J. Scattergood, 'The Originality of the *Shipman's Tale*', *ChR* 11 (1976–7), 210–31, is an excellent general study of the Tale.

The Tale in Context

There is no textual link between the Pardoner's Tale and the Shipman's, therefore no proof that Chaucer intended the two to be adjacent. The universal juxtaposition of them in the manuscripts may none the less be more than mere chance, and it is certainly suggestive. It is not in fact sex but love of money, the Pardoner's own theme, that is the ruling motive for the action of the tale. The merchant goes off to Flanders, the setting of the Pardoner's Tale, though we are assured that while he was there, unlike the rioters,

> He neither pleyeth at the dees ne daunceth.   (304/1494)

The line may simply pick up the reason behind the location of the story of the rioters —an association of Flanders with dissipation—but it does serve as a reminder of the Pardoner's Tale. The position of this amoral story of sexual gratification and profit-making between the Pardoner's sinister condemnation of avarice and the Prioress's praise of unworldly spirituality suggests the moral judgement that the tale itself withholds.

The relationships between the tales of Fragment VII are exceptionally unpredictable. Before the final tale, that of the Nun's Priest, there are none of the close echoes of motif or theme or phrase that characterize the other fragments. The tales do, however, gradually come together in terms of an idea examined at large in the *Canterbury Tales*, a concern with the nature and function of literature. This is never dealt with discursively in the Shipman's Tale, but Chaucer introduces here one crucial theme, of the slipperiness of language. The tale is riddled with words misused, abused, and misapplied, with speeches in which one thing is said and another intended. It is one of the clearest examples in the whole work of the shaping of an entire reading of life through the manipulation of language.

In its plot of the tricking of husband by wife and of wife by lover, the tale is one more statement to add to the many others on the nature of marriage, and a rather uncomfortable one. The merchant is presented too sympathetically as a husband to make the wife's adultery amusing even on the amoral level of fabliau: her complaints about him are not endorsed by the narrative. In a later story of a wife's unfaithfulness to a kind husband, the Manciple's, she is viciously condemned. Phebus is at least jealous; the merchant of St Denis, by contrast to John the carpenter or Simkin or January, is trusting, and he gives his wife the liberty advocated by the Franklin. The tale presents the wife without moral condemnation, and lets her come off better at the end than in any of the analogues, even though it has the potential for confirming the worst generalizations about women made in the *Tales*. That this does not happen, despite most tellers' fondness for generalizing about women, is probably due to its original ascription to the Wife of Bath. This would render such generalizations both gratuitous— she makes some of her own at the start of the tale—and redundant: she would by her very presence confirm all the antifeminist conclusions that might be drawn from it. In the Shipman's mouth, it comes over much more as a story about individuals (despite their lack of names: even 'John' is the standard type-name for a monk), and less as a tale that exemplifies universal principles of behaviour.

Style

The tale is written with a directness and a concentration on the narrative that also characterize the fabliaux of the Miller and Reeve. There is a minimal sense of a teller manipulating rhetoric and structure, but it is confined to the colloquial directions for shifts in the narrative, a few first-person comments at the start, and a single one at the end. It is also a story that observes the proprieties. It has none of the verbal obscenity of the other fabliaux; the characters are unfailingly polite to each other, whatever they may be thinking—

> Of his owene thought he wax al reed   (111/1301)

—and sexual invitations are rephrased, euphemistically and literally, in terms of money.

The way the semiology of finance takes over the sexual sphere is discussed above: it constitutes the main thematic movement of the tale. Other lexical areas take on a similar slipperiness. Words are used in the wrong contexts, to invalidate either the idea or the action they describe: it is impossible to read any spiritual activity into the monk's reading of his morning office when he is described as saying 'his thynges . . . ful curteisly' (91/1281), or to take his vocation seriously when he swears love for the wife by his 'professioun' (155/1345). Words such as *honour* and *worship* are used to mean putting on an expensive show, again corrupting chivalric virtues into monetary values (13/1203, 179/1369, 421/1611). 'Goods' are as much sexual as material (243/1433, 432/1622). The one factor that might possibly prevent the adultery, the blood relationship implied by the perpetual use of 'cosyn' between the merchant and monk, and, by extension, Daun John's use of 'nece' to the wife, turns out to be a pretence, as the monk hastens to assure her as soon as the possibility of a closer relationship comes up. 'Cosyn' and 'cosynage' threaten to take on the meaning attested only later in Middle English but familiar enough in French, of gulling—or, as Cotgrave nicely put it in his dictionary of 1611, 'to clayme kindred for aduantage, or particular ends'. The etymology may be false, but there is no doubt that this is what Daun John is doing:

> He is na moore cosyn unto me
> Than is this leef that hangeth on the tree!
> I clepe hym so, by Seint Denys of Fraunce,
> To have the moore cause of aqueyntaunce
> Of yow.   (149–53/1339–43)

By the time one reaches the monk's final farewell to his 'deere cosyn' the merchant, or the wife's declaration that he gave her the money 'for cosynage' (409/1599), it is hard to believe that the pun is not there. If the merchant's speeches are characterized by directness and honesty, Daun John specializes in deceit, flattery, and downright lies.

The style of the Tale is characterized by other features besides this pervasive *double entendre*. There are a number of localizing details—as in the Miller's Tale, though less pervasively; the characters swear by French saints, the husband calls 'Quy la?' when his wife knocks at the counting-house door. Like the other fabliaux, it draws some of its imagery from the animal world: birds at daybreak, the hare pursued by hounds (in a sexual context (103–8/1293–8), in keeping with the frequent sexual overtones accorded to the imagery of hares in the Middle Ages and elsewhere in the *Tales*), the wife 'as jolif as a pye' (209/1399; compare Symkyn's wife in the Reeve's Tale, I(A) 3950). Daun John tells the merchant that he needs the loan to buy 'certein beestes', in a direct equation of female with animal flesh. The other area of language that stands out from the tale is the vocabulary of finance: *countour-hous* and *countyng-bord*, accounts, treasure, *sheeldes* and francs, reckoning, borrowing, lending and *creauncing*, *reconyssaunce*, *chevyssaunce*, debt and winning.

All this means that moral comment is ruled out; the lexical range of the Tale has no room for it, and words that look as if they might have a moral charge have a much more practical weighting. There are none the less some wonderful effects made simply through juxtaposition of event and parallel syntax, even if morality is kept subordinate to comedy:

> Hastily a messe was ther seyd,
> And spedily the tables were yleyd,
> And to the dyner faste they hem spedde,
> And richely this monk the chapman fedde. (251–4/1441–4).

See also Richardson, *Blameth Nat Me*, ch. 5; Benson, *Chaucer's Drama of Style*, pp. 104–16; and David H. Abraham, '*Cosyn* and *Cosynage*: Pun and Structure in the *Shipman's Tale*', *ChR* 11 (1976–7), 319–27.

The Prioress's Tale

The Shipman–Prioress Link

Harry Bailly provides some kind of reaction to the amorality of the Shipman's Tale: he sees the monk as the villain of the piece, but also has some admiration for his trickery. The moral he draws,

> Draweth no monkes moore unto youre in, (442/1632)

recalls the theme of dangerous *herbergage* from the fabliaux of Fragment I.

His change of style when he turns from the Shipman to the Prioress, from boisterous masculinity to speaking 'as curteisly as it had been mayde', is an index of the shift of register between the two tales. The five lines of his speech to Madame Eglentine contain five subjunctives and a request, as well as a double 'my lady'.

Date and Text

The dating of the Prioress's Tale and its Prologue is an open question, but they were probably written as a single unit specifically for the *Canterbury Tales*. Some critics have read the tale as a satire on the Prioress, and therefore written with her in mind, but it is not so different from other Miracles of the Virgin (except in poetic quality) as to rule out independent composition. The use of Dante in the Prologue, and of rhyme royal throughout, makes any date after 1373 a possibility. It has been suggested that the poem might originally have been an independent work composed for the visit of Richard II to Lincoln in 1387. The double 'quod she', however, referring to a female teller (at 454/1644 and 581/1771), indicates at least revision, if not composition, for the Prioress, and the textual evidence suggests a common descent for the Prologue and Tale and for the preceding link.

The text presents no difficulties, though Hengwrt's heading to the start of the tale proper is worth note: 'heere bigynneth the Prioresse tale of Alma redemptoris mater'. Hengwrt and four other manuscripts gloss Chaucer's allusion to Revelation 14: 1–4 (580–5/1770–5) with its paraphrase from Jerome's *Adversus Jovinianum*, and quote generously from a hymn to the Virgin by John of Garland alongside the mass sung for the dead child (635/1825).

In addition to its appearance in manuscripts of the complete *Tales*, the Prioress's Tale was copied independently in five surviving manuscripts: twice with the Second Nun's Tale, once with the Clerk's, twice with assorted religious pieces. This figure is equalled by *Melibee* and surpassed only by the Clerk's Tale, suggesting a high popularity rating for the Tale in the Middle Ages.

Sumner Ferris, 'Chaucer at Lincoln (1387): *The Prioress's Tale* as a Political Poem', *ChR* 15 (1981), 295–321, suggests the 1387 Lincoln connection; if that was the occasion, however, one would expect the 'little' St Hugh of Lincoln to figure more centrally in the tale.
The textual tradition of the Tale is discussed in detail by Beverly Boyd (ed.), *The Prioress's Tale* (Variorum II 20, Norman, Okla., 1987).
On the glosses from Jerome, see John P. Brennan, 'Reflections on a Gloss to the *Prioress's Tale* from Jerome's *Adversus Jovinianum*', *SP* 70 (1974), 243–51.

Genre

The genre of the Prioress's Tale is precisely defined within the text, as a 'miracle' (691/1881). Miracles of the Virgin had been widespread across Europe as an expression of popular piety throughout the Middle Ages, and from early in the twelfth century they were gathered into collections (*mariales*). The three main groups of such stories, in Latin, all originated in England; various Anglo-Norman versions of these were made late in the century, and the first Middle English Miracles of the Virgin appear in the *South English Legendary* a hundred years later. The stories were written as aids to piety rather than as historical record, and their exemplary qualities tend to be stressed at the cost of any attempt at factual plausibility. The quality most valued in the recipients of the Virgin's miracles is simply devotion to her, which may well be divorced from full doctrinal understanding (as in the Prioress's Tale) or even from moral probity. The stories therefore rely on an appeal more to emotion and sentiment than to reason. The anti-Semitism of the Prioress's Tale is also a widespread feature of the genre: the deep cultural animosity of Christian towards Jew may have found particular expression in the Miracles because of specific doctrinal issues—Jewish thinkers found the notion of the Incarnation and Virgin Birth especially obnoxious—and because of such legends as the Jews' attempting to desecrate the Virgin's bier.

Doctrinal prologues of the kind prefixed to the Prioress's and Second Nun's Tales often introduced miracle collections and saints' lives.

R. W. Southern, 'The English Origins of the "Miracles of the Virgin"', *Mediaeval and Renaissance Studies*, 4 (1958), 176–216.
Robert Worth Frank, jun., 'Miracles of the Virgin, Medieval Anti-Semitism, and the "Prioress's Tale"', in Larry D. Benson and Siegfried Wenzel (eds.), *The Wisdom of Poetry: Essays in Early English Literature in Honor of Morton W. Bloomfield* (Medieval Institute Publications, Kalamazoo, Mich., 1982), pp. 177–88.
Beverly Boyd, *The Middle English Miracles of the Virgin* (San Marino, Calif. 1964)—a history and anthology.

Sources and Analogues

The story of the boy killed by the Jews in revenge for his singing of a hymn to the Virgin is found in numerous versions throughout Western Europe. It takes three main forms, in two of which the Virgin restores the child to life at the end. The group to which the Prioress's Tale belongs is distinguished from the others by generally specifying the 'Alma redemptoris mater' as the song; by having the body thrown into a privy; and by the different nature of the miracle, where the child sings during his funeral mass but is not brought back to life.

This version of the story seems to have been distinctive to England. Only one of the known analogues, which postdates Chaucer, was written elsewhere, and that locates the story in Lincoln (scene of a similar supposed martyrdom by the Jews of the boy saint Hugh mentioned by the Prioress, 684/1874), and connects it with the expulsion of the Jews from England. All the analogues are in Latin prose except one, in Middle English verse, which appears in a collection of vernacular Miracles in the Vernon manuscript (Bodleian Eng. poet. a. 1). Chaucer's version contains features found scattered across several of these analogues, and his precise source is unknown.

The Prioress's Tale has some unique elements which may derive from this missing source or may be original to Chaucer. One of these is the 'greyn' laid on the boy's tongue by the Virgin; the nearest equivalents are a lily or a precious stone, or in several of the analogues he simply sings until he is buried. He is made a seven-year-old only here, and is therefore too young to be learning his antiphoner in school and has to learn the hymn from an older boy. Most disconcertingly, the violence of the punishment meted out to the Jews is unparalleled. In the Vernon version the murderer is 'iugget', judged, presumably meaning condemned to death; in the Latin versions preceding Chaucer's, the worst fate mentioned for the Jews is that they cannot hear the miraculous song. In the legend as it appears in other forms, they are occasionally punished but more often converted. Given the closeness of Chaucer's adaptation of known sources in the two most similar tales, the Clerk's and Second Nun's, it is not safe to assume that these elements are added for the purpose of satire; one of the lines that seems to reflect most badly on the Prioress, for instance, the gratuitous definition of a cesspit (573/1763), appears in one of the analogues, and the punishment of the Jews may well be paraphrased from a source. The fact remains that if they were in his source, Chaucer did not exercise his freedom to change them.

The principal difference between the Tale and any of the analogues, and one which can safely be attributed to Chaucer, is the addition of a strong liturgical element. This is firmly established throughout the Prologue, which opens with a passage from Psalm 8 that was used in both the little office of the Virgin and the Mass of the Holy Innocents: 'O Lord our Lord: how admirable is Thy name in the whole earth . . . Out of the mouths of infants and of sucklings hast Thou perfected praise':

> O Lord, oure Lord, thy name how merveillous
> Is in this large world ysprad—quod she—
> For noght oonly thy laude precious
> Parfourned is by men of dignitee,
> But by the mouth of children thy bountee
> Parfourned is, for on the brest soukynge
> Somtyme shewen they thyn heriynge.   (453–9/1643–9)

The praise offered 'by mouth of innocentz' recurs later in the tale as well (607–8/1797–8). The Prologue's images of the lily and the burning bush are both traditional symbols for the Virgin (the bush that burned but was not consumed being taken to prefigure her unblemished virginity). The fourth stanza is based on St Bernard's hymn to the Virgin in the final canto of Dante's *Paradiso*, which Chaucer also used in the Prologue to the Second Nun's legend of St Cecilia.

The biblical references within the tale are given additional relevance by their use in the liturgy. The Gospel for the Mass of the Holy Innocents is the story of Herod's slaughter of the Innocents, concluding with the fulfilment of the prophecy of Rachel weeping for her children (Matt. 2: 13–18); the Prioress describes the Jews as 'cursed folk of Herodes al newe' (574/1764), and the boy's mother as 'this newe Rachel' (627/1817). The Lesson for this Mass, Revelation 14: 1–5, which tells of the virgins who had no knowledge of women singing a new song before the Lamb, is closely paraphrased in the description of the Innocents 'that nevere, flesshly, wommen they ne knewe', following 'the white Lamb celestial', and singing 'a song al newe' (580–5/1770–5). The Introit of the Mass uses the text that opens the Prologue on how the 'mouth of innocentz' praise God; it is also appropriate for the references to St Nicholas (514–1704), who when a baby (like those 'on the brest soukynge' of the Prologue, the 'sucklings' of the Psalm) refused to suckle on Fridays, and to St Hugh of Lincoln (684/1874). The blood crying out (578/1768) may be related to Psalm 78: 10, used as a response in the Second Nocturn for Holy Innocents, which calls on God to avenge the spilt blood of the saints.

The 'greyn' laid by the Virgin on the tongue of the murdered child may also have its source, and its explanation, in the connection of the tale with the Feast of the Holy Innocents. The analogues of the story contain nothing very similar—a lily or a gem—and the tale requires some mechanism to enable the child's spirit to depart. The Feast of the Innocents is also the eve of St Thomas of Canterbury; and the second vespers of the Innocents includes a responsory and a prosa in his honour in which the image of grain appears, as a symbol once of martyrdom, once of the soul released from the chaff of the body and gathered up to heaven. The soul of the martyred child of the Prioress's Tale is released to heaven only when the grain is taken from his tongue.

Carleton Brown, 'The Prioress's Tale', in *Sources and Analogues*, establishes the group of Miracles to which the tale belongs and prints all the known analogues.
On the liturgical elements in the tale, see: Beverly Boyd, *Chaucer and the Liturgy* (Philadelphia, 1967), and her discussion in the Variorum edition of the Tale, pp. 4–8; Marie Padgett Hamilton, 'Echoes of Childermas in the Tale of the Prioress', in Wagenknecht, *Chaucer: Modern Essays*, pp. 88–97; Sister Nicholas Maltman, OP, 'The Divine Granary, or the End of the Prioress's "Greyn"', *ChR* 17 (1982–3), 163–70; and J. C. Wenk, 'On the Sources of *The Prioress's Tale*', *MS* 17 (1955), 214–19.

Structure

There are two coexisting structures in the Tale. One is the formal construction of the prologue and the various sections of the story. The other, more significant structure lies in the idea of the child singing in praise of the Virgin and the Lamb. In the Prologue, the Prioress compares herself to a child incapable of speech before the 'worthynesse' of the Virgin, and prays for guidance in 'my song that I shal of yow seye' (481–7/1671–7). The boy in the Tale learns a song in praise of the Virgin, of which he is too young to have understanding; and after his death he joins the procession before the Lamb to 'synge a song al newe' (584/1774). Other tales of the Canterbury series open out into a sequence of stories within stories; here, the teller's own weak song tells of a song sanctified by miracle and transformed into the praise of the Church triumphant.

The Prologue serves at once as a liturgical introit, as a hymn, and as a prayer of invocation. Its five stanzas may be in honour of the five joys (or sorrows) of the Virgin, or the number may be coincidental: neither Chaucer nor medieval rhetorical handbooks ever suggest numerological principles of poetic composition.

The story itself consists of three parts, each leading up to the climax of a liturgical apostrophe or prayer. The first section describes the setting, the child's learning of the 'Alma redemptoris', and his murder, and immediately takes him beyond death to the New Jerusalem:

> O martir, sowded to virginitee,
> Now maystow syngen, folwynge evere in oon
> The white Lamb celestial.   (579–81/1769–71)

The short central section describes the mother's search for her child, culminating in

> O grete God, that parfournest they laude
> By mouth of innocentz, lo, heere they myght!   (607–8/1797–8)

—the 'myght' being shown in the miracle of the child's continued singing. The brief disposal of the Jews, the funeral, and the child's account of the miracle complete the tale, with a concluding prayer to St. Hugh.

    The bulk of the tale is narrative: the only direct speech consists of the brief exchange between the schoolfriend and the child on the nature of the song, the abbot's questioning of the martyred boy, and, the one significant speech of the tale, the child's account of the miracle. Satan is also given a semi-allegorical speech in which he incites the Jews to murder the child; this is matched by the Virgin's promise to protect the boy which he himself reports—

> Be nat agast; I wol thee nat forsake.   (669/1859)

Themes

The tale is not a comfortable one. It is sentimental—'litel' is its favourite word; it is highly selective in its expenditure of emotion, viciously inhumane punishment being meted out to the villains without producing any apparent ripple in the pathetic response demanded by the narration; it is crude—the definition of a cesspit is scarcely necessary; and it is deeply and mindlessly anti-Semitic. Jews' hearts are the natural habitat of Satan, and no humanity need be shown them. One is reluctant to father such characteristics on Chaucer, and the Prioress, with her sentimentality over trapped mice and attention more to the manners of religion than to its substance, provides an obvious escape route. There is no evidence, however, that the Tale was read, or could have been read, in Chaucer's own time as a satire on the Prioress— it was, for instance, copied independently a number of times—and there are genuine religious elements in the tale that militate against such an interpretation.

    The most significant of these is the Prologue. It is a superb piece of writing, perhaps Chaucer's finest religious poetry; and although it is put specifically into the mouth of the Prioress ('quod she' in the second line), there is no suggestion, or possibility, or irony. To follow such an opening with a satiric tale, to promise a song in praise of the Virgin in phrases drawn from the highest poetry of Christian tradition and then to produce a parody, would be little short of blasphemy. One might argue that the blasphemy would be the Prioress's and not Chaucer's, but then one still has to justify the discrepancy between the sublime vision of the Prologue and the Tale itself. But the discrepancies will not go away, however they are explained: between the Prologue and the Tale, or between the story and its liturgical climaxes.

The problems become less acute if one starts not from the teller but from the kind of story told. There is no incongruity in introducing a Miracle of the Virgin by a hymn in her praise; and this miracle is a serious one—that is, it deals with major issues of devotion, evil, salvation, and the power of divine intervention on earth. At the heart of the tale is one of the great paradoxes of Christianity, the power of God to make strength perfect in weakness. The idea is introduced in the Prologue, in the praise shown by nursing babies, in the Virgin's humility that enforces—'ravyshedest', almost 'rapes' (469/1659)—the Holy Ghost and conceives God's sapience, in the speaker's own childlike inability to express the Virgin's praise. The youth and innocence of the child are therefore crucial to the story, and are endorsed by association with the Holy Innocents. His devotion is a turning of the will— an *entente*, like the Pardoner's desire for money—towards the Virgin (550/1740). It precedes rational understanding of the grammar of the 'Alma redemptoris', and it runs counter to the adult-imposed disciplines of school life. He is prepared to suffer the small childhood martyrdom of beatings in order to learn the antiphon, and he hopes to know it 'er Cristemasse be went' (540/1730)—perhaps another reference to the Feast of the Holy Innocents, which falls on 28 December; the antiphon was also associated with Advent. He is three times described as an 'innocent', once in his readiness to suffer punishment, once when he is murdered, once when he is lying on his bier (538/1728, 566/1756, 635/1825). He is given only two direct speeches in the poem: the first one in a child's idiolect, when he determines to learn the antiphon; the second with a new authority, not as a child but as a teacher, as he describes how Christ wishes His glory to be made known 'for the worship of his Mooder deere' (654/1844).

At least some of the sentimentality of the tale, then, is thematically integral: that the child should be 'litel' shows forth the wonder of the miracle all the more. The destruction of the Jews may be connected with this. The verse 'Ex ore infancium' that starts the Introit of the Mass of the Holy Innocents (Ps. 8: 3) connects the praise of the innocent with divine punishment—'that thou mayst destroy the enemy and the avenger'. The setting of the tale in Asia allows the law to inflict a particularly horrific punishment; God's enemies come to a miserable end on this earth, the murdered child has his end not in the cesspit but in the procession before the Lamb. The Jews, like the Saracen mother-in-law of the Man of Law's Tale, are cast by definition as enemies of God. That neither Jews nor Saracens were known in England made it all the easier to treat them as something less than human, almost like evil androids in science fiction (or, with less excuse, like the Russians in some recent Western films). To be a Satan-inspired homicide, whether pagan, Jewish, or, like the Pardoner's rioters, professedly Christian, is enough to draw vengeance. The punishment here is at least confined to those directly implicated (630/1820). Certainly there were Christians in the Middle Ages who demanded a better deal for the Jews, but their place was not in the populist sensationalism of miracle literature.

The morality of the tale is not, even so, a simple opposition of Jewish evil to Christian good. The Christian lord of the city is corrupted by the same love of money as motivates the Pardoner or the Friar's summoner, and he protects the Jews 'for foule usure and lucre of vileynye' (491/1681). Chaucer thus gives the tale a grounding in hard economic fact, for the Church's prohibition of usury necessitated a Jewish presence to maintain financial liquidity; and though Christians were forbidden to lend at interest, it was common practice to take over the Jews' profits from usury through taxation or confiscation. Even within the Christian community, the boy is operating by an ethic in conflict with his society, which has painful sanctions for children who fail to learn their lessons and does not enquire into motive. No claim is made that the law applied to the guilty Jews is any better than this pragmatic morality. They are condemned on the Old Testament principle of an eye for an eye, measure for measure,

Yvele shal have that yvele wol deserve,   (632/1822)

but, unlike Shylock, they have not been offered mercy first.

The story does not, then, set up the Christians as ideal, even by the standards of a culture that was content to accept a definition of the Jews as enemies of Christ; nor does Chaucer put it into the mouth of one of his ideal characters, such as the Clerk or the Parson, either of whom could properly be given a devotion to the Virgin. By assigning it to Madame Eglentine, with her fondness for counterfeiting both courtly and ecclesiastical good manners and her inability to see that those are not the same as courtesy or spirituality, Chaucer passes judgement on the tale, and through it on the Miracles of the Virgin as a literary or devotional form. The Virgin is a proper subject of devotion—the Prologue makes that clear; but the legend of the boy offers none of the hard engagement with moral issues of the Clerk's or Parson's Tales. Aesthetically speaking, the Prioress's Tale is the best Miracle of the Virgin in existence; its development of the ideas of intuitive devotion and of innocence gives it a depth that few others achieve. But it is still a work of pious sensationalism, a Mills and Boon version of Christianity, and if it is the best that the Prioress can offer, Chaucer has other things to say.

In the Variorum edition of the Tale, Beverly Boyd divides critics into the 'unsympathetic' (who stress the bigotry), the 'sympathethic' (who stress the pathetic and devotional qualities), and those who stress the coexistence of both aspects. Modern criticism is increasingly reluctant to accept the simpler forms of sympathetic interpretation, but there is nothing resembling a consensus of interpretation.

Florence H. Ridley, *The Prioress and the Critics* (Berkeley and Los Angeles, 1965), discusses critical attitudes to the Prioress in the light of the Tale's anti-Semitism.

Of general studies of the *Tales*, Pearsall, *Canterbury Tales*, pp. 246–52, gives an especially illuminating reading.

The Tale in Context

The inclusion of the Tale in the Canterbury series and its assignment to the Prioress both limit its authority as religious statement. The genre does not invite any deep analysis of human wickedness or folly—the unsparing revelation of January's self-deception or the rigorous analysis of the rioters' sin would be out of place here—but that the story is seen against such tales reveals the inadequacy of its comic-strip conception of evil. Miracles of the Virgin may have a rightful function in stirring devotion, but there are other things than that in both the secular and the spiritual worlds: how much, is indicated by the rest of the *Tales*.

Chaucer's estimate of the intellectual rigour of the story may be indicated by its position between the Shipman's Tale and *Sir Thopas*. The Shipman's Tale portrays a realistic world, where religion functions as a quick hors-d'œuvre before the real business of eating, where a morally upright merchant can make a tidy thousand-franc profit on the international exchange market that falls outside the Church's ban on taking interest, and where the main commodity for sale is sex. *Sir Thopas* has entered completely the world of fairy-tale, where the ultimate object of devotion is not the Virgin but the Fairy Queen, and the opposition along the way takes the form of a three-headed giant. The Prioress's Tale asserts its distance from the mundane world of commerce of the Shipman's Tale in every sense: usury is condemned, childlike spirituality and not commercial acumen is the moral ideal, virginity the state sanctified by God and His Mother. In distancing itself from the everyday world, however, it takes a large step not just towards heaven but towards fairy-tale. The next tale after *Sir Thopas*, the *Melibee*, shows up its inadequacy in another direction, as it preaches the ethic of forgiveness in explicit contrast to the concept of returning evil for evil by which the Jews are condemned.

It would seem most likely that Chaucer assembled tales already written to form the group that runs from the Shipman to the Monk, but there is one phrase in the Prioress's Tale that makes best sense in this particular context: that monks are, 'or elles oght be', holy men (643/1833). It would fit with the universal medieval awareness of monastic imperfection, or with the presentation of Chaucer's own Monk in the General Prologue, but it derives a particular edge from its occurrence so soon after Daun John's thoroughly unholy activities in the Shipman's Tale.

The tale offers approaches to some of the more profound themes debated across the *Canterbury Tales*. The suffering of innocence is one, but here the form of the tale prevents its being treated as a problem: the providential turning of evil into good, murder into martyrdom, is the very point of the story. The slaughter of the Innocents is a part of Christian history, like the Passion and the sorrows of the Virgin, and the *litel clergeon* re-enacts the pattern.

The relationship of language to meaning, and the ways in which literary form can express meaning, are of concern in all the tales, but especially so within Fragment VII. The Prioress's Tale offers several thoughts on the matter. One is the inability of even the most sophisticated rhetoric to express adequately the 'grete worthynesse' of God or the Virgin; the words most acceptable as worship may be the babblings of an infant or the uncomprehended Latin of an anthem beyond a child's rational grasp. Such an idea suggests a profound reorientation of the conventional theory of the outward verbal form, the fable, as shell to the kernel of inner meaning. Here, the form is not something to be cracked open to obtain the moral nutrition within; it is a mere earthly vehicle, the thing that makes possible the expression of an ineffable or intuited truth but that encloses no allegorical substance. The metaphor that comes closer is that used by the Parson, of wheat and draff (X(I) 35); the chaff is there simply to be winnowed away. In the same image, the grain of the second vespers of Holy Innocents is the soul, preserved in God's granary when the body is winnowed through martyrdom. The grain laid by the Virgin on the child's tongue offers the possibility of bringing the various meanings together: it is at once the released soul, the childlike spirituality that precedes words, and pure meaning that can leave behind the draff of the physical form it has to take within this world.

Style

There is a narrow line between an affective appeal to devotion and an affecting appeal to sentiment, and the line is drawn differently now from in the Middle Ages. This does not necessarily mean that Chaucer simply endorses the Prioress's Tale as a model of pious storytelling: rather that the criticism of the form implied by the style is more delicate than it appears to modern readers, sensitized as we are by the Victorian sentimentalization of childhood. The Middle Ages possessed no literature of childhood as such: on the secular side, in romances, childhood was essentially a prelude to heroic maturity; in religious literature, it was associated with innocence, sanctity, and, by paradox, with the power and glory of God.

'Litel' is the dominant word of the first part of the tale, and its use is excessive—'this litel child, his litel book lernynge' and so on. The excess is not, I think parody or satire, so much as a demonstrated recognition of certain qualities—certain limitations—of the form itself, and which make such a tale especially appropriate for Madame Eglentine. Part of the point of the over-usage of the epithet is also to call attention to its absence in the second half of the tale: it is a little child who learns the song, who is murdered, and who is sought by his mother, but from the moment he starts his miraculous singing the adjective is dropped. He now has an exemplary and authoritative function in the tale that would make it inappropriate; he is an object not of pathos but of admiration. The epithet appears only twice more, once as a term of protectiveness from the Virgin (667/1857), once when his 'litel body sweete' is buried: only with the departure of the sanctified spirit can the pathos of the murdered flesh be reasserted.

The style of the Tale is poised between the childlike or childish, appropriate for the intuitive devotion of the sucking baby or the boy, and the more elaborate vocabulary and rhetoric appropriate for God's magnificence and its accompanying theology. There is one idiom of 'humblesse', another of 'sapience' (470–2/1660–2). The stanza form is especially suited to the heightened or lyrical sections of the poem—the Prologue, the apostrophes and prayers that conclude each of the narrative sections, the child's description of the miracle. The rhyme royal gives the whole poem a solemnity appropriate for the tales that demand an emotional response beyond the bare facts of the narrative: the Man of Law's, the Clerk's, the Second Nun's.

The sapiential voice in the tale is concentrated in certain sections: the Prologue, the devotional interjections. The language here is strongly Romance or Latinate: within three lines of the Prologue, *bountee, magnificence, vertu, humylitee, expresse, science* (474–6/1664–6). The syntactic unit tends to be the whole seven-line stanza, with the constituent clauses in a complex relationship of cause, effect, and qualification. Idiomatic word order can be disrupted, especially in biblical or liturgical paraphrase:

> Thy name how merveillous
> Is in this large world ysprad.   (453–4/1653–4)

The language is strongly allusive, symbolic, or metaphorical— 'O bush unbrent, brennynge in Moyses sighte' (468/1658), 'of martirdom the ruby bright' (610/1800). It can deal with theological paradox: the Virgin's humility ravishing the Holy Spirit, God's praise performed 'by mouth of innocentz'.

The humble style takes two forms. One is used for narrative; the other is a simplified version of the sapiential style, which appears in the last verse of the Prologue and in the boy's long speech. The close of the Prologue offers a linguistic change of key from the preceding high style into the simplicity of the tale. It moves from the verbal resources of the liturgy and Dante to an infant's linguistic incompetence and so to the simplicity of the final prayer,

> Gydeth my song that I shal of yow seye.   (487/1677)

The boy's account of the miracle offers a similar bridge between the childlike and the authoritative: it can encompass the symbolic depth of the sapiential style while retaining the lucidity of simplicity:

> This welle of mercy, Cristes mooder sweete,
> I loved alwey, as after my konnynge;
> And whan that I my lyf sholde forlete,
> To me she cam.   (656–9/1846–9)

This is very different from the childish impulsiveness of his first speech:

> Though that I for my prymer shal be shent,
> And shal be beten thries in an houre,
> I wol it konne Oure Lady for to honoure!   (541–3/1731–3)

The narrative itself has a steady forward movement mirrored in the syntax—it is much more paratactic than the sapiential passages, and where there is grammatical subordination it preserves the temporal linear sequence: 'while . . . and after that . . . and when . . . yet'. The stanzaic structure breaks up this sequence into separate images or episodes: the boy hearing the 'Alma redemptoris', his asking its meaning, the explanation, his determination to learn it, and so on. The quality that shifts the language decisively away from mere narrative is its repeated use of a narrow range of adjectives designed to produce an emotional response: about the boy and his murder, *litel*, *smale*, *yong*, *tendre*, *pitous*; for both himself and the Virgin, *deere* and *sweete*; for the Virgin alone, *meeke*, *kynde*, *blisful*. The Jews, by contrast, are consistently *cursed*.

Benson, *Chaucer's Drama of Style*, ch. 6, contains a stylistic study of the Prioress's Tale in contrast with the Second Nun's. See also Robert O. Payne, *The Key of Remembrance: A Study of Chaucer's Poetics* (New Haven, 1963), pp. 162–9.

The Tale of Sir Thopas

Prologue

The 'miracle', so defined in this link, leaves the pilgrims in a solemn mood, and so Harry Bailly calls for 'a tale of myrthe' from his next victim—Chaucer himself. He is undistinguished by any professional definition—'What man artow?'—but the Host has high hopes of his producing 'som deyntee thyng'. Harry Bailly also, in passing, makes some comments on the pilgrim Chaucer's portliness, his habit of staring at the ground, and his detachment from the company: the nearest thing we have to a portrait of Chaucer, if the Host (or the poet Chaucer) can be trusted. As with the Monk and Nun's Priest later in the Fragment, his comments extend from appearance to some hazards as to his sex life.

The pilgrim Chaucer declares himself ignorant of all stories except 'a rym I lerned longe agoon'—like the 'miracle' reference, an accurate enough description of the accompanying tale, except that this particular archaic rhyme is a brand-new forgery. The elvishness of countenance that the Host points out is a hint as to its fairy-tale subject: an elf-queen for an elvish man. In one key respect, however, the Prologue does not give any hint as to what is to come. Alone of all the links (except for the possibly cancelled stanza of the Host at the end of the Clerk's Tale), this one is written in rhyme royal, carried over from the Prioress's Tale. The ensuing shift from the formal and rhetorical stanza structure to the awfulness of tail-rhyme is all the more brutal when it comes.

Date and Text

There is no reason to doubt that *Sir Thopas* was written expressly as Chaucer's own tale. Its context is not any historical event to do with Flemings but the exploration of storytelling, poetry, language, and fiction that makes up the *Canterbury Tales*.

The traditional division into two fits is editorial. The manuscripts consistently indicate a three-part division, each beginning with an appeal for audience attention:

Listeth, lordes, in good entent	(712/1902)
Yet listeth, lordes, to my tale	(833/2023)
Now holde youre mouth, *par charitee*.	(891/2081)

Textual variants generally show the scribes struggling to cope with unfamiliar or abused word forms: the spelling *Thopace* is sometimes used, for instance, to avoid misspelling rhyming endings in *-as*. Such variants cast little doubt on what Chaucer wrote. The text is devoid of glosses, not least because in the early manuscripts there is no room for any: we tend to think of *Sir Thopas*, on the model of recent editions, as a *narrow* poem, but in Ellesmere, Hengwrt, Gg.4.27, and Dd.4.24—four of the seven earliest manuscripts—and in some others, it sprawls right across the page, threatening to fall off the right-hand side of the folio altogether. The layout is almost certainly Chaucer's own. It is the standard form of the earliest manuscripts; and scribal errors that appear in the stanzas with the extra short lines look like the result of difficulties in following the sense of the verse through the complexities of an existing layout, a pattern that is reminiscent of a schedule for a tennis tournament with an inconvenient number of players. Both Ellesmere and Gg, for instance, provide 'thyn hauberk' as the object of 'shal I percen' (823–4/2013–14), because the place of 'thy mawe' in the syntax has got so thoroughly lost through its placing on the page:

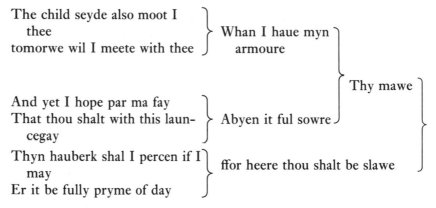

The first joke about *Sir Thopas*, in fact, is obvious before one starts to read, in its very appearance on the page. The layout also serves as a comment on the form, as the intellectual or narrative content of the columns dwindles towards nothing as one moves across the page.

Burrow, ' "Sir Thopas": An Agony in Three Fits', *Essays*, pp. 61–5 (repr. from *RES* 22 (1971), 54–8). 'Robinson 3' follows this layout.
Judith Tschann, 'The Layout of *Sir Thopas* in the Ellesmere, Hengwrt, Cambridge Dd.4.24, and Cambridge Gg.4.27 Manuscripts', *ChR* 20 (1985–6), 1–13; Helen Cooper, 'Chaucer and Joyce', *ChR* 21 (1986–7), 142–54.

Genre, Sources, and Analogues

Sir Thopas makes its genre explicit by aligning itself with 'romances' (897/2087), the only time the word is used in the entire *Tales*. It is not literally an old rhyme, as the pilgrim Chaucer claims; but tail-rhyme romances were abundant in Middle English, and Chaucer's is a brilliant parody of everything that can go wrong in them. Short as the truncated poem is, the section on *Sir Thopas* in *Sources and Analogues of Chaucer's Canterbury Tales* is longer than for any other tale. Almost all the details of the poem can be paralleled elsewhere, often many times over; a few cannot, and they show things going even more badly wrong.

There is no single source or model for *Sir Thopas*, but it may possibly offer one unique opportunity in Chaucer studies, of identifying not just works he used but one particular surviving manuscript. The Auchinleck manuscript, copied in London around the time of Chaucer's birth, is a miscellany of romances and other works that provides a number of parallels to *Sir Thopas* that are found nowhere else, and it is not impossible that Chaucer knew it—the one surviving artefact that could provide a direct physical link with him. It contains three of the romances cited at the end of *Sir Thopas*: *Horn Childe* (which survives in no other copy), *Beves of Hamtoun* (a widely popular poem which survives in various versions, but the one included here starts in a six-line stanza form close to that of *Sir Thopas* and with very similar opening lines), and *Guy of Warwick* (again extant in different forms in a number of manuscripts, but the unique Auchinleck tail-rhyme version contains significantly the largest number of verbal parallels to *Thopas*). It also contains *Sir Tristrem*, one of the rare metrical romances to use a bob (a two-syllable line, like Chaucer's 'In towne', 793/1983), though here it is an integral part of its verse form; and *Amis and Amiloun*, which offers some possible models of phraseology, and, perhaps more signifi-cantly, a character named Amoraunt, or Child Amoraunt—'Amoraūt' in the manuscript. There is also a giant of the same name in *Guy*. There are no known parallels for the name 'Thopas'; but 'amaraunt' and 'amyraud' are variant forms of 'emerald', and it is possible that Child Amoraunt inspired the naming of Child Thopas, after the somewhat similar, and highly valued, topaz.[1] (The child of the Prioress's Tale is also at one stage described as an *emeraude*, 609/1799.) Sir Thopas would thus be a jewel among knights as he is the flower of chivalry (901/2091), or as Gawain in *Gawain and the Green Knight* is like a pearl among white peas.

Chaucer clearly knew other romances in addition to these, and two further manuscript miscellanies, both copied too late for Chaucer to have seen them, though perhaps representing earlier prototypes, give some indication of the kind of form in which he might have come across such

---

[1] The 'topaz' interpretation of the name is universally accepted, the hard *t* being analogous to that in Thomas; but Thopas is invariably spelt *Th*- in the manuscripts, while the th-form of *topaz* occurs in the Middle Ages only as a rare scribal lexis in Latin.

works. The Thornton manuscript contains among other romances the only extant copy of *Sir Perceval of Gales*, the eponymous hero of which gets a mention from Chaucer; and the earliest surviving text of *Thomas of Erceldoune*, a romance in rhyming quatrains that shows some unusual verbal correspondences with *Sir Thopas*, in which Thomas meets and seduces a fairy in a forest full of singing-birds. MS Cotton Caligula A.ii contains *Libeaus Desconus*, Chaucer's 'Sir Lybeux', who acquires a mistress skilled in magic arts after defeating a giant; and also *Ypotis*, though that is not a romance but a didactic work in rhyming couplets, in which a wise boy—a literal 'child' Ypotys, perhaps, to pick up from the chivalric 'child' Horn of 898/2088—spells out the essentials of the Christian faith for the benefit of a Roman emperor and the pious reader. It also contains a number of other romances that offer verbal parallels to *Sir Thopas*, notably *Sir Launfal*, by Chaucer's near-contemporary Thomas Chestre. Launfal, like Thomas of Erceldoune, acquires a fairy mistress in a forest. The poem may also be the model for the particular form of tail-rhyme stanza used by Chaucer: other romances he drew on use slightly different forms—twelve-line stanzas in the Auchinleck *Guy*; a shorter, two-stress, b line within the same aabccb rhyme scheme in the Auchinleck *Beves*; triplets rather than couplets in *Sir Perceval*; stanzas of twelve lines of three stresses only in *Libeaus*.

Mixed in with the romances of both the Thornton and Caligula manuscripts are various pious vernacular works, a mixture which could perhaps have got Sir Thopas sufficiently confused for him to call for romances of popes and cardinals along with love-stories. These pious works do not make much impact on the tale itself. More significant may be popular ballads of the Robin Hood variety: certainly no self-respecting romance hero went in for wrestling or archery, or had a group of 'myrie men' at his disposal (740–1/1930–1, 839/2029). The ballad-style romance of *Gamelyn*, which survives only as a spurious Cook's Tale in a number of *Canterbury Tales* manuscripts, could be another source: Gamelyn wrestles for a ram and joins a group of archer-outlaws on the Robin Hood model. The poem is also distinguished by its repeated formula, 'Litheth and listenyth and holdith your tonge' (cf. 891/2081).

The vernacular romances affect Chaucer's choice of everything from word to episode. The linguistic effects are discussed below, in the section on style; here I will give only a sample of the kind of motifs Chaucer is parodying—though the originals are themselves sometimes so close to parody as perhaps to make 'imitation' a more accurate word.

Many of the romances start with appeals to the audience. Chaucer gives three, and the second is especially close to the opening of the Auchinleck *Beves*.

Lordinges, herkneth to my tale,
Is merier than the nightingale,
That y schel singe;
Of a knight ich wol yow roune . . .

Compare Chaucer's

Yet listeth, lordes, to my tale
Murier than the nightyngale,
For now I wol yow rowne
How sir Thopas . . .   (833–6/2023–6)

There are numerous analogues for the description of Sir Thopas's looks, clothes, pastimes, and accomplishments, though Chaucer sabotages many of the details. Sometimes the most ludicrous elements can be paralleled too closely for comfort in romances that expected to be taken seriously: if Sir Thopas spurs his horse until it sweats/bleeds so much it could do with wringing out, Amis in *Amis and Amiloun* spurs his until

The stede that he on rode
In a fer cuntray
Was ouercomen and fel doun ded.

A number of heroes wear themselves out with riding and rest in a forest. The Auchinleck Guy of Warwick

So michel he herd tho foules sing,
That him thought he was in gret longing,

just as Sir Thopas

fil in love-longynge,
Al whan he herde the thrustel synge.   (772–3/1962–3)

Thomas of Erceldoune is met by a fairy under similar circumstances, to the accompaniment of thrushes and papejayes (cf. *Thopas* 766–9/1956–9). Sir Launfal is accosted in a forest by the daughter of the 'kyng of fayrye', who asks him that

thou wylt truly to me take
And alle wemen for me forsake,

as Sir Thopas promises when he decides to love an elf-queen (794–5/1984–5).

Both the stanza form and the narrative threaten to part company from any models after the mention of the elf-queen, but the parody remains rigorous. The indiscipline of the verse goes beyond any parallels; giants appear in a number of romances, but not with three heads. Guy's giant is called

Amoraunt, which allows for him to swear in rhyme by 'Teruagaunt' just as Chaucer's Olifaunt does; *Libeaus Desconus* provides the further rhyme with 'geaunt' (807–10/1997–2000). Famous chivalric vows had been sworn on swans and herons, and various romance characters swear never to eat bread before they kill their enemy; Sir Thopas, less impressively, swears the giant's death on ale and bread, while snacking on wine, mead, gingerbread, and liquorice (851–6/2041–6, 872–3/2062–3). Lists of this kind are a widespread feature of *Thopas* and of its models: spices, birds, arms and armour, and directories of other romance heroes all make frequent appearances.

We are now, of course, dependent on manuscripts for our knowledge of these romances; but although the account I have given here has tended to stress romances concentrated in particular manuscript miscellanies, Chaucer might well have heard them rather than read them. These romances were not orally composed, but *Horn Childe* passed into oral tradition in ballad form, and *Thomas of Erceldoune* may have developed from a ballad original. As they can be understood by the illiterate who have no knowledge of Latin or court French, all of them may well have been more listened to than read on the page. The layout of *Sir Thopas*, however, is not paralleled in the major miscellanies of tail-rhyme romance; and it works as a joke only for a reader, not a listener. This is the tale that appears closest to oral traditions of poetry, but Chaucer's parody is enhanced by his returning it to written form.

Laura Hibbard Loomis's section on *Sir Thopas* in *Sources and Analogues* contains an excellent anthology of brief extracts paralleling the constituent elements of Chaucer's romance.

Complete editions of the principal romance analogues can be found as follows:

Middle English Metrical Romances, ed. W. H. French and C. B. Hale (New York, 1964) (*Gamelyn, Sir Launfal, Sir Perceval of Gales*); *Sir Launfal* is also edited by A. J. Bliss (2nd edn., Oxford, 1966).

Amis and Amiloun, ed. MacEdward Leach (EETS OS 203, 1937).

Guy of Warwick, ed. Julius Zupitza (EETS ES 42, 49, 54, 1883–91).

Horn Childe, in *King Horn*, ed. Joseph Hall (Oxford, 1901).

Lybeaus Desconus, ed. M. Mills (EETS 261, 1969).

Sir Beues of Hamtoun, ed. Eugen Kolbing (EETS ES 46, 48, 55, 1885–94).

Thomas of Erceldoune, ed. James A. H. Murray (EETS OS 61, 1875) (see also E. B. Lyle, 'The Relationship between *Thomas the Rhymer* and *Thomas of Erceldoune*', *Leeds Studies in English*, NS 4 (1970), 23–30).

Auchinleck manuscript: facsimile edited by Derek Pearsall and I. C. Cunningham (London, 1979).

Thornton manuscript: facsimile edited by D. S. Brewer and A. E. B. Owen (London, 1978).

Structure

The three-fit structure of *Sir Thopas* is described in the section on the text;

'fit' is itself a term borrowed from the romances, though something of a rarity even there. The events of each fit follow each other with a predictability that serves to emphasize their lack of internal logic; the hero's identity, place of birth and parentage, appearance and accomplishments, love-life (or lack of it), forest ride, decision to love an elf-queen, and encounter with a giant; his return, his home life—meinie, entertainments, and food—and arming; his riding back out again. The only action in the poem, and it is repeated in each section, is 'prikynge' or, as an alternative, riding on his way like a spark from a brand.

The first section contains eighteen verses, the second nine, the third $4\frac{1}{2}$, in a progressive halving. The threat of narrative interminability, in fact, is combined with a structural scheme that threatens the poem with an early death—which it does indeed receive, at the hands of Harry Bailly.

Themes and Style

Sir Thopas is one of those rare literary works where the words on the page state an entirely different meaning from their significance to the reader. The text is poetically appalling; one reads it as a *tour de force* of Chaucer's art, a virtuoso piece by an accomplished master. Chaucer exploits the difference by keeping his fictional audience blind to its virtues. To the Host, it is 'drasty rymyng . . . nat worth a toord' (930/2120). Generations of real readers have delighted in the brilliance of its awfulness, as they have in the mechanicals' play in *Midsummer Night's Dream*. The sense of a double text is far stronger in *Sir Thopas* than in other tales of the Canterbury sequence that are affected by their dramatic context: the text of the Pardoner's Tale, for instance, remains stable however much its *uses* may change, from being a 'moral thyng' to being an adjunct to the money-grabbing efforts of a 'vicious man'. Here, the fictional and real audiences construct two entirely different poems out of the same words.

The division between content, meaning and style is always an artificial one, adopted at best for critical convenience; in *Sir Thopas* the three are inseparable. The parody of vernacular romance involves all three, and the mindlessness of the events of the poem—to call them a plot would be too kind—cannot be divided off from its lack of any inner meaning or emotional coherence, or from the debasement of its verbal expression. Chaucer always writes with semantic and stylistic daring: it shows in his readiness to innovate in vocabulary and syntax, his pushing of the English language beyond any previous expressive limits, his fine control of rhetoric, his sensitivity to different lexical registers and stylistic effects. *Sir Thopas* turns backwards to the cramping mental universe of formula, cliché, and filler lines. When Emily is associated with roses, the convention gains resonance from every other courtly heroine or Maytime falling in love; Thopas's 'lippes rede as rose' is dead convention, cliché, that resonates neither intertextually nor within the tale—and where its very failure to do so, in the mouth of Chaucer's *alter ego*, is precisely the point. It is a tale that makes its effect in part by the absence of all those other effects that ought to be there. Speght admirably summed up the object of all this within the dramatic fiction of the storytelling context in his edition of 1598: it is 'purposely uttered by Chaucer, in a differing rime and stile from the other tales, as though he himself were not the authour, but only the reporter of the rest'. *Sir Thopas* decisively eliminates Chaucer from the competition.

The debasement starts at the level of vocabulary. Chaucer borrows words from the vernacular romances that he uses nowhere else in his works: *verrayment*, *listeth* (his usual word is 'herkneth'), *downe* (in the sense of 'hill'), *launcegay*, *auntrous*, *worly* (in the formula 'worly under wede', 917/2107, rationalized by some scribes into 'worthy'). Words are wrenched into dubious meanings for the sake of the rhyme: *roune* (835/2025) correctly means 'whisper', but the Auchinleck *Beves* had already abused it in the way Chaucer does. Word forms are similarly mistreated for the rhyme's sake: *slawe* as a dialect form of 'slain' (826/2016), *entent* for *entente* (712/1902), *gras* alongside *grace* to rhyme with *Thopas* (830–1/2020–1, cf. 723/1913), *plas* alongside *place* to rhyme with *gras*, 'grass' (779–81/1969–71, cf. 720/1910). *Gent*, *rode* ('face'), *love-longynge*, and *lemman* are used elsewhere by Chaucer in strictly demotic contexts, notably the Miller's Tale. 'Sir' Thopas is his only use of the title in naming a knight, though the Nun's Priest is given the honorific 'Sir John' (2820/4010).

Formulaic phrases that serve as ready-made metrical units are recurrent features of oral poetry, and had been retained in vernacular romances long after the justification of oral composition had ceased. *Sir Thopas* is full of them: doublets such as 'fair and gent'; alliterating phrases such as 'rede as rose', 'bright in bour', 'worly under wede'; minstrel tags that serve for nothing but to fill up a line and provide a rhyme, 'as I yow telle may', 'it is no nay'. The utter predictability of the phraseology can be seen from the uncompleted last line. We have had 'And so bifel upon a day' (748/1938); now we are given, requiring a rhyme with 'well',

Til on a day— (918/2108) .

One has already supplied the missing 'it so bifel' almost before one realizes that the poem has stopped: one's own version of the poem is a fraction more interminable than Chaucer's.

What is said in the poem is as devoid of significance as the way it is said; as Chaucer announces, it is a poem 'of myrthe and of solas', with any element of *sentence* or *doctryne* omitted. *Sentence* in romance is traditionally not allegory or separable moral, but an inner emotional logic or a pattern of ideal behaviour—all notably lacking from *Sir Thopas*. The resonance that might come from the use of widespread romance conventions serves only to belittle, not to enhance: they show, not the weight of tradition behind this romance, but the light weight of conventions that are so easy to parody. Aristocratic characters are one of the defining features of romance: Sir Thopas, with his suspiciously bourgeois-sounding lineage, barely passes muster (and the 'lord' of Poperinghe, whose son he is, was in historical fact an abbot). The settings should be exotic, removed either in time or 'in fer contree', for which Flanders will not do. Heroic perfection is represented by Thopas's 'semely nose', expensive clothing, skill at the country-fair sports of wrestling for the prize of a ram, and the chastity that leaves 'many a mayde' awake and mourning. The conventional romance subjects are love or chivalry, or both: in *Sir Thopas*, neither quite comes off—he may decide to love 'an' elf-queen (note the insouciance of the indefinite article, 788/1978, 790/1980), but he does not get beyond dreaming of her; and the great combat with a giant is postponed because he has left his armour at home.

The imagery is just as bad. There are some romance heroes, as well as many heroines, who have red-and white complexions, but 'payndemayn', the medieval equivalent of quality-controlled white sliced bread, is the wrong comparison. Bathos runs wild: the wild beasts in the forest prove to be bucks and hares; the herbs have practical domestic uses; the singing-birds include the raucously unmusical sparrowhawk and parrot; the romances Thopas calls for are to be about popes and cardinals; his bridle shines like the sun, or, by way of anticlimax, the moon.

The events of the tale alternate between such anticlimax and totally impossible hyperbole. Something nasty 'almost' happens to Thopas (758/1948), he cannot engage the giant in combat, God helps him escape the sling-stones. The great epic and romance set-piece of the arming of the hero starts with his underpants ('a breech', 859/2049). When his horse is not awash with blood and sweat from excessive spurring, it 'goeth an ambil', moving both legs on one side together to give an easy pace suitable for ladies (775–7/1965–7, 885–6/2075–6). In case an encounter with a giant is not sufficiently exciting to hold the audience's attention, Sir Olifaunt turns out four stanzas later to have three heads—or so at least Sir Thopas claims (842/2032). The pleas to the audience come with increasing frequency, and urgency: from the repetition of 'Listeth, lords' (712/1902, 833/2023), to the rather more desperate

> Now holde youre mouth, par charitee.   (891/2081)

The Host manages to keep silent after this for less than thirty lines.

If Harry Bailly simply condemns the poem, however, Chaucer does not do the same for his models. It is a parody that betrays as much affection as scorn. Chaucer, unquestionably, is thoroughly enjoying himself. The parody damns its own and others' abuses; it does not deny that the metrical romances can make fine effects, though those are not what he chooses to imitate. The dream of a fairy mistress has a deep imaginative potential, and if Chaucer deliberately sidesteps it, Spenser was to take it up.

E. Talbot Donaldson, *The Swan at the Well: Shakespeare Reading Chaucer* (New Haven and London, 1985), discusses the analogies between *Sir Thopas* and *A Midsummer Night's Dream*.

Burrow, 'Four notes on Sir Thopas', in *Essays*, pp. 60–78, discusses the use of 'sir' and the reading 'worly' (the latter reprinted from *ChR* 3 (1969)).

The Tale in Context

The Janus quality of *Sir Thopas*, its ability to be at once doggerel that writes Chaucer out of the competition and a technical masterpiece, makes it a perfect tale for the Canterbury series, and especially for this Fragment, with its particular concern for the potential and effect of poetic activity. It defines very clearly what Chaucer's poetic is not; he tells it himself to prove that he can do that too. Its opposite number would be the Nun's Priest's Tale, with its dazzling condensation of the full range of Chaucer's generic and rhetorical variety.

A romance such as *Thomas of Erceldoune* serves to illustrate the kind of relationships between *Sir Thopas* and other Canterbury tales perceptible to a medieval audience familiar with such romances. Thomas at first believes his surpassingly beautiful fairy queen to be the Blessed Virgin; after he has made love to her (seven times), she turns ugly. It would have made a wonderful tale to set against the Prioress's and the Wife of Bath's—perhaps too wonderful. Elf-queens are always dangerous mistresses; they are outside the theological structure of hell, heaven, and purgatory. Sir Thopas's sudden vision-inspired devotion threatens to parody the child's vision of a protecting Virgin in the Prioress's Tale. The hag of the Wife of Bath's Tale is also apparently a fairy, perhaps even the fairy queen (III(D) 860–1, 990–8); the knight's way to her sexual favours, however, lies not through combats with three-headed giants but through the absorption of an earnest discourse on the nature of true virtue. Both that and the Prioress's Tale show up nicely the cheerful haphazardry of Sir Thopas.

According to the tale orders found in all the manuscripts, *Thopas* is the last of the romances—after the Knight's, Wife's, Squire's, and Franklin's. The Knight's had expressed the highest reach of secular poetry: aspiring to the condition of epic, drawing on the finest Classical and modern Italian traditions, questioning the metaphysics of earthly life. *Sir Thopas* shows that doing the opposite is just as valid a poetic activity. It is insistently parochial, never seeking allusions beyond its own vernacular kind. Where the Knight's Tale discovered new poetic resources in the English language, *Sir Thopas* circumscribes itself linguistically as tightly as it can. That there might be any metaphysics beyond the possibility of a fairy mistress never crosses anyone's mind. The cousins' discovery that human relationships are difficult, painful, and contradictory is bypassed here by making Sir Thopas the only human character in the tale.

Chaucer was fully conscious of the greatness of his poetic powers: it shows most clearly in such moments as his attaching of himself to the poetic line of Homer, Virgil, Ovid, Lucan, and Statius at the end of *Troilus* (*Troilus* v. 1792), a genealogy imitated from Dante and perhaps also Boccaccio. The story-competition form of the *Canterbury Tales* enables him to show his mastery in every generic and rhetorical form: it is a kind of *ars poetica* that teaches by example rather than precept. It is typical of him that he should include a model of bad verse, and that he should put it in his own mouth. It is also important that alongside the tales that have their origin in French and Italian and Latin texts, there should be one that looks to vernacular traditions alone, and that the sophisticated criticism of such traditions offered by the cosmopolitan poet should double as unadulterated and naïve enjoyment.

The Tale of Melibee

Prologue

Here the hoost . . . biddeth hym telle another tale

It may be because the liveliness of the exchange between the Host and the hapless teller of *Sir Thopas* overshadows the enclosing tales that many manuscripts head the link with a summary of its contents rather than as the Prologue to *Melibee*. Just as Chaucer ran the Prioress's rhyme royal over into the following link, Harry Bailly is here allowed to participate in the idiom of *Sir Thopas*: 'the devil I biteche!' is just such another phrase from popular romance. His literary standards are outraged by Chaucer's 'rym'—used here apparently in a semi-technical sense, for a popular verse form with a high density of rhyming words. When the pilgrim Chaucer plaintively objects that it is the best he knows and that the Host hasn't stopped anyone else, he is invited to tell something 'in geeste' (possibly alliterative verse, in view of X(I)43) or prose. It is the latter suggestion that Chaucer takes up.

What follows is an elaborate apology both for the manner in which he will tell the next tale and for telling it at all. It 'oghte liken yow', he hopes; he describes it, correctly enough, as 'a moral tale vertuous' and, more euphemistically, as 'a litel thyng in prose' and 'a murye tale'. In particular, he apologizes for his version taking a different form from what his audience may be used to; he assures them that the 'sentence' of this version is the same as for every other, even if the words are different and there are more proverbs in it than they are used to.

It sounds like an approximation to literary criticism; certainly the distinction between *sentence*, inner meaning, and verbal expression is a recognized one, and the comparison of the case of the Gospels makes a serious point. But it is the wrong point to make here. Chaucer's translation is very faithful, at least to begin with, and at least so far as the proverbs go (he adds only three). What he does do, increasingly as the tale progresses, is simply to multiply the words of the original. A serious reading of his introductory speech is, I think, excluded by the dangerously bland Chaucerian innocence of 'Blameth me nat' (961/2151): a phrase he uses earlier when suggesting that it is his readers' fault if they find his stories offensive (I(A) 3181). He similarly denies responsibility for the words used by his own fictional creations (I(A) 726), and justifies speaking 'ful brode' by appealing to the example of Christ. When Chaucer excuses himself, something suspicious is always happening.

There are three possible explanations for his speech here. It is conceivable that he was aware of the differences between his immediate French source, which he translates fairly closely, and its Latin original, and is apologizing for that; but he never worries about such differences on any other occasion, and it is unlikely that his auditors or readers would know the Latin well enough to bother about the variation. Alternatively, he may perhaps have written a shorter version of the *Melibee* at an earlier stage in his career: this would explain why he seems to expect his audience—his real audience, addressed through the pilgrims—to know the 'litel tretys' already, and to know it in a briefer form. If this were so, the apology would suggest that he is calling attention to the elaboration of the language of the new version, and that the intention behind the inflation was mischievous.

The third possible explanation is more general. The 'litel tretys' itself can only be *Melibee*—attempts to argue that it refers to the whole of the *Tales* run counter to all normal linguistic usage, and such a meaning could not possibly be picked up without more cues—but the 'tretys' is cited as part of a larger argument about words and *sentence*. Chaucer's claim that different versions of a story proclaim the same message despite the verbal forms they take, as the Gospels do, is irrelevant to the change of language involved in his translation of *Melibee*. But the various tales of the Canterbury sequence very often rephrase existing stories, and if they prove one thing overwhelmingly, it is that the choice of words *does* alter the 'sentence'. Chaucer's literary vision of the world is also a linguistic vision, as tale after tale demonstrates. This does not for a moment deny the existence of an absolute truth behind the Gospels; but just as Christ will not do to authorize broad speech, so the Gospels entirely fail to prove that the meaning of a story remains constant regardless of the words.

Alan T. Gaylord, '*Sentence* and *Solaas* in Fragment VII of the *Canterbury Tales*: Harry Bailly as Horseback Editor', *PMLA* 82 (1967), 226–35, discusses the Fragment as 'the Literature Group' and central to Chaucer's aesthetic.

Date

The *Tale of Melibee* and its Latin and French originals are serious works of advice on personal and political right living. It would be an odd work to translate solely for the *Canterbury Tales*, and it has frequently been argued that Chaucer made the translation—either as it now stands, or in a briefer form—as a political tract. The most cogent evidence for such a purpose lies in its omission of the quotation from Solomon found in the original, that laments the state of the land where the king is a child: a text that would hardly have been tactful in late fourteenth-century England. The omission does not, however, help to date the work very accurately. It was clear by 1372, if not earlier, that the Black Prince was dying, and that the heir to the elderly Edward III would be the infant Richard. Even after Richard had reached the age of majority, the words might still have sounded too close to a prophecy of doom.

Attempts to tie the translation to a particular series of political events are frustrated by the generality of the advice: Albertanus had written the original with very different political circumstances in mind, and the blandness of much of the moralizing could be applied in all kinds of situations—the elderly 'goodman of Paris', contemporary with Chaucer, included it in his guide to good wifehood for his fifteen-year-old bride. The political message of the *Melibee*, on the superiority of reconciliation to war, could have had particular relevance to domestic or foreign affairs on several occasions during Chaucer's career, but it need not be tied to any specific series of events. Reasons have been educed for dating it to each of the last three decades of Chaucer's life, but hard evidence is lacking. The Man of Law's unfulfilled promise to speak in prose (II(B¹) 96) may refer to an original scheme whereby he would have told the *Melibee*, possibly even as the opening tale. This again suggests that Chaucer had the piece to hand in some form before work on the complete *Tales* had progressed very far.

The expansion of the closing section, on the primacy of the virtue of mercy in a ruler, could suggest that the tract was indeed written for Richard II, but the wayward king of the early 1390s rather than the child. One of Chaucer's few additions to his original runs as follows (italicized):

Ovyde seith that 'the litel wesele wol slee the grete bole *and the wilde hert.' And the book seith, 'A litel thorn may prikke a kyng ful soore*, and an hound wol holde the wilde boor.' (1325–6/2515–6)

The words may derive their point from the fact that Richard assumed the personal badge of the white hart in 1390. The image of the hart in *Melibee* would thus be a symbol picked up by the 'kynge' of the following sentence. The addition carries no special emphasis, and is a warning, not a threat; but it would none the less serve to place Chaucer among the wise counsellors of the treatise, not among the flatterers. His poem to the King on 'Lack of Steadfastness' confirms his readiness to take up such a role. If *Melibee* had had such a recent existence outside the *Tales*, it would explain the implication in the Prologue that the audience were already familiar with some form of the translation.

Richard Firth Green, *Poets and Princepleasers: Literature and the English Court in the Late Middle Ages* (Toronto, Buffalo, and London, 1980), argues the case for Chaucer's having written *Melibee* for the young Richard II.

Lloyd J. Matthews, 'The Date of Chaucer's *Melibee* and the Stages of the Tale's Incorporation in the *Canterbury Tales*', ChR 20 (1985–6), 221–34, outlines some considerations for the dating of the piece.

Anthony Tuck gives the dating of the distribution of the white hart livery in *Richard II and the English Nobility* (London, 1973), pp. 149–50.

Text

There is a handful of verbal variants, not greatly affecting the sense, in *Melibee*; the most interesting is the occasional Latinizing of Sophie's name into 'Sapience'. The thing that seems to have caused most trouble to the scribes was the sheer density of pagefuls of solid prose. Omissions resulting from eyeskip are frequent. Three passages found in the French that are necessary for the sense are omitted from all manuscripts (1062–3/2252–3, 1433–4/2623–4, 1664/2854), no doubt because of the same phenomenon early in the transmission of the text. The earliest copy of Chaucer's holograph may have failed to include them, Chaucer himself may have overlooked them, or they may have been missing from his source manuscript (some extant manuscripts of the French omit the second of these passages). Modern editions frequently provide the original French or a summary of these missing sections.

Where glosses exist, they consist of a listing of the authorities responsible for the maxims and quotations in the text.

Melibee survives in five manuscripts independently of the complete *Tales*—a number equalled by the Prioress's Tale and exceeded only by the Clerk's. It is accompanied on one occasion by the Monk's Tale, once by the Parson's.

Genre

Moral prose treatises were widespread in the Middle Ages. The generally secular emphasis of the *Melibee* and its sources, and its message of the superiority of peace to war and of reconciliation to vengeance, give it some affinities with tracts of advice to princes; if that was not Albertanus' direct purpose in writing it, it may have been Chaucer's in making the translation.

The slight narrative outline that provides the motive for the debate is a widely used device; so too is the debate itself as a means of presenting didactic material. 'Debate', as in this instance, is often something of a misnomer: Dame Prudence has things very much her own way. Albertanus' models are unlikely to be Socratic dialogues with their stooge figures—he shows no sign of knowing any Plato—but rather medieval works that made generous use of such one-sided instruction. These include one of the authorities he cites most frequently, the *Disciplina clericalis* of Petrus Alphonsus. This is a loosely framed story-collection in which a father gives advice to his son or a master to his pupil, and the recipient of the advice is given some opportunity to answer back. A more famous instance, though it is not used by Albertanus, is Boethius' *Consolation of Philosophy*, in which Lady Philosophy dominates the dialogue with the misguided prisoner.

A generic cousin to the treatise is the collection of proverbs and wise sayings, such as make up most of *Melibee*. The *Distichs of Cato* was a favourite medieval example; the wisdom-and-folly pairs of the dialogue *Solomon and Marcolphus* are of the same type. To set *sententiae* into longer speeches was also a widespread practice; the narrative of *Melibee*, however thinly spread it may be, serves as a kind of mnemonic or organizing device for its maxims. It is a *florilegium* of choice sayings organized into an argument.

Sources

The ultimate source of the *Tale of Melibee* is the *Liber consolationis et consilii*, a tract written by Albertanus, a judge at Brescia, in 1246. It was the last of three treatises he had written, each dedicated to one of his sons. It was immensely popular, no doubt in part because it brought together such a large number of wise sayings, *sentences*, for which the Middle Ages had an especial fondness. Translations were made into several languages, including four into French. The most widely known of these was composed around the middle of the fourteenth century by a Dominican friar named Reynaud de Louens. It is this version, also used by the 'goodman of Paris', that Chaucer translates: there is no sign that he knew the Latin original.

Reynaud's version of Albertanus is a good deal less faithful to its original than Chaucer's is to Reynaud, though Reynaud may have been working from a Latin text that had already been altered or abbreviated. He cut about a third of it, and added other, sometimes quite substantial, passages of his own. Apart from a tendency to expand on the French by the addition of synonyms, Chaucer makes no such drastic alterations. He omits a few sentences that his copytext may itself have lacked; his one excision that is clearly deliberate is Reynaud's, 'Doulente la terre qui a enfant a seigneur'— a sentiment that would have been highly impolitic to express, even if he felt its force. He adds very little; his version gives the appearance of containing several extra *sententiae*, but some of these are due to his turning Reynaud into an authority to be quoted—'the book seith' what in Reynaud was direct statement (e.g. 1177/2367). His actual additions consist of the proverb 'He hasteth wel that wisely kan abyde' and its paraphrase (1054/2244), the image of the 'hochepot' (1257/2447), and the images of the hart and the king discussed above in connection with the dating of the translation (1325–6/2515–16). It is Chaucer who provides the technical Latin terms for causality (1395/2585); and he translates the closing stages of the treatise, from the enemies' submission to Melibee (1818/3008) to the end, rather more freely than the rest, largely by elaboration, repetition, and paraphrase.

The many authorities quoted within the work are sources for Albertanus rather than for Chaucer directly. Many are biblical, especially Solomon, Jesus Syrak (supposed author of *Ecclesiasticus*), St Paul, and St James; a few *sententiae* are mis-attributed. Classical authors include Cicero ('Tullius'), Seneca, Cato, and Ovid, all favourite masters of morality in the eyes of the Middle Ages. The Church Fathers are represented primarily by Cassiodorus. Of medieval authors, Albertanus' favourite is Petrus Alphonsus, Chaucer's 'Peter Alfonce', a converted Spanish Jew who wrote a Latin story-collection to teach wise living through fable and exemplum.

Albertanus' original explains one point that remains obscure in French and English, and that is the reason for the choice of the name Melibeus. Every version offers an allegorical interpretation of this—'a man that drynketh hony' of sweet worldly goods (1410–12/2600–2)—but that is more a rationalization than an explanation of the choice of name. Albertanus seems to have adopted it from an epigram of 'Pseudo-Martial' that he includes in the *Liber*:

> Consilio juvenum fidis, Melibee; ruinam
> Expectare potes, dum sine consilio es.

You trust the advice of young men, Melibeus; you can expect your downfall, for you have no advice.

It is the task of Prudence to supply the advice that Melibeus lacks.

J. Burke Severs, in *Sources and Analogues*, prints the closest surviving text to Chaucer's copy of the *Livre de Mellibee et Prudence* of Reynaud de Louens; all my quotations are taken from this, and can be located by the Group B² numbers (i.e. the second half of the pair given here for each reference) provided by Severs in the left-hand margin.

Thor Sundby (ed.), *Albertani Brixiensis Liber consolationis et consilii* (London: Chaucer Society, 1883), gives Albertanus' Latin text and an invaluable, though in some respects outdated, introduction. The quotation is from p. 53. The existence of abbreviated Latin texts is discussed in *Sixty Bokes Olde and Newe*, ed. David Anderson (Knoxville, Tenn., 1986), item 42.

Structure

Albertanus wrote his treatise in separate chapters, with descriptive headings, but Reynaud did not adopt this layout. As the logic of the progression of *Melibee* can easily be lost beneath its sheer verbal density, I give here a guide to the main stages of its argument.

967–73 (2157–63) Melibee's foes break into his house, beat his wife and wound his daughter Sophie with five 'mortal woundes'.

974–1001 (2164–91) Prudence draws Melibee away from excessive grief.

1002–49 (2192–239) At her instigation, Melibee summons a large council of all kinds of people; he is given conflicting advice, but he decides to follow the prevailing voice to wreak war and vengeance.

1050–114 (2240–304) Prudence counters Melibee's reluctance to follow her own advice by a defence of women.

1115–231 (2305–421) She lays down principles of wise self-counselling and of prudent discrimination between good and bad counsellors and good and bad advice.

1232–354 (2422–544) She analyses Melibee's errors in his calling of counsellors, and in his interpretation of their advice.

1355–426 (2545–616) She analyses the true causes of Melibee's affliction, culminating in an allegorical reading of it.

1427–545 (2617–735) She urges the superiority of patience to vengeance.

1546–670 (2736–860) To counter Melibee's trust in wealth and might, she advises the careful use of riches, concern for one's good name, and a distrust of the chances of battle.

1671–725 (2861–915) Prudence overrides her husband's objections to a peaceful settlement and persuades him to seek reconciliation.

1726–69 (2916–59) She searches out his enemies and persuades them to submit to her husband; they, like Melibee, acknowledge her superiority.

1770–887 (2960–3077) Melibee agrees to her terms, and receives his enemies; she dissuades him from punishing them, and the treatise ends with his speech of forgiveness—'to this ende, that God of his endelees mercy wole at the tyme of oure diynge foryeven us oure giltes that we han trespassed to hym in this wrecched world'.

The points of transition from one area of debate to another are frequently marked by Melibee's speeches, as he capitulates on one point and raises a new set of objections.

The degree to which the tale is dominated by the debate is indicated by its failure to return to the opening narrative. If the daughter Sophie is indeed allegorical, the processes of argument will in themselves have restored her to health; if she is not, we are given no information as to her recovery from her 'mortal woundes'. The *sententiae* are both the point and the method of the story, and where other tales set one story within another in a receding series, the same happens here with the maxims. Chaucer's speech in the Prologue calls attention to the *sentence* of the tale; the function of Prudence is to utter sound moral apophthegms, *sententiae*; and her own authority is delegated in turn to all the authorities whose *sententiae* she cites. That Chaucer on occasion converts what in his source were her own statements into such authorized quotations—'the book seith'—underlines the interchangeability of Dame Prudence and the authorities she cites.

Themes

Whatever questions may be raised by its placing in the *Canterbury Tales*, the *Tale of Melibee* in itself must unquestionably be taken seriously. Albertanus of Brescia wrote it as a companion to treatises on the love of God and the control of speech; every other context in which the various versions of the treatise appear in the Middle Ages—in manuscript collections of didactic works, in the handbook of wifely behaviour by the 'goodman of Paris'— confirms its essential seriousness of purpose. It was the second favourite among the *Canterbury Tales* for independent copying. The need for wise counsel in government was a commonplace, as were the virtues of prudence. Conventional platitudes on the evils of war were backed up in Chaucer's own time by various movements that worked for harmony between Christian states, and he himself was involved in peace negotiations in the long-running hostilities with France.

Before one starts considering the implications of Chaucer's telling it as a Canterbury tale, there are still a number of oddities within the treatise itself. The most puzzling of these is the inconsistency of its allegorical subtext. That something other than literal narrative is in question is already implicit in the opening lines, as Melibee's daughter is wounded by three of his enemies 'in hir feet, in hire handes, in hir erys, in hir nose, and in hire mouth': in effect in the five senses. 'Feet', 'piez' is a variant of the French for Latin 'oculis', 'eyes'; it may be due to the moralists' widespread recognition of the tendency of the feet, as of the eyes, to wander off in a diversion of the soul from spiritual concerns. Prudence gives the obvious allegorical interpretation of this later in the work:

The three enemys of mankynde—that is to seyn, the flessh, the feend, and the world—thou hast suffred hem entre in to thyn herte wilfully by the wyndowes of thy body, and hast nat defended thyself suffisantly agayns hire assautes and hire temptaciouns, so that they han wounded thy soule in fyve places; this is to seyn, the deedly synnes that been entred into thyn herte by thy fyve wittes. (1421–4/2611–14)

Whether or not she sees this as representing the truth behind the allegory— she is, after all, herself a figure for Prudence as well as being called Prudence—or simply as a good opportunity to inculcate a moral lesson, it tends to make nonsense of the whole treatise, for the last foes with whom one should make peace are the world, the flesh, and the devil. Chaucer makes matters worse by one of his rare additions to the story, his naming of Melibee's daughter as Sophie—wisdom, one of the attributes of the soul closest to God. The name threatens to destroy the point of the treatise if prudence, expediency, makes peace with God's enemies regardless of the damage done to true wisdom.

It is easy to overstate the case for allegory, however; or rather, to push it too far in the wrong directions. The work is primarily about secular living, not spiritual—prudence rather than faith, political enemies rather than the devil. That political life can, allegorically speaking, be given a religious interpretation, would come as no surprise in the fourteenth century. To put it another way, the *Tale of Melibee* tells a literal story that invites a moral-allegorical reading, but which is also capable of an anagogical reading, to do with men's ultimate destination. That the moral and the anagogical interpretations are to some degree contradictory would likewise be no surprise to generations familiar with the traditions of moralizing Ovid, or with the rather startling moralities appended to fables by preachers. The point of Prudence's argument here is that Melibee must order himself aright, put his own spiritual house in order, before he can rightly order the affairs of his larger household. If that in itself restores him to wisdom, or wisdom to him, a physical recovery for Sophie in the narrative would be redundant.

For all its stress on the processes of taking counsel, *Melibee* emphasizes that wisdom and understanding are *a priori* qualities, pre-existing good advice. 'The heighe God' is the start of all good counsel (1116/2306), closely followed by a self purged of the sins. Such pre-conditions will enable advice to be rightly understood, in a way that may be in direct contradiction to what it says. The physicians are quite clear that 'right as maladies been cured by hir contraries, right so shul men warisshe werre by vengeaunce' (1917/2207). Melibee takes this to mean just what it says (1279-81/2469-71); Prudence accepts the premises but denies the conclusion:

Certes, the wordes of the phisiciens sholde been understonden in this wise: for good and wikkednesse been two contraries, and pees and werre, vengeaunce and suffraunce ... certes, wikkednesse shal be warisshed by goodnesse. (1288-90/2478-80)

For all the prudential grounding of the tale, the source of understanding is seen as being not in the philosophical arena of rational debate but in Christian values rooted in God.

The argument is, none the less, prudential—expediency and virtue are in this tale two sides of the same coin. There are a few moments when expediency wins—or at least, worldly prudence wins over ascetic spirituality. Riches should be acquired with care and shrewdly husbanded (1550/2740 ff.), an argument that has more to do with financial acumen than with charity. A man who cares about his conscience, his reputation in the estimate of God, at the expense of his good name in the world, 'nys but a crueel cherl' (1646-9/2836-9).

Prudence's prudential qualities extend beyond the advice she gives, to include her own actions. She is Dame Prudence, a wife with an awkward husband who has the temerity to have a will of his own; and she is a master at handling him—waiting for his initial grief to wear itself out (979/2169), or requesting his permission to speak (1064/2254), or, when he gets difficult, putting on a show of anger (1687–2877). She batters down his resistance to the principle of accepting advice from women, and expatiates generously on what Solomon really meant when he claimed that he had never found a good woman (1057/2247, 1076–80/2266–70). To a man who invented the Wife of Bath, Dame Prudence has possibilities that go beyond her semi-allegorical function.

This may be one clue as to what is going on when Chaucer puts *Melibee* into the *Canterbury Tales*, and into his own mouth. Like the Pardoner's Tale, its effect in isolation is decidedly different from its effect in context. In itself, as the individual copyings show, the treatise is a serious work. As a 'litel thyng in prose' told by the greatest living English poet as a follow-up to *Sir Thopas*, it falls far outside Chaucer's normal limits of subject and style. Its platitudes tumble out in an unceasing stream that overwhelms Melibee and audience alike; unquestioned within the treatise, they are taken to pieces in other tales (and especially where women are concerned). Narrative skill has no place at all; all originality is jettisoned, not only by virtue of the fact that it is a translation (and Chaucer insists in the Prologue that it is a work his audience may know already) but because it consists largely of a mosaic of quotations from other writers. The one thing that Chaucer might yet claim credit for is the style, but there too he counts himself out of the contest. Whoever is going to win the supper, it will certainly not be himself.

See p. 46 for the *Ménagier de Paris* (the *Melibee* is omitted from Eileen Power's translation).
Traugott Lawler's *The One and the Many* builds up a powerful case for a serious reading of the Tale.
Paul Strohm, 'The Allegory of the *Tale of Melibee*', *ChR* 2 (1967–8), 32–42, discusses the implications of allegory for the literal level of narrative.
On the connection of the eyes and feet in the sin of *curiositas*, see Christian K. Zacher, *Curiosity and Pilgrimage: The Literature of Discovery in Fourteenth-century England* (Baltimore, 1976), ch. 2. Richard L. Hoffman, 'Chaucer's Melibee and Tales of Sondry Folk', *Classica et medievalia*, 30 (1969), 552–77, suggests that the reading of 'feet' instead of 'eyes' may be due to association with the five wounds of Christ, the divine *Sapientia*.

The Tale in Context

One reason for the popularity of Albertanus' treatise was that it was a fine storehouse of moral truisms; it epitomized much of the received wisdom of the Middle Ages. Its overlap with the moral interpretations offered by other Canterbury tales is therefore inevitable. That Fortune should be distrusted is an idea inherent in the *Tales* from the very first story, the Knight's, and it is taken up most strenuously by the tale after *Melibee*, the Monk's. Patience, in its fullest sense, is of supreme importance (1505/2695 ff.), as both the Clerk and Franklin stress. That 'coveitise is the roote of alle harmes' (1840/2030) is a lesson thoroughly familiar from the Pardoner's Tale; that 'troubled eyen han no cleer sighte' (1701/2891) is the key theme of the Second Nun's and Canon's Yeoman's Tales; the importance of good name for the *gentil* man (1639/2829 ff.) is crucial to the Franklin's Tale; Innocent III's excursus on the harms of poverty is paraphrased both here (1567/2747 ff.) and in the Man of Law's Prologue.

It is, however, the Woman Question that relates *Melibee* most extensively to the *Canterbury Tales*. It is a question already present in Albertanus, and his use of the conventional materials of antifeminism ensures an overlap with the Wife of Bath; but Chaucer's translation sometimes goes out of its way to emphasize these. Reynaud's *seignorie*, 'lordship', for instance, is translated as 'maistrie', or as the doublet 'lordshipe and maistrie' (e.g. 1058–9/2248–9, 1082/2272). Prudence quotes the same proverbs as the Wife of Bath, that 'smoke, droppyng of reyn, and wikked wyves' drive a man out of his house (1086/2276, cf. III(D) 278–9), and the last phrase in particular recalls Jankin's favourite reading. Reynaud's Prudence goes on to declare that Melibee has never found her to be such a wife—'or scez tu bien que tu ne m'as pas trouvee telle'. Chaucer gives his Prudence a disclaimer that borrows the Wife of Bath's phrasing:

> And sire, by youre leve, that am nat I,   (1088/2278)

recalling Alison's denial of perfection:

> And lordynges, by youre leve, that am nat I.   (III(D) 112)

These are small matters, but they work in combination with the bigger issues under discussion—whether a man who takes his wife's advice is necessarily under her thumb, what Solomon meant by denying that it was possible to find a good woman, whether woman is man's help or his confusion, whether women can keep their mouths shut (all dealt with in the section 1055–111/2245–301). They cover the whole area of antifeminist debate, as it is found in the Wife's Prologue and Tale (including her inset story of Midas), in the discussion on marriage from the Merchant, January, Pluto, and Proserpina, and in the assorted views on women and 'wommenes conseils' put forward in the Nun's Priest's Tale. That this tale follows *Melibee*, with only the Monk's intervening, ensures that the treatise cannot be seen as giving any final answers.

The liveliness of the debate on women in the *Canterbury Tales* at large makes it impossible to read Dame Prudence simply as a personification: she is altogether too reminiscent of the Wife of Bath. Both have a vast range of learned arguments at their disposal; they have their own particular ways of managing their husbands, though the Wife is more ready to use defence against imagined attack as a means of aggression, while Prudence does at least wait until there is something to defend herself against. If the Wife is more of a virago, Prudence is also quite capable of reversing the normal male–female marital roles. This emerges in the very first saying that enters her mind,

He is a fool that destourbeth the mooder to wepen in the deeth of hire child til she have wept her fille as for a certein tyme. (977/2167)

In the circumstances of the tale, the genders are reversed: *she* would be a fool that would disturb the father weeping over the injury done to himself and his child. Her roles as counsellor and peacemaker are male ones; only Grisilde of the women elsewhere in the *Tales* is allowed any such function (IV(E) 430–1). That Harry Bailly should miss most of the point of *Melibee*, and take away only a vision of Prudence as a wife who bears patiently with her husband (1895–6/3085–6), is typical of his distorted interpretations of the tales he hears.

Hoffman, 'Chaucer's Melibee' (p. 319 above), includes a list of the major verbal parallels between *Melibee* and the other tales.

Style

The first thing that strikes the reader of *Melibee* is the clogged prose style. A comparison with Chaucer's French original strengthens the impression: Reynaud's treatise is not high art, but it moves fluently and sinuously. Chaucer's version is continually retarded by synonyms that add nothing to the sense—'no matiere ne cause' (1602/2792), 'spak and seyd' (1551/2741), 'wel and goodly' (1780/2970). Phrases are often both translated and paraphrased: 'celui qui est oiseux' becomes 'he that is ydel and casteth hym to no bisynesse ne occupacioun' (1591/2781). Redundant phrases abound: 'that is to seyn', 'but if so be that ye wenen sikerly' (for 'but if').

From the point where Prudence goes to meet with Melibee's enemies, all these characteristics are magnified. Chaucer's version at times parts company completely with his original in this last section, though never to add anything that has not already been said. Reynaud's enemies conclude their speech of submission thus:

Nous nous offrons a vous, appareilleiz d'obeir a tous voz commandemens, et vous prions a genoulz et en larmes que vous ayez de nous pitie et misericorde.

In *Melibee* this becomes:

We submytten us to the excellence and benignitee of youre gracious lordshipe, and been redy to obeie to alle youre comandementz, bisekynge yow that of youre merciable pitee ye wol considere oure grete repentaunce and lowe submyssioun and graunten us foryevenesse of oure outrageous trespas and offense. For wel we knowe that youre liberal grace and mercy strecchen hem ferther into goodnesse than doon oure outrageouse giltes and trespas into wikkednesse, al be it that cursedly and dampnablely we han agilt agayn youre heigh lordshipe. (1821–6/3011–16)

Unless there are political motives for laying such stress on the virtues of mercy, it is hard to believe there is not an element of parody in this, and especially to a man who has just so brilliantly exposed the hollowness of redundancy in *Sir Thopas*. But unlike in *Sir Thopas*, it cannot be meant to be funny: apart from anything else, it is simply too long. Even the sentences quoted are too lengthy to be witty, and the 'litel thyng in prose' is exceeded in word length only by the Parson's Tale. It has been argued that Chaucer is aiming at a certain kind of high prose style, the 'style clergial', or 'curial' and some of his effects—the many devices for amplification, for instance—do fit a textbook pattern for stylistic elegance. Attempts to demonstrate rhythmical patterns, on the model of Latin prose, have foundered on the uncertainty of prose stresses in English. But textbook models are not necessarily the same as good art, as Chaucer makes explicit with his take-off of Geoffrey of Vinsauf's treatise on the art of poetry in the Nun's Priest's Tale. It seems to me inconceivable that a poet with the sophisticated sense of good and bad style shown in those enclosing tales of *Thopas* and Chanticleer could have meant the *Melibee* to be taken at face value. Its message is serious; its manner, especially at the end, is designed to make one long for the next pilgrim, no matter whether churlish, *gentil*, pious, or opportunist, to take the next stage of the story-competition out of Chaucer's hands. In one respect it does work brilliantly, as an authenticating device for the other tales. That they are indeed told by the other pilgrims becomes a large step more credible when Chaucer demonstrates his incapability in two different media as strikingly as he does in *Sir Thopas* and *Melibee*. When the ghost writer behind the other tales manifests himself in physical form, it is quite enough to end one's belief in ghosts.

Diane Bornstein, 'Chaucer's *Tale of Melibee* as an Example of the *Style Clergial*', ChR 12 (1977–8), 236–54, sees the treatise as deliberate cultivation of high style. J. D. Burnley offers a modification of her views in 'Curial Prose in England', *Speculum* 61 (1986), 593–614.

Ralph W. V. Elliott, *Chaucer's English* (London, 1974), analyses *Melibee* as burlesque.

The Monk's Tale

Prologue

The first thirty lines of the *Melibee*–Monk link look backwards to the treatise, as the Host gives a vivid account of his own home life that stands in alarming contrast to Melibee's. His wife—Goodelief, if that is her name and not an epithet, 'goode lief'—'nys no thyng of swich pacience' as Prudence; instead of restraining him from vengeance, she encourages his violence to the point where he is afraid he will murder at her instigation (1917/3107). If Prudence adopted the male function of the dispassionate wise counsellor and governor, Goodelief invites a more domestic exchange of sexual roles:

> 'By corpus bones, I wol have thy knyf,
> And thou shalt have my distaf and go spynne!'
>
> (1906–7/3096–7)

Whether we are expected to believe in the fictional truth of this is less clear: Harry Bailly is enjoying himself enormously in the telling, and he is not going to spoil a good story.

The speech certainly makes a fine contrast to the obese prose at the end of *Melibee*: it is vigorous, colloquial, full of action and colour, with plenty of verbalized physical particularity to contrast with the relentless generalizations of the treatise. Even the barrel of ale by which Harry Bailly swears has a nice appropriateness for an innkeeper; and his mangling of his oaths ('corpus Madrian'), where the sound matters more than the sense, is a characteristic he has already displayed in the Physician–Pardoner link. Chaucer salvaged part of the Host's stanza from the end of the Clerk's Tale, in which he likewise wishes that his wife had heard the story, for use in this link: that stanza may have been rendered redundant by the introduction of the Merchant's Prologue, but an impatient Goodelief was too good an idea to jettison.

The next problem raised in the link is the notorious reference to Rochester—one of the very few allusions to the geographical route of the pilgrimage, and which, in conjunction with the Friar's remark about telling several stories before the pilgrims reach Sittingbourne (III(D) 847), has been seen as justifying the transposition of the whole Fragment out of the place universally assigned to it in the manuscripts to follow the Man of Law's Tale. One possible reason for the mention of Rochester at this point is rather different. What one would see first of a town that 'stant heer faste by' is its cathedral; Rochester Cathedral doubled as a monastic house, and Chaucer may be implying an association of Rochester with monks when he has the Host talk of both in the same breath. The cathedral, moreover, contained a wall-painting of the Wheel of Fortune—a rare subject in this form. It may be coincidence; but such thematic foreshadowing of the coming tales in their prologues is typical of the work, though Chaucer usually gives a clearer hint than this.

The Host next turns admiringly to the Monk—in admiration, that is, of all the un-monk-like things that the General Prologue describes with a similar admiration. He is well-fed, a 'maister' and a 'governour', and his vows of chastity are a great shame: he would be better at 'Venus paiementz' than such skinny secular folk as Harry Bailly—'we borel men be shrympes' (1955/3145), another rather questionable assertion, as innkeepers are not noted for their slenderness. The monk–sex–money connection is the same as that made in the Shipman's Tale, and the Host's first hazard at his name is 'daun John' (1955/3145). The apology with which he concludes is a decidedly backhanded one: he begs the Monk not to be angry at his fooling around, but notes that the truth can be spoken in jest.

The Monk's voice at once changes the style and tone of the link.

> I wol doon al my diligence,
> As fer as sowneth into honestee . . .   (1966–7/3156–7)

He will not align himself with the *cherles*: he has much too high an opinion of his own position. His first idea as to a tale, the 'lyf of Seint Edward', suggests that very clearly: his chosen saint will also be a king—very different from the Prioress's model of childlike saintliness. Then, as the first round of his 'two or three' tales, he decides to tell tragedies instead,

> Of whiche I have an hundred in my celle.   (1972/3162)

The Monk, once started, is going to be difficult to stop.

The lines in which he outlines his programme for the tragedies that follow belong properly with a discussion of his Tale. Of all the generic definitions of the tales given in the links, the Monk's is by far the most detailed.

Glending Olson, 'Chaucer's Monk: The Rochester Connection', *ChR* 21 (1986–7), 246–56, puts forward the argument about Rochester summarized above.

Date

The Monk's Tale has often been regarded as an early work, in existence before Chaucer started on the *Canterbury Tales*. It cannot have been finished before 1386, as the death of Bernabò Visconti, described among the latter-day tragedies, only took place in December 1385; but this stanza could have been added to a work already finished. It is possible that the group of four recent tragedies—those of Pedro of Castile, Pierre de

Lusignan (Peter of Cyprus), Bernabò Visconti, and Ugolino of Pisa—were composed after the rest, as their appearance at two different points in the various manuscripts of the Tale might indicate that they were at some time written on a separate leaf. Arguments for an early date for the Tale are however almost entirely hypothetical. There is no evidence for composition in the 1370s, and only one word, from the group of recent tragedies, that might suggest the 1380s. This appears as a variant reading in some manuscripts, where Pedro of Castile's 'brother' (2378/3568) can appear as his 'bastard brother'. The descendants of the two men were reconciled in 1386, when Pedro's granddaughter, daughter of John of Gaunt, married the grandson of the illegitimate half-brother, and if it is not simply a scribal variant the more damning phrase could have been changed for the occasion.

This is slim evidence, however, on which to base a hypothesis that the tragedies ever existed independently of the *Canterbury Tales*. Many features of the Tale—its repetitious moralizing, its relentlessly sequential structure—make best sense in the context of the larger work. At least one can say with certainty that if it does predate the *Tales*, Chaucer had a very different idea of what it meant at the time he wrote it from when he set it in the dramatic context provided by his Monk, Knight, Host, and Nun's Priest.

Text

The Monk's Tale raises more substantial textual problems than any other of the tales. Three of the early manuscripts omit the stanza on Adam, though the Hengwrt scribe added it later in the margin. The great majority of manuscripts, including the early Corpus manuscript, put the four recent tragedies, the 'modern instances', between those of Zenobia and Nero, but some of the most authoritative, including Hengwrt, Ellesmere, and Gg, place them at the end. The two different orders are as follows:

Hg, El, Gg and others	*Majority*
Lucifer	Lucifer
[Adam]	[Adam]
Samson	Samson
Hercules	Hercules
Nebuchadnezzar	Nebuchadnezzar
Belshazzar (Balthasar)	Belshazzar
Zenobia	Zenobia
Nero	*Pedro of Castile* (Peter of Spain)
Holofernes	*Pierre de Lusignan* (Peter of Cyprus)
Antiochus	*Bernabò Visconti*
Alexander	*Ugolino of Pisa*
Julius Caesar	Nero

Hg, El, Gg and others	Majority
Croesus	Holofernes
Pedro of Castile (Peter of Spain)	Antiochus
Pierre de Lusignan (Peter of Cyprus)	Alexander
Bernabò Visconti	Julius Caesar
Ugolino of Pisa	Croesus

The manuscripts that place the recent tragedies in the middle of the sequence all describe Pedro's brother as a bastard (2378/3568); he is simply his 'brother' in the manuscripts that place them at the end. There are two manuscripts that give the modern instances at both locations, and they too give the 'bastard brother' reading in the middle, 'brother' at the end.

If the 'bastard brother' represents an earlier reading, it might be taken as an indication that the early placing of the modern instances represents Chaucer's original plan; but the early position also makes good sense as representing his final plan, for the last line of the Croesus legend—the final line of the whole Tale in this majority order—is picked up by the Host in his remarks at the end. The transition from tale to frame is therefore smoother if Croesus appears last (though it can be argued that putting it earlier allows Harry Bailly to nod off through the rest—hence his complaint of audience inattention). Editors generally keep the Hengwrt–Ellesmere omission of 'bastard', but they keep the majority order to provide the transition to the link.

Fifteen manuscripts, including some from each group, provide as part of the title, as epigraph, or as an *explicit*, 'De casibus virorum illustrium'. Whether this is regarded as Chaucerian depends on the comparative weight attached to its omission from Hengwrt as against its appearance in a variety of other manuscripts, including Ellesmere. Apart from two recurrent and obvious errors (days instead of weeks at 2289/3479, the tautologous north instead of south at 2467/3657), there is only one minor variant that might be authorial: Ellesmere and others ascribe 'science', knowledge, rather than 'sentence' to Croesus' daughter (2748/3938).

Glosses consist mainly of marginal headings and explanatory notes; Hengwrt, Ellesmere, and others quote a verse from Judith at 2565/3755, and they gloss the incomprehensible 'Trophee' (2117/3307) with the equally incomprehensible note 'ille vates Chaldeorum Tropheus', 'this Trophee was a prophet of the Chaldeans'.

The Tale survives independently of the rest of the *Canterbury Tales* in two manuscripts, once in company with *Melibee*. In this manuscript (Huntington 144), a colophon invites the reader to relate the proverbs in *Melibee* to the downfalls of the Monk's Tale. The other items in both manuscripts include Lydgate's *Fall of Princes*: this is his version of

Boccaccio's *De casibus virorum illustrium*, the work that provided the epigraph and possibly the model for the Monk's Tale.

Genre

The Monk is determined to make sure his audience understands what he means by tragedy:

> Tragedie is to seyn a certeyn storie,
> As olde bookes maken us memorie,
> Of hym that stood in greet prosperitee,
> And is yfallen out of heigh degree
> Into myserie, and endeth wrecchedly.   (1973–7/3163–7)

The length of the definition was necessary because tragedy of any kind was not at this date a familiar form: there were scarcely any examples known of works that called themselves tragedies. Theoretical definitions were widely at odds with each other, agreeing only in their lack of reference to drama. Boccaccio's *De casibus virorum illustrium*, 'on the falls of great men', describes the same process of downfall as the Monk's Tale, but the term *tragedia* never appears in the work. The fullest definition of the form available to Chaucer comes in Boethius' *Consolation of Philosophy* and an accompanying gloss supplied by Nicholas Trevet: in Chaucer's own translation, which he paraphrases closely in the last stanza of the Croesus legend in the Monk's Tale (2761–6/3951–6):

What other thynge bewaylen the cryinges of tragedyes but oonly the dede of Fortune, that with an unwar strook overturneth the realmes of greet nobleye? (Glose. Tragedye is to seyn a dite of a prosperite for a tyme, that endeth in wrecchidnesse.) (II. pr. 2 67–72)

Boethius' text differs from the interpretation of *tragedie* given in the Monk's Prologue, in that it is 'realmes', not individuals, who are cast down by Fortune. The gloss suggests a definition by reference to an unhappy ending. The Monk appears to offer a conflation of the two.

Boethius presumably thought of tragedy as a dramatic form; medieval theorists did not. None of the definitions current in the Middle Ages makes any mention of drama. The clearest definition of tragedy in relation to an unhappy ending comes in the *Epistle to Can Grande* ascribed to Dante; an alternative tradition, mediated through Herman Alemannus' Latin translation of an Arabic commentary on Aristotle's *Poetics*, defines it as the praise of good men. In some medieval usages, the word seems to mean little more than 'tale'. It was only after Chaucer—because of the Monk's definition of tragedy, and Lydgate's adoption of it—that tragedy became synonymous with the *de casibus* tradition, the falls of great men through the instability of

Fortune, 'whan that Fortune list to flee' (1995/3185). The Monk's account of the genre appears platitudinous only because it was to become an established convention. Chaucer's definition remained the norm in England until the influence of the rediscovered text of Aristotle's *Poetics* made itself felt in the early seventeenth century.

The Monk tells, not just a tragedy, but a series of tragedies. As such, it represents the kind of story-collection that the *Canterbury Tales* is not: it assembles stories of a single genre, tone, and meaning, as do collections of saints' lives, animal fables, Miracles of the Virgin, or, from Chaucer's own works, the *Legend of Good Women*. The *Canterbury Tales*, on the other hand, stresses variety and multiplicity, moral, generic, and stylistic. The Monk's Tale is a story-collection that serves to define by contrast what is happening in the larger work to which it belongs.

H. A. Kelly has two seminal articles on medieval tragedy: 'Aristotle–Averroes–Alemannus on Tragedy: the influence of the *Poetics* on the Latin Middle Ages', *Viator*, 10 (1979), 161–209; and 'The Non-tragedy of Arthur', in Gregory Kratzmann and James Simpson (eds.), *Medieval English Religious and Ethical Literature* (Woodbridge, 1986), pp. 92–114.
Minnis, *Chaucer and Pagan Antiquity*, gives useful information on Chaucer's Boethius and its tragedy glosses.

Sources and Analogues

After giving his definition of *tragedie*, the Monk goes on to describe the literary forms it can take: hexameter verse, prose, rhyme ('meetre') (1978–81/3168–71). It is a small clue as to the enormous variety of forms from which Chaucer draws the tragedies, a variety almost as great as that from which he draws the whole *Canterbury Tales*—Latin prose and poetry, both ancient and modern; Italian poetry; French verse and possibly also prose. The Monk cites a good number of authorities along the way, though the names he gives are not always those of the sources Chaucer is using. He draws widely on works whose influence recurs throughout the *Tales*: the Bible, the *Roman de la rose*, Boethius, Dante, Ovid, Vincent of Beauvais's *Speculum historiale*, and possibly Valerius Maximus' *Factorum et dictorum memorabilium libri novem* (beloved of the Wife of Bath's fifth husband). Many of the general comments on Fortune, as well as some details of the stories, are derived from Boethius. It is also significant that not all his sources are written: the three most recent tragedies, of Pedro of Castile, Pierre de Lusignan, and Bernabò Visconti, almost certainly depend on knowledge acquired orally—Chaucer was, after all, an experienced diplomat close to the centre of affairs at court.

The heading that appears in a number of manuscripts, 'De casibus virorum illustrium', would suggest that Boccaccio's long Latin prose work provided the idea and the model for the Tale. It is very unclear, however, just how much Chaucer knew of it; at one point he appears to ascribe either it or the *De claris mulieribus* to Petrarch (2325/3515). Although the *De casibus* recounts a long series of falls of princes, the work is in many respects very different from Chaucer's. Boccaccio imagines those who have fallen from *prosperitee* into *myserie*, from Adam down to his own time, passing before him and telling their stories, with appropriate moralization. In contrast to the Monk, he emphasizes not so much the actions of a blind and undiscriminating Fortune as the protagonists' own rash or sinful acts that allowed Fortune to overthrow them: they are agents of their own tragedies, not mere victims. Chaucer appears to show an unequivocal knowledge of the *De casibus* in only a single stanza of the Tale, when he concludes the legend of Zenobia with the same series of contrasts as Boccaccio—the terror she held for kings against her becoming a spectacle for the people, her helmet against a woman's headdress, sceptre against distaff.

A different major source for the whole tale is Reason's discourse to the Lover in the *Roman de la rose*, a favourite quarry for Chaucer. Her speech on Fortune includes the story of Virginia adapted for the Physician's Tale, and it ends with the debate on the comparative verbal propriety of *coillons* and *reliques* that may underlie the close of the Pardoner's Tale. She demonstrates the instability of Fortune by telling the stories of Nero and Croesus, both used by the Monk, and she adds that if *ancienes estoires*, ancient stories, are not sufficient proof, the present time will provide equally convincing examples (*Roman* 6631–3): a cue that Chaucer also takes up.

The sources for the information contained in the individual stories are summarized below; all are paraphrased freely. Many of the details of the *tragedies* are found in numerous medieval works; as part of the attempt to limit Chaucer's reading to a plausible lifetime's quantity, I select works he is known from elsewhere to have read whenever these are on the list of possibilities.

Lucifer: Church tradition, itself based on a hint from the Bible (Isa. 14: 12).

Adam: The account owes nothing directly to the ultimate source, Gen. 1–3. The details come from more abstruse sources such as the *De casibus* or Vincent of Beauvais for the 'feeld of Damyssene', and Innocent III or Vincent (or homiletic tradition) for 'mannes sperme unclene'.

Samson: Judg. 13–16, supplemented by Vincent and perhaps the *Roman de la rose* 16677–88.

Hercules: Boethius, *Consolation* IV. m. 7, probably supplemented by Ovid (*Metamorphoses* ix, or *Heroides* ix).

Nebuchadnezzar and *Belshazzar*: Dan. 1–5. Some of the misinformation about Daniel in *Nebuchadnezzar* may derive from ambiguous phrasing in Vincent of Beauvais.

Zenobia: Boccaccio's *De claris mulieribus* (a series of Latin prose biographies of famous women), supplemented for the final stanza by the *De casibus*.

Pedro of Castile: Contemporary information.

Pierre de Lusignan: Contemporary information. The factually incorrect account of his death is common to both Chaucer and Machaut's *Prise d'Alexandrie*, but it is more likely that both poets drew on a version in oral circulation than that Chaucer copied Machaut.

Bernabò Visconti: Contemporary information. An English chronicler also records the lack of certainty as to the means of his murder.

Ugolino of Pisa: Dante, *Inf.* xxxiii; the variations are more likely to be due to memorial knowledge or deliberate alteration than to use of another source. Chaucer changes Dante's story drastically, making Ugolino a guiltless victim and omitting the cannibalism of his children at which Dante hints.

Nero: Primarily from the *Roman de la rose* 6183–488, which includes the reference to Suetonius repeated by Chaucer. The *Roman* does not include the details of the second stanza, most notably the imagination-catching 'nettes of gold thread' he used for fishing (2476), which may be derived from Vincent of Beauvais or the *De casibus* (though see p. 10 above).

Holofernes: Book of Judith.

Antiochus: 2 Macc. 9.

Alexander: As Chaucer says (2631–3/3821–3), the story was common knowledge. His version lacks particularizing detail from any specific source apart from 1 Macc. 1 (2655/3845).

Julius Caesar: Again, most of the material is commonplace; it is found, for instance, in Valerius Maximus and Vincent.

Croesus: *Roman de la rose* 6489–622.

Robert K. Root, 'The Monk's Tale', in *Sources and Analogues*, assembles material from the *Roman de la rose*, the *De casibus*, Boethius, the *Metamorphoses*, *De claris mulieribus*, Machaut's *Prise d'Alexandrie*, and Dante's *Inferno*. A facsimile of the 1520 edition of the *De casibus* is edited by Louis Brewer Hall (Gainesville, Fla., 1962). The *De claris mulieribus* is translated by Guido A. Guarini, *Concerning Famous Women* (New Brunswick, NJ, 1963); the standard edition is that of 1539 (Berne).

Pauline Aiken, 'Vincent of Beauvais and Chaucer's *Monk's Tale*', *Speculum*, 17 (1942), 56–68, gives the parallels from Vincent.

Piero Boitani, 'The *Monk's Tale*: Dante and Boccaccio', *MÆ* 55 (1972), 50–69, makes the fullest case for the use of the *De casibus*, and also discusses the Ugolino episode in detail.

Peter Godman, 'Chaucer and Boccaccio's Latin Works', in Boitani (ed.), *Chaucer and the Trecento*, includes an analysis of the Zenobia episode.

Structure

The Monk's Tale is a collection of tragedies, following each other sequentially, with a prologue—or a double prologue: one at the end of the preceding link in which the genre is defined, a second in the first stanza of the Tale that offers a moralization of the same material—but with no other linking or framing devices. Once again, it differs markedly from the organization of the larger story-collection of the *Canterbury Tales*, with its elaborate frame and numerous devices for relating or contrasting tales that are in themselves very different. The tragedies follow each other in a linear sequence, but with no sense of progression—an absence emphasized by the frequency of repetition in the Tale.

The tragedies vary in length from a single eight-line stanza (Lucifer, Adam, Peter of Cyprus, Bernabò Visconti) to sixteen stanzas (Zenobia). They typically introduce the protagonists in the first line, though a few delay the name for a few lines in order to describe first their height of power (Nebuchadnezzar, Holofernes, Julius Caesar). All emphasize in one way or another the height from which they fall; almost all end with a stanza, or a few lines, on the falsity of Fortune. That at the end of *Croesus*, which concludes the Tale in the majority of manuscripts, amounts to a *reprise* of the Fortune theme as it is set out in the first stanza of the Tale.

There are a few variations within this recurrent pattern. Two additional tragedies, those of Seneca and Pompey, are inset within the stories of Nero and Julius Caesar. Nebuchadnezzar's fall is told twice, once in his own tragedy, a second time in Daniel's speech in the tragedy of his son Belshazzar. More or less complete biographies are given for some characters (Samson, Zenobia, Nero), very general accounts provided for others (Adam, Alexander); most consist largely of single episodes, usually their deaths (Belshazzar and the writing on the wall, the four moderns, Croesus' dream).

Any play of voices within the Tale rests largely in the contrast between the narrator's apostrophes to Fortune and his historical material. There is a smaller proportion of direct speech here than in any other tale except the Parson's. Dialogue is almost non-existent. The story of Ugolino contains some disjointed speeches; Croesus' daughter is allowed a few lines to explain her father's dream. The one set-piece speech is Daniel's interpretation of the writing on the wall.

The basic structure of the Tale is chronological, especially in the Ellesmere order that puts the recent tragedies at the end; but Chaucer does not observe strict chronology, in particular in the series from Nero forward (i.e. after the point where the modern instances are intercalated). The sequence of biblical history is more accurately followed than that of pagan history. Of the recent tragedies, the earliest, that of Ugolino, is always placed after those of Chaucer's lifetime. The Monk himself apologises for not telling the tragedies *by ordre* (1985/3175).

The end of the last stanza of *Croesus* offers a *reprise* of the *tragedie*-Fortune theme given in the first verse, an epilogue to match the prologue.

The two contain almost identical material, about tragedies bewailing the strokes of Fortune, whom no man ought to trust. The structure is finally less a straight line or a heap than a closed circle.

Themes

The moral of the Monk's tragedies is set out in the introductory stanza: he will 'biwaille in manere of tragedie' how

> Whan that Fortune list to flee,
> Ther may no man the cours of hire withholde.
> Lat no man truste on blynd prosperitee;
> Be war by thise ensamples trewe and olde.   (1995–8/3185–8)

The 'ensamples' mostly repeat precisely the same point: of Hercules,

> Lo, who may truste on Fortune any throwe?   (2136/3326)

of Belshazzar,

> Whan Fortune wole a man forsake,
> She bereth awey his regne and his richesse;   (2241–2/3431–2)

of Pierre de Lusignan,

> Thus kan Fortune hir wheel governe and gye;   (2397/3587)

of Julius Caesar,

> Fortune was first freend, and sitthe foo,   (2723/3913)

and so on until the near repetition of the opening stanza at the end of the Croesus legend. The emphasis, in keeping with the presentation of the Monk in the General Prologue, is worldly: what interests him is high rank, and the workings of Providence play little part in his mental equipment.

The theme of Fortune is not however quite universal. On a few occasions the Monk does distinguish between the judgements of God and the arbitrariness of Fortune, though the distinctions can themselves be somewhat arbitrary. He correctly notes with reference to Lucifer that 'Fortune may noon angel dere' (2001/3191). Adam is driven from 'prosperitee' to 'meschaunce', but his fall is not ascribed to the agency of either God or Fortune. Samson's trust of his wife is blamed for his downfall; Nebuchadnezzar is both struck down and allowed recovery by God. Classical pagans are seen as subject to Fortune alone, but there is no corresponding consistency in biblical and Christian figures' being subject to God. Holofernes is presented as a victim of Fortune, Belshazzar and Antiochus are overthrown by a not very clearly distinguished combination of Fortune and God's vengeance. The Christians belong solely to the order of Fortune: Pedro of Castile is beloved of Fortune but brought down by Oliver Mauny (the *mau nid*, 'wikked nest', of 2386/3576); Pierre de Lusignan is slain for his virtues, his 'chivalrie', but he illustrates the instability of Fortune (2395–8/3585–8). There is no theological or philosophical differentiation offered of the two principles, nor much attempt to make the assignment of the downfalls to one or the other look anything but haphazard.

This lack of theological distinction is made worse by the lack of moral distinction. The good, the innocent, the high-born, and the evil are jumbled together, not to show the goodness of virtue or the viciousness of vice, but simply as *ensamples* of downfalls. Ugolino's infant children are set on a par with Nero, Holofernes with Zenobia. It is true that pride, pomp, murder, and the hatred of God's people are condemned, but it is Fortune and her actions that are made the moral and rhetorical focus of the Tale.

Only one other cause is specified: women. Remarkably, Eve does not get a mention (as she does in almost every other reference to the Fall in the whole *Canterbury Tales*: to miss her out altogether is perhaps the ultimate insult). But there is no doubt as to why Samson falls:

> To his wyves toolde he his secree,

as we are informed at the beginning, middle, and end (2021/3211, 2053/3243, 2092–3/3282–3), with the added assertion,

> Wommen shal hym bryngen to meschaunce.　(2062/3252)

The Monk is marginally kinder to Deianira ('I wol hire noght accusen', 2129/3319), and he is prepared to include an entirely worthy Zenobia; but the antifeminist bias of the Tale comes out most sharply in the most unlikely place, the story of Holofernes.

> And yet, for al his pompe and al his myght,
> Judith, a womman, as he lay upright
> Slepynge, his heed of smoot.　　　(2570–2/3760–2)

Judith is not here a mighty heroine, nor yet quite sunk to the level of 'Isbel, the woman' of *All's Well that Ends Well*: she is simply the extreme instance of how low Fortune can thrust a man. One needs to repunctuate the line to make sense of it:

> For al his pompe and al his myght,
> Judith—a womman!—

That Fortune too is a woman is of a piece with all this. Increasingly, as the Tale progresses, she moves from being a principle to a person. She is allowed her own thoughts and speeches (2522–6/3712–16). She will bring men to sorrow in just the same way as women bring Samson to mischance. She is cruel, fickle, and mocks at her victims (2662/3852, 2550/3740). She is a gambler (2661/3851), or a whore, who kisses Holofernes 'so likerously' that he does not notice he is dead until it is too late (2556–8/3746–8, paraphrased only slightly).

It was, according to the Bible, Judith, not Fortune, who was kissing Holofernes in order to kill him. The shift in moral ground is typical of the Tale. Both 'false fortune, and poyson' are blamed for the death of Alexander (2668–70/3858–60)—less a hendiadys than a confusion of categories. The philosophical basis that would distinguish between immediate and final causes, Providence and Fortune, righteous judgement and earthly wickedness, is missing. It is no wonder that Chaucer has the Knight, whose own tale presented such matters as deeply problematic, refuse to put up with these *tragedies* any longer.

William C. Strange, 'The *Monk's Tale*: A Generous View', *ChR* 1 (1967), 167–80, argues for a more consistent pattern in the meanings allotted to Fortune.

The Tale in Context

This will be a short section, not because the *tragedies* are unrelated to the rest of the *Tales*, but because they form a tale more acted upon than acting, just as their protagonists tend to be victims rather than agents. The Monk's Tale has very little to say about other tales, though they contain plenty of comment on it. Its discussions of 'wommenes conseils' and the untrustworthiness of Fortune are set between those of *Melibee* and the Nun's Priest's Tale; it is stopped by the Knight, to whom the Monk is set up as an antitype in the General Prologue. It refuses to admit the possibility of any other vision of the world, apart from its own narrow and belittling definition of tragedy: it is the other tales that provide such extras as human relationships, happy endings, searching philosophy, salvation. Only the Friar's and Pardoner's Tales offer as bleak a vision; all the rest acknowledge in some way the force of the Parson's dictum that 'prosperitee is kyndely matere of joy' (X(I) 491). It is a story-collection that could be expanded indefinitely—one wonders if the Monk need stop when his hundred is up—by a process of cloning. The *Canterbury Tales* assembles its stories to reflect the infinite variety of human life *sub specie aeternitatis*.

Style

The metrical form of the Monk's Tale is the most elaborate of the whole Canterbury series: an eight-line stanza rhyming ababbcbc, found elsewhere in Chaucer's works only in the *ABC* to the Virgin. The syntax tends to be complex, with only one or two sentences per stanza, and there is usually a strong syntactic link across the fourth and fifth lines where the verse might otherwise break in half. This in itself gives an impression of high style, of spaciousness and rhetorical elaboration, that is not consistently borne out at the verbal level. The language is often simple and direct, especially in the sections of unmediated narrative. Where interpretations of the material are being offered, on the other hand, whether in terms of God or Fortune, or where power or presumption is the subject, the vocabulary becomes correspondingly weightier and the rhetoric more overt.

These stylistic contrasts recur throughout the Tale. In the story of Zenobia, for instance, her sexual relations with her husband are described in euphemisms that border on the colloquial: 'doon his fantasye', 'pleyen thilke game' (2285/3475, 2288/3478). Their political activities are on an altogether grander scale:

> They conquered manye regnes grete
> In the orient, with many a fair citee
> Apertenaunt unto the magestee
> Of Rome.   (2313–16/3503–6)

Subtler distinctions are introduced alongside these major contrasts in the two accounts given of Nebuchadnezzar's madness, one from his own biography, the second as told by Daniel to Belshazzar in his prophecy of the king's downfall. Nebuchadnezzar's own fall is reflected in the collapse of the vocabulary from conceptual majesty to animal degradation:

> This kyng of kynges proud was and elaat;
> He wende that God, that sit in magestee,
> Ne myghte hym nat bireve of his estaat.
> But sodeynly he loste his dignytee,
> And lyk a beest hym semed for to bee,
> And eet hey as an oxe, and lay theroute
> In reyn; with wilde beestes walked hee
> Til certein tyme was ycome aboute.
>
> And lik an egles fetheres wax his heres;
> His nayles lyk a briddes clawes weere;
> Til God relessed hym . . .   (2167–77/3357–67)

The bathos of the moment of the downfall ('sodeynly he loste his dignytee') is typical of the Tale, and sometimes hard to justify (witness Holofernes, led up and down by Fortune 'in heigh presumpcioun', 'til that his heed was of, er that he wiste', 2555–8/3745–8). Daniel's restatement of Nebuchadnezzar's madness and repentance has a more consistent movement, the syntax pressing towards the culmination in God's mercy, as befits a prophet who can see not just a sequence of events but the divine logic behind them:

> 'He was out cast of mannes compaignye;
> With asses was his habitacioun,
> And eet hey as a beest in weet and drye,
> Til that he knew, by grace and by resoun,
> That God of hevene hath domynacioun
> Over every regne and every creature.'   (2215–20/3405–10)

The shift from an arbitrary to a providential reading of events is reflected in the style. For most of the Tale, it is the arbitrary that dominates.

The simple style is seen at its finest in the story of Ugolino and his children. The Fortune motif is itself here kept under restraint, being limited initially to the homely image of caged birds (2414/3604); and as Chaucer's Ugolino, unlike Dante's, is presented as guiltless, there is no motif of presumption to inflate the language at the start. It is a tale of pathos, reminiscent of the Prioress's Tale in its early pitching of tone by the use of the word *litel*. Here the first usage seems neutral, but the second gains an extra force from the repetition:

> Litel out of Pize stant a tour,
> In which tour in prisoun put was he,
> And with hym been his litel children thre.
>
> (2409–11/3599–601)

The terribleness of Ugolino's predicament is expressed through a rare virtue in the Monk's Tale, understatement:

> And on a day bifil that in that hour
> Whan that his mete wont was to be broght,
> The gayler shette the dores of the tour.
> He herde it wel, but he spak right noght.   (2423–6/3613–16)

Access to the characters' minds is equally rare outside this particular story. The longest speech of the whole Tale, excluding Daniel's prophecy, is given to Ugolino's three-year-old child, whose innocence is as appalling, in this context, as it is poignant:

> 'Fader, why do ye wepe?
> Whanne wol the gayler bryngen oure potage?
> Is ther no morsel breed that ye do kepe?
> I am so hungry that I may nat slepe.
> Now wolde God that I myght slepen evere!'   (2432–6/3622–6)

This is written with a sense of the human dimension of *tragedie* that is denied by the customary pat conclusion,

> From heigh estaat Fortune awey hym carf.   (2457/3647)

It is consistently the best written of all the tragedies, but the very quality of the writing serves to show up the inadequacy of the moral framework.

The Nun's Priest's Tale

Prologue: Text

The link between the Monk's and Nun's Priest's Tales exists in two forms.
The shorter of these has the Host, not the Knight, interrupt the Monk; it
omits lines 2771–90 (3961–80), passing straight from the idea of a little
'hevynesse' being enough for most people to there being no 'desport ne
game' in such dreary stuff. In the longer version, the Knight does the
interrupting on the grounds of his aversion to literary falls, and the Host
chips in with his disparaging comments on the final lines of the Croesus
legend and the 'peyne' of the whole series of tragedies. The shorter form is
found in twelve manuscripts, including Hengwrt; the longer in thirty-three,
including Ellesmere. As there is no reasonable way in which the missing
lines could represent scribal omission, both versions are presumably
Chaucer's. The link seems to have been added to Hengwrt, as the ink is of a
different colour from the rest of the text, so suggesting that the copytext for
the passage was written on separate sheets rather than being continuous
with the Monk's Tale. The circulation of an alternative form then becomes
all the more comprehensible.

There is, however, one oddity: although the single speech that constitutes
the shorter version unquestionably belongs to the Host (he refers to his task
of judging the story-competition, 2803–4/3993–4), a number of manuscripts, including Hengwrt, assign it to the Knight; and some manuscripts
of the longer form assign the first speech as well as the second to the Host.
These errors have customarily been explained by the hypothesis that
Chaucer made the additions, with the appropriate alterations, on a copy of
the shorter form; but this would not account for Hengwrt's having the
revised 'Knight' in the first line but then not including the rest of the
revision. My own guess would be that the shorter form was on one sheet, on
which Chaucer marked the points where revision was to be made; and that
the extra lines were on another sheet. The first sheet, with its Host/Knight
alteration in the first line, would then have been copied (as by the Hengwrt
scribe) without the second sheet attached.

The various manuscripts' placing of the 'modern instances' among the
Monk's tragedies bears a completely arbitrary relationship to the form of the
following link: that is, it is entirely haphazard as to whether a manuscript
includes the Host's reference to the end of the Croesus legend and also
places that legend last.

Prologue: Themes

The long version of the link presents a dramatic exchange between four of the pilgrims—the courteous Knight, who takes the responsibility for interruption on to his own preference for happy endings; the brusque Host, who is a good deal less tactful in his complaints; the injured Monk; and the 'sweete prest' who is quite ready to obey the Host's instruction to be 'murie'. In addition, the entire passage is concerned with literary issues, most particularly as to what literature ought to do or be, and the question of audience response. Chaucer has the Knight and the Host react in two contrasting ways to the Monk's Tale, and through them he raises wider questions as to the nature and function of literature that go beyond any dramatic consciousness that can be ascribed to the characters.

The Knight's excuse for interrupting is clearly not the whole truth on Chaucer's part. Chaucer's problem is to bring the tragedies to an end without disrupting the impression that they could go on indefinitely (as indicated by the hundred the Monk has in his cell); the Knight's problem is to do so politely. His distaste for tales of falls, and his reminder that stories of good fortune are also a possibility, need not therefore be read as indicating shallowness or escapism on his part; his own tale indeed bears witness that it should not be so read. The tale of Palamon and Arcite balanced the downward and upward movements of Fortune; and so it is the Knight who has the right to interrupt, for he has already shown that he can encompass the full vision of which the Monk can see only half. The antityping of Knight and Monk that began in the General Prologue reaches its climax here.

The Host is more outspoken, and his criticisms range more widely—over the high style of the Monk's Tale; the general uselessness of bewailing; that it is a 'peyne' and no fun; and that, since the function of literary activity lies in its effect on the audience, it is useless if their attention is lost ('as thise clerkes seyn'—he may have got the idea from *Melibee*, 1044–7/2234–7). It is, moreover, up to him to give the prize, and the Monk isn't doing too well. His suggestion that the Monk might 'sey somwhat of huntyng' is an invitation to him to live up to his General Prologue portrait, which the Monk tersely refuses.

So much serves more as epilogue to the Monk's Tale than as a prologue to the Nun's Priest's, but it is none the less important in setting certain conditions for the story that will follow. The Nun's Priest, up to this point of the *Tales*, has been without face or character; the little we are told about him now sets him in sharp contrast to the Monk. His horse is 'foul and lene', and the phrases 'sweete prest' and 'goodly man' have none of the irony of the 'fair prelaat' and 'manly man' of the Monk's portrait. We learn nothing else of him except for his readiness to play his promised part in the storytelling and to be 'murie' at the Host's order. There is little in this to indicate the kind of story he will tell, but the Host has decreed everything that it must not be: rhetorically elaborate, sad, or boring. The tale that follows is certainly never boring, and its potentially unhappy ending is neatly forestalled. Its rhetoric, on the other hand, is as amazing as anything in the whole Canterbury sequence, but if it does stray into high style the Host is much too enthralled to complain.

On the Knight's interruption, see R. E. Kaske, 'The Knight's Interruption of the Monk's Tale', *ELH* 24 (1957), 249–68.

Date and Text

The extensive appearance in the Nun's Priest's Tale of motifs found in other tales of the Canterbury collection indicates that it was written late—perhaps one of the last, after others such as the Wife of Bath's that are themselves second thoughts in the assembling of the series. Its references to the preceding tales, most particularly to *Melibee* and the Monk's Tale, suggest that it may have been written for its place at the end of this Fragment. Its internal evidence of date (after 1381, since it refers to the Peasants' Revolt) gives no more information than one would have guessed anyway, but a distance of some years between the Revolt and the writing of the Tale would make Chaucer's flippancy on the subject more explicable: it would be far enough away to be turned into a joke.

Textual variants are insignificant, though an extra couplet, almost certainly spurious, is occasionally found after 2870/4060 to give Chauntecleer a particularly hectic sex life—'He fethered hire an hundred tyme a day'. Glosses are limited largely to brief marginal finding-notes, though Dd.4.24 calculates the elaborate periphrasis for the date at 3190/4380 as 2 May. A final puzzling gloss in Hengwrt, Ellesmere, and Dd.4.24 identifies 'my lord' (3445/4635) as the Archbishop of Canterbury.

Derek Pearsall's Variorum edition, *The Nun's Priest's Tale* (Variorum II 9, Norman, Okla., 1984), is an excellent conspectus of all textual and critical issues raised by the Tale. Of the small editions, that by Kenneth Sisam (Oxford, 1927, repr. 1957) is especially notable.

Genre

The Nun's Priest's Tale is a beast-fable—not just a story about animals, but, as in every collection of fables from Aesop to La Fontaine, a story with a moral in which the animals stand in some kind of exemplary relationship to humans. Fable morals are traditionally concerned with practical homely wisdom: how things are, rather than how things ought to be—that the foolish are deceived by flattery just as cocks are carried off by foxes. There is, however, abundant room for exploring the incongruity between animals and men, and Chaucer carries this to unprecedented lengths. He is keenly aware that while the point of a fable may be its moral, animals in fact operate outside morality; and his treatment of the story calls attention to all the points that would be outrageously immoral in the human world but are mere facts of life in the barnyard, as, for instance, that Chauntecleer's seven hens are 'his sustres and his paramours'. Such an abundance of concubines transgresses all taboos on incest, fornication, and/or polygamy, but the effect is more to mock men's pretensions to morality than to reflect human promiscuity in the animal world. At the same time, Chauntecleer is emphatically not confined to any existence as mere cock: he is endowed with a complex matrimonial relationship, extensive book-learning, the ability to talk (2881/4071), and a psychology as highly developed as any of Chaucer's human characters. It would, in fact, be a far more sound and productive exercise to write an essay on the character of Chauntecleer than on that of the Nun's Priest, despite the continuing fashion, and deceptively greater plausibility, for doing the latter.

The beast-fable was an ambivalent genre in the Middle Ages. Its simplicity made it appropriate for elementary instruction, but it could also be used as a vehicle for sophisticated rhetoric; the Nun's Priest's Tale exploits the ambivalence to the full. Vincent of Beauvais, whose encyclopaedia probably provided material for part of the debate on dreams, includes a fable collection in the pedagogic section. The form also had a long association with more courtly literature, and lengthy elaborations of the fable after the manner of romances are found in beast-epics such as the *Roman de Renart*, itself probably Chaucer's main source. The label of 'beast-epic' is appropriate for such works in the first instance simply because of their length, but they also have a clear potential to become mock-heroic, and this too Chaucer exploits to the full. The courtly potential in the tale becomes explicit, only to be sabotaged by the barnyard setting. Something similar happens to the traditional wisdom of the fable. It is inflated into a philosophical debate on such matters as the prophetic qualities of dreams, predestination, and necessity, but the arguments are resolved by such unphilosophical considerations as Chauntecleer's hatred of laxatives.

Two other literary kinds act in effect as subgenres to the beast-fable: tragedy and romance, the two that together compose the Knight's Tale. There, the two protagonists were each allotted one of the generic patterns: Arcite falls at his moment of apparent triumph, Palamon recovers from apparent annihilation to achieve the happy ending of the tale. Similarly, the fox is the victim of the downward turn of Fortune's wheel at his moment of triumphal pride (3403–4/4993–4), while Chauntecleer escapes from what seems like certain death. Up until the end, it has seemed as if the cock is to be the tragic victim: his premonitions of doom, his downfall at his moment of most extreme self-congratulation, and the lamentations for his fall are all tragic motifs, and the point is driven home by references back to the Monk's Tale (e.g. 3205–9/4345–9). The relationship of the tale to genuine *tragedie* and romance is however one of parody, and indeed most genres of the *Canterbury Tales* come in for parodic treatment at some point.

Stephen Manning, 'The Nun's Priest's Morality and the Medieval Attitude Towards Fables', *JEGP* 59 (1960), 403–16, is informative on the fable background; and see also Walter Scheps, 'Chaucer's Anti-fable: *Reductio ad absurdum* in the *Nun's Priest's Tale*', *Leeds Studies in English*, NS 4 (1970), 1–10.

Sources and Analogues

The story of the cock and the fox was known in England before Chaucer used it, though his immediate source was apparently French. The plot, however, accounts for a remarkably small proportion of the Nun's Priest's Tale—not much over a tenth. The sources for the assorted discussions that make up the rest range from the Bible and the Classics to contemporary theology and oral tradition; but very often, the reasons for Chaucer's inclusion of such a wide scatter of material lie elsewhere in the *Canterbury Tales*. The themes and the rhetoric of the whole work are found in miniature in this Tale, all treated with the incongruity or irony or downright parody that comes from setting a story of potential romance and tragedy in a chicken-run.

The ancestors of the story lie in early fable collections, in tales such as the Fox and the Crow in Aesop. The double trick, in which the fox persuades his victim to close his eyes and the victim in turn tricks the fox into opening his mouth, is first found in a Latin fable collection made by Adhemar of Limoges early in the eleventh century. By the twelfth century, in the Latin poem *Gallus et vulpes*, the victim had been identified as a cock, the fox incites him to emulate his father in closing his eyes while singing, the cock persuades the fox to shout defiance at his pursuers, and each draws the appropriate moral, on keeping one's mouth shut or one's eyes open. Marie de France, who was probably writing in England, told the same story in French in her own collection of fables, possibly known to Chaucer.

The story also occurs in various of the beast-epics about the multitudinous adventures of the fox Reynard, and one of these, the second branch of the French *Roman de Renart*, was probably Chaucer's main source. This version of the tale includes a description of the fenced yard where the hens live (though it belongs to a rich landowner, not a poor widow), the cock Chantecler's favourite hen Pinte and their not entirely smooth matrimonial relationship, his prophetic dream, and, as in many of the fable versions, the double moral. The likenesses are reinforced by some verbal resemblances that go beyond coincidence of treatment, notably Pinte's 'Avoy!', which Chaucer takes over into English without translation (2908/4098). Other versions of the Reynard cycle that have been proposed as sources are unlikely despite similarities of detail; neither the German *Reinhart Fuchs* nor the French *Renart le contrefait* is likely to have been known in England. It has also been suggested that since so much in Chaucer's story is different from the *Roman de Renart* (including the names of Pertelote and Daun Russell) he may have known an intermediate version, whether written or oral, rather than the original *Roman*; but if the changes could be made by another poet, they could equally well be made by Chaucer. Whatever his source, he amplified and altered it extensively.

The story was also told in Chaucer's lifetime in John Bromyard's preacher's anthology, the *Summa praedicantium*. This version too may have been known to Chaucer, either indirectly through its use in sermons, or directly from a manuscript of the work. Both Bromyard and Chaucer stress guile, deception, and ambushes, *insidiae*. The Nun's Priest notes that the action of his story took place when birds could talk (2881/4071); Bromyard opens his cock's cursing of the fox with, 'The cock said—or might have said, if he had had reason and the power of speech—'. The final effect and point of the two versions are however very different. The appearance of the story in a preaching handbook underscores the deep association of fable with *moralitee* that Chaucer treats so equivocally at the end of the tale.

Oral tradition probably contributes at least one detail to the tale. Malkyn runs after the fox 'with a dystaf in hir hand' (3384/4574), as in the carvings of the chase of the fox with the goose on fourteenth-century misericords, or in the fifteenth-century lyric, presumably based on the same tradition, 'The fals fox came unto our croft'.

The longest passage in the Tale on a single theme has nothing to do with the basic story: it is concerned with the debate—if it deserves such a term, when Chauntecleer holds forth for so much of it—on the signification of dreams. There is a suggestion for this in the *Roman de Renart*, where Chantecler has a much more enigmatic dream than the open premonition of the Nun's Priest's Tale; but it is Chaucer who gives it such very extensive development. His main source for Pertelote's disquisition on the physical causes of dreams is probably derived from the *Speculum naturale* of Vincent of Beauvais, though the ideas were widely familiar in the Middle Ages. The list of purgatives and laxatives she prescribes to cure her mate's excess of choler is supported by many herbals and medicinal treatises, though some of them are exceedingly violent, and the total list might well have done

Chauntecleer more damage than the fox: it is just as well that he defies the whole lot. The possibility of divination through dreams was widely discussed in the Middle Ages, but the most likely major source of Chauntecleer's long speech on the subject is Robert Holcot, whose commentary on the Book of Wisdom included some of the same arguments as Chauntecleer gives, and also versions of the two stories of true dreams that he tells. Holcot's own source for these stories was Valerius Maximus' *Factorum et dictorum memorabilium libri* (I. vii. 10, 3), a text certainly known to Chaucer; Cicero also tells the stories in the *De divinatione*. Neither Holcot nor Cicero nor Valerius, however, gives the second story 'in the nexte chapitre after this' (3065/4255). In any case, Chauntecleer's versions are much more vivid and circumstantial than any of the earlier accounts: they become tales in their own right, not mere illustrative exempla. The stories are backed up by a host of other examples of significant dreams, from the Bible (David and Joseph), possibly reinforced by the Monk's reference to Daniel (2154/3344) and by Holcot's discussion of Pharaoh's dreams; from Cicero (whose *Dream of Scipio* is here wrongly ascribed to its commentator Macrobius, in whose work alone it was preserved in the Middle Ages: cocks can't get everything right all the time); from the post-Classical versions of the Troy story (Andromache, 3141–6/4331–6); from the legend of St Kenelm (current in both English and Latin versions, though Chaucer includes details not found in the English); and also the dream of Croesus, whose immediate source here is probably the Monk's Tale.

For the scatter of miscellaneous allusions throughout the tale, there is sometimes an embarrassment of choice as to source. The notorious complaint against Friday (3347/4537) is ultimately derived, as Chaucer says, from a specimen example of rhetoric in Geoffrey of Vinsauf's *Poetria nova*, but the passage was already famous enough to circulate independently. Of the tale's maxims, 'Evere the latter ende of joye is wo' (3205/4395) scarcely requires a source, but it is found in similar form in Proverbs 14: 13 (cited in a marginal gloss in Dd.4.24); Chaucer may also have had in mind the passage of Innocent III quoted as a gloss to the similar maxim in the Man of Law's Tale (II(B¹) 421–2). 'Mulier est hominis confusio' (3164/4354) was also widely known as a tag: it derived from a fictional dialogue between the Emperor Hadrian and a philosopher, but Chaucer may well have found it in Vincent of Beauvais, and in the *Canterbury Tales* it was last heard of in the course of *Melibee* (1106/2296).

The mixture of scholarly reference with allusion to the more immediate context of the *Tales* pervades the Nun's Priest's Tale. St Kenelm himself probably owes his inclusion less to his relevance for significant dreams than to the fact that he was a seven-year-old saint, like the Prioress's martyr. The question of predestination and free will, glanced at with reference to St

Augustine, the early fourteenth-century theologian Thomas Bradwardine, and, most particularly, Boethius (3243–50/4433–40), looks back to the Knight's Tale, as do the apostrophes to destiny and Venus (3338–46/4528–36). The archetype of all women in Eve (3257–9/4447–9), besides its obvious source in Genesis, has been called on frequently in earlier tales. The long simile on the lamentation at the fall of Troy includes its own footnote to the *Aeneid* (3359/4549), but its immediate antecedent lies in the Man of Law's Tale (II(B¹) 288 ff.). The similes in both tales extend to include the Punic Wars, though the Nun's Priest's reference to Hasdrubal's wife is probably derived from Jerome's *Adversus Jovinianum*. Nero's slaying of the senators was last heard of in the Monk's Tale, where it was described as having been done in order 'to heere how that men wolde wepe and crie' (2481/3671)—especially appropriate in view of its culminating position here in the similes on the racket made by the hens.

A few of the allusions in the Nun's Priest's Tale by contrast relate to this poem alone, and specifically to the animals who inhabit it. There is something deeply appropriate about Chauntecleer's singing 'murier than the mermayde in the see' (3270/4460) with an accompanying reference to Physiologus on sirens, for where other than in a bestiary would one expect to find authority on all matters relating to cocks? The fox claims to have read the satirical beast-poem of Nigel Wireker, 'daun Burnel the asse' (3312/4502), and summarizes its story of the cock that exacted its revenge for a broken leg by failing to crow and wake his injurer on the morning of his ordination. Little as Wireker's work contributes to the whole plot, it may have had a more extensive influence on Chaucer's treatment, for it is one of the finest medieval examples of the satiric exploitation of the incongruity between animals and the men they partly represent.

The tale also includes one of Chaucer's rare allusions to contemporary events, in the comparison of the noise of the chase to the din made by 'Jakke Straw and his meynee' (3394/4584) in the Peasant's Revolt of 1381. Even this, however, may have been influenced by a literary text as well as by historical fact, for John Gower, in a section of dream allegory in his Latin satirical work *Vox clamantis*, had described the peasants as being transformed into beasts, including a cock urged on by his mate (i. 7), and their din as being like the noise made by asses, oxen, pigs, dogs, foxes, geese, and wasps (i. 11)—compare the tale's dogs, cow, hogs, ducks, geese, and bees all contributing to the noise of the chase. Chaucer's list is, of course, derived from the farmyard setting, but the train of association that takes him from barnyard animals to rioting peasants might be the result of his knowledge of Gower's text.

James R. Hulbert, 'The Nun's Priest's Tale', in *Sources and Analogues*, gives extracts from the *Roman de Renart*, *Reinhart Fuchs*, and Valerius Maximus. Such studies supersede Kate

O. Petersen's *On the Sources of 'The Nonne Prestes Tale'* (Boston, 1898, repr. New York, 1966).

For 'Del cok e del gupil' of Marie de France, see her *Fables*, ed. and trans. Harriet Spiegel (Toronto Medieval Texts and Translations 5, Toronto, 1987), no. 60.

For Bromyard, see the *Summa praedicantium*, J. xiii. 28 (full reference on p. 12 above).

'The fals fox' is ed. Rossell Hope Robbins, *Secular Lyrics of the XIVth and XVth Centuries* (2nd edn., Oxford, 1955), no. 49.

Further possible sources are studied by Pauline Aiken, 'Vincent of Beauvais and Dame Pertelote's Knowledge of Medicine', *Speculum*, 10 (1935), 281–7; and Robert A. Pratt, 'Some Latin Sources of the Nonnes Preest on Dreams', *Speculum*, 52 (1977), 538–70, and 'Three Old French Sources of the *Nonnes Preestes Tale*', *Speculum*, 47 (1972), 422–4, 646–8.

Jill Mann, 'The *Speculum stultorum* and the *Nun's Priest's Tale*', *ChR* 8 (1974–5), 262–82, discusses Chaucer's links with, and differences from, Nigel Wireker and the beast-fable tradition. See p. 425 below for more on the story of the cock and the ordinand priest.

A. Paul Shallers, 'The "Nun's Priest's Tale": An Ironic Exemplum', *ELH* 42 (1975), 319–37, opens with an extensive discussion of the ancestors of the tale.

Structure

Two characteristics of the structure of the Nun's Priest's Tale have already been mentioned: first, the immense amount of amplification of the basic story, especially by the discussion of dreams; and secondly, the reversal that gives Chauntecleer an unexpected release and turns the fox into the victim of Fortune. It is unexpected, that is, in terms of farmyard probability; but there must be few readers who genuinely fear for Chauntecleer's life, partly because any reader, medieval or modern, is likely to have some knowledge of the plot in advance, and partly because Chaucer's elaboration of the role and character of his cock would make his consumption by the fox unthinkable— a breach of some kind of decorum of the imagination.

The opening sections of the poem would seem as if they ought to show a steady diminution of scale, moving as they do from the widow's household to the yard to Chauntecleer's relationship with his hens to the cock's own mind. The effect is in fact the opposite. The plain style of the opening enlarges to accommodate Chauntecleer's instinctive astronomical knowledge, the courtliness of Pertelote, and then the sententious and philosophical reach of the debate on dreams, which extends the range of reference of the tale as far as Cato, Cicero, Macrobius, and the Bible, and enlarges its world to include the 'fer contree' (3068/4258) of the exemplary tales, ancient Egypt and Troy. With Chauntecleer's recovery of composure, as expressed in his treading of Pertelote, the barnyard seems to return to its opening state of normality.

The main action of the tale opens with a line that one might have expected to find at the very beginning, 'Whan that the month is which the world bigan—' (3187/4377). Even after this dating of the fateful day, however (and the dating itself takes up four lines and remains ambiguous), it takes almost thirty lines of comment and chronology before the fox appears; and that is followed rapidly by a withdrawal from the story to the narrator, as he inveighs against treacherous homicides, discusses predestination and conditional necessity, and refuses to debate the question of how far women were responsible for the Fall of Man. Only after all this does the story really get under way, with the fox's flattery; and it does not go on for long before there are further rhetorical interruptions, on flattery, destiny, Friday, the fall of Troy, and a few other barely relevant topics. The racket of the hens opens out to the chaos of the chase, a brief closing section of narrative in which Daun Russell in his turn falls victim to Chauntecleer's tricks, the even briefer morals drawn by each of them, and the Nun's Priest's quiet conclusion.

If the two narrative climaxes of the story—the seizing of Chauntecleer and the hoodwinking of the fox—manage to stand out from all this, it is scarcely because of any emphasis they are given in terms of length. The Nun's Priest's Tale is 626 lines long, of which only about sixty are spent advancing the story; the debate on dreams, by contrast, occupies some 280. Others of the Canterbury Tales are almost equally disproportioned in narrative terms (the Wife of Bath's Tale offers some parallels, with its inset story of Midas and its disquisition on *gentillesse*), but the disproportion here calls attention to a second structure within the tale distinct from the one suggested by the plot. This is a structure of layers of fictionality.

It works like a series of Russian dolls. On the outside, the primary layer of fictionalizing, of storytelling, is the poet Chaucer. He is telling a story about his fictional self, the pilgrim Chaucer, who is in turn recording a story spoken by the Nun's Priest (making three layers so far). The Nun's Priest's story is about Chauntecleer; and he in turn has a story to tell, about the dream he has had (the fourth layer). Chauntecleer also tells of reading various authors who tell stories (the fifth layer) of men who have dreamed and therefore have presumably themselves recounted their dreams (a sixth layer), since dreams cannot be known about unless their narratives are told by their dreamers. The final and irreducible layer of storytelling, the Russian doll in the centre that will not take apart, occurs within these dreams, as figures appear to the dreamers to utter warnings—and the most incisive of these is cast explicitly in the form of storytelling;

> 'If thou tomorwe wende,
> Thow shalt be dreynt; my tale is at an ende.' (3081–2/4271–2)

This layering suggests a process of constant recession—the picture of a picture of a picture—but this is not quite the impression Chaucer gives. The outermost layers, of Chaucer the poet and pilgrim, are shadowy; and one is more conscious of Chauntecleer talking than of the presence of the Nun's Priest. Only within Chauntecleer's speech do the layers begin to recede, to appear miniaturized. The least equivocal meanings to be found beneath all these layers of fiction occur however at the very centre—'Thow shalt be dreynt', or the stories that 'prove' the significance of dreams. The further out one moves the more ambiguous or opaque do the meanings become. The tale does indeed offer two morals, but they are scarcely adequate to the fullness of the narrative development; if they are the kernel of truth within the shell of the fiction, the nut is only worth having for the shell. The 'truth' of even the inmost message is, however, at best contingent on the truth of the story of the drowned traveller, and one is scarcely being invited to take that at face value when it is presented as part of the intellectual equipment of a cock living at a time when 'beestes and briddes koude speke and synge' (2881/4071). Even he, moreover, forgets what his exempla are supposed to prove, concluding with a triumphant, and entirely irrelevant, 'Mordre wol out'. If even he cannot keep his intended *sentence* in mind, the intentions of the Nun's Priest, Chaucer the pilgrim, and Chaucer the poet as to the significance of the tale remain entirely obscure, as meaning is subverted by the insistent fictionality of the text.

Themes

The Tale's structure has major implications for interpretation. It suggests that, while there may still be themes in the story that are significant in themselves, there cannot be any decisive 'meaning', any direct linking of the story to life or to moral action, since all such ethical claims are enfolded within other layers that stress storytelling and fictionality. It still remains open to the individual interpreter, whether within the tale as a character or outside it as a reader, to derive a moral, as the fox and the cock each read off their own morals from the events; but the tale stresses that such moral readings are subjective, not inherent in the story. Chauntecleer gets so involved in rebutting his wife's accusation of indigestion that he forgets the point of his exempla on the significance of dreams except in so far as they enable him to defy her laxatives, and so fails to be on his guard against the fox. The morals offered by the narrator are no more trustworthy. His maxims on the mutability of earthly joy are backed up by an assertion that his story is as true as that of Lancelot, 'that wommen holde in ful greet reverence' (3205–13/4395–403): as a measure of authenticity, this leaves much to be desired. Other morals are no sooner proposed than they are withdrawn, especially if they tend to the antifeminist: 'Wommennes conseils been ful ofte colde', for instance (3256/4446), is hastily followed by the assurance that 'I kan noon harm of no womman divyne', which replaces the authority of aphorism with a personal apologia cast in such wide terms and so much at odds with the fictional context as to invite an ironic reading. That the ostensible narrator is the priest, and therefore confessor, to a convent, riding as an escort to its superior, underscores the doubt.

The relation of the tale to the Nun's Priest is at best marginal, however. It may appear momentarily in disclaimers such as that quoted, but Chaucer is as ready to make similar remarks when he is narrating in his own voice in *Troilus and Criseyde* or the *Legend of Good Women*, and he too tends to stress his disingenuous relationship to a female audience. There is some appropriateness in a priest's telling a beast-fable; this same one is, after all, included by John Bromyard in his handbook for preachers. Despite the tale's use of exempla, citation of authorities, and concluding prayer, however, it is very far from being a sermon, and Chaucer exploits the contrast between such an expectation of preaching and what actually happens, not least in the contingency of the *moralitee*. There are hints of a possible doctrinal interpretation of the tale as an allegory of the Fall of Man—its action is dated by reference to the Creation of Man (3188/4378), and furthermore

> Wommannes conseil broghte us first to wo,
> And made Adam fro Paradys to go,
> Ther as he was ful myrie and wel at ese;   (3257–9/4447–9)

but the insistent literalism of the tale keeps all such readings at bay, and this one in addition is foiled by Chauntecleer-Adam's personal success in foiling Daun Russell-Satan's triumph (the cock's retreat to a tree being scarcely sufficient to turn Chauntecleer-Adam into the second Adam of the crucified Christ). Traditional interpretations of the cock as preacher are similarly absorbed into the dominant reading of cock as cock; and moralizations for the benefit of human beings suffer a similar fate. Free will and predestination may be issues of colossal importance, but not when applied to a rooster.

The tale, in fact, refuses all attempts to turn it into something other than a superb story. The brilliance of the telling and the resistance it offers to possible audience expectations of what it 'ought' to do are both quintessentially Chaucerian. It is not reducible either to its ostensible teller or to the facts it purports to recount: any attempt to characterize the narrator produces only a portrait of Chaucer's own poetic genius, and even the solidity of the existence of the poultry or the certainty of moral truism are rendered unstable by the constant reference to other *texts* for authentication—the story is as true as that of Lancelot, the mutability of earthly joy appears to exist solely so that a chronicler can record it, God's foreknowledge is referred to 'certein clerkis', the hen's shrieks are measured

by reference to those of the Trojan women as recorded in the *Aeneid*. Both
its closeness to Chaucer and its constant textual reference are entirely fitting
for a tale that can claim to be the *Canterbury Tales* in miniature. Its layering
of stories within stories makes it a story-collection in itself, structured to
contrast with the linear sequence of the *Tales*. Its rhetorical pyrotechnics
and its inclusion of almost all the significant themes found in the rest of the
tales, both discussed below, make it an epitome of the larger work. The
sharp juxtapositions of different styles and different themes within a single
tale compress the relativism of the whole *Canterbury Tales* into downright,
and delightful, incongruity. The other priest on the pilgrimage, the Parson,
gives the ethical summary of man's life on earth; the Nun's Priest
summarizes the potential of language, of style, words, and text. The Parson
insists on unadorned meaning; the Nun's Priest insists that what a thing
means depends on how it is said. That too makes the Nun's Priest seem a
closer alias for Chaucer than the pilgrim-persona he assigns himself.

   There is one last trick that the tale has to play, in the least expected place:
the concluding prayer.

> Now, goode God, if that it be thy wille,
> As seith my lord, so make us alle goode men,
> And brynge us to his heighe blisse! Amen.   (3444–6/4634–6)

Who is 'my' lord that he should not be 'our' Lord? Modern critics have
made guesses ranging from God to the devil; some manuscripts identify him
as the Archbishop of Canterbury, so once again referring ultimate truth to a
more temporary, and temporal, authority. But the line remains baffling.
Like the figure who appears at Chaucer's shoulder to interrogate him in the
House of Fame, or the 'man of great auctorite' who never gets around to
speaking at the end of that poem, 'my lord' remains a shadowy figure who
casts things into doubt; but we are never quite sure what things, or how
much doubt.

Fine studies of the Tale include those by Mann and Shallers (p. 346 above); David, *Strumpet
   Muse*, ch. 15; Morton W. Bloomfield, 'The Wisdom of the Nun's Priest's Tale', in Vasta
   and Thundy, *Chaucerian Problems*, pp. 70–82; Susan Gallick, 'A Look at Chaucer and his
   Preachers', *Speculum*, 50 (1975), 456–76; and R. T. Lenaghan, 'The Nun's Priest's Fable',
   PMLA 78 (1963), 300–7.
On allegorical readings of the Tale, see E. T. Donaldson, 'Patristic Exegesis in the Criticism
   of Medieval Literature: The Opposition', in his *Speaking of Chaucer*; and Judson Boyce
   Allen, 'The Ironic Fruyt: Chauntecleer as Figura', *SP* 66 (1969), 25–35.

The Tale in Context

Read in isolation, the Nun's Priest's Tale is a superb beast-fable with two
explicit morals and a scatter of possible further latent meanings; read in
context, it subverts or parodies most of the other themes found throughout

the work. Its most obvious links are with the two tales that immediately
precede it, *Melibee* and the Monk's, but there are few that escape untouched.
It might seem impossible to parody fabliau, when it is already to a large
degree a parodic form; but that Chauntecleer's sexual frustration is due not
to an inconvenient husband but to the narrowness of his perch (3169/4359),
and that his glorious promiscuity with his seven concubines is his
undisputed function in life, triumphantly disprove the impossibility.

Sex and the Woman Question get as generous an airing in this tale as in
any outside the Wife of Bath's, but where other tales—hers included—tend
to present arguments that support a position already taken up, the Nun's
Priest's Tale argues on both sides at once. The result is very far from
anything resembling syllogistic impartiality, for the thesis and antithesis are
usually incapable of development into a single derived truth.

> *Mulier est hominis confusio,—*
> Madame, the sentence of this Latyn is,
> 'Womman is mannes joye and al his blis.'   (3164–6/4354–6)

Even those two propositions, however, are not as incompatible as they might
seem—if woman had not been so wholly man's 'blis', perhaps she might
never have been his confusion. That may be getting a little too subtle, but it
is the kind of subtlety on which this tale thrives; when the same issue is
debated in *Melibee*, there is no equivocation. There, Melibee accuses
women of being bad counsellors, and simply of being 'wikke'
(1057–8/2247–8); Prudence insists on women's skill in counselling and
reminds him that if it had not been so God would never have called them
'help of man, but rather confusioun of man' (1106/2296). The Nun's Priest's
method, like Chauntecleer's in his translation, is not to argue but to assert or
deny, or preferably both at once; women's counsels may have first brought
men to woe, but it is only the cock that says so. Melibee's arguments that a
man who follows his wife's advice is handing over the *maistrie* are acted out
in Chauntecleer's surrender to Pertelote in practice even while he is
announcing his refusal to be henpecked. Melibee's taking advice from his
wife shows him literally and metaphorically acting in accordance with
Prudence; Chauntecleer 'tok his conseil of his wyf, with sorwe' (3253). Once
Pertelote has been cast as Eve, who 'made Adam fro Paradys to go'
(3258/4448), she cannot put a wing right.

The great debate on sex is varied in this tale, in contrast to all the rest, by
focusing on the male. The Wife of Bath was all in favour of octogamy
(Jerome's word, coined in outrage, III(D) 33); Chauntecleer is only one
short of the required number. That the protagonists, being animals, are
outside normal moral paradigms becomes crucial here; a chaste cock would
be a contradiction in terms. Quite apart from the polygamy question (and in

any case the marital status of the hens is doubtful, as 'paramours' (2867/4957) or 'wyves' (2883/4073)), Chauntecleer's interest in sex,

> Moore for delit than world to multiplye,   (3345/4535)

puts him outside the requirements of correct Christian marriage as expounded by the Parson and others; but again, one can hardly expect conformity to such a model from a rooster.

Chauntecleer's sexuality marks him as a child of Venus (3342/4532), like the Wife or Palamon, but neither the gods nor astrology nor the metaphysical questions they invite are allowed a foothold. Chauntecleer's knowledge of astronomy is generous but instinctive, and limited to his knowing the time to crow. The sources of prophetic dreams are never discussed, as Pertelote brings the whole business of dreaming down to the digestive system that allows for excessive humours to cause dreams of black or red. The 'destinee, that mayst nat been eschewed' in this poem relates only to a fox's hunting; the problem of predestination and free will that has caused such wrestlings in the Knight's Tale here invites only a paragraph of name-dropping and the reminder that 'my tale is of a cok'; and the capricious and terrible Fortune that can turn hope and pride into disaster is called to bear witness to Chauntecleer's tricking of the fox. The Monk's version of tragedy is scaled down to Lilliputian size, and the aphorisms he has uttered as truths of the human condition, like the Nun's Priest's

> Evere the latter ende of joye is wo,   (3205/4395)

are shown up for the platitudes they are.

It is a tale, then, that encompasses practically everything; destiny and dreams, courtly love and unbridled sex, seven-year-old saints and the Fall of Man, Andromache, Judas Iscariot, Lancelot of the Lake, and Jack Straw. Its closing recommendation (from Romans 15:4) to find *doctrine* in 'al that writen is' casts its net widely. But however much it may be denied that the tale is merely a cock-and-hen story—and the denial is itself largely illusory (3438–40/6428–30)—too much of its proclaimed morality is contingent on the animal nature of its characters to stand independently, or to stand at all. However urgent the same issues may be in other tales, when projected on to the farmyard they lose any absoluteness they ever possessed. The great debates conducted between or within other tales are here compressed into a single vision that can yet see every side at once.

See also Gaylord, '*Sentence* and *Solaas*' (p. 311 above); and Cooper, *Structure*, pp. 161–95.

Style

In style as in theme and structure, the Nun's Priest's Tale is the *Canterbury Tales* in miniature—with one important difference: that although the rhetorical methods may be the same as in the whole range of other stories, their application is frequently ludicrous. The point is made explicit when 'Gaufred, deere maister soverayn' (3347/4537), the rhetorician Geoffrey of Vinsauf, is trundled on to bear witness to how splendidly it might be possible to lament the existence of Friday if only the narrator were equally capable (a *diminutio* of a type itself recommended by Geoffrey); or when the footnote to an epic simile on the fall of Troy is linked by rhyme to its referent in the narrative:

> Certes, swich cry ne lamentacion
> Was nevere of ladyes maad whan Ylion
> Was wonne, and Pirrus with his streite swerd,
> Whan he hadde hent kyng Priam by the berd,
> And slayn hym, as seith us *Eneydos*,
> As maden alle the hennes in the clos . . .   (3355–60/4545–50)

The lack of any inherent relationship between style and matter could scarcely be better demonstrated, but that is not the only point. Passages such as these turn the beast-fable into mock-heroic, but they also serve as a reminder of our own perversity in taking so much more lively an interest in Pertelote than in Hecuba. The simile does for the *Aeneid* what the Miller's Tale does for the Knight's; and the Nun's Priest's Tale can encompass the whole lot. If it is mock-heroic, it mocks everything else too.

There is a constant playing off of the barnyard register against the philosophical, the courtly, the theological, and the high rhetorical. The stylistic restraint of the opening lines of the tale allows the contrasts, when they come, to stand out all the more strikingly, technicolour against monochrome:

> Full sooty was hire bour and eek hir halle.   (2832/4022)
>
> Hir bord was served moost with whit and blak—
> Milk and broun breed.   (2843–4/4033–4)
>
> His coomb was redder than the fyn coral.   (2859/4049)

The simplicity of the widow's life is emphasized through the use of negatives—she had little in the way of goods and no more than three sows, she consumed no spiced sauces or dainty food or wine, she was never ill from over-indulgence or gout or apoplexy. For Chauntecleer, by contrast, negatives indicate not deprivation but the superlative:

> In al the land, of crowyng nas his peer.   (2850/4040)
>
> Thanne crew he, that it myghte nat been amended.   (2858/4048)

The factual particularity of the widow's household, with its 'sheep that highte Malle' and stick fence around the yard, gives way to a series of similes of an altogether different register: castle walls, jet, azure, lilies, gold. The domestic cows and milk are replaced by the technological jargon of ascensions and equinoctials, and the 'doghtren two' by the seven 'paramours' and 'faire damoysele Pertelote'. Such semi-naturalized French vocabulary emphasizes the shift to the courtly, though the courtliness can also embrace the language of more purely English love-lyrics—in the line from a song, 'My lief is faren in londe', or in the alliterative pairs of

> She hath the herte in hoold
> Of Chauntecleer, loken in every lith.   (2874–5/4064–5)

Above all, however, there are the constant bathetic reminders of what the real subject is: Pertelote may, like all the best courtly heroines, be courteous, discreet, and debonaire, but she has also been the object of Chauntecleer's love since she was 'seven nyght oold'.

All the animal characters occupy this ambiguous ground between the zoological and the courtly or chivalric. The opening imagery used for Chauntecleer may be high style, but it actually describes a cock's colouring very faithfully. The nasty look a cock can get in his eye is described by way of the ultimate simile of the fierce and noble beast used earlier about Palamon in battle, and his strutting is given a moral reading totally inappropriate to the animal world:

> He looketh as it were a grym leoun,
> And on his toos he rometh up and doun;
> Hym deigned nat to sette his foot to grounde.   (3179–81/4369–71)

In similar fashion, it is not enough for the fox to lie in wait in the cabbage-patch; he must be a 'homycide' and a murderer, inspired by Dantesque 'heigh ymaginacioun', and comparable to the worst traitors of Christian, Western European, and Classical history:

> O newe Scariot, newe Genylon,
> False dissymulour, O Greek Synon,
> That broghtest Troye al outrely to sorwe!   (3227–9/4417–9)

The only characters not to be subjected to this treatment are the humans. In other tales, the animal population is abundant in similes, sparse in the plots; here the poultry hold centre stage, while the widow and her daughters are fringe characters, and the similitudes teem with rioting peasants and lamenting women.

Within the main plot, only the animals are allowed to speak, and each one is allotted its own idiolect. The fox's is smooth, oily, and polite; he invariably uses 'you' to Chauntecleer, rather than the familiar 'thou'. It becomes clear in reading the tale aloud that his constant repetition of 'certes' and 'sire' shows him affecting a lisp, like Friar Huberd in the General Prologue, 'to make his Englissh sweete upon his tonge' (I(A) 265). Only his final curse of himself is more abrupt. Pertelote is the fussy wife, practical (if lethal) in her recommendation of laxative herbs, full of exclamations and imprecisions:

> Ye been a verray sleper; fy, for shame!   (2891/4081)

Her language to her husband is such as one would use to a child—'Swallow it down!':

> Pekke hem up right as they growe and ete hem yn.   (2967/4157)

Chauntecleer is much more on his dignity when he speaks. His colloquialisms are rare and ludicrously anthropomorphic:

> By God! I hadde levere than my sherte
> That ye hadde rad his legende, as have I.   (3120–1/4310–1)

Both birds consistently address each other as 'you', like the courtly lovers Troilus and Criseyde rather than the husband and wife John and Alison. Chauntecleer's exposition of dreams, however, and the inset exemplary stories, are distanced from the cock's voice to become miniature tales in their own right; only here do the kaleidoscopic variations in style cease, as Chaucer pays attention to the matter in hand rather than to the barnyard context of its telling.

Elsewhere the stylistic contrasts are unceasing, whether by the alternation of the idioms of romance and philosophy and the chicken-run, or by the undercutting of high style with a reminder that it is empty noise. The manner may be right, but the substance is not there:

> Now every wys man, lat him herkne me;
> This storie is also trewe, I undertake,
> As is the book of Launcelot de Lake.   (3210–12/4400–2)

The rhetorical climax coincides with the narrative climax of Chauntecleer's capture and the chase. The excuse for linking the two lies in the noise the hens make; the poem is filled out with over thirty lines of rhetoric devoid of substance—with apostrophes to an alarming mixture of the abstract and the literal, 'O destinee', 'O Venus', 'O Gaufred', 'O woful hennes'; with rhetorical questions:

> Why woldestow suffre hym on thy day to dye?   (3346/4336)

with anaphora and parallel syntax:

> Allas, that Chauntecleer fleigh from the bemes!
> Allas, his wyf ne roghte nat of dremes!   (3339–40/4529–40)

even with declarations of rhetorical inadequacy:

> Why ne hadde I now thy sentence and thy loore,
> The Friday for to chide, as diden ye?   (3350–1/4540–1)

The din of the hens is redoubled by the shrieking within the similes and amplified by the reverberating hollowness of the rhetoric, to reach its peak in the yells and barks and shouts of the chase.

Muscatine's *Chaucer and the French Tradition*, pp. 237–47, contains the classic study of style.

Endlink

The endlink is found in only nine manuscripts, the most authoritative being Dd.4.24. There is little doubt that the lines are Chaucer's, though the final couplet—

> And after that he, with ful merie chere,
> Seide unto another, as ye shuln heere   (3461–2/4651–2)

—must at best have been provisional. Scribes or editors who composed links of their own invariably included the name of the next pilgrim, and four manuscripts do indeed contain a six-line addition that is certainly not Chaucerian and that introduces the Second Nun.

  That the 'tredefowl' image is used both here for the Nun's Priest and for the Monk in the prologue to his own tale (1945/3135, 3451/4641) may suggest that Chaucer intended to cancel this passage. It is, however, a beautiful little piece, and clearly (with its reference to the Nun's Priest's ability to serve 'seven tymes seventene' hens) designed specifically to fit this tale. It may have been one of those passages on which Chaucer was keeping his options open. It is not finished, in that it does not function as a link; it did not circulate with the tale, and was presumably written on a separate sheet; but he obviously did not put it in the waste-paper basket, and he might yet have found a place for it in a finished version of the *Tales*.

FRAGMENT VIII(G)

The Placing of the Fragment

The Fragment of the Second Nun's and Canon's Yeoman's Tales has two alternative positions in the manuscripts, one before, and one after, the run of tales from the Physician's to the Nun's Priest's. The early placing, which puts it between the Franklin's and the Physician's Tales, is found in the majority of manuscripts, including Corpus; the later placing, where it comes between the Nun's Priest's and Manciple's Tales, has the support of some of the more authoritative manuscripts, including Ellesmere. Hengwrt is anomalous, and problematic: it places the Second Nun's Tale between the Franklin's and the Clerk's, and omits the episode of the Canon's Yeoman altogether.

The reference to Boughton-under-Blee (556) suggests that the later placing in the sequence is correct—Boughton is only five miles from Canterbury—but Chaucer had not completed the geographical framework of the pilgrimage, and it cannot be taken as unequivocal evidence of his final intentions.

The Second Nun's Tale

Date

The tale of St Cecilia that is assigned to the Second Nun is presumably the same 'Lyf of Seynt Cecile' that Chaucer lists among his works in both versions of the prologue to the *Legend of Good Women* (F. 426, G. 416). It must therefore have been written before 1386–7, and, in view of its borrowings from Dante in the Prologue, after Chaucer's first visit to Italy in 1373. Although there is no proof that Prologue and Tale were written as a unit, it is unlikely that the Tale was composed any earlier than this, since its use of rhyme royal is typical of Chaucer's work in the later 1370s and 1380s.

One suggestion has been made as to an occasion that might have prompted the work: an Englishman, Adam Easton, was installed as Cardinal Priest of the church of St Cecilia in Trastevere—the church whose consecration is celebrated at the end of the tale—some time between December 1381 and December 1384. Easton himself had a particular interest in the liturgy of the Virgin, echoed in the Prologue, as he was commissioned by Pope Urban VI, namesake of the pope in the tale, to compose a new Office of the Visitation of the Blessed Virgin. The evidence is entirely circumstantial, but the circumstances and the date would not be inappropriate.

Mary Giffin, *Studies on Chaucer and his Audience* (Quebec, 1956), ch. 2, proposes Easton's installation as the occasion for the poem.

Attribution and Text

The work shows no signs of having been revised for its inclusion in the *Tales*. Its attribution to the Second Nun does not affect the text of either the tale or the frame: it is given only in the heading, though some form of this is found in all the manuscripts. One detail, the reference to reading and writing (71), is more appropriate for an independent work than for a tale told as part of a storytelling contest. The narrator's description of him- or herself as an 'unworthy sone of Eve' (62) is a liturgical formula, and therefore effectively neutral as to gender.

Textual variants are minor. At 277, most manuscripts, and therefore probably Chaucer's own draft or an early archetype, associate Tiburce and Cecilia rather than Tiburce and Valerian as bearing witness to God; the latter reading is confirmed by Chaucer's source, the Life of St Cecilia in the *Golden Legend*. One interesting variant, though it is found in few authoritative manuscripts, is in line 82, where the source for the tale sometimes appears in the plural, 'hem' rather than 'hym'.

The division into Prologue and Tale is consistently observed in the manuscripts, by a subheading or a large capital or both. Hengwrt and Ellesmere further indicate the stages of the Prologue by noting 'Invocacio ad Mariam' at line 29, and the interpretation of her name at line 99, with the source attribution to the *Golden Legend*. There is only one other gloss of any substance or interest: Hengwrt provides at the start of the tale an excerpt from Gregory on the various methods of translation, whether sense for sense or word for word.

The Tale survives independently of the complete *Tales* in two manuscripts, once in company with the Prioress's Tale and saints' lives by Lydgate and others, once with other religious pieces, including several on the Virgin.

Genre, Sources, and Analogues

The genre of the tale is for once unproblematic: it is a saint's life, sufficiently summed up in the line after it finishes as 'the lyf of Seint Cecile'. It is decisively the best such life in Middle English, and far excels most of those written in any language, including its Latin prose sources.

The sources of the Prologue are more complex than those of the Tale. The opening four stanzas on the need to eschew idleness express a commonplace: there are a number of analogues but no known single source. That idleness is 'porter of the gate of delices' (3) recalls the *Roman de la rose*, though 'idleness' is here unambiguously a theological rather than a social concept. The opening stanzas of the Invocation to Mary (36–56) are freely based on St Bernard's prayer in the final canto of the *Divine Comedy*:

> Vergine Madre, figlia del tuo Figlio . . .   (*Par.* xxxiii. 1)
>
> Thow Meyde and Mooder, doghter of thy Sone . . . (36)

The 'Osanne–Anne' rhyme (69–70) may be based on Dante's similar rhyme in the preceding canto. The whole Invocation also draws on parts of the liturgy associated with the Virgin. A hymn of Venantius Fortunatus included in the Hours of the Virgin describes how the cloister of Mary bore the ruler worshipped by the threefold structure, *trinam machinam*, of earth, sea, and heavens:

> Withinne the cloistre blisful of thy sydis
> Took mannes shap the eterneel love and pees,
> That of the tryne compas lord and gyde is,
> Whom erthe and see and hevene out of relees
> Ay heryen.   (43–7)

The later part of this stanza (45–9) echoes evensong anthems. The liturgical associations continue after the influence of St Bernard's prayer ends. The unworthy sons of Eve crying from exile or the desert have a number of possible liturgical sources, including the 'Salve regina', and need indicate nothing as to the intended sex of the narrator; any nun would sing the phrase regularly. The story of the Canaanite woman, on the other hand, which might suggest association with a female speaker, is derived directly from the Bible (Matt. 15) and has no especial liturgical relevance.

The interpretation of Cecilia's name (85 ff.) is, as a gloss in Hengwrt and Ellesmere notes, part of Jacobus de Voragine's Life of St Cecilia in the *Golden Legend*. The same source also underlies the tale itself, though Chaucer changed sources half-way through (from line 345 forward) to a version of the *Passio* of St Cecilia now known only in a later recension. It is possible, though unlikely, that his source manuscript already contained a composite text of the two. Both Lives are longer than Chaucer's, the second (allowing for some uncertainty as to exactly what form it took) considerably so; Chaucer translates large parts of them in faithful detail, both the 'wordes and sentence', as he claims in the Prologue (81), and gives brief summaries of the rest. There is nothing of substance in the tale that is not found in his sources; St Ambrose's preface to the Mass for St Cecilia (quoted 271 ff.) is already present in the *Legend*.

G. H. Gerould, 'The Second Nun's Prologue and Tale', in *Sources and Analogues*, gives St Bernard's prayer from the *Paradiso*, Venantius Fortunatus' hymn, the 'Salve regina', and two more distant analogues. He also prints Jacobus de Voragine's *Legenda* of St Cecilia; and a fifteenth-century *Passio* composed or edited by Mombritius, to indicate the kind of text behind the later parts of the tale.

Sherry L. Reames, 'The Sources of Chaucer's Second Nun's Tale', *MP* 76 (1978–9), 111–35, identifies a different Latin *Passio*, edited by Antonio Bosio in 1600, as resembling more closely the source of the second half of the tale. She also presents the case against a composite source.

Structure

The structure of the Prologue is indicated by the subheadings given in some manuscripts: the eschewing of idleness, the Invocation to the Virgin, the etymologizing of Cecilia's name. The division into three parts is the first of many triplets in the structure and verbal detail of the poem: the three natures of the Virgin, as maid, mother, and daughter (36); her mercy, goodness, and pity (51); the 'trine compas' of heavens, earth, and sea (45–6); the conversions of Valerian, Tiburce, and Maximus; the three 'sapiences' of memory, imagination, and reason, themselves an analogy for the Trinity (338–41); the three strokes by which the executioner attempts to behead Cecilia, and the three days she survives in response to her prayer.

Cecilia's own story, of marriage and martyrdom, encloses the stories of conversion and deaths of the three male martyrs of the tale. The work describes successive aspects of her sanctity, which more or less correspond to the sequence of interpretations given to her name. Her own chastity is the subject of the opening, just as 'pure chaastnesse of virginitee' is the first etymology given (88). The second definition, that she is the way to the blind because of her 'good techynge' (92–3), is mirrored in the successive conversions of Valerian, Tiburce, and the officer Maximus. Her own lack of blindness and 'hir grete light | Of sapience' (100–1) of the fourth interpretation are revealed when she confounds Almachius with her learning and demonstrates his own spiritual blindness (499). That she is 'the hevene of peple' (104) is shown at the end of the tale, with her preaching, the consecration of her house as a church, and with her continuing witness to God from her own time to the present (545–53). That she is 'brennynge evere in charity' (118) is given physical expression in the flaming bath of her attempted martyrdom. The third and central etymology of her name (96), 'of "hevene" and "Lia"' (Leah), standing for 'thoght of hoolynesse' and 'lastynge bisynesse', is given expression over the whole tale, in her active preaching in the world in the service of contemplative devotion to God.

The pattern of tale within tale found in so many of the Canterbury series is appropriately varied here. Cecilia is an example of godly 'bisynesse' (98), and the translation is itself performed as an act of 'feithful bisynesse' (24). Here, instead of the teller affecting the tale, the tale affects the teller: Cecilia's life is told in response to the model of pious activity she sets within that life. Instead of Chaucer's usual series of Chinese boxes, this is a tale whose inside is bigger than its outside.

Themes

Structure and theme in this tale work in close harmony, to produce a single meaning. It lays a more direct claim to 'trouthe' than any other of the tales, and is treated accordingly. The lack of characterization of the teller rules out any possibility of distortion through a fallible narrator. The absence of a headlink to connect the tale to the pilgrimage, or of any reaction to the tale or its teller from the pilgrims afterwards, emphasizes its independence from any ironic or dramatic interpretations. It is rhetorically appropriate for a nun to tell of the life and martyrdom of a virgin saint, and thematically appropriate that it should be the anonymous Second Nun.

It is a much more intellectual story than its nearest generic equivalent in the *Tales*, the Prioress's Miracle of the Virgin. It is about the rational case for Christianity—Cecilia's explanation of the Trinity, her confounding of Almachius—though this case is made as a back-up to an impulse towards conversion initiated by the miraculous, as represented by the angel, the garlands, and the failure of the attempts to kill her. The learning expressed in the Prologue, with its theological definitions of the nature of the Virgin and its scholarly interpretations of Cecilia's name, is an appropriate introduction to the Tale. That the etymologies are all wrong is beside the point: they reflect Isidore's triple process of etymologizing by origin ('hevenes lilie'), by contrary ('*wantyng of* blyndnesse'), and something resembling cause ('the wey to [the] blynde'). The passage is far-fetched even by medieval standards—some manuscripts of the *Golden Legend* omit it— but it does represent an important area of belief, of how words can signify truth. A writer so keenly aware as Chaucer of the power of words to distort or substitute for truth can hardly have been unconscious of the degree of human ingenuity involved in the etymologizing, but his retention of the passage is further evidence for his interest in the theory as well as the practice of language. The stanzas stress the symbolic power of language— that a word's meaning can be infinitely greater than the sounds that make it up or its primary referent. The style of both Prologue and Tale exploits just such symbolic areas of language: well, lily, lamb; ideas of blindness and burning.

The *sentence* of the Tale is prefigured in the Prologue. There already are Cecilia's 'gerland wroght with rose and lilie' (27), her various qualities contained in her name, her 'brennynge evere in charite ful brighte' that takes physical form in the flaming bath of her martyrdom. That she burns in 'charite' and good works looks forward to the spiritual children this virgin bears to Christ,

> The fruyt of thilke seed of chastitee
> That thow hast sowe in Cecile.   (193–4)

The Blessed Virgin brings light and comfort to the soul imprisoned in the body (71–7), just as Cecilia calls on her brothers between their imprisonment and their martyrdom to

> Cast alle awey the werkes of derknesse,
> And armeth yow in armure of brightnesse.   (384–5)

The spiritual garlands of roses and lilies given by the angel to Cecilia and Valerian transcend the seasonal change of 'tyme of the yeer' (246); in martyrdom they are given their full symbolic meaning, as 'corone of lif that may nat faille' (388).

Of all the themes introduced in the Prologue, that of sight and blindness is the most important. Spiritual sight can take a literal dimension in the tale: only when Valerian is baptized can he see Cecilia's angel; the unconverted Tiburce is at first limited to the lower physical sense of smell—he can scent the garlands before he is able to see them. Visible physical reality, the stone idols, proves Almachius's blindness, and is a very poor second to

> thilke divinitee
> That is yhid in hevene pryvely.   (316–17)

At key moments of the tale, however, such things do not remain hidden. Valerian does see the angel, and also the strange and unexplained old man who carries a book summarizing the essence of the Christian faith (206–9). Tiburce too daily sees the angel of God 'in tyme and space' (355), in the order of the physical. Maximus sees the martyrs' souls departing to heaven (402). These are not illusions, but truth: it is the physical order that is illusory.

> 'In dremes,' quod Valerian, 'han we be
> Unto this tyme, brother myn, ywis.
> But now at erst in trouthe oure dwellyng is.'   (262–4)

Paul M. Clogan, 'The Figural Style and Meaning of *The Second Nun's Prologue* and *Tale*', *M&H*, NS 3 (1972), 213–40, is an admirable study of the tale and its background.
V. A. Kolve, 'Chaucer's *Second Nun's Tale* and the Iconography of St Cecilia', in Donald M. Rose (ed.), *New Perspectives in Chaucer Criticism* (Norman, Okla., 1981), pp. 137–58, studies the iconography of some of the major themes of the tale, especially the garlands and the flaming bath.
Sherry L. Reames, 'The Cecilia Legend as Chaucer Inherited it and Retold it: The Disappearance of an Augustinian Ideal', *Speculum*, 55 (1980), 38–57, analyses the emphasis Chaucer gives his version.

The Tale in Context

The relationships of the Tale to the other stories of the Canterbury sequence confirm its essential seriousness of purpose, but they do not unequivocally support its claim to represent a unique 'trouthe' in opposition to the 'dremes' of the physical world. It remains an exemplary tale of the workings of God; but Chaucer appears also to be aware of the fictive elements in it, the pious acceptance of miracle that takes it away from a deep engagement with the problems of living in the world. Cecilia's example is wholly admirable, but the average Canterbury pilgrim is not called to sanctity or martyrdom— few of them even to virginity.

It is paired with a single other tale, the Canon's Yeoman's, which may have been written specifically as a companion piece for it: certainly it gives in some detail the material or demonic opposite of the spiritual truths contained in the saint's life. The transmutation of metals, the damaged eyesight that results from alchemical experiments, the desperate pursuit of a wholly material end, the promptings of the fiend, the flaming baths used to try to find the ultimate secret of matter, all acquire an ironic power from their juxtaposition with Cecilia's shrugging off the mortal and the visible to achieve salvation through martyrdom.

The two alternative placings for the Fragment suggest other relationships. Its position late in the sequence, before the Manciple's and Parson's Tales, would suggest a move towards an analysis of the spiritual and fleshly lives as the pilgrimage draws towards its goal; but there is nothing in the links that would endorse such an interpretation. As I have discussed above (p. 272), its earlier position, preceding the pair of the Physician's and Pardoner's Tales, is in many ways more suggestive. Whatever the position of the Fragment in the final sequence, it is important that both the Second Nun's and the Pardoner's Tales should be a part of the same work. The three rioters are an unholy trinity to contrast with the three male martyrs of the Life of St Cecilia; the road they take leads to both physical and spiritual death. The old men who appear in the two tales have similar functions as teachers, and neither is fully explained; but where the old man in the Pardoner's Tale is associated with death, in the Second Nun's he is associated with eternal life.

The tale sets up further resonances with the Knight's. Emily too is compared to the lily, and weaves herself a garland of roses; St Cecilia's eternal garlands are a reminder that even the loveliest of courtly heroines is as subject to time as the spring, as the flowers that will not outlast the season. Valerian and Tiburce are blood-brothers as Palamon and Arcite are sworn brothers; Valerian's newly discovered love for God leads not to enmity with his brother but to a new spiritual companionship. God is no cause of jealousy; and neither is Cecilia, who can be chastely married to one and take the other for her 'allye', both in the love of Christ (295–7). The brothers become the upholders of a spiritual order of chivalry, 'Cristes owene knyghtes', armed 'in armure of brightnesse' (383–5): it is far different from the ritual armings before the combat in the forest or the tournament.

The metaphysical questions of the Knight's Tale can have no place in this story. Pagans here are blind, or at best short-sighted: Tiburce's worries before his conversion as to what might happen to him in this world are dismissed out of hand by Cecilia. It is a world in which Christianity has all the answers, ratified by miracle as necessary. As such, it is less than successful in providing answers in the wider context of the *Tales*. The world is a dream for the Christians of the tale; for the pilgrims, as for Palamon and Arcite, things are rather more problematic.

The tale also has a function within the context of the stories that take marriage as a theme, and again its solution—an uncompromising Christian chastity—is less, or more, than practicable. Not everyone, as the Wife of Bath points out, is called to such perfection, and for once the Parson is in agreement with her. The marriage of Cecilia and Valerian is so spiritual as to be effectively non-existent. Even the holy Custance had, however reluctantly, slept with her husband (II(B¹) 709–14). Valerian displays a moment of psychological plausibility rare in hagiography when he suspects that his bride's claims that an angel guards her chastity are not wholly truthful. The events of the tale show such plausibility to be outside the rules of the genre.

Cecilia herself is a woman of intellect and authority. Dame Prudence goes through the motions of deference to Melibee; the saint is always polite to her husband, but there is no question as to who gives the orders. Her spiritual authority is especially clear in her exhortations to the men in prison (383–90). She treats secular authority with overt scorn; Almachius comes out of the exchange as badly as the Wife of Bath's early husbands, and Cecilia has no need of the archwife's final resort to force, as she can run rings round him intellectually. Her own authority derives directly from God. She corrects her husband 'as God wolde' (162), 'conscience and good feith' supply her with answers to Almachius (434); but such behaviour cannot be a model for any woman who is not likewise a saint.

The tale stands in marked contrast to the other religious tales, and to those told by other tellers in religious orders, the Friar and the Monk. It lacks both the pious emotiveness of the Prioress's Miracle and the human pain of the Clerk's Tale. It gives a symbolic and religious value to virginity that is missing in the Physician's parallel tale of a governor who exercises his powers in the cause of evil. It provides a pervasive image of salvation largely missing from the Parson's Tale, though it also gives the impression—as the Parson's penitential treatise certainly does not—that leading the Christian life is miraculously easy.

Such a range of reference suggests that the Second Nun's Tale is thematically central to the *Tales*. It might therefore be of interest, given the current critical vogue for numerical centres, that the placing of the Fragment between the Franklin's and Physician's Tales puts the Second Nun's Tale as near as possible to the centre of the sequence of stories— thirteenth out of twenty-four (it is exactly central, twelfth out of twenty-three, if one discounts the fragmentary Cook's Tale). There is no evidence, however, that Chaucer intended such a placing, nor that any scribe or reader ever noticed its potential significance. Neither medieval theory nor practice seems to have worked by such principles.

Joseph E. Grennen, 'Saint Cecilia's "Chemical Wedding": The Unity of the *Canterbury Tales*, Fragment VIII', *JEGP* 65 (1966), 466–81, and Bruce A. Rosenberg, 'The Contrary Tales of the Second Nun and the Canon's Yeoman', *ChR* 2 (1967–8), 278–91, discuss the pairing of the two tales of the Fragment. Kolve, 'Chaucer's *Second Nun's Tale*', (p. 363 above), adds interesting detail on the contrast of spiritual and material weddings.

Style

There are two distinct styles within the Prologue, one for each section. The first, on idleness, is the most colloquial: it is about the conditions of living in the world, where the devil can catch you by the clothes in passing (12), where you eat, drink, and sleep. The final verse changes key in preparation for the magnificent *Invocacio ad Mariam* that is to follow:

> Right of thy glorious lif and passioun,
> Thou with thy gerland wroght with rose and lilie . . .   (26–7)

The new spaciousness ('glorious') and symbolism of the language opens the way for the hymn that follows, with its expression of the divine paradoxes of the Incarnation:

> Withinne the cloistre blisful of thy sydis
> Took mannes shap the eterneel love and pees.   (43–4)

The writer's apology at the end of the Invocation for not writing the work 'subtilly', appropriately brings the style back down in readiness for the exposition of Cecilia's name.

  The Tale itself is written throughout with a lucid directness that eschews ornament or rhetorical flourishes. Ambiguity and irony, which suggest alternative meanings to those contained in the words, are replaced by a symbolic use of language, which points to larger meanings behind the words. Metaphors in this tale are literal—the garlands, the crowns of life; or symbolic—the bee, the lion, the lamb (195–8). Comments from the narrator minimize any sense of her (or Chaucer's) contribution to the processes of composition: 'as I writen fynde' (124), 'to tellen shortly the conclusioun' (394). The emphasis therefore falls entirely on the materials of the story: the events, the symbols, above all on the speeches. Chaucer was well served in this by the *Golden Legend*, as Jacobus' version is already packed with direct speech.

  Speech has a clear function in the tale, for conversion. Only in the Prologue is it used for praise; even when Cecilia is singing in her heart to the accompaniment of the organs at her wedding, she is praying that she may not be confounded—that her chastity of body and soul will be justified by God. Her first words to her husband on their wedding night,

> O sweete and wel biloved spouse deere,   (144)

introduce not an expression of love but a 'conseil' that is to lead to his baptism. Every scene of the tale consists of dialogue: Valerian with, successively, Cecilia, Urban, the angel, and Tiburce; Cecilia with Tiburce, later with Almachius, and finally with Urban. Almachius' order to sacrifice to the pagan gods is given in direct speech, and so is Cecilia's exhortation to the men for faith in the face of martyrdom. Only the conversion of Maximus is done through narrative, in tactful contrast to the Latin sources.

The rhyme royal proves itself an unostentatious but supple verse form for containing all this. It can encompass the give-and-take of dialogue:

> Tiburce answerde and seyde, 'Brother deere,
> First tel me whider I shal, and to what man?'
> 'To whom?' quod he, 'com forth with right good cheere,
> I wol thee lede unto the Pope Urban.'
> 'Til Urban? Brother myn Valerian,'
> Quod tho Tiburce, 'woltow me thider lede?
> Me thynketh that it were a wonder dede.'   (302–8)

Any risk of slackness in this, of expanding a prose original to fill a complex verse form, is taken up by the play of tones of voice, of different kinds of surprise. The rhyme royal also enables instant shifts of register, to the lyrical or the symbolic or the epic. I have quoted some of the more compelling lines in discussing the tale's themes, and one could add many more—

> And whil the organs maden melodie
> To God allone in herte thus sang she.   (134–5)

> The sweete smel that in myn herte I fynde
> Hath chaunged me al in another kynde.   (251–2)

> Ye han for sothe ydoon a greet bataille,
> Youre cours is doon, youre feith han ye conserved.
> Gooth to the corone of lif that may nat faille.   (386–8)

These passages all describe states of mind; narrative, not least the account of Cecilia's martyrdom, is altogether sparer. She feels 'no wo' in the flaming bath, so emotive commentary would be beside the point, but even the 'torment' of her three-day survival with her neck half-cut is curiously painless—the emphasis to the last falls on her preaching, not on her suffering. The last line of the tale brings it full circle, back to the narrator's own act of translation done in honour of the saint:

> Men doon to Crist and to his seint servyse.   (553)

There is no talk here of humility, but it is implicit in the manner of the telling.

Benson, *Chaucer's Drama of Style*, ch. 6, contrasts the Second Nun's and Prioress's Tales.

The Canon's Yeoman's Tale

Date and Text

The episode of the Canon's Yeoman is normally divided in modern editions
into a Prologue and a two-part Tale. In the first part, the Yeoman recounts
his past life; the second part contains his story of a fraudulent alchemist. I
shall refer to these two parts as the *Life* and the *Tricks*, in the hope that the
blatant modernity of the titles will override the false impression, suggested
by Ellesmere's 'prima pars' and 'secunda pars', that the division must
necessarily be Chaucer's.

All three sections are concerned with the sham of alchemy. The Prologue
and the *Life* are especially closely connected: the Yeoman reveals his
master's true nature as an unsuccessful alchemist, and then describes their
past. His voice is continuous throughout both these sections, and it is likely
they were written as a unit.

The second part of the Tale, the *Tricks*, is more problematic. It has an
adequate structural unity of its own, independent of the preceding sections.
Its address to 'worshipful chanouns religious' (992–1010) is of a length and a
particularity not found in any of the rhetorical apostrophes to fictional
audiences elsewhere in the *Tales*; and the narrator speaks at the close with an
authority the Yeoman has never previously shown. All this suggests that the
Tricks could originally have been an independent composition, written for a
genuine audience of canons, and that the Prologue and *Life* could have been
added later to fit it to the Canterbury framework. There is however
negligible support for such a theory from the manuscripts. All signal the
Prologue as being separate from what follows, but most copy the two parts
of the Tale continuously, with no indication of a break between them. The
handful of manuscripts that indicate a division usually do so by no more
than a large capital. The only one to provide a full subheading is Ellesmere;
its exceptional generosity with tale divisions elsewhere (in the Knight's and
Man of Law's Tales, for instance) makes it rash to place too much weight on
this one.

An alternative theory would see the whole episode as having been
composed late, and perhaps designed specifically to pair with the life of St
Cecilia. The degree of dramatic development in the Prologue would support
a late date for the composition of both it and the related *Life*; the textual
evidence suggests that the *Life* and the *Tricks* belong together. The
Yeoman's own voice, as distinct from that of the more generalized first-
person narrator, is heard throughout all three parts; and though it is heard
less often in the *Tricks* (and Ellesmere omits one of the more distinctive

couplets, 1238–9), Chaucer never elsewhere seems to have revised a pre-existing tale to fit an individual teller.

The absence of the whole episode from Hengwrt may be further evidence that it was a late work, or at least given its place in the sequence late, and so may not have been available in a well-established copy as the more stable Fragment I(A) clearly was. Anomalies in Hengwrt's copying of the Second Nun's Tale suggest that the scribe was especially puzzled at this point as to what material might come to hand and how it should be fitted in. The rhythmical awkwardness of some of the lines may result from the fact that Hengwrt generally offers the best text, and for this tale we have to be content with what may be second best.

Textual variants in the *Tricks* are not sufficiently different in number or substance from those found in the Prologue or *Life*, or in the rest of the *Tales*, to make the case for early composition; Ellesmere's omission of 1238–9 is the most significant variant in the whole tale. There is a scatter of glosses in this and other manuscripts, most of them giving the Latin forms of proverbs or similar quotations found in English in the text.

Albert E. Hartung, ' "Pars secunda" and the Development of the Canon's Yeoman's Tale', *ChR* 12 (1977), 111–28, argues the case for early composition of the second part.

N. F. Blake has argued in numerous places for the non-canonicity of the whole section: see in particular *The Textual Tradition of the Canterbury Tales* (London, 1985). His theory has however been widely rejected by both critics and textual scholars. The state of the Hengwrt manuscript is discussed in Doyle and Parkes's introduction to the facsimile.

Prologue

The 'lyf of Seinte Cecile' is dismissed in a single line, and the rest of the Prologue—the longest in the *Tales* excluding only the Wife of Bath's—is devoted to the arrival of the Canon and his Yeoman, and the servant's gradual revelation of his master's alchemical practices. It is in some ways comparable with the 'confessional' prologues of the Wife and Pardoner, though here the Yeoman is revealing his lord's life as much as his own, and the process continues through the first part of his Tale.

The whole episode is more fully dramatic, in several senses, than any other section of the *Tales*. It is initiated by things actually happening to the pilgrims: they are overtaken by a new and unexpected character who has seen them ride off from the hostelry where they presumably spent the night. The interplay of characters is developed as much here as anywhere else in the frame story. Chaucer is not aiming at a full novelistic plausibility, however: there is no motivation for the Yeoman's shift from boasting at his master's skills, to his successive declarations that he is too clever for his own good and that the consistent failure of his experiments is likely to beggar them. The progress of revelation matters more than psychological consistency, just as it is to matter within the two parts of the Tale: the alchemist whose claims to knowledge initially look impressive is shown up as being little better than 'thise robbours and thise theves' among whom he dwells (659).

There are premonitions from early in the Prologue of what is to become evident only later. The horses of both the Canon and his Yeoman are sweating furiously, and so is the Canon himself, like a 'stillatorie' (580)—a vessel for distillation of the sort used in alchemy. Sweating over the fires needed for alchemical processes is to become a repeated image in the *Life*: it is only a few lines earlier, at the end of the Second Nun's Tale, that St Cecilia's flaming bath 'made hire nat a drope for to sweete' (522). The ironies within the Yeoman's speeches become explicit as the Prologue advances. The master whom he claims is able to pave the whole Canterbury road with gold and silver turns out to be well on the way to beggary (683). The efforts to transmute metals—a process that should change their colours towards red gold—have resulted only in the discoloration of the Yeoman's face.

Genre

The Tale falls outside any recognized generic patterns. It has often been described as journalism; as a classification, this has the advantage of declaring its anachronism, but the disadvantage of being anachronistic. The Prologue does, however, serve to root the whole episode in some such re-creation of 'real life'. It is a fictional re-creation, though both Prologue and Tale are apparently true to life—contemporary records indicate the accuracy of the whole presentation, both the endlessly frustrated search for the philosophers' stone, and the ease with which alchemy could become a cover for fraud. The initial horizon of expectation for Chaucer's audience would be set by the other links: the Yeoman's revelations are not so different in their starting-point from the confessions of the Wife of Bath or the Pardoner, though they lead from the 'real' world of the pilgrimage not to an overtly artistic world, but into the back alleys of the town, to the Yeoman's own past life, and to another 'chanoun of religioun' who shows what the Yeoman's Canon might yet become.

Three kinds of writings have some bearing on the Tale, though it does not belong to any of them. Treatises on alchemy are the first: these provide the jargon of the Tale and some longer passages. The second is fabliau: not the bawdy kind, for once, but the sort that demonstrates trickery and sharp practice such as make up the second part of the Tale, the *Tricks*. Also of relevance to the Tale are the prohibitions issued against alchemy. These regularly argued that alchemy fails, that it deceives its practitioners and others, and that therefore it must not be practised—a structural model repeated in the Tale.

Sources and Analogues

No stories resembling those in either part of the Tale were apparently known to Chaucer. His sources are historical, and can be glimpsed through condemnations of alchemy by the Church, through alchemical textbooks that urge the practitioners of the art not to give up hope, and through a handful of records of alchemists and their scientific failure or successful sharp practice.

Textbooks are the main contributors to the first part of the Tale, the *Life*, though Chaucer's presentation of their materials, as an undifferentiated mass of alchemical terms rehearsed by a 'lewed man' who has picked up the jargon but has no idea what it all means, prevents any easy identification. Alchemy textbooks, like chemistry textbooks, all tend to contain the same material. Chaucer's lists are closest to those given in Geber's *Summa perfectionis*, the standard alchemical work composed in the thirteenth century, though he could also have picked up most of his material from the *Speculum naturale* of Vincent of Beauvais. He cites two treatises by name at the end of the Tale, the *Rosarie* of 'Arnold of the Newe Toun' and the 'book Senior'. These apparently represent three texts. Arnoldus de Villanova did write a book called the *Rosarium*, but the jargon about the dragon and its brother is largely culled from another work of his, the *De secretis nature*, 'On the Secrets of Nature' (also known as 'On the Philosophers' Stone'). The 'book Senior' is a work derived from the Arabic, known in Latin as the *Epistola solis ad lunam crescentem*, 'The letter of the sun to the crescent moon'. Plato is cited in it just after the passage Chaucer quotes (1450 ff.), and one surviving manuscript identifies the 'senior', the old man mentioned in the *incipit*, as Plato, as Chaucer also does. Several treatises, notably the *De secretis*, stress the need for the alchemist to have some wealth before he starts, as his first attempts at transmutation are likely to lead to failure.

Prohibitions against alchemy were issued frequently, most particularly to the friars (cf. 1355). It was a distinctly clerical sin, as its practice required an education in Latin: the Yeoman describes its customary practitioners as 'monk or frere, preest or chanoun' (839–40), and populates his Tale with canons and priests. The most famous of the ecclesiastical condemnations was that issued by John XXII, pope between 1316 and 1334. All these prohibitions stressed alchemists' deception of themselves and others (as do the two parts of the Tale), and end, like the tale, with injunctions against its practice.

Fourteenth-century records of practising alchemists are sparse but interesting. Late in the century the chronicler William Walsingham reports how in 1319 William of Somerton, the prior of Binham, had been conned by a friar who pretended to be a practitioner. In 1374 it was claimed that a canon of Windsor, William Shuchirch, had counterfeited gold, pretending to 'multiply' it from a mixture of gold, silver, sal ammoniac, vitriol, and 'golermonik', Chaucer's 'boole armonyak' (790).

A few stories survive of the sharp practices of alchemists similar to those in the *Tricks*, but only one (from Ramon Lull's *Felix*) antedates Chaucer, and he is not likely to have known it. Sercambi tells another in his own story-collection (*c*.1400), and there are some later examples. The first two tricks played by Chaucer's criminal canon depend on genuine chemical knowledge, though it is used in the service of deception rather than science: as mercury vaporizes at a temperature lower than that at which silver melts, mercury in a crucible can be boiled away and replaced by silver running from a hollowed-out coal.

Chaucer's own attitude towards alchemy seems decidedly sceptical; surprisingly, in view of what he has to say about it, he was sometimes taken in the sixteenth and seventeenth centuries as being a master in the art—two alchemical recipes bear his name, and Elias Ashmole, in 1652, spoke of his expertise in glowing terms. The Yeoman himself never claims the theory behind it to be false: only that it is impossible to realize in practice, and sinful to try. A similar ambivalence lies behind many of the prohibitions of alchemy. John Gower, in his *Confessio amantis*, sums up what seems to have been the orthodox view:

> To gete a pound thei spenden fyve;
> I nat hou such a craft schal thryve
> In the manere as it is used:
> It were betre be refused
> Than forto worchen upon weene
> In thing which stant noght as thei weene.
> Bot noght forthi, who that it knewe,
> The science of himself is trewe.   (iv. 2591–8)

John Webster Spargo, 'The Canon's Yeoman's Prologue and Tale', in *Sources and Analogues*, gives extracts from John XXII's decree, Petrarch, Gower, Sercambi, and various alchemical works including 'Senior' and Arnoldus de Villanova's *De secretis*.

Edgar H. Duncan, 'The Literature of Alchemy and Chaucer's Canon's Yeoman's Tale: Framework, Theme, and Characters', *Speculum*, 43 (1968), 633–56, gives the fullest account of Chaucer's use of the alchemical treatises and the prohibitions, and describes his later reputation.

Pauline Aiken, 'Vincent of Beauvais and Chaucer's Knowledge of Alchemy', *SP* 41 (1944), 371–89, presents the case for the *Speculum naturale*.

Willa Babcock Folch-Pi, 'Ramon Lull's "Felix" and Chaucer's "Canon's Yeoman's Tale" ', *N&Q* 212 (1967), 10–11, mentions the analogue in Lull.

Structure

The Prologue and the two parts of the Tale are all concerned with the same subject: the failure of alchemy to produce what it promises. The Prologue demonstrates this by the collapse of the initially magnificent reports of what the Canon can do, the *Life* by the descriptions of the repeated disasters of his attempts to transmute metals, and the *Tricks* by the story of a con-man whose moral probity is as much a sham as the process of alchemy in which he claims expertise.

The three sections replay their common subject at different fictional levels. The first is the authentic-seeming level of the pilgrimage: the Canon is as solid a figure as any of the pilgrims, and the revelation of his inability to live up to his claims takes place in a conversation between the Yeoman and the Host reported as fact by the pilgrim Chaucer. When the Canon tries to silence his servant, Harry Bailly urges him to 'telle on' (697); and when his master has departed, he agrees to tell as much as he can of their past life. This is tale-telling in a different sense from the rest: not fiction as part of a story-competition, but fiction recounted as truth. The transition to the *Tricks* is signalled in a somewhat similar way: the pilgrims will know the truth of the Yeoman's moral conclusions

> By that I of my tale have maad an ende.   (971)

The *Tricks* combines being a tale with being reported 'fact':

> There is a chanoun of religioun
> Amonges us.   (972–3)

The introduction of this second canon marks the end of the Yeoman's confession, as the Wife's and Pardoner's autobiographical declarations end to give way to their stories. The Canon's Yeoman more properly tells a tale with a two-part prologue rather than a prologue and a two-part tale.

The structure of each half of the Tale is complete in itself. Each starts by introducing a dominant character—'this chanoun', a 'chanoun of religioun'. The *Life* then goes off into a long discourse on the nature of alchemy before the Yeoman gets back to his principal subject, his life story, with 'I go my tale unto' (888); the *Tricks* digresses into the apology to 'worshipful chanouns religious' before it returns to its main story. Both end with moralizing conclusions. The *Life* draws together the various lessons taught by the failure of alchemy into a series of aphorisms, the last of which serves as the hinge to the next part of the Tale:

> He that semeth the wiseste, by Jhesus,
> Is moost fool, whan it cometh to the preef;
> And he that semeth trewest is a theef.   (967–9)

The end of the *Tricks* denounces alchemy in still more uncompromising terms.

The structure of the Prologue, like that of the Second Nun, prefigures the structure underlying the whole Tale. It starts by introducing the Canon, unlawfully wandering from his order, and poor (his clothes are threadbare and he is travelling light); the Yeoman opens his *Life* by describing his own fall from well-being into poverty. His claims in the Prologue for his master's skills are echoed in the Tale in the long list of alchemical terms and equipment, a jargon designed to convince the ignorant of the wondrousness of the science. But the Canon is too clever for his own good in the *Life* as in the Prologue (645–9, 967–8); and for all their work, their experiments get nowhere, as the Yeoman states in the Prologue and recalls in the *Life*. Only at the end of the Prologue do suggestions of sharp practice creep in—'to muchel folk we doon illusioun' (673)—whereupon the Canon escapes with all the speed of a guilty conscience, just as the fraudulent 'chanoun of religioun' of the *Tricks* clears off with the cash and is never seen again (1380). The Yeoman ends the Prologue in relief that his addiction to alchemy has been broken; the Tale ends with an injunction to all and sundry to 'lete it goon'.

Themes

Since the subject of the Tale is how alchemy does not work, a detailed account of its theory and history is somewhat beside the point. Its jargon, as the Yeoman notes, never got anyone anywhere:

> Philosophres speken so mystily
> In this craft that men kan nat come therby,
> For any wit that men han now-a-dayes.
> They mowe wel chiteren as doon jayes,
> And in hir termes sette hir lust and peyne,
> But to hir purpos shul they nevere atteyne.   (1394–9)

Alchemical treatises themselves are by definition obscure to the point of impenetrability. Transmutation is, as they insist, a secret, and it was a secret nobody ever cracked.

A very brief summary of the main points in so far as they affect the Tale may none the less be useful. The two basic materials, according to Arabic alchemy, were mercury and its 'brother' sulphur (1431–9), sulphur being the only chemical with which mercury was known to combine to 'mortify', or produce a stable solid (mercuric sulphide). Our own two names for mercury are themselves alchemical: 'mercury' is derived from the planetary epithets assigned to the metals, or 'bodies', listed by the Yeoman at 826–9—

the other six being gold, Sol, the Sun; silver, Luna; iron, Mars; lead, Saturn; tin, Jupiter; and copper, Venus. Its other name, 'quicksilver', implies that mercury is the quick, living or unmortified, form of silver (1126–8). But since mixing mercury with sulphur results in mortification without producing silver, alchemical treatises insisted that the mercury and the sulphur of the philosophers were not the same substances as those commonly so called. Sulphur itself was one of the four 'spirits' that supposedly operated on the seven 'bodies' to transmute them; the others were sal ammoniac (ammonium chloride, which on sublimation produces a deposit that appears to colour things suspended in it white or silver), arsenic sulphide or orpiment (from 'auripigmentum', because by the same method it would colour things yellow or gold), and, again, mercury, which could produce a red deposit under certain conditions, and so counted as spirit as well as body.

The theory of transmutation depended on the notion that gold was a perfect blend or balance of other materials. If such a blend could be achieved, it would produce the philosophers' stone, which in turn would enable the blend to be 'multiplied'—perfection would be catching. The methods of producing such a substance required repeated distillation and sublimation; this often involved tightly sealing a vessel and heating it to very high temperatures, a procedure that invites explosion. That described in the *Life* is clearly only the most recent of many (766–7, 907 ff.). If the processes were going well, according to a theory derived from the Greeks, black (oxidized) matter would turn first white ('albificacioun', 805, related to silver) and then to yellow and red ('citrinacioun', lemon colour, 816, and 'rubificacioun', cf. 797, ultimately gold). The only success the alchemists of the Tale have had along these lines is an inverse one, by which the Yeoman's face, originally 'fressh and reed', has taken on a 'leden hewe' (727–8, 1095–100). This result is especially ironic since the perfect blend would also produce an elixir that combined the four elements—hot, cold, moist, and dry—in perfect proportions (862–3, 1460), so that it could restore the four humours within men to their proper balance, giving health and prolonging life.

The Yeoman consistently presents alchemy as 'madnesse and folye' (742), not necessarily because the theory is wrong, but because the end is unattainable. It is a science that blinds its practitioners both metaphorically and physically, renders them poor, gets them into debt, and can easily lead to fraud. He does not pretend to understand the materials or the processes he describes, but among the subliming, amalgaming, and calcining, the litharge, the porphyry, and the realgar, a casual mention of burnt bones, 'donge, pisse and cley', scarcely encourages belief or confidence.

The first part of the Tale is about matter, and its refusal to be transmuted.

Its sight never rises above the lists of materials that compose the poetry, materials that obstinately refuse to turn into anything better or higher. The only result of all the experiments is destructive, as pieces of shattered pot are blown through the walls by the force of the explosion, and the precious materials inside the vessel spattered all over the floor. The philosopher himself can get no further in his wisdom than his tired

> As usage is, lat swepe the floor as swithe.   (936)

The mess is gathered into a sieve and what remains of the precious elements picked out, in a process that, unlike Madame Curie's, never achieves its end.

The Yeoman's Canon may seem wise, but he is a fool; the canon of the *Tricks* talks a lot about trust—he even paraphrases Arveragus' best line, as 'Trouthe is a thyng that I wol evere kepe'—but he is a thief (967-9, 1044). He talks a gullible chantry priest into providing him with mercury and copper, and appears to transmute them into silver by means of adding a powder. He allows himself to be persuaded to sell the priest the recipe for the powder for a price of forty pounds, and then absconds with the money. The processes involved, needless to say, have nothing to do with the powder, or with the elaborate experiments of the *Life*. He uses three tricks: in the first two, the mercury evaporates unnoticed from the vessel and is replaced with molten silver concealed once in a hollow coal, once in a stick used as a poker; in the third, he makes a copper ingot, puts it into water to cool, and substitutes a silver ingot which he has in his sleeve while pretending to fish for it.

One question that the Tale leaves open by the very vigour with which it appears to close it is the relationship between the Canon of the Prologue and *Life*, and the canon of the *Tricks*. The Yeoman denies their identity, but there is no other narrative reason for them both to be canons, and many readers—perhaps most—feel that the Yeoman objects too much:

> This chanon was my lord, ye wolden weene?
> Sire hoost, in feith, and by the hevenes queene,
> It was another chanoun, and nat hee,
> Than kan an hundred foold moore subtiltee.   (1088-91)

Four lines later he describes himself as flushing 'evere whan that I speke of his falshede': a line that belies the detachment of his story of the *Tricks* from his own experience. He has spoken earlier of doing 'illusioun' to many people, and of how 'this folk bitrayen innocence' (673, 897). It is far from obvious that the Yeoman's Canon's conscience is clear: he, like the fraudulent alchemist, clears off fast when his secrets are revealed. Each of them, like mercury itself, 'is so variaunt, he abit nowhere' (1175), and cannot be caught up with. The structure of the Tale allows for the possibility that the Yeoman does not want to reveal his master's, or his own, direct complicity in fraud; it also allows for the canons to be seen as twins, rather than as a single figure. The comment that most urges a distinction between them is that the first is too much of a fool to profit from his deception: he is self-deceived more than he deceives others (967–9).

The Prologue and Tale show three successive kinds of deception: the false claims made by the Yeoman about his master; their common deception by the false hopes held out by alchemy; and the sham alchemist's deception of the priest. The three parts are given a single impulse by the repeated exhortations to turn away from such a devilish business as alchemy. Both canons are dispatched to the 'foule feend' (705, 1159); alchemists are 'feendly' and Judas-like (1303, 1007). The science itself is a 'cursed craft', and its jargon would be sufficient to conjure the devil (830, 860–1). You can recognize its practitioners a mile away by the smell of brimstone, a smell traditionally associated with the fires of hell (885–9, cf. X(I) 841). By the end of the Tale, the fires of the alchemical processes and the damage they cause the eyesight take on apocalyptic overtones, of hell and spiritual blindness (1407–23). The final lines insist that those who try to find the secret of the stone make God their adversary. It is not accident that the Canon refuses to join the pilgrimage. It may not appear a very religious outing, but it does have a spiritual aim that the Canon does not share.

The Yeoman does not doubt that the philosophers' stone could exist; the pervasiveness of the theme of deception holds the Tale back from endorsing his views. Chaucer himself seems to have regarded the whole paraphernalia of alchemy as a sham, whatever he may have thought of the theory behind it. The give-away line is one that he slips into what in other respects is a close translation from the 'book Senior'. The pupil asks his master the name of the stone, and is told that it is called Titanos; when he asks what that is, he is told it is Magnasia. At this point, his patience begins to run out:

> This is *ignotum per ignocius,* (1457)

explaining one unknown by means of a yet more obscure one. The Yeoman accepts the master's conclusion, that Christ does not wish it to be discovered. The possibility remains open that Chaucer regards the whole business as blundering further and further into the dark.

Muscatine, *Chaucer and the French Tradition*, pp. 213–21, contains the classic study of the tale. See also Lawler, *The One and the Many*, ch. 6 and Duncan, 'The Literature of Alchemy' (p. 372 above).

The Tale in Context

The juxtaposition of the Canon's Yeoman's Tale with the Second Nun's calls attention to the dimension it lacks, that of spirituality. The physical world is described by Valerian as 'dreemes'; the alchemical world, the world of matter, is here similarly illusory, but these illusions lead not to the reality of salvation, but to the devil. The story of St Cecilia explores the themes of spiritual vision, of a life lived uniquely for God, of the faith that could quench the heat of the flaming bath; the Canon's Yeoman describes physical blindness, the pursuit of Mammon, the fires that explode the experiments and that threaten to turn into the fires of hell. Red and white in the saint's life are the colours of the roses and lilies of martyrdom and chastity; here they are the deceptive signs of a material transmutation that never actually happens.

The Pardoner's Tale is the other story that takes as its theme the pursuit of gold at the cost of all spiritual life, and the alternative placing of the Second Nun–Canon's Yeoman Fragment immediately before the Physician–Pardoner is an interesting one. The Pardoner's Tale describes the failures of transubstantiation in cookery and in the bread and wine fetched by the youngest rioter; the Eucharist offers the only worthwhile transmutation of substance, but it is one in which the Canon has no possible interest.

The Tale is the extreme example of a theme first sounded in the Knight's Tale:

> We seken faste after felicitee,
> But we goon wrong ful often, trewely.   (I(A) 1266–7)

Here too, the pursuit of false felicity ends in failure:

> The philosophres stoon,
> Elixer clept, we sechen faste echoon.   (862–3)
> We faille of that which that we wolden have.   (958)

The Miller's Tale varies the theme in John's story of the clerk who failed to see the pit at his feet while walking in the field to watch the stars, and concludes that it is unsafe to know too much of 'Goddes pryvetee' (I(A) 3454 ff.). The Canon's Yeoman proposes a serious reading of the same ideas: alchemists blunder around like blind horses, trying to discover what God chooses to keep secret (1413–14, 1467–8, 1471–5).

On the links with the Second Nun's Tale, see the bibliography on p. 365.

Style

The central concern of the Tale with matter is apparent throughout the *Life*. It contains a sheer density of *things* unparalleled elsewhere in Chaucer's work:

> Unslekked lym, chalk, and gleyre of an ey,
> Poudres diverse, asshes, donge, pisse, and cley,
> Cered pokkets, sal peter, vitriole,
> And diverse fires maad of wode and cole;
> Sal tartre, alkaly, and sal preparat,
> And combust materes and coagulat;
> Cley maad with hors or mannes heer, and oille
> Of tartre, alum glas, berme, wort, and argoille ...   (806–13)

The very lack of order or scheme in the tumbling list mirrors the impossibility of ever arriving at the perception of the stone through such means. The Second Nun's paradoxes of the Incarnation or St Cecilia's explanation of the unity of the Trinity are of a limpid simplicity beside all this.

It is easy to forget, in reading the Tale, that a medieval listener would have been as much in the dark as the typical modern reader.

> We semen wonder wise,
> Oure termes been so clergial and so queynte.   (751–2)

It is a jargon that sets out to blind with pseudo-science those who are not initiates; Ben Jonson's *Alchemist* later uses identical techniques. Most of Chaucer's original audience, hearing the passage quoted above, would pick out as fully understood only a handful of words, and those are the 'wrong' ones: egg-white ('gleyre of an ey'), dung, piss, clay, wood, coal, horses' or men's hair. All the passages in the Tale that operate on these lines are meant to be semi-comprehensible at best. Chaucer himself seems to know what he is talking about, but he is taking some care to disguise the fact.

Like the passage describing the clerk of Orleans's skill in astrology in the Franklin's Tale, the alchemical sections of the Canon's Yeoman's Tale are something of a rhetorical *tour de force*—virtuoso writing for its own sake. It is hard to know whether medieval poets and audiences believed such subjects to be inherently unpoetic—the belief that makes Tom Lehrer's song of the periodic table of the elements so ludicrous—but they were certainly not the conventional elements of poetry. There are stylistic variations even within the most technical sections, however. Parts are sheer poetic mischief, as if Chaucer had a bet with himself as to whether it were possible to put this jargon into rhyme. Others read like nursery-rhyme mnemonics, like 'Thirty days hath September', which as poetry leaves as much to be desired as does the list of the spirits and bodies:

> The firste spirit quyksilver called is,
> The seconde orpyment, the thridde, ywis,
> Sal armonyak, and the ferthe brymstoon.
> The bodyes sevene eek, lo, hem heere anoon:

> Sol gold is, and Luna silver we threpe,
> Mars iren, Mercurie quyksilver we clepe,
> Saturnus leed, and Juppiter is tyn,
> And Venus coper, by my fader kyn!   (822–9)

There is a hint that the lines may indeed be intended as a mnemonic, for the Yeoman repeats them to the pilgrims 'as was me taught also' (819).

The Yeoman's voice is more consistent throughout all this than anywhere in the *Tales* outside the links and confessional prologues. The *Life* is indeed effectively confession rather than story; when he comes on to his tale of the fraudulent canon, his own voice still surfaces, though less frequently. The initial address to good canons is more Chaucer's than his, whether it was intended for a specific ecclesiastical audience, for any canons who might read the *Tales*, or as rhetorical colour. The long moralizing conclusion (1388–481) is also spoken with an authority that goes beyond dramatic plausibility in the mouth of a man as ignorant as the Yeoman has claimed to be. Some of the rhetorical flourishes are also distinctly more Chaucerian than yeomanlike—lines such as these would not be out of place from the Nun's Priest or the Pardoner:

> O sely preest! o sely innocent!
> With coveitise anon thou shalt be blent!
> O gracelees, ful blynd is thy conceite.   (1076–8)

In contrast to these outbursts are the interjections plainly in the Yeoman's own voice: the denial that the canon of the *Tricks* is the same as his own, the explanation of his complexion, his dismissal of the contents of the powder, his wish for vengeance, his exclamation that of course—'devel of helle!'— silver is silver, and a scatter of imprecations (1088–100, 1148–50, 1172–5, 1238–9).

The stories of the two canons are contemporary tales of town life; the seond is set in London, like the unfinished Cook's Tale. Unlike the fabliaux of Oxford and Cambridge, the Canon's Yeoman's Tale claims to be reporting fact. The paraphernalia of alchemy substitutes for the minutely realized settings of the fabliaux, but Chaucer does carry over from them the fine modulations of colloquial speech. The Yeoman's own voice is thoroughly individualized, sometimes at some cost to the tautness of the verse. He is full of exclamations, most often to the devil; and he is given an abundance of nonce-phrases, occasionally empty but often precisely to the point: 'I dar seyn boldely' (902), for instance, refers to his freedom to speak out now his master is gone. He can put things with delightful conciseness, as after the explosion:

> Somme seyde it was long on the fir makyng;
> Somme seyde nay, it was on the blowyng—
> Thanne was I fered, for that was myn office.   (922–4)

Other speaking voices are equally clearly individualized: the quarrelling servants; the patient plainness of their master—a plainness in marked contrast to the rigmarole the Yeoman has been spilling out; and in the *Tricks*, the unctuousness of the fraudulent canon, who overwhelms the gullible priest with his articulateness and his constant appeals to God.

In other respects there is a marked contrast between the styles of the two parts of the Tale. The density of material things in the *Life* gives way in the *Tricks* to a small but repeated set: silver, gold, quicksilver, copper, crosslet (crucible), coals, ingot. The moral vocabulary, by contrast, is much enlarged: a vocabulary of sleight and falsehood, confusion, destruction, treachery, dissimulation, subtlety, and cursedness. The Prologue and Tale move from the neutrality of the Canon's first arrival on the scene, where appearance can be sufficient, through the grappling with the intransigence of matter, to a revelation of the moral and anagogical implications of engaging in a work associated with the devil.

The Manciple's Tale

Prologue

The Manciple's Prologue is one of the liveliest exchanges between the pilgrims, and the only one, apart from the arrival of the Canon and his Yeoman, to contain any action or to give any sense of context for their speeches. Its fit as part of the whole work is more awkward, and raises a number of problems of consistency. The Host wants the Cook to tell a tale, but he has already been given a portion of one at the end of the Fragment I. The exchanges between the Host and the Manciple make it sound as if a number of tales are still to come, but in the Parson's Prologue only one is left; and the time has moved on from morning to near sunset.

The traditional solution to these latter problems is to separate the Manciple's and Parson's Tales into separate Fragments, though the manuscripts consistently connect them, and the geography of the pilgrimage supports the connection. 'The Blee', where the Manciple's Tale is told, is the Blean forest, only a short distance from Canterbury (though 'Bobbe up and down' has resisted firm identification). The Parson's Tale seems to be intended for the final approach to the destination of the pilgrimage, though Chaucer in effect moves its telling beyond topographical location. The two prologues and tales were presumably not written as a sequence (as the Miller's and Reeve's may have been), or the inconsistencies would never have appeared; but their juxtaposition could still be intentional and not an accident of transmission, the discrepancies being evidence of the unrevised state of the *Tales*. There is also no way of knowing whether the Manciple's Prologue and Tale were written as a pair, though they appear to share a common manuscript tradition, and the tale's moral, on the dangers of loose talk, follows appropriately from the Manciple's anxious withdrawal of his sneers at the Cook.

The quarrel between the Cook and the Manciple has its roots in the same kind of professional rivalry as that between the Miller and the Reeve; potentially they know too much about each other, and their professional malpractices. The Cook's have been listed by the Host in the Prologue to his earlier fragmentary story, and the Manciple prevents any threat of the drunken Cook's revealing his own abuses by plying him with yet more wine. Unlike the Miller and carpenter-Reeve, or the Friar and Summoner, he does not build the rivalry into his tale; it is curious, however, that his method of proceeding, by giving a moralizing commentary on every aspect of his narrative, is most closely matched elsewhere in the *Tales* by the constant interjection of moral aphorisms in the Cook's Tale.

Compared with other quarrels among the pilgrims, that between the Manciple and the Cook remains curiously isolated. It does not, as the *Tales* stand, develop into anything, and the Cook's fall from his horse likewise leads nowhere. He gapes as if he would swallow the whole company, possibly like hell-mouth—

The devel of helle sette his foot therin!   (38)

—but the effect is more of Rabelaisian grotesque than of anagogical allegory. Potential thematic connections with the rest of the work remain undeveloped: drunkenness had previously been associated with anger and seen as unremittingly sinful (notably by the Pardoner—who insists on wetting his own whistle—and the friar of the Summoner's Tale); here, the Cook's anger is due to the insults, not the alcohol, and the Manciple uses yet more wine as a cure. If the episode has any more specific relevance to his tale than the notion that talk is dangerous, it lies in the Host's reference to Bacchus at the end of the Prologue (99–101). The introduction of a pagan god is hard to justify on any dramatic grounds; but the god of wine can turn 'rancour' to 'love' as the god of poetry in the tale signally fails to do.

John Norton-Smith, *Geoffrey Chaucer* (London, 1974), suggests (p. 151) that the drunken Cook's fall from his horse is meant to introduce the Ovidian material of the Tale by recalling Silenus' similar fall in the *Ars amatoria*; but there is minimal evidence of Chaucer's direct knowledge of the work, and there is no obvious point in the allusion.

Date and Text

There is no external evidence as to the date of the Tale. It used to be thought an early work, in view of its use of the *Roman de la rose* and Ovid and its rhetorical elaboration. Recent criticism has stressed its appropriateness as the tale preceding the Parson's, and has accordingly assigned it a late date in the composition of the *Tales*. The sophistication with which it debates questions of language and style and the freedom with which it treats its source both render the earlier arguments inadequate; and it is extremely hard to imagine any context for it outside the *Canterbury Tales*.

The text of both Prologue and Tale is unusually consistent across the manuscripts. There is only one widespread variant, 'for naught' in line 147, where Ellesmere and Gg.4.27 read 'in ydel'. There is a handful of scribal glosses, mostly marginal notes of content or source—the *Distichs of Cato* at 333 and 360, Proverbs at 337; Hengwrt also quotes from Jerome–Theophrastus for 148–54, though the idea may have been proverbial. Ellesmere and others note that the Manciple's denial that he is referring to women (187) is spoken 'per antifrasim', and have a disapproving (or perhaps licentious) 'Nota malum quid' by the word 'swyve' (256).

Donald C. Baker (ed.) *The Manciple's Tale* (Variorum II 10, Norman, Okla. 1984), discusses the dating and the textual tradition.

Genre

At one level the tale is a just-so story, a *pourquoi*:

And for this caas been alle crowes blake.   (308)

In Classical or medieval terms, it is a metamorphosis on the Ovidian model, a myth of origin, but the transformation of the crow takes up very little of the space or emphasis of the tale. The stress on the dangers of speaking turns it into an extended 'ensample' (309) or a moral tale, as does its fondness for moralizing digression. It has been compared to a sermon, and while that is perhaps going too far—there is no resemblance in either structure or Christian content—sermons did frequently use beast-fables to illustrate the moral point at issue. Its affinity with the beast-fable is however limited by the large part played by human (or quasi-human) characters. It could better be regarded as an antitype to the genre created in the *Legend of Good Women*: there, largely Ovidian material is played for pathos to tell the stories of women wronged by treacherous men; here, a story from Ovid is used to denigrate women through one wife who betrays her husband, and the tone is stripped of any sentiment.

Sources and Analogues

The basic story of Phoebus and the crow is derived from the *Metamorphoses* (ii. 531–632), but Chaucer makes numerous alterations and omissions. Some of these may be due to the influence of other versions, but most seem to be his own idea. He may have known the version in the *Ovide moralisé*, though, given the thinness of other evidence of his acquaintance with this work, the case is not strong; it does, however, contain a lengthy passage of moralization on the dangers of *jenglerie*. Machaut also told the story, with similar moralizing digressions, in his *Livre du voir dit* (7773–8110), and Gower, very briefly, in the *Confessio amantis* (iii. 768–817). The formula 'My son—' repeated in the moralizing at the end of the tale could be taken over from Gower's use of the phrase as a confessional formula; it is hard to think of other excuses for dragging in so superfluous a character as the Manciple's mother.

The present state of scholarship agrees that Ovid was not Chaucer's only source, and this may be correct; but the only reason for looking elsewhere lies in the extensive differences between Ovid and Chaucer's version, so the argument rests largely on the fallacy that Chaucer was less capable of altering his source than were earlier redactors. None of the rival versions on offer makes such extensive changes to Ovid, and most of the alterations are indeed unique to Chaucer; so it would seem not unreasonable to ascribe them provisionally to him.

The differences affect both the plot and its handling. The bird in Ovid is a raven, in Chaucer a crow. The change may have been influenced by Ovid's inset narrative of a maiden transformed into a crow for tale-telling, or it may simply be Chaucer's translation of *corvus*; crows are after all commoner birds. It is Chaucer who makes the woman in the story Phebus' wife, rather than mistress, and his version alone never names her—changes that lessen the particularity of the story and make it serve more as an exemplum in the continuing debate on the virtue (or otherwise) of married women. That she is pregnant, and that Phoebus rescues her child Aesculapius, are crucial to the end of the story in Ovid, but are omitted by Chaucer. Ovid's Phoebus repents of killing her, but never doubts her guilt; Machaut's Phebus notes the possibility that the bird might have lied; Chaucer's Phebus convinces himself that his wife is innocent and spends twenty lines on the crow's linguistic treachery. Chaucer alters the crow's punishment to fit with this. In his version alone, Phebus had taught the bird to speak, and it can also sing better than a nightingale; at the end, he deprives it of the powers of speech and song, and this is stressed far more than its accompanying Ovidian metamorphosis from white to black. It is also condemned to 'crie agayn tempest and rayn' (301). This has been seen as derived from another moralized Ovid, the *Integumentum Ovidii*, or from a chough's complaint of a storm in a more distant analogue in the *Seven Sages of Rome*; but it was a commonplace of bestiary lore (it appears in Isidore's *Etymologiae* with a reference to Virgil's comment on the same phenomenon in *Georgics*, i. 388) and need have no very learned source.

The extent of the concern with the dangers of speech and tale-telling, even if the tale is true, is unique to Chaucer, and is reinforced by two of the non-narrative sections of the tale, on the way language itself can lie—that there is no difference between a *wenche* and a *lady*, an *outlawe* and a *captayne*, except rank and success—and the warning against speaking. Neither passage appears to have any single source. Warnings against loose speech were common, not least, as the Manciple indicates (344–5), in Proverbs and the Psalms. The theme is also present in Ovid's version of the story, and is developed in the *Ovide moralisé*. The notion that

> The firste vertu, sone, if thou wolt leere,
> Is to restreyne and kepe wel thy tonge,　　(332–3)

would have been known to Chaucer from the *Distichs of Cato*, where the glosses use the 'My son—' formula; and from the *Roman de la rose*, which itself cites Cato (7053–7). This passage in the *Roman* occurs in the course of Reason's discourse on giving things their true names and avoiding euphemisms; the arguments and examples are different from the Manciple's, but the passage does constitute an analogue to Chaucer's discussion, and his interest in it is indicated by the end of the Pardoner's Tale. The importance of restraining the tongue is also a widespread motif of sermons and penitential literature; the Parson includes a related discussion of the 'sins of the tongue' under his heading of Wrath, though his emphasis is less purely prudential than the Manciple's. The distinctive image of the tongue being walled with the teeth and lips (323) was likewise widely known. It is used, for instance, by Gower in the *Vox clamantis* (v. 901–10), and in a widely disseminated preacher's manual, the *Fasciculus morum*.

The *Roman* contributes to the tale in various further ways. In the course of the Friend's speech recounting the complaints of a jealous husband—a passage on which Chaucer also draws in the Wife's Prologue and the Shipman's Tale—white crows are declared to be more common than honest women (8695), and the image could have served to draw Chaucer's attention to a story that turns the analogy into a narrative. The work also provides models for the exempla of the bird that prefers freedom to caged luxury (*Roman* 13941–58; also in Boethius, III. m. 2. 17–26); the cat that abandons its special petfood to chase a mouse (*Roman* 14039–52); and the she-wolf who prefers the worst mate (*Roman* 7761–6). The example of the bird also appears in the Squire's Tale (V(F) 610–18), and its further use here may be one of those instances where Chaucer uses himself as source.

Phebus' divine nature is remarkably little stressed in the tale; it is interesting that the moralization in the *Ovide moralisé* gives a historical interpretation here, relating the story simply to 'uns jovenciaux prisiez'. Some of the detail of the opening description of the god could however be drawn from the mythographic tradition, from Bersuire's *De formis figurisque deorum*, which describes him as a 'nubilis iuvenis', skilled at archery and *mynstralcie*, and victor over the serpent Phyton. He is also accompanied by a raven, said to be the bearer of evil rumours and signifying detractors and backbiting gossips.

James A. Work, 'The Manciple's Tale', in *Sources and Analogues*, gives extracts from Ovid, the *Ovide moralisé*, Gower, Machaut, the *Integumentum*, and the *Seven Sages*, with shorter extracts illustrating the exempla. For Bersuire, see p. 11 above.

On Chaucer's probable ignorance of the *Ovide moralisé*, see Cooper's 'Chaucer and Ovid' (p. 14 above).

On the connection between the *Distichs of Cato* and the Gower parody, see Richard Hazelton, 'Chaucer and Cato', *Speculum*, 35 (1960), 357–80.

On the *Fasciculus morum*, see Siegfried Wenzel, *Verses in Sermons: Fasciculus morum and its*

388 *IX(H) The Manciple's Tale*

Middle English Poems (Medieval Academy of America 87, Cambridge, Mass., 1978), pp. 50–1, and his edition (University Park, Penn., 1990), I.iv (p. 49).

Structure

The oddities of the structuring of the Manciple's Tale are obvious on first reading, and comparisons with other versions of the story emphasize its strangeness. The main story opens the work, and, with the final injunction to 'thenk upon the crowe', concludes it; but the effect is more of a structure that falls in half. The first part contains the series of *ensamples* of women's vice and the disquisition on language, the second the single *ensample*, told with more detail and at a length sufficient to balance the first half, of what happens to the crow.

The tale starts briskly enough, in Chaucer's favoured manner, with a description of the authority figure of the story, in this instance Phebus, followed by the crow and the wife. After this, the narrative progression settles down to taking two steps sideways for every step forwards. 'Now to purpos', announces the Manciple (155), but he veers off into three exempla designed to show that women always prefer the worse to the better, then denies the application. Thirty-five lines of this are followed by a nine-line return to the story, but the mention of the wife's 'lemman' diverts him for another thirty lines on the nature of language. This passage marks a divide in the morality of the tale as in the structure: before it, women's lewdness is the subject; afterwards, the nature and consequence of speech. Next there follows the entire action of the story, concluding with Phebus' complaints. At the end comes the moral—appropriately enough, except that the warning to the 'lordynges' of the assembled company is supplemented by the tautologous harangue ascribed to the teller's mother, which rings endless (and very minor) changes on the advice already given to keep your mouth shut. This runs for forty-five lines, and is unparalleled elsewhere in Chaucer's works, where morals, even in the more didactic tales, tend to be sharp and to the point. The Nun's Priest takes under three lines to make the identical moral point (VII. 3433–5/B². 4623–5).

The looseness of overall structure is in marked contrast to the concision of the main narrative (238–70, 303–6). Ovid's inset story of the girl turned into a crow is removed; and everything that would divert attention from Chaucer's central theme of report and disbelief goes too, not least the birth of Aesculapius. Phebus is given two speeches that stress this central theme, the first a lament for his wife containing its own moral conclusion—

O every man, be war of rakelnesse! (283)

—and the second a condemnation of the crow for lying. It is in keeping with this theme that so much of the narrative is converted from Ovid's third-person narration to direct speech, in the exchange between Phebus and the crow as well as in the god's complaints. The change makes for a very lively piece of storytelling. This advantage cannot be claimed for the views of the Manciple's mother, though the fact that her warnings are again given as direct speech, as well as at inordinate length, underlines the ironic contrast of manner versus message.

Themes

There are two sets of thematic concerns in the Manciple's Tale, each occupying half the work. The first hundred lines culminate in an exposition of the viciousness of women, the last hundred are concerned with the dangers of speech; between the two comes a passage where the two overlap, on how lexical choice imposes an unjustified moral interpretation, in which the key example is that

> Ther nys no difference, trewely,
> Bitwixe a wyf that is of heigh degree,
> If of hir body dishonest she bee,
> And a povre wenche, oother than this—
> If it so be they werke bothe amys—
> But that the gentile, in estaat above,
> She shal be cleped his lady, as in love;
> And for that oother is a povre womman,
> She shal be cleped his wenche or his lemman.
> And, God it woot, myn owene deere brother,
> Men leyn that oon as lowe as lith that oother.   (212–22)

The focus in this shifts from its ostensible subject of female vice to the processes of language.

The first theme is introduced along with the first mention of the wife. Phebus may be a 'lusty bachiler', but in one respect he resembles the elderly husbands of the Miller's and Merchant's Tales:

> Jalous he was, and wolde have kept hire fayn.   (144)

After a passing nod to virtuous wives, the Manciple homes in on the impossibility of keeping a wife under control. He argues from those qualities

> which that nature
> Hath natureelly set in a creature,   (161–2)

as illustrated by three analogies from the animal world. The first is the caged bird's preference for freedom over luxury; this is paralleled most closely elsewhere in the *Tales* not in the Franklin's aphorism on caged love flying away, but in the Squire's Tale (V(F) 610–20), where the bird's wish for liberty is taken to show 'newefangelnesse'. If the cage represents faithfulness, or the yoke of matrimony, any desire for freedom must be vicious. The next example is of a cat that abandons 'every deyntee' in favour of a mouse, which concludes (somewhat unfairly on the cat),

> Lo, heere hath lust his dominacioun,
> And appetit fleemeth discrecioun   (181–2)

—at which point it is not unreasonable to believe that the moral is leading the exemplum by the nose. The final illustration is condemnatory in substance as well as in moral: it describes the 'vileyns kynde' of the she-wolf, which always takes the 'lewedeste wolf' as her mate.

This is as unpleasant a view of women as any in the *Tales*, and it is followed by some hasty backtracking reminiscent of the Nun's Priest's denial of antifeminism:

> Alle thise ensamples speke I by thise men
> That been untrewe, and nothyng by wommen.   (187–8)

This is as flagrant a contradiction of the tenor of the *ensamples* as is the application of the *moralitee* to the bird or the cat. There is no overt recognition of the fact that bad analogies make bad arguments, although the passage is followed closely by the discussion on how 'the word moot cosyn be to the werkyng' (210).

It is advice that the crow takes all too literally.

> This crowe sang 'Cokkow! cokkow! cokkow!' (243)
> 'On thy bed thy wyf I saugh hym swyve.'   (256)

But neither innuendo nor plain speaking saves him from the accusation of lying, or from the punishment of loss of song and speech. These are new elements in Chaucer's handling of the story, and serve to extend the implications of Ovid's simpler warning against gossip. In the discussion of vocabulary, falsification is seen as inherent in lexical choice, and therefore in stylistic variation; and even unvarnished truth is indistinguishable from falsehood, since words are no guarantee of fact. In so far as language is metaphorical—'cosyn to the werkyng', not the thing itself—it is in itself neutral: it has no inherent quality to show whether it signifies something or nothing. It is up to the hearer to make that decision, and Phebus gets it wrong. The consequences for the crow are dire—nothing less than the loss of all capability of language, true or false. The pilgrims of the frame story had used one fiction to 'quite' another; Phebus' requital for what he sees as the crow's fictionalizing—'I wol thee quite anon thy false tale' (293)—is altogether more drastic.

The implications of this go far beyond the warning against scandal-mongering—how far, is indicated by a couplet close to the very end of the long final moralization:

> My sone, be war, and be noon auctour newe
> Of tidynges, wheither they been false or trewe.   (359–60)

The last time Chaucer wrote of 'tidynges . . . of fals and soth compouned' was in the *House of Fame* (1027–9), where they are associated with the tales told by 'shipmen and pilgrimes' (2108–24). That the phrase is crucial to the whole conception of the *Canterbury Tales* is reinforced by the reappearance of the idea of true and false tidings at this point of the *Tales*, and by what happens to it next, in the Parson's Prologue.

The tale has little obvious relevance to the Manciple in professional terms, but it does fit the non-portrait of him given in the General Prologue. The description there gives nothing away; the Prologue to the Tale shows the Manciple narrowly avoiding giving anything away; his tale illustrates the need for such avoidance. The moral he himself draws is a narrow one:

> Ne telleth nevere no man in youre lyf
> How that another man hath dight his wyf.   (311–12)

His mother is introduced five lines later to generalize the moral. If there is any reason within the confines of the tale for bringing her in—excluding, that is, any possible reference by Chaucer to Gower—it would seem to be that a man may be sure of his mother, but paternity remains an open question. The tale closes with a speech in praise of motherhood in both the literal and the satiric sense. The Manciple is the only pilgrim to derive his moral stance from his mother; he does so in a context that insists on women's immorality. We are all in favour of virtue, or, in the context of the tale, against loose speech; but the reasons for favouring virtue, or for holding one's tongue, may be less than virtuous. It is a tale against tale-telling, which denies validity to its own language, and which urges a morality grounded in expediency.

Baker, *The Manciple's Tale* (p. 385 above), summarizes scholarship and criticism on the Prologue and Tale.
Richard Hazelton, 'The *Manciple's Tale*: Parody and Critique', *JEGP* 62 (1963), 1–31, is an interesting study of generic and thematic aspects of the Tale. See also Howard, *Idea*, pp. 298–306.

The Tale in Context

There are both textual and thematic reasons for regarding the prologues and tales of the Manciple and Parson as constituting a single fragment. The speech of the Manciple's mother rejects the telling of any 'tidynges', false or true, along with gossip; the only form of speech allowed, and that in a subordinate clause, is 'to speke of God, in honour and preyere' (331). The Parson refuses to tell 'fables', regarding them as the opposite of 'soothfastnesse': 'fable' was a common Middle English (and French and Latin) synonym for lying, and the Parson uses it to stress the fabrication of fiction. According to conventional literary theory in the Middle Ages, the fable was the fictional cover for the truth within—the shell of the kernel, the chaff to the grain. It was a principle most fully elaborated in the commentaries on the *Metamorphoses*, and although Chaucer does not belong with the allegorizing school of Ovidian scholars, the method of the Manciple's Tale is largely similar. In rejecting *fable* for *soothfastnesse*, *draf* for *whete* (X(I) 33–6), the Parson is rejecting fiction, even down to the use of such *ensamples* as were recommended in every preacher's manual and constitute so much of the Manciple's Tale.

The Manciple's Tale begins the process of closing down the *Tales*; and it does so by reference to Ovidian themes on poetry and speech. The Introduction to the Man of Law's Tale, which may once have been designed to begin the *Tales*, uses a related theme from the *Metamorphoses*, of chattering birds and the deities of poetry, to open up the work:

> Me were looth be likned, doutelees,
> To Muses that men clepe Pierides—
> *Methamorphosios* woot what I mene.   (II(B¹) 91–3)

The Man of Law is suggesting that he risks being compared unfavourably with Chaucer, just as the daughters of Pierus strove with the Muses in song and were turned into chattering magpies; but it seems not to have escaped Chaucer's notice that 'Pierides' is a name for both the true and the false Muses. Their potential for being two aspects of the same identity is carried through in Chaucer's being the voice behind the Man of Law: muse and magpie are the same poet. The Manciple's tale is likewise told by Chaucer, just as the crow could 'countrefete the speche of every man' when he would 'telle a tale' (134–5); but it ends with a withdrawal from speech. The tale undoes the identification of muse and talking bird, as the god of poetry deprives the crow of his powers of speech and song and himself breaks his instruments of music. The first passage enables the *Tales* to be written; the second signs them off.

The General Prologue also contains a discussion on the nature of true speech analogous to that in the Manciple's Tale, but that too opens up possibilities where the tale forecloses on them. It is an argument, like the Manciple's, that 'the woordes moote be cosyn to the dede' (I(A) 742), but the defence of broad speech is there applied, not to denying the validity of stylistic variation, but to the true reporting of a tale in its teller's words.

Chaucer's apology is disingenuous—again, it is he who puts the words into the mouths of the speakers in the first place—but the difference in the interpretation of the relationship of word and thing is instructive. The 'dede' of the General Prologue to which the words must be true is the telling itself; in the Manciple's Tale, it is the physical fact, taken at its coarsest common denominator and denying any variability of perspective.

Alongside all this, the Manciple's Tale continues the great debate that runs through so many of the tales, on the Woman Question. As so often, women are seen as polarized into good versus bad, but the good are allotted a bare two lines:

> A good wyf, that is clene of werk and thoght,
> Sholde nat been kept in noon awayt, certayn.   (148–9)

Phebus is 'jalous', but that attribute seems to be included to explain the violence of his actions at the end, not to indicate anything about how he treats his wife. The tale presents a two-dimensional antifeminism very different from the ideals put forward by tales such as the Franklin's or even the Wife of Bath's, of mutual forbearance fostering respect and love. That Ovid's Coronis is turned into Phebus' wife, not mistress, that she is designated only as 'his wyf', and that he himself displays much more of the aggrieved husband than the affronted god, all serve to alter the balance of Chaucer's original to fit with the patterns of the rest of the tales. The gods elsewhere in the *Tales* may act unreasonably and arbitrarily, but they do not act by mistake.

Style

Stylistic variation and incongruity in this Tale are closely related to the Manciple's argument that language can falsify—that the differences of connotation between 'ladye' and 'wenche' are lost in their common denotation of woman as sexual object. This in turn implies that low style is a closer representation of the physical fact than high style, and the Tale's excursions into rhetorical elaboration similarly represent departures from both realism and reality.

One of the clearest illustrations of the method comes in the sharp drop in style at the end of the crow's speech to Phebus, after its taunting 'Cokkow!':

> 'Phebus', quod he, 'for al thy worthynesse,
> For al thy beautee and thy gentilesse,
> For al thy song and al thy mynstralcye,
> For al thy waityng, blered is thyn ye.'   (249–52)

The syntactic patterning of the first three lines, their focus on beautiful and attractive virtues, is undone by the bluntness of the conclusion—

though it is a conclusion that works not by statement but by distasteful innuendo. The god of poetry, in this phraseology, is as indistinguishable from the dotard January as the lady is from the wench. The crow's account of the adultery has the same summary pointedness as the brisk narrative that recounts it in the first place:

> Anon they wroghten al hire lust volage.   (239)
>
> 'On thy bed thy wyf I saugh hym swyve.'   (255)

There is still a touch of French euphemism in the first of these lines; the second is as brutal as it could be. The Manciple's Tale equates such brutality with realism, to claim it to be a faithful representation of reality. The same pattern of exposing rhetorical elaboration as sham reappears throughout the tale. It is present even before the disquisition on linguistic falsification, in the series of exempla of animals. The dialectical opening of these *ensamples*, 'Lat take—', suggests formal logic, but their content of cats and mice and wolves aligns them with fabliau. The lack of congruence between the moral and the illustrative example indicates the distance of the argument from the rational: the tale's cynicism about virtue in general and women in particular is a gut attitude inadequately justified by pseudo-logic, a fabliau reading of the world purporting to be truth. The Manciple will not endorse anything as truth, however, and hastily withdraws the application he has just proposed (187–8).

Anything that pretends to be higher or nobler is equally hollow. Phebus' first lament is the most rhetorically elaborate passage in the whole Tale, but the point of it is that it is wrong: his grief results from his self-deception that his wife was in fact innocent. He fires off apostrophes in every direction— 'Traitour', 'o deere wyf', 'o rakel hand', 'o trouble wit, o ire recchelees', 'o wantrust, ful of fals suspecion'—but every one of them is grounded in a false belief. Everything about the god of poetry is a lie; only the physical facts of the punishments he inflicts on the crow have any reality, when he turns it black and deprives it of speech. Language is untruthful, or even if it is true it is dangerous: the Manciple's mother gives the logical conclusion, that one should avoid speech altogether. What is not logical is the manner in which the moral is presented. Her advice takes the form of a string of some twenty-two maxims from one to three lines in length, any of which would serve to make the point. To devote a full fifth of the Tale to the dangers of prolixity is too much. The final contradiction of the substance of the speech by its manner is still more drastic: if the word were truly 'cosyn to the werkyng', it would be impossible to enjoin silence at all.

V. J. Scattergood, 'The Manciple's Manner of Speaking', *Essays in Criticism*, 24 (1974), 124–46, analyses the Manciple's tendency to express things in such a way as to deny what is being said.

The Parson's Tale

Prologue

All the manuscripts of any significance follow the Manciple's Tale with the Parson's, as the first line of the Prologue indicates. The editorial habit of dividing the pair into individual Fragments is due to the inconsistency of the indicators as to the time of day in the prologues of the two tales: it is early morning, 'morwe', in the Manciple's Prologue (IX(H) 15), but four in the afternoon in the Parson's Prologue—a time confirmed by the calculation Chaucer gives, though most manuscripts specify ten o'clock, the Roman numeral 'X' presumably representing a miscopying of 'IV' or the tilted medieval form of the Arabic 4. In addition, Hengwrt substitutes 'Manciple' in the first line for an erased name. Given the uncertainty of the references to time and place in all the other links, the inconsistencies do not justify disregarding the overwhelming manuscript evidence that the two tales belong together.

The reference to the time of day is not the only temporal inconsistency: the Prologue also makes possible a calculation of the date, and it produces a different dating for the pilgrimage from that given in the Introduction to the Man of Law's Tale, of 18 April. According to Nicholas of Lynn's *Kalendarium*, a six-foot man would cast an eleven-foot shadow at 4 p.m. on 16 or 17 April, a date that fits with the ascent of Libra. (If, as has been argued, Chaucer meant to indicate that it was Good Friday, as 17 April was in 1394, there would have been some hundreds of more direct ways of saying so.) If there is any significance in the mention of the ascent of Libra, it might refer to the scales of justice that the Parson's tale could be held to symbolize.

If the timing of the tale is contradictory, the placing of its telling on the road to Canterbury is so unspecific as to suggest a different order of reality altogether. The pilgrims are entering a 'thropes ende'; if they have moved on from the Blean Forest where the Manciple's Tale is told, they are close to reaching their goal. But Chaucer does not give them the city of Canterbury as their final destination. They are still on the road, and the Parson reminds them that their physical pilgrimage runs concurrently with a spiritual one:

> Jhesu, for his grace, wit me sende
> To shewe yow the wey, in this viage,
> Of thilke parfit glorious pilgrymage
> That highte Jerusalem celestial.   (48–51)

The sun is about to set (70); the Parson is concerned with the ultimate destination of humankind. The prologues to the other tales often give a foretaste of what is to follow; the Parson's Prologue gives such foreshadowings a new significance, as the opening text of his tale takes up the theme of journeying, and the bulk of it shows his audience the ways that lead to hell and heaven.

Whatever plans Chaucer may have had for the work, it is clear that by the time he wrote this Prologue, the Parson's was to be the final tale. The Host declares,

> Almoost fulfild is al myn ordinaunce . . .
> Thou sholdest knytte up wel a greet mateere.   (19, 28)

The Parson agrees in the same terms, that he will 'knytte up al this feeste, and make an ende'.

He will not, however, have anything to do with Harry Bailly's invitation to him to tell a 'fable'. It is a reasonable enough suggestion: fables were not just fictions, but frequently fictions that conveyed truths, exemplary stories, such as were a preacher's stock in trade. The Parson's reply indicates that all fables to him are on a par with those of the Epistle to Timothy that he goes on to cite, where St Paul

> Repreveth hem that weyven soothfastnesse
> And tellen fables and swich wrecchednesse.   (33–4)

He will not supply the chaff or the nutshell to disguise the fruit within; he will sow pure wheat, 'moralitee and vertuous mateere'. Along with fiction, he rejects poetry—both rhyme and the 'rum, ram, ruf' of alliterative verse. He will speak the truth and he will speak it in prose.

Chaucer's own audience did not have a footnote to direct them to a particular verse of Timothy, nor did verse numberings exist. The Parson's reference sweeps in the whole context of both Epistles along with the verse he paraphrases; and St Paul in fact says similar things several times (1 Tim. 1: 4, 4: 7; 2 Tim. 1: 13, 2: 16, 4: 4). The second Epistle is largely about true preaching as opposed to fables, sound words against empty speech, 'profana et vaniloquia' and *fabulae*. The choice of this particular tale for the Parson reinforces the definition of him in the General Prologue as a true minister of God. It also, however, opens the possibility that the rejection of fable and fiction, of verse and all the artistic elaboration it invites, is not only the Parson's but Chaucer's. The Epistle to Timothy, like the Manciple's Tale, warns against careless speech: the Manciple takes this further to warn against all speech except prayer. The last two tales in effect represent a closing down of the work, with the Parson's Prologue expounding the theory that its enclosing tales present in practice.

The Parson does not, even so, have things all his own way. At this point, as one reads through the work, his words are the dramatic voice of one character, not Chaucer's own; whether the voices merge in the Retractions is not yet an issue. The signs of closure are clear; but it is not possible to forget that a different ending had once been suggested, an ending not at the geographical goal of the shrine, nor the spiritual goal of 'Jerusalem celestial', but back in the Tabard for a grand secular supper, where judgement would be pronounced not on the pilgrims but on the stories. There can be no doubt that Chaucer regarded God's judgement as supremely important; that is why he ends with the Parson's Tale. But the Parson is still one pilgrim among many, telling a tale that is rhetorically and dramatically appropriate for him; one voice to set besides all the others.

The two interpretations need not part company completely, and the text indeed suggests at least a partial reconciliation between them. The pilgrims, for once, stop quarrelling; they are all in agreement, *gentils* and *cherles* speaking with a single voice, through Harry Bailly—he 'hadde the wordes for us alle'. What he actually says, however, is obscured in almost all modern editions by a rearrangement of the lines unauthorized by any manuscript. What the manuscripts say, and what Chaucer therefore presumably wrote, is as follows (I give the editorial line numberings alongside):

'Sire preest,' quod he, 'now faire yow bifalle!	(68)
Sey what yow list, and we wol gladly heere.'	(73)
And with that word he seyde in this manere:	(74)
'Telleth,' quod he, 'youre meditacioun.	(69)
But hasteth yow; the sonne wole adoun;	(70)
Beth fructuous, and that in litel space.	(71)
And to do wel God sende yow his grace.'	(72)

The last four lines, in other words, are Harry Bailly's afterthought: he does not want anything too long (having already borne with Chaucer's 'litel' prose piece of *Melibee*), but, more importantly, he ends with the secular world's blessing on the Parson. Secular and spiritual are not in opposition; they are all travelling the same road, they are all eager to end 'in som vertuous sentence'. The Parson's Tale ends with the word 'synne'; but the last word in the *Canterbury Tales* that Chaucer lets us hear from the secular world is the word 'grace'.

Eisner's introduction to Nicholas of Lynn's *Kalendarium* argues for the Good Friday dating (full reference on p. 125).

Rodney Delasanta, 'The Theme of Judgement in the *Canterbury Tales*', *MLQ* 31 (1970), 298–307, discusses the astrology and number symbolism of the Prologue. I have reservations about his idea that the significance of 6 and 11 lies in their being one short of the perfect numbers 7 and 12, because the sinking sun would have already passed such a 'perfect' ratio (which would have corresponded with its 30° angle, the number of the pilgrims).

Emerson Brown, jun., 'The Poet's Last Words: Text and Meaning at the End of the *Parson's Prologue*', *ChR* 10 (1975–6), 236–42, points out the significance of the unedited form of the text.

All critics of the *Tales* have to take up some position on the degree to which they see the Parson's Prologue as representing Chaucer's own beliefs, and a full list would amount to a bibliography of Chaucer studies. Arguments for a reading that allows some degree of distancing include: Judson Boyce Allen, 'The Old Way and the Parson's Way: An Ironic Reading of the Parson's Tale', *Journal of Medieval and Renaissance Studies*, 3 (1973), 255–71; John Finlayson, 'The Satiric Mode and the Parson's Tale', *ChR* 6 (1971–2), 94–116; Carol V. Kaske, 'Getting around the Parson's Tale: An Alternative to Allegory and Irony', in R. H. Robbins (ed.), *Chaucer at Albany* (New York, 1975), pp. 147–77; and Whittock, *Reading*.

Critics who argue for the Parson's Prologue and Tale as Chaucer's final words include Baldwin, *Unity*; Howard, *Idea*, pp. 376–87; Jordan, *Chaucer*, ch. 11; and Paul G. Ruggiers, 'Serious Chaucer: The *Tale of Melibeus* and the Parson's Tale', in Vasta and Thundy, *Chaucerian Problems*, pp. 83–94.

Date

On the face of it, the *Parson's Tale* would seem as good a candidate as the *Melibee* for having originally been an independent work that was imported into the *Canterbury Tales*. Some details of the text, however, suggest that it was written with the *Tales* in mind, and written at quite a late stage: of the handful of statements in it that have not been traced back to Chaucer's major sources, several bear some striking resemblance to other parts of the *Tales*—the wish to take precedence in going first to the offering, for instance, as an example of pride (407, cf. I(A) 449–52, 377), or the comparison of too great desire of one's own wife to cutting one's self with one's own knife (859, cf. IV(E) 1839–40).

An alternative reading of the Tale, which would suggest not just a late but a last minute date, connects it with the Retractions, so that the two together become Chaucer's palinode, a rehearsal of the nature of penitence made as a penitential act. The writing of it, with its summarizing of a number of sources, could scarcely have been a deathbed activity, but this interpretation would underline the qualities of closure that it suggests: it would be the point at which Chaucer closed down not only the *Tales* but his whole poetic career. Such a reading, however, can never be more than a tentative extrapolation from a text that presents itself as dramatic. The Parson may not be as fallible a narrator as most, but he is still a narrator, a figure standing between the poet Chaucer and the tale.

An alternative hypothesis is that the Parson's Tale got into the *Tales* by mistake: that Chaucer left the Parson's Prologue with nothing following it, and an enterprising editor attached the treatise to the end. The work might still be Chaucer's, but it would not be the Parson's, and it would not be the intended ending of the *Tales*. This theory was popular among the critics of the 'genial Chaucer' school of criticism until the middle of this century: Manly and Rickert, for instance, were inclined to accept it (and to deny that the work was Chaucer's at all), although they admitted that the textual evidence for the integration of the treatise into the *Tales* was as strong as for any tale. More recent criticism has tended to regard the piece as of key significance, and the exegetical school of interpretation would have disposed of any other tale rather than the Parson's; but the theory of its being an editorial addition has been revived in connection with the categorization of the *Tales* as a compilation, a collection which in effect invited supplementation.

The impulse for such a hypothesis lies in the sense that a rebellion of Carnival against Lent is appropriate for the *Canterbury Tales*. It is unsupported by any evidence either from the state of the manuscripts or from within the Tale; and the treatise follows too consistently from its foreshadowings in the Prologue for such a theory to be convincing. It is, as the Parson warns, a non-fiction prose piece of 'vertuous sentence' about choosing the right way to 'Jerusalem celestial', and the theme is repeated from the Prologue in the opening lines of the Tale (51, 80). The probability that it is Chaucer's, and that he intended it for this placing, is as strong as such things can be.

A. J. Minnis argues the case for the late addition of the Tale, by Chaucer or someone else, in his *Medieval Theory of Authorship* (London, 1984), pp. 207–9. See also David Lawton, 'Chaucer's Two Ways: The Pilgrimage Frame of the *Canterbury Tales*', *SAC* 9 (1987), 3–40; and Manly and Rickert, *Text*, iv. 527 (p. 3 above).

Text

The Tale was a regular part of manuscripts of the *Canterbury Tales*, but a number have lost some or all of it through damage to the final leaves. Most manuscripts mark a division at 315/16, between the discussions of Contrition and Confession, and at 1028/9, where Confession ends and Satisfaction begins, and the divisions are probably Chaucer's own. He may well also have provided a general heading for the discussion of the sins at 386/7, which again appears in most manuscripts; Ellesmere's addition of a formal division of the text at this point is the result of scribal over-eagerness—his fondness for sectionalizing is attested elsewhere in the manuscript, and this one, in the middle of the Confession, does not make sense.

Glosses consist of marginalia indicating the individual sins and their subdivisions, the remedial virtues, and such things as 'How contricion destroyeth the prisoun of helle' (Ellesmere, at 311). There are often marginal notes of authorities cited in the text. Ellesmere also warns 'Notate

vos mulieres et cauete'—'Take note, you women, and be careful'—by one of
Solomon's rude remarks about women (155). All these glosses are likely to
be scribal.

There is a large number of small textual variants, some resulting from
scribes' adding words of explanation; as in *Melibee*, eyeskip also seems to
have been a problem. A few words or phrases were troublesome: Christ's
speech in 273 seems to have lacked an introductory phrase, which different
scribes supplied in different ways; 'nigromancye' (605) accounts best for the
assorted variants for the word, though it often appears as 'geomancye'. At
several points the archetypal manuscript seems to have been in error, giving
such readings as 'discordaunces' at 275, where 'disordinaunces' would make
better sense, and 'confession' at 134, where the source text, by Raymund of
Pennaforte, authorizes 'confusion'. Most manuscripts read 'beautees' at
858, but both the sense and the source confirm some such word as 'bushes'
to be correct.

The Parson's Tale was copied independently twice: once with the
Retractions, alongside *Melibee*, some of Chaucer's shorter poems, and some
Lydgate; and once in a collection of moral and religious pieces, where it
appears anonymously and with no reference to its origins.

Genre, Sources, and Analogues

Although the Tale starts with a text, in the manner of a sermon, it is in fact,
as it rapidly announces, a treatise on Penitence. Such treatises had become
widespread after the decision of the Lateran Council in 1215 that oral
confession should be made at least once a year. Chaucer appears to draw on
several such works.

His material on the nature of penitence, contrition, the conditions of
confession, and satisfaction (80–386, 958–1080) is adapted from the *Summa
de poenitentia* of the Dominican Raymund of Pennaforte, written in the
1220s.

The account of the sins (390–955) is ultimately derived from an
encyclopaedia of the vices, the *Summa vitiorum*, written by another
Dominican, William Peraldus, in 1236. This in turn was twice reworked in
shortened versions, known from their first words as *Primo* and *Quoniam*,
both made in England in the third quarter of the thirteenth century; the
Parson's Tale is more closely related to these shorter treatises than to
Peraldus' original. The case is marginally stronger for Chaucer's using
Quoniam, but the Tale contains some material unique to each; his actual
source may have been a different redaction as yet undiscovered, possibly a
compilation made from both.

Chaucer also used the *Summa virtutum de remediis anime*, a work on the remedial virtues—the virtues, that is, that correct the sins: humility against pride, and so on. This work is often found in manuscripts following the *Primo* text on the sins; it is also known by its first word, *Postquam*—'*after* describing the diseases of the soul, that is, the sins, we must add their remedies, the virtues'.

So far as is known, it was Chaucer himself who combined these three works—the *Summa de poenitentia*, the *Quoniam* or some form of it, and the *Postquam*—into a single work. Both Raymund and Peraldus were widely read and imitated, but no work has been found, in Latin or any vernacular, that would serve as a single source for the Tale as it stands.

Chaucer treats his three sources in very different ways. He uses a single chapter of Raymund's *Summa*, 'de poenitentiis et remissionibus' (Book 3, chapter 34), but reduces its length comparatively little—by about a third. He selects and abbreviates much more rigorously from the *Quoniam–Primo* texts, though he keeps their ordering of the sins (which differs from that in Peraldus' *Summa*), and there are many correspondences of verbal detail as well as of basic material. The degree of his indebtedness varies from sin to sin: all of Chaucer's Gluttony can be paralleled there, but parts of his Sloth and Avarice are independent, and everything of significance in Pride; Wrath is assembled from various parts of this and other treatises. He abbreviates the *Postquam* even more drastically, using only about a fortieth of it; that fortieth, however, supplies over two-thirds of his own analysis of the remedial virtues.

Some of the most striking parallels to the other tales do not appear in these Latin sources, but they do sometimes figure in other penitential works. The image of a man's lust for his wife being like cutting one's self with one's own knife, for instance, occurs in the French *Somme le roy* and its Middle English translation in the context of a discussion of Lust, and it also appears to have been proverbial (859, cf. IV(E) 1840).

Chaucer mentions none of these sources by name: in contrast to the Clerk and Monk, the Parson claims no general authority for his speech apart from its self-evident 'soothfastnesse'. The treatise does, however, contain a large number of quotations, usually adopted direct from its sources, and it frequently names the authors of these 'sentences'. The New Testament is the most frequent source, then the Old Testament and Apocrypha, then the Fathers of the Church, especially Augustine, Gregory, and Jerome. The use of non-Christian authorities is rare: it is consistently a treatise not of secular wisdom, but of the Word of God.

Kate O. Petersen, *The Sources of the Parson's Tale* (Boston, 1910), first identified the *summae* of Raymund of Pennaforte and Peraldus as models. Her work is summarized by Germaine Dempster in *Sources and Analogues*, where extracts from the *summae* are given along with others from analogous Anglo-Norman and French penitential treatises. See also the

Summa Sancti Raymundi de Peniafort Barcinonensis de poenitentia et de matrimonie (Rome, 1603; repr. Farnborough, Hants, 1967).
Siegfried Wenzel, 'The Source of Chaucer's Seven Deadly Sins', *Traditio*, 30 (1974), 351–78, identifies the *Primo–Quoniam* text as most closely resembling the Tale. Chaucer's debt to the *Postquam* is discussed in the introduction to his edition of the *Summa virtutum de remediis anime* (Athens, Ga., 1984).

Structure and Themes

The theme of the Parson's Tale is Penitence, and it is treated under the three main heads of Contrition, Confession, and Satisfaction: of being sorry, making a formal confession to a priest, and making amends. The moves from one to another are indicated by subheadings in the manuscripts. The three topics are compared to a tree, Contrition being the root, Confession the trunk from which spring various branches and leaves, and Satisfaction the fruit.

The clarity of this outline is somewhat blurred by a mass of smaller subdivisions, and in particular by the large proportion of the Tale taken up by the analysis, in the course of the Confession section, of the seven deadly sins and their remedial virtues. The image of the tree is repeated for the sins (388–9): pride is the root, the other six the branches, and each of these branches in turn produces its smaller branches and twigs.

Contrition, Confession, and Satisfaction are themselves subdivisions within the framing scheme of the treatise. It opens, sermon-style, with a text: 'Stondeth upon the weyes, and seeth and axeth of olde pathes (that is to seyn, of olde sentences) which is the goode wey'—the good way, which will lead humankind to 'Jerusalem celestial', being the way of Penitence. The Parson then announces the different aspects of Penitence he will discuss (82–3), and the rest of the treatise more or less fulfils these divisions. The first is 'what is Penitence' (84–94). Next comes the etymology, 'whennes it is cleped Penitence': this is not given a separate discussion, but it is covered by implication in 86, where the English, 'a man that *halt* hymself in sorwe and oother *peyne* for his giltes', disguises the Latin *poena* and *tenere*. The third and fourth divisions are 'in how manye maneres been the acciouns or werkynges of Penitence', and 'how manye speces ther been of Penitence' (95–101, 102–6). The next section, 'whiche thynges apertenen and bihoven to Penitence', namely Contrition, Confession, and Satisfaction, forms the bulk of the treatise (127–315, 316–1028, 1029–56), and is discussed further below. The last section, 'whiche thynges destourben Penitence', is dealt with much more briefly (1057–75). The final 'fruyt of penaunce' is described in the last few lines (1076–80): this is the 'endeless blisse of hevene' promised in the opening exposition of the text, a goal reached through 'mortificacioun of synne'.

Contrition itself is divided into four main heads (128). First is 'what is Contricioun' (129–32); next 'whiche been the causes that moeven a man to Contricioun', discussed in turn in six parts—remembrance of sin, disgust at sin, fear of Judgement and hell, sorrow for good not done, the recollection of the Passion, and hope for forgiveness, grace, and glory (133–291). The third head is 'how he sholde be contrit' (292–307), the fourth 'what Contricioun availeth to the soule' (308–15).

Confession is still more complicated. The Parson announces a three-part division: 'what is Confessioun, and wheither it oghte nedes be doon or noon, and whiche thynges been convenable to verray Confessioun' (317). Confession is defined as a true showing of one's sins to the priest with all their circumstances; this in turn requires an exposition of the sources of sin (322–49), how they grow (350–7), and what they are—whether venial (371–86) or deadly (387–955), with their appropriate remedies. The circumstances of a sin are explained in 960–79. The treatise then returns more briefly to the other two divisions of Confession, whether it is necessary (980–1, without any textual indication of the new section), and what is necessary for a true confession (982–1027: Chaucer announces a four-part treatment of this, but the numbering system becomes incoherent after the first two).

The origin of this material, in the penitential literature that sprang up in response to the decree of 1215 that required regular confession, explains some features of the treatise that might otherwise appear strange. The much greater emphasis on sin than on virtue and grace, for instance—an emphasis that has been estimated to give a ratio of fourteen to one of vice to goodness—is inevitable in writings of this kind: penitents have to learn to recognize what their sins are before they can make a full confession or properly repent. It does all the same make for a very negative view of humankind. The remedial virtues get little space, and are sometimes hurried over (as witnessed by Chaucer's drastic cutting of his original for these sections, or his passing mention of 'mo speciale remedies' that get minimal elaboration, 738). Sometimes, too, these sections are partly taken up with further discussions of sin—a third of 'misericorde and pitee', the virtue counterbalancing Avarice, is devoted to 'fool-largesse, that men clepen wast', which is itself damnable (813–17).

The penitential treatise is an appropriate form to give to the Parson, in terms of both dramatic and rhetorical decorum. His portrait in the General Prologue stresses his teaching by example rather than by precept, but his Tale does both at once: it is a set of instructions, but he also puts into practice a storytelling of 'vertuous mateere' that shows up the moral shortcomings of most of the other tales as strikingly as the goodness of his life shows up the imperfection of most of the other pilgrims. The Tale shows him ready to 'snybben' sinners sharply where appropriate, but with the emphasis on castigating the sin rather than the sinner (I(A) 523, 516; cf. 'nat wrooth agayns the man, but wrooth with the mysdede of the man', 540). The fit of the Tale to the General Prologue portrait is closer than for many of the pilgrims: a fact which makes the treatise one more tale among the many that are filtered through a narrator distinct from Chaucer, and at the same time privileges it by relating it to so explicit an ideal of the Christian life as the Parson represents.

By the time the Retractions are reached, Chaucer and the Parson are speaking with a single voice; and this makes it especially hard to be sure of the status of the narrating voice within the Tale. Most of it is written in the voice appropriate to a preacher. There is a liberal sprinkling of exclamations—'lo', 'allas!', 'certes'—and the standard transition formulae are used for new sections, 'Now wol I speken of—'. Problems in identifying the narrator come when the authority of the preacher gives way to expression of uncertainty or inability. He says of unwilled sins of pride that they may be grievous but 'I gesse that they ne been nat deedly' (449); of the fruit of virginity, 'I ne kan seye it noon ootherweyes in Englissh, but in Latyn it highte *Centesimus fructus*' (869); he apologizes for not including a discourse on the ten commandments, 'but so heigh a doctrine I lete to divines' (956–7). Neither the Parson nor Chaucer is a professional theologian, and all such expressions can be paralleled elsewhere in the *Tales*; but they still suggest that the dramatic voice has not yet been abandoned completely.

Lee Patterson, 'The Parson's Tale and the Quitting of the *Canterbury Tales*', *Traditio*, 34 (1976), 331–80, gives a detailed analysis of the structure and themes of the treatise and its significance for the *Tales*.

Howard, *Idea*, pp. 376–87, discusses the various ways the Tale can be interpreted in the context of the *Tales*, the fourteenth century, and the modern world.

The Tale in Context

The Parson is the last of a number of pilgrims who have not only told stories but have given their own discursive expositions of Scripture or of Christian doctrine to the assembled company. Their preachings were, however, very differently motivated from the Parson's. The Wife of Bath is concerned to justify her own way of life; the Pardoner is out to fill his pockets. Within the stories told, characters such as the Summoner's friar likewise exploit Scripture for their own ends. Other uses of the Bible inside the tales serve all kinds of worldly purposes: the Song of Songs becomes a lecher's seduction platform, Old Testament narratives prove to the Monk the dominance of Fortune. Only the Parson's Tale consistently expounds the Word of God for the sole end of bringing its hearers to salvation. In contrast to the Pardoner, he will not let souls go blackberrying if he can prevent them. His allusions in his Prologue to the Second Epistle to Timothy serve to confirm his office as a true preacher, in contradistinction to the vicious man who can yet tell a moral tale.

It is impossible for the descendants of Adam and Eve to live without venial sin: 'this thyng may nat faille as longe as he lyveth' (340). A penitential treatise is in effect a compendium of human actions, for all actions performed in the world and for the world are tainted by the Fall. The treatise therefore inevitably overlaps with the earlier tales, and with the pilgrims themselves. The penitential stress on sin connects with the rest of the *Tales* most closely at those points where the various characters have stepped out of the 'good way' to heaven.

This does not mean that the Parson's Tale was deliberately written to show up such errors, nor that the earlier tales were written as exempla of the various ways of sinning. The aim of both the tales and the treatise is encyclopaedic; the viewpoints on life offered by the individual stories are as many and various as the pilgrims, but the whole *Canterbury Tales*, like the Parson's Tale, is concerned with the process of living in the world. As a *summa* in miniature, the Parson's Tale in one sense encapsulates the various *moralitees* of the whole work into a single treatise, just as the tale of the other priest on the pilgrimage, the Nun's Priest, encapsulates the aesthetics of all the tales, their styles and genres. The Nun's Priest's Tale, however, preserves the variety of the complete work, its interplay of voices and styles, its refusal to stand still. The Parson's Tale pins every attitude, every action, into a fixed place on the various twigs of the branches of his tree of Penitence.

Not all of what Chaucer says in the Tale is critical of what he has said elsewhere: there is indeed as much reinforcement of moral messages already given as there is reappraisal of the amoral or immoral. That sinners should 'forlete synne er that synne forlete hem' (93) is the same moral as the Physician had thrown in to his tale; that one should not trust in fortune or riches (471–2) is a theme first sounded by Arcite and repeated constantly; that *gentrie* comes from virtue and not birth, and that patience enables people to live in harmony with each other and to withstand the adversity contingent on living in an unstable world, are two of the key ideas of the whole *Tales* (461–2, 654–61). That one should do good to one's enemies is the message of *Melibee* (522–5); that 'the roote of alle harmes is Coveitise' (739) is as clear to the Parson as to the Pardoner. In both approval of virtue and castigation of vice, the Parson's Tale can endorse what has gone before.

It can also, of course, criticize. It would be possible to arraign a good many of the pilgrims under one form or another of sin—the Wife with her insistence on precedence (407), the Monk with his gay bridle (433), the Franklin's interest in food (444, 829—though the elaboration of feasting described by the Parson goes beyond the Franklin's practices). The content of many of the stories is also put in a new light by the rigorous appraisal of sinful behaviour, which includes just about every form of sexual activity— among them, the procreation of children, and being raped (920, 942, 872). On the status of women, the treatise is not quite as patriarchal as it at first appears. It insists, as the whole culture requires, that women should be subject to their husbands, but it insists too that Eve was made from Adam's rib, and not his head or his foot, to show that 'womman sholde be felawe unto man' (634, 922–3, 928). The treatise has harsh words for the 'desray' visible 'day by day' that results from the woman's having the *maistrie* (927); and it notes the fallacy of wives' pretending they can please their husbands by 'queyntise of aray' (932)—both closely relevant to earlier parts of the work, and both apparently Chaucer's own additions. Most of the variations on the sources that have to do with lechery and its corresponding virtue are inversely paralleled in the Merchant's Tale, in January's views on sex (1446–56, 1838–40); much of the Parson's lengthy discourse on the subject could indeed serve as a commentary on January's delusions.

The treatise insists, however, on its generality. Just as it reserves its anger for the misdeed and not the man, so only a tiny fraction of its teaching bears any close relevance to the rest of the *Tales*. For every opportunity taken, Chaucer lets pass a dozen others: 'espiritueel marchandise', for instance, is limited to simony, and not extended to the Pardoner's malpractices (781); the section on the sins of the tongue (580–653), assembled from various points in the sources, never meshes closely with the Manciple's condemnation of loose speech or the Parson's own insistence on truth-telling. The *Tales* offer an abundance of qualifications that the Parson overlooks— reluctance to sleep with one's husband, for instance, is scarcely a virtue where May is concerned (941); Cecilia's spiritual authority over her husband is in no sense sinful; Chauntecleer's preference for delight over procreation, and his readiness to mate with his sisters, invites a reading of the anthropomorphic condition not quite covered by the Parson's dismissal of the incestuous as 'lyk to houndes' (907). The treatise's flat condemnation of all questioning of divine Providence (500–1) does not provide any answer to the questions posed by the Knight's Tale, or by any of those tales that concern themselves with the suffering of the innocent, beyond its insistence on the value of patience.

The bulk of the treatise is taken up with matters that have only an oblique application to the rest of the work, or none at all. Its focus is different from that of the *Tales* at large, and if in most respects it is narrower—in its condemnation of most human activity, its refusal to admit any aesthetic or

407

literary values, its joylessness—in other ways it looks more widely, to the world rather than the *Tales* alone. The General Prologue offered a cross-section of society, of the different estates representing earthly institutions and ranks of all kinds, each embodied in a distinctive individual. The Parson's Tale turns away from both individuality and social and professional distinctions; for him all men are descendants of Adam, and difference of estate lies in the eyes of God.

> Certes the estaat of man is in three maneres. Outher it is th'estaat of innocence, as was th'estaat of Adam biforn that he fil into synne . . . Another estaat is the estaat of synful men, in which estaat men been holden to laboure in preiynge to God for amendement of hire synnes . . . Another estaat is th'estaat of grace, in which estaat he is holden to werkes of penitence. (681–4)

These estates are not the contingent professions of a society in flux, where rank and wealth and self-esteem struggle for dominance, but God-given conditions through which humankind can rise. Innocence may be less possible to regain even than a society in perfect hierarchical order, but the way from sin to grace is an open one, and the Parson is the spiritual guide.

The Parson's Tale is the last word of the *Canterbury Tales*; it is not the only word. Its timelessness, paradoxically, has stood the test of time worse than those distinctively fourteenth-century figures of the crusader Knight, the well-mannered Prioress, and the Pardoner of St Mary Rouncesval. Modern taste ranks the literary dazzle and the wit of the Nun's Priest above the scholastic moralizing of the Parson. To Chaucer, both were valid. We live in a world that allows for beast-fables and the Wife of Bath, but that has little time for saints' lives and penitential treatises. The narrowing is ours, not Chaucer's.

Robertson, *Preface*, pp. 317–36, discusses 'Chaucer's exegetes'.
See Patterson, 'The Parson's Tale' (p. 404 above), for Chaucer's additions to his sources, and Baldwin, *Unity*, pp. 99–104, for links with the earlier tales.
See the bibliography on p. 398 for rival interpretations of the function of the treatise within the *Canterbury Tales*. Lawler, *The One and the Many*, chs. 5 and 7, is especially good on the Tale's features of closure, and its counterpointing of the *General Prologue*.

Style

'I wol nat glose', the Parson declares in his Prologue (45), and he is true to his word. The treatise is relentlessly expository, with none of the evasion of awkward prescripts that the glossing friar John of the Summoner's Tale specializes in, none of the self-serving selection from Scripture of the Wife of Bath, none of the rhetorical fireworks of the Pardoner. The Parson rejects fables as untruthful, and so rules out one of the main devices of the preacher to hold his auditors' interest. The play of voices found everywhere else in the *Tales*, including the dialogue of *Melibee*, here comes down to a single voice of authority.

The Tale is not so consistently drab as this might make it sound, however. The Parson does not scorn quoting 'thilke newe Frenshe song' to drive a point home (248); and one exemplary tale does manage to creep in, in the shape of the child who reproves his master for losing patience (670–3). There are some striking similes, some already present in Chaucer's models, but which lose nothing in the translation: external pride as a sign of spiritual pride, 'right as the gaye leefsel atte taverne is signe of the wyn that is in the celer' (411); tight hose looking from the rear like 'the hyndre part of a she-ape in the fulle of the moone' (424); Envy as a blacksmith, who 'holdeth the hoote iren upon the herte of man with a peire of longe toonges of long rancour' (555); old lechers past the age of performance like a hound, 'whan he comth by the roser or by othere [bushes], though he may nat pisse, yet wole he heve up his leg and make a contenaunce to pisse' (858); that the chaste should avoid company that might tempt them to sin, for a wall can be blackened by a candle though it may not itself catch fire (954). Such imagery is always closely integrated with the message of the treatise. Sin is associated with the dominance of the flesh over reason, as wine and drunkenness overcome rationality, or as animals lack the godlike faculty of intellect; it is a foretaste of the burnings of hell, and substitutes darkness for light.

The treatise is written in the plain style appropriate to exposition, where understanding is more important than persuasion. In keeping with the emphasis on sin as the subordination of reason, the appeal is to the intellect, not the emotions. This accounts in part for the emphasis on enumeration and subdivision. It may hinder the reader's being moved, but it serves as a kind of mnemonic structure, and moreover it reflects the order of God:

God hath creat alle thynges in right ordre, and no thyng withouten ordre, but alle thynges been ordeyned and nombred. (218)

There are however a few moments where the language becomes more highly charged, and where Chaucer's prose can briefly take its place beside that of that later master of religious rhetoric, Donne. On the Passion,

Thanne was he byscorned, that oonly sholde han been honoured in alle thynges and of alle thynges. Thanne was his visage, that oghte be desired to be seyn of al mankynde, in which visage aungels desiren to looke, vileynsly bispet. (278–9)

On Adam,

And therfore, he that first was so myghty that he sholde nat have dyed, bicam swich oon that he moste nedes dye, wheither he wolde or noon, and al his progenye in this world, that in thilke man synneden. (324)

On the state in hell of those who loved fine clothing,

Naked shul they been of soule, as of alle manere vertues, which that is the clothyng of the soule. Where been thanne the gaye robes, and the softe shetes, and the smale shertes? (197)

The end of the Tale is its rhetorical as well as spiritual climax:

Ther as the body of man, that whilom was foul and derk, is moore cleer than the sonne; ther as the body, that whilom was syk, freele, and fieble, and mortal, is inmortal, and so strong and so hool that ther may no thyng apeyren it; ther as ne is neither hunger, thurst, ne coold, but every soule replenyssed with the sighte of the parfit knowynge of God. This blisful regne may men purchace by poverte espiritueel, and the glorie by lowenesse, the plentee of joye by hunger and thurst, and the reste by travaille, and the lyf by deeth and mortificacion of synne. (1078–80)

Chaucer's Retractions

The Retractions are an integral part of the *Tales*, or at least of the Parson's Tale. They appear in all manuscripts of the complete *Tales* that have not lost the end through damage, and in one of the independent copies of the Parson's Tale. The case for their being Chaucer's is as strong as for the Parson's Tale itself.

The question remains as to how the passage fits into the work—whether it concludes the entire *Tales*, or the Parson's Tale alone. The heading 'Heere taketh the makere of this book his leve' is found in fifteen manuscripts; another places the heading as if to indicate a subsection of the Parson's Tale, two leave a space and give no rubric, two copy the Retractions continuously with the Parson's Tale. Chaucer's intentions for a heading are not known. Hengwrt, which seems the most likely to preserve authorial details of this kind, has its final folios missing. Reading on from the end of the penitential treatise, without any rubrics as a clue, one would take the opening words of the Retractions, 'Now preye I to hem alle that herkne this litel tretys or rede', as the Parson's own signing off; it is only when Chaucer begins to list his works that the voice becomes unmistakably Chaucer's own. It is conceivable that these lines (1085–90a) are an interpolation, by Chaucer himself or someone else, into what was originally the end of the Parson's treatise. The reference to 'reading' the treatise, however, the apology for possibly displeasing some of his audience—a thing that the Parson is quite prepared to do in the service of God—and the closing prayer for his own salvation rather than that of the pilgrim company would all make better sense if the voice were Chaucer's and not the Parson's. In his Prologue, the Parson had announced the rejection of fiction and poetry; his Tale further rejects any voice other than his own and those of ecclesiastical authority. By the time one reaches the Retractions it is not illogical that there should be only one voice left, and that that should be the non-fictional voice of the man who wrote the Parson's Tale, the Retractions, and all those 'enditynges of worldly vanitees'. The Parson himself is a fiction rejected along with the rest, and there is no distinction to be made now between the author and the voice in which he speaks.

There are some oddities about the Retractions that have made some critics read even this as ironic. It is not odd, however, that it is there: such retractions are so recurrent a feature among medieval writers as to amount to a literary convention. As with all the conventions Chaucer uses, this does not mean that it is merely formulaic, or insincere. One of his greatest strengths as a poet is his ability to bring out the resonances behind a convention, the truth behind the truism; here, he achieves the same effect by linking the Retractions to the penitential treatise. He prays for 'verray penitence, confessioun and satisfaccioun': the satisfaction is partly achieved in the writing of the treatise, the Retractions themselves contain his confession. It is made, too, in accordance with the principles laid down in the Parson's Tale. Chaucer's use of confessional formulae—sins remembered and unremembered, 'many another book, if they were in my remembrance'— makes clear the nature of the Retractions as confession, however curious it may seem for an author to forget his own works. The precision with which he lists the poems of which he repents compared with the generality of 'othere bookes of legendes of seintes, and omelies, and moralitee, and devocioun' is likewise in keeping with the instructions for a good confession laid down in the treatise: one should confess every detail of one's sins without mitigation, excuse, or justification (319–20, 586, 983–8). The details of his sinful works are accordingly listed; the others are a cause of thankfulness to 'oure Lord Jhesu Crist and his blisful Mooder', and a further list, in this context, would be pride.

We do not know when the Retractions were written: they need not have been his final work. A legend was current by the middle of the fifteenth century that Chaucer underwent a deathbed repentance of this kind, though no specific mention of the Retractions is made in the story. Such an idea could none the less have been the result of this passage rather than its cause. The piece follows thematically and logically from the Parson's Tale, however much at odds it may be with the whole dramatic conception of the pilgrimage. But drama, along with tale-telling, the sins of the tongue, and any 'ydel wordes of folye or vileynye' (378), has been rejected in the course of the closing sections of the work, from the Manciple's Tale forward.

Intention, 'entente', has been at the heart of tale after tale: Arcite's desire for felicity by way of Emily, the Wife's for sovereignty, that of the Friar's summoner, the Pardoner, and his rioters for money. The *entente* of an author was traditionally to teach and delight, and the stress in the Middle Ages fell strongly on to the first element—hence the classification of literature as a branch of ethics. This is the theory by which Chaucer measures himself in the Retractions—if the line is not part of the Parson's orthodox reference to the Word of God:

Oure book seith, 'Al that is writen is writen for oure doctrine,' and that is myn entente. (1083)

By the late fourteenth century it had become a deeply ambivalent quotation. St Paul had been referring to the Scriptures; but it was on occasion applied much more widely in the Middle Ages, being used, for example, by the author of the *Ovide moralisé* to justify the reading of pagan authors—so long, again, as the *entente* was edifying. The words were last heard in the *Canterbury Tales* in the mouth of the Nun's Priest; and if the story of a cock and his paramours can be justified in such terms, so indeed can 'al that is writen'. Chaucer requests forgiveness for 'the tales of Caunterbury, thilke that sownen into synne', but he does not deny the possibility that *doctrine* might be found even there. The complete and self-accusing confession he correctly makes admits both the difficulty of distinguishing motive and the range of interpretation beyond his control, where readers may find *doctrine* or *synne*. How great the range of interpretation can be has been abundantly demonstrated over the last six centuries, and never more intensively than in our generation.

Unlike Virgil, Chaucer made no recorded effort to have his masterwork destroyed, on the grounds of either sinfulness or incompleteness. The Retractions may be penitential, but they do also serve as a record of the canon, of the works that have established Chaucer in the eyes of the world. That Lent should be allowed its say, as Carnival had been allowed earlier, and that its voice should take this form, is both proper and, in the context of fourteenth-century culture, right. The rest of his works record his exploration of the balance between the world, art, human nature, secular idealism, and the claims of God. However deep the questions, however much the processes of history and the development of Western culture may validate Chaucer's asking them, for him there could only be one answer. The Retractions may not have been the last thing he wrote; they do show that for all the relativism of which he was so conscious, for all the different readings of the world embodied in the various tales and all his other works, he never lost sight of the Boethian belief that God's vision was single.

Olive Sayce, 'Chaucer's Retractions', *MÆ* 40 (1971), 230–48, presents the strongest case for Chaucer's using the *retractio* formula primarily as a way for him to establish the canon of his works.

Douglas Wurtele, 'The Penitence of Geoffrey Chaucer', *Viator*, 11 (1980), 335–59, gives a survey of opinion from the fifteenth century forwards, including Thomas Gascoigne's account of the deathbed repentance (which is told as a dreadful warning of repentance made too late, and sets Chaucer alongside Judas as an example). He makes a strong case for the interpolation of the central section into the Parson's conclusion.

Imitations of the *Canterbury Tales* 1400–1615

The Parson's Tale and Retractions may imply closure, but the *Canterbury Tales* is an unfinished work, and a work, moreover, that is effectively a *compilatio*, a collection to which other items can be added. In the course of the two centuries after Chaucer's death, a number of writers responded to Chaucer's work by providing endings to unfinished tales, or by producing further Canterbury tales of their own, sometimes as additions to the sequence, sometimes as autonomous imitations. In addition, a number of the individual tales were reworked in various forms, including several dramatic versions to provide food for the insatiable appetites of Elizabethan theatregoers.

I give an account below of these various kinds of afterlife enjoyed by the *Tales*. I stop around 1615, the year of John Lane's Squire's Tale, and just after Shakespeare and Fletcher's Knight's Tale, because that more or less represents the last point when Chaucer is admired and imitated in terms of a living tradition of English poetry. The next major poet to turn his attention to imitating Chaucer is Dryden; and for him, Chaucer has become an antiquarian interest.

Filling in the Gaps: The Cook's and Squire's Tales

The commonest way round the abrupt ending of the Cook's unfinished tale was to supply a brief link, usually of two lines, in which he decides to tell a different story altogether, and then to give him the ballad-like *Gamelyn*. One manuscript (Lansdowne 851) has him break off 'for schame of the harlotrie'. *Gamelyn* is certainly not by Chaucer, though it survives only through its connection with the *Tales*; it tells the story that becomes the Orlando half of *As You Like It* (Lodge's *Rosalynde*, which adds the love interest, being the intermediary).

Twenty-five manuscripts of the *Tales* contain *Gamelyn*. Two have an altogether more laconic way of finishing off the Cook's Tale, and Perkin and his associates with it:

> And thus with horedom and bryberye
> Togeder thei used till thei honged hye;
> For who so evel byeth shal make a sory sale.
> And thus I make an end of my tale.

One other manuscript, Bodley 686, contains some thirty extra lines

interpolated at various points in the tale, and another dozen at the finish that
bring Perkin and his 'felawe' to an equally moral end:

> The tone ydampned to preson perpetually,
> The tother to deth for he couthe not of clergye.
> And therefore, yonge men, lerne whil ye may,
> That with mony dyvers thoghtes beth prycked al the day,
> Remembre you what myschefe cometh of mysgovernaunce.

The versification may be clumsy—the longer version uses the tumbling
verse characteristic of many of the morality plays with no apparent sense of
its incongruity here—but both endings catch the tale's sententiousness very
accurately.

The Squire's Tale was usually left in its unfinished state, but Lansdowne
851 provides a brief epilogue in which the Squire deliberately breaks off
until his next turn to tell a tale comes round. It was not until the sixteenth
century that anyone attempted to finish it, and then two versions were
written within a few years: one by Edmund Spenser in Book IV of the *Faerie
Queene*, one by the minor poet John Lane. Spenser takes up a single thread
from the plot summary contained in the Squire's final words, of the combat
over Canacee between Cambalo and the 'bretheren two' (whom Spenser
increases to three). Spenser has the fight end when his Cambello and the last
surviving brother, Triamond, into whom the other brothers' souls have
transmigrated, are reconciled through the magic caduceus and potion of
Triamond's sister Cambina. Triamond marries Canacee and Cambello
Cambina; the men become the model friends who embody the principle of
Friendship that is the subject of Book IV. The Squire's stories of
Cambyuskan and the flying horse, and his promised story of Cambyuskan's
other son Algarsif and Theodora, are beyond Spenser's scope here. The
shift from Chaucer's characteristic love-triangle, of the girl with two rival
lovers, to a quartet, is typical of Spenser's methods in the *Faerie Queene*: a
poem about the harmony of the virtues cannot afford jealousy among its
allegorical or model lovers. Spenser's continuation indeed has little in
common with the original except for the names of Cambello and Canacee;
the opening stanzas of the section contain a tribute to Chaucer that the
narrative does not substantiate.

Lane's version, which remained in manuscript, was written in 1615 and
revised in 1630. This adds an extra ten cantos to the two parts of the original
Tale to bring it up to the epic number of twelve. Even with so much room at
his disposal, he finds difficulty in bringing in all the motifs given in the
Squire's concluding summary, and he invents some more of his own.
Algarsif is here a prodigal, led astray by a new character, a witch named
Videria. Other additions include Cambuscan's death and revivification

through the virtue of an elixir mixed by the sender of the magic gifts, and a singing-match between Canacee, Theodora, and two 'bowncinge gearles' who turn up at the tournament held for the hand of Canacee. She herself is finally married to her father's High Admiral, Akafir. Both the magic horse and the deceived falcon are relegated to the sidelines, though Canacee is given a quick spin through the universe on the horse, and the birds are reunited at the very end of the last canto. Lane ends by declaring,

> This, or like this, th'ingenious Chaucer wrought.   (xii. 551)

He was perhaps over-optimistic.

The continuations of the Cook's Tale are given in J. M. Manly and Edith Rickert, *The Text of the Canterbury Tales* (Chicago, 1940), ii. 169 (the four-line version, found in two mid-fifteenth-century manuscripts, Rawlinson poet. 141, in Oxford, and Chicago 564, formerly the McCormick MS), and v. 432–7 (the longer version). For a discussion, see Kolve, *Chaucer and Imagery*, ch. 6.

Edmund Spenser, *The Faerie Queene*, ed. A. C. Hamilton (London and New York, 1977), IV. ii. 31–iii. 52.

John Lane's Continuation of Chaucer's Squire's Tale, ed. Frederick J. Furnivall (London: Chaucer Society, 1888, 1890).

Tales for the Pilgrimage: Beryn, The Siege of Thebes, *Two Ploughman's Tales*

Two tales, the anonymous *Tale of Beryn* and Lydgate's *Siege of Thebes*, were written in the course of the fifteenth century as additions to the stories told on the pilgrimage. Besides these, two works (one of them by Thomas Hoccleve) were provided with prologues to turn them into tales told by the Ploughman, who is the most interesting of those pilgrims who figure in the General Prologue but do not tell tales. The chief interest of all these pieces lies not in their narrative content, but in the strikingly different interpretations of Chaucer they suggest. To the author of *Beryn*, he is the master of lively comedy, of character, and naturalistic action. To Lydgate, he is the supreme rhetorician. To the author or redactor of the anonymous *Plowman's Tale*, he is a spokesman against ecclesiastical corruption, even a Lollard. There are some grounds for all these readings of Chaucer in the *Tales*; that none of these early authors apparently put allegory on the programme of Chaucerian fiction is a salutary warning to modern critics.

The *Tale of Beryn* is not the earliest imitation of the *Tales*—the *Siege of Thebes*, of 1420–2, has that honour—but it is the only one that is not disappointing when read beside Chaucer, and so deserves pride of place. It is preserved in a single, highly disordered manuscript of the late fifteenth century, Northumberland MS 455, where it is given a place between the Canon's Yeoman's Tale and *Melibee*. Its main interest lies not in the story of

Beryn itself, but in the lengthy prologue, which does what Chaucer fails to do: it describes the pilgrims' arrival in Canterbury and their adventures while they are there. It gives a surprisingly modern, novelistic treatment to the pilgrims such as the General Prologue and links never quite supply.

The poet has none of Chaucer's skill with prosody or language, but he has read the *Tales* very carefully indeed. The pilgrims are all given activities that are plausible in terms of the characters Chaucer gave them: the Miller steals a heap of pilgrims' tokens, 'Cauntirbury brochis' (175), and the Summoner, catching sight of him, demands half shares; the Knight takes his son around the town's fortifications to show him the strengths and weaknesses of its defences; the Wife of Bath, feeling tired, takes the Prioress into the garden of their inn and promises her wine with the host's wife in the parlour afterwards—a nicer touch for the woman who enjoys the company of her 'gossib' (III(D) 529) than the more obvious husband–chasing. The Clerk is given a speech to the Summoner in which he tries to soothe his quarrel with the Friar: he urges, in an appropriately ethical use of logic, that it is right for the Friar to know of evil so that he can eschew it and choose the good, and that his story was no personal disgrace to the Summoner

> ffor, of alle craftis, and of eche degre,
> They be nat al perfite.   (261–2)

All this shows an impressive attention to the detail and subtlety of Chaucer's text.

The *Beryn* prologue is also a fabliau in its own right. It tells the story of the Pardoner's determination to make love to Kitt the barmaid, and of how he is foiled at her bedroom door, in a state of high expectation, by the presence of her own paramour inside. The whole affair ends with a chase through the inn, in the course of which the paramour is hit on the nose with a ladle, the tavern-keeper cuts his shin, and the Pardoner suffers a head-wound from a stick and a bite on the thigh from the tavern dog. It is a little like a slapstick compound of the Miller's and Reeve's Tales. The care with which the poet has read the *Tales* means that his testimony should weigh heavily in a crux of interpretation in Chaucer's work, the question of the Pardoner's sexuality. This Pardoner is emphatically neither homosexual nor eunuch.

The prologue ends with the pilgrims setting off on the return journey, and the Merchant volunteering a story. This is a folktale, ultimately Oriental but mediated through a French source, about how a young prodigal named Beryn loses a fortune, and regains a greater one by turning the tables on those who have tricked him. He is helped in his recovery to riches by the ingenuity of a man named Geffrey, who has disguised himself as a cripple after suffering at the hands of the same tricksters: the name is already present in the French, and makes no allusion to Chaucer. The story makes a competent narrative, but it has none of the specific interest of its prologue.

The prologue to Lydgate's *Siege of Thebes* is also set in Canterbury, but it does not involve any of the pilgrims' own goings-on. Lydgate himself takes the place of Chaucer as the first-person author; Chaucer is indeed absent from all these tales associated with the pilgrimage—no other poet will assume his persona, and he is never described as present among the pilgrims. Lydgate claims to have been making his own pilgrimage in gratitude for recovery from sickness, and to have come upon the Host and the rest of the company at their inn; and he is called on to tell the first tale of the homeward journey.

There is some dramatic development in his prologue, but not much. Lydgate imitates not the 'life' of the *Tales* but Chaucer's language, and of that it is the aureate 'rethorike and eloquence' (42) that interest him. His first sentence attempts to epitomize the *Tales*: it contains a description of the season, a summary of the pilgrims (in which the Pardoner and Summoner are hopelessly confused), an account of the variety of the stories matching the 'degre' of the various 'estatis' of the pilgrims, and a tribute to Chaucer's poetic skill. This takes up the first sixty-five lines, and never gets around to a main verb.

The tale itself shows a similar lack of shape. It is told as a pair to the most ambitious of Chaucer's own tales, the Knight's: the return journey, like the outward, will start with the story of Thebes. It recounts the entire history of the city, from its founding by Amphion, through the stories of Oedipus, Polyneices, and Eteocles, down to the killing of Cappaneus and his companions by Creon—the point at which the Knight's Tale starts. The work enjoyed some popularity in the fifteenth century—it survives in almost thirty manuscripts, sometimes in company with the Knight's Tale—but its 4,500 lines lack Chaucer's conciseness and sense of shaping, and its occasional virtues of phrasing are well buried. Lydgate did not have the advantage of knowing Sophocles, but it is still hard to forgive a man who can read the story of Oedipus as (*a*) a warning to princes against incest, and (*b*) an exemplum of a man cast off Fortune's wheel.

Two different tales were assigned to the Ploughman over the years. Both reflect the piety Chaucer ascribes to him, but in very different ways. One manuscript of the *Tales*, Christ Church 152, has him tell a Miracle of the Virgin actually written by Hoccleve, in which a monk's praying of extra *Aves* adds sleeves to the Virgin's otherwise sleeveless garment. Hoccleve's poem is supplemented by two anonymous stanzas that link it to the framework of the pilgrimage, and the tale is slotted in between the Squire's and Second Nun's—the tale order in this manuscript being unusually erratic.

The other *Plowman's Tale* consists of a prologue and what is apparently an early fifteenth-century Lollard tract, both in eight-line stanzas (though with slightly different rhyme schemes). The prologue opens with the ploughman in his village, deciding to leave his plough and go on pilgrimage; he meets up with the company, catches the eye of the Host, and is asked for a story. It is never completely clear whether the author intends this ploughman to be the same as the one who figures in the General Prologue; the most obvious link is that Chaucer's Ploughman is brother to the Parson, whom the Host suspects of Lollard sympathies. The tale consists of a dialogue between a pelican and a griffin, representing 'these lollers' and 'the Popes syde', on the wealth and corruption of the Church.

The history of the work is obscure. There are no surviving manuscripts; it was first printed about 1536 by Thomas Godefray, and was introduced into the *Tales* in the 1542 and later editions of Chaucer's works. It is possible that the prologue, and perhaps three stanzas that lack the refrain lines found elsewhere throughout the tale (205–28), are sixteenth-century additions. The debate would in this case have been conceived without any connection with Chaucer in mind; its ascription to the Ploughman would be a Reformation invention designed to give the work a spurious authority by association with England's master poet. Whatever the date of the prologue that relates the work to the *Tales*, it provides evidence of how seriously Chaucer's own condemnation of ecclesiastical abuses was taken. The inclusion of the *Plowman's Tale* among his genuine works in turn encouraged the Elizabethan interpretation of Chaucer as a proto-Protestant: he figures as a forerunner of the Reformation in Foxe's *Book of Martyrs* largely on the basis of this poem.

The Tale of Beryn as edited by F. J. Furnivall and W. G. Stone (EETS ES 105, 1909) is a less
    fanciful text than in Furnivall's original edition for the Chaucer Society (1876).
Lydgate's Siege of Thebes is edited by Axel Erdmann and Eilert Ekwall (EETS ES 108, 125,
    1911, 1930); for critical comment, see A. C. Spearing, *Medieval to Renaissance in English
    Poetry* (Cambridge, 1985), pp. 66–88.
For Hoccleve's Miracle, see *A New Ploughman's Tale*, ed. Arthur Beatty (London: Chaucer
    Society, 1902).
The Plowman's Tale is included in vol. vii of Skeat's *Works of Geoffrey Chaucer*, 'Chaucerian
    and Other Pieces', No. ii. For the possibility of Reformation additions, see Andrew N.
    Wawn, 'Chaucer, *The Plowman's Tale* and Reformation Propaganda: The Testimonies of
    Thomas Godefray and *I Playne Piers*', Bulletin of the John Rylands Library, 56 (1973),
    174–92. Wawn's further argument that the work was known to the anonymous author of
    the *Pilgrim's Tale* (on which see below) is based on very slender evidence. See also John
    Foxe, *Ecclesiasticall History* (1570 edn.) pp. 965–6 (quoted in Brewer, *Critical Heritage*, i.
    107–9).

The Non-Canterbury Tales: The Pilgrim's Tale, The Cobbler of Canterbury, Greene's Vision

The sixteenth century saw a handful of works written in imitation of Chaucer but not intended as part of the pilgrimage sequence. The earliest of these, the *Pilgrim's Tale*, written between 1536 and 1540, survives in a single fragmentary copy of the 1540 print of the *Courte of Venus*. In substance it is similar to the *Plowman's Tale*, with its attack on the established Church. The unidentified first-person narrator arrives at the abbey of Sempringham in the course of a pilgrimage to Walsingham—a pilgrimage undertaken, like Chaucer's, for less than fully devotional reasons—and indulges in some abuse of monks and friars, some of it echoing similar passages in the *Tales*. He is joined in the abbey church by a priest, who declares that the religious orders are the invention of man, not God, and spends several hundred lines (some of them in rhyme royal) associating 'thes ydell lobers' (366) with Antichrist and the Whore of Babylon. In the course of it he quotes six lines from the Middle English *Romaunt of the Rose*, which he describes as 'chaucers awn hand wark' (740).

The *Cobbler of Canterbury*, first printed in 1590, is the earliest attempt to write a whole collection of Chaucerian stories. It contains six prose tales, told by the passengers—a cobbler, a smith, a gentleman, a scholar, an old woman, and a summoner—who find themselves together in a barge travelling between Billingsgate and Gravesend. The narrators are all described, in octosyllabics, before they begin their tales, but the portraits are little differentiated; most of the travellers display the effects of an over-fondness for drink. The tales show equally little variety: only one, the scholar's tale of two faithful (but unmarried) lovers, is not a fabliau. The author's imitation of some of Chaucer's methods of interrelating tales is more interesting. The cobbler tells a tale against a smith and a prior, the smith responds with a tale against a cobbler, and the summoner ends with a tale of an abbot to match the opening story of the prior, and so 'keep decorum'.

The work is written in part as an 'invective' against another story-collection that had recently appeared, *Tarltons Newes out of Purgatorie*, which derived its tales largely from the *Decameron* and Dante. The author of the *Cobbler*, and his characters, insist that Chaucer's tales are as good as anything in the Italian tradition (though some of the plots of their tales in fact originate in the *Decameron*). The whole work, it is claimed, is written in imitation of 'old father Chaucer, who with the like Method set out his Caunterbury tales'.

The *Cobbler* appeared anonymously, but it was rapidly fathered on Robert Greene, who denied any responsibility for it in a work that includes his own imitation of Chaucer, *Greene's Vision* (though the authorship of this too is not altogether certain). The *Vision* describes how Greene himself has a dream in which Chaucer and Gower argue the respective cases for wantonness and gravity in poetry. Both poets are given octosyllabic portraits, like those in the *Cobbler* (and in various of Greene's other works).

Chaucer's sounds a little as if it describes a manuscript illumination to the *Tales*, where the pilgrims are shown with the tools of their trade, and, since they are on horseback, with disproportionately short legs. There is no attempt to convey anything beyond appearance:

> His stature was not very tall;
> Leane he was; his legs were small,
> Hosd within a stock of red . . .
> His Inckhorne at his side he wore,
> And in his hand he bore a book.

Despite Greene's rejection of the authorship of the *Cobbler*, the tale he gives Chaucer to tell is remarkably similar to the prose fabliau told by the gentleman on the barge, though it is less bawdy. The gentleman tells of the tricks a girl from Cherryhinton plays on a doting Cambridge scholar and of his revenge; Greene's Chaucer tells of the trick played on her husband by the young wife of a Grantchester wheelwright to convince him that he has no need to be jealous of her friendship with the scholars of the university. The conclusion of the *Vision* none the less endorses Greene's supposed refusal to countenance stories of this type: he adjudicates the debate between the poets in favour of Gower's sententious tale, and Solomon makes an appearance to approve his judgement and to note that 'all learning except Theologie, be meere foolishnesse and vanitie'. It is a neat way for Greene to write a fabliau while paying lip-service to the highest moral principles.

All that survives of the *Pilgrim's Tale* is edited by G. H. Kingsley in *Francis Thynne's Animadversions upon Speght's First Edition of Chaucer's Works* (EETS OS 9, 1865), pp. 77–98.

The Cobler of Caunterburie and Tarltons Newes out of Purgatorie, ed. Geoffrey Creigh and Jane Belfield (Medieval and Renaissance Texts 3, Leiden, 1987), contains a discussion, necessarily inconclusive, as to authorship: common authorship of the two works is considered, and the case for Greene is reopened. A new recension of the *Cobler* appeared in 1630 under the title *The Tinker of Turvey*: this contains new prefatory material, a tinker's tale as a new opening story, and a seaman's tale at the end in place of the stories of the old woman and the summoner.

Greene's Vision is in *The Life and Complete Works of Robert Greene*, ed. A. B. Grosart (London, 1881–6), xii. 201–81.

The Afterlife of Individual Tales

Later writers found inspiration in various areas of the *Tales*. The seasonal opening of the General Prologue was echoed or approximately imitated many times over; the Knight's and Clerk's Tales, the Wife of Bath's Prologue and Tale, and *Sir Thopas* enjoyed a particularly lively literary afterlife. Other tales were cannibalized or imitated more sparingly. I list the most notable descendants of the individual tales below; a complete account of the imitation of particular motifs and phrases would of course be much longer.

Of the various works that recall the opening of the Prologue, one in particular deserves special mention: Barclay's winter introduction to his Fourth Eclogue (1512–13). The description of the season forms a companion piece to Chaucer's, of 'colde Ianuary' instead of April,

> What time the verdure of ground and euery tree,
> By frost and stormes is priuate of beautee,
> And euery small birde thinketh the winter longe
> Which well appeareth by ceasing of their songe . . .   (5–8)

The passage introduces two shepherds who are described in something of the manner of the portraits: one 'formall and proper in his geare' who has enjoyed a wild life in London until forced to flee through debt; the other, like Chaucer's Ploughman, 'content with his estate'. A portrait that gives more of the traditional iconography of the shepherd introduces of the First Eclogue.

The Knight's Tale was imitated, after a fashion, in Lydgate's *Siege of Thebes*, and was reworked in various forms later. A fragment containing five quatrains of a fifteenth-century stanzaic version survives in a manuscript in Trinity College, Dublin (MS D.4.18): Emily in the garden is described in this fashion:

> Goyng merely in a garden grene,
> Singyng herself, this lady bright,
> She ravisshed bothe the hertes, I wene,
> Of Palamon and his brother Ersyte.

The tale was also dramatized several times, though only one such version, Shakespeare and Fletcher's *The Two Noble Kinsmen*, survives. Richard Edwardes's two-part *Palamon and Arcite* was played before the Queen in Christ Church when she visited Oxford in 1566, a production notable less for its literary qualities than for the fact that three spectators were killed on the first night by the collapse of a wall (the play went on). It contained some fine showpiece hunting scenes for Theseus in the wood, and apparently also a Vice figure. Henslowe recorded a new, and therefore presumably different, play of *Palamon and Arcite* as being presented by the Admiral's Men in 1594. The Shakespeare–Fletcher version probably dates from 1613, though it was not printed until 1634. It adds a subplot of the passion for Palamon suffered by their gaoler's daughter (who runs mad, Ophelia-style, but finally happily marries the man who loves her), and some other episodes of more interest as a commentary on Chaucer's original: a debate, for instance, between Palamon and Arcite as to whether they should fight for the tyrant Creon in support of their native city (I. ii); and the love of Emily for her dead 'playfellow', which forms the stable equivalent of the shattered sworn brotherhood of the cousins and the agonies of heterosexual love. Venus is even more of a perilous influence in the play than in Chaucer. The dramatic high points of the Tale—the disruption of Theseus' marriage festivities by the mourning queens, the arming in the wood—are preserved and developed; and further moments of suspense and tension are introduced, notably by Palamon's already lying with his head on the block, awaiting the death promised to the loser in the tournament, when messengers rush in with the news of Arcite's death.

The Knight's Tale also influenced two earlier plays of Shakespeare's, *Two Gentlemen of Verona* and *A Midsummer Night's Dream*. These are obviously not based on the Knight's Tale to the same degree as *The Two Noble Kinsmen*, but they all take as their theme the clash of passion and friendship when two friends love the same person. The debt of the *Dream* to the Knight's Tale extends considerably further. Shakespeare takes over from Chaucer the character he accords to Theseus, his hunting, and the names Philostrate, Egeus, and Hippolyta for Theseus' bride; and some of the principal motifs of the play are also Chaucerian—the battling of the lovers over their ladies in the wood outside Athens, and the illusory nature of free will and free choice in a world inhabited by a second order of beings. Titania and Oberon are modelled not on the gods of the Knight's Tale but on Chaucer's parody of them, the underworld gods of the Merchant's Tale who have themselves become king and queen of the fairies with their own marital quarrels. The origin of Shakespeare's couple in Pluto and Proserpina re-emerges in the *Dream* in the dire effects of their quarrel on the seasons. E. Talbot Donaldson also suggests that the mechanicals' play of Pyramus and Thisbe (who get a mention in the Merchant's Tale) was inspired by *Sir Thopas*, or was at least the offspring of a related inspiration: Shakespeare, like Chaucer, will prove that he can write excruciating verse.

A further possible area of influence from the *Tales* on Shakespeare emerges in the last plays. The theme of women's endurance of undeserved suffering in *Henry VIII*, *The Winter's Tale*, and *Pericles* may owe something to the Clerk's and Man of Law's Tales. Catherine of Aragon, who had been presented earlier in the century as a second Griselda, is given a maid called Patience solely to allow such lines as 'Patience, be near me still' (*Henry VIII* IV. ii. 76). *Pericles* is explicitly based on Gower—it tells the story of Apollonius of Tyre that the Man of Law condemns so fiercely (II(B²) 81–5)—but the stress on patience in the play has far more in common with the similarly plotted tale of Custance. This may also have been the source for the lost play of *Fair Constance of Rome*, written by Dekker and others in 1600; the title recalls a modernized version of the Tale of c. 1520.

The Wife of Bath is the most frequently mentioned of all the pilgrims—by Hoccleve and Lydgate, for instance, as a woman who will stand up for female rights, by Skelton as a kind of epitome of the *Canterbury Tales*, by Nashe as an example of the fame poetry can bestow. Her tale was reworked as a broadside ballad by Richard Johnson in 1612, and John Fletcher made a free dramatization of it under the title of *Women Pleased*. Here, the hag turns out to be the hero's own true love in disguise; and a subplot is added, drawn, interestingly, from the old woman's tale in the *Cobbler of Canterbury*. The Wife's own moment of glory, and the strongest evidence of her continuing power for subversion, comes from a long-lived broadside called *The Wanton Wife of Bath*, which survived numerous attempts through the early seventeenth century to suppress it. The poem shows an unusual creative engagement with its original: it tells of how, after her life of pleasure described by Chaucer, the Wife approaches the gates of heaven and points out the error of their ways to all the patriarchs and saints who try to keep her out, including Solomon (guilty of polygamy and fornication), Judith (throat-cutting), and St Paul (a 'lewd desire' of persecution). She acknowledges her own weakness only to Christ, who allows His prodigal daughter admission.

The story of Griselda inspired a wide range of forms—broadsides in verse and prose, Latin and English plays, a panegyric verse history of Catherine of Aragon; by the nineteenth century there were apparently puppet-plays on the subject. A number of these adaptations were derived from French or Italian versions of the story, not from Chaucer's; but the two earliest were based directly on the Clerk's Tale. The first was a Latin play, no longer extant, written about 1550 by Ralph Radclif for the school he founded in a former Carmelite convent at Hitchin; he also adapted the *Melibee* for his pupils to act. The second was the account of Catherine of Aragon as 'Grisilde the second', written in 1558 for her daughter Queen Mary, by Mary's chaplain William Forrest. Forrest probably knew Petrarch's version—his comment, 'Many imagyne that Petrarke dyd but fayne' (p. 132), suggests that he had read the account in the *Epistolae seniles* of the reactions of two of Petrarch's friends to the story—but his poem is in rhyme royal, the metre of the Clerk's Tale, and Forrest's knowledge of Chaucer is further attested in his other works. Much of Queen Catherine's biography correlates smoothly with the Griselda model: her son died, her daughter was disgraced and excluded from the succession, and she herself divorced, after negotiations with Rome, in favour of a younger and more beautiful bride. Forrest never claims that she accepted all this with Griselda's unquestioning equanimity, but when it comes to a comparison between the two, he gives the reward to Catherine, for her sufferings were not feigned—neither a temporary testing, nor fictional. For the same reasons, Henry is cast as Walter because of his 'muche vnkyndenes' (p. 5), but his cruelty is worse than Walter's. There is no restoration for this second Grisilde, nor any reclothing with a jewelled crown; she achieves 'perdurable Coronation', but only in heaven.

The first English play to take Griselda as its subject, *The Commodye of Pacient and Meeke Grissill* by John Phillip, probably dates from the early 1560s; the forms of names it uses, however—Gautier for Chaucer's Walter, Pango for Chaucer's Panik—suggest that Phillip was working from a continental source. A second play of *Patient Grissil*, by Dekker, Chettle, and Haughton, which may owe something to Chaucer, followed in 1599–1600. The threat of dramatic redundancy in the repeated taking of the children is solved here by making them twins; the same feature is found in the earliest surviving broadside ballad, which probably antedates the play. The more appalling aspects of the story are bowdlerized: Grissil is never faced with any really serious threat that her children will be murdered, and the play gives a running insight into Walter's mind, so his fiction of the test is stressed at the expense of her genuine suffering. A subplot is provided that includes a 'froward' woman to serve as foil to Grissil. The whole play can thus become sententious in a very unexacting way, and it loses all the depth and difficulty of its original.

Unlike the Knight's and Clerk's Tales, *Sir Thopas* was not accorded the accolade of popularity indicated by independent manuscript copyings, but it produced three notable descendants besides 'Pyramus and Thisbe'. The first was William Dunbar's burlesque on James IV's court fool, 'Sir' Thomas Norny:

> Now lythis off ane gentill knycht
> Schir Thomas Norny, wys and wycht
>   And full of chevelry,
> Quhais father was ane giand keyne—
> His mother was ane farie queyne
>   Gottin be sossery.

Drayton's *Dowsabell*, a shepherd's song inset in the Eighth Eclogue of *Idea the Shepheards Garland*, makes its ancestry explicit: of Dowsabell's father,

> Fell was he and eger bent,
> In battell and in Tournament,
>   As was the good sir Topas.

Dowsabell herself falls in 'love-longing' for a shepherd, with a happier, and quicker, result than Sir Thopas's love-longing for an elf-queen. The most unexpected reworking of that theme is in Spenser's *Faerie Queene*, where it is of crucial importance for the whole poem: Arthur, like Sir Thopas, lies down to rest from riding, and has his own dream of a Fairy Queen that is to be the inspiration for the whole action of the work.

Other tales were imitated more sparingly. The Nun's Priest inspired Henryson's own superb little beast-fable of the Cock and the Fox. Another Scottish beast-fable retells Nigel Wireker's story of the cock and the ordinand priest to which Chauntecleer refers (VII. 3312–6/B². 4502–6, p. 345 above); its cock, like his Chaucerian prototype, enjoys a lively matrimonial relationship, and the action of the story is relocated in Kent, near Rochester, where the Nun's Priest told his own tale. The Monk's Tale had some influence on Lydgate's *Fall of Princes* and, through that, on the Elizabethan *Mirror for Magistrates*, though neither is a direct imitation. The Monk's account of *tragedie* did however become the standard definition in England for most of two centuries, and so had a major, though indirect, influence on the development of Elizabethan dramatic tragedy (Aristotle's *Poetics* did not reach England until later). The Canon's Yeoman's Tale was never imitated complete, but some sections of its alchemical jargon were adopted by Reginald Scot in his *Discouerie of Witchcraft* (1584), and John Lyly took them over from there—with further recourse to Chaucer—for the subplot of his *Gallathea* (1585?). It is also probable that Ben Jonson had the Tale in mind when he wrote *The Alchemist* (1610). Specific echoes are lacking here, but all three authors, like Chaucer, present the language of alchemy as a pretentious sham.

Two further tales were given dramatic form. The Physician's Tale was reworked as the moral interlude *Apius and Virginia* (1567), a version that remains blissfully impervious to any moral questions raised by the story (it describes itself as a 'tragicall comedie'). Webster also dramatized the story, but there is no sign that he used Chaucer as a source. The one-act *Triumph of Honour* of Beaumont and, possibly, Fletcher (*c.*1612) is based on the much distorted plot of the Franklin's Tale. One quotation from this Tale is given so important a literary place as to deserve special mention: Spenser's Britomart, his knight of Chastity in the sense of good love, includes three lines from the Tale in the first direct speech she is given, and they therefore to some degree serve to define Spenser's ideal of human love:

> Ne may loue be compeld by maisterie;
> For soon as maisterie comes, sweet loue anone
> Taketh his nimble wings, and soone away is gone.
> (III. i. 25 (cf. V(F) 764–6))

Some sections of the *Tales* that might seem to have the greatest potential for development, such as the fabliaux or the confessional prologue of the Pardoner, were used less than one might expect. The Pardoner of John Heywood's *The Pardoner and the Frere* (possibly written before 1521) quotes generously from the Pardoner's Prologue; but other dramatic pardoners—Heywood's other one in *The Four PP*, Lindsay's in *The Satire of the Thrie Estatis*—draw on the same traditions as Chaucer but not on his text. There are more imitations of Chaucer's use of the fabliau as a genre than of his own bawdy stories. The main exception is a tail-rhyme version of the Reeve's Tale, entitled *A Mery Jest of the Mylner of Abyngton*, first printed *c.*1533. This retains the Cambridge setting and some details of the story unique to Chaucer; but the plot diverges sufficiently to indicate that its author also knew some version resembling analogues now known in Breton or Danish, in which the clerks seal the sack so that the miller has to beat it to get the flour out, and the daughter is provided with a lover of her own— named in the *Jest*, unoriginally, as Jankyn. In addition to this poem, the gentleman's tale in the *Cobbler of Canterbury* and 'Chaucer's' tale in *Greene's Vision*, both discussed above, clearly owe their university settings to the models of the Miller's and Reeve's Tales.

The interest in the fabliaux shown in the 1590s is however the first indication of the way in which the 'merry' or improper Chaucer was to become the conventional image of the poet—an image that bedevilled him throughout the nineteenth century and into the twentieth. The unknown author of the *Cobbler* signs his introductory Epistle 'Robin Good-fellowe'. Perhaps it was one of Puck's more successful pieces of mischief-making to set up the bawdy Chaucer—the Chaucer who lacks high seriousness, in Arnold's notorious phrase—as a changeling in the place of England's greatest non-dramatic poet.

A conspectus of Renaissance dramatizations of the *Tales* is given in Ann Thompson, *Shakespeare's Chaucer: A Study in Literary Origins* (Liverpool: Liverpool Texts and Studies, 1978), ch. 2.

The following bibliography cites the tales in the editorial order used in this book.

General Prologue: *The Eclogues of Alexander Barclay*, ed. Beatrice White (EETS OS 175, 1928).

Knight's Tale: the *Palamon and Ersyte* fragment is given in *Essays on Chaucer*, Part IV (London: Chaucer Society, 1878), p. 418. On the plays, see E. K. Chambers, *The Elizabethan Stage* (Oxford, 1923), ii. 143, iii. 311, and N. W. Bawcutt's introduction to *The Two Noble Kinsmen* (Harmondsworth, 1977). On Shakespeare's links with Chaucer, see Harold F. Brooks's Arden edition of *A Midsummer Night's Dream* (London, 1979); E. Talbot Donaldson, *The Swan at the Well: Shakespeare Reading Chaucer* (New Haven and London, 1985); and Piero Boitani, 'The Genius to Improve an Invention', in *Chaucer Traditions*, ed. Ruth Morse and Barry Windeatt (Cambridge, 1990), pp. 185–98.

Miller's and Reeve's Tales: see pp. 419–20 above.

Reeve's Tale: *A Mery Jest of the Mylner of Abyngton* (first printed 1532–4, reprinted *c.*1575) is edited by Joseph Raith, 'Die Geschichte von der vertauschten Wieger: The Mylner of Abyngton', *Aus Schrifttum und Sprache der Angelsachsen*, 4 (Leipzig, 1936), pp. 125–60.

Cook's Tale: see pp. 413–14 above.

Man of Law's Tale: on *Fair Constance of Rome*, see Thompson, *Shakespeare's Chaucer*, pp. 30–1; on *Pericles*, ibid. pp. 83–4. See also Franklin B. Williams, jun., 'Alsop's *Fair Custance*: Chaucer in Tudor Dress', *ELR* 6 (1976), 351–68, and the colophon on p. 368.

Wife of Bath's Prologue: *The Wanton Wife of Bath* is preserved in various prints in most of the major broadside collections, e.g. *The Roxburghe Ballads*, ed. J. W. Ebsworth (Ballad Society, Hertford, 1890–3), vii. 213–15. See also Helen Cooper, 'The Shape-shiftings of the Wife of Bath, 1395–1670', in Morse and Windeatt, *Chaucer Traditions*, pp. 168–84.

Wife of Bath's Tale: Richard Johnson's *New Sonet of a Knight and a Faire Virgin* appeared in *A Crowne-garland of Goulden Roses* (1612; repr. Percy Society VI, 1842). *Women Pleased* appears in vol. v of *The Dramatic Works in the Beaumont and Fletcher Canon*, ed. Fredson Bowers (Cambridge, 1982). Its date is uncertain: it may be *c.*1620, or earlier (pp. 443–5). It is discussed by Thompson, *Shakespeare's Chaucer*, pp. 51–7.

Clerk's Tale: for a discussion of the broadside and dramatic versions, including Radclif, see Cyrus Hoy, *Introduction, Notes, and Commentaries to Texts in The Dramatic Works of Thomas Dekker edited by Fredson Bowers* (Cambridge, 1980), i. 129–43; Bowers (Cambridge, 1953) gives the text of *Patient Grissill*, i. 207–98. The earliest extant broadside ballad (*c.*1600, but there may have been earlier examples) is printed in *The Roxburghe Ballads*, ed. William Chappell (Ballad Society, Hertford, 1872), ii. 269–74; two prose texts, one with the ballad inset, are edited by J. Payne Collier (Percy Society III, 1841). The puppet-plays are mentioned as a contemporary phenomenon by W. Carey Hazlitt in his edition of Thomas Warton's *History of English Poetry* (London, 1871), ii. 350. Forrest's *History of Grisild the Second* is edited by W. D. Macray (London: Roxburghe Club, 1875); the manuscript that seems to have been the original presentation copy is in the Bodleian, MS Wood empt. 2. See also *Henry VIII*, II. iv. 19–37, III. i. 129–37, IV. ii. 76, 165–6. Phillip's play is edited as *The Play of Patient Grissell* by R. B. McKerrow and W. W. Greg (Chiswick: Malone Society Reprints, 1909).

Merchant's Tale: see Brooks, *Midsummer Night's Dream*, under Knight's Tale above.

Squire's Tale: see pp. 414–15 above.

Franklin's Tale: *The Triumph of Honour* is part of *Four Plays or Morall Representations in One*, *The Works of Beaumont and Fletcher* vol. x, ed. A. R. Waller (Cambridge, 1912, repr. New York, 1969: for a discussion, see Thompson, *Shakespeare's Chaucer* (p. 426 above), pp. 44–51. On the *maisterie* theme in the *Faerie Queene*, see A. C. Hamilton, *The Structure of Allegory in the Faerie Queene* (Oxford, 1961), pp. 180 ff.

Physician's Tale: editions of *Apius and Virginia* include those by W. W. Greg and R. B. McKerrow (Chiswick: Malone Society Reprints, 1911), and Peter Happé, *Tudor Interludes* (Harmondsworth, 1972).

Pardoner's Prologue: John Heywood, *The Pardoner and the Frere*, ed. John S. Farmer (London: Tudor Facsimiles, 1909).

Sir Thopas: 'Schir Thomas Norny' is no. 27 in *The Poems of William Dunbar*, ed. James Kinsley (Oxford, 1979); 'Dowsabell', *The Works of Michael Drayton*, ed. William Hebel (Oxford, 1961), i. 88–91; Spenser, *Faerie Queene*, I. ix. 12–15. See also John Burrow, 'Sir Thopas in the Sixteenth Century', in Douglas Gray and E. G. Stanley (eds.), *Middle English Studies Presented to Norman Davis* (Oxford, 1983), pp. 69–91.

Melibee: see the entry on Radclif for the Clerk's Tale above.

Monk's Tale: *Lydgate's Fall of Princes*, ed. H. Bergen (EETS ES 121–4, 1924–7); *The Mirror for Magistrates*, ed. Lily B. Campbell (Cambridge, 1938, repr. New York, 1960).

Nun's Priest's Tale: 'The Cock and the Fox' in *The Poems of Robert Henryson*, ed. Denton Fox (Oxford, 1981), pp. 19–27 (Fables III); 'The Unicornis Tale' on the cock and the ordinand priest in *Colkelbie Sow and The Talis of the Fyve Bestis*, ed. Gregory Kratzmann (Garland Medieval Texts 6, New York, 1983), Talis 135–280. The rationale for the unicorn may be heraldic (p. 32). For Chauntecleer and Pertelote's birth and a justification of their morality, see *Colkelbie Sow* 898–922.

Canon's Yeoman's Tale: see Reginald Scot, *The Discouerie of Witchcraft*, ed. Brinsley Nicholson (London, 1886), Book XIV, chs. 1–3; and *Gallathea* II. iii in *The Complete Works of John Lyly*, vol. ii, ed. R. Warwick Bond (Oxford, 1902, repr. 1967).

GENERAL BIBLIOGRAPHY

THIS bibliography contains a selection of works of importance for the whole *Canterbury Tales*. Criticism that relates to specific areas of the *Tales* is listed in the bibliography of the appropriate section. A bibliography of editions of the *Tales* is given on pp. 3–4, and of recurrent sources on pp. 11–15.

Further bibliographical information can be found in John Leyerle and Anne Quick, *Chaucer: A Bibliographical Introduction* (Toronto Medieval Bibliographies 10, Toronto, 1986); in forthcoming volumes of the *Chaucer Bibliographies* (general editors A. J. Colaianne and R. M. Piersol, Toronto); and, for general updating, in *Studies in the Age of Chaucer*.

AERS, DAVID, *Chaucer, Langland and the Creative Imagination* (London, 1980).

ALLEN, JUDSON BOYCE, and MORITZ, THERESA ANNE, *A Distinction of Stories: The Medieval Unity of Chaucer's Fair Chain of Narratives for Canterbury* (Columbus, Ohio, 1981).

ANDERSON, J. J. (ed.), *Chaucer: The Canterbury Tales: A Casebook* (London, 1974).

BALDWIN, RALPH, *The Unity of the Canterbury Tales* (Anglistica 5, Copenhagen, 1955).

BENSON, C. DAVID, *Chaucer's Drama of Style: Poetic Variety and Contrast in the Canterbury Tales* (Chapel Hill and London, 1986).

BENSON, LARRY D. (ed.), *The Learned and the Lewed: Studies in Chaucer and Medieval Literature* (Harvard English Studies, Cambridge, Mass., 1974).

—— and ANDERSSON, THEODORE M. (eds.), *The Literary Context of Chaucer's Fabliaux* (Indianapolis and New York, 1971).

BIRNEY, EARLE, *Essays on Chaucerian Irony*, ed. Beryl Rowland (Toronto, 1985).

BLAMIRES, ALCUIN, *The Canterbury Tales* (The Critics Debate, London and Atlantic Highlands, NJ, 1987).

BLOOMFIELD, MORTON W., *Essays and Explorations* (Cambridge, Mass., 1970).

BOITANI, PIERO (ed.), *Chaucer and the Italian Trecento* (Cambridge, 1983).

BREWER, DEREK, *Chaucer: the Poet as Storyteller* (London, 1984).

—— *Tradition and Innovation in Chaucer* (London, 1982).

—— (ed.), *Chaucer and Chaucerians: Critical Studies in Middle English Literature* (London, 1966).

—— (ed.), *Chaucer: The Critical Heritage* (2 vols., London, Henley, and Boston, 1978).

—— (ed.), *Writers and their Background: Geoffrey Chaucer* (London, 1974).

BRYAN, W. F., and DEMPSTER, GERMAINE (eds.), *Sources and Analogues of Chaucer's Canterbury Tales* (1941, repr. Atlantic Highlands, N.J., 1958).

BURLIN, ROBERT B., *Chaucerian Fiction* (Princeton, 1977).

BURNLEY, DAVID, *A Guide to Chaucer's Language* (London, 1983).

BURROW, J. A., *Ricardian Poetry* (London, 1971).

—— *Essays on Medieval Literature* (Oxford, 1984).

COOPER, HELEN, *The Structure of the Canterbury Tales* (London and Athens, Ga., 1983).

CRAMPTON, GEORGIA RONAN, *The Condition of Creatures: Suffering and Action in Chaucer and Spenser* (New Haven, 1974).

CROW, MARTIN M., and OLSON, CLAIR C. (eds.), *Chaucer Life-records* (Oxford, 1966).

CURRY, WALTER CLYDE, *Chaucer and the Medieval Sciences* (rev. edn., London, 1960).

DAVID, ALFRED, *The Strumpet Muse: Art and Morals in Chaucer's Poetry* (Bloomington, Ind., and London, 1976).

DINSHAW, CAROLYN, *Chaucer's Sexual Poetics* (Madison Wis., 1989).

DONALDSON, E. TALBOT, 'Designing a Camel: or, Generalizing the Middle Ages', *Tennessee Studies in Literature*, 22 (1977), 1–16.

—— *Speaking of Chaucer* (London, 1970).

ELBOW, PETER, *Oppositions in Chaucer* (Middletown, Conn., 1975).

ELLIOTT, RALPH W. V., *Chaucer's English* (London, 1974).

ELLIS, ROGER, *Patterns of Religious Narrative in the Canterbury Tales* (London and Sydney, 1986).

FICHTE, JOERG O., *Chaucer's 'Art Poetical': A Study in Chaucerian Poetics* (Studies and Texts in English 1, Tübingen, 1980).

HAMMOND, ELEANOR PRESCOTT, *Chaucer: A Bibliographical Manual* (New York, 1908).

HOWARD, DONALD R., *The Idea of the Canterbury Tales* (Berkeley, Los Angeles and London, 1976).

JORDAN, ROBERT M., *Chaucer and the Shape of Creation: The Aesthetic Possibilities of Inorganic Structure* (Cambridge, Mass., 1967).

JOSIPOVICI, GABRIEL, *The World and the Book* (2nd edn., London, 1979).

KEAN, P. M., *Chaucer and the Making of English Poetry*, ii: *The Art of Narrative* (London and Boston, 1972).

KELLOGG, ALFRED L., *Chaucer, Langland, Arthur: Essays in Middle English Literature* (New Jersey, 1972).

KOLVE, V. A., *Chaucer and the Imagery of Narrative: The First Five Canterbury Tales* (Stanford and London, 1984).

LAWLER, TRAUGOTT, *The One and the Many in the Canterbury Tales* (Hamden, Conn., 1980).

LAWTON, DAVID, *Chaucer's Narrators* (Chaucer Studies 13, Cambridge and Dover, NH, 1985).

LINDAHL, CARL, *Earnest Games: Folkloric Patterns in the Canterbury Tales* (Bloomington, Ind., 1987).

LOWES, JOHN LIVINGSTON, *Convention and Revolt in Poetry* (2nd edn., London, 1930).

McCALL, JOHN P., *Chaucer among the Gods: The Poetics of Classical Myth* (University Park, Pa., and London, 1979).

MANDEL, JEROME, and ROSENBERG, BRUCE A. (eds.), *Medieval Literature and Folklore Studies: Essays in Honor of Francis Lee Utley* (New Jersey, 1970).

MERSAND, JOSEPH, *Chaucer's Romance Vocabulary* (2nd edn., New York, 1939).

MILLER, ROBERT P. (ed.), *Chaucer: Sources and Backgrounds* (New York, 1977).

MINNIS, A. J., *Chaucer and Pagan Antiquity* (Chaucer Studies 8, Cambridge and Dover, NH, 1982).

MITCHELL, JEROME, and PROVOST, WILLIAM (eds.), *Chaucer the Love Poet* (Athens, Ga., 1973).

MUSCATINE, CHARLES, *Chaucer and the French Tradition* (Berkeley and Los Angeles, 1957).

NORTH, J. D., *Chaucer's Universe* (Oxford, 1988).

OWEN, CHARLES A., *Pilgrimage and Storytelling in the Canterbury Tales: The Dialectic of 'Ernest' and 'Game'* (Norman, Okla., 1977).

PAYNE, ROBERT O., *The Key of Remembrance: A Study of Chaucer's Poetics* (New Haven, 1963).

PEARSALL, DEREK, *The Canterbury Tales* (London, Boston, and Sydney, 1985).

RICHARDSON, JANETTE, *Blameth Nat Me: A Study of Imagery in Chaucer's Fabliaux* (Mouton Studies in English Literature 58, The Hague, 1970).

ROBERTSON, D. W., jun., *Essays in Medieval Culture* (Princeton, 1980).

—— *A Preface to Chaucer: Studies in Medieval Perspectives* (Princeton, 1962).

ROWLAND, BERYL, *Blind Beasts: Chaucer's Animal World* (Kent, Ohio, 1971).

RUGGIERS, PAUL G., *The Art of the Canterbury Tales* (Madison, Milwaukee, and London, 1965).

SALTER, ELIZABETH, *Fourteenth Century English Poetry: Contexts and Readings* (Oxford, 1983).

SCHOECK, RICHARD J., and TAYLOR, JEROME (eds.), *Chaucer Criticism*, i: *The Canterbury Tales* (Notre Dame, 1960).

Sources and Analogues: see Bryan, W. F., and Dempster, Germaine.

STROHM, PAUL, *Social Chaucer* (Cambridge, Mass., 1989).

VASTA, EDWARD and THUNDY, ZACHARIAS P. (eds.), *Chaucerian Problems and Perspectives: Essays Presented to Paul E. Beichner* (Notre Dame, 1979).

WAGENKNECHT, EDWARD (ed.), *Chaucer: Modern Essays in Criticism* (New York, London, and Oxford, 1959).

WASSERMANN, JULIAN N., and BLANCH, ROBERT J. (eds.), *Chaucer in the Eighties* (Syracuse, NY, 1986).

WHITTOCK, TREVOR, *A Reading of the Canterbury Tales* (Cambridge, 1968).

ZACHER, CHRISTIAN K., *Curiosity and Pilgrimage: The Literature of Discovery in Fourteenth-century England* (Baltimore, 1976).

INDEX

Virgil 169, 412
  Aeneid 64, 345, 353
  commentaries 21
  Georgics 386
  see also *Troilus*: list of poets
Virgin 39 n., 131, 134, 176, 191, 196, 205, 211, 256, 288, 289–98 *passim*, 362
  Annunciation 97
  and Eve 134, 199, 210, 212
  Invocation 359, 360, 366
  liturgy of 358
  sufferings 135, 190
  and *Thomas of Erceldoune* 308
  see also Miracles
Visconti, Bernabò 324, 328, 330, 331

Wanton Wife of Bath 423, 427 n.
Webster, John 425
Weddynge of Sir Gawain and Dame Ragnell 157–9, 161
Wife of Bath 28, 47, 50–2, 86, 181, 198, 320, 404, 405–6, 411
  and Clerk 51, 186, 188, 197–8
  imitations 416, 423; old woman 419
  past life 18, 27, 104, 141, 143–55
  as sample wife 93, 134, 193, 209, 212, 234, 256, 364
  as teller 156, 157, 162, 166; of Shipman's Tale 139, 278, 284

Wife of Bath's Prologue 139–55, 181, 202
  Samaritan woman 51
Wife of Bath's Tale 156–66, 172–3, 308, 347
  copyings 63; Fragment III 140
  ideals in 196, 242
  imitations 420, 423, 427 n.
  as romance 63, 64, 218
  what women desire 104, 278
Wireker, Nigel 345, 425
women 17, 28, 47, 51, 94, 104, 150, 158, 217, 333–4, 348, 406
  antifeminism 87, 141, 144, 149, 199, 204, 234, 280
  marriage 18, 70–1, 86, 134, 144–5, 147–9, 151–2, 153 n., 198, 202, 203, 204–5, 206, 207–9, 214–5, 284
  moral status 93, 134, 142, 152, 162, 188, 190, 198–9, 205, 210–11, 212, 227, 256, 320, 351, 385, 389–90, 393
  sexuality 131, 134, 145, 148, 149, 152, 210, 252–3, 255, 364 5, 406
  sovereignty 86–7, 149, 151–2, 158, 161, 163, 198, 237, 318–19, 320–1, 351, 365, 406
  submission 134, 191, 195, 197, 199, 238, 240, 241
Wyatt, Thomas 76
Wyclif, John 5

Yeoman 37, 174
Ypotis 302